HENRY WINTER DAVIS.

Charles Sumner.

SPEECHES AND ADDRESSES

DELIVERED IN THE CONGRESS OF THE UNITED STATES,

AND ON SEVERAL PUBLIC OCCASIONS,

BY

HENRY WINTER DAVIS,

OF MARYLAND.

PRECEDED BY A SKETCH OF HIS LIFE, PUBLIC SERVICES, AND CHARACTER,

BEING AN ORATION BY THE HON. J. A. J. CRESSWELL,

U. S. SENATOR FROM MARYLAND.

With Notes, Introductory and Explanatory.

NEW YORK:

HARPER & BROTHERS, PUBLISHERS,

FRANKLIN SQUARE.

1867.

PREFACE.

THE friends of the late HENRY WINTER DAVIS have thought it due to his memory, and to the remembrance of the public service which he fulfilled both in the Congress of the United States and before the people of Maryland, especially in behalf of emancipation, that all such adequate and proper account of it as could be had should be put into some convenient shape, and published, as a contribution to the history of the times, as well as constituting a suitable record of that service.

To this end they have collected all the reports and accounts of the speeches and addresses delivered by him, and, upon examination of them, it was resolved to publish all such as were regularly and correctly reported, and which he had gathered or retained, precisely as they were printed and as he left them, without correction and without omission, except in two instances alone, where direct allusion by name was made to persons, which allusions they believe Mr. Davis would have omitted if he had lived to correct these speeches for the press.

In this collection have also been included such documents and reports as were wholly written by him, although the course recommended in such papers was not adopted, or the measures or men condemned thereby were approved, by the party he supported or by the people to whom he appealed. For it has not been thought admissible to correct any part of the account, nor to withhold any part of it, unless by reason of an insufficient and inadequate report it was plainly no true record of what was said.

It is to be regretted, of course, that these speeches and documents should not have received final revision by the author's hand; but, in the absence of that, the only proper emendation, it has been thought improper to substitute the corrections of any other.

They have gladly used the permission of the Hon. Mr. CRESSWELL to include here, as a sketch of the life and services of Mr. Davis, the admirable Oration delivered by him in the hall of the House of Representatives on the occasion of the commemorative services held there by the senators and representatives on the 22d of February, 1866.

Short notes have been prefixed or annexed to each speech or paper, explanatory of the allusions made in it—recalling contemporary events, or the circumstances under which, and the time at which, it was delivered. The intention has been to confine those notes to that purpose alone; and the statements made have been verified by a recurrence to the daily record of such events printed or made at the time of their occurrence.

CONTENTS.

THE LIFE AND CHARACTER

OF

HENRY WINTER DAVIS.

AN ORATION BY

HON. JOHN A. J. CRESWELL,

U. S. SENATOR FROM MARYLAND.

Delivered in the Hall of the House of Representatives,

FEBRUARY 22, 1866.

The death of Hon. Henry Winter Davis, on the 30th of December, 1865, for many years a distinguished representative of one of the Baltimore congressional districts, created a deep sensation among those who had been associated with him in national legislation, and they deemed it fitting to pay to his memory unusual honors. They adopted resolutions expressive of their grief, and invited Hon. John A. J. Cresswell, a senator of the United States from the State of Maryland, to deliver an oration on his life and character in the hall of the House of Representatives on the 22d of February, a day the recurrence of which ever gives increased warmth to patriotic emotions.

The hall of the House was filled by a distinguished audience to listen to the oration. Before eleven o'clock the galleries were crowded in every part. The flags above the Speaker's desk were draped in black, and other insignia of mourning were exhibited. An excellent portrait of the late Hon. Henry Winter Davis was visible through the folds of the national banner above the Speaker's chair. As on the occasion of the oration on President Lincoln by Hon. George Bancroft, the Marine band occupied the anteroom of the reporter's gallery, and discoursed appropriate music.

At twelve o'clock the senators entered, and the judges of the Supreme Court, preceded by Chief Justice Chase. Of the cabinet, Secretary Stanton and Secretary McCulloch were present. After prayer by the chaplain, the Declaration of Independence was read by Hon. Edward McPherson, Clerk of the House. After the reading of the Declaration, followed by the playing of a dirge by the band, Hon. Schuyler Colfax, Speaker of the House of Representatives, introduced the orator of the day, Hon. J. A. J. Cresswell.

REMARKS

OF

HON. SCHUYLER COLFAX,

SPEAKER OF THE HOUSE OF REPRESENTATIVES.

Hon. SCHUYLER COLFAX, Speaker of the House of Representatives, said:

LADIES AND GENTLEMEN,—The duty has been devolved upon me of introducing to you the friend and fellow-member, here, of HENRY WINTER DAVIS, and I shall detain you but a moment from his address, to which you will listen with saddened interest.

The world always appreciates and honors courage: the courage of Christianity, which sustained martyrs in the amphitheatre, at the stake, and on the rack; the courage of Patriotism, which inspired millions in our own land to realize the historic fable of Curtius, and to fill up with their own bodies, if need be, the yawning chasm which imperiled the republic; the courage of Humanity, which is witnessed in the pest-house and the hospital, at the death-bed of the homeless and the prison-cell of the convict. But there is a courage of Statesmen, besides; and nobly was it illustrated by the statesman whose national services we commemorate to-day. Inflexibly hostile to oppression, whether of slaves on American soil or of republicans struggling in Mexico against monarchical invasion, faithful always to principle and liberty, championing always the cause of the downtrodden, fearless as he was eloquent in his avowals, he was mourned throughout a continent; and from the Patapsco to the Gulf the blessings of those who had been ready to perish followed him to his tomb. It is fitting, therefore, though dying a private citizen, that the nation should render him such marked and unusual honors in this hall, the scene of so many of his intellectual triumphs; and I have great pleasure in introducing to you, as the orator of the day, Hon. J. A. J. CRESSWELL, his colleague in the Thirty-eighth Congress, and now senator from the State of Maryland.

ORATION

OF

HON. JOHN A. J. CRESSWELL.

The Hon. Mr. CRESSWELL rose and spoke as follows:

MY COUNTRYMEN,—On the 22d day of February, 1732, God gave to the world the highest type of humanity in the person of George Washington. Combining within himself the better qualities of the soldier, sage, statesman, and patriot, alike brave, wise, discreet, and incorruptible, the common consent of mankind has awarded him the incomparable title of Father of his Country. Among all nations and in every clime, the richest treasures of language have been exhausted in the effort to transmit to posterity a faithful record of his deeds. For him unfading laurels are secure so long as letters shall survive and history shall continue to be the guide and teacher of civilized men. The whole human race has become the self-appointed guardian of his fame, and the name of Washington will be ever held, over all the earth, to be synonymous with the highest perfection attainable in public or private life, and coeternal with that immortal love to which reason and revelation have together toiled to elevate human aspirations—the love of liberty restrained and guarded by law.

But in the presence of the Omnipotent how insignificant is the proudest and the noblest of men! Even Washington, who alone of his kind could fill that comprehensive epitome of General Henry Lee, so often on our lips, "First in war, first in peace, and first in the hearts of his countrymen," was allowed no exemption from the common lot of mortals. In the sixty-eighth year of his age he too paid the debt of nature.

The dread announcement of his demise sped over the land like a pestilence, burdening the very air with mourning, and carrying inexpressible sorrow to every household and every heart. The course of legislation was stopped in mid career to give expression to the grief of Congress, and by resolution, approved January 6, 1800, the 22d of February of that year was devoted to national humiliation and lamentation. This is, then, as well a day of sorrow as a day of rejoicing.

More recent calamities also remind us that death is universal king. Just ten days ago our great historian pronounced in this hall an impartial judgment upon the earthly career of him who, as savior of his country, will be counted as the compeer of Washington. Scarce have the orator's lingering tones been mellowed into silence, scarce has the glowing page whereon his words were traced lost the impress of his passing hand, yet we are again called into the presence of the Inexorable to crown one more illustrious victim with sacrificial flowers. Having taken up his lifeless body, as beautiful as the dead Absalom, and laid it in the tomb with becoming solemnity, we have assembled in the sight of the world to do deserved honor to the name and memory of HENRY WINTER DAVIS, a native of Annapolis, in the State of Maryland, but always proudly claiming to be no less than a citizen of the United States of America.

We have not convened in obedience to any formal custom, requiring us to assume an empty show of bereavement, in order that we may appear respectful to the departed. We who knew Henry Winter Davis are not content to clothe ourselves in the outward garb of grief, and call the semblance of mourning a fitting tribute to the gifted orator and statesman, so suddenly snatched from our midst in the full glory of his mental and bodily strength. We would do more than "bear about the mockery of woe." Prompted by a genuine affection, we desire to ignore all idle and merely conventional ceremonies, and permit our stricken hearts to speak their spontaneous sorrow.

Here, then, where he sat for eight years as a representative of the people; where friends have trooped about him, and admiring crowds have paid homage to his genius; where grave legislators have yielded themselves willing captives to his eloquence, and his wise counsel has moulded in no small degree the law of a great nation, let us, in dealing with what he has left us, verify the saying of Bacon, "Death openeth the good fame and extinguisheth envy." Remembering that he was a man of like passions and equally fallible with ourselves, let us review his life in a spirit of generous candor, applaud what is good, and try to profit by it; and if we find aught of ill, let us, so far as justice and truth will permit, cover it with the veil of charity, and bury it out of sight forever. So may our survivors do for us.

The subject of this address was born on the 16th of August, 1817. His father, Rev. Henry Lyon Davis, of the Protestant Episcopal

Church, was president of St. John's College at Annapolis, Maryland, and rector of St. Ann's parish. He was of imposing person, and great dignity and force of character. He was, moreover, a man of genius, and of varied and profound learning, eminently versed in mathematics and natural sciences, abounding in classical lore, endowed with a vast memory, and gifted with a concise, clear, and graceful style; rich and fluent in conversation, but without the least pretension to oratory, and wholly incapable of *extempore* speaking. He was removed from the presidency of St. John's by a board of Democratic trustees because of his Federal politics; and, years afterward, he gave his son his only lesson in politics, at the end of a letter addressed to him when at Kenyon College, in this laconic sentence: "My son, beware of the follies of Jacksonism."

His mother was Jane Brown Winter, a woman of elegant accomplishments, and great sweetness of disposition and purity of life. It might be truthfully said of her that she was an exemplar for all who knew her. She had only two children, Henry Winter, and Jane, who married the Rev. Edward Seyle.

The education of Henry Winter began very early, at home, under the care of his aunt, Elizabeth Brown Winter, who entertained the most rigid and exacting opinions in regard to the training of children, but who was, withal, a noble woman. He once playfully said, "I could read before I was four years old, though much against my will." When his father was removed from St. John's, he went to Wilmington, Delaware, but some time elapsed before he became settled there. Meanwhile Henry Winter remained with his aunt, in Alexandria, Virginia. He afterward went to Wilmington, and was there instructed under his father's supervision. In 1827 his father returned to Maryland, and settled in Anne Arundel County.

After reaching Anne Arundel, Henry Winter became so much devoted to outdoor life that he gave small promise of scholarly proficiency. He affected the sportsman, and became a devoted disciple of Nimrod; accompanied always by one of his father's slaves, he roamed the country with a huge old fowling-piece on his shoulder, burning powder in abundance, but doing little damage otherwise. While here he saw much of slaves and slavery, and what he saw impressed him profoundly, and laid the foundation for those opinions which he so heroically and constantly defended in all his after life. Referring to this period, he said, long afterward, "My familiar association with the slaves while a boy gave me great insight into their feelings and views. They spoke with freedom before a boy what they would have repressed before a man. They were far from indifferent to their condition; they felt wronged, and sighed for freedom. They were attached to my father and loved me, yet they habitually spoke of the day when God would deliver them."

He subsequently went to Alexandria, and was sent to school at Howard, near the Theological Seminary, and from Howard he went to Kenyon College, in Ohio, in the fall of 1833.

Kenyon was then in the first year of the presidency of Bishop McIlvaine. It was the centre of vast forests, broken only by occasional clearings, excepting along the lines of the National Road and the Ohio River and its navigable tributaries. In this wilderness of nature, but garden of letters, he remained, at first in the grammar-school, and then in the college, until the 6th of September, 1837, when, at twenty years of age, he took his degree and diploma, decorated with one of the honorary orations of his class on the great day of commencement. His subject was "Scholastic Philosophy."

At the end of the freshman year a change in the college terms gave him a vacation of three months. Instead of spending it in idleness, as he might have done, and as most boys would have done, he availed himself of this interval to pursue and complete the studies of the sophomore year, to which he had already given some attention in his spare moments. At the opening of the next session he passed the examination for the junior class. Fortunately I have his own testimony and opinion as to this exploit, and I give them in his own language:

> "It was a pretty sharp trial of resolution and dogged diligence, but it saved me a year of college, and indurated my powers of study and mental culture into a habit, and perhaps enabled me to stay long enough to graduate. I do not recommend the example to those who are independently situated, for learning must fall like the rain in such gentle showers as to sink in if it is to be fruitful; when poured on the richest soil in torrents, it not only runs off without strengthening vegetation, but washes away the soil itself."

His college life was laborious and successful. The regular studies were prosecuted with diligence, and from them he derived great profit, not merely in knowledge, but in what is of vastly more account, the habit and power of mental labor. These studies were wrought into his mind and made part of the intellectual substance by the vigorous collisions of the societies in which he delighted. For these mimic conflicts he prepared assiduously, not in writing, but always with a carefully adduced logical analysis and arrangement of the thoughts to be developed in the order of argument, with a brief note of any quotation, or image, or illustration on the margin at the appropriate place. From that brief he spoke. And this was his only method of preparation for all the great conflicts in which he took part in after life. He never wrote out his speeches beforehand.

Speaking of his feelings at the end of his college life, he sadly said:

"My father's death had embittered the last days of the year 1836, and left me without a counselor. I knew something of books, nothing of men, and I went forth like Adam among the wild beasts of the unknown wilderness of the world. My father had dedicated me to the ministry, but the day had gone when such dedications determined the lives of young men. Theology, as a grave topic of historic and metaphysical investigation, I delighted to pursue, but for the ministry I had no calling. I would have been idle if I could, for I had no ambition; but I had no fortune, and I could not beg or starve."

All who were acquainted with his temperament can well imagine what a gloomy prospect the future presented to him, when its contemplation wrung from his stoical taciturnity that touching confession.

The truth is, that from the time he entered college he was continually cramped for want of money. The negroes ate every thing that was produced on the farm in Anne Arundel, a gastronomic feat which they could easily accomplish without ever having cause to complain of a surfeit. His aunt, herself in limited circumstances, by a careful husbandry of her means, managed to keep him at college. Kenyon was then a manual-labor institution, and the boys were required to sweep their own rooms, make their own beds and fires, bring their own water, black their own boots, if they ever were blacked, and take an occasional turn at grubbing in the fields or working on the roads. There was no royal road to learning known at Kenyon in those days. Through all this Henry Winter Davis passed, bearing himself manfully; and knowing how heavily he taxed the slender purse of his aunt, he denied himself with such rigor that he succeeded, incredible as it may appear, in bringing his total expenses, including boarding and tuition, within the sum of eighty dollars per annum.

His father left an estate consisting only of some slaves, which were equally apportioned between himself and sister. Frequent applications were made to purchase his slaves, but he never could be induced to sell them, although the proceeds would have enabled him to pursue his studies with ease and comfort. He rather sought and obtained a tutorship, and for two years he devoted to law and letters only the time he could rescue from its drudgery. In a letter written in April, 1839, replying to the request of a relative who offered to purchase his slave Sallie, subject to the provisions of his father's will, which manumitted her if she would go to Liberia, he said: "But if she is under my control" (he did not know that she had been set to his share), "I will *not consent to the sale*, though he wishes to purchase her subject to the will." And so Sallie was not sold, and Henry Winter Davis, the tutor, toiled on and waited. He never would hold any of his slaves under his authority, never would accept a cent of their wages, and tendered each and all of them a deed of absolute manumission whenever the law would allow. Tell me, was that man sincere in his opposition to slavery? How many of those who have since charged him with being selfish and reckless in his advocacy of emancipation would have shown equal devotion to principle? Not one; not one. Ah! the man who works and suffers for his opinions' sake places his own flesh and blood in pledge for his integrity.

Notwithstanding his irksome and exacting duties, he kept his eye steadily on the University of Virginia, and read without assistance a large part of its course. He delighted especially in the pungent pages of Tacitus, and the glowing and brilliant, dignified and elevated epic of the Decline and Fall of the Roman Empire. These were favorites which never lost their charm for him. When recently on a visit at my house, he stated in conversation that he often exercised himself in translating from the former, and in transferring the thoughts of the latter into his own language, and he contended that the task had dispelled the popular error that Gibbon's style is swollen and declamatory; for he alleged that every effort at condensation had proved a failure, and that, at the end of his labors, the page he had attempted to compress had always expanded to the eye when relieved of the weighty and stringent fetters in which the gigantic genius of Gibbon had bound it.

About this time—the only period when doubts beset him—he was tempted by a very advantageous offer to settle in Mississippi. He determined to accept; but some kind spirit interposed to prevent the dispatch of the final letter, and he remained in Alexandria. At last his aunt—second mother as she was—sold some land, and dedicated the proceeds to his legal studies. He arrived at the University of Virginia in October, 1839.

From that moment he entered actively and unremittingly on his course of intellectual training. While a boy he had become familiar, under the guidance of his father, with the classics of Addison, Johnson, Swift, Cowper, and Pope, and he now plunged into the domain of history. He had begun at Kenyon to make flanking forays into the fields of historic investigation, which lay so invitingly on each side of the regular march of his college course. As he acquired more information and confidence, these forays became more extensive and profitable. It was then the transition period from the shallow though graceful pages of Gillies, Rollin, Russel, and Tytler, and the rabbinical agglomerations of Shuckford and Prideaux, to the modern school of free, profound, and laborious investigation, which has reared immortal monuments to its memory in the works of Hallam, Macaulay, Grote, Bancroft, Prescott, Motley, Niebuhr, Bunsen, Schlosser, Thiers, and their fellows. But of the last-named none except Niebuhr's History of Rome and Hallam's Middle Ages were accessible to him in the backwoods of Ohio. Cousin's Course of the History of Modern Philosophy was just glittering in the horizon, and Gibbon shone alone as the morning-star of the day of historic research, which he had heralded so long. The French Revolution he had seen only as presented in Burke's brilliant vituperation and Scott's Tory diatribe. A republican picture of the great republican revolution, the fountain of all that is now tolerable in Europe, had not then been presented on any authentic and comprehensive page.

Not only these, but all historical works of value which the English, French, and German languages can furnish, with an immense amount of other intellectual pabulum, were eagerly gathered, consumed with voracious appetite, and thoroughly digested. Supplied at last with the required means, he braced himself for a systematic curriculum of law, and pursued it with marked constancy and success. While at the University he also took up the German and French languages and mastered them, and he perfected his scholarship in Latin and Greek. Until his death he read all these languages with great facility and accuracy, and he always kept his Greek Testament lying on his table for easy reference.

After a thorough course at the University, Mr. Davis entered upon the practice of the law in Alexandria, Virginia. He began his profession without much to cheer him; but he was not the man to abandon a pursuit for lack of courage. His ability and industry attracted attention, and before long he had acquired a respectable practice, which thenceforth protected him from all annoyances of a pecuniary nature. He toiled with unwearied assiduity, never appearing in the trial of a cause without the most elaborate and exhaustive preparation, and soon became known to his professional brethren as a valuable ally and a formidable foe. His natural aptitude for public affairs made itself manifest in due time, and some articles which he prepared on municipal and state politics gave him great reputation. He also published a series of newspaper essays, wherein he dared to question the divinity of slavery; and these, though at the time thought to be not beyond the limits of free discussion, were cited against him long after as evidence that he was a heretic in pro-slavery Virginia and Maryland.

On the 30th of October, 1845, he married Miss Constance T. Gardiner, daughter of William C. Gardiner, Esq., a most accomplished and charming young lady, as beautiful and as fragile as a flower. She lived to gladden his heart for but a few years, and then,

> "Like a lily drooping,
> She bowed her head and died."

In 1850 he came to Baltimore, and immediately a high position, professional, social, and political, was awarded him. His forensic efforts at once commanded attention and enforced respect. The young men of most ability and promise gathered about him, and made him the centre of their chosen circle. He became a prominent member of the Whig party, and was every where known as the brilliant orator and successful controvertist of the Scott campaign of 1852. The Whig party, worn out by its many gallant but unsuccessful battles, was ultimately gathered to its fathers, and Mr. Davis led off in the American movement. He was elected successively to the Thirty-fourth, Thirty-fifth, and Thirty-sixth Congresses by the American party from the fourth district of Maryland. He supported with great ability and zeal Mr. Fillmore for the Presidency in 1856, and in 1860 accepted John Bell as the candidate of his party, though he clearly divined and plainly announced that the great battle was really between Abraham Lincoln, as the representative of the national sentiment on the one hand, and secession and disunion, in all their shades and phases, on the other. To his seat in the Thirty-eighth Congress he was elected by the Unconditional Union party.

Since the adjournment of the Thirty-eighth Congress he had been profoundly concerned in the momentous public questions now pressing for adjustment, and he did not fail, on several fitting occasions, to give his views at length to the public. Nevertheless, he frequently alluded to his earnest desire to retreat for a while from the perplexing annoyances of public life. He had determined upon a long visit to Europe in the coming spring, and had almost concluded the purchase of a delightful country-seat, where he hoped to recruit his weary brain for years to come from the exhaustless riches of nature. When the Thirty-ninth Congress met, and he read of his old companions in the work of legislation again gathering in their halls and committee-rooms, I think, for at least a day or two, he felt a longing to be among them. During the second week of the session he again entered this hall, but only as a spectator. The greeting he received —so general, spontaneous, and cordial—from gentlemen on both sides of the House, touched his heart most sensibly. The crowd that gathered about him was so great that the party was obliged to retire to one of the larger anterooms for fear of interrupting the public business. A delightful interview among old friends was the reward. He was charmed with his reception, and mentioned it to me with intense satisfaction. Little did you, gentlemen, then think that between you and a beloved friend the curtain that shrouds eternity was so soon to be interposed. His sickness was of about a week's duration. Until the morning of the day preceding his death his friends never doubted his recovery. Later in the day very unfavorable symptoms appeared, and all then realized his danger. In the evening his wife spoke to him of a visit, for one day, which he had projected, to his old friend Mrs. S. F. Du Pont, when he replied, in the last words he ever uttered, "It shows the folly of making plans even for a day." He continued to fail rapidly in strength until two o'clock in the afternoon of Saturday, the 30th of December, when HENRY WINTER DAVIS, in the forty-ninth year of his age, appeared before his God. His death confirmed the opinion of Sir Thomas Browne, who declared, "Marshaling all the horrors of death, and contemplating the extremities thereof, I find not any thing therein able to daunt the *courage* of a *man*, much less a *well-resolved Christian*." He passed away so quietly that no one knew the moment of his departure. His was

"A death-like sleep,
A gentle wafting to immortal life."

Mr. Davis left a widow, Mrs. Nancy Davis, a daughter of John B. Morris, Esq., of Baltimore, and two little girls, who were the idols of his heart. He was married a second time on the 26th of January, 1857. His nearest surviving collateral relation is the Hon. David Davis, associate justice of the Supreme Court of the United States, who is his only cousin—german. To all these afflicted hearts may God be most gracious.

Thus has the country lost one of the most able, eloquent, and fearless of its defenders. Called from this life at an age when most men are just beginning to command the respect and confidence of their fellows, he has left, nevertheless, a fame as wide as our vast country. He died nineteen years younger than Washington, and eight years younger than Lincoln. At forty-eight years of age Washington had not seen the glories of Yorktown even in a vision, nor had Lincoln dreamed of the presidential chair, and if they had died at that age they would have been comparatively unknown in history. Doubtless God would have raised up other leaders, if they had been wanting, to conduct the great American column, which he has chosen to be the body-guard of human rights and hopes, onward among the nations and the centuries; but in that event the 12th and 22d days of February would not be, as they now are, held sacred in our calendar.

Mr. Davis had gathered into his house the literary treasures of four languages, and had reveled in spirit with the wise men of the ages. He had conned his books as jealously as a miner peering for gold, and had not left a panful of earth unwashed. He had collected the purest ore of truth and the richest gems of thought until he was able to crown himself with knowledge. Blessed with a felicitous power of analysis and a prodigious memory, he ransacked history, ancient and modern, sacred and profane; science, pure, empirical, and metaphysical; the arts, mechanical and liberal; the professions, law, divinity, and medicine; poetry and the miscellanies of literature; and in all these great departments of human lore he moved as easily as most men do in their particular province. His habit was not only to read, but to reread the best of his books frequently, and he was continually supplying himself with better editions of his favorites. In current, playful conversation with friends he quoted right and left, in brief and at length, from the classics, ancient and modern, and from the drama, tragic and comic. In his speeches, on the contrary, he quoted but little, and only when he seemed to run upon a thought already expressed by some one else with singular force and appositeness. He was the best scholar I ever met for his years and active life, and was surpassed by very few, excepting mere book-worms. He has for many years been engaged in collecting extracts from newspapers, containing the leading facts and public documents of the day, but he never commonplaced from books. His thesaurus was his head.

I have but little personal knowledge of Mr. Davis as a lawyer. It was never my good fortune to be associated with him in the trial of a cause, nor have I ever been present when he was so engaged. But at the time of his death he filled a high position at the bar, and was chosen to lead against the most distinguished of his brethren. On public and constitutional questions, as distinguished from those involving only private rights, he was a host, and in the argument of the cases which grew out of the adoption of the new Constitution of Maryland he won golden laurels, and drew extraordinary encomiums even from his opponents in that angry litigation. He was thoroughly read in the decisions of the federal courts, and especially in those declaring and defining constitutional principles.

Possessed of a mind of remarkable power, scope, and activity; with an immense fund of precious information, ready to respond to any call he might make upon it, however sudden; wielding a system of logic formed in the severest school, and tried by long practice; gifted with a rare command of language and an eloquence wellnigh superhuman, and withal graced with manners the most accomplished and refined, and a person unusually handsome, graceful, and attractive, Mr. Davis entered public life with almost unparalleled personal advantages. Having boldly presented himself before the most rigorous tribunal in the world, he proved himself worthy of its favor and attention. He soon rose to the front rank of debaters, and whenever he addressed the House all sides gave him a delighted audience.

I shall not attempt a review of the topics discussed in the Thirty-fourth and Thirty-fifth Congresses. The day was fast coming when contests for the speakership and battles over appropriation bills—ay, even the fierce struggle over Kansas, would sink into insignificance, and Mr. Davis, with that political prescience for which he was always remarkable, seemed to discern the first sign of the coming storm. The winds had been long sown, and now the whirlwind was to be reaped. The Thirty-sixth Congress, which had opened so inauspiciously, and which his vote had saved from becoming a perpetuated bedlam, met for its second session on the 3d of December, 1860, with the clouds of civil war fast settling down upon the nation. In the hope that war might yet be averted, on the fourth day of the session the celebrated committee of thirty-three was raised, with the lamented Corwin, of Ohio, as chairman, and Mr. Davis as the member from Maryland. When the committee reported, Mr. Davis sustained the majority report in an able speech, in which, after urging every argument in favor of the report, he boldly proclaimed his own views, and the duties of his state and country. In his speech of 7th February, 1861, he said,

"I do not wish to say one word which will exasperate the already too much inflamed state of the public mind, but I will say that the Constitution of the United States, and the laws made in pursuance thereof, *must be enforced;* and they who stand across the path of that enforcement must either *destroy* the *power* of the *United States*, or it will *destroy them.*"

For such utterances only a small part of the people of his state was on that day prepared. Seduced by the wish, they still believed that the Union could be preserved by fair and mutual concessions. They were on their knees praying for peace, ignorant that bloody war had already girded on his sword. His language was then deemed too harsh and unconciliatory, and hundreds, I among the number, denounced him in unmeasured terms. Before the expiration of three months events had demonstrated his wisdom and our folly, and other paragraphs from that same speech became the fighting creed of the Union men of Maryland. He farther said on that occasion:

"But, sir, there is one state I can speak for, and that is the State of Maryland. Confident in the strength of this great government to protect every interest, grateful for almost a century of unalloyed blessings, she has fomented no agitation; she has done no act to disturb the public peace; she has rested in the consciousness that if there be wrong, the Congress of the United States will remedy it; and that none exists which revolution would not aggravate.

"Mr. Speaker, I am here this day to speak, and I say that I do speak, for the people of Maryland, who are loyal to the United States; and that when my judgment is contested, I appeal to the people for its accuracy, and I am ready to maintain it before them.

"In Maryland we are dull, and can not comprehend the right of secession. We do not recognize the right to make a revolution by a vote. We do not recognize the right of Maryland to repeal the Constitution of the United States; and if any Convention there, called by whatever authority, under whatever auspices, undertake to inaugurate revolution in Maryland, their authority will be resisted and defied in arms on the soil of Maryland, in the name and by the authority of the United States."

In January, 1861, the ensign of the republic, while covering a mission of mercy, was fired on by traitors. In February Jefferson Davis said, at Stevenson, Alabama, "We will carry war where it is easy to advance, where food for the sword and torch await our armies in the densely populated cities." In March, the Thirty-sixth Congress, after vainly passing conciliatory resolutions by the score—among other things recommending the repeal of all personal-liberty bills, declaring that there was no authority outside of the states where slavery was recognized to interfere with slaves or slavery therein, and proposing by two-thirds votes of both houses an amendment of the Constitution prohibiting any future amendment giving Congress power over slavery in the states—adjourned amid general terror and distress.

Abraham Lincoln, having passed through the midst of his enemies, appeared at Washington in due time and delivered his inaugural, closing with these memorable words:

"In your hands, my dissatisfied fellow-countrymen, and not in mine, is the momentous issue of civil war. The government will not assail you.

"You can have no conflict without being yourselves the aggressors. You can have no oath registered in heaven to destroy the government, while I shall have the most solemn one to 'preserve, protect, and defend' it.

"I am loth to close. We are not enemies, but friends. We must not be enemies. Though passion may have strained, it must not break our bonds of affection.

"The mystic chords of memory, stretching from every battle-field and patriot grave to every living hearth and hearthstone all over this broad land, will yet swell the chorus of the Union, when again touched, as surely as they will be, by the better angels of our nature."

Words which, if human hearts do not harden into stone, through the long ages yet to come

> "Will plead like angels, trumpet-tongued, against
> The deep damnation of his taking off."

The appeal was spurned; and, in the face of its almost godlike gentleness, they who already gloried in their anticipated saturnalia of blood inhumanly and falsely stigmatized it as a declaration of war. The long-patient North, slow to anger, in its agony still cried, "My brother—oh, my brother!" It remained for that final, ineradicable infamy of Sumter to arouse the nation to arms! At last, to murder at one blow the hopes we had nursed so tenderly, they impiously dragged in the dust the glorious symbol of our national life and majesty, heaping dishonor upon it, and, like the sneering devil at the Crucifixion, crying out, "Come and deliver thyself!" and then no man, with the heart of a man, who loved his country and feared his God, dared longer delay to prepare for that great struggle which was destined to rock the earth.

Poor Maryland! cursed with slavery, doubly cursed with traitors! Mr. Davis had said that Maryland was loyal to the United States, and had pledged himself to maintain that position before the people. The time soon came for him to redeem his pledge. On the morning of the 14th of April the President issued his proclamation calling a special session of Congress, which made an extra election necessary in Maryland. Before the sun of that day had gone down this card was promulgated:

"*To the Voters of the Fourth Congressional District of Maryland:*

"I hereby announce myself as a candidate for the House of Representatives of the 37th Congress of the United States of America, upon the basis of the *unconditional maintenance of the Union.*

"Should my fellow-citizens of *like views* manifest their preference for a different candidate on *that basis*, it is not my purpose to embarrass them.

"H. WINTER DAVIS.

"*April* 15, 1861."

But dark days were coming for Baltimore. A mob, systematically organized in complicity with the rebels at Richmond and Harper's

Ferry, seized and kept in subjection an unsuspecting and unarmed population from the 19th to the 24th of April. For six days murder and treason held joint sway; and at the conclusion of their tragedy of horrid barbarities they gave the farce of holding an election for members of the House of Delegates.

To show the spirit that moved Mr. Davis under this ordeal, I cite from his letter, written on the 28th, to Hon. William H. Seward, the following:

> "I have been trying to collect the persons appointed scattered by the storm, and to compel them to take their offices or to decline.
>
> "I have sought men of undoubted courage and capacity for the places vacated.
>
> "We must show the secessionists that we are not frightened, but are resolved to maintain the government in the exercise of all its functions in Maryland.
>
> "We have organized a guard, who will accompany the officers and hold the public buildings against all the secessionists in Maryland.
>
> "A great reaction has set in. If we *now* act promptly, the day is ours and the state is safe."

These matters being adjusted, he immediately took the field for Congress on his platform against Mr. Henry May, Conservative Union, and in the face of an opposition which few men have dared to encounter, he carried on, unremittingly from that time until the election on the 13th of June, the most brilliant campaign against open traitors, doubters, and dodgers, that unrivaled eloquence, courage, and activity could achieve. Every where, day and night, in sunshine and storm, in the market-houses, at the street corners, and in the public halls, his voice rang out clear, loud, and defiant for the "unconditional maintenance" of the Union. He was defeated, but he sanctified the name of *unconditional union* in the vocabulary of every true Marylander. He gathered but 6000 votes out of 14,000, yet the result was a triumph which gave him the real fruits of victory; and he exclaimed to a friend, with laudable pride, "With six thousand of the working-men of Baltimore on my side, won in such a contest, I defy them to take the state out of the Union." Though not elected, he never ceased his efforts. With us it was a struggle for homes, hearths, and lives. He said at Brooklyn,

> "You see the conflagration from a distance; it blisters me at my side. You can survive the integrity of the nation; we in Maryland would live on the side of a gulf, perpetually tending to plunge into its depths. It is for us life and liberty; it is for you greatness, strength, and prosperity."

Nothing appalled him; nothing deterred him. He said at Baltimore in 1861,

> "The War Department has been taught by the misfortune at Bull Run, which

has broken no power nor any spirit, which bowed no state nor made any heart falter, which was felt as a humiliation that has brought forth wisdom."

He also said, speaking of the rebels, and foretelling his own fate if they succeeded in Maryland,

"They have inaugurated an era of confiscations, proscriptions, and exiles. Read their acts of greedy confiscation, their law of proscriptions by the thousands. Behold the flying exiles from the unfriendly soil of Virginia, Tennessee, and Missouri."

And so he worked on, never abating one jot of his uncompromising devotion to the Union, like a second Peter the Hermit, preaching a cause, as he believed, truly represented by insignia as sacred as the Cross, and for which no sacrifice, not even death, was too great.

But his crowning glory was his leadership of the emancipation movement. The rebels, notwithstanding "My Maryland's" bloody welcome at South Mountain and Antietam, claimed that she must belong to their confederacy because of the homogeneousness of her institutions. They contended that the fetters of slavery formed a chain that stretched across the Potomac, and held in bondage not only 87,000 slaves, but 600,000 white people also. Their constant theme was "the deliverance" of Maryland. We resolved to break that last tie, and to take position unalterably on the side of the Union and freedom, and thus to deal the final blow to the cause and support of rebellion. We organized our little band, almost ridiculous from its want of numbers, early in 1863. A Sibley tent would have held our whole army. Our enemies laughed us to scorn, and the politicians would not accept our help on any terms, but denied us as earnestly as Peter denied his Lord. Mr. Davis was our acknowledged leader, and it was in the heat and fury of the contest which followed that our hearts were welded into permanent friendship. He was the platform maker, and he announced it in a few words:

"A hearty support of the entire policy of the national administration, including immediate emancipation by constitutional means."

It was very short, but it covered all the ground. The campaign opened by the publication of an address, written by Mr. Davis, to the people of Maryland, which, I venture to say, is unsurpassed by any state paper published in this age of able state papers for the warmth and vigor of its diction, and the lucidity and conclusiveness of its argumentation. It is a pamphlet of twenty pages, glowing throughout with the unmistakable marks of his genius and patriotism, and closing with these words of stirring cheer:

"We do not doubt the result, and expect, freed from the trammels which now bind her, to see Maryland, at no distant day, rapidly advancing in a course of unexampled prosperity with her sister *free* states of the *undivided* and *indivisible* republic."

Mr. Davis was ubiquitous. He was the life and soul of the whole contest. He arranged the order of battle, dictated the correspondence, wrote the important articles for the newspapers, and addressed all the concerted meetings. In short, neither his voice nor his pen rested in all the time of our travail. He would have no compromise, but rejected all overtures of the enemy short of unconditional surrender. On the Eastern Shore he spoke with irresistible power at Elkton, Easton, Salisbury, and Snow Hill, at each of the three last-named towns with a crowd of wondering "American citizens of African descent" listening to him from afar, and looking upon him as if they believed him to be the seraph Abdiel. His last appointment, in extreme southern Maryland, he filled on Friday, after which, bidding me a cordial God-speed, he descended from the stand, sprang into an open wagon awaiting him, traveled eighty miles through a raw night-air, reached Cambridge by daylight, and then crossed the Chesapeake, sixty miles, in time to close the campaign with one of his ringing speeches in Monument Square, Baltimore, on Saturday night. In this, our first contest, we were completely victorious.

But we had yet a weary way before us. The Legislature had then to pass a law calling a Convention. That law had to be approved by a majority of the people. Members of the Convention had then to be elected in all parts of the state, and the Constitution which they adopted had to be carried by a majority of the popular vote. He allowed himself no reprieve from labor until all this had been accomplished. And when the rest of us, worn out by incessant toil, gladly sought rest, he went before the Court of Appeals to maintain every thing that had been done against all comers, and did so triumphantly.

Let free Maryland never forget the debt of eternal gratitude she owes to HENRY WINTER DAVIS.

If oratory means the power of presenting thoughts by public and sustained speech to an audience in the manner best adapted to win a favorable decision of the question at issue, then Mr. Davis assuredly occupied the highest position as an orator. He always held his hearers in rapt attention until he closed, and then they lingered about to discuss with one another what they had heard. I have seen a promiscuous assembly, made up of friends and opponents, remain exposed to a beating rain for two hours rather than forego hearing him. Those who had heard him most frequently were always ready to make the greatest effort to hear him again. Even his bitterest enemies have been known to stand shivering on the street corners for a whole evening, charmed by his marvelous tongue. His stump efforts never fell below his high standard. He never condescended to a mere attempt to amuse. He always spoke to instruct, to convince, and to persuade through the higher and better avenues to favor. I never heard him deliver a speech that was not worthy of being printed and preserved. As a stump orator he was unapproachable, in my estimation, and I say that with a clear recollection of having heard, when a boy, that wonder of Yankee birth and Southern development, S. S. Prentiss.

Mr. Davis's ripe scholarship promptly tendered to his thought the happiest illustrations and the most appropriate forms of expression. His brain had become a teeming cornucopia, whence flowed in exhaustless profusion the most beautiful flowers and the most substantial fruits; and yet he never indulged in excessive ornamentation. His taste was most austerely chaste. His style was perspicuous, energetic, concise, and, withal, highly elegant. He never loaded his sentences with meretricious finery, or high-sounding, supernumerary words. When he did use the jewelry of rhetoric, he would quietly set a metaphor in his page or throw a comparison into his speech which would serve to light up with startling distinctness the colossal proportions of his argument. Of humor he had none; but his wit and sarcasm at times would glitter like the brandished cimeter of Saladin, and, descending, would cut as keenly. The pathetic he never attempted; but when angered by a malicious assault, his invective was consuming, and his epithets would wound like pellets of lead. Although gallant to the graces of expression, he always compelled his rhetoric to act as a handmaid to his dialectics.

Style may sometimes be an exotic; but when it is, it is sure to partake more and more, as years increase, of the peculiarities of the soil wherein it is nurtured. But the style of Mr. Davis was indigenous, and strongly marked by his individuality. Although he doubtless admired, and perhaps imitated, the condensation and dignity of Gibbon, yet it is certain that he carefully avoided the monotonous stateliness and the elaborate and ostentatious art of that most erudite historian. I look in vain for his model in the skeptical Gibbon, the cynical Bolingbroke, or the gorgeous Burke. These were all to him intellectual giants, but giants of false belief and practice. Not even from Tacitus, upon whom he looked with the greatest favor, could he have acquired his burning and impressive diction.

Henry Winter Davis was a man of faith, and believed in Christ and his fellow-man. His heart and mind were both nourished into their full dimensions under the fostering influences of our free institutions, so that, being reared a freeman, he thought and spake as became a freeman. No other land could have produced such dauntless courage and such heroic devotion to honest conviction in a public man, and even our land has produced but few men of his stamp and ability. His implicit faith in God's eternal justice, and his grand moral courage, imparted to him his proselyting zeal, and gave him that amazing, kindling power which enabled him to light the fires of enthusiasm wherever he touched the public mind.

To show his power in extemporaneous debate, as well as his determined patriotism, I will introduce a passage from his speech of April 11, 1864, delivered in the House of Representatives. You will remember that the end of the rebellion had not then appeared. Grant, with his invincible legions, had not started to execute that greatest military movement of modern times, by which, after months of bloody persistence, hurling themselves continually against what seemed the frowning front of destiny, they finally drove the enemy from his strong-holds, made Fortune herself captive, and, binding her to their standards, held her there until the surrender of every rebel in arms closed the war amid the exultant plaudits of men and angels. Our hopes had not then grown into victory, and we looked forward anxiously to the terrible march from the Rappahannock to Richmond. Thinking that perhaps our army stood appalled before the great duty required of it, and that the people might be diverted from their purpose to crush the rebellion when they saw that it could only be accomplished at the cost of an ocean of human blood, a call was made on the floor of the American Congress for a recognition of the Southern Confederacy. Speaking for the nation, Mr. Davis said:

"But, Mr. Speaker, if it be said that a time may come when the question of recognizing the Southern Confederacy will have to be answered, I admit it. * * * * When the people, exhausted by taxation, weary of sacrifices, drained of blood, betrayed by their rulers, deluded by demagogues into believing that peace is the way to union, and submission the path to victory, shall throw down their arms before the advancing foe; when vast chasms across every state shall make it apparent to every eye, when too late to remedy it, that division from the South is anarchy at the North, and that peace without union is the end of the republic, *then* the independence of the South will be an accomplished fact, and gentlemen may, without treason to the dead republic, rise in this migratory house, wherever it may then be in America, and declare themselves for recognizing their masters at the South rather than exterminating them. Until that day, in the name of the American nation; in the name of every house in the land where there is one dead for the holy cause; in the name of those who stand before us in the ranks of battle; in the name of the liberty our ancestors have confided to us, I devote to eternal execration the name of him who shall propose to destroy this blessed land rather than its enemies.

"But, until that time arrive, it is the judgment of the American people there shall be NO compromise; that ruin to ourselves or ruin to the Southern rebels are the only alternatives. It is only by resolutions of this kind that nations can rise above great dangers and overcome them in crises like this. It was only by turning France into a camp, resolved that Europe might exterminate but should not subjugate her, that France is the leading empire of Europe to-day. It is by such a resolve that the American people, coercing a reluctant government to draw the sword and stake the national existence on the integrity of the republic, are now any thing but the fragments of a nation before the world, the scorn and hiss of every petty tyrant. It is because the people of the United States, rising to the height of the occasion, dedicated this generation to the sword, and pouring out the blood of their children as of no account, and vowing before high Heaven that there should be no end to this conflict but ruin absolute or absolute triumph, that we now are what we are; that the banner of the republic, still pointing onward, floats proudly in the face of the enemy; that vast regions are reduced to obedience to the laws, and that a great host in armed array now press with steady step into the dark regions of the rebellion. It is only by the earnest and abiding resolution of the people that, whatever shall be our fate, it shall be grand as the American nation, worthy of that republic which first trod the path of empire, and made no peace but under the banners of victory, that the American people will survive in history. And that will save us. We shall succeed, and not fail. I have an abiding confidence in the firmness, the patience, the endurance of the American people; and, having vowed to stand in history on the great resolve to accept of nothing but victory or ruin, victory is ours. And if with such heroic resolve we fall, we fall with honor, and transmit the name of liberty, committed to our keeping, untarnished, to go down to future generations. The historian of our decline and fall, contemplating the ruins of the last great republic, and drawing from its fate lessons of wisdom on the waywardness of men, shall drop a tear as he records with sorrow the vain heroism of that people who dedicated and sacrificed themselves to the cause of freedom, and by their example will keep alive her worship in the hearts of men till happier generations shall learn to walk in her paths. Yes, sir, if we must fall, let our last hours be stained by no weakness. If we must fall, let us stand amid the crash of the falling republic and be buried in its ruins, so that history may take note that men lived in the middle of the nineteenth century worthy of a better fate, but chastised by God for the sins of their forefathers. Let the ruins of the republic remain to testify to the latest generations our greatness and our heroism. And let Liberty, crownless and childless, sit upon these ruins, crying aloud in a sad wail to the nations of the world, 'I nursed and brought up children, and they have rebelled against me.'"

Mr. Davis's most striking characteristics were his devotion to principle and his indomitable courage. There never was a moment when he could be truthfully charged with trimming or insincerity. His views were always clearly avowed and fearlessly maintained. He hated slavery, and he did not attempt to conceal it. He remembered the lessons of his youth, and his heart rebelled against the injustice of the system. His antipathy was deeply grounded in his convictions, and he could not be dissuaded, nor frightened, nor driven from expressing it.

He was not a great captain nor a mighty ruler; he was only one of the people, but, nevertheless, a hero. Born under the flag of a nation which claimed for its cardinal principle of government that all men are created free, yet held in abject slavery four millions of human beings; which erected altars to the living God, yet denied to creatures formed in the image of God, and charged with the custody of immortal souls, the common rights of humanity, he declared that the hateful inconsistency should cease to defile the prayers of Christians and stultify the advocates of freedom. No dreamer was he, no mere theorist, but a worker, and a strong one, who did well the work committed to him. He entered upon his self-imposed task when surrounded by slaves and slave-owners. He stood face to face with the iniquitous superstition, and to their teeth defied its worshipers. To make proselytes he had to conquer prejudices, correct traditions, elevate duty above interest, and induce men who had been the propagandists of slavery to become its destroyers. Think you his work was easy? Count the long years of his unequal strife; gather from the winds, which scattered them, the curses of his foes; suffer under all the annoyances and insults which malice and falsehood can invent, and you will then understand how much of heart and hope, of courage and self-relying zeal, were required to make him what he was, and to qualify him to do what he did. And what did he? When the rough hand of war had stripped off the pretexts which enveloped the rebellion, and it became evident that slavery had struck at the life of the republic, unmindful of consequences to himself, he, among the first, arraigned the real traitor and demanded the penalty of death. The denunciations that fell upon him like a cloud wrapped him in a mantle of honor, and more truthfully than the great Roman orator he could have exclaimed, "*Ego hoc animo semper fui, ut invidiam virtute partam, gloriam non invidia putarem.*"

This man, so stern and inflexible in the execution of a purpose, so rigorous of his demands of other men in behalf of a principle, so indifferent to preferment and all base objects of pursuit, had a monitor to whom he always gave an open ear and a prompt assent. It was no demon like that which attended Socrates, no witch like that invoked by Saul, no fiend like that to which Faust resigned himself. A vision of light, and life, and beauty flitted ever palpably before him, and wooed him to the perpetual service of the good and true. The memory of a pious and beloved mother permeated his whole moral being, and kept warm within him the tenderest affection. Hear how he wrote of her:

"My mother was a lady of graceful and simple manners, fair complexion, blue eyes, and auburn hair, with a rich and exquisite voice, that still thrills my memory with the echo of its vanished music. She was highly educated for her day, when Annapolis was the focus of intellect and fashion for Maryland, and its fruits shone through her conversation, and colored and completed her natural eloquence, which my father used to say would have made her an orator, if it had not been thrown away on a woman. She was the incarnation of all that is Christian in life and hope, in charity and thought, ready for every good work, herself the example of all she taught."

It was the force of her precept and example that formed the man, and supplied him with his shield and buckler. His private life was spotless. His habits were regular and abstemious, and his practice in close conformity with the Episcopal Church, of which he was a member. He invariably attended divine service on Sunday, and confined himself for the remainder of the day to a course of religious reading. If from his father he drew a courage and a fierce determination before which his enemies fled in confusion, from his mother he inherited those milder qualities that won for him friends as true and devoted as man ever possessed. Some have said he was hard and dictatorial. They had seen him only when a high resolve had fired his breast, and when the gleam of battle had lighted his countenance. His friends saw deeper, and knew that beneath the exterior he assumed in his struggles with the world there beat a heart as pure and unsullied, as confiding and as gentle, as ever sanctified the domestic circle, or made loved ones happy. His heart reminded me of a spring among the hills of the Susquehanna to which I often resorted in my youth; around a part of it we boys had built a stone wall to protect it from outrage, while on the side next home we left open a path, easily traveled by familiar feet, and leading straight to the sweet and perennial waters within.

He lived to hear the salvos that announced, after more than two centuries of bondage, the redemption of his native state. He lived to vote for that grand act of enfranchisement that wiped from the escutcheon of the nation the leprous stain of slavery, and to know that the Constitution of the United States no longer recognized and protected property in man. He lived to witness the triumph of his country in its desperate struggle with treason, and to behold all its enemies either wanderers, like Cain, over the earth, or suppliants for mercy at her feet. He lived to catch the first glimpse of the coming glory of that new era of progress that matchless valor had won through the blood and carnage of a thousand battle-fields. He lived, through all the storm of war, to see, at last, America rejuvenated, rescued from the grasp of despotism, and rise victorious, with her garments purified and her brow radiant with the unsullied light of liberty. He lived to greet the return of "meek-eyed peace," and then he gently laid his head upon her bosom, and breathed out there his noble spirit.

The sword may rust in its scabbard, and so let it; but free men, with free thought and free speech, will wage unceasing war until truth shall be enthroned and sit empress of the world. Would to God that he had been spared to complete a life of threescore and ten years, for the sake of his country and posterity. When I think of the good he would have accomplished had he survived for twenty years, I can say, in the language of Fisher Ames, "My heart, penetrated with the remembrance of the man, grows liquid as I speak, and I could pour it out like water."

At the portals of his tomb we may bid farewell to the faithful Christian, in the full assurance that a blessed life awaits him beyond the grave. Serenely and trustfully he has passed from our sight and gone down into the dark waters.

> "So sinks the day-star in the ocean bed,
> And yet anon repairs his drooping head,
> And tricks his beams, and with new-spangled ore
> Flames in the forehead of the morning sky."

From this hall, where as scholar, statesman, and orator he shone so brightly, he has disappeared forever. Never again will he, answering to the roll-call from this desk, respond for his country and the rights of man. No more shall we hear his fervid eloquence in the day of imminent peril, invoking us, who hold the mighty power of peace and war, to dedicate ourselves, if need be, to the sword, but to accept no end of the conflict save that of absolute triumph for our country. He has gone to answer the great roll-call above, where the "brazen throat of war" is voiceless in the presence of the Prince of Peace. Let us habitually turn to his recorded words, and gather wisdom as from the testament of a departed sage; and since we were witnesses of his tireless devotion to the cause of human freedom, let us direct that on the monument which loving hearts and willing hands will soon erect over his remains, there shall be deeply engraved the figure of a bursting shackle as the emblem of the faith in which he lived and died.

For the Christian, scholar, statesman, and orator, all good men are mourners; but what shall I say of that grief which none can share—the grief of sincere friendship?

Oh, my friend! comforted by the belief that you, while living, deemed me worthy to be your companion, and loaded me with the proofs of your esteem, I shall fondly treasure, during my remaining years, the recollection of your smile and counsel. Lost to me is the strong arm whereon I have so often leaned; but in that path which in time past we trod most joyfully together, I shall continue, as God shall give me to see my duty, with unfaltering though perhaps with unskillful steps, right onward to the end.

Admiring his brilliant intellect and varied acquirements, his invincible courage and unswerving fortitude, glorying in his good works and fair renown, but, more than all, *loving the man*, I shall endeavor to assuage the bitterness of grief by applying to him those words of proud, though tearful satisfaction, from which the faithful Tacitus drew consolation for the loss of that noble Roman whom he delighted to honor:

"Quidquid ex Agricola amavimus, quidquid mirati sumus, manet mansurumque est, in animis hominum, in æternitate temporum, fama rerum."

SPEECHES AND ADDRESSES

OF

HENRY WINTER DAVIS.

A PLEA FOR THE COUNTRY AGAINST THE SECTIONS.

Mr. DAVIS was elected, in November, 1855, by the American party, from the fourth district of Maryland, to the Thirty-fourth Congress, and commenced his service there on the 3d of December following.

So soon as the House met began that memorable contest for the election of Speaker, which continued from that day till the 2d of February, 1856, when, upon the hundred and thirty-third vote (being the fourth after the adoption of the plurality rule, on motion of Mr. S. A. Smith, of Tennessee), Mr. Banks, of Massachusetts, was declared to be elected. Throughout all those votes Mr. Davis steadily refused to support any of the candidates named by either the Democratic or Republican parties, and persistently voted for Mr. Fuller, of Pennsylvania, upon the final and decisive roll-call, when his colleagues from Maryland passed over to the support of Mr. Aiken, of South Carolina, then the Democratic candidate. During that long struggle, the gentlemen named for that place were interrogated as to their political views and opinions, and their intentions in regard to the organization of the House. As the candidates of the two great parties had declined or evaded the questions, a resolution was proposed on the 11th of January "that it was the duty of all candidates for political position frankly and fully to state their opinions upon important political questions involved in their election, and especially when interrogated by the body of electors whose votes they are seeking." In giving their votes upon this resolution (adopted by one hundred and fifty-five to thirty-eight), many of the members made short statements of their reasons therefor. In so doing, Mr. Davis first invited the House to hear him in such manner as to command its marked attention, and to confirm among the members the impression as to his powers which had preceded him there.

Mr. Davis was named, although this was his first term of service, on the Committee of Ways and Means; and his first speech in the House was delivered on the 12th of March, 1856, upon a resolution reported from the Committee of Elections, in the contested election case from the Territory of Kansas, empowering that committee to send for persons and papers. The argument was confined to the points of parliamentary practice, due order of proceeding, and to the questions of administration of political law. It may be found reported in the *Congressional Globe*, vol. xli., p. 227; and as it did not refer, except incidentally, to the political condition of the country, it has not been thought proper to be included in this collection. During the same session he also took some part in the discussions in regard to the proposed amendment of the Naturalization Laws (March 25), the Election Bill for the District of Columbia, the Deficiency Bill, the bill for the remission of duties on goods destroyed (in warehouse) by fire, and the Civil and Legislative Appropriation Bills.

The three great political parties, American, Democratic, and Republican, had now (July, 1856) nominated Mr. Fillmore, Mr. Buchanan, and Mr. Fremont as their respective candidates for the Presidency. The election was to be held in November. The country was excited to the highest degree. In the Southern States threats of revolution and secession were openly made; and secret meetings of the governors of those states were held, at which measures were concerted for joint action and a separate confederacy in case of the election of Mr. Fremont. The Congress was about to rise, after a most protracted and excited session. The bitterness and exasperation of party feeling was daily increasing; it had shown itself not only in violent recrimination and abusive language in debate, but in disgraceful scenes of personal violence on the floor of the House. The members were anxious to return to their homes, and to begin there the work of stirring up anew the passions and prejudices of each section for the great contest in November.

It was when this feeling had nearly reached its height, and under such a condition of affairs, that Mr. Davis, in the evening session of the House on the 7th of August, 1856 (the House being in Committee of the Whole on the State of the Union), spoke as follows:

"Is Philip dead? No, by Jove! but he is sick." Such was the chatter of the factious demagogues of Athens, chilled by the shadow of the coming Cheronea.

Will Fillmore decline? "No; but he is too weak to get a single state!" say Democrat and Republican, shivering before the blast of the coming November.

Mr. Chairman, they consult prophets who prophesy pleasant things. Their hopes are the oracles speaking by the inspiration of their interests; and yet, while they trust to the prophecy to produce its accomplishment, they confidentially sigh, "Would it were bedtime, Hal, and all well!" That bedtime will surely come, but whether the couch of victory or the bed of death be spread—ah! that's the question. Sir, a party at brag and bluff is a suspicious witness to the goodness of his own hand, and the bystanders, I believe, do not usually regard him as a better witness of the badness of his adversary's.

If Democrat and Republican have conspired together to play by-bidder at each other's mock auction—to put off on the country plated brass for gold—the people will have the sagacity to see that, though *Liberty* be on one side, the image and superscription of the *Union* is not on the other, and the lacking weight will reveal the counterfeit.

I desire to make this discrimination. I wish to inquire into the weight of this style of brag, which has, to my poor understanding, exhausted the resources of opponents.

Say the Democrats, "Do not vote for Mr. Fillmore, because he can not get a single state at the North." Say the Republicans, "Do not vote for Mr. Fillmore, because he can not get a single state at the South." And both are so simple as to suppose, by thus excluding him from the regions of their opponents, that they have finally dealt with his pretensions.

Why is it that two parties, as wide apart as the southern and northern poles, have conspired together, in this significant and novel way, for the purpose of denying to their most dangerous opponent strength in the regions where the adversary of each is strong? There are two organized parties in this country which claim to represent adverse local interests. The Democratic party rests itself on its boasted and self-arrogated privilege of supporting and sustaining the peculiar institution of the South. Its strength, and its whole strength, consists in its assertion that it alone is the defender of Southern rights. It is therefore dangerous to them for any thing to arise within the limits of the South, and claim a hearing from the Southern people, which touches more nearly the rights of the people, and appeals to the more elevated and noble sentiments of devotion to the Constitution and the Union. The gentlemen of the Republican party of the North aspire to represent that sentiment which is likewise local and peculiarly confined to the boundary of the North, and having no power beyond it. They likewise are jealous of the intrusion on their domain of any topic of such stirring interest as will call the minds of the North away from the contemplation of the perpetual cry, "Freedom is national, and slavery is sectional;" "The rights of man;" "The oppressions of the South;" "The equality of the negro race."

All these minister to the excitement in the North. They are subjects in themselves neither interesting nor attractive—not so interesting or attractive but that an appeal to the great interests of the country, the great fundamental principles of the Constitution, to the great danger of the agitation of these topics, may possibly reach the ear of the most besotted, and startle the reason of those who are still rational, that they whose talk is of negroes, and who think that the servants at the altar should live of the altar, may find themselves preaching to empty benches. One, therefore, and the other, each within his own region, seeks to drive out every thing that may sow wheat among his tares. They may touch any thing else but these rights of sovereignty; but put forth your hand and touch them in the very body of their power, and they arise and curse you to your face.

The Democrat is jealous of any thing which impeaches the high duty of extending *the institution*, and is impatient of men who accept it as an existing institution, to be protected as any other industrial interest is to be protected.

The Republican tolerates no man who questions the practical honesty of the higher law, and suggests the conscientious duty of conformity to the practical enforcement of the Constitution. Both cry out "No compromise;" both execrate all adherence to the existing condition of affairs as wisest and best. Each boasts conquests in the future over his antagonist; each lives, and moves, and has its being in an atmosphere confined to its own region; it can not breathe a moment the air on which the other thrives. Neither has any representative in the region of its adversary to soften their antagonism. They are both strictly sectional parties, tending to bring into collision hostile opinions, feelings, and interests, concentrated without mixture at the opposite poles of the country; each intensified, like opposite electricities, by the intensity of the other, and threatening, if brought into contact, an explosion that may shake the foundations of the republic. Each knows that, unless it can keep exclusive control of the whole region, there is no hope of triumph or even of a collision.

In this lies at once their strength and their weakness. Unless Mr. Buchanan can carry the whole South, and trust—not to party discipline, for that has died away, but—to the chance of the bribe of high office to persons in the North to make up the deficiency of the Southern vote, they have not the most remote prospect of succeeding in carrying him to the presidential chair; and our Republican friends on the other side, with equal reason, based on equally notorious facts, know, if the State of New York is stricken from them, they are a powerless minority out of doors, and that no nominee of theirs can darken the doors of the White House. It is, therefore, not because of their *strength*, but because of their *weakness*, that the one and the other seek to produce the impression which it is possible, and in charity ought to be conceded, each believes, but which it is difficult for men who, like myself, hold a moderate and middle position, not to regard in a very different light. It is for this reason that each party, deluded into the idea that it is enthroned in the exclusive control of its own sectional interest and its own sectional power, attempts the vain task of persuading the country that a man like Mr. Fillmore, resplendent with the glories of a great administration, which appeals to those pervading and national considerations which wake responses in the hearts of the people, must be left in the insignificant minority of a few rational men of the North and the South.

Mr. Chairman, long lists of names have been paraded of new converts to Mr. Buchanan. Letters have been spread before the public, urging arguments with all the authority of names entitled to the profound respect of the House and the country. I know in these lists, whether they relate to Maryland or elsewhere, of no man who, at the fall election, earnestly supported the American cause. I see, in most of them, neophytes of Democracy, those hardened sinners against its benign rule who were baptized last fall, whose tender faith has been duly instructed by the sponsors at their baptism, and whose public and formal declaration now is nothing but the ceremony of confirmation to the world of their earlier conversion. There is nothing in that list which need shake the confidence of the American party. There is nothing which makes the scale of Mr. Fillmore vacillate for a single instant in its inclination in the State of Maryland. There is nothing that in the slightest degree increases the difficulty of repeating, with larger majorities and greater éclat, the triumph of the past year. But, sir, I rise to test the argument thus supported by great names and widespread authority. We are not to vote for Fillmore because a *majority* at the North are opposed to his wise and patriotic administration — so runs the reason; because the *majority* of the North are not favorable to compromise and conciliation—so runs the reason; because the *majority* of the North regard the time as come when they must get a scourge for the South; because the *majority* of the North are of that opinion, therefore, in this contest, which they superciliously assume is to be between the Northern and the Southern candidates, all men must desert the candidate who is alone the candidate of the Constitution and the Union. The argument is hollow and insidious. If the *majority* of the North be such, *then the time for voting is past.* It is no longer a question whether we will vote for Fillmore or Buchanan as President of the United States, because the South is in a pitiable minority in the electoral college, and every vote cast there leaves her where she is, and without the power of self-protection. If the hour of madness be come; if reason be dead in her chosen seat; if the conservative North has ceased to be conservative, and is inspired by the hatred this argument ascribes to her people, then we have no election on the 4th of November for President of the *United* States. Mr. Buchanan will be ineligible as a foreigner to rule the South. We have passed by the time of the election of that man whose name is to close the fasti of that illustrious line.

The people of 1852 divined well that they were choosing the Honorius of the republic, and fitted the man to the station. The argument proves too much, if it is true. If it is not true, it is trash.

But the argument is put into a different shape, and pointed directly at Mr. Fillmore. His merits are made his incapacities. His truth to the Union is made the reason why Southern gentlemen, for whom he ran the greatest risk against the opinion of his own region of country, are to turn against him;—desert him, for a man who has encountered nothing for them or for the Union. The majority of the North are opposed to Mr. Fillmore because of *his wise and patriotic administration.* They will then vote for Buchanan because his administration will not be so wise and patriotic. They are opposed to Fillmore because they are opposed to conciliation and compromise. They will vote for Mr. Buchanan because he and his party have said, "No more compromise, and no more conciliation." They will not vote for Fillmore because they want a scourge for the South. Unwittingly the argument pictures the result of that policy which our Democratic friends have inaugurated and followed out to its bitter end. The majority of the Northern allies of the Democrats are supposed very likely to vote for Buchanan because he *will be a scourge to the South.* If that be not the argument, then the argument is unmeaning.

Well, if that be the foundation of the argument, will not gentlemen who appreciate the force of reasoning cease to use it? Will they not give some better reason why Mr. Fillmore can get no strength at the North?

Will they not say, "Come, let us reason together;" and say that Mr. Buchanan better respects the great fundamental principle of the Constitution, and not base their argument on the revolutionary assumption that the majority of the men of the free states are run mad against the men of the South? It is very tempting, I know, to Southern Democrats. If the majority of the North are madly bent on punishing the South, they will pass Mr. Fillmore by, and inflict on it Mr. Buchanan as the more cruel scourge. The argument is good, sir; the fact on which it rests is not true.

Far different is my estimate of my Northern brethren. I am not aware of any acts of the North, as they appear upon our statute-books, or as executed from the executive chamber, however wild may have been the votes occasionally of a majority upon this floor, or however dangerous the arguments pressed into their support, which in the slightest degree has sullied the honor or injured the interest of the South. They have differed upon industrial questions, and decided them by party tactics; they have been set one against the other in party manœuvre, party triumph and domination; but I say that, during the eighty years of the republic, there is no portion of this great land which has reason to cast into the teeth of either the North or the South that any great right of either section has been trampled down—any great right of the Constitution deliberately violated—any fact showing that madness rules the majority either at the North or at the South.

But there is a solemn fact which my Democratic friends admit. There is *hostility* at the North. They adroitly point it at the South. *They vainly strive to place the South between themselves and the shaft that has already smitten them to the earth.* There is wrath boiling up at the North, but it is a wrath which boils against *them.* There is a hostility at the North, but it is a hostility which *they* have aroused, which has stricken *them* down, and will keep them *down.*

I wish to feel the pulse of the North to-night; I wish to see whether there be reason or madness throbbing there; whether it be the rational wrath of men who believe they have been outraged in their dearest rights, or whether it be the madness of men who have flashed into fury causelessly.

Sir, there are a series of great facts which strike us wheresoever we turn our eyes. In 1853, the present incumbent of the presidential chair was elevated on the shields of twenty-seven states, and borne to the White House amid the acclamations of an exultant people, rejoicing in the advent of an era of peace. Three suns have run their course, and now "he is at supper; not where he eats, but where he is eaten; for a certain body of politic worms are e'en at him." When he ascended the chair of state, a great majority of seventy in this House obsequiously awaited his will. The sun had not thrice run his course ere that majority had shriveled to seventy-four men. Their place knows them no more. This side of the House is a charnel-house of dead Democrats. The few survivors tread mournfully as they pass it—as a Roman might walk over Cannæ. "The bloody ghost of the murdered Wright" still to the eye of the gentleman from Georgia (Mr. Cobb) disputes the stool with his successor of flesh and blood (Mr. Fuller); and many other spectres have left untimely graves to warn the pale survivors of their fate.

My honorable friend from South Carolina was early at the sepulchres of the righteous in New Hampshire, vainly seeking signs of the day of the resurrection of the body; but the snow still lay on the marble. The crocus of the early spring had not pushed itself through the frozen soil, and he returned chanting sadly,

> "A cold, deceitful thing is the snow,
> Though it come on dove-like wing.
> The false snow,
> 'Tis but rain disguised appears,
> And our hopes are frozen tears—
> Like the snow."

Indeed, sir, the resurrection of the Democratic party at the North is an event not at all anticipated there. It has sunk from view, like water spilled upon the ground, not to be gathered again.

A stubborn resolution has been manifested at the North. Since that great day there has been nothing which shows that my honorable friends on the Democratic side of the house have a majority in one single state north of Mason and Dixon's line. There is not one single fact that shows that they can carry a state north of Mason and Dixon's line on national politics even on a plurality. The account of loss and gain stands as a set-off. If, in Pennsylvania, Democrats, and Whigs, and Americans have combined to elect a canal commissioner by a plurality only, in Maine Democrats and liquor-men have united, and carried a local election by a plurality. In New Hampshire and Connecticut the Americans have carried the local elections by pluralities. If New Jersey has given a Democratic majority in a local election, California has come to the Americans by a large majority.

The faithful fondly hoped that some of these elections indicated a change of tide. They forgot that Falstaff "parted just between twelve and one, e'en at turning of the tide." If there be any compunctions of conscience forcing them to cry out, "God! God! God!" let them beware of those Dame Quicklys who, to comfort them, bid them not think of God, and hope there is no need to trouble themselves with such thoughts yet; for when the parting Falstaff so cried and was so comforted, and had more clothes laid on his feet, the comforter, Dame Quickly, knew there was but one way; and when she had put her hand into the bed and felt his feet, they were cold as any stone; and then she felt to his knees, and so upward and upward, and all was cold as any stone.

Sir, the fatal hour has come. Even while I speak the stricken field of Iowa brings to them defeat and disaster, crushed hopes and cruel disappointment. Their feet are already cold in the North, and we feel upward, and upward, and upward toward their head in the South—all is cold as any stone. 'Tis vain to ask for more clothes on the feet, for their passing bell is already tolling that men may pray for the parting soul. But, sir, they are not without consolation. There are true Bardolphs, who, when told of their death, will exclaim, "Would I were with them, wheresoever they be—either in heaven or in hell." Now, sir, why is all this? We need no election statistics for the response. They were the triumphant and dominant party at the North ere this great flood. None so sound, none so unshaken, none so true to defend the South through thick and thin, at all hazards and to the last extremity, as the Democrats of the North. Where are they gone? "Are they asleep, or on a journey, or at a feast?" or have they forgotten their duty, or have they become mad? or have they played like children, casting one vote for my honorable friend and another for their honorable opponents?

Sir, the American people have been bred in American habits. They are not in the habit of capricious and causeless change. I mean to speak the *cause* of that change out loud. It is *the repeal of the Missouri Compromise, the enactment of the Kansas-Nebraska Act, and the outrages in the Territory of Kansas*, denied or defended by my honorable Democratic friends. They were here warned by the honorable senator from Illinois, who reported that measure, *in his first report against it*, of the dangerous consequences, and they would not heed the warning. In an evil day for his reputation, he allowed himself to be overcome by party and personal ambition, and to be deluded by the hopes of party domination. He allowed himself to be deluded by the supposition that he could bring to the support of that measure the great body of Southern men, Whigs and Democrats, and that the temporary excitement would only raise the froth upon the surface, while the depths of the ocean would roll on in their sluggish sleep. Sir, he cast a javelin into the cave of Æolus, and all the winds of strife have rushed forth across the ocean and cast up a tempest which leaves of the Democratic party nothing but scattered and broken fragments, cast on the shores for the wreckers to collect, and, as they measure the dimensions of mast and spar, to wonder what great admiral it was that has gone down in that terrific sea. Sir, is not that the reason? I do not ask gentlemen to tell me whether it is an adequate reason. I do not ask gentlemen to say if the North is reasonable in its anger. I simply ask gentlemen, upon their candor and honor, if that is not *the reason of the existing condition of things?* There is no gentleman here whose heart does not echo that it is; and I venture little when I say there is scarcely one of my Democratic friends who can appreciate the position in which it has placed them, who does not from the bottom of his heart curse the day on which he was so misled. If they adhere still to the Kansas-Nebraska Act, it is from necessity, and not from choice. My honorable friends, finding themselves at the bottom of the water, have, like Cooper's sailor in the Western lake, seized a root to keep themselves there. It is from necessity, and not from choice, that, with a millstone around their necks, they march down to the water for a swimming-match with light men having floats on.

Why, sir, what are their apologies—their *apologies to the North*, their apologies to *their Democratic friends, whom they have slain*, murdered, and sent to the land of ghosts, for whose absence my friend from Georgia weeps? The Missouri Compromise, say they, was unconstitutional. "But since when?" say the North to them. That does not rest well, gentlemen, in your mouths, for it was a Democratic majority that passed it. It was the great men of the Democratic party, and, more than all others, the great Marylander, William Pinckney, who proposed, and advocated, and carried that great measure of healing in that day. The great argument which he addressed to vindicate the *sovereignty of a state* from the binding control of conditions imposed by Congress, is the argument, misunderstood, broken into small fragments suitable to the strength and stature of those who use them, and misapplied now by gentlemen to disprove the power of Congress to pass the very Missouri restriction *on a Territory*, which he all along advocated at the very time of that great argument, and incorporated into the very act which is his triumphal monument to the peace which he conquered and perpetuated by it; and Mr. Monroe, *their President*, signed it—signed it, not hastily, but after consulting his cabinet, in which was Mr. Calhoun, on the precise question of constitutionality. Is that long ago? Has wisdom arisen in a later generation? Have new lights been discovered in the Constitution? Have judicial decisions cleared away the difficulty?

It was in 1845 when the great *Democratic measure was passed* by which Texas was annexed to this Union; and my honorable friends, or their predecessors, then in a majority in both branches of Congress, passed the Texas resolution, which enacted the *very thing* against which Pinckney directed the argument which they now make the arsenal for weapons to assail what he advocated. They cast their votes for it, and President Tyler on the 3d of March signed it. "Oh, but Tyler was not a Democrat." Yes, but he was, by conversion, or perversion, or treachery, or desertion; he was by acceptance and adoption; he was by his cabinet and his administration; he was doubly so by the presence and counsel of Calhoun, the incarnation of the very idea of Southern strict construction; and it is understood that the resolutions came down from the secretary of state, who was *Mr. Calhoun*—that it was his influence which dispatched the resolutions to Texas for acceptance on the last day of President Tyler's term; and Mr. Polk, though on the spot, did not recall them.

That resolution declares that all the territory south of 36° 30′, whenever Texas should be divided, should come into the Union, with or without slavery, as the states may determine, and *that in such state or states* (I ask gentlemen to bear the word *state* in mind)—in those *states* which shall be formed out of the Texan territory as lies north of 36° 30′—in those *states* (I wish the word to burn itself into their seared consciences; it is *the thing* which was in issue in the Missouri struggle; it was the only thing which was there disputed; it is *the thing* which was decided in the Missouri controversy in favor of the South to be an unconstitutional limitation on the *sovereign equality of the states*)—in those states which shall be formed of the territory north of that line, slavery and involuntary servitude *shall be prohibited;* and James Buchanan was one of the Democratic majority who advocated and passed it.

Time rolled on, and another Territory was to be organized. Again, with that remarkable luck which has followed them—which has misled them to their deep undoing—they had the majority in this hall; they had a majority in both branches of the councils of the nation when the Territory of Oregon was to be organized; and again that majority adopted that restriction—word for word—the ordinance of 1787. Again a Democratic President, Mr. Polk, signed it, and not merely so signed, but with a farther declaration, not that he expected *this to be the last of it*—not merely that slavery was there impossible or improbable, but on the expectation *that it would be again passed by that or another Congress, adopted, and incorporated into the acts for the settlement of the Mexican conquests!*

I neither affirm the correctness or the incorrectness of this view. I simply urge the *fact* which Northern Democrats pleaded against the Southern Democrats.

But, said my honorable friends upon the Democratic side of this hall to their friends from the North—for *there* is where the defection arose; *there* is where the strength of the Republican party comes from—out of their own side came that portentous creation whence comes this sin and all our woe into our happy world. "We say that we have reversed all that, and those laws and compromises are void by reason of *being inconsistent with the compromise* measures of 1850. Those measures have repealed it." "Ah! but," said their Northern Democratic friends, continuing their remonstrance, "the law which organized the boundary of Texas declared in so many words that nothing therein contained should be construed to repeal or modify any thing contained in that very clause of the Texas resolutions."

These Northern Democrats still farther mercilessly press their Democratic brethren, as if to leave my honorable friends on my left no escape from the most awkward of dilemmas. If it be true that the principle of popular sovereignty was settled by the compromise measures of 1850, how came it to be omitted in the legislation of 1853, since the acts of 1850 were enacted? The Congress of 1853, with a great Democratic majority, organized the Territory of Washington out of a territory over which the ordinance of 1787 had been *by them* in 1848 extended; and that Congress, in the year of grace 1853, and of the era of the new dispensation of the 3d, not merely failed to remove that restriction, but declared that the laws of Oregon should be enforced in the Territory of Washington, *which laws included slavery by special enactment*, in flagrant conflict with the principles which they now declare to have been the very vital principle embodied in and pervading the acts of 1850. You know as well as we do that these compromise measures of 1850 have always been regarded and treated as *a finality*—the end of controversy; that this last compromise, this great compromise of 1850, was settled on the basis of *all the preceding compromises.*

On the assumption and the concession, as stated by Mr. Webster, that every foot of territory in the United States was finally settled by laws irrepealable, and that it was only on that supposition that the laws of 1850 became laws at all, only last session you passed a bill creating a government over all the territory now embraced in the Kansas and Nebraska Act, without opposition, merely by common consent; and no man of any party discovered, or, if he had discovered, revealed, still less attempted to declare the novel dogma of a latent principle, not even *expressed* in an act, being effectual to annul another law enacted on another principle. From argument they passed to entreaty and pathetic appeal. These thirty years we have lived under this law; it has injured no man. No Southern state protested against its enactment; none in 1850 demanded its repeal; many Southern men pressed its extension to the Pacific; no Southern state now demands it; no tempest agitates the popular mind which its repeal can quiet; no great national necessity compels the statesman, in the high election between evils, to tread this untrod path. You say your object is not a new slave state; then let it be as it is. You say the Northern tide of emigration will insure its freedom. Then why do the nugatory act of repealing a law which changes no result? Why disturb the peace of the country by this wound inflicted on the prejudices of your Northern brethren? Deliver us not over into the hands of the Abolitionists. They are ever watchful to rebel against the overthrow of 1850. We stood by you then; will you BETRAY US NOW?

Well, sir, this bill passed, I come to the deplorable sequel: it was an invitation for all the elements of strife to concentrate in Kansas. The executive, representing the combined factions of both North and South, ought to have been doubly careful to have taken some man from the North or South who was far above suspicion, strong to resist solicitations, strong to repel menaces, magnanimously above private, personal, and pecuniary considerations. He could have taken such a man as my friend from Oregon (Mr. Lane), now in my eye. They should have taken a man with nerve enough not to be frightened by threats or menaces, and honest enough not to be moved by promises. They should have taken a man who knew of border life, with military experience enough to set a battalion in the field—whose head would not be dizzy at the flash of steel—who would have said to all invaders—emissaries of aid societies or marauders from the Missouri border—"Pass not hither;" who would have seen that the great tourney between the champions of freedom and of slavery was fairly fought, with equal wind and sun, and a truncheon swayed by no partiality. There are men within the sound of my voice, of that party, who would have cut off their right hand rather than allow the violent overthrow of a law they were ordered to execute—whose cheek would burn with shame at the unchecked insolence with which Governor Reeder's authority was derided or eluded; men who would have bitten out their tongues ere they made the confessions poured by Governor Reeder into the President's ear, or, hearing them, would have held a parley with the confessor, proposed honorable banishment on a foreign mission to coax a faithful but obnoxious instrument out of the way, to avoid the scandal of a public dismissal, and the greater scandal of a confession of blunders worse than crimes, and weakness worse than wickedness.

If there were no such men within the party, it is unfit to guide the destinies of the country; and if there were, then are they thrice unworthy to hold a power they have so grossly abused. Sir, that scene in the executive mansion—the proconsul of the President narrating that he let the life-blood of the province he ruled run unavenged and unstanched, the very flowers of her franchises be trampled down at the sacred ballot-box, marauders from either pole run a muck over her peaceful population, himself buried to the eyes and ears in private speculations in public lands over which he ruled of questionable legality and of unquestionable evil example, and deaf to the cry of helpless agony that rang through his domain, content to leave his people to their enemies, if the protector and the President could agree on the color to be put on the scandal and adjust the division of the responsibility, confessing these things to the President of the republic, and that President driving a bargain for a foreign mission instead of instant and ignominious expulsion from office, and the negotiation failing, dismissing him gently for illegal speculation, silent as the tomb to the civil war that he allowed to rage, the outraged law he failed to avenge, the rights of suffrage violated with impunity, and the yoke of a legislation born in violence and fraud by his judgment fastened on the necks of American freemen—these things, established by a vast mass of resistless testimony, form a new and melancholy chapter in the history of the republic.

Sir, the party whose policy, however well intended, has given occasion to stain the American name with civil blood by the repeal of the Missouri Compromise, is not likely to stand well with the men of the North, whose brethren have been the sufferers. Their denial of the outrages, their extenuations, their apologies, day after day, in this House, till the stupendous mass of the committee's evidence overwhelmed them, and their cavils at the evidence—to my judgment unimpeached, and, if so, of crushing weight—scarcely tends to improve the odor of the Democratic party in the Northern nostrils. That is my opinion of the result of the Kansas investigation: I dare not impute perjury to men by the hundred; the concurrence of so many is itself conclusive against the hypothesis of fabrication; and I must be pardoned if my legal habits will not allow me to weigh partisan denials against testimony sworn in the face of cross-examination. I make no plea for some strained or one-sided inferences which my friend from Ohio has drawn from that evidence. I tender no apology for the one-sided results drawn by my friend from Missouri. I am here, sir, for no party. I am speaking this day for the Constitution and the Union; I am pleading for the great rights of American citizens; I am pleading for the honor and integrity of the American government and the American name. I will set down no word in malice that would tinge the honor of the country, or hide one dark trait which the people of the country ought to know. The reason that the North is opposed to the Democratic party is that *they* have done *these things*.

Now, sir, perhaps we begin to see why the Northern people will not support Mr. Buchanan. Why will they not support him? Why will not the Conservative vote be given for him?—for there is a Conservative majority. They will not vote for the Democratic party, or for the Democratic nominee, because they have been guilty of these things. They will not vote for them because they have never repented in sackcloth and ashes. They will not vote for them because they have denied the wrongs before the proof, and defended them after the proof. They will not vote for them because they have reiterated the insult. They will not vote for them because they have blazoned on their banner the very words of the ambiguous oracle of the Kansas-Nebraska Act, the very cause and declaration of war, now no longer deluding any one, but plainly, and in bloody letters, interpreted on the fields of Kansas.

These are reasons they think sufficient, and they are likely to continue to think them sufficient. If Mr. Fillmore were in that position they would not vote for him. Ay, sir, even a conservative Northern man, tempted by a spirit of revenge and retaliation, would have to argue with himself a long time before he could bring himself down to vote for this man, who has outraged all the feelings with which these men have been brought up. The best and most conservative of them—thousands of degrees from abolitionism — men who are supporting the Constitution and the Union—men who are willing to support and defend the institution of slavery—men like those of Boston, who execute the Fugitive Slave Law, marched down the streets of that city with loaded arms to shoot down their own citizens, that you, men of the South, might be protected—these are the men you have driven from you. Where will they go if Mr. Fillmore were not offered to them as the symbol of peace?

Sir, I put it to my honorable friends to apply to them the arguments they hold valid at the South. The Northern men are of like passions with us, moved by insult, not above revenge, and not given to prefer, in a sectional contest, the candidate of their opponents. My Democratic friends from every hustings in the South exhort the people to vote for Mr. Buchanan *because he is the Southern candidate*—because he is for the *Kansas-Nebraska Act*—because he is *against compromise* in a Southern sense—because he is the *strongest man opposed to the Northern sectional candidate;* and by this sort of argument they admit that the sectional candidate at the North represents the same class of men at the North that they represent at the South—men who are no more unreasonable in a Northern than they in a Southern sense. As they appeal to the South, so do the men who support Mr. Fremont appeal to the North. Gentlemen of the Democratic party, *judge ye how far* they are entitled to weight. Are they conclusive? Do they compel me to yield my political preferences? Is it right that I shall go for Mr. Buchanan? Am I bound to bow the knee to him? Is it so desperate a case that I must stomach the slurs and imputations which were hurled on me and the American party during two or three months of this session? Shall I, for these considerations of a merely sectional character, because he is, as you say, the candidate of my section, abandon those who stood by us? I pray you to recall to your memories, and weigh well the obloquy cast on the American party. We were, you say, an unconstitutional party—yea, the very enemies of the Constitution. We were opposed to civil and religious liberty; we were for depriving men of equal rights; we were for driving the honest foreigners from our shores; we were midnight assassins, stained with the blood and dirt of riotous mobs; we had taken unconstitutional oaths not to obey the Constitution; we could not be touched in the speaker's contest; no compromise could be made with us; no exchange of candidates could be thought of for a moment. The honorable gentleman from Pennsylvania (Mr. Fuller), who better accords with their notions on slavery, in theory and in practice, than the honorable member from Illinois, so long their candidate, could not be touched. The very meeting in Convention—the very meeting in caucus—ay, sir, the very meeting for open consultation, was scorned, and flung back in our faces. They could not touch such political lepers. A plurality rule was an alternative they preferred, knowing the consequences of the vote would be to place the present speaker in the chair.

Such was their conduct to us—so conciliatory, so amiable, so loving, so winning; yet, in the face of this rough wooing, they urge us, *because of our connection with the South*, to abandon Mr. Fillmore, the choice of our hearts, for Mr. Buchanan, because Mr. Buchanan is the safe and strong man for the South, the *representative of Southern interests.* So intensely did they hate us—so much more did they hate us than the gentleman from Massachusetts (the speaker); yet so paramount do they regard the allegiance to the sectional candidate that they ask us to sacrifice our personal preferences, our political connections, our outraged dignity, for *their* triumph.

Be it so. Is that the intensity of their sectional devotion? I ask them to apply the argument north of Mason and Dixon's line, and tell me who, if he is not utterly abandoned and degraded, can, under these circumstances, vote for that candidate who holds the position their candidate holds at the South, and toward the South. I make here no argument of my own. I take honorable gentlemen upon their principles. I commend to their lips the chalice they mixed and poisoned for mine, and I dare them to the task. I know that my friends, in rashness and in hot party strife, have done many things to endanger the Constitution. I do not believe they wish to elect Fremont; but, sir, if they had been bent directly on that purpose, no man could find out any manner which would more directly and more inevitably accomplish that result than that which has been pursued.

I wish to free it from all collateral issues, and put this one great argument before the country, so that there shall be an end; to get rid of Mr. Fillmore by this appeal to Southern prejudices, I wish to deal with that and nothing else to-night. I say, sir, if Mr. Fillmore be not supported by the South, the whole North, and every state of it, must and will, conservative men and madmen, vote for Mr. Fremont, by the very same reason that Southern Democrats urge to induce Southern gentlemen to abandon

Mr. Fillmore for Mr. Buchanan. There needs but these words to accomplish it: "Fillmore is deserted by the South he saved." That one line would be a quietus undoubtedly of this contest. Democrats must accept that result of their own reasoning. They claim every Southerner in the name of sectional interest. The Republicans will claim every Northern man in the name of Northern interests. If he must obey, they must obey. Is the North, will the Democrats admit, less excitable, less hostile than themselves? If not, the sectional feeling must press them at least equally. Will they be likely to listen more readily to reasons for Mr. Buchanan than Southern men to reasons for Mr. Fremont? Or will not *both* be more accessible to arguments for Mr. Fillmore than either? Do they suppose the Northern laborer to be less interested than the Southern planter in the question of free and slave labor? or is he more cool and unprejudiced, when his livelihood and personal dignity are involved, than the Southern planter, whose property only is affected?

The argument, therefore, must be abandoned, or it must be admitted as unquestionably true that the logical result is to drive the whole North, not into the arms of Mr. Buchanan, but into the arms of Mr. Fremont.

The Democratic party at the North has melted away into the Fremont party. They form its strength. They have done so because they were specially grieved by the use made of *their* representatives in the Kansas-Bill conflict. They had always been what in other people the Southern Democrats called Free Soil. That shone out in the remarks of the honorable gentleman from Ohio (Mr. Leiter), whose series of resolutions for fifteen years spoke the language—beginning in the Democratic Conventions and ending in the Republican Conventions—with a unity of sentiment and language defying the detection of the point where the Democrat shaded off into the Republican. It is for this reason that this blow has been so fatal to the Democratic party of the North—that the hatred of the North is so deadly against it, and yet is confined to it, and yet so sagaciously under control, so much of method in their madness, that they will not allow a chance to Mr. Buchanan of the election by pluralities, but will defeat that by any combination.

This view should determine the South to disentangle its cause from the fragments of the broken, powerless, and obnoxious Democrats. The Democratic party are no longer fit mediators between the North and South. How can they exact performance of the Texas Compromise? how protest against a repeal of the Fugitive Slave Law? how demand that the Wilmot Proviso be not extended to all the Territories? how claim the admission of more slave states? *Their* mouth is sealed on these topics before the revenge of the Republicans. By the law of retaliation, these things would be natural and just punishments to that party which has swept away the compromises and denied the principles on which all these rights rested. The Republican closes his mouth with the reply, "*You* (the Democratic party) have no right to appeal to us."

It is only in the name of the Southern people—of the men who do not join in the outrage—that these dire consequences can be surely avoided. The repudiation of the Democratic party is the first condition and best security for peace and safety. It silences the plea of revenge and retaliation. The people of the South owe it to themselves and to their future as completely to discard the Democrats as the people of the North have withdrawn from them their confidence.

But there are Democratic gentlemen who anticipate the success of the argument in driving every body to support Mr. Fremont, and who speculate on the consequences. There are men who go about the country declaiming about the inevitable consequences of the election of Mr. Fremont, and the question is asked whether that simple fact is not sufficient, not merely to justify, but to require a dissolution of the Union. The question has been asked of me to-day. That is a question which I do not regard as even a subject of discussion. It never will be done while men have their reason. It never will be done until some party, bent upon acquiring party power, shall again, and again, and again exasperate, beyond the reach of reason, Northern and Southern minds, as my Southern friends have now exasperated the Northern minds. It would be an act of suicide, and sane men do not commit suicide. The act itself is insanity. It will be done, if ever, in a tempest of fury and madness which can not stop to reason. Dissolution means death—the suicide of Liberty without the hope of resurrection—death without the glories of immortality, with no sister to mourn her fate, none to wrap her decently in her winding-sheet and bear her tenderly to her sepulchre—dead Liberty left to the horrors of corruption, a loathsome thing, with a stake through the body, which men shun, cast out naked on the highway of nations, where the tyrants of the earth, who feared her living, will mock her dead—passing by on the other side, wagging their heads and thrusting their tongue in their cheek at her, saying, Behold her! how she that was fair among nations is fallen! is fallen!—and only the few wise men who loved her, out of every nation, will shed tears over her body to quiet her manes, while we, her children, stumble about her ruined habitations, to find dishonorable graves wherein to hide our shame.

Dissolution! How shall it be? Who shall make it? Do men dream of Lot and Abraham parting, one to the east, one to the west, peacefully, because their servants strive? That states will divide from states, and boundary-lines will be marked by compass and chain? Sir, that will be a portentous commission that will settle that partition, for cannon will be planted at the corners, and grinning skeletons be finger-posts to point the way. It will be no line gently marked on the bosom of the republic—some meandering vein whence generations of her children have drawn their nourishment—but a sharp and jagged chasm, rending the hearts of great commonwealths, lacerated and smeared with fraternal blood.

On the night when the stars of her constellation shall fall from heaven, the blackness of darkness will settle on the liberties of mankind in this Western world. This is dissolution. If such, sir, is dissolution, as seen in a glass darkly, how terrible will it be face to face? They who reason about it are half crazy now; they who talk of it do not mean it, and dare not mean it.

They who speak in earnest of a dissolution of this Union seem to me like children or madmen. He who would do such a deed as that would be the maniac, without a tongue to tell his deed or reason to arrest his steps; an instrument of a mad impulse, impelled by one idea—to smite his victim. Sir, there have been maniacs who have been cured by horror at the blood they have shed.

Gentlemen ask, "If Mr. Fremont be elected, how will Maryland go? what will Maryland do?" I do not allow that question to be asked. She knows but one country and but one Union. Her glory is in it; her rights are bound up in it. Her children shed their blood for it, and they will do it again. Beyond it she knows nothing. She does not reckon whether there is more advantage in the Union to the North or to the South; she does not calculate its value; nor does she cast up an account of profit and loss on the blood of her children. That is my answer to that question. But, sir, it is portentous to hear the members of a party contesting for the presidency menace dissolution and revolution as the penalty they will inflict on the victors for defeating them. People who do not hold the Union worth four years' deprivation of office are scarcely safe depositaries of its powers.

But if these are to be the bloody consequences of a successful concentration of the Northern vote for Mr. Fremont, will not my Democratic friends, as the result of the argument, allow the moderate and conservative men of the North and South a chance to cling to those around who, being open to reason, yet doubt how they shall vote, and reiterate in their ears reasons why they should not drive this dangerous issue to a decision? They suppose that because, in the wreck of parties, they must go to the wall or to the bottom unless Mr. Fillmore can be gotten rid of, that which is necessary to save them is necessary to save the Union. "*We are the state;*" what is good for us, therefore, is good for the state, is their reasoning, and the Kansas Act and civil war is the conclusion. Self-love, party devotion, have misled them. Their safety and their success involve great danger to the republic, and in *their ruin lies the safety of the republic.*

Sir, they boast at the South, and it is their *Io triumphe*, that they have defeated and overthrown *abolition.* Is it from this great struggle, then, that the Democratic ranks are weak, and wan, and thin? Why, sir, the Abolition party fell beneath the blows of Millard Fillmore, leading the conservative men of all parties—the Clays, the Websters, the Footes, the Bentons of that great era of 1850, and was laid in a tomb inscribed with those acts, and bearing on its base the words *Millard Fillmore fecit. Their* leaders covered the journals of the Senate with their protests against those wise but obnoxious concessions which laid the evil spirit. But when the monster was overthrown and the field deserted, they dug up the dead body, and laid it at the feet of the South, and claimed their reward:

"Lo our trophy! lo our scalp! to you be the spoil of our sword and spear."

Why, sir, they "fought a long hour by Shrewsbury clock." When Prince Hal made Percy food for worms, Falstaff counterfeited death; and when the fight was over and the victor gone, Falstaff, thus soliloquizing—

"Zounds, I am afraid of this gunpowder Percy, though he be dead. Therefore I'll make him sure; yea, and I'll swear I killed him. Nothing confutes me but eyes, and nobody sees me"—

stabbed the dead body in the thigh, shouldered it, and cast it at the feet of the victor:

"There is Percy; if your father will do me any honor, so; if not, let him kill the next Percy himself. *I look to be either earl or duke, I can assure you.*"

The prince turned away, Falstaff following:

"I'll follow, as they say, for reward. He that rewards me, God reward him!"

Mr. Chairman, I have but a few words more to say. Whose cause am I pleading? I speak here in behalf of that vilified party, representing the great mass of the American people in revolt against the domination of effete parties, which is willing, irrespective of the chances of defeat or success, like its great leader, to devote itself to the Constitution and the Union. I am bound to see, and will see that contending factions do not make the *foreign vote* the balance of power in this country. I have resolved that, so far as in me lies, religion shall be banished from politics, and no man shall attempt to invoke the religious prejudices of any man. Sir, I will devote myself to weeding out these transactions, with the Secession party of the South, with the Abolition party of the North, with religious parties aspiring to political power, be they Methodist or Catholic, with foreign votes that can be bought, with the venal of all parties, who play the game of power with the interests of the people, and light the war of sectional interests that they may be sutlers to the camp. And whether we succeed to-day or not until to-morrow, time is for us, the future is ours. The young American cries the name of the American party, and imbibes its principles, in his earliest and pristine vigor. These sentiments will not die out for a generation, and in less than a generation the republic can be saved. I, sir, shall abide by that candidate who has been selected by this party to protect the interests of this country.

Between the candidates of rival factions I will not select. I can accept no statesman of twenty days, whose only principle is the forcing of the Topeka Constitution on the necks of the Kansas people, without pledges to the future for good behavior, or a past to read the future by. I marvel at my Republican friends, still smarting under the experience of what one unknown man may do, walking with their eyes open into the same trap. I can accept no man whose tortuous career touches alternately each extreme of the political sphere, his political life merged in a party platform, and chosen of the leader of the Democratic party to torment the North to madness, and to follow in the footsteps of this administration on the bloody ground of Kansas. I have no preference between two men who dispute the doubtful honor of applying the torch to the temple of the Constitution.

No law can quiet Kansas unless a soothing administration soften the exacerbated feelings of the people. With such an administration no law is needed. If Mr. Buchanan be elected, he will follow the bloody policy of this administration, whose sins and glories—Greytown, Ostend, Kansas, and all—decorate and oppress him. If Mr. Fremont be elected, he will be the hero of a counter-revolution, fierce and merciless as is the retaliation of the oppressed—the sport of fierce passions, to which he will owe his power, and which he can not and dare not control.

I shall, in this crisis, adhere to Millard Fillmore, who knows not where the South ends or the North begins, equally above fear or flattery, decorated with the glory of an illustrious administration, saluted "Pacificator" by the acclaim of the people, and now alone capable of restoring peace to this distracted land. He has been tried on each extreme of fortune. He has passed through the torrid zone of heady and tempestuous youth without excess; he has trod the temperate zone of matured manhood, where ambition burns with strongest flame, and reason stands ready to minister to its bidding, unswayed by any temptation; and now, near the close of a great career, in that last zone when the head is covered with the snows of many winters and the sun of reason knows no setting, when there is no mist to cloud the eye and no passion to lead astray the heart, the past of life is more than the future, temptation jeopards more than it can promise, and only posterity and the throne of God are before him, he can do justice in the face of temptation, and between contending factions who can not do justice to themselves. To him I shall adhere in every extremity. To him I summon my countrymen in the name of the Union he saved. And in this great issue I put myself on God and my country.

THE PRESIDENT'S MESSAGE (1856).—THE TEACHINGS OF THE LATE ELECTION.

MR. DAVIS took an active part in favor of Mr. Fillmore in the canvass preceding the election for President held in November, 1856, and which resulted in the choice of Mr. Buchanan. At the following (third) session of the Thirty-fourth Congress (December, 1856, to March, 1857) Mr. Davis was named on the Special Committee of Investigation into alleged corrupt practices of certain members, and took part in the House in the debates on the reports and conclusions of that Committee; on the bill to guard against corruption and corrupt practices in legislation, and on the bill to refund duties on goods destroyed in (United States) warehouses by fire. On the 6th of January, 1857, the question of referring the President's Message to the Committee of the Whole on the State of the Union being under consideration, Mr. Davis, of Maryland, said:

MR. SPEAKER,—Grave perplexities have arisen in interpreting the teachings of the late election. A singular diversity of views has been revealed. Gentlemen of the same party have differed as widely as those of opposite parties. The gradually widening circle of debate has drawn in great numbers on every side. As Democrat and Republican have been crippled in the conflict, fresh friends have poured in to the rescue; and the result of every addition has been that doubt has been piled upon doubt, confusion has become worse confounded, until he who attempts to read the recent election by the recent debate in this House will find himself with authorities for any opinion, with testimony for any fact, with views confounded and unintelligible, in endless mazes lost.

The gentlemen of the administration have exhibited some sensitiveness on the question who opened the debate. Wherever the responsibility rests, the great differences of opinion that it has elicited more than justify me, now that the debate has raged for weeks, in reviewing the field, summing up the results, and pointing the attention of the people to the great diversity with which the question they have decided, and the judgment they are supposed to have pronounced, has been interpreted. Sir, this discussion was not opened either by the gentleman from Ohio [Mr. Campbell] or by another gentleman in the other wing of the Capitol, now not far distant [Senator Wilson]. It originated neither in this House nor in the Senate. *Its first word is found in the President's Message.* He was justly fearful that the people might mistake their approval for a rebuke; that their unaided vision might not discover the comfort under the castigation, nor be quite aware that behind a frowning Providence they hid a smiling face; and therefore he wisely availed himself of his constitutional privilege to lead their tottering steps in the way he would have them go. So witless is the fling, that the vanquished have reopened a closed controversy!

Far be it from me to imitate the spirit which breathes through that extraordinary document. They only can fitly apologize for it who can estimate the bitterness of a spirit broken by such a fall! I do not care to open any controversy either with its statements, its reasonings, or its scoldings; but I may be allowed to use it for instruction, and the country to profit by its teachings. It reveals some facts of sinister import. The President first teaches us:

"That as senators represent their *respective* states, and members of the House of Representatives their *respective* constituencies in each of the states, *so the President represents the aggregate population of the United States!*"

Napoleon Bonaparte said to an insubordinate assembly, "You are only the deputies of single provinces—*I represent the nation!*" Thus to compare small things with great, our President respectfully assigns us our lower sphere, wherein we should behave not unseemly. Be it so, Mr. Speaker. Amid all the diversities, there is one fact which no one has controverted. It was fairly stated by the gentleman from Tennessee, and is apparent on every return of the aggregate vote. Mr. Buchanan ascends the chair of state against the will of a majority of about four hundred thousand of the people of the United States. If, therefore, the President represents the aggregate population of the Union, Mr. Buchanan does not represent, but misrepresents the people of the United States!

The President farther instructs us in what the people have decided in the election of Mr. Buchanan. "They have asserted," he says, "the constitutional equality of each and all of the states of the Union, *as states.*" He means that they who by their votes elected Mr. Buchanan, voted for that principle contested by their opponents, or he means nothing. If it has settled that principle, it proves *that a majority of the people of the United States are opposed to the equality of the states!*

"They have affirmed," says the President, "the constitutional equality of each and all of the citizens of the United States as citizens, whatever their religion, wherever their birth or their residence." If so, then it proves that a great majority of the people of the United States *deny the equality of the United States—deny their equality by reason of their religion*—deny their equality by reason of their residence—deny their equality by reason of their birth!

"They have asserted," says the President, "the inviolability of the constitutional rights of the different sections of the Union." Then a majority of the people of the United States have in the late contest been inimical to the constitutional rights of the states, and have been endeavoring to break them down!

The President farther informs us that "they have proclaimed their devoted and unalterable attachment to the Union and the Constitution, as objects of interest superior to all subjects of local or sectional controversy, as the safeguard of the rights of all, as the spirit and the essence of the liberty, peace, and greatness of the republic."

If so, then a majority of the people of the United States have declared against those great principles; they are inimical to the existence of this Constitution; they are inimical to the rights of some great sections of the country; they are bent on war and not on peace; for a great majority of the people have voted against the man who, the President says, is the symbol of this decision. Sir, if the President's opinion is right, that those great and vital principles were in contest, then the vote of the people is more full of awful portent than any they have ever cast, and the day of our dissolution draws nigh. If they were not in contest, then that message is the most ungracious sarcasm ever flung by a President on the people who lifted him above his fellows.

It is of evil example for the President to have departed, in the language of his message, from the severe courtesy, the respectful reserve, the passionless dignity observed by his predecessors in alluding to the conduct of sovereign states, or the motives of great bodies of the people in the highest function of their sovereignty. It is of all things most deplorable that, elevated above the turbulent atmosphere of a popular canvass, the President should have stooped to the region of the storm, been swayed by the passions of the strife whose excesses it was his high duty to have restrained, and that, stung by the great condemnation of the vote of the people, should have poured out the bitterness of his heart in sharp vituperation of his judges, forgotten the President in the partisan, and inflamed the passions already consuming the vitals of the republic.

But, Mr. Speaker, the people have taught some lessons worthy of being learned—not those the President would inculcate, nor such as are grateful to Democratic hearts—yet fruitful of warning and admonition, and quite visible to the dullest eye.

It proves that a minority of the people desired to see Mr. Buchanan President of the United States. Nobody ever doubted that.

It proves that a minority of the people were in favor of the Kansas-Nebraska Act. Nobody ever questioned that.

It proves that a minority of the people approve of President Pierce's administration. Nobody ever doubted that; but nobody knows how small that minority is.

It proves that a minority of the people are content that his system of misrule may be prolonged for another four years. Nobody ever doubted that.

It proves that the minority which preferred Mr. Buchanan was so located in various states, that under the Constitution it could cast a majority of the votes of the electoral college; *and this is the only point touching that minority about which there was ever much doubt.*

It proves farther, Mr. Speaker, that a majority of the people have condemned the Democratic party.

It proves that a majority of the people are opposed to that administration of President Pierce, which a minority propose to continue for four years.

It proves that a majority of people of the country think it time that the misgovernment of Kansas should cease.

It proves that no diversity of interpretation can extort any thing but condemnation of the principles and the purposes of the Kansas-Nebraska Act from a majority of the people of the country.

It proves that Mr. Buchanan comes into power with a decided majority of the people against him; with every proposed principle of his administration condemned beforehand; with the great Democratic majority in the Senate narrowed to the very verge of a bare working majority; with the House of Representatives, so far as any experience teaches, against him; with only about one third of the representatives from the North in his favor, and they chiefly representing minorities, and chosen by the divisions of their opponents; and thus that, for all his cherished purposes of mischief, his administration is paralyzed before its birth.

Still more, sir, it dissipates the sweet delusion of the dead heroes of the Nebraska Act, that there was a day of resurrection for them. It demonstrates that the blast which prostrated its friends in the North was no passing squall; that no sober second thought has changed their first thought; but that a settled and unchangeable hostility through all the North condemns them to a hopeless and pitiable minority. The death-wound, I rather think, has been dealt to that party which insolently boasted itself a perpetual plague to the republic, but now—worse than the scotched snake—staggers to its grave like a wounded gladiator, whose fall, even in the arms of victory, wins for him neither pity nor a crown.

These are some of the lessons about which I think there can be very little difference of opinion. They need only the teaching of numbers. They need only to count the results of the ballot-box. They depend on no adjustment of the difference of principle between the different portions of the party. They are irrespective of the question whether the approval of President Pierce's administration was made or evaded north of Mason and Dixon's line. They still stand, no matter what meaning was assigned to the Kansas-Nebraska Act any where. On a simple count of the voices of the judges—even admitting a Northern and a Southern Democrat to mean the same thing—it appears that the great majority of the country are tired of its men, are hostile to its principles, condemn its measures, mock at its blunders, are weary of its agitations, abhor its sectional warfare, and have ordered hue and cry to be made against every thing bearing the name of Democrat as a disturber of the public peace. Instead of repentance and reform under the discipline administered two years ago, the majority of the people of the country have beheld with alarm every element of electioneering torture applied to wring from the terrors of the country an approval, real or apparent, of the conduct of the administration; and they have by this great vote indicated their abiding hostility to a policy which has brought the republic to the verge of ruin. This, I take it, is the judgment of the American people—only *they were so unfortunate as to differ as to the measures of redress; and the penalty of this blunder is the continuance of that domination in the executive chair for four years more.*

Thus condemned by the popular vote, these gentlemen of the minority are ingenious in extracting an approval of their policy and principles, but in the vain effort they have revealed that the minority itself is divided as much with itself as from its opponents. While claiming an approval of their principles by the country, the minority is itself wrangling as to what those principles are.

The world has long known that they were divided on every question of domestic policy—that their harmonious ranks included protectionists and anti-protectionists. The last session exhibited great internal improvement bills passed over the veto by Democratic votes. But still they boasted that on the slavery question —the shibboleth of their faith—Democrats were every where the same faithful friends of the Southern and Northern rights—alone at the North worthy of trust. *They* passed the Kansas Act to vindicate the right of the South to enter Territories with their slaves; *they*, therefore, alone, are worthy of Southern countenance! *They* have wrung from the country the approval of the principles of that act; *they* have vindicated the equality of the states; *they* have asserted the right of the people of a Territory to frame their own domestic institutions; and for these things the country has conferred power *on them!*

Sir, the Kansas Act was an enigma till read by the light of the late election. What my opinions of it are is immaterial. I desire now to deal with it *historically*—to deduce some conclusions from the discussion that has rolled around me for so long.

The Kansas-Nebraska Bill was introduced, it is said, to vindicate the equality of the states, and the right of the South to carry their slaves into the Territories. That act conferred on the Territorial Legislature power "over all proper subjects of legislation;" and its framers, for fear that there might be one subject of legislation that was withdrawn from their consideration, in extending over them the laws of the United States, said, "Excepting the law of 1820, which, being inconsistent with the principles of the legislation of 1850, is hereby declared inoperative and void, it being the true intent and meaning of this act"—as if there might have been doubt in the mind of the country as to what that act intended to confer on the people—"it being the intent of this act to leave the people of the Territory [ay, sir, 'of the Territory'] perfectly free to form their own institutions to suit themselves." Early in the last session of Congress it became apparent that there was a diversity as to the object and effect of that act. As the session progressed, that diversity grew wider. Those same words were carried into the Democratic platform; they were carried into the discussions before the people; and I now desire to ask, in the face of gentlemen, how far there is any conformity of views between the two wings of the Democratic party? I aver at the outset that they are as widely divided as is the Republican party from the Democratic party, and upon exactly the same question of constitutional power that rests at the bottom of the words of the Kansas-Nebraska Act.

There can be no controversy, I presume, among gentlemen here as to this great fact, that the language of the Kansas-Nebraska Act confers by *grant*, as the gentleman from Georgia [Mr. Stephens] so accurately described it this morning, upon the people of the Territories all the legislative powers that Congress can confer; and as the Constitution says that "all legislative power herein granted is vested in the Congress, which shall consist of a Senate and House of Representatives," it is plain that, unless the doctrine of squatter sovereignty as expounded by the gentleman from Georgia be accurate, then this Congress has conferred all the power upon the people of the Territories which can exist under the Constitution, and that they have, and can have, no power from any other source. Now the pinch arises. One set of gentlemen say, "Oh, that bill does not authorize the people of the Territories to exclude slavery." Another set of gentlemen say, "Oh, that bill does authorize the people to exclude slavery." Then we have explanations from the Southern wing of the party that it authorizes them to exclude it only when they come to form their state Constitution. "No," say Democratic gentlemen from the North, "the language is universal; it authorizes the people of the Territories to exercise all legislative power consistent with the Constitution, and we say that they can exercise it *now, in their Territorial condition.*" As a mere question of legal interpretation, there can be no dispute as to the meaning of the words. There may arise a question whether Congress have power to confer that authority; but if Congress have it, then unquestionably it has been conferred.

There is, therefore, a difference between the two wings of the Democratic party. It is not, Mr. Speaker, a mere difference of interpretation. It is not a mere dispute about the legal meaning of the words they have used. It is not a mere accident of legislation which a scratch of the pen could change. It is not something which has been sprung upon them by accident, of which they had no notice before its arrival. But upon that most delicate of all questions—that one on which the minority boast themselves the special defenders of the South, and in reference to which they say their Northern brethren are more faithful than other gentlemen at the North—on that question, and not upon the interpretation of the language of the Kansas-Nebraska Bill, there is a radical, inherent, profound difference, splitting them from top to bottom, as irreconcilable as any other diversity of party views that can be exhibited in the history of the republic. It can not be pushed aside as a mere diversity of opinion on the Kansas-Nebraska Act, because it is carried back to the very foundation of the Constitution. And then we can understand, what otherwise, perhaps, we might not so well be able to understand, how it is that the Northern gentlemen of the Democratic party have supported the principles of the Kansas-Nebraska Act, and have united in the election of a President. Why, Mr. Speaker, the propriety of that act was not submitted to the people now at this election. That question was passed upon in the election of this Congress; and this side of the House gives the answer of the whole North as to whether it ought or ought not to have been passed. No one proposed its repeal, and the restoration of the compromise, but Mr. Dunn, and *that* was made a ground of attack by Northern Democrats on Republicans. The question at the North was one of reprisal and retaliation, revenge and conquest—not defense and restoration; and Democrats and Republicans only argued the question, which of the two best represented the North *in that contest* for the Territories.

But then another question arose, whether there could not be such an interpretation put upon that act as would enable gentlemen at the North still to stand with the Democratic party, and cast their votes for the same man, although differing in principle and pursuing a policy not merely different from, but hostile to, the purpose of the Southern Democrats. Therefore it is, that while at the South we have heard a universal interpretation that that act does not confer upon—that there is no power in the people of a Territory to exclude slavery—and I speak now in the face of a great majority of Southern gentlemen who were active in the canvass, and who can correct me if wrong—I say there was a unanimous interpretation by Democratic gentlemen throughout the South as to the purpose, meaning, and effect of the Kansas-Nebraska Act—we can understand how it was that, while throughout the whole South that law was claimed as a great Southern triumph, not merely in point of principle, but in point of policy and fact, as opening a hitherto barred territory to slavery, and giving a chance for another slave state to restore the disturbed equilibrium of the Union—as something to bind the South to the Democratic party forever for the great boon conferred upon them, the Democrats of the North could say, "We will accept with them that measure, not that we would have dared to have voted for it—not that we would have dared to have advocated it; but now that the thing is done and can not be undone, preferring the Democratic party to any other party, and seeing their strength at the South, we are willing to aid that party at the South, and we are willing to adopt the principles of the Kansas-Nebraska Act—*with a gloss*, yielding none of our principles, not admitting, for a single instant, that Congress has not the power to legislate upon the subject of slavery in the Territories—not breathing such a suggestion, yet we are willing to abide by the principles of the Kansas-Nebraska Act as *we shall interpret* it." How interpret it? "It is the best measure for freedom; it breaks down all the compromises; it leaves the question open; it confers legislative power upon the people of the Territory. We will agree that the people of a Territory have power over the question of slavery. You will never hear of another slave state: we will make Kansas a free state; and therefore we are willing to abide by the principles of the Kansas-Nebraska Act, because, although it ought not to have been passed, it perhaps will do no harm. While our Southern brethren say it is a Southern triumph, we will claim it as a Northern one. That will enable us to maintain our position at the North in the party, and give us the full advantage of our overwhelming power to vote slavery from the Territories." Why, sir, in more than one handbill, and in more than one newspaper, how many it boots not to inquire, it has been seen—yea, I have seen with my own eyes, in Pennsylvania and New York, Republicans taunted by Democrats with being opposed to freedom for having voted for Dunn's bill. I saw in more than one place—in more than one handbill—proclaimed "Buchanan, Breckinridge, and Free Kansas!" and the result of the colloquy which took place upon this floor between two gentlemen from Illinois the other day, shows how far authorities can agree as to what position was assumed by the Democratic party in that state.

I have nowhere here heard it asserted that it was any where maintained as an accepted dogma of that party at the North, that Congress had no power over the question of slavery in the Territories; that the people had no power over it in the Territories; that the people ought not to exclude slavery from the Territory of Kansas; that they were opposed to the people doing it; and unless there be gentlemen who can reconcile and justify all those things, then there is as great and wide a gulf in point of policy, as there is in point of constitutional principle, between the Democrats of the North and the Democrats of the South. For what matters it to the South that Congress shall not interfere if another instrument is substituted which will interfere? Is it more humiliating to the South to have a line of fair division, like that of 1820, giving part to the South and part to the North—a line and boundary of peace forever established here by the Congress of the United States—than to be rudely expelled by a Congress of Kansas squatters?—here, where she is represented by her eloquent sons; in the Senate, where she is protected by her equal vote; by the President, armed with the veto against all oppression, rather than there, where she is not represented, has no voice, and no veto? Or are her interests more likely to be tenderly dealt with by the rude backwoodsman or the European Red Republican? Or, if she may be excluded, is it so much more to her taste, or does it better comport with her dignity, that a few rambling emigrants get together in a log cabin by our authority—ay, under that bulwark of Southern rights, the Kansas Act—and, to improve the price of land, proclaim that slavery shall not exist—that at the line a man in a hunting-shirt, with a rifle on his shoulder and a bowie-knife at his belt, shall flaunt a blotched copy of the Wilmot Proviso in the face of the Southern emigrant, and bid him back in the name of the squatter kings—than that here, on solemn consultation, such partition be made that peace, and not war, may reign in the republic? Does that mode of settling the matter touch the dignity of the South less; or, rather, does it not touch it more? Or is justice more or less likely to be done?

"Oh, but it's of no consequence at all," say the gentlemen from Tennessee and South Carolina, "for if the people are opposed to slavery they won't protect it!" Indeed! then it is only more apparent that the only point of agreement between the Northern and Southern Democrats is in the fact that directly or indirectly, by law or without law, they both admit slavery may be excluded. One would suppose the South had small favor to be grateful for. A right without a remedy is the lawyer's absurdity; yet for *this* the country has been brought to the verge of civil war!

Prostrated in one effort, they try their limping logic on another. Their merit and unity consist in their assertion of the equality of the states and the right of the people of a Territory to form their own domestic institutions—the principles of the acts of 1850 violated by that of 1820, and restored and reinaugurated by the Kansas-Nebraska Act, its vivifying principle.

Sir, the President libeled the living, and his friends rob the dead to cover his nakedness. The very purpose and principle of the act of 1820 were to vindicate the equality of the states, and the right of the people to form their own Constitution without control; it was signed by Mr. Monroe for that very reason; and they doubly blunder in law and history when under pretense of those principles they repeal it.

The acts of 1850 inaugurated no new principle. They were acts of compromise—giving and taking, like that of 1820—wisely suited to the *present necessity*, leaving unrepealed the laws of the central government of Mexico, and, if Congress could pass them, in full force as laws of Congress, just as the French and Spanish laws were left in full force in Florida and Louisiana when repealed north of 36 deg. 30 min. by the act of 1820.

If the acts of 1850 provided for the admission of states with or without slavery as the people might prefer, then that was the very principle consecrated forever as the law of the republic by the act of 1820; for the one purpose of the law of 1820 was to divide the territory between the North and the South, and by the same authority to make one part slave and the other part free territory, while a Territory; and the other thing settled in that law—and from that day down to the Kansas-Nebraska Act never assailed or controverted by any party known to the history of the republic, and remaining now the accepted and conceded law of the Constitution every where, except among a few wild abolitionists of the Garrison and Beecher school—was, that the people of the Territory could, and alone could, frame their own institutions when they come to form their state Constitution; and that Congress could neither impose a condition precedent, nor bind by a compact their absolute sovereignty over the matter. The effort in the Missouri contest was to place an inhibition on the State of Missouri—to cause the people of that Territory to provide specially in their Constitution against the existence of slavery. It was that which was voted down—voted down, as I have said before, on the immortal argument of William Pinckney, of Maryland, who then stood as Maryland would always have her sons to stand, defending the constitutional rights of the weaker against the aggressions of the stronger; whose words of glory, vindicating the absolute equality of the states against the usurpation of the United States, form the fit prelude to that equal argument of the man of Massachusetts, who, ten years after, maintained the supremacy of the United States against the encroachments of the states. On those cyclopean foundations have ever rested, and still unshaken rest, those two pillars of the Constitution, the absolute and inalienable equality of the states in their sovereign functions, and the equally absolute supremacy of the United States within the sphere of their conceded powers; the one unquestioned except by the Democrats of the State-rights and Secession school, the other never violated except—by whom?—by the Democratic party in their Texas resolutions, which imposed, carelessly or deliberately, but expressly, upon future states—yes, states by name and not by implication—the very inhibition which Pinckney and Clay excluded from the statute-book by the act of 1820—the gentlemen of that party who now impeach that great act, and its great authors, of violating the equality of the states, and invading the right of the people to form their own Constitutions; for, unless the act of 1820 *did those things*, the Kansas-Nebraska Act is *defenseless and senseless*. Sir, are they not content to have pulled down the monument and decorate themselves with its rifled trophies, without staining the memory of the great dead with the reproach of the very thing they prevented others from doing?

But, they say, if there be differences, yet we agree in this—not to agitate the question *in Congress*—forsooth where their divisions are inconveniently visible, and bring scandal at the South—but to refer it to the Territories, where the two wings can privately fight it out! How will the two divisions of the minority silence the majority? Or is the President's Message an illustration of their silence? or do they expect the North to keep silence before it? or are they ignorant that they would die of silence in a year?

These were not the purposes of the Kansas Act, Mr. Speaker, in my opinion. I think it was an electioneering manœuvre. That has been, at least, its effect, and its only effect. To the South it has secured neither a Territory, nor a state, nor a constitutional principle, nor peace. Its authors tear each other about its meaning, and pursue diametrically opposite purposes under its cover. They have accomplished nothing but to reopen a dangerous agitation—to bring themselves into hopeless minority, crippled by internal divisions.

There is another lesson taught by this election. The Democratic party has ceased to be a homogeneous body. It is bound together by no unity of principle. It is a conglomerate of incongruous materials—Whigs and State-rights men, and Secessionists, and Democrats, and Free-Kansas Democrats, and Free-Soilers, and Union men—not a mosaic, for that is a work of art—but huddled together by the confusion of the conflict. The Irish brigade stood firm, and saved them from annihilation; and the foreign recruits in Pennsylvania turned the fate of the day. They have elected, by these foreigners, by a minority of the American people, a President to represent their divisions!

The first levee of President Buchanan will be a curious scene. He is a quiet, simple, fair-spoken gentleman, versed in the by-paths and indirect crooked ways whereby he met this crown, and he will soon know how uneasy it sits upon his head. Some future Walpole may detail the curious greetings, the unexpected meetings, the cross purposes, and shocked prejudices of the gentlemen who cross the threshold. Some honest Democrat of the South will thank God for the Union preserved. A gentleman of the disunionist school will congratulate the President on the defeat of Mr. Fillmore, whose quiet administration might have postponed the inevitable day. The slavery propagandist will vaunt his triumph over the unwieldy North, and boast of conquered Kansas; while the Northern gentlemen will whisper "Buchanan, Breckinridge, and free Kansas" in the presidential ear, and beg without scandal the confirmation of their hopes. Some Whig will remind him of the California letter, and exact the Pacific Railroad at his hands; while the strict construction Democrat will execrate the usurpation, and cast sinister innuendoes against the mail which would not reveal its contents this side the Pacific. Pennsylvania will be touching in the cause of iron, and plead the merits of the October election; while Democrats from the South and West plot the treason of free railroad iron, and carefully adjust the loss and gain in votes. The Ostend Manifesto will be respectfully spoken of, and a Northern and Southern Democrat in a corner will nicely balance free trade against a slave state, and suggest that an imprudent steamer may favor the application of the principles of the manifesto, the President the while repeating to some enthusiastic Free-Soiler his resolution of 1819, to "prevent the existence of slavery in any of the Territories or *states* which *may be erected by Congress!*"

But how to divide the spoils among this motley crew—ah! there's the rub. There are gentlemen who have united from every creed and every party, and who make up this conglomerate of the present Democratic party, having changed no principles, still holding jealously the position of allies, not being embodied into the party, but maintaining their own individuality. Sir, I envy not the nice and delicate scales which must distribute the patronage amid the jarring elements of that conglomerate—as fierce against each other as clubs in cards are against spades—which must decide whether the gentlemen of the Whig party who only acted as allies should be received and accepted as candidates for high office; whether gentlemen of the Free-Soil school should sit down with gentlemen of the Cincinnati school; whether the past shall be *rasa tabula*, or the criterion of acceptance or exclusion. There will be required a nice discrimination and a careful adjustment by some skillful accountant in party politics, in that curious chancery for the distribution of the spoils, to determine the shares of Northern Democrats who were faithful, but failed, and Northern Free-Soilers who were heretics, but useful;

of the Whig convert and the Whig ally; of Whig gentlemen of name — leaders who left their followers in their transition; of Whig leaders in states where they were zealous but not needed, and in states where they were zealous and needed, but powerless. And long ere this can be adjusted the clamors of the foreign legion will add to the interest of the scene—the vision of King George's judgment over again:

> "There crashed a sturdy oath of stout John Bull,
> Who damned away his eyes as heretofore.
> Here Paddy brogued 'by Jasus.' 'What's your wull?'
> The temperate Scot exclaimed; and, 'mid the war,
> The voice of Jonathan was heard to express,
> 'Our President is going to war, I guess.'"

They may not be disregarded, for but for them Pennsylvania was lost, and with it the day. Yet what will satisfy those indispensable allies, now conscious of their power? That, sir, is the exact condition of things which will be found in the antechamber — exorbitant demands, limited means, irreconcilable divisions, strife, disunion, dissolution — whenever the President shall have taken the solemn oath of office, and darkened the doors of the White House.

And there are lessons taught to the Republican gentlemen of this House as well as to the Democrats. They have been taught that, great as was the wrong; blundering as was the policy of the Kansas and Nebraska act; earnest as are the Northern people against the extension of slavery; resolved as they are that no more slave territory shall be added to this country, they have likewise shown that there is still one principle which they will not sanction. They will not sanction a merely sectional canvass for the presidency, nor intrust with the government a party whose whole power is confined to one half the states, whatever their purposes may be. They will not sanction retaliation as the spirit in which wrongs is to be redressed; they will not allow wrongs committed by a party of the South and of the North to be visited on all their Southern brethren, nor sanction retaliation as a fit political remedy. They have settled the policy, that if wrong has been done, reciprocal wrong is not redress. They have put the seal of their condemnation on revenge as a principle of legislation, and have refused letters of marque and reprisal against the South for wrong *legally* done, and requiring the remedy to be pursued by other means than a raid against Southern institutions. They think that the evils of civil war are greater than the evils of another slave Territory; and the policy of the Republican party, while it did not justify, did tend to kindle civil war. They have resolved that there shall be no attempt to grasp the reins of power on principles which tend to exclude every Southern gentleman from office, and necessitate a decision by the country of the great question whether one half of the people of the Union will be governed by the other half—for that was the only *practical* result of the success of the Republican party. Honest though their purpose may have been—as devoted to the Union as the friends of Mr. Buchanan, their position was unsocial, and their success dangerous.

The great argument at the South has been—and there is no Democratic gentleman here who has not heard it, and I will venture to say there are very few who have not used it—the argument every where used at the South was, that it was a question of independence, and not of administration; that it was a question, not whether the majority should rule according to the great constitutional principle, but whether a majority obtained under the forms of the Constitution, in such a manner as practically excluded all Southern gentlemen from a participation in the conduct of affairs, ought to be submitted to? Not that there were no friends of Mr. Fremont to fill the offices, for his fifteen hundred votes would pretty well answer that purpose; nor that there was any reason which peremptorily forbade any one from accepting office, though inclined so to do; nor that, in point of fact, it was at all certain that there could not be found men enough who would fill them—Northern emigrants would fulfill that condition; but because the condition on which alone any party can fitly and safely be intrusted with the government is the possession of power, and friends enough *every where* to carry on the government with the men of the state to be governed, so that a domestic government shall not assume the form of a foreign domination. Instruments of any power may always every where be found; but the office in such hands partakes of the nature of despotism, and such men alone were at the disposal of the Republican party in one half the states of the Union. They would doubtless have tendered high office to men of high position in the South, but the condition precedent of conformity of political views and principles was wanting. They could not aid in forming an administration to whose creation and whose policy they were radically opposed. Thus, practically, the Republican party must have employed Southern men who represented no body of Southern supporters, or Northern men, to conduct the government; and that is what is meant by a purely sectional party—their radical and incurable defect. They, by the simple statement of their position, confined themselves to the free states. Equal candor would have equally confined the Democratic party to the Southern States; for the objects and principles of the Southern Democrats found, so far as I can see, no supporters in the North. They owe their little remaining power there to a common name and an ambiguous resolution covering a radical hostility of purpose and principle; but, honestly or not, they fulfilled that indispensable condition of carrying on the government, that in most of the Northern States there were a minority content to vote for the candidate of the coalition of the Northern and Southern Democrats, and to be silent about their differences—the sole distinction between the sectionalism of the Democrat and the sectionalism of the Republican.

The great lesson is taught by this election that both the parties which rested their hopes on sectional hostility stand at this day condemned by the great majority of the country as common disturbers of the public peace of the country.

The Republican party was a hasty levy, *en masse*, of the Northern people to repel or revenge an intrusion by Northern votes alone. With its occasion it must pass away. The gentlemen of the Republican side of the house can now do nothing. They can pass no law excluding slavery from Kansas in the next Congress, for they are in a minority. Within two years Kansas must be a state of the Union. She will be admitted with or without slavery, as her people prefer. Beyond Kansas there is no question that is practically open. I speak to practical men. Slavery does not exist in any other Territory—it is excluded by law from several, and not likely to exist any where; and the Republican party has nothing to do, and can do nothing. It has no future. Why cumbers it the ground?

Between these two stand the firm ranks of the American party, thinned by desertions, but still unshaken. To them the eye of the country turns in hope. The gentleman from Georgia saluted the Northern Democrats with the title of *heroes*—who swam vigorously down the current. The men of the American party faced, in each section, the sectional madness. They would cry neither free nor slave Kansas, but proposed a safe administration of the laws, before which every right would find protection. Their voice was drowned amid the din of factions. The men of the North would have no moderation, and they have paid the penalty. The American party elected a majority of this House; had they of the North held fast to the great American principle of silence on the negro question, and, firmly refusing to join either agitation, stood by the American candidate, they would not now be writhing, crushed beneath an utter overthrow. If they would now destroy the Democrats, they can do it only by returning to the American party. By it alone can a party be created strong at the South as well as at the North. To it alone belongs a principle accepted wherever the American name is heard—the same at the North as at the South, on the Atlantic or the Pacific shore. It alone is free from sectional affiliations at either end of the Union which would cripple it at the other. Its principle is silence, peace, and compromise. It abides by the existing law. It allows no agitation. It maintains the present condition of affairs. It asks no change in any Territory, and it will countenance no agitation for the aggrandizement of either section. Though thousands fell off in the day of trial—allured by ambition or terrified by fear—at the North and at the South, carried away by the torrent of fanaticism in one part of the Union, or driven by the fierce onset of the Democrats in another, who shook Southern institutions by the violence of their attack, and half waked the sleeping negro by painting the Republican as his liberator, *still a million of men, on the great day, in the face of both factions, heroically refused to bow the knee to either Baal.* They knew the necessities of the times, and they set the example of sacrifice, that others might profit by it. They now stand the hope of the nation, around whose firm ranks the shattered elements of the great majority may rally and vindicate the right of the majority to rule, and of the native of the land to make the law of the land.

The recent election has developed, in an aggravated form, every evil against which the American party protested. Again, in the war of domestic parties, Republican and Democrat have rivaled each other in bidding for the foreign vote to turn the balance of a domestic election. Foreign allies have decided the government of the country—men naturalized in thousands on the eve of the election—eagerly struggled for by competing parties, mad with sectional fury, and grasping any instrument which would prostrate their opponents. Again, in the fierce struggle for supremacy, men have forgotten the ban which the republic puts on the intrusion of religious influence on the political arena. These influences have brought vast multitudes of foreign-born citizens to the polls ignorant of American interests, without American feelings, influenced by foreign sympathies, to vote on American affairs; and those votes have, *in point of fact*, accomplished the present result.

The high mission of the American party is to restore the influence of the interests of the people in the conduct of affairs—to exclude appeals to foreign birth or religious feeling as elements of power in politics; to silence the voice of sectional strife—*not by joining either section*, but by recalling the people from a profitless and maddening controversy which aids no interests, and shakes the foundation not only of the common industry of the people, but of the republic itself; to lay a storm amid whose fury no voice can be heard in behalf of the industrial interests of the country, no eye can watch and guard the foreign policy of the government, till our ears may be opened by the crash of foreign war waged for the purposes of political and party ambition, in the name, but not by the authority nor for the interests, of the American people.

Return, then, Americans of the North, from the paths of error to which in an evil hour, fierce passions and indignation have seduced you, to the sound position of the American party—silence on the slavery agitation. Leave the Territories as they are—to the operation of natural causes. Prevent aggression by excluding from power the aggressors, and there will be no more wrong to redress. Awake the national spirit to the danger and degradation of having the balance of power held by foreigners. Recall the warnings of Washington against foreign influence—here in our midst—wielding part of our sovereignty; and with these sound words of wisdom let us recall the people from paths of strife and error to guard their peace and power; and when once the mind of the people is turned from the slavery agitation, that party which waked the agitation will cease to have power to disturb the peace of the land.

This is the great mission of the American party. The first

condition of success is to prevent the administration from having a majority in the next Congress; for, *with that*, the agitation will be resumed for very different objects. The Ostend Manifesto is full of warning; and they who struggle over Kansas may wake and find themselves in the midst of an agitation compared to which that of Kansas was a summer's sea; whose instruments will be, not words, but the sword.

AGAINST THE LECOMPTON FRAUDS.

In November, 1857, Mr. Davis was elected (for the second time) to the Thirty-fifth Congress. Mr. Orr, of South Carolina, was chosen Speaker, and by him Mr. Davis was again named on the Committee of Ways and Means. He was heard during that session on the Treasury-note Bill, on the Pacific Railroad Bill, on the bill relating to the reappointment of officers dropped or retired by the Naval Board of Inquiry, and who had not been restored by the Revising Board, and on the Report of the Kansas Conference Committee. In that debate he stated correctly, and proved, from the records and from the argument of William Pinckney, of Maryland, the point settled by the Missouri Compromise—to wit, "That it assumed that *there could be a restriction upon a Territory while it remained a Territory*, and it settled that there could be *no* restriction, no condition imposed *upon a state*, not merely upon the subject of slavery, but upon any subject." He also spoke on the Ohio Contested Election Case, the Washington City Election Bill, and on the Civil and Legislative Appropriations.

On the 30th of March, 1858, he spoke as follows against the admission of Kansas under the Lecompton Constitution:

Mr. Chairman,—The earlier explorers in high northern latitudes were perplexed at beholding great icebergs mysteriously making their way to the north against current, and wind, and tide. Philosophers in the closet divined from the strange phenomenon the existence of an under current running counter to that of the surface, that bore them along. The disinterested spectator, Mr. Chairman, of the course of this debate, ignorant of our history for four years, and of who now holds the helm, would find himself similarly perplexed, and perhaps he might surmise a similar solution.

That an administration which professes to be the godfather of "*popular* sovereignty" should oppose the submission of a Constitution to the *popular* vote; that an administration which is in name Democratic should propose to impose upon the majority the will of the minority; that an administration elevated to power by the South, against the will of the North, should urge, as the shortest way to accomplish the great purpose of making Kansas a free state, her admission as a slave state; that the administration, which professes anxiety to preserve the peace of the country, should say that the shortest way to restore the broken peace is, not to remove, but to fasten, by irrevocable laws, in the form of a state Constitution guaranteed by the united power of the country, that hateful oligarchy upon a people, whose neck was too tender to bear the weight of their territorial yoke, which Congress could at any moment alleviate; that these methods should be taken to accomplish these purposes, may well puzzle the speculator in exploring the hidden reasons that drive men thus contrary to what apparent reason—the ordinary method of guiding the commonwealth, the ordinary propelling powers of the government—would seem to dictate. And possibly, Mr. Chairman, he might not be very far from solving the problem if he were to assume that the question is, not so much how to accomplish the pacification of Kansas, or to make legislation square with the dogma of "*popular sovereignty*," or to secure the right of the people to form their own domestic institutions in their own way, which we are taught to believe is a new revelation of the year of grace eighteen hundred and fifty-four—not so much any of those reasons as to prevent the administration, which boasted itself the omnipotent pacificator, from being brought to lick the dust, now, ere the termination of the first session of its first Congress—to lick the dust before the will of that majority which it is defying in one of the Territories—before the will of that majority of the people of the United States, against which Mr. Buchanan ascended the presidential chair, and amid the irreconcilable diversities of opinion of the people who were combined to elevate Mr. Buchanan to the Presidency—but here that men and parties are brought face to face—can no longer coalesce in the policy he would have them pursue.

We are debating the recognition of an independent state.

The administration produce a piece of parchment with a form of government written on it, and a certificate of one John C. Calhoun, that it is the Constitution adopted at Lecompton by a Convention of the people of Kansas; and on *this* evidence the President and his friends demand the recognition of the State of Kansas.

We respectfully ask for the proof that the piece of parchment contains the will of the people of Kansas.

We are told the Territorial Legislature took, by law, the sense of the people, and 2670 voted to call a Convention; that 2200 persons voted, *in all*, for the members of the Convention; that the Convention, whose journal no one here has seen, voted the Constitution; that it was not submitted to the people for their ratification, and that the vote of the 4th of January, of 10,000 against it, is of no legal relevancy to the question before us.

On this state of facts, Mr. Chairman, we are besought, on behalf of the administration, to vote for the admission of Kansas under the Lecompton Constitution for the sake of the *principle* involved. Sir, I confess myself the servant of principle; and I respectfully ask gentlemen what principle they ask me to sanction?

Is it that a minority in a Territory constitute the people, and so must make their will the law over the majority? If so, I respectfully dissent from the principle.

Is it that the people of a Territory, with or without previous authority of Congress, have a *legal* right themselves to take the initiative, and to lay upon your table a Constitution which they are entitled to demand at our hands that we shall accept? If so, then I respectfully dissent from the principle.

Is it, on the part of our Southern friends, that any Constitution which may be laid upon our table containing, no matter how put there, a clause sanctioning slavery, is to shut the eye to every other circumstance connected with it, and to drive us to the admission of that people as a state merely because that provision is in the Constitution? If so, then I respectfully dissent from the principle.

Is it that they mean that gentlemen may look into the Constitution for the purpose of seeing that slavery *is* there, and when they find it there are bound to vote for the admission? If so, then the gentlemen upon the other side of the house, by exactly the same reason, may look into that Constitution to see that slavery is there; and, if they think it the more logical conclusion, may vote to refuse admission upon that ground. But as I do not understand the gentlemen on the other side to admit the latter alternative as one fit to be embraced, they will indulge me in the logical consequence of not regarding the former as a proper consideration to weigh at all with me upon the question that is before the House.

That slavery is embraced in that Constitution, is certainly, Mr.

Chairman, in my opinion, no ground at all for the rejection—no ground at all for any difficulty about admission. If put there by the will of the people, it ought not to weigh with the weight of the dust in the balance upon the question; for to allow that to be a ground of exclusion, while it would be within the legislative discretion of Congress, would be, in my judgment, unwise, tending directly to consequences that all of us are most anxious to avoid, and would exhibit an unsocial disposition in behalf of the majority which might come to such a conclusion, which, whether rightfully or wrongfully, the past history of the nation teaches us only too well will lead to nothing but disastrous civil collisions; which, in their result, if not immediately, will first undermine, and then bring down in ruin, the whole fabric of our liberties.

Then, if these be not the principles which ought to commend themselves to the judgment of a right-judging man, is there any other? Is it that because the Territory has proceeded under a law of a Territorial Legislature, with all the regularity and formality, as the President tells us, that any territory has ever proceeded, we are *bound* to accept what they send to us, blindly and without looking beyond it? Is it the principle of this government not only that we *may* stop, but that we are *bound* to stop, at what the Territory sends to us? Then, Mr. Chairman, I do not assent to that proposition; and it is to that proposition that I desire chiefly to draw your attention now.

Upon that question I am freer than most of the gentlemen upon either side of this House. I voted with my Southern friends against the Topeka Constitution, being a free Constitution formally sent here by the majority of the then inhabitants of the Territory. I am, therefore, free to raise the question whether there is legal authority at the bottom of that Constitution now presented to us? They protested against the admission of California because there was no evidence that a majority of its people had assented; because there was no formality of law preceding its Constitution; because there were no protections to the ballot-box. I am, therefore, now free to ask those who did protest to join me in inquiring whether there be here legal authority; whether here the ballot-box has been protected; whether here we have the will of the people ascertained in legal form which we not only may accept, but which we are bound to accept?

This assumes the validity of the laws of the Territorial Legislature calling the Convention, and the proceedings under them in point of law; and that the legal effect of those proceedings is to clothe this parchment with all the attributes of a state Constitution, and that we are not entitled to inquire who voted for or against it; how many staid from the polls, or why they did so; nor whether fraud or force have decided the result; but that the legal certificates preclude inquiry into every thing beyond.

I respectfully deny the validity in point of law, and farther say that if they were as valid as if authorized by act of Congress, they could to no extent exclude the legislative discretion of Congress as to the fitness of recognizing the new state.

Mr. Chairman, in my judgment, all that is necessary to the admission of a state is a concurrence of the will of the people of a Territory and of Congress. Prior to such concurrence there is no state. After that concurrence there is a state. The application of a Territory to be admitted as a State is only a petition upon your table—an offer upon their part which we may accept or which we may reject at our pleasure. After that concurrence it has been ingrafted into the living body politic of the country, bone of our bone, flesh of our flesh, to share with us for good or evil, to the end of time, the blessings or misfortunes of the republic—to be severed by nothing except that external violence which shall lop off some living limb of the republic, or that civil strife which the chief of the republic is so rashly provoking.

Enabling acts, whether contained in the organic law of the Territory, or in special acts authorizing the formation of a Constitution, providing for the formalities of election, the protection of the polls, the expression of the popular will under the forms of law, are only the guarantees that Congress in its wisdom throws around the expression of the popular will. They are only methods of ascertaining that will; and when that will is ascertained, Congress has every thing that is indispensable, and all the Territory can supply. The will of Congress to concur with the will of the people is expressed in the act of Congress admitting the state; and it is that concurrence, no matter how ascertained, by what forms, or with the omission of what forms, which makes the distinction, and alone makes the distinction between a Territory of the United States and a state of the United States.

There is no such thing in our system as an incipient state—a state whose federal relations are undefined, a state of uncertain federal relations, as Mr. Calhoun once expressed himself. I respectfully submit that there is no intermediate condition between a Territory and a state; that a state whose federal relations are undefined is a state of which the Constitution of the United States knows nothing. Uncertain federal relations are no federal relations. Unless the state be in this Union, the state is out of this Union. Unless the state be bound by the Constitution, the state is independent of the Constitution. Unless the state have a right to be here represented, the state has no right to be represented any where. It is a state under the Constitution, or it is a state independent. If, therefore, any proceeding create a state which does not simultaneously bring it within, and make it one of, the United States, that state may as well form an alliance with the incipient confederacy of Canada and New Brunswick as enter this confederacy. It may levy war against the United States, and you can not punish its people for treason. It may appropriate the territory of the United States, and it is beyond your power. In a word, by the public law of the United States, all the territory within their jurisdiction is either a Territory of the United States or a state of this Union.

If, then, that be the case, we are brought at once to the question of the relation of Congress to the Territories in the formation of states. What are the respective parts belonging to the people of the Territory and to the Congress in the creation of a new state?

With the dogma of sovereignty I do not deal here. I leave that to the schools or to the gentlemen who meddle with metaphysical disquisitions. What sovereignty is I shall not attempt to define. The word is not used in our laws; it is not found among the wise words of our Constitution. It is the Will of the Wisp, which they who follow will find a treacherous guide through fens and bogs. We are not engaged in defining that "popular sovereignty" with which gentlemen on the other side have been so much plagued for the last year or two. Popular sovereignty is only a demagogue's name for the foundation principle of all our institutions. It is only a demagogue's name for the right of the people to govern themselves—not that popular sovereignty which is limited by, and springs from, an act of Congress—not that mushroom growth, bred in the hot-bed of political corruption as a dainty delicacy for the people's palate, under the sedulous care of my honorable friends opposite—which, now that it is grown, is found to be nothing but toad-stools, whereof the body politic is now sick—but that right of the people to govern themselves, recognized by the fundamental law as the very corner-stone of the republic, which in this case the President violates and denies.

I here this day would deal in legal language; and in legal language there is such a thing as the people of the United States, of which the people of a Territory form the subjects. And there is known in the law of the United States such a thing as the right of the people of a state to form their own government. And it is assumed that every state which can form, at any time, a part of these United States, shall have emanated spontaneously from the people, whose affairs it regulates, and shall have been received voluntarily into the United States by the authority of Congress.

Now, sir, what is the relation of Congress to the Territories? Have the Territories—I do not say any *natural* right, for I am not here upon a philosophical dissertation—have they any *legal* right to initiate proceedings to form a Constitution? I do not ask whether they may not come here and ask, by petition, Congress to receive them, for that does not meet the difficulties of the case; but I ask whether the people of any Territory, by their simple volition, can meet in Convention, and assume to themselves such legal powers as shall compel Congress to recognize them as a legal body. Certainly those gentlemen who protested against the admission of California because there had been no preceding law can not maintain that proposition. Certainly gentlemen who voted against the Topeka Constitution can not maintain that proposition. Certainly the gentlemen who signed what purported to be a report of the Committee of Investigation of this House can not maintain that proposition. Certainly the President, who devoted a great part of his message to demonstrate that it is only through legal channels, by legal forms, and under legal authorities that a Constitution could be formed, can not maintain that proposition.

Neither can we, in point of sound sense and reason, maintain it, because that assumes there is a power in the people of some portions of the Territory not derived from the Constitution of the United States—since the Constitution says nothing upon the subject, except that Congress may admit new states. And if they have any inherent power, by the same reason they have all power;

in other words, we are upon revolutionary ground, and not legal ground. It is to confound a right by law under the Constitution with the natural right mentioned in the Declaration of Independence, of people to alter and change their government to suit themselves. But we are not dealing with revolutionary, but with legal rights. We live and were born under the Constitution, and to us that is the ultimate criterion of legal rights; it is our embodiment of natural right in a living practical form of government; beyond it we recognize no natural right as a source of legal right, and he who can not deduce his claim of right under it has none. I submit, therefore, that by the law of the United States the people of a Territory have no original right or authority to form a state government. No public man of position and character of any party has ever ventured to maintain such a proposition distinctly. The distinguished head of the State Department has fallen into expressions which seem to imply it; he has hastened to repel the inference, but, in his haste, has involved himself and his opinions in inexplicable perplexity and mystification, whence nothing can rescue him.

Then, if there be no inherent legal right in the people of a Territory to form a state government, how is it to be accomplished? They *must* form it; Congress can not do it for them; yet Congress is the only legal authority, the only source of law for the Territories. Where, then, does it exist? I maintain that, so far as legal authority is asserted of, or essential to, any proceeding for a Convention, it must flow from Congress, because here only is any government over the Territories in the eye of the law of the United States. The Supreme Court, which even State-rights gentlemen nowadays regard as the ultimate arbiter upon all questions, has settled some other things besides the relation of slavery to the Territories, and among them it has settled that Congress alone governs the Territories—whether under the clause which authorizes them to make all needful rules and regulations for the Territory of the United States, or under some unwritten clause implied by the strict constructionists, it is needless here to inquire. It can flow from nowhere else, because a state, in the view of the Constitution of the United States, means a body of people within a particular Territory, and that Territory belongs to the people of the United States; and the people who live upon a particular portion of that Territory have no right to assume to themselves, without our assent, any portion of it. A state involves the idea of a certain population inhabiting and possessing a certain Territory; and if the people can not get the Territory without the assent of Congress, they can not make themselves a State without the assent of Congress, nor take any steps toward it essential to its existence, which can exclude the control of Congress. Congress, it is true, can not make a Constitution for a Territory. It can only throw around the people of a Territory a legal protection, authorize them to proceed, and give them the guarantees of law in their proceedings; but beyond that I apprehend Congress can do nothing, and, excepting Congress, nobody can do that. What I wish here to maintain is, that that is the fundamental principle of all the legislation of Congress upon that subject. All the history of the republic is in its favor; it has all authority in its favor; and there is no precedent which raises even a doubt against it.

Now, sir, I ask the attention of the Committee very briefly to the law—for I rose to-day to deal with the legal position of gentlemen on the other side. They have not been willing to enter the controversy with their opponents on the question of fraud in the formation of the Constitution, or whether it be the fair and *bona fide* expression of the will of the people. They have insisted that these things were concealed from them by a screen of legal technicalities, and it is to tear down that screen that I now address myself.

In the absence, therefore, of any special act of Congress, authorizing a Convention, the *only* question is the construction of the Kansas-Nebraska Act of 1854. Does *that* act confer on the Territorial Legislature power to call a Convention to form a Constitution?

There have been many states admitted into the Union, and under diverse circumstances, but much the greater number of them have been admitted under the express and precedent authority of laws of Congress. And, sir, you will perceive at once —if the authority can only come from Congress to take the initiative steps—that it is immaterial whether that authority be contained in the organic act or in a special act. In either case it is our authority that they are exercising. In every instance they are our agents. In every instance they have only the authority that we give them. And, therefore, it comes exactly to the same thing whether there was an enabling act to authorize the Territory to proceed to form a state Constitution and government, or whether the authority was given under its organic act. This can never be a judicial question; but it is settled by every form of political authority. The states of Vermont, Kentucky, Maine, and Texas have been admitted into the Union, but not, as has been erroneously stated, without precedent legislation. If it were so, it would not affect the argument, for they were never Territories of the United States. But the assumption is historically erroneous. Vermont went through the Revolution without any defined relations to the other colonies, claiming independence at the time of the Revolution under no colonial government; and as a state by its own inherent power, it acceded to and adopted the Constitution of the United States, exactly as the other states did. It is no case of the formation of a state out of a Territory of the United States. Texas was likewise an independent republic, acknowledged by the United States, and afterward received into the Union. Kentucky proceeded under a law of the State of Virginia, whose territory it then was, and on that authority formed its Constitution, and was admitted into the Union. Maine proceeded under the authority of a law of Massachusetts, whose territory it was, and by that means formed its state government and was admitted into the Union.

But the argument is irrelevant; for the question is not whether Congress *may* in its discretion recognize constitutions formed by the people *without* authority of law, but whether a Territorial Legislature was *in point of law* authority to legalize the election of a Convention, to give the Convention itself a *legal* existence, to vest *it* with *legal* power to bind not merely the *people*, but the *Congress*. No one denies the power of Congress to admit Tennessee and Florida, yet nobody ever asserted any legal validity in their proceedings before admission.

The language of the organic acts and the proceedings of Congress thereupon are decisive.

The Territories divide themselves into two great classes. In Ohio, Illinois, Indiana, Missouri, Mississippi, Alabama, Arkansas, Tennessee, and Michigan, the Legislatures had "power to make laws in *all cases* for the good government of the people of the said Territory not repugnant to or inconsistent with the Constitution and laws of the United States."

In Wisconsin, Minnesota, Oregon, Florida, Iowa, the power of the Legislatures were declared to extend—in the identical words of the Kansas-Nebraska Act—"to all rightful subjects of legislation not inconsistent with the Constitution and Laws of the United States."

Congress has construed *both* forms of expression by passing enabling acts for both classes. Not only for Ohio, Louisiana, Missouri, Mississippi, Alabama, Illinois, Indiana, but also for Wisconsin, Minnesota, and Oregon, did Congress pass acts specially *authorizing* them to call a Convention and form a state government; and in every instance, excepting Wisconsin, these bills provided all the details of the Convention, the number of delegates, its time of assembling, the modes under which the delegates should be elected. It is plain Congress thought the power "to make laws in all cases" necessarily extended it "*to all rightful subjects* of legislation." It is plain Congress thought neither form of expression authorized the temporary Territorial government to create a Convention to form a Constitution which would begin to operate only after the Territorial Legislature itself had ceased. Its power to govern was confined to the Territory—a temporary contrivance for a temporary purpose—involved in all the local interests and conflicts of Territorial politics—and not safely to be intrusted with the providing for a Constitution. In a word, they were authorized to make laws to govern *the Territory;* but a law for a *Constitution* was no law for governing a *Territory* at all.

The case is stronger under the Kansas Act, for it reserves to Congress the power to make two or more states or Territories out of that Territory; and if Congress have the right to make *two* states, it is absurd to suppose it gave the Legislature power to make *one* state of it.

But there are cases of Territories which have spontaneously petitioned for admission under Constitutions framed without an enabling act, and they are fruitful of authority.

The proceedings for the admission of Arkansas, Michigan, and Iowa—where there were no acts of Congress authorizing Conventions—are decisive.

The law admitting Arkansas declared *the boundaries of the state.* That, I suppose, establishes the fact that nobody then maintained that there was any authority in her Constitution prior to her admission. The territorial limits of a state are essential to her existence; till they are defined there can be no state; after there is a state, Congress can not determine its right of territory. On the Territory depend the counties, the election districts, the judicial divisions, the apportionments of representation, the very people who are entitled to be heard on the adoption of the Constitution.

If the Territorial law can authorize a Convention which can adopt a Constitution having any *legal* force prior to the recognition of Congress, it must have the right to define and appropriate the territory of the state it creates; and if it have not *this* power, it can not create a state in the eye of the law *at all;* for Congress may destroy its identity by taking away a half, or two thirds, or *all* its territory, and give it to another state.

Congress recognized the State of Michigan upon the condition that her people should accept the boundaries Congress prescribed; and on their acceptance only was Michigan admitted.

Iowa was declared to be admitted as a state in 1845, under her Constitution of 1844, Congress declaring her boundaries, and requiring the assent of her people to them. But in August, 1846, Congress prescribed by law *other* boundaries for Iowa, and by that law recognized the validity of the proceedings of the Legislature of the *Territory* of Iowa of the 17th of January, 1846, submitting the boundary between the *Territory* and Missouri to the Supreme Court; and finally, in December, 1846, Congress declared Iowa admitted into the Union under a Constitution formed in May, 1846, and with the boundaries of the law of 1846.

The case of Wisconsin is still more decisive. The Territorial legislative power extended to all proper subjects of legislation; yet Congress passed an enabling act, and it defined the boundaries of the future state, on the 6th of August, 1846. The people formed a Constitution on the 16th of December, 1846, and Congress admitted the state on condition the people assented to other boundaries. Instead of merely assenting to the boundaries, they formed a new Constitution on the 1st of February, 1848, and on their application were admitted as a state with the boundaries of the enabling act, on the 29th of May, 1848.

These cases demonstrate that, whether a Constitution be formed by the people, under or without an enabling act, the Constitution has *no force of law*, over either person or territory, till the final and complete admission of the state. Till her senators and representatives are entitled to their seats, the Territorial authorities continue, the organic law is operative and supreme, the Territorial Legislature retains its legislative power, Congress can absolutely dispose of the Territory, assign its limits, and exercise its discretion whether to admit the people as a state or to retain them as they are. In a word, these cases display the great fact lost sight of in this controversy, that, till actual and final admission as *a state*, the Constitution *is not a law;* it is merely a *proposition* which will become operative only when Congress recognizes the existence of the state.

With reference to Michigan, a controversy arose in the Senate which elicited some salutary opinions. We have first of all the statement of his excellency the President, then in the Senate. When Michigan was applying for recognition, the exact question arose whether there was a legal power in the Territorial Legislature to proceed, their powers being as I have stated them. Mr. Buchanan then said:

"We have pursued this course [that is, to disregard informalities] in regard to Tennessee, to Arkansas, and even to Michigan. *No senator will pretend that their Territorial Legislatures had any right whatever to pass laws enabling the people to elect delegates to a Convention for the purpose of forming a state Constitution. It was an act of usurpation on their part.*"

This was said in the hearing of the whole Senate, that *no senator would contend* that they had legal authority, and he asserted that it was an act of usurpation! And, so far as the record shows, no man rose to controvert the authority of this distinguished expositor of Democratic doctrines of that day. Well, sir, that covers the three cases of proceedings by Territorial Legislatures without authority from Congress by special act. That destroys the whole argument which has been attempted to be founded upon them. With reference to Arkansas, I am protected by the authority of a name dear to the party which he founded. The governor of that Territory applied to General Jackson to know whether the Territorial Legislature had any authority to pass an act for the purpose of taking the sense of the people on the subject of a state Constitution. General Jackson took the opinion of his attorney general, Mr. Butler, and the opinion of that distinguished lawyer, acquiesced in by the whole administration, was, that there was no legal authority in the Territorial Legislature, but that it was beyond their temporary functions; that there was no authority inherent in the people, but that they were subordinate to the power of Congress, governed, as he says, under that clause of the Constitution which gives Congress power to make all needful rules and regulations for the territory of the United States. The new lights had not risen in their day. And, as if no authority should be wanting entitled to command respect with every division of the various opinions that are entertained now in this House, we have the farther authority of a gentleman from whom, in many respects, it is my misfortune to have differed in political opinion, but who, in my judgment, was one of the ablest gentlemen that ever graced the councils of this country—more conservative, manly, and upright in his views, and convictions, and conduct, than almost any man of his party; always ready to sacrifice party allegiance upon the altar of truth; always following the dictates of an independent judgment, as well in his votes as in his reasoning, and, for that reason, justly the worshiped idol of the great Southern section of this country. I suppose that the strict constructionist gentlemen of this House will not accuse me of any sympathy for dangerous dogmas from Federal quarters when I quote the authority of Mr. Calhoun:

> "My opinion was," said he, "and still is, that the movement of the people of Michigan in forming for themselves a state Constitution, without waiting for the assent of Congress, was revolutionary—"

What does the incumbent of the executive chair say to that now? Why were not the military forces of the United States directed, instead of guarding and protecting the Lecompton Convention, to turn them out, as they were directed to turn out the Topeka Convention, equally illegal or equally legal?

Mr. Calhoun proceeds to assign the reason:

> "As it threw off the authority of the United States over the Territory."

That he regarded as necessarily involved in the very idea of their assuming to themselves to take the first step, in a legal form, toward the establishment of a state government.

He proceeds to say:

> "And that we were left at liberty to treat the proceedings as revolutionary, and to remand her to her Territorial condition."

For doing which, with reference to Kansas, we are now threatened with the direst consequences by the gentlemen who then concurred in this opinion:

> "Or to waive the irregularity."

Now all the argument of our friends on the other side is to follow the *regular* course, and break down the irregular course—only they have agreed to call the *regular course* that which Mr. Calhoun called the *irregular* course. He proceeds to say:

"And to *recognize* what was done as *rightfully done—as our authority alone was concerned—my impression was that the former was the proper course;* but I also thought that the act remanding her back *should contain our assent in the usual manner for her to form a Constitution, and thus leave her free to become a state.*

And so a distinguished gentleman in another place [Mr. Crittenden] thought, not long since, and possibly there are some here who may think like him.

Well, sir, no gentlemen can rise here and cite any administration that has ever existed in this republic, down to the beginning of Mr. Buchanan's administration, that has ever so flagrantly violated the laws of the republic as to recognize any proceeding of a Territorial Legislature on this subject as having *authority of law.* No man can name any high officer of the government that has ever said so, as no man can show any vote of Congress that has ever looked to such a recognition. It was, sir, the first blunder —to be followed up consecutively and logically by other blunders in law, in policy, as well as in morals—that this administration made when it recognized the *legal authority of the Lecompton Convention*, assembled under the Legislature of Kansas. It was the last of the novelties which have been palmed on the country as sound law, to break the fall to which the inventors of the Kansas-Nebraska Act have been staggering for the last four years. Sir, it was new in this administration. No member of either house of Congress, at the last Congress, thought that there was any authority in the act of 1854 for the people to proceed, or for the Territorial Legislature to proceed. That law reserved to Congress the right to divide the Territory. How, then, could it authorize the people of that Territory to form themselves into one state? Did it contemplate that the wandering rabble that was there when that law was passed had then the right? And if they had nôt the right, pray how and when was the construction of the law changed, so far as the legal meaning is concerned, by the accession of population?

Did President Pierce, when he requested Congress to settle the difficulties of Kansas by passing a law authorizing them to form a state Constitution when they should have ninety-three thousand inhabitants, think the people of Kansas *then had* that authority? Did the gentleman [Mr. Toombs] who, in another place, during the last Congress, moved a bill authorizing them, when they should have ninety-three thousand inhabitants, to form a Constitution, and providing all the detailed organization of the Convention, think that without that law they had the authority *then?* Did this House, when it passed Mr. Dunn's bill, suppose they were doing then what the Territorial Legislature had the right already to do, although that bill postponed the exercise of the authority it conferred until their population had reached the requisite point? If they did not, then we have the concurrent opinions of all departments of the government during the last administration—nay, of every member of the last Congress of both sides, Democratic and Republican, as well as of all previous administrations—of the statute-book speaking for itself no less than the reason and nature of the proceeding against the possibility of any legal validity being imparted to the Convention and its proceedings by virtue of the Territorial laws; and those things of themselves ought to be sufficient, in my judgment, to settle the principle that *there is no legal authority in the Territorial Legislature to proceed in the matter.*

But it is perfectly clear that the law of the Legislature of Kansas itself has not been executed. It required a census to be taken in all the counties. It was not taken in half of them. It required the appointment of delegates to be made after the census was "completed" and "returned." It was made before the census was more than half taken. The law contemplated an apportionment on the basis of a completed census of the whole Territory, and of course, till that was *done*, there was no authority to make any apportionment. The causes of failure are immaterial to the *legal* point, but they are certified officially, by the governor and secretary, to have been the neglect of the local officers, and not the hostility or opposition of the people. It required the apportionment to be made by the governor and the secretary: it was made by the secretary *alone*, who was acting governor at the time. It required counties not having population enough for a delegate to be attached to some district. The fourteen counties excluded from the census were not attached to any district; they, therefore, had neither vote nor representation, actual or constructive, in the Convention. This failure to execute the law alone is fatal to every idea of legal validity in the proceedings.

If there was no legal authority in the Legislature, then I suppose that the fabric of my honorable friends on the other side tumbles about their ears. What becomes of the argument that we can not look behind the certificates? Why, the certificates have no legal authority. What becomes of the argument that these people who staid at home authorized those who voted to vote for them? If there was no legal election, they were not bound by it. If there was no law requiring them to attend, staying at home was their duty. They were only not participating in a usurpation. The foundation for a presumption of the assent of those who staid at home is, that the law required them to be at the polls. The good old law of Virginia, as my honorable friend in my eye will remember, made it a punishable offense to stay away from an election; and though there may be no law punishing it, yet it is a violation of law, and of the duty of the citizen, to stay away from an election. It is the duty of the citizen to cast his vote; and if the citizen does not cast it, he is held to authorize those who do; but that can not be where the proceeding has no legal validity—that presumption can not arise where it is merely a voluntary collection of a portion of the people of the Territory to signify their willingness to admit a certain form of Constitution without their having any authority to bind any body else. I suppose, then, that in that point of view, the whole argument upon the other side is in ruins. All their barriers of laws and certificates, presumptions against fact, and acquiescences extorted from protests and denials, are swept away.

We are at liberty to see that only two thousand six hundred and seventy people voted on calling a Convention; that only two thousand two hundred people elected the Convention; that the census shows only nine thousand two hundred and fifty-one voters, and twenty-four thousand seven hundred and eighty people in the Territory which has transformed itself into a state. And if they who hitherto insisted on confining us to legal returns and certificates now suggest the imperfections of the census and registry, I agree we may go farther and see that there may be twelve thousand voters, and from thirty-seven thousand to forty-two thousand people in the Territory; but of them not three thousand voters modestly ask the powers of a state government against the votes of ten thousand, and the protest of seven thousand. Nay, sir, emancipated from every trammel, we are at liberty and bound to go farther, and to inquire whether there has been in this Territory such fierce collisions, such hostile passions, so much of rebellion against the regular government, such an absolute division of the people with reference to their government, so much of civil bloodshed, so much of military control, such an absence of the ordinary political virtues, of calmness, of consideration, of deliberation as the President describes; whether an overwhelming majority of the people are opposed to the thing that is now sought to be forced or foisted upon them and devoted to another form of government. It relieves us from the fear of encountering the dangers intimated and vaguely hinted at by gentlemen upon the other side in the event of our venturing to do our duty. It leaves us free to determine whether, under all these circumstances, it is not a fair case for legislative discretion to pause and ask the people again what they say, upon "a sober second thought," about it—to see whether the people are likely to submit or likely to resist—whether any such great good is to be accomplished by now forcing this Constitution upon them that inevitable civil war will be compensated by it.

We are told by the President that this is the shortest way to settle the agitation. Mr. Chairman, I confess myself astonished at such an opinion from a gentleman who has seen so much of public service, has so long filled distinguished positions, and also knows, or ought to know, so much of human nature. Why, what has been the difficulty in that unfortunate Territory? Was it not that their Territorial Legislature was usurped? Is not that the reason that, from the foundation of the Territory to last October, the people refused to recognize any authority under the laws emanating from that Legislature? Have they not been quieted only by the earnest efforts and warm appeals, backed by the military power, of Governor Walker? Were they not quieted alone by the assurance which he gave them that they should have an opportunity of expressing their opinion on the law which was to govern them? Did they not join in the October election because they had confidence in his assurances? Was it not the first time that the people of that Territory had ever met, face to face, in an American manner, at the common ballot-box? Was it not the first time that they had stood in any other attitude except that of hostility, with arms in their hands and hatred in their hearts? And are we to be told by the President that the way to pacify them is to subject them permanently to the hateful domination of the handful of men from whose hands they would have wrested the government—as the President tells us—but for the United States troops; that the whole sanctity and authority of a state government shall remove them from all the power of Congress to redress their grievances; that they shall be admitted as a state, and thereby be delivered over to the legal authorities under the Constitution which they protest against, which Congress can not repeal, and will be bound to enforce if resisted? for, if the state be admitted, Congress has then no discretion but to follow the legal line of authority, and to put down every thing else as rebellion. But has not the President learned enough from the experience of the last three years to make him pause ere he pushed the country upon this dangerous experiment, or is he madly bent on a party triumph at the risk of civil war, forced on people of Anglo-Saxon blood as the only alternative to a tame surrender of their right of self-government?

The President's policy is high treason against the right of the people to govern themselves. His apology for his conduct is insulting to the victims of his usurpation.

Is it true that the dividing line is between those who are loyal to this Territorial government and those who endeavored to destroy it by force and usurpation? Then the *latter* have been no parties to the proceedings for a Convention, yet are to be subject to the Constitution.

Is it true that the Territorial government would long since have been subverted had it not been protected from their assaults by the troops of the United States? Then the stronger part of the people is against the proceeding for a Constitution, and it is to the weaker part the President proposes to confide the powers of state government over the stronger. Is not this to deliver the state into the hands of its enemies? or will the rebels submit when the United States withdraw its troops? or are they to *guarantee* the new usurpation?

Is it true that Secretary Stanton was obliged to summon the Legislature as the only means whereby the election of the 21st of December could be conducted without collision and bloodshed? Then why was Mr. Stanton dismissed for summoning them? Was it in furtherance of the same policy which then refused the people an opportunity to speak, and, now that they have spoken, refuses to hear them? Or, if that election could not be conducted without collision and bloodshed because the people were subjected to an authority they defied, is it the purpose of the President to insure the collision and bloodshed Stanton avoided by forcing on them a government which they have protested and remonstrated against, and are ready to defy and destroy? Is *that* the readiest method of *settling* the Kansas question?

Is it the truth that, up till the present moment, the enemies of the enabling government adhere to their Topeka revolutionary Constitution? Then *they* are not likely to receive the Lecompton Constitution.

Is the reason the people refused to vote for delegates to the Convention that they have ever refused to sanction or recognize any other Constitution than that of Topeka? Then surely *they* are not among those who sanction the Lecompton Constitution. It is not by their will it is put over them. It was not from *acquiescence* they refrained from voting. Their silence is their *dissent;* the President tells us so. He says they would have voted against it had it been submitted. Surely, then, silence is as instructive as their voice.

Sir, in my judgment, the passage of this law is a declaration of civil war. The history of the last three years in Kansas leaves no doubt that the people will not submit to this Constitution. It can not legally be changed before 1864. I think it a fair case for disregarding the form of law and the substance of law. If the constitutional authorities should concur in the change, peace may be preserved. I trust they will concur, and that peace will be preserved. But if they do resist the change which the mass of the people will demand, if we *now* refuse to listen to their protest, then, in my judgment, the shortest remedy is the best.

Free government is a farce if men are required to submit to usurpation such as has here been perpetrated, and I fear the people of Kansas are not in a mood to assist at the farce. They will turn it into tragedy. Having heretofore resisted, we ought to suppose they will resist again. We ought to act wisely and carefully, and, if we have discretion now, we will not drive this people upon revolutionary courses. Give them a mode of relief, and allow them to follow that peaceful course which they are inclined to follow, according to all reports from that Territory. Give them the opportunity of expressing their will as to the law under which they are to live; and, having expressed their will—whether it be for slavery or against slavery, is, in my judgment, absolutely immaterial—allow them to come in at a proper time, with a proper population and with reasonable boundaries and a rich dower, as one of the sister states of the republic.

REMARKS

AT THE COMMENCEMENT OF THE EASTERN FEMALE HIGH SCHOOL OF BALTIMORE.

DELIVERED IN BALTIMORE, MD., NOV. 10, 1858.*

YOUNG LADIES OF THE GRADUATING CLASS:

WHEN the devotee of the Ganges would seek the favor of her God, at eventide she commits to the current of the river a lighted lamp, and watches with beating heart its course and its fate. If it sinks she returns sorrowing, for her God is not with her; if it floats till lost in the distance and darkness, she returns rejoicing, for her offering is accepted.

You are those lamps which the people of Maryland have committed to the stream of time, their offering to that God who rules its current, to test his favor for this their highest sacrifice before him. If you shall fail, amid the temptations or the trials of life stray from the paths of truth and virtue, their offerings will stand condemned; but if, so long as life shall last, your lights shall shine on your fluctuating voyage, the examples of virtue, the guide of innocence, the illuminators of youth, then will the people of Maryland know that their sacrifice was well pleasing to the God of nations.

Before him they offer this their service in the cause of morals, light, and religion; and by its fruits they shall divine whether it be a true or false way which they have chosen to serve him.

To your conduct is committed this great religious service; at your hands will the future demand it.

And you, FATHERS, MOTHERS, FRIENDS of these maidens, to whose bosoms the state now restores them, how do you receive them? tarnished or purified? dimmed or brightened? For these are the fruits of our "infidel" free-schools. These are fruits of that smattering education, that surface-culture, that varnish over poor material, whose only tendency is to beget vanity, to engen-

* Mr. Davis was invited to address the graduating class of young ladies at this Commencement.

der self-conceit, to turn the head with teaching above their station, to unfit them for the duties of the matron, and consign them to the life of the butterfly till they sink soiled into corruption! Then let the system be judged by these its fruits.

This is an American spectacle; the image of the national genius; the handiwork of the utilitarian republic.

Well, let England glory in her Crystal Palace and its industrial splendors. Let France boast the camps of Boulogne and the miracles of her Cherbourg: we of this republic prefer to polish these diamonds.

They are from our mine. We first discovered that gold lies rather in the plains than on the mountains. We first explored the levels of creation for nature's richest treasures. We first discovered the hidden value of the common mind. We first proclaimed that the impartial hand of the Almighty had sown his precious pearls of reason and affection in every vale as well as on the hills, as he did his dew, it may be in darkness, yet awaiting only the rising sun to reveal each blade of grass, however lowly, flashing with its morning offering of beauty. We first saw that the beauty was all there, and that, though the sun touched the hills first and the vales last, he touched *all* in his course; and we are now displaying to the world the treasure we have found, some deep in the vales, which otherwise would never have been known.

And what say you for the culture—its breadth, its depth, its purity, its genuineness. Is it likely to promote the cause of knowledge, of patriotism, of domestic virtue, of holy religion in life and works?

If you have followed these exercises with as quick an ear, as appreciating a mind, as lively an interest as I have, you can now answer that question. The tree has shown its blossoms and its fruits—are the former only beautiful, and the latter bitter?

Surely these exercises have revealed a comprehensiveness and a thoroughness of instruction, a degree of attainment, and a modesty of bearing seldom combined. They who have traced before us here this evening, with steady hand, the succession of "historic cities" from buried Nineveh, through ruined Athens and the lone mother of dead empires, to the teeming abodes of our republican glory; or, treading the "starry path to the Temple of Truth," have reviewed the great results of Herschel or of Franklin; or, alive to the glories of mechanical skill, have pointed out with accuracy what has been accomplished by their countrymen's enterprise; or have touched with caustic finger the enervating follies of the day with equal judgment and wit; or embodied in poetic numbers, with accuracy and ease, at once poetic thought and graceful pleasantry—are no smatterers in knowledge; and any lady in the land may well be proud of daughters who can write their native tongue with simplicity and grace characteristic of the compositions we have heard; and if the hand of the master may have purified *them* from occasional errors, the tone and cadence of the recital, the enunciation and pronunciation are at least their own, and the first were just and spirited, and as to the latter, if there was more than one word mispronounced, my ear was not quick enough to catch it.

Not only were Milton and Byron aptly quoted by some, but the tone and style of sentiment pervading the productions revealed the influence of such companionships.

Nor are knowledge and intellectual culture all, but these, the future matrons of the republic, even now give evidence of fitness for their high mission as prophets of patriotic inspiration to the young men of the land; for who did not hear in those glowing words on the "March of Mind" the tramp of patriotic hosts fired by their enthusiasm in defense of the republic? And when, with kindling eye and earnest voice, she devoted to execration the cravens who should allow the fabric of our liberties to be torn asunder, did we not see in her all of that matron who bade her son, going forth to battle, return with his shield or upon it?

Nor did the sterner virtues exclude the womanly virtues; for what do we recognize as worthy of the woman in every station, from motherly tenderness and domestic duties up to their source in religious inspiration and trust in God, which was not comprised in that touching portraiture of "The True Woman," which fitly and beautifully closed this farewell to girlhood?

That outpouring of pious feeling expressed in words what the sacred anthems which every voice joined to swell had sent in music to the skies.

They were the *infidelity* inculcated by our public schools!!

They are *infidel*, because the clergy are excluded from inculcating sectarian dogmas, just as our republic is *anarchy*, because kings are not invited to teach us civil obedience!

The objection comes from no republican lips. It reveals a

profound ignorance of the foundations of our republic. They who utter it have yet many a fathom deep to penetrate ere they sound the depth of the American principle of the *freedom* of thought, the *freedom* of religion, the *right* of every citizen to unchecked freedom in forming his religious opinions, and the deep interest of the state in securing him not only *freedom*, but the *means* of enlightened judgment, and that greater, deeper, and holier faith in the sufficiency of every enlightened mind to read for himself in the Word of God the will of God, whose *practice* is *religion.*

We of America have our own peculiar mode of cultivating religion as well as of guiding the state, and that is *freedom.*

There are other methods which older nations have tried and still cling to, but we have discarded them; and they who assail our system would bring us back to those. It is well to know what they are.

There is one which assumes the supremacy of the spiritual over the civil power; asserts the right of the Church to define and of the state to enforce the true faith; prohibits free judgment, or punishes its errors as crimes.

This was the law of old Europe; the principle has never been abandoned; the perversity of modern times has greatly limited its enforcement. It is still the law of Italy, Spain, and Turkey.

There is another which professes toleration for all opinions, declares the state the patron of all the sects whose ministers it pays and controls as a part of the machinery of government, and seeks the quiet of the state in the stagnation of opinion and the hereditary descent of creeds.

This is the system of England and Prussia, and, since the Revolution, of France and Belgium. It is the boasted system of toleration.

There is a third system which asserts the right of each man to absolute freedom in belief and worship, which denies to the state and to the Church all power to coerce in matters of religion, which declares absolute freedom of thought the only security for religion.

It is not *toleration*, for that implies *indulgence*, a privilege which may be regulated or revoked. It is *freedom* of the individual in matters of religion.

It denies to the state all power over it except the necessary right to determine the limits of the domain of conscience and the state.

This is our American freedom of religion.

It proclaims to every conscience freedom for its worship, but not freedom to control any other conscience, nor to exclude any other conscience, young or old, from seeking in its *own way* its own satisfaction. It does not recognize in the parent any more than in the state any right to coerce the convictions of the child, to exclude it from the light, to impair its freedom in matters of religion. On the contrary, it pledges to all alike, of every age, equal freedom; offers to *all* the means of thought and education; but forces none, and allows none to be forced, either into darkness or light.

It is the profound idea of the American people, which those not reared under its influence find it difficult to conceive. It is peculiar to this people. It is *our* principle, and we alone profess it, and we alone practice it; we alone have staked the very existence of the government on its truth. We have boldly released religion from the control of the state, and the state from the control of the Church, and the people from the control of the clergy; declared not merely the right, but the duty of all men to worship God according to their own conscience, and offered to every human being the freedom and the means of so doing, with a firm conviction that God has conferred on every mind power to understand his duties toward Him not less than toward his neighbor, that each human being has within him the capacity for himself to learn the path of duty from that book which God gave to be the guide of all men, and not merely to teach the clergy to guide them. The American principle is not *neutrality* between religion and irreligion, between faith and infidelity. It is not merely abstinence from state control in affairs of religion, leaving the people to the power and control of the clergy or of the Church. On the contrary, the American people, by their laws and Constitutions, every where avow themselves for religion and against irreligion. They every where assert the freedom of each conscience as well from clerical as state control, the capacity of each man for himself to determine his religious condition, and they deny the right, not merely of the state, but of the Church or the clergy, to dictate his belief and exact conformity to their rules.

This is the logical consequence of the freedom of speech and of the press, the freedom of thought and religion as expressed or implied in our laws; and it is illustrated by every statute-book, and by every Constitution in the United States, not merely in the freedom they assert, but in the bulwarks they every where throw up for its protection against not merely the power of the state, but the undue spiritual influence of the clergy and the Church.

Nor do the American people content themselves with barren declarations. Every where the public schools attest their efforts to make freedom of thought and religion not merely the *right*, but the *habit* of the nation. The state throws open the field of knowledge, and declares the right of every one freely to enter and enjoy its fruits. Strange and inconsistent would it be if, where every science and all history find a voice, and the children are to be trained for the public service, the Bible alone were silent. The common fountain of every creed, in either version a fertile source of religious life, the American people see no departure from their ideas of religious freedom in opening its simple text in the public schools. It adds no sectarian exposition; that it leaves to the discretion of the parent. It listens to no sectarian complaint at its admission; for it is asserting the right of the child to the means of forming its own judgment, and freedom of thought is a farce without knowledge.

Do any maintain that ignorance is better than knowledge without sectarian teaching? Then the American people think otherwise. They can regard no such protest without abandoning the holy cause of free instruction, without surrendering their faith in the sufficiency of every mind to learn the path of duty in the Word of God. A right to deprive children of all instruction not sectarian is not a right of conscience in the American sense, and they who first declared the principle may well be allowed to construe and apply it. As well elevate absolute ignorance to the dignity of a religious dogma, and in its name call on the state to close the public schools. If the interests of any sect suffer by free investigation, it is its misfortune, but confers no right to keep men in ignorance; for the state asserts the right of freedom of thought and religion against all who impeach it—as a right of man against the arrogant usurpations of those who would rule them.

Far from admitting the right of any one to object to free instruction, the principle of freedom is asserted in opposition to that very assumption. It is to elevate to the dignity of a religious right the very power over the human mind against which we protest, and which drove our fathers into exile. As soon suspend the Habeas Corpus Act that some sect may perform the religious duty of coercing its members. As soon fail to punish those who, in the name of spiritual discipline, imprison a citizen of the republic, or devoutly burn a witch or a heretic. If the state yield the freedom of instruction to one sectarian prejudice, it must yield it to all; and that is to abandon the education of the children of the state for the education of the children of the sects by the sects.

Nay, more, it is an abandonment of the right of the people to freedom of thought, of opinion, and of instruction; for the state yields to the sectarian only because he denies the right of the state to teach any thing he disapproves. It is a confession that there is something which the people have no right to know—at least without its antidote. Our principle is the right of each individual to know all things, to prove all things, and to hold fast what *to him* seems good.

If nothing can be taught which any sect would rather not have taught, narrow indeed would be the field. There are few on whose history there is no blot, and scarcely one which, left to itself, would not tear out some page of history, expunge some scientific truth, or close some department of discovery. How many would protest against geology, because they fear it conflicts with the books of Moses? One sect might insist that Newton's system of the heavens be excluded, or taught merely as a hypothesis and not as a truth, because they think the Bible teaches that the earth is stationary and the sun moves; or others exclaim against a book on moral philosophy, which teaches the freedom of the will—in conflict with their views of predestination taught in the Bible. While one may object to classic authors, because in conflict with Christian morals, another will ostracize half of English literature by referring to the Index Expurgatorius as the criterion of the lawful; and the Atheist may join the chorus of complaints for the invasion of the rights of conscience, and insist that the name of God shall be suppressed, or taught only as a myth.

The state asserts the right of her children to judge of all these things *for themselves*—to know the evidence on which they rest. It teaches no dogmas, to be received on authority blindly, but it aspires to place in every hand the means of judging every thing; and while it will enforce or teach no creed or worship, it will recognize no right in any one to exclude any department of knowledge from the teachings of the public schools. The people reserve to themselves the sole right of defining the limits of the domain of conscience and of the state, to be determined by the common conscience of mankind, and in the honest purpose of promoting human freedom.

The people must adhere to this free system of state education, or abandon the education of the people of the Church.

All history can not show the mass of any people ever educated by any Church. Schools have been frequently recommended, and sometimes established under the shadow of the Church, but they have never gathered within them the mass of the children of the people; they have been partial, exceptional, inadequate—a part of the Church machinery, and never dedicated to freedom of thought; and the mass of every people remained in ignorance till America set the example which churchmen now carp at.

They who would know what education under Church auspices is can learn it in Italy, or England, or Spain. Let them who are in love with it adopt it. For ourselves, we glory in having both proclaimed the principle and perfected the system of free instruction.

And if, the purpose being the same, the objection be varied, and the system be impeached for irreligion because no creed is taught, then the American people reply religion is one thing and creeds are another thing. The republic cherishes religion; it has no concern with sectarianism but to see that it does no mischief. It remembers it rather as the instigator to strife than to love, the cause of wars and bloodshed, the fruitful source of heart-burnings and alienation among fellow-citizens—the opposite in all things to that religion which is pure, and peaceful, and gentle, which is the inspiration of public virtue and the best guardian of the public peace; and thus remembering the historic character of religious sects, it has no interest in promoting either at the expense of the other, and will not subsidize universal war among them by recognizing them as elements in the adjustment of its system of public schools.

The American system proceeds on the assumption of the capacity of each man and each woman to learn the will of God from the Word of God. The American people place their faith, not in teachers of religion, or in speculative or traditional creeds, but in the nature of man and the good inspiration of God. They spread the Bible before the youthful mind, and when it is read they close it; and they look for spiritual nourishment to flow as freely from it to the open mind, as the milk from the mother's breast to the infant that clings there. They think that the sun is visible without telescopes, and that the colored glasses of sectarian instructors may impair its glory, but can not add to its brightness or its warmth. They cherish religion such as it blazes from the heavens, such as it is reflected from the Bible, shining into the heart of man from either source, needing no creed to define it, allowing no sectarian anathema to limit it—cheerfully greeting it wherever the life exemplifies the spirit of the Bible, however the disciple may stammer in the recital of crabbed catechisms or stumble in the darkness of theological metaphysics. And while the American people profess to be a religious people, and would shrink with horror from any system which encouraged irreligion, yet they remember that their republican government has been assailed on the same ground. They feel that their system of liberty and religion must flourish or fall together; and whether they now flourish or languish, they will judge only by the fruits. We are no wiser than the apostles, who knew that their religion was universal, because they saw its fruits among the Gentiles who professed it. We do the like. We point to the churches that every where decorate the land—the thousands who daily crowd them for humble worship—to the spontaneous and free reverence for things divine, which bows every head and bends every knee before the Supreme—to the perpetual fountain of pious teaching which flows from the mother's lips—to the orderly march of free millions, with no guide but their conscience and the law, in peace and order—to the overflowing charities which every where attest the reality of Christian love—these things are the *proofs* of the religion which the American people cherish; and they are the proofs that it does flourish and not languish. We think these better tests than a theological inquiry as to how many believe in predestination, or transubstantiation, or episcopal succession.

This is the reply of the American people to those who impeach their system for infidelity. To these results they point to prove that religion flourishes better when free than when controlled—under the air of heaven than in sectarian hot-houses or under the deadly shadow of state protection, and the reply is decisive.

They respect the ministers of religion of every sect—seek willingly and freely their spiritual aids and consolations; but they do not regard them as either the sole or the best instructors of youth, whether in matters of religion or matters of science. They have a firm conviction of the sufficiency of laymen to regulate affairs of education, and they prefer to confine the minister to the service of the altar. They think the less their children are taught why they turn their backs on each other when they pray to the same God, the better for them.

They look to other sources of religious instruction for the young, which they are careful to provide.

They think the first lispings of infant piety are best poured forth at the mother's knee; that the first inspirations of spiritual truth flow best from the mother's lips; that the earliest guides in religious conduct are the living examples of the mother's walk and conversation, aided by the free Sunday-schools conducted by the people, and not by the clergy. They think that the best instruction for a religious life flows directly from the Bible, which God gave to guide men, and which He therefore supposed them able to understand. This the American people spread before the minds of the young, without note or comment, and in either version, that its teachings, instilled in earliest youth, may influence the life and conduct long ere the maturity of mind tends to theological speculations, and instruct and comfort thousands who may never comprehend a single sectarian theory.

But this free system can exist only where cultivated and pious mothers preside over the family. That is the purpose of this beneficent institution at whose celebration we have been this evening assisting, and these maidens are its flowers, woven by its hands into a crown worthy of the brow of Eve.

These maidens are the missionaries of the state.

Yes, it is to you, future mothers of the republic, that its destinies are committed. This high cultivation has been bestowed on you, not to promote vanity or frivolous dissipation, or the rivalries of social ambition, but to make you the lights and guides of the next generation in the paths of religious and civil prudence. You are not called to mingle in the turmoil of public life, nor to assist at the wrangling of synods, nor to flame in the front of war, but you are the sent to outwatch the stars for the safety of the life of the republic, the virtue and truth, the patriotism and devotion, the religion and morals of those to whom the destinies of the republic are committed—the people who will constitute and rule it. Your life and station find their fittest symbol in that glorious path which spans the arch of night, thick sown with blazing stars, but more beautiful still by the clouds of trembling light amid which they shine—the blended beams of innumerable but invisible stars, deep hidden in the recesses of the heavens till explored by the great astronomers of modern times. It is not yours to glitter in the eye of the world as those leaders of the starry host which first arrest the gazer's eye, or guide the mariner on the deep; but, hidden within the heaven of your homes, invisible to every eye but those who penetrate there, the pathway of the republic will glow with your light, a visible halo from invisible stars, whose glory is not to be seen, but to wrap all things else in your light.

So, when in after ages the eye of the world shall marvel at the dazzling destinies of the republic culminating in splendor and triumph, let them be taught that it is not the glory of industry, or arts, or arms, but the light which the matrons of a nation shed around its path.

THE REOPENING OF THE SLAVE-TRADE.

The case of the slave-trader *Wanderer*, and the harangues of Messrs. Spratt, of South Carolina, Yancey, Ruffin, and other extremists in the South in favor of repealing the United States enactments against the slave-trade; the exhibition, at an agricultural fair in South Carolina, of an "imported laborer of African origin," to whose owner was awarded a silver prize; the serious discussions as to the necessities of the South for a class of "immigrants from Africa" suited to her climate and productions, and the boldly-declared doctrine of the "divinity" of slavery, and the rightfulness and Christian duty of its extension and increase, had begun to awaken the fears of even the least thoughtful.

In August, 1859, Mr. Davis wrote for a daily journal the following article on THE REOPENING OF THE SLAVE-TRADE.

It is time that the insidious advances toward this nefarious and unchristian traffic which a large and influential party are making should attract the attention of Maryland. Her people should not be taken unawares, as they were by the repeal of the Missouri Compromise under the same false pretexts. The preparation of men's minds for the grand end has already begun, either consciously or unconsciously.

The grand and humane policy of Maryland—the colonization scheme—is insinuated to have failed. The ideas and sentiments from which it springs are said to have been shown false. Journals talk of the great revulsion of public opinion among the leading men of England on the question of emancipation, which has no existence out of their imaginations, to lend respectability to the change of men's opinions of the honesty, morality, humanity, and policy of the slave-trade, already begun, and which they wish to foster. While they do not venture to recommend the reopening of it, they suggest that it exists now, in fact, more than ever, though we are deprived of its benefits.

That the fleets of England and the United States do not prevent or suppress, but aggravate it. That interest which would be equal to humanity in securing good treatment to the candidates for civilization and heaven, is now expressed by terror, and converted into cruelty by the fear of capture, the ignominy of exposure, the menace of punishment. It is plausibly argued that the removal of the cruisers would remove the terrors of the trader, and the captive, no longer a source of danger to the thief, would become an object of interest.

Good food, water, and air, all the delights of a pleasure voyage, would obliterate the ill renown of the "middle passage;" and, after a charming voyage of a few days or a week, the neophytes of Christianity would land on the celestial shores of the New World disenthralled from barbarism, and, under the training of Christian masters and ministers, learn at once the way to cultivate cotton and the Christian life. The question of morals is passed in silence. These ingenious gentlemen assume the *existence* of the trade, and their philanthropic purpose is to ameliorate the condition of the slaves.

In aid of this argumentation, others insist strenuously on the entire unfitness of the negro for freedom; for of course, if he is nowhere fit for freedom, he must be slave to somebody, and if any body's, why not *ours*, the Southern fire-eaters will in due time exclaim.

Of course, this view is expressed with great moderation, great candor, great independence—nay, philosophically, simply as an ethnological question; or piously, as an attempt to purchase the divine counsels touching the negro race, and to become the humble instrument of His will, which, of course, can be only good! His will is learned, not in the Bible, but in the British West Indies. The great English experiment of emancipation is loudly proclaimed a failure. The opinion of English statesmen is said to have changed. The very emancipationists are claimed as converts to the system they ignorantly overthrew. Statistics are paraded to corroborate the proof of failure, and adjective is piled on adjective to describe how, in the lowest deep of slavery, a lower deep of ignorance, idleness, worthlessness, was found in freedom by the English experiment.

If the writers draw no conclusion, every reader can draw it without much trouble. It is an ally to the argument of the universal unfitness of the negro for mere personal civil freedom any where; that is, the mere exercise of the right in subordination to the laws of the land to dispose of his own labor, to enjoy the fruits of his own toil.

It is the exact course of reasoning which was heard in the late Slaveholder's Convention in Baltimore. The resolutions proposed to be adopted by the extreme men of that Convention were merely the formal expressions of the above reasoning, yet no such conclusions are hinted at, but the dissertations usually close with some general and edifying remarks about the inequality of the races, the absurdity of attempting to give negroes equal privileges with whites, about which nobody differs, and could have been deduced from much more accurate premises than those employed. But the mind of the reader is sent far beyond the conclusions of the writer.

If we turn our eyes southward, we shall get more light there. Men's opinions are more pronounced. It is now a political question. Large masses of the Democratic party openly avow themselves in favor of reopening the slave-trade, and greater multitudes sympathize with them, but prefer the safer course of insinuation and circumvention. They assume the Southern disguise which cheated the country into the repeal of the Missouri Compromise. They suggest, assert, maintain the unconstitutionality of the laws prohibiting the slave-trade. They do it under divers pretexts, but all end in one point. Some merely wish the laws repealed, not to reopen the trade, but to leave it to the several states to say whether they will allow it, just as Congress was to allow each Territory to decide on slavery for itself; others think the laws ought to be repealed because the penalty of death is too severe to be enforced against the innocent, mild, and moral captains and crews of the slavers; while others, more practical and more logical, say, if the laws be unconstitutional, there is no need of a repeal—they are nullities. Juries, grand and petit, may and must disregard them.

The courts have no power to enforce unconstitutional laws—nay, the courts are not even to decide the question of constitutionality; it is too plain for question; each juror must decide for himself. Grand juries must refuse to find indictments for slave-trading, though the facts be admitted; petit juries must acquit any one indicted by the usurpation of a grand jury. We have seen within the last year both grand and petit juries in Southern states disregard both evidence, and law, and court, and refuse to find indictments, or, where found, acquit the prisoner in the face of uncontradicted testimony of the officers of the navy making the arrest, and of the jail full of stolen negroes—for the laws are unconstitutional. The latter is now the view prevalent among the Democrats of the South. The majority in some states are openly and avowedly of that opinion. In other states the minority are loudly in favor of it, and the majority is silent and sympathizing, but restrained by prudence until after 1860. In some states it is the question underlying the apparent topics in contest, as in Texas. Mr. Stephens more than insinuates his inclinations toward those views in his late speech. In Mississippi most of her public men have made profession of their faith. The question is upon us, *Is it the great Democratic bait to catch the South in* 1860, *or to concentrate the South for an act of rebellion?* The repeal of the laws is the legalization of the slave-trade. No law affirming its legality is needed. It revives by the *simple repeal*, under the law of nations. The Democratic party is now ready at the South to make the issue—repeal or rebellion. It touches their honor, they say, as they said the Missouri Compromise touched their honor. The laws are a slur on their institution and on their ancestors, therefore they will have repeal or blood. What does Maryland say?

THE QUESTION IN THE TERRITORIES.—UNION OF ALL OPPOSED TO THE DEMOCRACY.

DURING 1859 Mr. Davis had been active in endeavoring to bring about a union or fusion of the two parties—the Republican in the Northern and Western, and the American and Union parties in the Middle and Southern States—equally opposed to the continuance in power of the two factions which, having coalesced under the name of Democratic, had, in consequence, carried the election of 1856, and now claimed, under the usual penalty, to be allowed to carry the election in 1860.

In various letters to individuals and to journals, written during that year, he set forth his views as to the necessity, the expediency, and the feasibility of such a union; and he was unremitting in his efforts to bring about such a state of opinion as should induce those parties in opposition to agree upon a candidate for the presidency in 1860 upon his past record and position, and without any platform or declaration as to *legislation* in regard to slavery in the Territories. He was in favor of the nomination, in that way, of Judge Edward Bates, of Missouri; and he afterward endeavored (in 1860, at Chicago) to induce the Republican party to offer him as a candidate who could be accepted and voted for by Southern Whigs and the opponents of Southern pro-slavery Democracy.

In November, 1859, Mr. Davis addressed to the Editor of the New York *Tribune* the following letter upon this subject:

SIR,—The Republican party is the expression of the Northern opposition to the extension of slavery into the Territories.

All the Territories are now by law, and in fact, free, for there are slaves in none. No law establishing it or regulating it has been passed by Congress, nor by any Territorial Legislature to which Congress has delegated the power; and the act of New Mexico, being in conflict with the decree of Mexico abolishing slavery, is for that reason void.

In this state of the case, your Republicans insist on declaring it the right and duty of Congress to interdict slavery by law in a platform, and to make the enactment of such a law a cardinal point of policy in the canvass of 1860.

Others, who see in such a policy an end of every hope of union with the Southern opposition, and a strong improbability of uniting the Northern opposition in Pennsylvania, New Jersey, and Indiana for the election of a President in 1860, think that the election of a President by the opposition, holding the views of Mr. Clay on that question, and in character above the necessity of pledges or platforms, insures every thing that is necessary to satisfy reasonable men to arrest permanently the slave propaganda.

To obtain security by legislative restriction, the Republicans must elect a clear majority of both House and Senate, and the President, and hold them long enough to change the Supreme Court. The Republicans must first get a clear majority of the whole House of Representatives. Not merely an opposition majority against the Democrats, but a Republican majority against both the Northern Democrats and the whole body of the vote from the slaveholding states; and that Republican majority must be more radical than any ever seen in the House of Representatives.

They must also have a like majority in the Senate, where the free states lose their numerical advantage, and where any two free states in Democratic hands prevent the possibility of success.

They must at the same time have the President, for a Democratic President would veto any bill excluding slavery from the Territories.

They must, after all those unprecedented conditions, still, in addition, either reorganize the Supreme Court, or hold all that power long enough to change it by appointments not Democratic. This is plainly so; for, as now constituted, or as hereafter filled by *any* Democrat, any law of Congress restricting slavery will be declared void.

This can not be avoided by districting the country and assigning to the free states a number of judges proportioned to their population, for any Democratic President can find discarded anti-Lecomptonites enough to fill the bench from every district for a full generation.

Neither can this be avoided by any law, for the appointment of the judges must remain in the President's hand, according to the Constitution.

But if such a reorganization were attempted, it would so rouse or frighten the timid or Conservative men as almost inevitably to restore the Democrats to power.

The Republicans, then, to restrict slavery by law, must have every department of the government, and hold them long enough to reorganize the Supreme Court, and still hold power to prevent the work being undone.

Such majorities they have not now even in the House of Representatives. The Republicans have no majority at *all*, not even with the eight anti-Lecompton men, for any such purpose. In the Senate they are in a great minority, and the President is against them.

Is there any prospect of their ever within this generation holding such power under the condition above framed?

No prudent man can say there is; and if not, then the attempt to adopt a restriction law is wholly futile. No matter how much men may wish it, the thing is, humanly speaking, impossible.

But, on the other hand, the election of a President in 1860, of itself, silences and arrests the slave propaganda, if he be elected by a combination of the opposition in a manner so free as to insure a permanent union of the Republican and American voters in the Northern and Western states.

We say the President alone is sufficient, and without him every thing else is perfectly worthless.

With the President an adverse majority in Congress is worthless.

The President appoints the Territorial judges and removes them at his pleasure, as well as the United States attorneys, and the marshals who summon the juries, and the governors of the Territories, and these *constitute* the Territorial governments in fact.

The President appoints the judges of the Supreme Court, and between now and the end of next term a majority of those judges now on the bench must, in the course of nature, be substituted by others.

The Dred Scott case is a Democratic case, decided by Democratic judges, resting on Democratic party political views of the Constitution and laws, and inspired by Democratic prejudices and sentiments. It would have been rendered by no judge whom either Harrison, or Taylor, or Fillmore would have appointed.

It would have been rendered by any Democratic judge appointed by any Democratic President in the last ten years.

Now the old Whig view of the relation of slavery to the Territories was this—that it existed only by virtue of the positive law of the land on which it was attempted to be enforced. So that, if forbidden by Congress, or if neither forbidden nor sanctioned by Congress, it did not exist; and if Congress has no power over the subject at all, then that of itself made all the Territories necessarily and forever free, till they both became states and adopted slavery.

Now suppose such a man as all the opposition could unite on —a man holding Mr. Clay's views, and honest enough to trust without the distracting pledge of a platform.

He will name judges for the Territories holding like constitutional views with himself.

Mr. Clay, *e. g.*, thought the Mexican laws excluded slavery, and a judge so thinking would declare the law of New Mexico, or any other establishing or so regulating slavery, void.

The United States attorneys and marshals would be instructed to institute no prosecutions, and to enforce no laws of that character.

In civil suits a master would have no remedy against his slave, for he could institute no suit against him. The marshal and his force would not lend the public force to secure his authority over a slave voluntarily carried into the Territory.

No indictment would be preferred for any rescue of such a slave; and if the negro were not interfered with by the people, it would be merely a question *between* the claimant's power to *guard* and his power to go off.

If a civil suit for a rescue were instituted, a judgment might be brought to the Supreme Court.

In such a case, the Supreme Court, as now constituted, or as constituted by any Democrat, will decide for the master; but as constituted by any President elected by the opposition, the decision would necessarily be against him.

Three new appointments will change the complexion of the court. There are more than three very old men whose places must be filled by the next administration, and that will determine the complexion of the court for the next generation, in all probability, if made by a Democrat.

Now, to accomplish a rehearsal of the Dred Scott folly no pledge is needed, no platform, nothing but a President holding Mr. Clay's views. Judges appointed by such a President will instantly repudiate that ridiculous farago of bad history, worse law, and Democratic partisanship.

The decision was made only because the people had been quarreling for twenty years, and the Democrats had been allowed to hold the President because the people could not agree to turn them out of the presidency, and, like the Democrats, quarrel about matters of policy while sheltered against disaster by the power of the President.

We repeat that, without the President, every thing else is worthless; with the President, every thing else follows; for the President gives all the offices at home and abroad; thus *his* will inspires every act of the government, even the very courts, on political and constitutional subjects.

A majority in Congress with him consecrates his will and that of those who elect him as law, and he executes and construes it in the spirit of its authors.

His veto protects his policy against an adverse majority in both houses, and gives his friends time to rally and restore their majority in the next Congress.

He is omnipotent against every thing but a two-third's vote of both houses, so that his administration may be censured, but can not be arrested by any less number *by law.*

The possession of the President, except under great abuse of power, draws to it generally the majorities of both houses, from the natural tendency of the people to make a complete government while they are about it.

But, with the President alone in such hands as we have indicated, the slave propaganda is forever broken down.

It can pass no slave code for its Territories.

It can not repeal the laws against the slave-trade. It can not repeat the scenes of Kansas, for President Pierce could at any moment have ended those invasions and those frauds by the appointment of his marshals and governors, or, if necessary, by the troops.

Thus paralyzed, the black Democrats could not agitate the country; the progress of population would settle the condition of the Territories for their transformation into states without any farther legislation.

On these principles the opposition can unite, for they are simply a cessation of the propaganda. They only assume that whoever the opposition may agree on will be one holding Mr. Clay's views, and known to do so, without any pledges or questions. Such a person *only* can unite the opposition.

Such an administration inaugurated in 1860 gives the Conservative body of the people—now unhappily divided on the issue, shown above not to be material, *i. e.*, not necessary to be raised in order to accomplish *all* which moderate men ought to want, and do want—the possession of the government for a generation at least, if wisely conducted.

On the other hand, if the opposition fail in 1860, they may roll up the map of the United States for twenty years.

ON THE RESOLUTIONS OF CENSURE BY THE MARYLAND LEGISLATURE ON ACCOUNT OF MR. DAVIS'S VOTE FOR MR. SPEAKER PENNINGTON.

At the second session of the Thirty-fifth Congress (December, 1858, to March 4, 1859) Mr. Davis spoke against the proposed resolution to impeach Judge Watrous, of Texas (which was rejected), and on the bills for the Indian, Civil, and Naval Appropriations.

In the month of October, 1859, occurred the outbreak at Harper's Ferry, and attack on and capture of the United States Arsenal there by John Brown and his associates, who attempted also to cause and lead an insurrection of the negro slaves. The excitement caused by this invasion of Virginia by twenty men was only less in certain parts of Maryland than the terror it occasioned in the state first named. It was instantly asserted every where as the deliberate act of a great political party in the North, and for which they were responsible, and was held forth as the convincing reason why the only safety of the South was in the party whose excesses had provoked it.

Notwithstanding the efforts of the missionaries who preached this new doctrine in Maryland, Mr. Davis was again elected, for the third time, in November, 1859, to the Thirty-sixth Congress, which met on the 5th of December. There were returned to the House one hundred and nine Republicans, one hundred and one Democrats, twenty-six Americans, and one Whig (Mr. Etheridge, of Tennessee).

For the speakership, at first Mr. Bocock was supported by the Democrats, Mr. Sherman by the Republicans, and Mr. Gilmer and Mr. Boteler by the Americans. A resolution was introduced by the Democrats, in hopes of compelling the Americans to side with them, that "no indorser or advocate of the 'Helper Book' (The Impending Crisis of the South, by H. R. Helper, of North Carolina) was proper to be placed in the chair of the House." This was aimed against Mr. Sherman, whose name appeared in a list of those who recommended the distribution and reading of that volume. The discussion was long and violent, and after many ineffectual efforts, and the withdrawal of Mr. Sherman and others, on the 31st of January, 1860, Mr. Davis, when his name was called, voted for Governor Pennington, a member from New Jersey. Governor Pennington was a Whig, who had been elected as a Republican, and who had been supported as their candidate for the speakership by the Republicans only when they found it impossible to elect one of their straitest sect, and "an indorser or advocate of the 'Helper Book.'" This vote gave to Mr. Pennington one hundred and sixteen votes, *within one* of the required number. This was secured next day, February 1, by the arrival of Mr. Briggs, and thereupon Mr. Pennington was conducted to the chair.

There was a furious clamor raised in the Legislature of Maryland, then in session at Annapolis, and attempted to be raised among the people of the state, and of the city of Baltimore especially, upon the announcement of the vote cast by Mr. Davis for Mr. Pennington.

The most abusive articles were printed in the daily papers of Baltimore; insulting and threatening anonymous letters were sent to Mr. Davis, and violent efforts made to hold him up as "a traitor to the South, and renegade to the political, commercial, and social interests of Baltimore."

In the Maryland Legislature enough members were found of the party which had sent Mr. Davis to Congress, and who had been elected from their own counties partly through his efforts, to join with the pro-slavery Democracy in denouncing this vote, by resolutions declaring that he had therein misrepresented the sentiments and feelings of the state.

After these resolutions had been presented to the House of Representatives, Mr. Davis took occasion, on the 21st of February, 1860 (the House being in Committee of the Whole on the State of the Union), to set forth his opinions of them and their contrivers and supporters in the following speech:

MR. CHAIRMAN,—The honorable the Legislature of Maryland has decorated me with its censure. It is my purpose to acknowledge that compliment.

It is long, sir, since the party which now controls the Legislature of Maryland has been so fortunate as to have a majority in both its branches, and it has so conducted itself that it is probable it will be long ere again it succeeds in getting that control.

If one may judge from the course and conduct of that body, the gentlemen who compose it are perhaps more surprised at their present power than their opponents. They do not appear to be less bewildered or more to have changed their original nature than Christophero Sly, when waking up, after his debauch, in the nobleman's chamber, dazzled with the unaccustomed elegance which surrounded him, he began to question himself thus:

"Am I a lord? and have I such a lady?
Or do I dream? or have I dream'd till now?
I do not sleep; I see, I hear, I speak;

I smell sweet savors, and I feel soft things;
Upon my life, I am a lord indeed,
And not a tinker, nor Christophero Sly.
Well, bring our lady hither to our sight:
And once again, a pot o' the smallest ale."

Sudden elevation has never changed the character of the person accidentally raised to a position he was never intended by nature to occupy; and those who imagine it ever can may free themselves from that delusion by looking at the Legislature of Maryland. That majority, which now presumes to represent the people of Maryland, are as much out of place in her legislative halls as was Christophero in the lordly chamber; and they retain and reveal their natural instincts and ability as did Christophero his preference for a pot o' the smallest ale.

There is no department of legislation to which, in the brief period of their power, they have not applied their fingers, and it would be doing them injustice to say that there is any they have adorned.

Greatly deficient in that first quality which constitutes the legislator—sound practical common sense—they abound in that genius of ignorance which so amazed and delighted Montesquieu's Persian in the Parisian professors—a genius which enabled them to undertake to practice and teach, with the utmost confidence, arts and sciences of which they knew nothing.

Inexperienced in the forms of legislation, it was certainly prudent that they should be attended in the caucus, where, instead of the committee, their laws are matured, by learned attorneys, not members of either House, for else their blunders might *betray* their ignorance; yet, in spite of this wise precaution, this Legislature has worthily earned for itself a place beside that lack-learning Parliament where Lord Coke says there was never a good law passed.

Not elevated to the full sense of the dignity and responsibility of their high place by the great memories which surround them in the State House where daily they meet—where once the great Congress of the Revolution sat, and where George Washington surrendered his sword, that the law might thenceforth reign—the caucus is the Legislature, the Legislature the recording clerk for the dictates of the caucus; debate is silenced and consideration is banished. At a suggestion from partisans out of doors, the sacred rights of a great city are sacrificed; every responsibility surrounding legislation is gone; and the result has been such a series of legislative measures as will, perhaps, revive in the memories of the people of Maryland the fading sense of the greatness of the calamity inflicted upon them when Democrats control a majority in both branches of their Legislature.

Since, sir, they have seen fit to honor me with their censure, it is fit that this high and honorable body should have the means a little more in detail of appreciating the weight of that censure.

Ambitious of the reputation of Justinian, and not enlightened by the great jurists which surrounded his throne, the General Assembly of Maryland, in the first few days, not of their consultation, not of their consideration, but of their session, adopted, without reading it, and in profound ignorance of its provision, a code defining the rights of person and of property of every citizen of the State of Maryland, and a great part of the residue of the brief period assigned them by the Constitution has been occupied in repealing and altering the code they had just adopted.

Anxious to overrule the popular will and touch the fruits of political success, where political success is not likely to be attained by the will of the people, they have been exceedingly desirous to empty some of the offices which, in Baltimore, were filled by the popular vote; and evidence having been taken in contests between members of the Legislature and persons claiming their seats, the honorable the committee of the body of which I am speaking, so cognizant of the laws of the land, so aware of the rights of justice, and so anxious to give them full effect, allows that evidence, taken behind the backs of gentlemen whose offices are contested, to be put in against them, upon the witnesses merely identifying their depositions formerly taken. Perhaps they were conscious, Mr. Chairman, that some witnesses can not safely be resworn after the lapse of a reasonable time.

In the midst of the excitement in the country upon the Negro Question, it is not surprising that they have some men among them anxious to follow the deplorable example which has been set recently elsewhere, shocking to the sensibilities of the great mass of the people of Maryland, of reducing into slavery the men that our fathers freed. That such a measure is now depending before that Legislature, and receiving such consideration as it can give to any thing, instead of having been instantly rejected, or leave to bring it in refused—this, sir, would be cause of great surprise *in any other* Legislature assembled in Maryland. But, sir, I fear that nothing but the unanimous shriek of indignation which rung from one end of Maryland to the other averted the danger of the passage of some such despotic and oppressive measure, and one seriously and rashly unsettling the industrial interests of Maryland.

From these few circumstances, perhaps, we may begin to divine something of the character of that honorable body and the scope of its legislative sagacity. They are still more careful of Southern rights. They boast themselves their sole guardians in Maryland. They are diligent and not unsuccessful students of the debates of this House. They were smitten with admiration of the resolution offered—and so long debated in this House—by the honorable gentleman, my friend from Missouri [Mr. Clark]. A bill was pending before the Legislature of Maryland for the purpose of disfranchising a great city refractory to the Democratic yoke. Certain respectable attorneys, knowing as much of constitutional law as is comprised in the art of special pleading, aspired to apply these microscopic principles of their favorite art to the construction of the Constitution, and the result of that novel application was a bill which annulled by evasion, and repealed by direct enactment of the Legislature, some of the most fundamental provisions of the Constitution itself. Accepted at the hands of its legal originators by the caucus—if ever read, yet never understood by the majority in either House—it was about to receive the confirmation of the Legislature, when a grave omission was discovered. It said nothing about the Negro Question. That was beyond the province of special pleading; and the Legislature rashly tried their 'prentice hand on a proviso. They solemnly incorporated in the bill the following clause:

"*Provided*, That no Black Republican, or indorser or supporter of the Helper book, shall be appointed to any office under the said board."

Upon its passage, the yeas and nays were called and recorded; but I should not perform a grateful task were I to rescue their names from their native oblivion and spread them on the face of the debates of this House.

The proviso was the fit cap and bells for such a bill. Its provisions deprived a great city of their constitutional right to self-government by a flagrant usurpation. It was fit that the men who were ambitious of the honor of passing that act should likewise place in the bill the measure of their capacity, by enacting what they, with the same breath, condemned. Perhaps the most obnoxious portion of Helper's book is the proscription of fellow-citizens for their opinions on slavery; and the proviso, for the first time in American legislation, excludes by law from a municipal office all the members of the most numerous political party in the United States by their party name, and because of their political opinions ascribed to them by their enemies. The proviso does not confine its exclusion to the approvers of Helper's work—itself sufficiently ridiculous—but deprives the honorable gentleman from Ohio [Mr. Corwin] and the Speaker of this House, and the governor of almost every free state, and over a million of voters, from all chance of promotion in the Police Department of Baltimore. Possibly the people might not have selected them, but the Legislature apparently feared that their Board of Commissioners might.

Their vigilance having been once awakened, they were not content with having thus protected the institutions of the people of Maryland against the wiles of this great Northern party by excluding them from the high and lucrative position of policemen. They were called upon shortly afterward to pass upon another measure—a city railroad for Baltimore—a dangerous contrivance of Northern ingenuity, which would cover with its network of tracks that great city, on whose cars thousands of people might come in contact daily with the conductors and directors, and by them, if not *sound*, the subtle poison of anti-slavery sentiment might be diffused through all the streets and alleys of Baltimore, without any body being the wiser. That sagacious and learned body, the Senate, having hurried through the code for the purpose of getting at those things which touch the vital interests of the country, having before them this bill for the inauguration of that great modern convenience in the city of Baltimore, thought that there likewise they should protect themselves by law against this poison in the atmosphere. And therefore it was provided, and now stands as a part of that bill,

"That no *Black Republican*, or indorser or approver of the Helper book (laughter) shall receive any of the benefits and privileges of this act, or be employed in any capacity by the said railway company." (Renewed laughter.)

I want honorable gentlemen upon this side of the House, the Helperites as well as others, to know, that when they pass home through the city of Baltimore they must be prepared, at the car doors, to deny their political principles, or lose the lightning train. (Laughter.) Disappointed office-seekers here can find employment there only by apostasy, and secret trusts alone can secure Black Republican capital in this lucrative investment.

Sir, in the course of a few days there was before the Legislature another bill for the purpose of endowing an agricultural society for the state. An energetic, but not discreet representative of the dominant party rose and moved to apply this proviso to that bill. We all know that contamination does not spread so rapidly in the rural districts as in our great cities, and some legislator, more sagacious than his brethren, reflected that there are Black Republicans who raise Morgan horses, and Durham cattle, and Southdown sheep, and Alderneys, and that occasionally a Black Republican invents a plow, and that these things lessen the burden or enhance the profits of agricultural labor, and in singular contrast to the rest of their conduct, in a lucid interval, they actually voted down the proviso!

But the Senate, having at this point made themselves, as the Frenchman would say, suspected, in spite of their earnest and disinterested guardianship of Southern institutions, even at the expense of making themselves ridiculous, the House of Delegates next assumed the guardianship of the representative upon this floor. They had passed a resolution, prior to the election of speaker, which was intended to condemn beforehand any vote which should not be for some one of the honorable gentlemen from the Democratic party. I knew it was aimed at me; for they knew that, highly as I respect those gentlemen—eminently fit by knowledge and experience for that position as I know many of them to be—entire as is my confidence in their personal honor, to the extent of trusting my fortune, my life, and my honor in their hands, yet I did not consider them safe depositors for any of the political powers of this government, and that all they could do would not make me waver one hair's breadth from what they knew was my firm resolve.

But it is unfortunate that the gentlemen upon that side of the legislative body are more devoted to study the Cincinnati platform than Blair's Rhetoric or Whately's Rules of Logic, and they became afflicted with that entire incapacity of saying any thing which has not two meanings which so singularly characterizes the authors of that remarkable platform. They moved a resolution in such ambiguous terms that my honorable friends in the Maryland Legislature thought it was a condemnation of the gentlemen on the administration side of the House for not having elected the gentleman from North Carolina, for whom I cast my vote so perseveringly and so fruitlessly. I had intended to waive the benefit of the ambiguity. I intended to have responded to them in the sense of the gentleman who moved them; but events were so rapid that, before I could have an opportunity to express my opinion of them, I was overwhelmed and oppressed by another. The elevation of the gentleman from New Jersey to the speaker's chair instantly revived all their earnestness for the protection of Southern rights.

My vote recalled to them that they were committed by what they had said before to follow it up with an explicit condemnation of the act which had now been perpetrated. And thereupon the honorable the House of Delegates of Maryland thus resolved:

"*Resolved, by the General Assembly of Maryland*, That Henry Winter Davis, acting in Congress as one of the representatives of this state—"

Sir, it is greatly to be regretted that those gentlemen do *not* act in the Legislature of Maryland as representatives of Maryland—

"by his vote for Mr. Pennington—"

They did not know his Christian name—

"the candidate of the Black Republican party—"

Think of it, Mr. Chairman! spread upon the statute-book of Maryland forever! "of the Black Republican party—"

"for the speakership of the House of Representatives, has misrepresented the sentiment of all parts of this state, and thereby forfeited the confidence of her people."

I respectfully tell the gentlemen who voted for that resolution to take back their message to their masters, and say that I speak to their masters face to face, and not through them. Sir, it has always been the striking and marked peculiarity of that party which now accidentally, and only temporarily, predominates in the councils of Maryland, that they will allow no opportunity to pass of what they call "indicating their entire fealty to the South;" and that, sir, always consists in exciting sectional strife, in mooting matters which men ought not to argue, in libeling their neighbors, in endeavoring to make them hateful and disgusting to their fellow-citizens, in giving an advertisement to the whole country that every body that is not a Democrat is an Abolitionist; and that, if any fanatics shall see fit at any time to come within the limits of a Southern state for the purpose of shaking and unsettling the solid foundations of society, there would be found men who, if they feared to join them, would yet sympathize with them. Their whole policy is to poison the minds of our people against every man not a Democrat in the free states, to inspire them with distrust, apprehension, and terror, to teach them to look on the accession to power of any one called by the name of Republican as not merely a change of power from one to another political party, differing in principle and policy, but equally loyal to the United States, but as not far removed from such oppression and danger as to furnish just cause of seeking revolutionary remedies. Their hope seems to be to retain power by the fears of one half the people for the existence of slavery, and of the other half for the existence of the Union. Agitation, clamor, vituperation, audacious and pertinacious, are their weapons of warfare. Of this spirit the Legislature of Maryland, as now constituted, is the incarnation. It stands the embodiment of that terrific vision of the Portress of Hell gate, who, to the eye of Milton,

> "Seemed woman to the waist, and fair,
> But ended foul in many a scaly fold
> Voluminous and vast—a serpent armed
> With mortal sting; about her middle round
> A cry of hell-hounds never ceasing barked
> With wide Cerberean mouths full loud, and rung
> A hideous peal; yet when they list would creep,
> If aught disturbed their noise, into her womb
> And kennel there, yet there still barked and howled
> Within unseen."

And they, as false to their mission as the Portress of Hell to hers, stand ready, for the purpose of retaining their hold of power, to let loose on this blessed land the Satan of demoniacal passion.

And then, sir, in the midst of these more noisy, boisterous, and disturbing elements, there is a certain number of small, shriveled, restless beings, incapable of wielding the arms of logic or of reason, yet skillful to scratch with poisoned weapons. Of such are the honorable gentlemen who contrived the resolution.

They supposed that I was so weak before my friends in Maryland that they could take from me the confidence of that constituency that has stood by me through good report and through evil report, while it blew a storm as well as when it was calm. Sir, I REPRESENT MY constituents; and I *know* the people of Maryland even beyond the limits of my constituents better than these dabblers in eternal agitation; and I say that, right or wrong, wise or unwise, honest in its motives or unfaithful in its motives, that vote of mine is, to-day, not only approved, but honored and applauded by every man whose opinion I regard. (Applause in the galleries.) I say that now, this day, I am stronger in my district and in the State of Maryland, in any appeal I may see fit to make to the people, on my vote for speaker, than all the banded body of the Legislature bound into one man. And, sir, unless I am greatly deceived by the press of the Southern opposition, the American members of the Legislature are as little in sympathy with their political friends of the South as they are with the people of Maryland.

Why, sir, what are the circumstances of that election? I, sir, have no apologies to make. I have no excuses to render. What I did, I did on my own judgment, and did not look across my shoulder to see what my constituents would think. I told my constituents that I would come here a free man, or not at all; and they sent me here on that condition. I told them that if they wanted a slave to represent them, they could get plenty, but I was not one. I told them that I had already passed through more than one difficult, complex, dangerous session of Congress; that I had been obliged, again and again, to do that which is least grateful to my feelings; to stand not merely opposed to my honorable political opponents, but to stand alone among my political friends without the strength and support which a public man receives from being buoyed up breast-high by men of like sentiments, elected on like principles, and who, if there be error, would stand as a shield and bulwark between him and his responsibility. I foresaw then, exactly as it resulted, that the time would come when I would be obliged again to take that stand; and I wanted my people to know it, so that if they chose to have another one, who would go contrary to his judgment, and bend like a willow when the storm came, they might pick him out, and choose the material for their work.

Mr. Chairman, they sent me here, and I have done what I *know* was my duty. Sir, it is my proud satisfaction at this moment that, having given no side-wind reasons, having made no apologetic statement, spontaneously, without asking, I know this day that my constituents approve what I have done; and that, if not the fit reason for my doing so, is at least a consolation after doing it.

The honorable gentlemen of the Legislature presume to know better what my constituents think than I do. They possibly will find out that they do not know so much about the honorable gentleman who occupies the speaker's chair as my constituents know. The objection made to me in the Maryland Legislature by the mover of one of the resolutions was, that I had not voted for my friend from North Carolina. The rapidity of the transit of information from Washington to Annapolis is apparent to any one. The diligence with which these self-constituted judges of my conduct make themselves acquainted with it, adds greatly to the weight of their condemnation. The care with which they studied the code before its passage leads me to fear that they learn our proceedings chiefly from expurgated editions in their country newspapers, *via* Alleghany and St. Mary's. Not only no Democrat, but no American, could, or ventured, or cared to correct the blunder.

Thus ignorant of contemporary events, it were unreasonable to expect them to know events twenty years old—to them a period beyond the memory of man or newspaper—the subject of tradition merely.

It is not to be supposed that they could identify the honorable gentleman who so worthily fills the speaker's chair with that Whig governor of New Jersey, whose broad seal was discarded by the Democrats of this House when they wished to usurp the speakership of the House, and had not the votes to do it without rejecting the votes of the New Jersey members. They did not, but my constituents do know that fact; and they think that his elevation is a righteous rebuke, after long delay, for that usurpation. They know—though it can not be supposed the Legislature do—that the Governor of New Jersey of that day was a Whig in the day of Whig greatness. The gentlemen of the Legislature can not be expected to know, but my constituents know, that General Taylor appointed to a high office, in his gift, the same distinguished gentleman, and that, though the Senate of the United States unanimously confirmed him, he declined the honor. The gentlemen of this Legislature can not be expected to know that Millard Fillmore, whose name at this day, in Maryland, stands second only to that of the immortal Clay, appointed him likewise to another high and responsible office, which he declined to accept. Perhaps his contempt for office excites their indignation. They, of course, can not be expected to know that the distinguished gentlemen to whom I refer is a Whig in his politics, now called a Republican, in favor of the enforcement of every law that any Southern state has any interest in, and of that one in which Maryland, more than any other, has a direct and practical, not a political and party interest. The gentlemen of the Legislature could not be expected to know—but my constituents know—that this honorable gentleman is sound on all those more practical questions touching the protection of American industry and river and harbor improvements, in which they have so direct and deep an interest. They know full well that it is by the votes of such men we must secure the inauguration of that policy, so essential to the industrial interests of Maryland.

The gentlemen of the Legislature may not know—but my constituents know—that, above and beyond all other things, the gentleman whom I aided in elevating to the chair is of moderate views, in favor of silence on the slavery question, of putting an end to the internecine strife of sections that has raged for years, and, therefore, of all men the man to sit in that chair—at once the symbol and the pledge to the country of the peace that is before us, if we will only not repel it. It is because my constituents know and approve these things that they approve my vote.

I supposed that there would be clamor over that vote. I did not intend to trouble myself about it. I knew the quarter from which it was likely to come. I knew that the majority of the gentlemen of the Legislature would adopt some such resolution. I confess myself surprised that my own friends, excepting four of them, voted for it. I fear that in an evil hour some of them allowed themselves to be frightened. I suspect some of them were afraid that they should be called "Abolitionists." Subjected to the torture of voting against a resolution which was supposed to be in favor of Southern rights, or of deserting a friend, they could not be expected to regard justice to me rather than safety to themselves. So every man took care of himself. Some voted for the resolutions who went through their election on my shoulders. They did not know that when they saw away the bough between themselves and the tree they must fall. (Laughter.) But, sir, it was a curious scene, that vote. The clerk called the name of an American in the Legislature once, and there was a pause; twice, and there was a shuffling; thrice, and there was a hesitating response. Then there was a period of blessed repose, when certain Democratic names were called, and were responded to with that earnestness with which Democrats always respond when aiming a blow at a political adversary. Then some unfortunate Americans were called upon to vote. The gentlemen stood first on one leg, and then on the other, in sad doubt on which to rest; gentlemen looked over their shoulders to see if there were not some dust of a coming reprieve; some rushed to inquire of friends whether they ought or ought not to vote for the resolution; while there sat their inexorable and determined opponents, with their eyes glaring upon them and their mouths open, sure of their prey after the fluttering was over; and in they went. (Laughter.) The scene I am sure I should never have been able to describe had it not been for the torture and agony which certain honorable gentlemen upon the other side of the House suffered when called upon to cast a patriotic vote for my friend from North Carolina. (Renewed laughter.) Sir, I admire the audacity of the Maryland Democrat as much as I deplore the weakness of the Maryland American.

Mr. Chairman, I know that I have to meet—and I shall meet with all equanimity—all the obloquy that is attached to the course that I have felt it to be my duty to pursue, and I know that, so far as I am worth pursuing—a gentleman in the Legislature had difficulties about passing the resolution for fear it should give me too much importance—so far as I am worth pursuing, I do not doubt that I shall be well hounded. I remember that a great many years ago, not this hall, but the old Hall of Representatives, was the scene of a great struggle, which excited the country at that day as much as the one through which we have just passed excited us in our day; and I remember, sir, that there was an illustrious individual who there found himself bound by his duty to the country to depart from his personal preferences, and, to some extent, from his political friends, and to cast a decisive vote for John Quincy Adams, of Massachusetts, for President; and from that day to the day of his death there was no time that the howl of "bargain and corruption" did not pursue him to his grave. Sir, I have sat at his feet and learned my political principles. I can tread his path of political martyrdom. Before any cry of Legislatures or people I will not yield; they may pass over my prostrate body or my ruined reputation, but step aside I will not to avoid either fate. I care not, sir, whether it be in one shape or another that the danger may come. I am aware that we all this day regard the Negro Question as that which is decisive, important, and controlling. There have been others at other times equally important, equally exciting, equally controlling. There have been Legislatures that have been anxious to strike down a political opponent. There have been timid constituencies who have deserted their representatives for serving them too faithfully; there have been stormy constituencies which demanded humiliating things of their representatives. The special trial of our day comes from the feverish excitement on the Slavery Question, and the despotic intolerance of any deviation from the extremest views of either side. For myself, sir, on every question I mean to assert my independence, awed by no authority into acts which I disapprove—

> "Non civium ardor *prava* jubentium,
> Mente quatit solida—*neque auster*"—

no, sir, not even the *south wind*. Whether it relate to a matter of financial policy or to a matter of sectional strife, no man is fit for this place who is not willing to take his political life in his hand, and, without looking back, go forward on the line of what he regards as right, and, sir, whether it relates to the material interests of my constituents, or to those great political interests which are supposed to be bound up with the existence of slavery in the slave states, I trust I shall never allow myself, by any clamor or by any storm, however loud or however fierce, for an instant to be made to veer from that course which strikes me to be right. I am not here merely as a member from the fourth congressional district of Maryland. I am not here merely to represent the residue of the State of Maryland. I am not entitled to consult their prejudices as only worthy of regard. I am bound to look to a wider constituency, to a higher duty. If my duty to that wider constituency can be made to promote the interests of my local constituency, then my duty to the two coincides. But, sir, in the great necessities of public life, there have been heretofore, and there may be again, occasions on which I may be called upon, as other public men have heretofore been, to make the painful decision that the interest of the nation requires that I shall disregard the opinions, unanimous, firm, repeatedly expressed, of my constituency. I humbly pray that that may not occur, but that, if it do, I shall have strength equal to the occasion; at least such now is my resolution.

Mr. Chairman, I had intended, but I have not time, to speak to one or two other points. (Cries of "Go on!") I think that the spirit which lies at the bottom of the resolutions which the lower House of the Legislature of Maryland in an evil hour has adopted, is of sinister import to the people of this country. I wish, sir, I had time to develop how sinister it is.

They were extraordinary circumstances under which the election of speaker took place, which is summarily condemned by that Legislature. We had met, and been struggling for eight weeks, I think. At the meeting of this session of Congress, an explosion of passion of revolutionary intensity—beyond any thing it has been my fortune to see here or to read of outside of the revolutionary assemblies of Paris—greeted us upon our advent. One great body of gentlemen, evidently deeply in earnest, however much I may deplore that earnestness, and however much I may think them in error in their estimate of the causes of their indignation, manifestly felt themselves to be upon the brink of great, decisive, and revolutionary events. One portion of this House, day after day, branded the representatives of the great majority of the people of the free states as traitors to the country, instigators of assassination, bent upon breaking up and destroying slavery in the states, carrying into the midst of our families the torch and the knife of the assassin and incendiary. Great states, moved from their propriety, passed beyond what hitherto they had done, and adopted resolutions which, however moderate in their tone, looked revolutionary in their aspect, and must, in their execution, have been revolutionary. For the first time, I believe, in the history of the government, a great and patriotic state was so deeply moved as to be forgetful of that clause of the Constitution which forbids the entering of one state into compacts or agreements with another, and to send one of her justly-distinguished citizens to the capital of Virginia for the purpose of arranging a common consultation among the Southern States—not one of those Conventions which from time to time have met under the usurped authority of a governor; not one of those commercial conventions which from time to time have been the result of a movement on the part of a certain portion of the Southern people—but a mission assuming all the solemn forms of an embassy, speaking the tones of the last hour before the revolution breaks out, appealing to the people of Virginia, in their sovereign capacity as represented in their Legislature, by reason of a melancholy event which had just transpired, to send delegates *by law* to a Convention of states which, if it did any thing, must assume the form and functions of that great revolutionary Congress which took the earlier steps to break the bonds that bound our fathers to the throne of Great Britain.

I do not agree with those gentlemen as to the cause of that excitement. I profoundly regret the steps that those various Legislatures thought fit to take, as much as I deplore the intense agitation of the popular mind which tolerated or favored their adoption. But, sir, I stand here sworn to support the Constitution of *these* United States—not of any other confederacy which a future sun may rise upon—to support the Constitution of these United States; and, under these circumstances, was it to be expected, or did the people of Maryland expect, that their representative here should, when his vote would elevate to the speaker's chair a gentleman, personally and politically, in every way so far as I am acquainted with his character and previous conduct, a symbol of peace—of peace to those very states that were so excited and revolutionary in their measures—that I should allow the opportunity to pass of placing that olive-branch where men all over this wide land could see it? Or, sir, to take another alternative, if the dire day must come that peaceful secession shall be attempted, and it shall be found that peaceful secession means the arrest of the United States marshal in the execution of his office, the driving of the United States judge from the seat of justice, the taking possession of the Custom-houses of the United States, the arresting the execution of all the laws of the United States—sir, was it in accordance with my duty here to allow this government to be caught in circumstances so grave, in a crisis so imminent, without a House of Representatives competent to sanction measures which then might be necessary? Was it not a still higher duty to avert the very possibility of collisions so disastrous by removing the apprehensions which might precipitate them? And how could that be so well accomplished as by the elevation to the contested chair of a gentleman whose previous political relations, whose known character for moderation, whose opinions on the most vexed and delicate questions of an administrative character touching the sensitive interests of the slave states, whose gray hairs, crowning a long life of honor, all gave assurance to those who looked with undefined apprehension to a different result of the contest for speaker—that under his auspices there might be peace—that at least there is time for reflection—that at least there is an hour before strife, when men may pause and become cool?

The honorable the House of Delegates thought otherwise. Such considerations were wholly beneath their view—that anarchy had better reign than that any one called by the name of Republican should be elected speaker; than that the people of Maryland should see the sad example of the whole body of the Republican representatives uniting to elect a gentleman known and formally declared, in their hearing, to favor the enforcement of every law, and the protection of every interest they are represented to be bent on destroying; nay, for the overthrow and ruin of which their very party is pronounced a conspiracy.

Sir, there is no act of my life I less regret, none more defensible on high and statesmanlike reasons, none where the event has more promptly indicated its wisdom. Even now its fruits are, if I mistake not, visible. The people are relapsing into repose in the country. Chafed passions explode less violently in the House.

I trust that now the calmer judgment of the other side of the House will modify their views heretofore expressed, and limit and soften the sweeping judgment which impeached a whole political party of conspiracy to promote servile insurrection.

I think they will be inclined to take a somewhat different view of the origin, the character, and the scope of John Brown's crime.

It was no invasion of Virginia at all, still less an invasion of Virginia by or from a free state. It was a conspiracy to free negroes, arrested in the attempt, defended with arms, stained with murder, and punished with death. It was a crime to be dealt with by judge, and jury, and sheriff.

The utmost vigilance of two governments has failed to trace a single connection with any body of men in any state. Two of Brown's confederates were arrested in Pennsylvania without warrant, and carried without a guard to jail in Virginia. His arsenal contained two hundred Sharpe's rifles and something over a thousand pikes; his army consisted of about twenty men: such were the means provided by eighteen millions of people for the invasion of ten millions; for, though rumor promised him succor, no one ever saw a body of men or a single man marching to join him or to rescue him. Not a slave joined him voluntarily; not one lifted his hand against his master; all were anxious to return to the bosom of their masters' families.

Atrocious as was the crime, and great as is the cause I have to deplore some of the best blood shed, that crime has revealed a state of fact and of feeling, both among our own population and that of the free states, on which our eyes ought to rest with satisfaction in view of the future.

It negatives the existence of any conspiracy against our peace in the free states of the Confederacy. Neither the plan nor the execution revealed any higher intelligence or greater power behind the crazy enthusiasts who acted in the tragedy. To lay this blood at the door of a great political party of our fellow-citizens, who now control the government of every free state except two, in spite of the indignant denial of all their representatives here, and without a particle of proof, in fact, is not reasonable. It is to call Dirk Hatterick's defense, in his lair, an invasion of Scotland! It is to lay the bloody deeds of Balfour of Burleigh on the whole body of the Protestants in Scotland!

But the keenness with which gentlemen feel this crime against the peace of a slave state may well enable them to appreciate how the more aggravated events in Kansas inflamed the minds of men in the free states, and fired the fanaticism of Brown to the point of bloody revenge.

That men and women of like mind, in whom, on one subject, the ideas of right and wrong are sadly disordered, sympathized with the convicts; that some papers applauded his deed, and some pulpits echoed his eulogy, are certainly symptoms of no sound state of morals in the actors; but they are of no political significance in the populous North. On this floor they have no representative. That bloody type of fanaticism is, of all things, most rare among the Abolitionists; and they are a body of enthusiasts who have never, to my knowledge, had ten representatives in this hall. But to sympathize with a criminal, to pity a convict, to consider the conviction an expiation, and the execution a martyrdom, is too common at this day to excite surprise in any case. Even with the ministers of religion, the ascent to the scaffold is Jacob's ladder—the gallows is the very gate of heaven; and the old formula of *pax et misericordia* is changed for one in the spirit, if not in the words, of Edgeworth, "Son of St. Louis, ascend to heaven!"

I dwell on these matters the more, because they have been made the occasion of exaggerated inferences and the proofs of unfounded fears, which a more thorough or a cooler contemplation of the manifestations of thought and feeling in our free American society will dispel. I seek for signs of peace. I will explore every region for ground of returning confidence. I think there is no ground for the excitement which has prevailed. I think the longer gentlemen look at the facts, they will the more surely see that their feelings led them to extremes which they will not be inclined to repeat.

In this spirit, I feel sure they will now be inclined to accept the formal declaration of the gentleman from Ohio, who was the first candidate of the Northern opposition for speaker, at its full value and scope:

> "I say now, that there is not a single question agitating the public mind; not a single topic on which there can be sectional jealousy or sectional controversy, unless gentlemen on the other side of the House thrust such subjects on us. I repeat, not a single question."

He so spoke while a candidate; and had he said exactly the opposite, there is not a gentleman on the administration side of the House who would not have rung it in the ears of his constituents as the authorized and formal avowal by the Republican candidate of all his enemies impute to his party. But, being a declaration of peace instead of one of war, shall we impeach its faith that our fears may not subside? or ought we not rather to read this text—authoritatively spoken in the presence of the gentlemen whose candidate he was, and who sanctioned it by their continued support for nearly two months afterward—by the light of that magnificent oration of his distinguished colleague [Mr. Corwin], which won the heart of every hearer by its genial and comprehensive spirit, and inaugurated in this hall, after the silence of years, the example of great parliamentary eloquence!

These declarations are reiterated assurances that there is no intention of invading the rights or quiet of any slaveholding state; that there is no design or desire to tamper with or trouble slavery where it exists; that they are willing to let the subject alone, if others are willing to let things stand as they are.

Are declarations like these to be encountered and outweighed by the irresponsible clamors of scattered newspapers, by trumpery resolutions at excited town meetings, or by the ambiguous, contradictory, and shifting platforms hastily contrived for an emergency, and then forgotten? It was one of Mr. Calhoun's profound and sagacious remarks, that there was a strong tendency to confound the machinery of parties with formal bodies known to the law, and to treat the latter like the former. The debates of this session have been one perpetual illustration of its truth. They have repeated here the discussions of the hustings, dealt here with the contrivances of party warfare, and invoked such proofs to repel and annul the formal representations of the constitutional representatives of the people touching their purposes.

I invoke gentlemen to accept the declaration of the legal representatives touching the purposes of the people who sent him here to represent them in that very thing. Men may clamor, partisans may propose, papers may print a thousand things, and no one care to explain or contradict them; for no one is responsible for them. Silence is no consent; it is mere indifference or contempt. It is the conduct of the representative to which the people look when they would know if they were truly represented, and it is to that representative we should look when we wish to know the spirit and policy his constituents contemplate.

There will always be more or less of that vague dissertation on impractical theories, such as the possibility of property in man, or whether slavery be hateful to God, and the like, and those views will always have, as they have heretofore had, their eight or ten representatives on this floor; but surely we can afford to leave such dissertations unanswered, and without an answer they will soon die out. Politically, they are of no decisive importance, and involve no such danger as to keep gentlemen always on the alert with a response. But the records display the purposes of parties in the government; and if we there investigate the signs of the times, we will find, I think, that from 1855 to this time, there has been no single bill proposed contemplating a change in the condition of affairs touching slavery as it existed before the repeal of the Missouri line. I had meant to develop that as a word of peace, but I have not time. The first controversy of the Thirty-fourth Congress related to the seat of the delegate from Kansas. The first bill was to repeal the laws of Kansas passed by the Legislature whose legality was contested. The next was Mr. Dunn's statesmanlike bill to reorganize the Territory of Kansas. The third was to admit Kansas under the Topeka Constitution. The fourth was to abolish the existing laws, and to reorganize the Territory of Kansas, without one word of slavery on one side or the other; and you know very well, gentlemen, that at the last Congress no proposition was entertained, excepting the question, which you argued and which we argued, whether we had a right to remit to the people the Lecompton Constitution, to be decided upon by the people who were to be bound by it. Up to this time, while there has been excitement at the North and at the South—while gentlemen have made offensive speeches here and elsewhere, there has been no measure of practical legislation proposed in this House that has not been defensive in its character; not one that has looked beyond retaining the Territories free which were already free.

We have, then, peace before us, if we will only accept it. The free states ask no new law. Their representatives tell us there will be no sectional questions mooted by them unless forced on them by others; and if we close with such declarations in the spirit of the declaration of the honorable gentleman from Ohio, and of the patriotic speech of his distinguished colleague, we may banish from our minds those "gorgons, hydras, and chimeras dire," amid whose hideous forms we have so long pursued our weary way.

SPEECH BEFORE THE ELECTORS OF THE FOURTH CONGRESSIONAL DISTRICT OF MARYLAND.

Congress rose on the 25th of June, 1860, and all parties prepared for the great struggle in the approaching election for President of the United States. The excitement was greater than ever before throughout the country. The threats made in 1856, by the Southern States-rights Democracy, that the election of a "Black Republican" and sectional "Abolitionist" should be the signal for the secession of the South and the disruption of the Federal Union, were renewed with still more frequency and violence. The united and indivisible Democracy, after wrangling confusion and ineffectual efforts to unite upon a nomination at Charleston in May, had hopelessly split, and separated into the factions headed respectively by Mr. Douglas and Mr. Breckinridge. Each of these fragments claimed to be the whole; and each, as the exclusive and infallible authority, denounced and excommunicated the other half.

The Convention of the National Union and American party met at Baltimore, and efforts were made to procure the nomination of Judge Bates, of Missouri, with a view to his acceptance also by the Republicans. But the candidates named were John Bell, of Tennessee, with Edward Everett for the vice-presidency. It was afterward known that this position was assigned to Mr. Everett against his wishes, and he was with difficulty restrained from publicly disavowing it.

At Chicago the Republican Convention came together in the highest spirits. It seemed now, after the Kansas and Nebraska iniquities, and the openly-avowed intention of the Southern and Democratic parties to carry the blessings of slavery into all the Territories of the United States, as if the defeat of the party in 1856 had only rallied the resolution and moral sense of the North and West to the determination that the limit of endurance had been reached. It was confidently expected that the nomination there would naturally fall upon Ex-governor William H. Seward, the senator from New York, who had formed, organized, and led the great party of national defense in the North and West against the aggressions of the pro-slavery Democracy. His friends thought him entitled to this nomination by great ability, by long experience in the public service, by the eminent positions he had held, and by the fact that he was its acknowledged chief, and the leader of its success.

But, through causes not necessary to be related here, the choice fell upon Abraham Lincoln, of Illinois, a man then comparatively unknown outside of his own state, but who was widely popular there, and who had gained great reputation at home by his contests with Mr. Douglas. To him was added Mr. Hamlin, of Maine, as candidate for the vice-presidency.

And now the contest began. In Maryland all four parties had some supporters; but it was soon evident that the question in this state would be between Mr. Breckinridge, as the representative of the extreme Southern and States-rights party, and Mr. Bell, who was a Southern Whig, opposed to the Kansas-Nebraska Bills, and of that party also which, although in fact opposed to the extension of slavery, wished to be "neutral," and was forced to be silent on that question.

Mr. Davis took an active part in the campaign, and spoke before the electors of the Fourth Congressional District of Maryland as follows:

FELLOW-CITIZENS OF BALTIMORE,—I regret that absence on public duty has prevented my being with you to celebrate the first note of triumph over the dissolution of the Democratic party.

When the resolution of the American members of the Legislature of Maryland, which has just been read to you, was passed, there *was* a Democratic party; one which was an "Old Bruiser" (laughter), as Mr. Thompson described Great Britain, roaming about the world, thrashing whomsoever it pleased, and shaking its fist in the face of all creation, domineering over every body, impudent, intolerant, and tyrannical. *Now*, the Democratic party is disputed between the warring elements, headed by Mr. Douglas and by Mr. Breckinridge. Who will have the honor of burying the body is not for us to determine. That will be left to whichever of these two fragments shall turn out to be the stronger at the end of this contest, and in that way to arrogate to itself to be the sole, united, undivided, universal, national, omnipotent Democratic party. (Laughter.) Our Democratic brethren last year, at Frederick, passed a resolution saying that upon the integrity of the Democratic party depended the integrity of the Union. The party is gone — where is the Union? (Laughter.) That where went its fragments must likewise go the fragments of the Union; and in accordance with the unfulfilled but anxiously-desired prophecy, one large portion of that party is now engaged perpetually in prophesying that if *they* happen to be defeated, that result will still follow. Gentlemen, it is matter of profound gratitude in my mind that, whatever else turn up, there is an end of that intolerable domination (applause)—than which none, *without exception*, can be worse; than which none can be more inimical to the peace, the happiness, the integrity, and the great interests of this country; than which none can ever push this country nearer to the brink of the precipice of disunion; and the death of which confers more strength upon it than the death of *all* other political organizations that have ever existed. (Great applause.)

It is time there should be a change. Maryland has thought so long, and she struggled long and heroically. She struggled under the heroic Scott, and failed. She struggled under the conservative and statesmanlike Fillmore (great applause), and failed—failed, not by any fault of hers—failed, because there were "weak knees" elsewhere; because men were afraid to meet the Democratic party on its own ground, and hold it responsible for its own principles. Maryland alone, of all the states, kept her banner floating in the breeze, and stands to this day with her escutcheon more brilliant than any other in the United States (applause) for heroic devotion, for unshaken pluck, for perfect resolution to do as she pleases, and leave the rest of the country to do as it pleases. (Applause.) And now, under another leader, equally acceptable, of wider public experience, of old Whig antecedents, holding the most intimate relations to that great statesman to whom Maryland was always only too proud to give her voice; first in every department of the public service, true upon every great question that touches the *real* interests of the country, Maryland places the names of John Bell and Edward Everett before her people. (Tremendous applause.) And I take it that, deeply as she feels the necessity of a change, just so deeply and firmly is she resolved that for them, in November, her vote shall be cast. (Applause.) Whatever timid men may do elsewhere, whatever coalitionists and fusionists may do elsewhere, whatever doubt and hesitation may drive other people to do, let what will come, the vote of Maryland will, in November, be cast for these two men; and then Maryland will have discharged *her* duty, and her skirts will be free from the responsibility of whatever may occur.

I know, fellow-citizens, the deep feeling which pervades you upon the condition of the national government. I know that you, as I do, think that the most important of all things is a change in the government; and, having come to that conclusion, that it is our duty to do our best to effect that change, in such manner as shall best secure the peace and the happiness of the country; but that *in no contingency*, under no combination of circumstances, for no purpose, are we to aid, directly or indirectly, in continuing in power those whom we now have a chance of ejecting.

Why is a change so necessary? Is that Democratic party fit to be trusted with the power of the sword, which has allowed innocent and honest American citizens to be shot down in the streets of Washington by American soldiers? ("No, no.") Is it fit to be trusted with the sword, which has converted the army of the United States into a *posse comitatus* to enforce the service of process, and to subject the people of the Territories to military rule? Are they fit to be trusted with the power of the sword who have wielded it so weakly in Utah, so illegally in Paraguay? Are they fit to be trusted with the power of the sword who, forgetful of all the obligations of international law, have fired into the neutral vessels in or near the fort of Vera Cruz—an act so flagrantly illegal, that the courts of this country had to discharge the captured vessels as not legal prize? Are they fit to be trusted with the power of the sword who have sought at the hands of Congress authority to use it, "whenever, in the opinion of the President," American citizens may be injured, or American interests may in his discretion require it, abroad, against any of our South American republican sisters? Are they fit to be intrusted with the sword who desire the privilege, and have endeavored to get it, of protecting the transit routes, without the authority of Congress given at the particular time, but according to the mere will and humor of the President? Are they fit to be intrusted with the power of the sword who have recommended to Congress that the President should be allowed, in time of profound peace, without any serious provocation, to take military possession of, and hold for an indefinite time, two great states of the Mexican republic—Chihuahua and Sonora? ("No, never.") Why, my friends, we had better at once give the whole power of war to the President. They have forgotten here all the limitations upon the executive power, and they are grasping at the right to wield the sword at the pleasure of the President, irrespective of the will of the people, whenever or wherever it may suit his discretion.

Are they fit to be trusted with the direction of the finances and the commercial interests of the country who, in time of profound peace, have ran up a debt of some forty millions of dollars for the ordinary expenses of the government, rather than vary the tariff to supply its wants; who have swollen its expenses during one year to nearly or over eighty millions of dollars; who thought that the crisis of 1857 was a passing breeze, that ruffled the surface merely of our mercantile transactions—that terrific storm which turned up from its depths the sea of commerce, and left strewn all along the coast of this republic the fragments of our greatest fortunes?

Are *they* fit to be intrusted with the administration of the government? Read the Fort Snelling Report. Read the Willett's Point Report. Read the Covode Committee's Report. Read Mr. Sherman's report on the navy yards and their corruptions. Read of the political brokerage for contracts. Read of the distribution among members of Congress of the patronage of the navy yard in Brooklyn, divided up between the Democratic Representatives from the city of New York. Read of the navy yard at Philadelphia made a receptacle of illegal voters to return Democratic members to Congress. Read of the reckless use of public money in the elections. Read of the President himself directing the distribution of the surplus compensation from one of the printing departments, for party purposes among party papers, instead of recommending that the ratio of compensation should be reduced by Congress.

Is any party fit to be intrusted with the government which not only thus abuses its powers, but asserts its freedom from congressional investigation into acts so detrimental to the public service?

Fellow-citizens, are these gentlemen fit to be intrusted with the government of a free republic after their conduct in Kansas, where they attempted to force by violence upon the people a Constitution that they utterly repelled and abhorred; then attempted to force through the two houses of Congress a law to make that Constitution the Constitution *of Kansas*, when its people had utterly repudiated it; and then, when Kansas adopted *another* Constitution, allowed it to lie for months upon the table of Congress without its having been taken up for action in the Senate? Are they fit to be intrusted with the conduct of the government who could so far forget the interests of the great agricultural classes as to allow to be vetoed (after voting against it in the lower House) the Agricultural College Bill of Mr. Morrill, of Vermont, which would have given the State of Maryland $150,000 to endow her new agricultural college? Are they fit to be allowed to take care of the public interests who prefer to go on borrowing money day after day, and year after year, rather than remodel the tariff so as to protect all the varied interests of American industry? (Great applause.) Even Mr. Douglas, in his campaign through Pennsylvania, found it essential to make a slight reference to the condition of the revenue laws and the tariff as a condition precedent to asking a vote in that great State. And yet the Democratic majority in the Senate allowed a tariff bill, passed by an overwhelming vote of the lower House, to lie on their table for weeks and weeks, at any moment of which they could have taken it up and passed it, and thus restored to life and energy all the great material interests of the American republic. But there it rests, and there it is likely to rest.

Fellow-citizens, these are the reasons why we want a change of government. These are the reasons why we want to oust from position those who have abused or neglected properly to exercise the powers of the government, and to place some gentleman there who will, in these respects at least, restore the government to its original basis; restore to the commerce of the country the protection of the Federal government; give us the laws which are essential to the prosperity of the industry of the country; execute that great and necessary improvement, the Pacific Railroad; reinstate the system of improvements of rivers and of harbors throughout the whole country; reorganize and recreate the navy, which has been allowed to rot to pieces under their neglect (applause); place the army upon a footing that will enable it to be the nucleus around which the volunteer sons of the republic may rally in the event of any great public necessity; sweep out from office the flocks of "unclean birds" that have there been nestling for the last eight years (tremendous applause), and put in their places men who will *honestly* discharge their duties; men who will honestly *devote their time* to the public interests; men who will cease to strive over the matters which now divide the Democratic party, and will allow the voice of the people, calling on the government for the protection and aid to their industry which it requires, to be heard and answered.

In my judgment, that never can be so long as the Democratic party is allowed to remain in power. So long as the Democratic party shall remain in power, so long there will be nothing but one eternal howl on the Negro Question to keep themselves in. There is no remedy for that old conflict except turning them out, neck and heels, "to get an airing," as a Virginia friend said; and, I take it, when they are turned out, there will be a rest on that subject.

Now, gentlemen, we in Maryland, and our true political friends every where, are doing what in them lies to give to John Bell the glory of doing this. We make this effort, perhaps, under adverse circumstances. We have encountered adverse circumstances before. We are not to be discouraged by any odds that stand before us. We mean to cast our votes and to get our friends to cast their votes to secure, as far as in us lies, that great result. We trust that the division of the Democratic party may enable us to take great steps toward the accomplishment of that high purpose. We trust that they will be broken down in a great portion, if not in every one, of the Southern States. We trust that the State organizations will be transferred from the hands of the Democratic party to the hands of their opponents, and that again there will be an opportunity to hear the voices of Whig senators from the South debating in the Senate, as Mr. Clay and Mr. Berrien debated in former days. (Great applause.)

Fellow-citizens, there are before the country four candidates for the presidency. I wish to call your attention to-night, without indulging in any bitterness toward either gentleman or either party, to the real political opinions of all these four gentlemen, and I beseech your attention. I rise here this night not to add bitterness to any controversy. I will join my voice to no portion of any party, the tendency of which is to widen existing diversities, to indurate existing prejudices, to influence existing passions, to mislead the public from the truth in order to gain a political advantage; but, stating every thing fairly and fully, I shall leave you to form your own judgment as to how far different representations are well founded, as to how far a different policy comports with the interests and peace of the republic, as to how far partisan influences or personal ambition may have tended to mislead gentlemen, or to cause them to mislead the public. I desire to misrepresent nobody; and I shall not hesitate to state whatever can be stated, fairly and freely, to set the opinions of every one of these four gentlemen honestly and truly before you, and then possibly we shall be able to form a judgment of the propriety or impropriety of certain modes of conducting the canvass, which I have observed in the newspapers to have become very common. It has not been my fortune heretofore in this canvass to have the privilege of addressing any of my fellow-citizens here or elsewhere. I have been engaged in arduous public duty assigned to me by those in authority, and I have had no opportunity even to attend a political meeting elsewhere; but I have had my eye upon the current of public affairs. I have had my ear open to the echoes of what has been said elsewhere; and while I allow no one to speak for me either here or elsewhere (great applause), and while I regard no insinuations from any quarter ("that's right"), I likewise am never afraid to say exactly what I think upon public affairs. I am no boy in politics, that I should be afraid to make a declaration of what I think. I am no child of yesterday, that I should be frightened by popular clamor out of telling my constituents what I know to be for their good. I am not eaten up by any personal ambition that would lead me to hide, in any particular, any opinion of mine. (Great applause.) I have met the clamor of Democrats, in their highest rage, in the Hall of Representatives, when I dared to do what other men did not choose to do (vociferous cheering), and I am not afraid, before you my constituents, to avow that act, and to say that, were it to go over again, I would repeat it. (Renewed cheering.) I am not afraid here, this evening, before my fellow-citizens of Baltimore, to say that I do not hesitate now to proclaim before you *all* my opinions with reference to this pending controversy. If it is supposed that any amount of intimidation, or threat, or insinuation can make me say that I am willing to make *any* combination with a Democrat, to aid a Democrat to his election, I tell them they mistake the man. (Great applause.) I will do every thing *that is honorable* to elect John Bell; I will do nothing to prevent the defeat of a Democrat by *any body*. (Renewed applause.) Aid the Democrats! (laughter)—so courteous—so forbearing—so respectful—so considerate of the "Know-Nothing" party! (laughter)—so ready to coalesce with "the enemies of civil and religious liberty!" (laughter)—so ready to shake hands with "bloody midnight assassins!" (laughter)—so content to accept our votes; so unwilling to reciprocate the compliment, as in the great contest of Fuller, Banks, and Richardson (applause)—so truthful in their representations of my position in that great controversy, and so considerate in their expressions of opinion touching my conduct in the last great controversy! Of course, gentlemen, I am a Christian man, and I *ought* to coalesce with them. (Laughter.) No; they may get along as they can. I see, gentlemen, and you see, every where in the newspapers, "the wing" of the Democratic party led by Mr. Breckinridge, and "the wing" of the Democratic party led by Mr. Douglas; but there is no "body" of it spoken of any where. These "wings" are good for flight, but poor for battle. The claws are not there. The beak is not there. They are powerless—the shadow of what they were. Now this great Cæsar, in its most miserable estate, shaking with its last ague, cries out,

> "Like a sick girl,
> Give me some drink, Titinius!"

(laughter); but, I take it, there will be some one else who will minister to its thirst in its dying hour than myself or my political friends.

But, gentlemen—to come back to plain matters—let us consider calmly the condition in which we are. Unfortunately, the great body of the opposition to the Democratic party, which concurs in every principle that I have stated to you, which is in favor of *every* measure that I have indicated as necessary for the public weal, the representatives of which have struggled through long months in Congress, shoulder to shoulder, for the purpose of accomplishing these things, have stood together in exposing the corruptions of the administration, and in rebuking its high functionaries by votes of the House—that great body of the opposition, representing the great body of the once powerful and dominant Whig party, is divided, like the Democratic party, from top to bottom; and this is the great misfortune of the times. Whose fault is this? I shall not stop to inquire. Whose misfortune? That of all of us. There are those who seek to widen this division. There are others who know that *no* opposition administration can be powerful, enduring, and national, unless it combines both these elements in its support. If Mr. Lincoln shall be President, how can he carry on the government without the support of the opposition representatives from the South, in the Senate and in the lower House? If John Bell shall be President, how can he carry on the government with only twenty-three members in the House and with two senators to support him?

Agreeing upon every measure of public policy, agreeing upon almost every vote they will be called upon to pass in either House, touching the great interests of the country, how will it be possible for either of these gentlemen to carry on the administration, with the friends of the great measures that they both must advocate, to which both are committed, in virtue of having been Old Whigs, as well as in virtue of their present avowals, divided among themselves? Will any body tell me?

I say, then, if there is one thing to be struggled for more than another, it is the obliteration of the lines of demarcation; it is the bringing together men who think alike upon the great public interests of the country; it is, as far as possible, to push into the background, to silence forever, to put out of men's view, and (if God will only allow it) out of men's thoughts, the *only* element of distraction of a national or party character, which prevents the organization of a great and powerful party, which can hold the government for a generation, if only the present causes of division can ever be gotten rid of.

There are those who wish to widen the division. My sense of public duties require me, first of all, to see how wide it is—whether it be a division of principle too wide to be bridged, or a division occasioned by temporary passions, and susceptible of adjustment, consistently with the honor and interest of every section. And if so, then I am for *that* party really of the Union and of the Constitution—a party united and powerful over the whole republic—devoted to the interests of the whole country—which will inflict wrong or insult on the sentiments, the feelings, the rights, the interests of none. And I say that now, instead of attempting to excite the passions, arouse the hostility, and cast violent imputations upon one great portion of the opposition now struggling against the Democratic party in the North, it would be wiser not to mislead the people too far, because there may be contingencies in which to have misled them may be dangerous. You can easily arouse the passions of men; but when their passions are aroused, it is very difficult to calm them. You can easily excite the fears of men; but when their fears are excited, they are not in a condition for calm conduct. You can very easily lash them into a fury, but then you can not control them. The representations as to the course of the canvass in certain portions of the United States do, in my judgment, in certain contingencies which are within the bounds of possibility, at least as the end of this political contest, tend to create a state of feeling in the public mind which may prove beyond the control of those who have lashed it into fury. To you, my fellow-citizens, to whom I am responsible for my public conduct, and to whom I am bound to tell the whole truth touching the affairs of the country, I desire to say what I think with reference both to the individuals and the parties that are struggling for the supremacy.

Yielding to none in devotion to the interests of the candidate whom my friends support, and whom I shall support—earnestly, and heartily, and resolutely—I am determined here, as I have been resolutely in the House of Congress, never for an instant to allow myself to join in a clamor which I know to be baseless, which I believe to be in a great measure dishonest, and which I am convinced is dangerous to the best interests of the country—(applause)—however certain portions of the opposition may, for local and temporary purposes, find it to their interest to exaggerate the points of diversity, to keep up the sectional temper, to blacken their political opponents with virulent abuse, to make the people of the South believe that the North is filled with John Browns, to make them believe that the Republicans are not merely a political party, *differing from you as the Democrats differ from each other*, but that they are traitors to the Constitution, hostile to your interests, bent on servile insurrection, endeavoring to invade your State institutions, and make your families insecure and your lives a torment—that is a policy to which I will never give my assent, and against which I have struggled always. It is a misrepresentation of the condition of affairs in more than one half of this country, against which I feel called upon, by my highest duty here before you this night, face to face, as I did in the House of Representatives when responding to the impertinent resolutions of the Maryland Legislature (great applause), to declare that they who attempt to excite these passions are doing it for no patriotic purposes. They are doing it to facilitate a party triumph. They are doing it to blacken and render hateful their fellow-citizens in the eyes of *their* fellow-citizens. They are playing into the hands of that element of disunion which exists at the South, and which rejoices in having the chorus of "disunion if Lincoln is elected" rung all over the South, because, if the contingency should occur, they can appeal to men's pride and their consistency to precipitate them into a revolution.

Now I say that these representations are *mis*representations of the condition of affairs at the North. What is the great point of diversity? In Congress, after the election of speaker, there was scarcely a whisper about "John Brown." He had served his purpose and was dropped. There was scarcely a whisper about "disunion." It would serve no purpose. On the other side, the talk among the men of the opposition, from the South as well as from the North, was of the corruptions of the government, of the necessity of a change, of the anxiety of getting somebody who could accomplish that change. *Now* the tone seems to be different. What are the opinions which prevent their acting together? Not that a man's opinions are at all the criteria by which we are to be guided in voting for him or refusing to vote for him. If that were the case we never could elect a President, because there is no one with whom we concur in every particular. We must guide ourselves according *to the policy* we know they are going to pursue, and allow their abstract opinions to remain abstract opinions, unless they are called into active practice, and are matters directly in issue. I say that, at this moment, according to the avowal of every party *not Democratic*—mark the limitation—according to the avowal of every party excepting the two wings of the Democratic party, THE SLAVERY QUESTION IS ABSOLUTELY SETTLED if the Democracy will let it alone. In the language of Mr. Webster, "There is not a foot of territory within the jurisdiction of the United States, the condition of which, as slave or free, is not now irrevocably settled by some law; and if that be the case, there are some misrepresentations afloat which require to be corrected.

First, gentlemen, what are the opinions of the opposing candidates—Mr. Breckinridge, Mr. Douglas, Mr. Lincoln—upon this great question? Fortunately, the gentleman who prepared the Address of the Union Party, my personal and political friend, Mr. Boteler, of Virginia, than whom there is no sounder Whig, no more chivalrous gentleman, no more earnest friend of John Bell, no more pertinacious, undying enemy of the Democratic party existing (applause), has in one portion of that admirable address used these words: "The more conservative portion of the Republican party have tacitly acquiesced in the Fugitive Slave Law, in the existence of slavery in the District of Columbia, and in the right to carry slaves from one State to another." That indicates that the whole of that wide field is covered and out of controversy. You are safe, then, at home. You are safe in carrying, if you choose to carry, your slaves to Mississippi, to sell them. You are safe from the example of freedom in the District of Columbia. There is nothing of that kind open at all. When he said they had "acquiesced in the Fugitive Slave Law," he did not state it strongly enough, because the statements are, from Mr. Corwin last winter in the House, and others, Mr. Lincoln himself included, that it must be executed, "not grudgingly, but fully and honestly." (Applause.) Does any body take the trouble to repeat these sentiments when talking about politics before the people of Maryland? Then my friend Mr. Boteler proceeds in another sentence to say this:

"At this moment no one will question the correctness of the statement that there is not a foot of the territory of the United States, the condition of which in reference to slavery is not already fixed by law, and there is no place within the federal domain upon which the abstract theories of the extremists of either section, in regard to the exclusion of slavery from the Territories or its introduction into them, can be practically applied."

That is what I have been saying before you, people of the Fourth Congressional District, for five long years, and there *is* no question now open except such as the Democracy may see fit to open, that the way to settle the Slavery Question is to be silent on it; and it is greatly to be regretted, it is with me a matter of profound regret, that my friend Mr. Boteler, in the residue of that document, should have allowed himself to go into a discussion as to the responsibilities for the opening of the question, and to lay it perhaps at certain doors where it was not altogether justly due. But, taking this starting-point, that it is a question of abstractions, that there is no Territory to which mere theories are required to be applied, does not that at once end the whole matter? Is it not of itself an absolute confession that there is no ground for the imputation upon the people of the North in general, that there is no ground for fear in the event of Mr. Lincoln's succeeding in lieu of Mr. Bell, that there is no fear of a dissolution of the Union by reason of any thing these gentlemen may do if they happen to get possession of the government? Is not that distinctly the confession of that statement, that in reference to the substantial questions I have indicated there is an absolute concurrence, and in reference to the others in the Territories they are questions of abstractions? I could not have my own opinion more felicitously, more accurately, or from a more authoritative source, stated for the information of my constituents and of the country.

Now, what are the individual opinions of the gentlemen who are before the country for the votes of the people? First, for Mr. Breckinridge. We all know that he is the seceding candidate of the Democratic party. We all know that his friends seceded because of an inability to agree upon the Slavery Question. We find him and Mr. Douglas equally the victims of that element of distraction with which they first broke up the Whig party, then severed and broke up the American party, and to which they have themselves, by a righteous judgment, at last fallen victims. (Applause.) What are Mr. Breckinridge's opinions? The most extreme, untenable, and dangerous of all; yet people, half of them, are afraid to controvert them. He maintains that the Constitution of itself carries slavery into all the Territories; that under it any individual has a right to carry his slave there *without any law;* and that laws must be passed by Congress, as they may become needful, for the purpose of protecting it. The result, therefore, of the election of Mr. Breckinridge is, that there will be a perpetual struggle in the Congress of the United States, by persons who desire to carry negroes into the Territories, and do not wish to do so until they are protected by law, to secure the passage of laws by Congress to protect them there. There is not the remotest probability that such a law can ever be passed through both houses of Congress. It is therefore, in its very statement, an element of perpetual discord, of perpetual strife, of perpetual alienation, perpetually tending to widen still farther apart the two portions of the Union, until possibly, on some great day, a dissolution *may* follow, in the heated state of the public mind under some casualty of the moment.

What are Mr. Douglas's opinions? They have been variously stated by himself in his wide circuit through the country; yet I take it that, for this purpose, there can not be any great difficulty in describing them with accuracy. I desire to do him no injustice; I desire to do Mr. Breckinridge no injustice. I merely wish to inform my constituents what are the things which politicians try to conceal. Mr. Douglas has shown, with great emphasis and great point latterly, in a speech, that the Constitution does *not* carry slavery into the Territories. Of course it would be beyond the control of the people of a Territory, exactly as any provision of the Constitution applicable to a State is beyond the control of the people of the State; but Mr. Douglas's opinion is, that the inhabitants of a Territory have themselves the absolute right to introduce and allow slavery if they see fit, or to prohibit and exclude it if they see fit. Whether they have this power by reason of some inherent right, or by reason of the acts of Congress organizing the Territories, his language is doubtful; sometimes he seems to say one thing, and sometimes the other. At any rate, he contends that they may pass what law they please in reference to slavery, and may make their domestic institutions to suit themselves.

The great struggle in the Democratic party, and that on which it has gone to pieces in the great storm, is, which of these two opinions is the orthodox doctrine of the party. Now, while I am very unwilling to undertake to decide questions of party history or of party law for the Democrats, I rather fear that my friend, Mr. Douglas, has the better of his antagonist as a question of political history. I rather fear that he is not merely the regular nominee of the Democratic party, but that he likewise is the representative of the regular Democratic opinion. I rather think that if there has been a change, the change has been *from* him, and not *by* him from his companions. I rather think that in his great speech in the Senate toward the end of the last session he arranged an amount of authority which ought to have satisfied, or at least tended strongly to satisfy my mind, and probably satisfied a good many others, that under the ambiguous phrase "non-intervention" was couched the very dogma that he himself proclaimed. And certainly it looked as if he rather had his enemies on the hip when he quoted the language of the Kansas-Nebraska Act, "it being the true intent and meaning of this act not to legislate slavery into any Territory, nor to exclude it therefrom, but to leave the people thereof perfectly free to regulate their domestic institutions in their own way, subject only to the Constitution of the United States." I take it that these words will scarcely bear any other interpretation than that the people of a Territory, before they become a State, have a right, according to the views of the gentlemen who drew and passed that act, to introduce or exclude slavery. I rather think that he had the "old public functionary" on the hip when he went farther, and quoted from his letter of 1856, in which he said that the people of a Territory, like the people of a State, had a right to regulate the question of slavery for themselves.

Whatever may be the truth between those two divisions of the Democratic party, I do not desire to cast any more confusion into their midst than is there now. (Laughter.) I do not know how they will ever be able to solve the great problem as to what are their opinions, unless they shall bring an action in the United States Court on a wager, and carry it to the Supreme Court, and have it there decided. (Laughter.) Or, if the spoils should ever be divided again, there should be a suit brought in equity to determine which of the two portions is the real seceder, and which is entitled to the whole of the property. (Laughter.) That is a problem that I do not mean to touch; it is a controversy in which I have no interest; the farther and bitterer it is waged, the better probably for the country. But there is at least one good and patriotic thing that Judge Douglas has done in his life. Having lent himself to the extreme Southern portion of his party to do their work, when his turn came they would not lend themselves to him; they thought they had been dealing with a tool, and they found they had been dealing with a master, and they determined to break him; and he reciprocated the compliment by breaking up the Democratic party. (Applause.)

There is another good thing that he has done. The doctrine of Mr. Breckinridge to which I have referred, it is claimed, rests upon the decision of the Supreme Court in the Dred Scott case; although Mr. Reverdy Johnson, who argued that case, said that really the Supreme Court never passed upon any such question—and it is difficult for any one who knows any thing about the legal points really involved in the record before the court to surmise how it was possible for them even to have gotten at it—yet this theory, bolstered up by the perpetual assertions of political men, has been adopted by the great body of the Democratic party at the South, and some of our friends are gradually gliding into it, until I suppose it will come, after a while, to be a great piece of treason to the South, a great invasion of Southern rights, something dangerous to her internal condition, to venture to moot a question which is only ten years old, and to say that you do not believe in any such legal absurdity as that the Constitution (which says nothing about slavery in the Territories) has extended it to the Territories—an opinion as absurd as that Congress can not establish slavery in a Territory if it see fit.

The Democratic party has lived upon its boasted orthodoxy for the last twenty years. It has been "out at the elbows" in every thing else; its reputation is all gone for every thing except impudence and audacity; but, by holding itself out as the special protector of Southern institutions, it has been enabled to stand upon its legs. It has asserted its own exclusive orthodoxy, always putting up the most extreme and untenable pretensions, and always smearing every body else over with the brush of abolitionism who did not see fit to agree with it. Did any body happen to quote the resolutions of the Legislature of Ohio, or the nice family quarrel between the Hards and Softs of New York, or any other of the wranglings and diversities in the free States, over this "hard doctrine and difficult to be received" by Northern men, he was told, "You must not pretend to discuss differences in the Democratic party; it is one and indivisible." (Laughter.) But Judge Douglas has done this patriotic service; he has carried from Maryland to Louisiana, through every slave State, the elements of division upon that new dogma; and when it is attempted to assail others for expressing their opinions on the Slavery Question, who avow that they hold, as I avow that I hold, all the opinions of Henry Clay (applause)—a little out of fashion in divers particulars in this day, but I am getting to be old-fashioned —they can not turn and say, "You are an Abolitionist, and the united Democratic party is the only one that is faithful to the South;" because, in every neighborhood, in every town, in every parish, in every county, rise up the friends of Stephen A. Douglas, and say, "The Constitution does *not* carry slavery into the Territories, but the people have a right to exclude it if they choose." (Applause.) It is no longer treason to say that, for their own men say it; and now, in the Commonwealth of Virginia, the Breckinridge men are on their knees to the Douglas men, and say, "Oh, don't divide, and give the state to Bell." (Laughter.) The governor of the State, holding all the powers of the State, the man who must call out the Virginia militia "to arrest the march of the United States troops in case of a rebellion farther South," is tainted with the heresy of Douglasism.

(Laughter.) They have ceased to be powerful; they have ceased to be dangerous; there is again freedom of opinion; men can speak above their breath; men can read history, and repeat it, without the fear of being tarred and feathered, in any neighborhood in the South. (Applause.) If Mr. Douglas shall never do any thing more than that, if he shall fail to be elevated at any future period to that glittering height which is the object of his ambition, I desire to say that future generations will owe him a debt of gratitude for having, in the course of the internecine struggles of the Democratic party, and perhaps without meaning it, but from the necessities of the case, been instrumental in restoring free speech, free opinion, and a right to think as the fathers thought upon the Constitution of the United States, though he does not happen to think with them. (Applause.)

Now, what are Mr. Bell's opinions on these subjects? He avows, like an honest man, his opinions, and they substantially concur as a matter of abstract opinion with those of Mr. Breckinridge. That is, he thinks that, without a law of Congress, under the Constitution there is a right to take slaves into the Territories; but he differs from Mr. Breckinridge in this: that he has been nominated by a party calling itself the Constitutional Union party, and that party proclaims itself, in its address from which I have read to you, an enemy of slavery agitation, in favor of things remaining as they are, opposed to any farther legislation, for the doctrine that I have so often inculcated in your hearing, of silence upon the Negro Question. Let it die the death; let the Territories remain as they are; let there be no effort to change their condition, and there can be no controversy. That is a position which a gentleman holding any abstract opinion whatever may very well come up to, and that is the opinion which the brief and pointed platform of the Constitutional Union party assigns to both its candidates, wholly independent of what their individual opinions may be. They are what Mr. Boteler in his address most appropriately terms mere abstractions, abstract opinions that are not required to be acted on at this time, and can only be called into living existence by an attempt to put them in practice, and change the existing condition of the Territories; and if I understand the opinion of all the gentlemen who, with myself, advocate the election of Mr. Bell, it is, that he may silence that controversy, and not reopen it; leave things as they are, and not attempt to vary them. If that be not the view with which he was nominated, if that be not the purpose of his friends, then it will be the most pitiable farce, and I should be the last man in the world to ask any one here to vote for John Bell as a person who was going to quiet the Slavery Question. It can not be quieted as long as there is an effort to change any thing, for that raises the question. When any body proposes that any thing in the Territories, no matter what it may be, no matter for whom it may operate, or against whom it may operate, should be otherwise than it is, that instant he opens the controversy; and when the controversy is opened, no one knows where or how it will be ended.

Next, with reference to Mr. Everett. He holds, or did hold in former days, opinions upon exactly the other extreme. You remember that Mr. Fillmore was impeached of abolitionism because, at a former time, when a candidate for Congress, he had declared himself in favor of the abolition of slavery in the District of Columbia; and yet, in spite of that, because men knew what his policy would be, the people elected him Vice-President; and all the people rose up to do him honor when he passed out from the discharge of the duties of his high office. That is only another illustration of how false a guide mere abstract constitutional opinions are when you are selecting a President. The question is, never what he may *think* as a question of law, but what he will *do* as an administrator of the law. (Applause.) There can not be a more striking example of that than in the case of Mr. Everett, one of the most distinguished, patriotic, conservative, and moderate men in the United States, perfectly orthodox in his old Whig policy and principles, having filled some of the high stations of the nation, and now not, perhaps, without a prospect of filling the highest itself. That gentleman was sent many years ago, I think by General Harrison, as minister to England. It appeared, as well as I remember the circumstances, that he had previously been a candidate for some office in Massachusetts, and there he had questions thrust at him to which, in the heat of the canvass, he responded, and it seemed that he avowed himself in favor of abolishing the slave-trade between the States, of the immediate abolition of slavery in the District of Columbia, and against the admission of any more slave States. Nowadays people would open their eyes with horror at the mere mention of opinions like these; and in that day they wanted to injure that great and distinguished man because he entertained these opinions, and the action of the Georgia Legislature was invoked because Mr. Berrien had voted for his confirmation. Now, Edward Everett is the candidate of the Constitutional Union party for the purpose of stopping agitation on the Slavery Question (applause), and in my judgment they could have got no fitter candidate in the United States. (Great applause.)

I say that a man's abstract opinions have little or nothing to do with his discharge of the high functions of either President or Vice-President; and when they are invoked by political partisans, they are invoked to distract the timid, to divide their opponents, to draw off votes, to enable themselves to elect some person of less position, without expressed opinions, by the prejudices that they excite, by quotations of antiquated opinions, or opinions intended for another era, applicable to a different combination of circumstances, having no relation to those things that are now to be done, and therefore impertinences, so far as the political canvass is concerned. Are we to be prevented from voting for Mr. Everett because some Democratic orator down in the slaveholding counties may rake up that question and the response, and say, "You are voting for an Abolitionist?" I have seen the day when men who were Whigs were fools enough to be frightened at that howl. I take it that now they have learned that it is merely a howl, and nothing else, and they treat it accordingly. (Applause.)

Both Mr. Everett and Mr. Bell, by virtue of the simple declaration that they are in favor of the Constitution, the Union, and the enforcement of the laws, have pledged themselves to silence, to quiet, to leaving things as they are, to the faithful and honest execution of every law, and from such men in these days that is ample. It is impossible to go back into the history of any man who has filled public station in this country for twenty years, and not find that in the sharp struggles of parties here he has uttered an obnoxious sentiment, that there he has been guilty of an imprudent or unpopular vote, that here he has answered a question thrust at him in the heat of a canvass, which, pushed to its logical consequences, would involve a great error. If you allow yourselves to be misled by that style of canvassing, you will strip the country of the services of nine out of every ten of its best men, confine it to people who have been so insignificant that they have never been called upon to make a declaration upon any great controverted question; who have all the time been skulking along, endeavoring to get upon the popular side for the time being, eschewing pen, ink, paper, and printing, as if they were the inventions of Mephistopheles, and trusting by their very insignificance to worm themselves up into high station, as I have seen divers in these latter days, even to the presidential chair. It is this sheer cowardice, this fear to take gentlemen upon their course and conduct, and not upon their expressions and their abstract opinions, that has driven great men from the presidential chair. It is because gentlemen are afraid of being turned out of Congress, are afraid of going before their constituents, and being hissed for making the avowal of obnoxious opinions, that you have weak men in public life, and the race of great men has gone to the grave. (Applause.)

Well, now, what are the opinions of Mr. Lincoln? Let us meet the question right in the eye: What are the opinions of Mr. Lincoln, because there are certain parties in this country who say that if he is elected they will dissolve the Union. I do not assert that all Mr. Breckinridge's friends say so. I believe that the vast majority of them have no such idea. I believe that very many of them who say so would not attempt it when the time came. (Laughter.) I believe in the "sober second thought." I believe that the difficulties of the practical execution, that horror at shedding fraternal blood, would make the boldest pause. I do not fear the result. I am confident that Mr. Breckinridge himself entertains no such policy. I am not here to misrepresent any political antagonist. I am not here to sow dissensions between any regions of the country. I merely say that there are parties who declare that that event will be cause for a dissolution of the Union; and that declaration on their part is made the pretext of an echo from other quarters, that if Lincoln be elected, such will be the result. Now I say that will not be the result, and in my judgment it will not be tried; but since it is said that in that event they are going to take steps at least to break up the confederacy, let us see upon what ground they are going to do it.

Mr. Boteler says, in his address, in the most authoritative manner, that on the really great questions, among the conservative portions of the Republican party, there is an acquiescence in what we suppose to be essential to our safety—the right of slave-trade between the States, the right to continue slavery in the District of Columbia, and the execution of the Fugitive Slave Law. What else is open? Nothing, literally nothing, excepting the mere condition of the Territories. Then, what now is the condition of the Territories? Absolutely free in point of fact; no slave in them, remaining as they were at the time of the repeal of the Missouri Compromise—in spite of that repeal, remaining as free from slavery as if that compromise had never been repealed. What is there, then, to change? From the extremest point of view, nothing. It is only with reference to the question of slavery in the Territories that we are told, by the address from the National Committee of the Union party, that there is a controversy open, and as to them it is said that the controversy is a controversy of abstractions. But it can be stated stronger than that. So far as the opinions of Mr. Lincoln and his friends go, the Territories are in the exact condition in which they want to keep them. They say, "Let the subject alone, and they have nothing to say; if you attempt to carry slavery there, we will attempt to exclude it; if you attempt to extend it, we will oppose the extension; if you attempt to plant slavery in territory which we think is now free, we not only will not vote with you, but we will vote against you, and we will use the power of the government for the purpose of keeping it where it is." It is not necessary, even if it was their design, now to propose the passage of any law on the subject of slavery at all. The Territories are practically in the exact condition that they were when Mr. Clay introduced his great Compromise Bill, which was the foundation of peace until the controversy was reopened by the Democrats in 1854. The condition of the Territories remains as it was when Mr. Clay had his bills passed, saying not one word on the subject of slavery, but resting on his resolutions. What were his resolutions? The second of the resolutions which Mr. Clay brought into the Senate on the great occasion in 1850 runs in this wise—I pray you, gentlemen, be not shocked because I told you that Mr. Clay held some old-fashioned notions, but this resolution was the foundation of the legislation of that day; it was attacked by the extreme Southern men in the Senate, it was denounced as being no compromise at all; but it was the view on which great men, such as Mr. Benton on one side, and Mr. Clay and Mr. Webster on the other side, concurred for the settlement of the Territorial difficulties, and therefore it bears a historic significance even beyond the vast authority of the name of the man who reported it. It runs in this wise:

> "That as slavery does not exist by law, and is not likely to be introduced into any territory acquired by the United States from the Republic of Mexico, it is inexpedient for Congress to provide by law either for its introduction or exclusion from any part of said territory."

Silence upon the Slavery Question, leaving the Territory as it was, and nothing more, was the great wisdom of that compromise. (Applause.) Here you see what Mr. Clay thought. He thought slavery did not exist there, because the laws of Mexico excluded it. The Missouri Compromise of 1820 excluded it from all the residue of the territory. It was on that basis, coupled with the unfitness of the country for slave labor even if the laws did not exclude it, that Mr. Webster made the great declaration that there was an irrepealable law, of one kind or another, which forever settled the condition as to slavery of every foot of territory in the United States.

Now, gentlemen, what Abraham Lincoln thinks is what Mr. Clay thought with reference to slavery and the condition of the Territory—that it is free. It is therefore needless to pass any law upon the subject. He thinks it is time, and so do a great many others who bear Mr. Clay's memory in high esteem—not with Mr. Douglas, that a bunch of squatters, congregated under a bush, can pass a law to determine the condition of the Territory for you and me—but that the great National Legislature, which under the Constitution has the power "to make all needful rules and regulations concerning the Territory," has the power, if it see fit, to exclude or to admit slavery in any Territory, and that, in the absence of a statute, there is no law to authorize it; and then slavery can no more exist than a man can exist without air to breathe. Here is the language of Mr. Clay upon that subject—that it is an evil, and ought not to be extended voluntarily:

> "I am extremely sorry to hear the senator from Mississippi say that he requires first the extension of the Missouri Compromise line to the Pacific, and also that he is not satisfied with that, but requires, if I understood him correctly, a positive provision for the admission of slavery south of that line. And now, sir, coming from a slave State as I do, I owe it to myself, I owe it to truth, I owe it to the subject to state, that no earthly power could induce me to vote for a specific measure for the introduction of slavery where it had not before existed, either south or north of that line. Coming as I do from a slave State, it is my solemn, deliberate, and well-ma-

tured determination that no power—no earthly power—shall compel me to vote for the positive introduction of slavery either south or north of that line. Sir, while you reproach, and justly too, our British ancestors for the introduction of this institution upon the continent of America, I am, for one, unwilling that the posterity of the present inhabitants of California and New Mexico shall reproach us for doing just what we reproach Great Britain for doing to us. If the citizens of those Territories choose to establish slavery, I am for admitting them with such provisions in their Constitution; but then it will be their own work, and not ours, and their posterity will have to reproach them, and not us, for forming Constitutions allowing the institution of slavery to exist among them. These are my views, sir, and I choose to express them; and I care not how extensively and universally they are known. The honorable senator from Virginia has expressed his opinion that slavery exists in these Territories, and I have no doubt that opinion is sincerely and honestly entertained by him; and I would say with equal sincerity and honesty, that I believe that *slavery nowhere exists within any portion of the territory acquired by us from Mexico.* He holds a directly contrary opinion to mine, as he has a perfect right to do; and we will not quarrel about that difference of opinion."

Then, again, touching the power:

"The power, then, Mr. President—and I extend it to the introduction as well as to the prohibition of slavery in the new Territories—does exist with Congress. I think it is a power adequate either to introduce or exclude slavery. I admit the argument in both its forms of application."

Judged by the standard of Henry Clay, the opinion of Mr. Lincoln, together with the opinion of all the great men of the North, excepting, possibly, a few Democrats, for aught I know to the contrary, is, that slavery is an evil which they are unwilling to extend, and that the power of exclusion exists, leaving open the question of the necessity or expediency of exercising it. Now, what with reference to the expediency of exercising it? The opinion is expressed, as distinctly as can be, that since slavery does not, in point of fact, exist in the Territories, and since they think it can only exist by affirmative legislation, they have no legislation to ask unless legislation is asked on the other side; and hence that great declaration of Mr. Sherman, when he was candidate for Speaker in the House of Representatives, in the face of the storm of vilification and abuse with which he was assailed by the Democrats during the whole of that long controversy—a declaration which gentlemen may not be willing to repeat, but which it behooves every man who wishes to know the truth of the history of the country to bear in his mind and ponder—in substance, if not in words, was, "I tell gentlemen now here that there is not one subject of sectional controversy which can possibly arise unless it is thrust on us by our opponents." That was said when he was the candidate of the Republican party for Speaker of the House of Representatives. It was said in the face of the Republicans who were voting for him. It was a sentiment that I knew he had entertained ever since I had the honor of sitting in the House with him. It might have been thought of some persons a rash declaration for a man in the doubtful and ticklish condition of a candidate for Speaker, within three or four votes of an election, and therefore the more manly, and also the more significant. It was received in silence by his party, and he received again and again their votes for that position.

Does that look like reopening the Slavery Question? Every body who knows any thing about the history of the country must know that, from the first day of the repeal of the Missouri Compromise down to this time, whatever of excitement there has been in the country, and especially in the North, however much of exaggerated sentiment there may have been uttered, however furious the onslaughts of their newspapers and speakers on the South and its institutions—never more violent, never more excited, never more outrageous than the retorts and retaliations of Southern Democrats upon them—judging by the record (the only way to judge of the purposes of political parties), there never has been an act attempted that looked beyond reinstating things as they were prior to the repeal of the Missouri Compromise. There were measures which I thought were unwise; there were some which I thought were imprudent; they were all, I thought, unnecessary, because I knew they never could become laws, even if ill results would not have followed from them if they had become laws; because the fixed Democratic majority in the Senate prevented their enactment; but the scope of these proposed laws was confined to the reinstatement of things as they were before the repeal of the Missouri Compromise. The controversy has raged about the Territory of Kansas. The struggle has been on the part of the administration, in Democratic hands, to force slavery into it, against the will of the people. The struggle on the part of the whole body of the Northern people has been to prevent slavery from being forced into Kansas. Nobody can doubt that that is an extension of slavery. Nobody can doubt that that is carrying slavery where it has not heretofore existed. Nobody can doubt, therefore, that it is within the position that leading

Northern gentlemen, Mr. Lincoln among them, take with reference to slavery, and especially the opinion of that great man, Mr. Edward Bates, that they are opposed to its extension, to its going where it is not now, and that is all.

I happen to have been a party to all this controversy, sometimes voting in a manner that did not satisfy some of my friends, and sometimes, perhaps, voting in a manner that did not altogether satisfy me on cooler reflection subsequently; at all times, however, struggling to do what I thought was best under the circumstances, and with the little power that I had. But I was at least a witness of them; I saw what passed; I heard the argument; I think I remember the history. Turn to the journals of Congress, and you will find, I think, that that controversy sums itself up in these several points:

The first bill was a bill to repeal the laws of Kansas passed by the Legislature whose legality was contested. You remember that it was supposed—nay, asserted and proved; there is no supposition about it now; every body admits it and every body knows it, since the great investigation ordered by the first Congress in which I was by your votes—that that Legislature was elected by Missourians and others out of the Territory of Kansas. A bill was introduced to repeal the laws of that Legislature forced on the people by non-residents of the Territory. Was that agitating the Slavery Question? The next was a bill introduced by my friend, Mr. Dunn, now deceased, reorganizing the Territory of Kansas, reinstating the Missouri Compromise, and providing that any slaves which might be there might be removed within one or two years after the passage of the bill, which bill was met by the Democrats in the North with an attack upon the Republicans for establishing slavery in the Territory, and more than one member of Congress lost his election by reason of that Democratic argument. That, you, see, merely went to reinstating the Missouri Compromise line. The third was the bill to admit Kansas under the Topeka Constitution. That failed; but it was only to make it a free State. It was an unwise bill—a bill that ought not to have become a law, because there was a mere handful of people in the Territory; but it did nothing so bad as what the Democrats tried to do the next year, when they framed the Lecompton Constitution by a minority of the people, and attempted to force that on the people of Kansas. The next bill was to abolish the existing laws, and to reorganize the Territory of Kansas without one word relating to slavery in any way. In other words, as the contest progressed, the hot blood cooled, and the whole body of the Northern representatives began to see that all they wanted was to wipe out the Territorial laws, leaving the Territory to the people, and they stopped there in that bill.

The only other controversy that arose was in reference to the Lecompton Constitution. The Democratic party had again taken the lead in forcing a slave Constitution upon the people against their will, and I, together with other Southern representatives, Mr. Marshall (now supporting Mr. Breckinridge), Mr. Gilmer, of North Carolina, Mr. Underwood, of Kentucky, Mr. Harris, of Maryland (applause), and one or two others, concurred in defeating it, under the lead of Mr. Crittenden. I take it that it was not agitating the Slavery Question. If it was, it was agitating it in very strange company and under very singular auspices.

Now, gentlemen, the statement I have just made covers the history of the controversy in Congress, since I went there, up to the beginning of the last session, on the subject of the Territories. The wild platform adopted at Philadelphia in 1856 said, "It is both the right and duty of Congress to prohibit in the Territories those twin relics of barbarism, polygamy and slavery." At Chicago (to show what men do when they become cool) all that resolution is wholly left out, and there is in it no declaration of a duty to pass any law at this time on the subject. They declare the condition of the Territories to be free in their opinion, in the absence of any law on the subject, just as Mr. Breckinridge declares them to be slave in the absence of a law on the subject. But they proposed no action on the subject, and they repealed and omitted that resolution which was in the platform of 1856. If any thing more significant could be required, it is that in the three, or four, or five bills which were introduced during the last session by Mr. Grow, of Pennsylvania—in all conscience, a stiff Free-Soiler enough for any body—as chairman of the Committee on Territories, to organize certain new Territories, there was simply a declaration, in the precise spirit of the resolution which I have read as reported by Mr. Clay, that nothing in these bills, which were absolutely silent on the subject, should be taken to authorize slavery in the Territories—a simple declaration of opinion, needless, in my judgment imprudent, because liable to be distorted and misrepresented, but not at all amounting to a law of affirmative exclusion, but leaving the law as it stood at the time of the passage of the bills.

Well, gentlemen, how are you to judge of the purposes of a party? By hunting up the speeches of small men who want to carry a neighborhood vote? By extracts from furious editors of small papers, who think they are never safe unless they are beyond the most extreme in their neighborhood? Are we to judge of men's opinions by the imputations of their enemies and their exaggerations for a purpose? Are we to suppose that our friends are black because their enemies daub them black? Or are we not rather to look at the facts, and to remember that among the millions of the North there are men as wise as we are, as honest as we are, as well educated as we are, having as great interests at stake in the perpetuity of the Union as we have, and as earnestly and honestly devoted to the integrity of the Constitution as we are, and that they are not likely deliberately to invite civil war, deliberately to moot questions which are wholly needless, whatever their opinions may be on them? Let us at least give them credit for common sense, and take their declarations rather than the declarations of their enemies and of our enemies. Is a Democrat's impeachment evidence against any body on a question of politics? (Laughter, and cries of "No, no.") Now we all know that there are men who are furious at the South on the Negro Question, and there are men at the North who are furious on the Negro Question. I am thankful that they are in an equally small minority in both sections. Their power is clamor. I do not believe that between them they could set a regiment in the field, even if they desired to do so.

And, gentlemen, if a collateral proof was required of how far the conservative masses of the North, the conservative leaders of the Republican party, or, rather, of the whole body of the opposition in the North to the Democratic party, are misrepresented, there would be no better or more convincing proof than in the fact that while the whole body of the Republican party are denounced as Abolitionists, the Abolitionists themselves have very quietly refused their support, and are organizing separate tickets for themselves. (Laughter and applause.) Can Mr. Breckinridge's friends say as much of the disunionists? Why are not the Abolitionists satisfied with the representations of our Southern brethren? They can not want any thing more than to invade the South; they can not want any thing more than to disturb our firesides; they can not want any thing more than to break up the slave-trade between the States; they can not want any thing more than scenes of blood and destruction throughout the country; they can not want any thing more than to repeat John Brown's crazy and bloody exploit by the thousand times a year. That is what we are taught by leading orators of the Democrats to expect, if not the result of a set purpose, the tendency of the conduct of the conservative millions of the North; and that in the face of the fact that, great as was the storm raised by that insanity of John Brown, and reckless as were the imputations upon gentlemen of certain political opinions throughout the whole North, yet, with all the powers of the United States to rake evidence from one end of the country to the other, with a diligent examination, extending through months, by the Senate of the United States, by an able and honorable committee, headed by Mr. Mason, of Virginia, and after a careful examination by the Legislature of Virginia, there was no evidence found that implicated any body of confederates, or any man holding political position, or aspiring to hold any position, any where in the North, with that insane performance. It is, as I have said before, instead of being a source of disquietude, the most quieting of all the occurrences of the last half century. It has lifted the veil of misrepresentation, and enabled us to see what men are doing. Till that event occurred, and till these investigations were had, such was the uniformity of the imputation of extreme anti-slavery opinions to a great body of men at the North, and of an earnest determination to intermeddle with Southern institutions to their damage, that gentlemen, even of calm minds, were perhaps justified in having a doubt, or even perhaps in forming opinions adverse to them upon the subject. But when investigations were made, after that occurrence, subsequent to all the provocations, all the series of outrages in Kansas Territory, where Northern men were allowed to be hunted down by the hundred, during, I believe, more than a year, for the express purpose of extending slavery into it, by border ruffians —notwithstanding all that excitement, nobody could be found implicated, except those at Harper's Ferry, directly with Brown, and one or two accomplices, who had fled. No man of name, not even any of the leading Abolitionists at the North, was found concerned in it. Why, it is, as a general thing, true, that the Abolitionists of the North, so far from exciting rebellion, are of the Quakers' opinion, that it is wrong to shed blood, and are the most peaceable and quiet, if the silliest and most misled, of people in the world. (Laughter.)

Gentlemen, I have stated what I believe to be the condition of affairs at the North. If, with these views of Mr. Lincoln and his leading friends, they should succeed in reaching power, my opinion is that they will act upon these opinions; and unless the question is forced on them by being raised by Democratic agitation, they will let it rest where it is, because they have nothing to accomplish, and there is no reason why they should reopen the question, and they declare that their only purpose is to oppose the extension of slavery into territory now free; or, in the words of Mr. Bates—who is entitled to speak for them—in enumerating the opinions of Mr. Lincoln, his personal and political friend, "his opinions are, that slavery is an institution in the States, of the States which choose to have it, and it exists within these States beyond the control of Congress; that Congress has supreme legislative power over all the Territories, and may at its discretion allow or forbid the existence of slavery within them; that Congress in wisdom and sound policy ought not so to exercise its power, directly or indirectly, as to *plant and establish* slavery in any territory theretofore free, and that it is unwise and impolitic in the government of the United States to acquire tropical regions for the mere purpose of converting them into slave States."

Then, gentlemen, over all the present Territories of the United States, unless Democrats agitate to extend slavery in fact, it is settled, according to the confessions of the Union party, according to the confession of every body excepting Mr. Douglas upon one side and Mr. Breckinridge upon the other. Who is in favor of acquiring more territory to reopen the question? I am not. Are you? ("No, no.") Is John Bell? Is Edward Everett? Is Mr. Lincoln? Not one of them. Which is the party that does not frown on the filibusters; or, if not quite that, what party claims to be the party of expansion; what party proposed to buy Cuba at an expense of $300,000,000—a small item of $18,000,000 interest per annum to be saddled on you and me? Who proposed to take military possession of Sonora and Chihuahua, which, if once gotten, would never be given up? Who was negotiating a treaty which virtually inaugurated a protectorate over Mexico, which must sooner or later resolve itself into a conquest and annexation? Not those opposed to the Democratic party.

The Democratic leaders are the persons who alone propose to acquire additional territory. If they do acquire it, they must take the responsibility of the agitation that will arise out of it. That it will be fierce is certain; that it can be settled is uncertain. That the acquisition can be prevented, and ought to be prevented, is of all things the most clear. If great international necessities should force upon us, contrary to our will, additional territory, I take it that, irrespective of the abstract opinions of this party or that, it will be apt to settle itself according to the existing condition of the territory when it is acquired. I doubt very much, if you were to acquire the *Tierra Caliente* of Mexico to-morrow, with the Mexican population densely filling it, slavery could ever be carried there; for it could only be carried there by consent of the people, if at all; and the Mexicans, having abolished it once, would not be likely to reinstate it. On the other hand, if you acquired Cuba with its immense negro population, no amount of opposition could prevent its admission into the Union with its slaves, as it stood. When acquired, in other words, the law of settlement would be the statesman's law applied by Mr. Clay to the territory acquired from Mexico—the *status quo*, the condition in which it is when acquired. If it is free, it is impossible in this country ever to make it slave, for the whole body of the Northern vote is irrevocably committed against it. If it is slave, the body of the Northern as well as of the Southern vote is committed against an abolition of slavery in a State; and Cuba must be acquired as a State, if acquired at all. The whole conservative body of the country would be resolutely and positively opposed to freeing the mass of negroes in that island, against the will of the people of the island, just exactly as they would be to freeing them in Louisiana itself. So I take it that if, in future years, we should be driven upon the acquisition of farther territory, the question will be settled as it was settled in 1850, and that no power in this country can prevent its being so settled, if, indeed, it be adjusted at all. If you acquire territory free, it will remain free. If you acquire the island of Cuba, slavery will remain the law of the land until the inhabitants change it.

Gentlemen, we have in the threats against the Union, in the

event of the election of one of the candidates, only another instance of that persistent agitation of the Slavery Question, and appealing to men's fears, and attempting to shake their nerves, which has been the policy, in my judgment, of the Democratic party for a great many years past. Break up the government! Why, gentlemen, who are going to do it? Mr. Douglas is not, for his whole charge against his Democratic opponent is that he is a Disunionist. Mr. Bell is not, because he is named as the Union candidate. Mr. Lincoln is not, because one of the grounds of charge against him is that he says the South shall not secede if she wants to do so. (Laughter and applause.) Mr. Breckinridge disavows being a secessionist, and I believe him. The great body of his followers, I believe, disavow it likewise. I believe them. As to the remaining small body of noisy Disunionists—I have no doubt there are such persons in the United States, but I think that now, as heretofore, in the event of no great grievance occurring, of no great outrage being perpetrated, of no war being made on the Southern States and their institutions; upon every thing being allowed to continue as it has been hitherto, and to go on as it has proceeded heretofore; the sun being allowed to rise not covered with blood, and the moon being allowed to rise not turned to darkness—if these things shall continue, my impression is, that the hottest of the Disunionists will count their numbers, and they will count the numbers on the other side, and they will prudently, upon a reconsideration of the whole matter, wait for a more convenient season. (Great laughter and applause.)

Then, gentlemen, is there any thing to be afraid of? Are we surrounded with terrific forms and shapes, that haunt us as we pass along the streets, and make the merchant tremble for his ship upon the ocean, and the person holding stocks fear lest the stock board should show a decline in his favorite securities? Or are persons who want to speculate in property calculating the duration of the Union, to see whether land be worth a year's value in fee, or whether there will be so many people engaged in war that possibly rents will not be so high as they expected? Are these the considerations that we are now called upon to weigh? Are we on the borders of a civil war, or are we merely determining a question of political parties? If we are in the former, then, gentlemen, it requires very different methods from any that have been taken heretofore. It is not a New York or New Jersey contract for fusion that will avert that danger. Is there so near a prospect that the Union will be broken up in the event of the triumph of Mr. Lincoln? Then why do you not all turn in and vote for Mr. Breckinridge, who has the Disunionists in his ranks?—for they will be quiet if he be elected. Why does not Mr. Douglas cease his clamor about disunion, and get his friends to unite throughout the South, and likewise in the North, with his political opponents? Or, gentlemen, if we are not to be so generous as that, and can higgle over a matter of men when the existence of the government is at stake, as the Democrats say they are the only party competent to preserve the Union, and they are now in an unfortunate and distracted minority, why do they not hold out the olive-branch to us and say "Know-Nothings as you are—enemies of civil and religious liberty, stained with midnight assassination—still, to save the government, we will even vote for you?" (Great applause.)

That would be a coalition equal to the occasion, as the alarmist and agitators state it. There would be a necessity which would justify it. That would be the subordination of every political division to the existence of the government. But this puling question, "Shall I join with you," "Why, then, don't you join with me?" this miserable question as to who shall have the honor of saving the government and who shall make the sacrifice, is unworthy of the crisis that Disunionists and Union savers assert to be at hand, and which the latter profess to desire to avert. In my judgment the Union receives more discredit from being saved all the time than it would from being let alone to save itself. (Applause.) Thank Heaven, it is not a Maryland idea; we do not deal with politics in that way in Maryland; we do not make bargains with our political opponents, and lie down in the same bed, after they have spit at us, over us, for years. (Applause.) It is a New York idea, originating in local hostilities and interests—which has migrated into New Jersey, and tends to spread. It originated since the Baltimore Convention, since the nomination of Mr. Bell. "Oh! let us make a fusion to beat Mr. Lincoln—not to elect Mr. Bell"—observe the phrase—"to beat Mr. Lincoln," because all these evils will follow on his election! What good is that going to do Mr. Bell? ("That's it.") If there are these dangers, the men who cry out against them ought to be consistent in their proposals for fusion; it should be carried into every Northern State; Mr. Breckinridge, Mr. Douglas, and Mr. Bell ought to unite there. Every gentleman in the South ought to be willing to abandon his political diversities of opinion with his neighbor, and sacrifice them on the altar of his country, if the *country* demand the sacrifice; for when the struggle is for life or death, for peace or civil war, it is out of place to allow political divisions of opinion to keep asunder lovers of the country. All parties should be merged in the presence of the overruling necessity of the country. And when gentlemen make an argument which should lead them to subordinate their individual opinions, and lay them down in that way in order to induce others to make political sacrifices, and yet show no desire themselves to make them, I say it is a cry of wolf, with no wolf threatening the fold at all. "Oh! fuse in New York and New Jersey, or Pennsylvania, for there they are weak!" How about Georgia? What does Mr. Breckinridge say to that? How about Virginia? How about South Carolina? What of Alabama? What of Mississippi? There is no fusion there; it is war to the knife between the Union savers on both sides. (Laughter.) But up in one or two doubtful States in the North, where men are given to bargaining, and where political principles are only the counters laid down on the gambling board, there they can make bargains and fuse to save the Union (laughter) and their customers.

Gentlemen, I am disgusted at the suggestion, and I think the honorable gentlemen who have given it their assent will regret it when it is too late. I will do any thing that is honorable to aid the election of John Bell to the presidency. (Great applause.) I will not give the lie to all political truth by casting a vote or half a vote for men with whom I differ on every political question. (Continued applause.) In the presence of a common enemy, politics is silent; but as long as it is a question of politics, my duty requires me to vote for men in whom I have confidence personally, who I suppose will pursue those views of policy that I and my friends believe to be right, and to vote against all who are opposed to them. To that extent I will support John Bell; but I will not vote for Mr. Douglas to defeat Mr. Lincoln, nor for any other purpose. (Renewed applause.)

Gentlemen, what good is fusion going to do Mr. Bell? If they really want to elect him, and not merely to frighten weak people into giving a Democrat a chance of being elected before the House of Representatives or before the Senate, they have a short way to do it. If the case is as grievous as they say, and they believe it, then it is to them a bagatelle whether Mr. Breckinridge or Mr. Bell be President; and if the Breckinridge men and Douglas men throughout the whole body of the South will, upon that one ground (thus marking the earnestness of their belief, that the only way to avert revolution and disaster, and to keep their homes unsullied and free from the blood of their wives and children, is to defeat Mr. Lincoln, and elect somebody that is safer and better), vote for John Bell, it would be something that I could appreciate. They can mark that feeling in a manner which will speak in tones of thunder to every man of common sense north of Mason and Dixon's line; they can do it by just casting their votes for John Bell, and by making the avowal that he shall be President if their united votes can make him so. And they can say that if they fail there, then, if Mr. Lane does not come before the Senate, but Mr. Everett does, they, the Democrats, will vote Mr. Everett into the presidential chair. (Great applause.) Let them say it, and we shall begin to believe that they are in earnest.

New York politicians are very well content, as they say, to defeat Mr. Lincoln, and let a Democrat be elected. They are not proposing to aid Mr. Bell, nor can it. It only humbles his party; it deprives it of power in the future; it almost puts an end to the possibility of its ever being powerful in a State where it has been made a subject of barter and sale upon 'change. Who can fling back a Democrat's charge of bargain and corruption? Who hereafter can ever cast in the teeth of the Democrats their covering up their divisions by compromises? What becomes of the perpetual assault upon them, that in the South they have one opinion, and in the North another; that in the South they are extreme slavery men, and in the North have Free-Soilers in their ranks, who receive their highest honors? Who hereafter can ever cast the imputation on them that the Kansas-Nebraska Act was supported with one signification in the North and another in the South? Are not the mouths of those who, differing from Mr. Douglas and Mr. Breckinridge on these very points, yet agree to give Mr. Douglas say twenty-five votes, in order that they may buy ten votes for Mr. Bell—are not their mouths sealed forever?

Let us work it out, gentlemen, in a national point of view. Is it wise thus to act? Where does it send the election? If successful, it sends it to the House of Representatives. There was a time—I hope it has not passed, but I fear that the course of policy which has been pursued by a portion of Mr. Bell's friends has rendered it now almost impossible—there was a time when, had the election failed out of doors, and Mr. Lincoln been defeated, Mr. Bell would have gotten, in my judgment, and gotten cheerfully, the vote of every Republican State in the lower House. The insane method of assault upon and misrepresentation of Mr. Lincoln's opinions, of the purposes of his party, have, I fear, put an end to the possibility of a single vote from that quarter, if the election should go to the House of Representatives. In my judgment, it will be an impossibility to elect any body there, such is the division of parties. The Republicans have not a majority; the Democrats have not a majority; the Americans have not a majority.

The Republicans and the People's party have fifteen States. Possibly they might buy two, under the enormous pressure of the occasion. (Laughter.) The Democrats have enough to elect, *if* they can get all the American States, together with Oregon and California, which now belong to them in the House. Whether they will go that way or not, it is not my province here to say; but it is perfectly certain that the Democratic States will not go for Mr. Bell. Does any body think they will? Look at the speaker's election. Do not forget things that have occurred within a few months past. Go and examine that list, and tell me whether there is a single Democratic State that, under these circumstances, will cast its vote in the House for John Bell. Then there is no election, and this accompanied, probably, with such scenes of violence and tumult as possibly men of greater firmness than I have may desire to encounter, but from which I pray to be delivered. I have gone through two contests in the House of Representatives for the election of the comparatively unimportant office of speaker with the House divided as it is divided now. I have seen these scenes of violence; I have heard words of menace; I have looked from day to day to some outbreak that would drench that hall in blood, and be the beginning of a real (and not a newspaper) revolution in the country; but, by the infinite blessing of Providence, that danger has been averted. I will not rush upon the bosses of His buckler, and tempt Him too far. I will not try that House of Representatives again to do the business which the *people* ought to do, in their majesty and in their calmness. (Applause.) I will not tempt them with the immense bribes that can be urged—with the intensity of political passions excited to the uttermost—with the fierceness of men, some of them, possibly, only too willing to convert a political into a revolutionary strife in that hall. I do not wish to see the immense temptations of a presidential election forced on the House of Representatives without a necessity, and only in the last resort—something to be shunned, and not to be sought for—something to be trembled over whenever it comes—something to be thankful to God for if it shall pass without civil violence.

And what next? If there be no election by the House when the 4th of March comes, who is the President? The Vice-President, elected by the Senate. Who are in the Senate? A clear Democratic majority. If Mr. Lane's name goes to the Senate, of course he will be by them cheerfully elected President. But suppose Mr. Everett's name goes to the Senate? Oh, say the confiding New Yorkers, he will be elected by the Democratic senators. Well, gentlemen, I should go for credulity somewhere else than the stock exchange. Expect them to elect Edward Everett! Why, gentlemen, they have the game in their own hands. I do not expect so much from their liberality. I should rejoice in such a result. Nothing, after the terrific scenes in the lower House, could give this country such peace, and quiet, and relief as to know that, when the wished-for 4th of March shall come, such a man as Edward Everett will be in the presidency, no matter by whom or how chosen. (Applause.) But I have not that faith in the Democratic senators, and I am not sure they would make an election in the Senate, if his name and Mr. Hamlin's should be alone before them.

I think they might prefer rather to wait until the 4th of March, let the presidential office be vacant, have a year of interregnum, and a new election, in the midst of which, without a head to the government, who will tell me what would occur? Or they might take the other alternative, doubtful in law, but which they may undertake to solve, and therefore may solve to suit themselves; and, instead of having an interregnum, Mr. Breckinridge being then a member of the Senate, they may elect him President of that body, and treat him as President of the United States after the 4th of March. The Constitution of the United States appears to have left a very unfortunate, it may prove some day a very dangerous gap. It is possible that a construction may close that gap, but none has closed it yet. It declares, in the event of the death, resignation, or disability of the President and Vice-President happening after entrance into office, Congress may declare what officer shall discharge the duties of President till removal of the disability, or an election.

Congress has provided that the President of the Senate becomes, for the time being, the President, and in his absence the Speaker of the House of Representatives becomes the President. But there seems to be no provision for a *failure to elect* both President and Vice-President. The Constitution—and the law which was intended to provide for the vacancy of the presidency follows the language of the Constitution—does not authorize Congress to provide for that case. There seems to be no provision any where for the case of the presidential office being absolutely vacant at the commencement of a term—the case of an absolute failure to elect either a President or Vice-President. Whether, in that contingency, the President *pro tempore* of the Senate would assume to exercise the powers of President of the United States, or whether it would be treated by the Senate (the only legal body existing on the 4th of March) as vacant, no mind can now determine; and legal arguments may possibly be adduced on both sides. We may very well rest assured that the majority of the Senate will settle it in whichever way will best suit their interests. It rests with them; it rests with no one else; you and I have no power over it. When the matter goes to the Senate, if they see fit to make no election, we are pushed upon this dangerous alternative, a vacant or a disputed presidency.

If the people wish to run afoul of these difficulties, well and good. They were not originally intended to be made by bargaining politicians. The provision of the Constitution is for a case of accident or failure, after a *bona fide* effort of the people to elect, not for a conspiracy of a few politicians in a corner, in one State of the United States, to adjourn their political difficulties and their personal hatreds into the halls of Congress. I therefore enter my protest solemnly against any such style of electioneering. Others may engage in it. In the State of New York it is none of my business. I am not called upon to vote for Mr. Douglas or Mr. Breckinridge, and I have nothing more to say about it, except that it is with them; but it is not our style, here in Maryland, of standing to our principles, and conducting our canvass, and doing our best to elect our own candidates. (Great applause.)

What I have said, gentlemen, covers the exposition I desired to make to you this evening. I am aware that there is a great cry about sectionalism, and a great scramble for the vacant title of national. I wish, gentlemen, that there were a national candidate for the presidency. I wish there were a really national party—not merely one which has principles that will suit the whole land, but one whose power extended unbroken from North to South, as did the Whig party in its days of glory. (Applause.) I trust that, ere I die, I shall again see the lines of these divisions obliterated. But when people talk about sectionalism, and one party casts upon another the imputation of being sectional, I am free, for my part, to say that they are all sectional, in any proper sense. Mr. Douglas—is he a national candidate? He is, it would seem, the regular nominee of the Democratic party; but the Democratic party is not the nation; for the regular Democratic party is as much a whole party as a man is whole when cloven by a sabre from head to heels. Where is his strength? In the North! He has a few supporters in the South, it is true. Mr. Breckinridge—is he a national candidate? He has great strength in the South. Whether it will be as powerful there as he supposes, remains to be seen. Circumstances now indicate that somebody else will have a say in political matters in the South besides the Democrats hereafter; but his strength is in the South. In the North, it is the shrunk shank of a decrepit old man. Mr. Lincoln's strength is undoubtedly in the North; he has supporters in some of the border slave States. Is not Mr. Bell's strength in the South, although he has supporters sporadically over the whole North?

Gentlemen, it is the misery of our condition that, turn wherever we may, we find that this infernal strife has split every body into a thousand pieces, and no man can tell where to find the piece that belongs to him. (Laughter.) Nay, more, gentlemen, if I may be allowed to quote words which I heard in a sacred place, from a very eloquent gentleman [Rev. Mr. Stockton], whom doubtless many of you have heard in the pulpit here in Baltimore, I say of the condition of the people of this country and its party, especially of that great opposition party to the Democrats which now is rent into fragments and struggling together, as he said of the Christian religion—that the vase in which the precious spirit of Christianity was held had been broken by sectarian strife into so many pieces, that not only was its beauty marred and gone, and its precious essence poured out and lost, but that he who, on a mission of love, attempted to collect its fragments and put them together, was in danger, in the attempt to reconstruct the vase, of cutting his fingers. It is the danger—it is the sickness of the times; and, instead of attemptng to cure it, men who ought to know better are acting so as to aggravate it. The patient is in a fever, and they wrap him up in blankets. His blood is boiling, and they dose him with strong drinks and fire-water, and call that—curing!

Gentlemen, there is a degree of timidity that is, of all things in my judgment, the most dangerous in political life. Half the blood that was shed in the French Revolution was shed from sheer terror. It was not courage, it was not ferocity, it was sheer terror, that made them cut their neighbors' throats to-day, lest those neighbors should cut theirs to-morrow. That is the state of mind in which the conduct of too many in this canvass tends to throw the people of the United States. I lift my voice against it.

Whether these sentiments are popular here or not is to me a matter of secondary moment. I have a duty to perform to myself as well as to you. I agree with that most honorable and distinguished gentleman, my friend, Mr. Millson, of Norfolk, who, in his late letter, said, if I am not mistaken, that he thought it his duty to warn his constituents, as well when there *was* danger of invasion of their rights as when, in point of fact, there was *none*. And, acting upon that high principle, I say here now, this night, that peace is within our grasp, if we only see fit to hold fast to it. If we choose to encourage war, we may encourage it too far.

Gentlemen, there has been a sort of hesitation on the part of the opponents of the Democratic party to meet them directly in the eye, to make formally the issue with them as to the correctness and safety of their principles and policy, and their mode of conducting the government. And the reason the opposition have failed in other parts of the South is, in my judgment, because they have *not* met the Democrats in that way; the reason that we have not failed in Maryland is because we have not been afraid to strike a blow that would overthrow our enemy. (Applause.) It only requires that there should be energy and union, and the day is ours.

Gibbon tells us that, as Christianity progressed and spread as far as Egypt, the idols roused the ire of the faithful. There was at Alexandria an image of Serapis, which superstitious faith in ancient prophecies protected from their iconoclastic rage.

"It was confidently affirmed that, if any impious hand should dare to violate the majesty of the god, the heavens and the earth would instantly return to their original chaos. An intrepid soldier, animated by zeal, and armed with a mighty battle-axe, ascended the ladder; and even the Christian multitude expected with some anxiety the event of the combat. He aimed a vigorous stroke against the cheek of Serapis; the cheek fell to the ground; the thunder was still silent, and both the heavens and the earth continued to preserve their accustomed order and tranquillity. The victorious soldier repeated his blows; the huge idol was overthrown and broken in pieces, and the limbs of Serapis were ignominiously dragged through the streets of Alexandria. His mangled carcass was burnt in the amphitheatre, amid the shouts of the populace; and many persons attribute their conversion to this discovery of the impotence of their tutelar deity."

Gentlemen, smite fearlessly the Democratic party! The Union will survive its fragments. (Enthusiastic applause.)

ADDRESS TO THE VOTERS OF THE FOURTH CONGRESSIONAL DISTRICT.

The election in November, 1860, resulted in the choice of Mr. Lincoln, and the success of the Republican party. The leaders in the South now set about the work of making good the threats which had thus proved useless for again driving the North and West to submission. Unwilling to afford a breathing space or moment for reflection to the people, which they knew must prevent the consummation of such suicidal folly, they at once, the result of the election being ascertained, proceeded to carry out the conspiracy. The first cry was raised in Charleston, and the Governor of South Carolina at once recommended to the Legislature that steps should be taken for the assembling of a "Sovereign Convention." Similar proceedings were had in the Gulf States, and every where throughout the South the emissaries of sedition, secession, and disunion were traveling to and fro to finish the work they had undertaken. The Secretary of War of the United States (Floyd) had joined the conspiracy, and had accumulated large quantities of arms and munitions of war at the arsenals, forts, and military posts belonging to the United States in the Southern States, and had, at the same time, in pursuance of the wishes of the Southern conspirators, removed all the larger garrisons from those posts, and sent them to the Northwest, and to other remote and not easily accessible points.

The militia in the Southern States were called out, were armed, uniformed, and drilled. Their cities and chief towns were filled with volunteers and armed men, called out "to defend the State from invasion," and "to drive back the Abolition and Black Republican hordes."

The people of the Northern and Western States could not at first be brought to believe that the attempt at disunion would really be made. They had heard, on many previous occasions, the same threats by South Carolina, which had failed either before the resolution of Andrew Jackson or the good sense of the Southern people. And now they saw no more cause for alarm in the South than before; they readily, therefore, supposed the tumult would be quieted by the firmness of the federal government and on appeal to the Southern popular vote. They were ignorant of the extent, of the violence, of the intimidation of the conspiracy, of the numbers of the conspirators, of their positions in the cabinet, and in the highest offices of the government. To this state of ignorance rapidly succeeded one of alarm and anxiety, as other Southern States prepared to abet South Carolina, when the Congress met on the 3d of December. When the President's Message was delivered, the country was surprised by the announcement that, if federal officers within a State should all resign, or *be prevented by state legislation* from executing the laws of the United States, and such State should undertake to withdraw from the confederacy, there was no power given to the Executive, or "delegated by the Constitution to the Congress," to use force, in case of necessity, to compel the execution of the federal laws; that, even if Congress possessed this power, "the object of which doubtless would be the preservation of the Union," yet the exercise thereof, when indispensable, would be the surest means of destroying what it alone could uphold; and that the "confederacy" (meaning the United States) was afflicted with a deep-seated inherent defect, or fatal mistake, as regards the propriety of the power, if given, in its Constitution. To remedy this, after quoting the Virginia Resolutions of 1799, Mr. Buchanan thought "an explanatory amendment" of the Constitution was advisable, and exhibited the following prescription:

1. An express recognition of the right of property in slaves in the States where it now exists, or *may hereafter exist.*

2. The duty of protecting this right in all the common Territories, throughout their territorial existence, and until they shall be admitted as States into the Union, with or without slavery, as their Constitutions may prescribe.

3. A like recognition of the right of the master to have his slave, who has escaped from one State to another, restored and "delivered up" to him; and of the validity of the Fugitive Slave Law, enacted for this purpose, together with a declaration that all State laws impairing or defeating this right are violations of the Constitution, and are consequently null and void.

On the 4th of December the House resolved that so much of the President's Message as relates to the present perilous condition of the country be referred to a special committee of one from each State. On the 6th Mr. Davis was named as the member from Maryland, and Mr. Corwin, of Ohio, was chairman.

On the 21st the representatives from South Carolina announced their withdrawal, as a consequence of the ordinance by which "the people of South Carolina, in their sovereign capacity, had resumed the powers heretofore delegated by them to the Federal government of the United States." The same performance was gone through by the Mississippi delegation on the 12th of January; by the majority of the Alabama delegation on the 21st; by Georgia (Mr. Hill *resigned*) on the 23d; by Florida (in the Senate) on the 25th; and on the 5th of February by the Louisiana representatives, with the exception of Mr. Bouligny.

In view of the condition of affairs at New Year, 1861, Mr. Davis wrote from Washington the following letter to his constituents of the Fourth District of Maryland:

January 2, 1861.

It is my right and my duty as your representative to warn you of the danger which threatens the destruction of the government, and to overwhelm you beneath its ruins.

The first act of the drama of revolution was opened in South Carolina.

Ambitious and restless men, availing themselves of factitious fear which they have inspired, and sectional passions which they have inflamed, are conspiring the overthrow of the government. They hope to found a Southern Confederacy on the fragments of the United States of *America.*

Maryland has been formally asked to join a Southern Confederacy. The advocates of ruin speciously deny their treasonable plans under the form of Southern prejudice, and ask if Maryland will desert the South and join the North. But that is not the question which Maryland is called on to answer.

Maryland is now joined to both the free and the slave States, under the wisest Constitution, and by the best government the world ever saw.

That government has never wronged her, or failed to protect her. The formation of a Southern Confederacy must be preceded by the destruction of that government. Till it is broken up and its armies defeated, there can be no Southern Confederacy. Maryland is therefore asked, not whether she prefers to enter a Northern or a Southern Confederacy, but she is asked to form a coalition to break up and destroy the Constitution which Washington founded, and to plunge into the horrors of a civil war, for the purpose of creating a Southern Confederacy.

That is the true question you have to consider, for peaceful secession is a delusion; and if you yield to the arts now employed to delude you, the soil of Maryland will be trampled by armies struggling for the national capital. The only question is, Will you fight to maintain or to destroy the existing government?

The interests of Maryland are indissolubly connected with the integrity of the United States; any division of the confederacy is to her fatal.

Maryland has not an interest that will survive the government under the Constitution. No matter what new combinations arise, whether Maryland stand alone, or unites her fate to any new confederacy on her northern or her southern border, she is utterly ruined and prostrate for this generation at least. When she will revive, God only knows.

If the present government be destroyed, Maryland slaveholders lose the only guarantee for the return of their slaves. Every commercial line of communication is severed. Custom-house barriers arrest her merchants at every frontier. Her commerce on the ocean is the prey of every pirate, or the sport of every maritime power. Her great railroad loses every connection which makes it valuable. If two republics divide the territory of the United States, Maryland is ruined whichever she join. If the South, her slaves will walk over the Pennsylvania line unmolested. The African slave-trade will reduce their market value below the cost of raising or supporting them; and, if they did not abscond, they would be abandoned by their masters.

Free trade will open every port, and cotton and woolen factories, and the iron and machine works of Maryland would be prostrate before European competition. The expenses of government must be doubled by the necessity of a large standing army, for all the conditions of present security will be gone; and a great Northern power, divided from us by an air-line, will be an ever-impending danger.

In the war of separation, and even after, Maryland will be an outgoing province, without a fortification or a natural boundary, always overrun at the first sound of arms, incapable of being defended by the weaker power, of which she will form a part, whose natural line of defense must be the Potomac, and on this side of which no Southern army would venture a decisive battle.

The hope that Baltimore will be the emporium of such a republic is a delusion too ridiculous to need refutation. Nothing intended for the *South* will ever pass Norfolk, and from the West we will be severed by custom-houses, duties, and political antipathies in favor of New York.

Is not a Southern republic ruin to Maryland? Joining a Northern one is equally so, if stated lines define the limits of the two republics. The slave interest will be immediately destroyed; the great railroad to the West is cut off at Harper's Ferry; and Baltimore becomes a tributary to the Central Pennsylvania Road.

All the Southern and Southwestern trade is gone, and her foreign commerce can seek the ocean only by favor of Virginia, or under the guns of a powerful navy. In war still we are the frontier, and our soil will be desolated by the contending armies.

Our manufacturing interests will be better secured, our military frontier better protected by the Potomac, our foreign commerce will have the protection of a maritime power, and we shall be free from the humiliation of a European protectorate; but the sudden and absolute destruction of the slaveholding interest, and the radical change in the relations of our population, will give a shock to our internal quiet and prosperity that neither this nor the next generation will recover from.

But there can be no such division of this Confederacy by existing State lines. The present territory has been acquired and divided to be used as a whole, bound by the common ties of the Constitution, and the course of trade is arranged accordingly. Break it in any part, and it will fly into a thousand pieces like a Prince Rupert's drop.

Western Virginia belongs to the Valley of the Mississippi. Virginia can never withdraw from the existing Confederacy undivided; her western boundary will be the Blue Ridge. Maryland will be swayed by adverse forces, which will probably give her northern and western counties to Pennsylvania; her peninsular to Virginia, unless a civil war shall first have desolated and subdued them.

Whatever the *sympathies* of her commercial emporium may be in the present political heats, yet, when the conditions which gave rise to them are gone with the present government, her *interests* will find a voice, and a decisive voice, in determining her future relations. What they shall be I trust in God may never be decided.

With these consequences before their eyes, there are yet men in Maryland who seem madly bent on revolution, and conspirators beyond her limits instigate and aid their efforts. To the success of their schemes the convocation of the Legislature is essential.

In securing that object many unite who are strangers to their purposes, and blind to the consequences of what they are doing —men who honestly think there is danger it might avert, or that there ought to be an agreement or understanding with Virginia, or who are moved by sympathy with neighboring agitators, or wish to gain party advantages, or play a political game, or are interested in the corrupt and active lobby. They are all the allies, conscious or unconscious, of the revolutionists.

The revolutionary agitators, existing elsewhere in the republic, will be aggravated by a call of the Maryland Legislature. It will look like sympathy with the revolutionary States. It will dishearten the friends *of the government* in those States. It will inspire the revolutionists in the Central States, now in hopeless minority, with new hopes. It will tend to destroy the moderate feelings of the free States in dealing with the existing discontent. It will greatly embarrass the President, who must maintain the authority of the laws, and is entitled to the undivided support of the people of Maryland for that purpose.

The halls of legislation will immediately become the focus of revolutionary conspiracy. Under specious pretexts, the people will be implicated, by consultations with other States, by concerted plans, by inadmissible demands, by extreme and offensive pretensions, in a deeply-laid scheme of simultaneous revolt, in the event of the inevitable failure to impose on the free States the ultimatum of the slave States. Maryland will find herself severed from more than half the States, plunged in anarchy, and wrapped in the flames of civil war, waged by her against the government in which we now glory.

In the face of such consequences, what justification, what excuse is there for convening the Legislature? Within its constitutional powers it can do nothing, and there is nothing for it to do.

The only danger to Maryland in the present crisis is that rebellious States may destroy the United States, and that to her is absolute ruin; but against that her only and sufficient security is the power of the United States government, supported by the loyal devotion of the people outside of the disaffected States. Maryland can not suppress revolution in South Carolina, and neither South Carolina nor any other State threatens Maryland with invasion or any other danger. Congress and the President are vested exclusively with the power to enforce the laws of the Union, and every person in Maryland, as in all the other central slave States, is bound to obey the laws of the President for that purpose, any thing in their laws to the contrary notwithstanding. The Legislatures can, therefore, do nothing in the matter.

But many persons clamor for the Legislature in order that it may *agree* with Virginia, or with other slave States, on a course of conduct.

The Constitution forbids any agreement between Maryland and any other States for any purpose.

Not only does the 10th section of the first article of the Constitution declare that "no State shall enter into any treaty, alliance, or confederation," but it also says "no State shall, without the *consent of Congress, enter into any agreement or compact with another* State, or with a *foreign power;* and Article VI. declares this Constitution to be the supreme law of the land of *Virginia* as well as of *Maryland;* and that the members of the several State Legislatures, and all executive and judicial officers of the *several States,* shall be bound by oath or affirmation to support *this Constitution.*"

Are the members of the Legislature to violate their oath? If not, there can be no consultation; if they *are,* then it is not to preserve the Constitution, but to promote its destruction by *revolution,* that the Legislature is to be convened.

The Legislature can, within its constitutional power, do nothing. It is as unconstitutional to make an agreement with Virginia as it would be with France.

An agreement to consult to have any common purpose, any concerted action, is expressly forbidden; for, if allowed, the United States might be defied by a coalition too powerful to be suppressed without arms, and the laws of the Union be enforced only at the hazard of civil war.

The prevailing discontents, the inflamed state of public feeling, which now prompt men and states to consult, are the very dangers the constitutional prohibition was intended to guard against. Southern States only now think of a coalition; but what should we say of a free-state coalition to repeal the constitutional guarantee of the slavery interest?

A Convention of the central slave States is equally unconstitutional, dangerous, and needless. Whatever it can do, which is not unconstitutional and mischievous, can be better done without it. Is it to propose amendments to the Constitution? No body authorized to amend could even consider the proposal.

But Congress, on the application of the Legislatures of two thirds of the States, can call a Convention of ALL the States, and that can remedy every grievance. Is it to secure agreement on the same amendments? Their representatives in Congress are the constitutional representatives of the States in the only body where the States are permitted to consult, and they can *there* move any amendments they may concur in thinking necessary; and those amendments will, under the Constitution, be formally sent for approval to *all* the States. Is it to agree upon demands to be made on the free States, on refusal of which nothing is to follow? Then why assemble it?

But is the purpose of it to combine the central slave States in demands on the free States, accompanied with the menace of revolution, in the event of their refusal to submit to the dictation? Then the Convention is a treasonable assembly to levy war for the overthrow of the government.

Such a consultation among the central slave States, where no voice from the free States will be heard, and their feelings and wishes will be wholly disregarded, and where the more extreme opinions of the slave States will predominate, is likely to result in a demand of concessions wholly impossible to be maintained, accompanied by the implied pledge not to be satisfied with any thing less; and on the refusal of the free States to submit to terms thus dictated without any consultation with them, the revolutionists will precipitate the whole of the consulting States into revolution. This I believe to be the most natural result of the proposed consultation. I presume the revolutionists have not been so dull as to overlook it.

Maryland is not ready to be entrapped. Her people are the best guardians of their own interests, duty, and honor. It is for them *now* to demand of those who counsel a Convention of the central slave States to specify whether there are, in the words of President Jackson, "*any acts so plainly unconstitutional and so intolerably oppressive*" *to them* that they are willing to tear the government to pieces in the pursuit of redress.

If there be such acts, then convene the Legislature; assemble a Convention; concert with Virginia measures of resistance in default of redress; but also let the people prepare their hearts for WAR, and their fields for desolation, and their children for slaughter. Let them prepare for an era of proscriptions, confiscations, and exiles, to be followed by anarchy, and be closed by the rude despotism of the sword.

But if there be no such grievances which justify, in the eye of reason, encountering those consequences, then let the people of Maryland not allow themselves to be seduced by insidious wiles, under plausible disguises, into measures which, whatever may be their professed objects, *tend* to such results, and must bring them forth.

Will any one propose gravely to rush on such ruin because a few negroes have run away and not been caught—because some liberty bills have been passed and never acted on—because a mob, once in a while, has resisted an unpopular law—because Maryland has been in a minority on a presidential election? Or are there any other grievances for which revolution is considered the only adequate remedy?

Is it the personal liberty bills?

They exist in only a few of the free States. They do not exist in any one of the free States coterminous with the slave States. They are all remote from us, where a negro hardly ever goes. It is not known that they ever aid a single negro to escape. The courts of the United States have always declared them void, and it is only in the courts that a free country enforces any law. It is probable they soon will be repealed, and vanish with the temporary excitement which occasioned them.

They have been suffered to exist more than two administrations without any one in Maryland dreaming of revolutionary redress.

Is it the failure to enforce the Fugitive Slave Law?

The States are not charged with that duty at all. It is imposed on the United States government, and the right to claim fugitive slaves exists only so long as the Constitution exists. It is certain that the dissolution of the government repeals and annuls this law, and that is therefore no redress.

If mobs have occasionally interfered to rescue fugitives, they have been successful only occasionally. The guilty parties have frequently been punished by both State and federal courts, and it is probable that they can be entirely avoided by a reasonable change in the law itself. Is a government to be *destroyed* because a mob makes a rescue?

Are we to make a revolution because we can not catch a fugitive in a free State, whom we have already failed to catch in a slave State?

But the Territories, they must be adjusted; the *rights* of the

South must be acknowledged. Are the people of Maryland dreaming of a revolution in the event of a failure to *resettle* the Territorial Question to the satisfaction of *Southern secessionists?*

Is Maryland so discontented with the *actual* condition of the Territories that she will aid in destroying the government unless it be changed? I will not believe in such madness.

No change has taken place since Mr. Clay's adjustment of 1850 but at the instance of the slave States; that change was the Kansas-Nebraska Act of 1854, which repealed the Missouri line, in order to substitute what was called the principles of the act of 1850; and at that time all the Territories were in fact free.

Slavery has, in point of fact, been introduced into New Mexico by the people under the act of 1850. Slavery has not been introduced into Utah, nor Kansas, nor Nebraska, under the law of 1854. The only Territory south of 36° 30′ is New Mexico; all the residue of the Territories are north of that line. Now we are in danger of civil war unless, by an amendment of the Constitution, we establish slavery south of 36° 30′—not merely in New Mexico, but in all territory hereafter to be acquired. No man who values the peace of the country can assent to that bribe to filibustering.

But, touching the Territory now to be disposed of, while the people of the free States will refuse the proposed amendment because it makes *them establish* slavery, they will probably agree to make New Mexico a State, and that removes it beyond the meddling of Congress.

The Committee of Thirty-three have, on motion of Mr. Adams, agreed to recommend it, and New Mexico includes all the territory south of 36° 30′.

Shall we break up the government because the free States refuse to do what Mr. Clay refused to do touching this Territory?

Fellow-citizens, the Territorial Question is of no practical importance to you; it is merely the pretext to entangle you in the plots against your peace. If by common consent any change can be made which will silence clamor, or soothe the sensibilities, or satisfy the jealousies excited by recent contest, let *that* change be made. But that is the only interest you have in any change; and if none can be obtained of *that character*, it is our policy to let the question alone, and to make others let it alone.

The existing condition of the Territories is better than agitation for any change.

If discontented men attempt to destroy the government because it is not changed to suit them, the right and the duty, the highest interest and the loyal honor of Maryland, require her to sustain the laws of the United States and the Constitution, which are her only safety. Let us not countenance revolutionary violence to redress imaginary wrongs by impossible measures.

Mr. Adams's proposition to admit New Mexico as a State, and to amend the Constitution so as to *prohibit* any chance in it hereafter by which slavery in the States can be affected, unless upon the proposal of a slave State, concurred in by all the States; the repeal of the liberty bills; and a just modification of the Fugitive Slave Law, ought to close the Slavery controversy forever—certainly till some rash conquest shall reopen it.

Or are we to destroy the Constitution because Mr. Lincoln has been elected according to its provisions?

The existing prostration of commerce and industry; the idle ships; the accumulated merchandise and produce; the unemployed artisans, laborers, and mechanics; the stinted allowance of their families; and the desolate prospect of the winter—these are the points, not of the acts of South Carolina, nor of the threatened revolution in two or three of the Gulf States, but of the doubtful loyalty of the Central States—of the threats of designing politicians to resist the government unless their extreme pretensions are acknowledged—of the agitation of men's minds occasioned by extraordinary elections — the assembling of Legislatures—the meeting of State Conventions—and the menace of a Convention of the central slave States to array them in opposition to the United States. Maryland alone is guiltless of this great error. Her laboring people are the victims of agitations for which they are not responsible, aggravated by the restless and ambitious policy of certain of their fellow-citizens.

The firm attitude of Maryland is now the chief hope of peace. If you firmly adhere to the United States against all enemies, resolved to obey the Constitution and see it obeyed, your example will arrest the spirit of revolution, and greatly aid the government in restoring, without bloodshed, its authority. If Maryland yield to this revolutionary clamor, she will be overcome in a few months in the struggle for the national capital; and her young men, torn from the pursuits of peace, excluded from the closed work-shop and counting-house, must shoulder the musket to guard their homes at the cost of fraternal blood.

I confidently trust that the people of the Fourth Congressional District will, in this grave emergency, give new proofs of their devotion to the Constitution, and their superiority to envy, fear, and delusion.

Your fellow-citizen, HENRY WINTER DAVIS.

THE REPORT OF THE COMMITTEE OF THIRTY-THREE.

On the 14th of January the special Committee of Thirty-three presented their Report, and the discussion thereon began on the 21st. In that committee, on the 7th of January, an amendment proposed by Mr. Davis was adopted to the Fugitive Slave Bill (afterward reported to and rejected by the House), securing to the fugitive slave a *trial by jury in the state* to which he was returned. On the 18th of December the committee had previously adopted, on motion of Mr. Davis, a resolution, to be reported to the House, calling upon the several states to revise their statutes, with a view to repeal such as clearly conflicted with the Constitution or laws of the United States (Personal Liberty Bills).

On the 28th the President submitted the propositions from the Virginia General Assembly, adopted on the 19th, proposing a Peace Conference of commissioners from each of the states, to be holden in Washington on the 4th of February, and declaring that the proposition for amendment of the Constitution, submitted in the United States Senate by Mr. Crittenden, "*so modified* as that the first article proposed shall apply to all territory of the United States now held *or hereafter acquired* south of latitude 36° 30′, and that African slavery shall be protected therein while a Territory; and that the fourth article shall *secure to the owners of slaves the right of transit, with their slaves, between and through the non-slaveholding states and territories*, constitute the basis of such an adjustment as would be accepted by the people of Virginia."

On the 31st of January Mr. Charles Francis Adams, of Massachusetts, delivered a speech, remarkable for ability, candor, and moderation, *in support* of the propositions submitted by the Committee of Thirty-three, including an amendment to the Constitution in these words:

"*Article* XII. *No amendment of this Constitution having for its object any interference, within the states, with the relations between their citizens and those* described in section second of the first article of the Constitution as 'all other persons,' shall originate with any state that does not recognize that relation within its own limits, or shall be valid *without the assent of every one* of the states composing the Union."

The Peace Conference met on the 5th of February.

Seven states had now passed formal ordinances of secession, and their senators and representatives had withdrawn. Major Anderson was beleaguered in Fort Sumter. The "commissioners" from South Carolina had come to Washington, "authorized and empowered to treat with the government of the United States for the delivery of the forts, magazines, light-houses, and other real estate, with their appurtenances, in the limits of South Carolina; and also for an apportionment of the public debt, and for a division of all other property held by the government of the United States as agent of the confederated states, of which South Carolina was recently a member; and generally to negotiate as to all other measures and arrangements proper to be made and adopted, in the existing relation of the parties, and for the continuance of peace and amity between this commonwealth and the government at Washington." They demanded of the President the immediate withdrawal of the United States troops then in Charleston Harbor. Castle Pinckney and Fort Moultrie were occupied by South Carolina militia. The "Palmetto" flag was raised over the United States Custom-House and Post-Office in Charleston. The United States Arsenal there was "taken by force of arms," and on the 9th of January the steamer Star of the West having the *United States ensign* at the fore, *was fired into* from a masked battery on Morris Island. The navy yard at Pensacola, Forts Barrancas and Pulaski, the United States Arsenal at Augusta (Georgia), the United States Mint and Custom-House at, and the forts below New Orleans, and the United States revenue cutters, had been seized. The rebel Convention had met at Montgomery (Alabama), and even North Carolina had threatened, by a unanimous declaration of her House of Commons, "to go, if reconciliation fails, with the other slave states."

Such was the condition of affairs when Mr. Davis addressed the House on the 7th of February, 1861, as follows:

MR. SPEAKER,—We are at the end of the insane revel of partisan license which for thirty years has in the United States worn the mask of government. We are about to close the masquerade by the dance of death. The nations of the world look anxiously to see if the people, ere they tread that measure, will come to themselves.

Yet in the early youth of our national life, we are already exhausted by premature excesses. The corruption of our political maxims has relaxed the tone of public morals, and degraded the public authorities from the terror to the accomplices of evil doers. Platform for fools—Plunder for thieves—Offices for service—Power for ambition, unity in these essentials—Diversity in the immaterial matters of policy and legislation—Charity for every frailty—The voice of the people is the voice of God: these maxims have sunk into the public mind—have presided at the administration of public affairs, have almost effaced the very idea of public duty. The government, under their disastrous influence, has gradually ceased to fertilize the fields of domestic and useful legislation, and pours itself, like an impetuous torrent, along the barren ravine of party and sectional strife. It has been shorn of every prerogative that wore the austere aspect of authority and power. The President, no longer preceded by the fasces and the axe, the emblems of supreme authority, greets every popular clamor with wreathed smiles and gracious condescension, is degraded to preside in the Palace of the Nation over the distribution of spoils among wrangling victors, dedicates his great powers to forge or find arms to perpetuate partisan warfare at the expense of the public peace. The original ideas of the Constitution have faded from men's minds. That the United States is a government entitled to respect and command; that the Constitution furnishes a remedy for every grievance, and a mode of redress for every wrong; that the States are limited within their spheres, are charged with no duties to each other, and bear no relation to the other States excepting through their common head, the government of the United States; that those in authority, alone, are charged with power to repress public disorder and compose the public discontents; restrain the conduct of the people and of the States within the barriers of the Constitution—these salutary principles have faded from the popular heart with the great interests which the government is charged to protect, and has gradually allowed to escape from its grasp. Congress has ceased to regulate commerce, to protect domestic industry, to encourage our commercial marine, to regulate the currency, to promote internal commerce by internal improvements—almost every power useful to the people in its exercise has been denied and abandoned, or so limited in its exercise as to be useless—its whole activity has been dedicated to expansion abroad, and acquiring and retaining power at home till men have forgotten that the Union is a blessing, and that they owe to the United States allegiance paramount to that of their respective States.

The consequence of this demoralization is, that States, without regard to the federal government, assume to stand face to face and wage their own quarrels, to adjust their own difficulties, to impute to each other every wrong, to insist that individual States shall remedy every grievance, and denouncing their failure to do so as cause of civil war between the States; and as if the Constitution were silent and dead, and the power of the Union utterly inadequate to keep the peace between them. Unconstitutional commissioners flit from State to State, or assemble at the national capital to counsel peace or instigate war. Sir, these are the causes which lie at the bottom of the present dangers. These causes, which have rendered them possible and made them serious, must be removed before they can ever be permanently cured. They shake the fabric of our national government. It is to this fearful demoralization of the government and the people that we must ascribe the disastrous defections which now perplex us with the fear of change in all that constituted our greatness. The operation of the government has been withdrawn from the great public interests in order that competing parties might not be embarrassed in the struggle for power by diversities of opinion upon questions of policy; and the public mind, in that struggle, has been exclusively turned on the Slavery Question, which no interest required to be touched by any department of this government. On that subject there are widely marked diversities of opinion and interest in different portions of the Confederacy, with few mediating influences to soften the collision. In the struggle for party power, the two great regions of the country have been brought face to face upon this most dangerous of all subjects of agitation. The authority of the government was relaxed just when its power was about to be assailed, and the people emancipated from every control; and their passions, inflamed by the fierce struggle for the presidency, were the easy prey of revolutionary audacity.

Within two months after a formal, peaceful, regular election of the chief magistrate of the United States, in which the whole body of the people of every State competed with zeal for the prize, without any new event intervening, without any new grievances alleged, without any new menaces having been made, we have seen, in the short course of one month, a small portion of the population of six States transcend the bounds, at a single leap, at once of the state and the national Constitutions, usurp the extraordinary prerogative of repealing the supreme law of the land, exclude the great mass of their fellow-citizens from the protection of the Constitution, declare themselves emancipated from the obligations which the Constitution pronounces to be supreme over them and over their laws, arrogate to themselves all the prerogatives of independent power, rescind the acts of cession of the public property, occupy the public offices, seize the fortresses of the United States confided to the faith of the people among whom they were placed, embezzle the public arms concentrated there for the defense of the United States, array thousands of men in arms against the United States, and actually wage war on the Union by besieging two of their fortresses, and firing on a vessel bearing, under the flag of the United States, re-enforcements and provisions to one of them. The very boundaries of right and wrong seem obliterated when we see a cabinet minister deliberately, for months, engaged in changing the distribution of public arms to places in the hands of those about to resist the public authority, so as to place within their grasp means of waging war against the United States greater than they ever used against a foreign foe; and another cabinet minister, still holding his commission under the authority of the United States, still a confidential adviser of the President, still bound by his oath to *support* the Constitution of the United States, himself a commissioner from his own State to another of the United States for the purpose of organizing and extending another part of the same great scheme of rebellion; and the doom of the republic seems sealed when the President, surrounded by such ministers, permits, without rebuke, the government to be betrayed, neglects the solemn warning of the first soldier of the age, till almost every fort is a prey to domestic treason, and accepts assurances of peace in his time at the expense of leaving the national honor unguarded. His message gives aid and comfort to the enemies of the Union by avowing his inability to maintain its integrity; and paralyzed and stupefied he stands amid the crash of the falling republic, still muttering—not in my time—not in my time—after me the deluge!

Sir, history, by her prophet Tacitus, has drawn his character for posterity—*major privato visus dum privatus fuit et consensu omnium capax imperii nisi imperasset.* Yes, sir, *nisi imperasset*, James Buchanan might have passed to the grave as one of the men of the republic, equal to every station he filled, and not incompetent for the highest. The acquisition of supreme power has revealed his incapacity, and crowns him with the unenviable honor of the chief destroyer of his country's greatness.

We have, Mr. Speaker, this day to deal in a great measure with the consequences of his incapacity. Persons usurping power in six or seven States have thrown off their allegiance to the United States. It was fondly hoped that it was only temporary—possibly a desperate contrivance to restore the chief actors to power; but we are now authoritatively informed by the response of South Carolina to the kindly messenger from Virginia that their position is permanently fixed; that they desire to have, and will have no farther political connection with the United States; and a distinguished gentleman, until within one month a member of the cabinet of the United States, recently elected President of the revolutionary Convention at Montgomery, has informed us in his inaugural speech that it is their purpose finally to sever their connection with the United States, and to take all the consequences of organizing an independent republic.

Mr. Speaker, we are driven to one of two alternatives; we must recognize—what we have been told more than once upon this floor is an accomplished fact—the independence of the rebellious States, or we must refuse to acknowledge it, and accept all the responsibilities that attach to that refusal. Recognize them! abandon the Gulf and coast of Mexico; surrender the forts of the United States; yield the privilege of free commerce and free intercourse; strike down the guarantees of the Constitution for our fellow-citizens in all that wide region; create a thousand miles of interior frontier to be furnished with internal custom-houses, and armed with internal forts, themselves to be a prey to the next caprice of State sovereignty; organize a vast standing army, ready at a moment's warning, to resist aggression; create upon our southern boundary a perpetual foothold for foreign powers whenever caprice, ambition, or hostility may see fit to invite the despot of France or the aggressive power of England to attack us upon our undefended frontier; sever that unity of territory which we have spent millions, and labored through three generations to create and establish; pull down the flag of the United States and take a lower station among the nations of the earth; abandon the high prerogative of leading the march of freedom, the hope of struggling nationalities, the terror of frowning tyrants, the boast of the world, the light of liberty, to become the sport and prey of despots whose thrones we consolidate by our fall; to be greeted by Mexico with the salutation, Art thou also become weak as we? art thou become like unto us? This is recognition.

Refuse to recognize! We must not coerce a State in the peaceful process of secession. We must not coerce a State engaged in the peaceful process of firing into a United States vessel to prevent the re-enforcement of a United States fort. We must not coerce States which, without any declaration of war or any act of hostility of any kind, have united, as have Mississippi, Florida, and Louisiana, their joint forces to seize a public fortress. We must not coerce a State which has planted cannon upon its shores to prevent the free navigation of the Mississippi. We must not coerce a State which has robbed the United States Treasury. This is peaceful secession!

Mr. Speaker, I do not design to quarrel with gentlemen about words. I do not wish to say one word which will exasperate the already too much inflamed state of the public mind; but I say that the Constitution of the United States, and the laws made in pursuance thereof, must be enforced; and they who stand across the path of that enforcement must either destroy the power of the United States, or it will destroy them. (Loud applause in the galleries.) I trust in God that any such collision is years, centuries, yea, thousands of years off. I see no necessity for it. I think it may be avoided by prudent administration, till the people shall come to themselves. But the laws of the United States provide their own method of enforcement, and when they are enforced, those who resist must take the consequences.

I think the revenues may be collected in disaffected ports on board United States ships. I think the laws of commerce may be enforced by allowing no vessel to pass out unless she has papers of the United States on board. The postal routes and arrangements may be sustained or suspended, as the interests of the government or the disturbed condition of the localities may require. The courts of justice, if needs be, may be supported as they were in Utah; or we may remove the courts, extend the districts over several States, and locate the courts in States which are not disturbed. These are the regular peaceful methods of enforcing the laws of the United States. These methods, if pursued, will allow time for reflection—cooling time to the people excited by a fierce political canvass, and surprised on a sudden unprepared, by revolutionary contrivances prepared beforehand. We can await the inevitable time of division, discord, and resistance to taxation and military exactions.

But the government of the United States is vested by the Constitution with adequate power to meet every emergency. It is required to guarantee a republican form of government to every State. A government whose executive Legislature and judicial officers are not sworn to support the Constitution of the United States is mere usurpation, and not a republican government. It will never be recognized for any purpose. If the loyal citizens of any State, whose authorities have usurped the prerogative of repealing the Constitution of the United States, shall see fit to organize for themselves a government, the President can recognize them, and the President can support them. Among the powers granted by the Constitution is the power to suppress insurrection; it does not except insurrections ordered by State authority, and they will be suppressed as promptly as others. The Constitution authorizes Congress to provide for calling forth the militia to enforce the laws, and it makes no exception of those laws which a State may see fit to oppose; and if to the regular execution of the laws of the United States armed resistance shall be made, the government has authority to disperse those who oppose the enforcement. The Constitution forbids any State to keep troops or ships of war in time of peace; and if troops be organized by any State, the United States have power to require them to be disbanded, and to disperse them if they be not disbanded. If ships of war shall be built, they have a right, under the Constitution, to require them to be disposed of, or, if that be refused, they may sink them. Whether that shall be done is a matter of discretion. If States levy troops and attack no one, the United States may well let them eat their own heads off. The cost will soon disperse them. But if they assail the United States, or other States, or loyal citizens of the United States in the disaffected State, then the blame of collision rests on those who compelled the United States to resistance. In this manner, without any thing like war upon States, without any attempt to do damage to any citizens excepting those who may have arrayed themselves in arms against the United States, the government can vindicate its authority and maintain its power. This is not war. The Constitution calls it enforcing the laws. It is no more war than arresting a criminal is war. It is supporting the civil power by the military arm against unlawful combinations too powerful to be otherwise dealt with. The guilt of the actors is not extenuated by State authority, still less by that of the revolutionary conventions. By their sanction they become participators in the guilt, and liable to the punishment of the armed actors. War is the struggle between two powers to do each other the greatest possible harm, subject only to international law. But when the United States suppress an insurrection or enforce the laws, they harm only those *actually* resisting, and them only so far as to remove their resistance to the *civil* arm. Its *end* is *their dispersion*. The United States carry the Constitution before their arms; its provisions hedge in their bayonets; and every weapon sinks when its authority is admitted. Conquest in war is absolute despotism; the triumph of the United States is the restoration of *constitutional* liberty.

But, Mr. Speaker, the marvel still remains to be explained how it is that, in this free republican land, over so wide a region of country, people hitherto loyal to the United States have so suddenly taken such strange and revolutionary courses.

First, sir, it is because there is, and has been for years, a revolutionary faction in many of them, disguised by being mingled in the ranks of a great political party, but always working to accomplish its treasonable purposes.

It is because of the tenacity with which defeated politicians—not revolutionists, but acting with them—cling to power, determined to rule or to ruin the government.

They have the power to bring these great disasters upon the country only because the popular mind has been aroused and excited by fierce discussions upon the topic of slavery, on which the Southern people are so justly sensitive. By the grossest misrepresentations of the purposes of the great body of the Northern people, by perpetual and reiterated misrepresentation and exaggeration of their feelings, a hostile state of feeling has been created throughout a great portion, if not throughout the whole of the South, which borders upon revolution itself. A state of fear, an undefined dread, a sense of insecurity, has been inspired by the course of the political canvass in the South. The mischief has been done at home. The mischief has been done by the violent struggles of parties for supremacy. Both have striven each to blacken their common opponents at the North, by imputing to them opinions and purposes which both execrate; and one has imputed sympathy with the same opinions to their political opponents at the South. Whatever disturbance exists there, the great, the main, the substantial cause of it is not the conduct of the people of the free States, but the conduct of the political canvass at the South, the course of the debate by Southern gentlemen in this House, the mode in which they have, consciously or unconsciously, exaggerated and blackened the purposes of gentlemen upon the other side of the House, and habitually circulated at home inflammatory speeches of certain Northern gentlemen, which I submit they ought to have known did not represent the feelings of the great body of the people of the North, however well they may represent that small faction called there "Abolitionists." I say that is the real, the chief, the exciting cause of the existing disturbances; and, sir, in my judgment, without constitutional amendments, or the passage of one law, if gentlemen will only remove the impression that they have erroneously left upon their people's minds, if they will only go and say to them what they have heard said again and again on this floor by the distinguished gentleman from Massachusetts [Mr. Adams], by the distinguished gentleman from Ohio [Mr. Corwin], so often and by so many of his colleagues upon this floor, and what is now said still more formally by the resolutions adopted by Republican votes in the Committee of Thirty-three, and reported by the distinguished gentleman from Ohio, that there exists no purpose, directly or indirectly, to disturb or interfere in any manner with the institution of slavery within the States, and that the only question is whether it shall go into the poor, miserable, worthless Territory of New Mexico or not; if they will go and tell the people that, there would be peace and quiet throughout the whole South within a month after they made the explanation. But, sir, from the course of debate in this House, I have small hope of that natural, prompt, and honest remedy. They who profit by the error will not correct it.

A committee has been raised charged with devising such measures as will at once assuage the existing discontents, avoid the occasions of future irritation, and tender such guarantees to the sensitive interests of the South as, in the absence of those just recantations by politicians of the South, will still give peace, quiet, and security to the Southern people. I desire, Mr. Speaker, to lay before the House, in as plain and brief a manner as I can, the results to which the committee charged with that duty have come; to *compare* the remedies that the majority and the minority of the committee respectively propose, and to contrast the *complaints* and the *remedies* of the minority with themselves.

The first cause of irritation is the Personal Liberty Bills. Both portions of the committee propose a recommendation that they shall be repealed. The votes of the committee and of the House on that subject ought to remove every trace of dissatisfaction or suspicion.

Great irritation has grown out of the obstructions to the execution of the act for the delivery of fugitives from service. The repeal of those bills ought to be accompanied by an amendment of that law. The minority of the committee, headed by the gentleman from Louisiana [Mr. Taylor], who took his leave of us the other day, propose on that subject an amendment of the Constitution requiring that when fugitives are rescued by violence, the United States shall pay the value to their owner, and have the privilege of suing the county or district permitting the rescue for the amount. Sir, this is to perpetuate, and not to close the slavery controversy. The only effect of the adoption of such an amendment of the Constitution would be to make this hall every session, on every bill to pay for negroes rescued, the scene of fierce strife upon the very subject of slavery. Another objection is equally fatal. It brings the United States into direct collision with an organized political division of a State, which the Constitution of the United States was most carefully devised to avoid. The right of action against a county for so harsh a cause could scarcely be enforced by any process known to the law. Success would itself cause great discontent among large masses of people, and resistance to their execution could only be removed by armed force. In other words, the amendment prepared by the minority of the committee would plunge us here into the perpetual discussion of the Slavery Question, and would require the government to enforce against communities numerous, and powerful, and innocent responsibilities for acts which they have not done, but have only failed to prevent. The bill reported by the majority of the committee is very different in its purposes and in its policy. It assumes that the law for the rendition of fugitive slaves ought to be so modified as not to give cause or pretext for the fears which it has occasioned at the North, and then when that exciting cause of discontent is removed, the law can be executed. The danger which the Northen people feel is that their own free resident colored people may, under summary process, be arrested, carried off, and sold into slavery. The law of 1850 provides no remedy for cases of that sort. We propose that where there is a claim of freedom, the negro shall be surrendered to the marshal of the United States, and carried back to the slave State from which he is ascertained to have come, and there shall have the privilege of a trial before a court of the United States in that State. A trial there can not be objected to by Southern gentlemen; Northern gentlemen ought to be satisfied that his claim to freedom, brought in a formal and public manner before a judicial tribunal of the United States, will be decided according to its merit. Surely no one can hesitate between the cumbersome and anomalous plan of the minority, and the simple and just bill of the majority of the committee.

The next subject is that of the Territories. Mr. Speaker, it is certainly marvelous that, having settled this very question touching this very Territory by Mr. Clay's acts in 1850, and no intermediate law having been passed by any body excepting the law of 1854 repealing the Missouri Compromise, so as to allow slavery to exist north of the line of 36° 30′, the South having boasted of the laws of 1850 as their triumph, and every party in the country having pledged itself to stand by them, it is of all things most strange that we are now told that this Union can not endure unless those laws themselves are repealed; and the very principle of the Missouri Compromise, so far as it was objected to by the South, that is, the exclusion of slavery beyond the line which they denounced as unequal, shall be not only restored, but ingrafted forever on the Constitution of the United States! It was denounced and branded by Southern men all through the debate which resulted in its repeal as a badge of inferiority, a mark of inequality, a stain of dishonor to the South. And now they demand that it shall be restored, not by a temporary act of legislation, but by the sanction of the people in the supreme law of the land. A more flagrant, inexplicable, unintelligible case of capricious inconsistency is unknown to history. But, sir, the gentlemen who assume to speak for the South have changed their notions of equality and honor, and of course the world must change too. The proposal is made on the part of the minority of the committee that there shall be a division of territory, and that all the region north of 36° 30′ shall be dedicated to freedom, and in all the region south to Cape Horn, slavery of the African race is "*hereby recognized as existing*"—existing over the whole of Mexico—over all the regions of Central America, skipping Brazil, I suppose, where slavery already exists, and going down to the extremest regions of South America by virtue of our Constitution. Now, Mr. Speaker, the gentleman who proposed that ought to know something of the history of the last few years at least, and if there is one thing which ought to be understood as absolutely impossible, it is ever to get a law through this House, or even through the Senate, by a simple majority, establishing slavery in any inch of territory where it does not already exist. Be it right or be it wrong, be it liberal or be it illiberal, every gentleman here must know that that is one of the things which are impossible. But in what method do the gentlemen of the minority propose to do this? By a constitutional amendment requiring two thirds of this House—where it could not get one third—and two thirds of the Senate; and when it has gone through these impossible ordeals, it has to go before the people of the United States, and get, not *two thirds* but *three fourths* of the Legislatures of the several states. Scale the heavens, if you please, without wings; pass the abyss which divides heaven from hell, but do not talk about a thing like this. And what in the mean time, Mr. Speaker? Agitation, violence, recrimination, not merely on the question of the *policy* of slavery, but compelling the Northern people, whether they will or not, to go into the very question of its *merits*, moral and religious, not leaving them where they are willing to leave you—as they have said over and over again—within the impassable barriers of the Constitution of the United States, made tenfold higher and tenfold stronger by the provision of the gentleman from Massachusetts [Mr. Adams]—but asking the people of the North to declare that they have been hypocritical in their opinions that African slavery is not merely impolitic, but immoral; a thing which they ought not to sanction—to reverse all their judgment on that subject, and themselves ingraft in the Constitution a doctrine which you accuse them of hating so eternally that they are struggling to destroy it illegally and unconstitutionally. You ask them to save and protect that very thing which, for two years past, you have stood here and denounced them for intending to destroy; by exciting servile war; by insidious appeals to the non-slaveholding white people of the South; by the hands of such incendiaries as John Brown. In the most of these appeals, while their echo is still ringing in my ears, while I have before me the scenes that I witnessed last year on that side of the House, when men, raging and furious as the revolutionary assemblies in France, hurled the epithets "traitor" and "incendiary" against their equals from the free states thick as arrows in a Parthian battle-field, gentlemen now ask those very men, to whom such opinions have been imputed, to turn round and forget all, and, as honest men, conciliatory men, wise men, do the very thing which they have told you for the last eighty years they could not in their consciences do.

Very different is the mode of disposing of the territory that has been fallen upon by the majority of the committee, anxious to remove the pretext for contention, and striving as far as they could to avoid the difficulties in the plan demanded of them, and that in no conciliatory tone, but with the air of dictating an ultimatum! They propose this. All the territory now held by the United States south of 36° 30′ is the Territory of New Mexico extending a little north of it. In that Territory, under the law of 1850, which is now so fiercely assailed, the people within one year have themselves adopted a slave code as rigorous as any in existence in any of the Southern States. The law of 1850 secured to that people the right to admission into the Union with or without slavery, as their Constitution might provide. With eminent liberality, in mere execution and not in repeal of that law, the gentleman from Massachusetts [Mr. Adams], whose position on the subject of slavery all the world knows, as if to put forever to silence imputations of any design in any portion of the Northern people to invade the rights of the South, comes forward now and proposes to pass a law creating New Mexico a state. If it see fit to adopt slavery, then it will be a slave state. If it see fit to forbid it, then it will be a free state. In either event, it removes the subject of controversy. In either event, it puts it beyond the power of any one to touch this domestic institution by constitutional guarantees as irrepealable, as unchangeable as the minority demand. That would remove the controversy from Congress, not by a compromise, but by removing the whole subject from Congress and *the people* forever by a simple majority of this House and of the other House, and the signature of the President, leaving the whole subject in controversy to be decided, as Southern gentlemen must see it must ultimately be decided, by the Constitution of New Mexico. If I am correctly informed by the gentleman who has so honorably represented that Territory here, the people are likely to require a decision themselves within a year; proceedings are now pending before the Legislature for the purpose of asking their recognition. I ask, therefore, whether it is not wise, before we have still farther revolutionary complications forced upon us, to tell them at once to form their Constitution, and thus take away the *subject* of the controversy now and forever. With regard to the other portion of the territory, Northern gentlemen ask no exclusion of slavery by law or Constitution. The perpetual imputation is that they are for prohibition every where. South Carolina has elevated that to a chief place in her travesty of the Declaration of Independence. During the two months that we have been here, no gentleman heard such a thing urged as a proposal to exclude slavery from the northern portion of the Territory. If I am rightly informed, the Senate, by a Republican majority, has, within the last two days, passed a bill organizing the western portion of Kansas as a Territory, and there is not one word in it on the subject of slavery, so that the proposition of the gentleman from Massachusetts is to place the Slavery Question beyond the possible reach of Congress south of 36° 30′, and in the residue to leave it to the administration of the law. He says: "We all agree as to what that law is. We will not attempt to change it by leglslation. And as you desire the southern portion of it set apart for your patrimony, in God's name take it, and let us be at peace." Any man who is not wholly blind to the great interests at stake would accept such an offer as that as an eternal adjustment, not only in spirit, but in fact, of this whole controversy. After that, no imputation of a desire on the part of the North to interfere with slavery ought to pass Southern lips.

Sir, I know that these propositions will be received with a shrug of the shoulders, and a suggestion that they are not *satisfactory*, by gentlemen of the South. But, sir, I tell them that if they do not satisfy them, they will satisfy the *people*, and that they will find out before they are many months older. The great State of Virginia has told them within the last three days that the heart of the people of the Commonwealth still beats true to this Union; and though they may for a moment be deluded, they can not be forced into revolutionary violence for the difference between the measures of the majority and the minority of the committee.

If their representatives here, or at Richmond, or in their unconstitutional Convention, called for unconstitutional purposes, shall, after the adoption of these proposals, venture to advise resort to revolution, they will speak to deaf ears and hard hearts. I do not envy the lot of any one who advocates an ordinance of secession on such grounds. I think he will meet with small favor who, rather than create New Mexico a State, presents to the people of Virginia the awful alternative of tearing down the fabric built up by our fathers, of making war upon their Northern brethren, of blotting out the great memories of the past, of striking out their star from the galaxy of this great Confederacy, formed under the auspices of Washington, to become the small sun of a secondary constellation, dependent on the caprice of greater powers for justice and safety. I am under no delusion about the meanings of the vote in Virginia. I think the failure of these measures will create serious disappointment, and gravely aggravate existing discontents; but I am confident that, however politicians may regard them, they will be hailed with delight by the great mass of the *people* of Virginia, as well as of the other central slave States, and will strip the enemies of the United States of all power for mischief.

But, sir, there is one State I can speak for, and that is the State of Maryland. (Applause in the galleries.) Confident in the strength of this great government to protect every interest, grateful for almost a century of unalloyed blessings, she has fomented no agitation; she has done no act to disturb the public peace; she has rested in the consciousness that, if there be wrong, the Congress of the United States will remedy it; and that none exists which revolution would not aggravate.

Mr. Speaker, I represent here the Fourth Congressional District of Maryland only; but, though I am not elected by the State of Maryland, I am entitled to speak here, and I will speak *what I know* to be the sentiments of the State of Maryland. (Applause on the floor and in the galleries.)

Mr. Speaker, I am here this day to speak, and I say that I do speak, for the *people* of Maryland, who are loyal to the United States; and that when my judgment is contested, I appeal to the people for its accuracy, and I am ready to maintain it before them. (Great applause.)

In Maryland we are dull, and can not comprehend the right of secession. We do not recognize the right to make a revolution by a vote. We do not recognize the right of Maryland to repeal the Constitution of the United States; and if any Convention there, called by whatever authority, under whatever auspices, undertake to inaugurate revolution in Maryland, their authority will be resisted and defied in arms on the soil of Maryland, in the name and by the authority of the Constitution of the United States.

A majority have no more right than a minority. The right of a majority is a constitutional, not a natural right. For the destruction of the Constitution they can have no right. The whole mass of the nation alone has the right to alter the fundamental law by common consent. The right of resistance to oppression attaches to the oppressed, whether a majority or a minority of a state, a country, or a nation, and success vindicates the right. The assumption of the revolutionary bodies to bind the people of a State by the formalities of a vote is as ridiculous as it is impotent; their law directing the vote is a nullity; and the result expresses the will only of those who concur in it. If by the usurpation they can beat down domestic opposition, and defy the United States, they vindicate their right by power; if they fail, they pay the penalty of failure. We in Maryland will submit to no attempt of a minority or a majority to drag us from under the flag of the Union. The Committee of Thirty-three have carefully considered the proposed restrictions on the change of certain articles in the Constitution of the United States.

The minority propose to prohibit by amendment the abolition of slavery in the forts, dock-yards, and District of Columbia, and of the slave-trade between the slave States; and to make those prohibitions, and also the article touching the ratio of representation and fugitives from labor, unchangeable.

But no party from any quarter now proposes to touch them, and the committee thought a simple declaration of that fact more satisfactory and prudent than to open the agitation by asking three fourths of the States to agree not to do what no one proposes to do. Those topics are agitated, not at the North, but at the South, and merely for political effect.

But the question of the immunity of slavery in the States is very different. It exists by state authority. When established, the Constitution guarantees it. And the impression having been studiously made on the minds of the people of the slaveholding states that the North design at some future time to destroy slavery, the majority of the committee propose to quiet forever that apprehension, and anew to consecrate the principle of state rights in internal matters by forbidding any change in the Constitution affecting slavery in the States.

That guarantee, as proposed by the gentleman from Massachusetts [Mr. Adams], in my judgment, is more ample and more satisfactory than the corresponding proposition offered by the minority. They propose that no alteration of the Constitution shall be made authorizing *Congress* to abolish slavery. The proposition of the gentleman from Massachusetts is, that there shall be no amendment affecting the relation of persons held to labor within a State at all, whether directly through the Constitution, or indirectly through the Congress, unless by the consent of all the States, and upon motion of a slave State; so that, with extreme astuteness, the amendment of the gentleman from Massachusetts guards against that which is really our greatest evil, the beginning of agitation for the purpose of varying the Constitution in this respect. The motion can only be made by a slave State. No free State can ever open the question of the repeal, or change that article of the Constitution. I submit, therefore, that the report of the majority, in that respect, is far more satisfactory than that of the minority.

The failure to surrender fugitives from justice, when the crime is connected with slavery, has been a topic of endless crimination. The report of the minority refers to the complaint. But not only does it propose no remedy, but actually passes in silence the very important bill of the majority of the committee, effectually ending the controversy by transferring from the executive of the State to the judiciary of the United States the power and duty of making the surrender. This is a step in the right direction—resuming by the United States the right to administer its own laws, and freeing itself from all dependence on State officers whom it can not control.

There are, Mr. Speaker, other complaints mentioned by the minority of the committee for which they have proposed no remedy. We have seen what remedies they propose. And they think the adoption of their propositions ought to give peace and quiet to the country. Yet there are other topics treated in their report quite as significant as those; other grounds of discontent and apprehension for which the minority have proposed no remedy, against which they ask no guarantee. The causes of complaint left without redress are vastly more important than those covered by the enactments proposed. They are wholly unaffected by them; yet the minority of the committee, while devoting whole pages to the development of dangers and outrages consummated or apprehended, leave them without any suggestion for redress or protection. They think "the object aimed at can be accomplished by the adoption of the series of amendments to the Constitution rejected by the committee, and now reported to the House"—that "they afford such a basis of an adjustment as they would all cheerfully accept, with a strong conviction that, if the proposed amendments were adopted by the Northern States, harmony and peace would be restored to our people."

Sir, nothing in legislative history is more instructive than these declarations, compared with the narrative of wrongs and apprehensions which precede them, and the remedies which I have enumerated.

They have complained that the right of transit is refused, yet there is no proposal that it be granted.

The gentleman from Louisiana [Mr. Taylor] heads the list of wrongs in his report with the refusal to protect slaves upon the ocean and in foreign countries. I presume, to the extent of international law, they are now so protected; but whether they are or not, that was not apparently considered of sufficient importance to justify any recommendation on the subject, and the complaint merely swells the list of irritative topics.

The minority bitterly complain of the Northern hostility to slavery, the circulation of incendiary pamphlets, the perpetual appeal through the pulpit and the press, the never-ceasing activity of the abolition societies, and the doctrine of the irrepressible conflict so much invoked during the last few years for the purpose and with the effect of heating the public mind. If these complaints be true—if they are the causes of the present discontent—if they have shaken the security of Southern society, then how can peace and harmony be restored by measures which have no relation to the cause of discontent and apprehension? If they have caused the excitement which threatens the integrity of the government, how is it that gentlemen, after enumerating the grievance, propose to rest content without redress? No guarantee of slavery will silence *agitation*, or the pulpit or the press, or incendiary publications, or incitements to revolt, or the organized invasion of States. Yet so important is this topic considered, that one of the gentlemen who signed the minority report, in default of adequate proof, argued the ineradicable hostility of the North to slavery, and their resolution to exterminate it in spite of every constitutional guarantee—even those which would "restore peace and harmony to our people"—because their party platforms opposed it, and they were honorable men, and therefore must, in the face of their disclaimers and denials, and of the very declarations of the platform itself, consistently go on and—despite the Constitution and contrary to its provisions—attempt to break up the relation of master and slave in the slave States.

Mr. Speaker, I suppose that if, as the gentleman who made that argument said, they are honorable men, then of course their word is to be taken rather than the inference from a doubtful political platform. Political platforms are entitled to small respect from any quarter. They are, sir, nothing but sails spread to catch the popular breeze. It depends upon the pilot whether the ship shall sail before the wind, or close-hauled and in a different direction. Least of all does it become gentlemen who first agreed that a Territory should be allowed to regulate its own institutions in its own way, and then considered the forcing of the Lecompton Constitution on the people against their will a fair execution of that policy, to argue that any very rigid consistency between the platform and the policy of a party is to be expected in the course of political strife; yet to such shifts are gentlemen driven in their efforts to show—in spite of the resolutions of the majority of the Committee of Thirty-three and their unanimous disavowal—that the Northern people do contemplate disturbing slavery in the States. The importance of retaining that impression is not overestimated; for if it be yielded, the revolutionists will have few followers, and peace and harmony will be restored to our people in spite of every effort to disturb them.

[The following, owing to interruptions, was not delivered in the House of Representatives:]

A more marvelous contrast awaits us.

The minority report with great elaboration depicts the rise of a purely sectional party, determined to rule the Southern States by the Northern votes, united by hostility to slavery alone; declared that its triumph reduces the people of the South from citizens to subjects; and that by the late election the work of sectionalism was completed, to the apprehension of the people of the South; and if that apprehension be not speedily removed, the days of the Republic are numbered. They find countenance for this view in the South Carolina and Alabama ordinances. Read the remarkable recital of the Alabama ordinance:

"Whereas, the election of Abraham Lincoln and Hannibal Hamlin to the offices of President and Vice-President of the United States by a sectional party avowedly hostile to the domestic institutions and peace and security of the people of the State of Alabama, following upon the heels of many and dangerous infractions of the Constitution of the United States by many of the States and people of the Northern section, is a political wrong of so insulting and menacing a character as to justify the people of the State of Alabama in the adoption of prompt and decided measures for their future peace and security."

The revolutionists of Alabama for those causes tear themselves away from the government; the minority of the committee reiterate the complaint, and leave it unredressed. They are *silent* on the remedy for the *great grievance*—the *accomplished fact* of sectional domination—the inauguration of a party bent on reducing the people of the South from citizens to subjects—that great political wrong of so "insulting and menacing a character," the election of a President "by a sectional party avowedly hostile to the domestic institutions, peace, and security of the people" of the South. They leave it unredressed—unless a right to expand into new territory be a compensation for the right of self-government, or absolute security for existing rights touching *slavery* be an indemnity for the loss of "a voice in the management of the national affairs, in which they have a common interest with their Northern brethren."

Sir, that is impossible. We know that the Southern people and those gentlemen who signed the report count the right of self-government infinitely above all rights of property and all personal security. If they really feared such a domination, they would spurn accommodation on any terms.

Sir, the majority must rule. Particular interests will aggregate in particular localities, and parties will group themselves around interests; the East will be manufacturing, the West agricultural,

New York commercial, and Pennsylvania interested in iron and coal; Alabama will grow cotton, and Louisiana sugar; Virginia will grow tobacco, wheat, and corn; but a coalition of such interests to *oppress* others is without example in our history, and if effected, could be only temporary. Such a coalition of the free States is absolutely absurd. The South has always been able by its *one* common interest to impose on the divided North its policy and views; the North has no bond of Union, no one pervading and common interest so controlling as to concentrate its power and dictate its policy. It unites only in the *negative* interests of *repelling* the *intrusion* of slavery on its borders. It never united for that defensive purpose till the South united to invade the domain secured to it by the Missouri Compromise. This defensive and reluctant union, only partially effected, is the pretext for these exaggerated and sombre pictures of political subjection. Webster, failing to unite them in defense of their interests, exclaimed, "There is no North." Southern politicians have created a North. Let us trace the process and draw the moral.

The laws of 1850 calmed and closed the slavery agitation; and President Pierce, elected by the almost unanimous voice of the States, did not mention slavery in his first two messages. In 1854, the repeal of the Missouri Compromise, at the instance of the South, reopened the agitation.

Northern men, deserted by Southern Whigs, were left to unite for self-defense.

The invasion of Kansas in 1855 and 1856 from Missouri; the making a Legislature and laws for that Territory by the invaders still farther united the Northern people. The election of 1856 measured its extent.

The election of Mr. Buchanan and his opening policy in Kansas soothed the irritation, and was rapidly demoralizing the new party, when the pro-slavery party in Kansas perpetrated, and the President and the South accepted the Lecompton fraud, and again united the North more resolutely in resistance to that invasion of the rights of self-government.

The South for the first time failed to dictate terms, and the people vindicated by their votes the refusal of the Constitution.

Ere this result was attained, the opinions of certain judges of the Supreme Court scattered doubts over the law of slavery in the Territories; the South, while repudiating other decisions, instantly made these opinions the criterion of faithfulness to the Constitution, while the North was agitated by this new sanction of the extremest pretensions of their opponents.

The South did not rest satisfied with their judicial triumph.

Immediately the claim was pressed for *protection* by Congress to slavery, declared by the Supreme Court, they said, to exist in all the Territories.

This completed the Union of the free States in one great defensive league, and the result was registered in November. That result is now, itself, become the starting-point of new agitation—the demand of new rights and new guarantees. The claim to access to the Territories was followed by the claim to congressional protection, and that is now followed by the hitherto unheard-of claim to a constitutional amendment establishing slavery, not merely in territory now held, but in all hereafter held from the line of 36° 30′ to Cape Horn, while the debate foreshadows in the distance the claim of the right of transit and the placing of property in slaves in all respects on the footing of other property—the topics of future agitation. How long the prohibition of the importation of slaves will be exemplified from the doctrine of equality it needs no prophet to tell.

In the face of this recital, let the imputation of autocratic and tyrannical aspirations cease to be cast on the people of the free States; let the Southern people dismiss their fears, return to their friendly confidence in their fellow-citizens of the North, and accept as pledges of returning peace the salutary amendments of the law and the Constitution offered as the first fruits of reconciliation.

ADDRESS TO THE CITIZENS OF BALTIMORE ON THE PRESENT STATE OF THE NATION, OCTOBER 16, 1861.

IMMEDIATELY upon the election of Mr. Lincoln, and on the news of the first movement toward rebellion in South Carolina, efforts were made by those parties in Maryland who approved of or sympathized with those movements to induce Governor Hicks to call an extraordinary session of the General Assembly. As he knew the views and wishes of very many of such parties, and there was an intention expressed, by even the more moderate of them, of associating this state in any action which might be taken by the Commonwealth of Virginia, and as he felt convinced, from his own knowledge and observation, as well as from the numerous counter-memorials (against such call), that the great majority of the people of the state were opposed to such a session at that time, he steadily refused to yield. He also declined to take any part in any joint action, conference, or league with the States of Mississippi and Alabama, whose commissioners visited Annapolis to confer with him. When it was found the governor was not likely to yield to these, a "State Conference Convention" was called and held, by parties in favor of such assembling of the Legislature, on the 18th of February, in Baltimore. This Convention issued an address to the people of the state, declaring it to be the duty of Maryland, if conciliation should fail, to follow such course as might be adopted by Virginia. Some members of this Convention reassembled on the 12th of March, and, after reiterating their resolutions of the 18th of February, appointed a committee of six to visit and confer with the Virginia Convention.

Amid increasing excitement throughout the country, the rebel batteries erected in Charleston Harbor opened their fire against the United States garrison in Fort Sumter on the 12th of April.

On the news of that disgrace the North and West arose. The President issued (April 15th) his call for seventy-five thousand volunteers, and called the Congress of the United States for the 4th of July.

On the same day Mr. Davis announced that he "would be a candidate for the Thirty-seventh Congress, on the basis of an unconditional support of the Union and the government; but that if his fellow-citizens of like views should declare in favor of any other candidate *on that basis*, it was not his intention to embarrass them."

A Union mass meeting had been called in Baltimore for the 22d of April, when, on the 19th, the mob, incited by some of the secessionists, attacked the troops from Massachusetts (Sixth Regiment) proceeding to Washington in response to the President's call. The track over which the cars containing those troops were to pass was torn up or obstructed, and an assault was made on them with stones and discharges of fire-arms as they attempted to march to the Washington Station. Several persons and some of the soldiers were killed, and a number of these who failed to get through to the train for Washington retreated toward Philadelphia. The wildest excitement prevailed in the city, and an attempt was made to organize an armed opposition to the passage through Baltimore of United States troops.

In the afternoon the mob and its leaders reigned supreme, and on that night the bridges on the railway leading to Harrisburg and Philadelphia were burned by order of the parties who had assumed control in Baltimore. The telegraph wires were cut, and all communication of the government at Washington with the North was intercepted. The Board of Police Commissioners laid restrictions on the commerce of the port, forbade the display of flags of *any* description, distributed arms to volunteers, and appointed a commanding general. It was the evident determination of the secessionists and their friends to prevent the passage of United States troops to Washington through Baltimore. Secession flags were displayed on the 18th on Federal Hill, and on the 20th at the Southern head-quarters on Fayette Street; and it had previously been hoisted on a merchant-vessel at the Point. The governor returned to Annapolis on the 20th, and, yielding at last to clamor and threats, protested, on the 21st, against the landing there of "Northern troops" (meaning the United States troops who had come down the bay from Perryville, opposite Havre de Grace), gravely proposed to the President to refer all matters then in dispute to the arbitrament of the British minister, and finally, next day, issued his call for the General Assembly, which was to meet on the 26th at Frederick.

An election of delegates in Baltimore was held on the 24th, while the city was still under the effects of the mob of the 19th, was yet without communication with the seat of government, or with the North and West, and yet under the control of the military authorities appointed by the Police Commissioners. At this election 9249 votes were cast, all for the only set of candidates named. As soon as this result was known affairs began rapidly to mend; and on the 5th and 13th of May, when the United States troops occupied the heights at the Relay, on the Washington Railway, and on Federal Hill, it was seen that the minority was not to determine the fate of Maryland.

On the 17th of May Mr. Davis was nominated for Congress, his competitor being the Hon. Henry May, who accepted an independent nomination as a friend of the Union, in favor of conciliation, compromise, and settlement, and entirely opposed to the Republican party. Mr. Davis during the canvass openly declared himself in favor of coercion, and the maintenance of the federal authority by force, if necessary. He boldly avowed that he had voted against the proposed "Crittenden" Compromise (which was undoubtedly the preference of the people of Maryland), because he thought it impracticable, and imposed terms to which the free states ought not to be asked to, and could not submit.

The election took place on the 13th of June, and Mr. May was elected (8335) over Mr. Davis (6287) by a majority of 2048.

During the summer of 1861 the country suffered the humiliations of Bethel, Manassas, and Ball's Bluff. Then the administration began to perceive the necessity of organization, and of an army that should be of better material than undrilled recruits and parade militiamen. General M'Clellan was appointed to the command in chief, and the country began to awake to the reality—to a sense of the resources, the valor, and determination of the Southern States. These, now completely united among themselves, and encouraged by the failure of the first federal efforts against them, firmly believed they could obtain, and resolutely carried on the war for their independence.

Mr. Davis was invited in October, by a large number of the principal citizens, merchants, mechanics, and business men, to address them on the condition of affairs. He complied, and spoke on the 16th as follows:

Mr. President and Fellow-citizens of the United States (applause),—Time and events, the great instructors, have dispelled many a delusion, stripped off many a mask, and reduced to certainty many things about which men some months ago might have ventured to doubt. Who now talks of reconstruction as the purpose of secession? Who now talks of peaceful secession? Who now dreams of secession as a constitutional right to be determined at the ballot-box and to be acquiesced in, now that invading armies are trampling down the soil of Kentucky, and marching through and through the territory of Missouri, in spite of the repeatedly expressed will of their people? The mask of hypocrisy has been stripped from those pretenses.

There have been expectations, likewise, disappointed. There were those who, when they raised the standard of rebellion against the government of the United States, fondly supposed that cotton was king. (Laughter.) They dreamed that his upstart majesty would bring to their knees Great Britain and France, incapable of controlling their laboring population without that aliment of their industry. They dreamed that if a blockade should interpose an obstruction to the free exit of cotton, English and French fleets would sweep the ships of the Union from before the Southern ports; that if armies of invasion should venture to touch "the sacred soil" of the cotton-field, that imperative necessity would require that England and France should retaliate by blockading Boston and New York, and that if these gentle measures were not sufficient, their armed intervention here would be required to secure them peace at home. Whether the six months during which this contest has progressed have been sufficient yet to remove these delusions from the minds of those who fondly reposed in them as a source of strength, you now can judge. Nay, those who led in that rebellion misled their deluded fellow-citizens into supposing that it was not an organized resistance to the government in only one portion of the Union, but that disintegration had wrought its work from one end to the other of the republic, and that whenever there should be any attempt on the part of the government to strike a blow for the maintenance of its integrity, it would not be the rebellious States of the South alone that would have to meet the brunt of the contest, but that "the Northern myrmidons of Abraham Lincoln" (laughter), his "hireling men" sent to trample down the South, would be met, arrested, and overthrown by the faithful Democrats of the North (laughter), subservient for a long generation to Southern dictation, as they fondly supposed their allies, not merely in the pursuit of political power by the ballot-box, but also in arms of rebellion, having no purpose but to elevate some man to power, who might share the plunder with them, and ready to imbrue their hands in their neighbor's blood rather than allow insurrection to be suppressed by military power. (Applause.) It is probable that, however any other delusion may still cling around their vision, that one, at least, has faded away.

And then, fellow-citizens, events have taught us something more. Men have waked from the dream of that millennium of a Southern republic peaceful in guise, merciful in disposition, resting upon the unconstrained will of its people, carrying out an industrial theory amid its patriarchal institutions, coercing nobody, doing violence to nobody, peacefully pursuing its commercial and industrial interests! They who so dreamed and so spoke, and felt a soft inclination toward "our Southern brethren," have had some rather rude instruction upon that topic. (Laughter.)

They have inaugurated instead an era of confiscations, proscriptions, and exiles. Read their acts of greedy confiscation, their laws of proscription by the thousand. Behold the flying exiles from the unfriendly soil of Virginia, Tennessee, and Missouri. Andrew Johnson an exile from Tennessee! (Applause.) Emerson Etheridge (great applause) dare not go home for fear of arrest, prosecution, and death by the hangman, if the swifter and more congenial assassin leave him to their mercy. Thomas A. R. Nelson seized on his transit to the capital of the United States, incarcerated, and compelled by threats to his life to forego the allegiance to his native land. John S. Carlisle (great applause) pursued by a writ for his arrest because he would not be a traitor. And the partisans in Maryland of the men who do these things make our streets hideous with their howl about "oppression," and invoke all the principles of the Constitution that their allies have spent now nearly a year in making a dead letter, to secure their immunity here and convert this heaven into their hell. (Applause.)

Fellow-citizens, these events have worked another and a remarkable change here. They have disposed of nearly the whole of that wretched class of middle-men; men who are secessionists with Union proclivities (laughter), or Unionists with secession proclivities (laughter); men who are for the Union and against coercion (laughter); who are opposed to the dissolution of the Union and equally opposed to having it maintained; who think the government ought to assert its authority if men will submit to it, but if not, that it ought to submit to them; men who think that rulers do bear the sword in vain; men who confess with a sigh their allegiance to the government, but that their hearts are with the South—the men of compromise, the men of concessions, the men of "Southern" feelings, the men of "Southern" proclivities, and sympathies, and inclinations. All that class of men who concealed their treasonable purposes under the flimsy disguises that recently deluded our people no longer deceive any one. The enemy is at the door, and the people of Maryland know that they who are not their friends are their enemies ("That's so." Applause); that they who are not upon the side of the government are against it ("That's so"); that they who are not for repelling the invader mean to invite him here; that they who do not wish the rebellion stamped out in Virginia mean that it shall cross the Potomac into Maryland; they who do not wish M'Clellan to winter in New Orleans want Jefferson Davis to winter in Baltimore. They have known all along, and we know now, even the most doubting of us, as well as they know, who are our enemies and who are our friends; and if we have treated some of our enemies to their deserts, let not those who walk at large and insult the mercy of the government suppose that there is any impassable barrier between them and the companionship of their friends. (Great applause.) They have no right to complain. In the face of the mercy of the government which they perpetually abuse, they insolently meet patient Union men upon the corners of the streets, in their counting-rooms, and in the parlor, and on the Merchants' Exchange, and wherever men "most do congregate;" and while they writhe under the blow that has stricken them down here and taken from them the fruits of their treason before they could fully enjoy them, their only comfort is to appeal to the future, to promise retribution, to intimate that assassination may cut short those who treat them as traitors; that if ever they get the upper hand the lamp-post will be graced by individuals that they name; that they will not be as insanely merciful as the government of the United States is; and these things while they venture to impeach the government for harsh and oppressive measures!

Gentlemen, we have great patience. With the liberty of every one of these individuals in the grasp of the government if it choose to close the hand upon them — with their lives at our mercy if we only choose to invoke their precedent and set loose the mob that they organized upon the 19th of April—with the example of their avowed confederates, who have exiled our friends, confiscated their property, outraged and scourged our flying sisters—with these provocations, these men have so little of prudence or such profound conviction that loyal men differ from traitors in that they execute the law in mercy and forbearing kindness—these men venture to tell us that our time will come when they get the uppermost. I doubt not, gentlemen; but *when!* (Laughter.) When? "Two weeks" has been the period of expectation of the prophets of the Southern millennium for the last six months (great laughter), and still time drags slowly on to the movable feast of the secession. Two weeks is marked for the crossing of the Potomac from day to day, and still the water rolls on unpolluted by a traitor's foot. (Applause.) Nay, it is even said that gentlemen traitors, of delicate breeding and aristocratic pretensions, whose patriotism always assumes the form of a supper (laughter), have already spoiled one through the watches of one long wearisome night in the vain expectation that the lips of the deliverer might taste their wine. (Laughter.) Will these prophets tell us when?

Fellow-citizens, the time for doubting men has gone; even the time for "peace" men has gone. (Laughter.) They have invoked every thing else, and now they can scarcely find advocates to invoke peace. "Blessed peace" goes begging in the midst of this warlike state. "Blessed peace" can find no advocates now that her advocates are incarcerated. "Blessed peace" is no argument to urge now in the presence of embattled hosts. And why? Not because there are not people who want peace; peace, accompanied even with the triumph of the traitors; peace at the expense of the integrity of the government; peace at the cost of every interest of the State of Maryland; peace, though it soil our national escutcheon with degradation and defeat. There are men who will crawl in the dirt still for peace; but there is nobody now who can be deluded into believing that peace means any thing but humiliation, disgrace, degradation, national dissolution, the end of the republic, the beginning of the scorn and contempt of the world. (Great applause.) Ye men of Maryland who will crawl to the altar of peace, crawl there; but ye men of Maryland who remember that your forefathers thought seven years of war better than peace with submission and degradation, I appeal to you here this night to revive the recollection of those great days, and act upon their inspiration. (Great applause.)

And Maryland, too, is she disloyal? (No, no.) There are those who say so. There are those who say so in our State; there are those who say so abroad; there are those in power who believe it, and there are those who are not in power, but who skulk about in the darkness of the alleys of this great city, and carry whispering to the ear of power their slanders on their fellow-citizens, or spread them broadcast by the press all over the country, until Maryland stands almost in as ill repute as if she had lifted her hand in arms against the government that she adores and will maintain; and because of one deplorable and humiliating event, the result of weakness in some of our rulers and of treachery in others, there are those in one great region of this country who treat the State of Maryland as the whole South lately treated the whole North. The time was when one fanatic, inflamed by hatred, started out to make war upon the State of Virginia and set its negroes free, with twenty men at his back. (Laughter.) He was seized and hung. All the South with one acclaim laid that dastardly and crazy deed at the door of every man throughout the great regions of the civilized and Christian North; and there was no voice from the South in the House of Representatives but one, and that one ventured it at the peril of his political existence, to defend the North from that imputation. (Applause.) And now the city in which he lives has yet to find one defender in all the region of that North from complicity with the equally dastardly crime of the 19th of April. (Applause.) Great masses of men, when their passions are aroused, and when the judgment is asleep, when great events are transpiring, forget the rules of justice and of discrimination, and one portion of the country is just as liberal and just as illiberal as the other under analogous circumstances. I have defended my fellow-citizens of the North. I can venture now to defend my fellow-citizens of Maryland, and demand to be heard elsewhere than here. (Applause.)

Is Maryland, then, disloyal? Has she ever, for a moment, hesitated even? It is more than can be said for any other State south of Mason and Dixon's line but Delaware. Have the *people* of Maryland ever hesitated as to the side they should take in this great struggle? ("No, no.") Did she hesitate when the commissioners from Alabama and from Mississippi sought to associate her to the plotting of their treason? Did she hesitate when her governor resolutely, for three decisive months, refused to convene her traitorous Legislature (applause), lest they might plunge her into the vortex of rebellion? Did she ever hesitate when cunning politicians pestered him with their importunities, when committees swarmed from every disloyal quarter of the State, when men of the first position sought him and attempted to browbeat him in his mansion? Did she swerve when they, failing to compel him to call the Legislature, attempted the vain formality of a mock vote throughout the State to call a sovereign Convention by the spontaneous voice of the traitors of Maryland? Did they hesitate when in almost every county, even in those counties which were strongly secession, at the election for that Convention, the disloyal candidates were either defeated or got votes so insignificant as to create nothing but disgust and laughter throughout the State? Did they hesitate when that wretched remnant of a Convention met here, amid the jeers and the scoffs of the people of Baltimore, at the Maryland Institute—to do nothing and go home? What was it that enabled the governor to resist the pressing applications for the convocation of the Legislature? Are we to suppose that he had courage and resolution to face down and overbear the will of the great majority of the people of Maryland? Or was it not because, knowing the people who had elected him, their temper and their purposes, he felt that, however severe the pressure might be on him, where one person sought the meeting of the Legislature, there were thousands who stood by him in his refusal to convoke them? (Applause.)

Gentlemen, if the country will only go back to that critical period, the period of the opening of the electoral votes in the House of Representatives in February, and the inauguration of the President on the 4th of March, they who know most about that period will know best that the destiny of the capital of the United States lay in the hollow of the hand of Maryland? And had Maryland been *then* as people now presumptuously assert that she is, Abraham Lincoln might have taken the oath before a magistrate in the corner of some magistrate's office in Pennsylvania, but he would not have been then inaugurated where his predecessors were inaugurated, in the august presence of the Capitol of the country. I pray gentlemen to reflect, when they think of subsequent events, that if disloyalty had lain as a cankering worm at the heart of Maryland, then was her time. She could have made something by being false then. She could have presented herself before her Southern sisters dowering them with the capital of the country; and there was no power that could have prevented that gift, however the returning tide of events might have shown it to be as unwise as it was treacherous.

Then, fellow-citizens, what next? The bombardment of Fort Sumter, the uprising of the North, the call for troops which Marylanders stood ready to respond to (applause), when their ardor was damped by the proclamation of the governor, and the disloyal mayor of Baltimore—not the disloyal governor, but the governor and the disloyal mayor of Baltimore ("that is it")—informing the people that no troops should be sent out of the State of Maryland for any other purpose than the defense of the capital. That was the equivalent of telling the traitors of Maryland that the loyal men of Maryland were afraid to do their duty, and they acted upon it instantly. That proclamation appeared upon the 18th of April, and on the very evening of that day was held the meeting at which Parkin Scott, and Mr. Carr, and Mr. Burns, and other men of that stamp, prepared the hearts of the mob for the 19th of April. ("True.") And then, gentlemen, came that eternal stain upon the memory of those engaged in it—not a stain upon the memory of Baltimore—not a stain upon the memory of her loyal governor—not a stain upon the memory of her disarmed loyal citizens—a stain upon those who vilely and perfidiously perverted the trust given to them by the people of Maryland for the preservation of the peace of this city into an instrument of revolution, treacherously begun, treacherously carried on, until it fell before the scorn and wrath of the people of Maryland.

Then, gentlemen, the governor, with the commissions already signed lying upon his table, with the officers standing around him waiting to receive their commissions—the governor, suddenly smitten by an inexplicable terror, forgetting that the majority of the people of Baltimore were loyal and were around him, and, if summoned, could support and would support him; forgetting that on Federal Hill the very night before, even after his damaging proclamation of the 18th, when some traitors attempted to raise a secession flag there, the loyal working-men pulled it down and tore it to tatters (great applause); forgetting that these men were within five minutes' walk of where he sat, and that their breasts were such a protection as all the secessionists of Baltimore could not have marched over to assail him; forgetting that the voice of authority can paralyze in its incipient stages civil outbreak; forgetting the great example of which history gives us so many—more especially forgetting the great example of Cardinal Richelieu, when the enemy was almost at the gates of Paris, and the populace of Paris thought it was there through his neglect and were calling for his blood, the old cardinal, unarmed and without guards, went to the *Hotel de Ville* in the midst of the excited and infuriated multitude, and besought them to come to his aid and not to his overthrow, and every rebellious arm sank before his patriotic appeal—forgetting great examples like these, the governor, failing to rise to the height of the occasion, went to the *Hotel de Ville*, and threw himself into the arms of his enemies, and became from that time but their instrument, graced by his presence their disloyal and degrading meeting, stood in their midst while they uttered disloyal sentiments, uttered no word of disapprobation when they, the mayor at their head, falsified events that had occurred under their own eyes that day, and allowed them to treat as an assault on the people of Baltimore the act of self-defense of our fellow-citizens of Massachusetts against the traitorous assassins that assailed them without warning as they marched peacefully on their way for the defense of the Capitol. Then came the calling out of the military, two thirds of them secessionists, under officers many of whom were known then to be traitors, and who have since signalized their treachery by leaving Maryland, in pursuit of military service in the Confederate States. Then it was that here in Baltimore even strong men's hearts failed them for fear. Then it was that we saw the Chief of Police, and the Commissioners of Police, and Trimble, the "general commanding" (derisive laughter), and his aids innumerable, and his adjutant general (continued laughter), disporting themselves through the streets in gaudy colors, arraying armed men in Monument Square, first their trained volunteers, and then the rabble and the mob not to do their behests, and then arresting the commerce of the port, and then seizing upon the military stores of the United States, and then forbidding the display of the national flag, and then arresting people for spies, cutting off the transit of troops to the Capitol by breaking up the railway communications, arming steamers to ply in the port to arrest the free transit of Maryland commerce—all these things done by the *Chief of Police* and the *members of the police of Baltimore* and the organized mob—the loyal men informed that their lives were not safe—men insolently warned to leave the city if they would be safe—men thinking that it was "too good news to be true" that the Virginians were coming down to aid us; communication opened, formal embassies sent up to Harper's Ferry to invite John Letcher's 6000 men to come down and help the Marylanders to be free (laughter), and empty cars mysteriously gliding, in spite of the President, for a whole day toward Harper's Ferry—a peace-offering to our Southern brethren ("that's so") which might prevent their destroying the road and could not embarrass their march to Baltimore—the correspondence opened with John Letcher for muskets to be put into the hands of our "loyal citizens"—quarreling between General Steuart and certain members of the Police Board and Mr. Trimble for the possession of the precious deposit of 2000 arms sent down here from Harper's Ferry to keep the peace—Bradley Johnson, with an "invincible legion" of thirty men, rushing to defend Baltimore against "the Northern hordes" (laughter)—Marshal Kane making the mountains and the valleys of Virginia and Maryland hideous with his cry for help, which did not come (great laughter)—the Vansville Rangers scattered all along the way, forty men full (renewed laughter), from Washington to Baltimore, to guard the road—"loyal men" from Harford County, in equally overwhelming masses, rushing in to defend Baltimore against "Lincoln's hirelings" (laughter)—all these things are represented by the *intelligent* Northern press as the doings of the *people* of Maryland!

And on Wednesday an election was called (great laughter), and it was supposed that the unanimous voice of "an oppressed people" would signalize this day of their deliverance.

* * * * * * *

Had they not taken every possible pains to "obliterate all past differences" by the organizing of 3000 sharp bayonets to argue with the refractory? Was there not, therefore, every reason to suppose that there would be entire unanimity; nay, that these people, trodden down to the earth, trembling before the advent of "fresh hordes," wishing to place the mild and peaceful government of Jefferson Davis between their threatened bosoms and the Northern onslaught, would rush as one man to elect these gentlemen, the symbols of Southern sympathy, as their protectors in the day of their distress? The morning of election came, and one third of the people of Baltimore, under the influence of pressure, and persuasion, and delusion, and a little coercion (laughter), signified at an illegal election that they thought ——— and his colleagues fit associates for the rest of the majority of the House of Delegates. (Laughter.)

On Thursday morning, when men woke and walked down the streets, they found that a revolution had occurred, although they did not know it. Gone was the elastic step, gone was the uplifted eye of insolence, gone was the jeering scoff with which Secessionist met Union man, gone was the half menace with which loyal men were met, gone was the nod of fate that told them that their hour was coming. They fell by their victory; they died of their vote; the silence of two thirds of Baltimore stripped the revolutionists of their power, and consigned them to ignominy. (Applause.) Half the votes of a people do not make a revolution. One third may make a rebellion, but two thirds on the spot can put it down; and they felt it. ("That's so.") Gradually troops disappeared from Monument Square; gradually the arms were placed in their armories; gradually there were fewer and fewer "orders from head-quarters," "Trimble commanding" (laughter); gradually the steam-tug which constituted the navy of the incipient republic (laughter) ceased to send forth its black smoke, and vessels could venture to leave Baltimore without having a pop-gun fired at them (laughter); and even the Union men that had been frightened awoke to the consciousness that where they thought they were slaves they were masters, and from that day to this there has been nothing in Baltimore to make any man afraid, except one who has violated the laws of the land.

B—— J—— was seen almost immediately after that election, having accomplished the purpose of his visit, to return to Frederick; and on the 9th of May, "the defenders of Maryland," "the defenders of Baltimore," the candidates for immortality in the coming revolution, the men who were to fill the places in the niche of history corresponding to those filled by Williams and Smallwood of the Revolution—those men had tramped way-worn and weary to Frederick, and in that loyal town were guarded by the police through the town on their way to Dixie's land, without any music accompanying. (Laughter.) And B—— J——, with his thirty heroes, not one fallen in conflict with the "Northern invaders," joined them and marched to defend Harper's Ferry!

Now, upon the simple statement of that series of facts, is there any man who needs any thing else to be told him to convince him that the outbreak of April was a mob and not a revolution; that it received importance from the fact that the traitorous authorities attempted to use it for traitorous purposes; and without the firing of a gun, without the approach of a Northern soldier, without the menace of force, without the necessity even of a count of noses, without even the advent of an election in the State, they recognized that their time was come and gone; that they were powerless, and in the hands of the civil authorities; that they must gain immunity by good behavior; that Maryland was so loyal that they could not make her even appear to be disloyal;

and the arms dropped from their hands, and they began to seek mercy of their traitorous confederates at Frederick by begging and accepting a bill of indemnity for their criminal acts? Look at the counties. Was there any one of them that met to pass resolutions approving of what proceeded in Baltimore, or poured forth their thousands to support the revolution? If there was, let some one better versed in the history of the State than I am name it. If not, how came the whole State, being filled with traitors (!), to be silent when Richmond was ringing with the joyous acclamations that saluted the narrative of ——? How is it that Virginia appreciates our "deliverance" more than we do ourselves? How is it that we can find no tongue to celebrate the glories that they are rejoicing over? Why, gentlemen, not only was there no county that expressed any such approval, but even in St. Mary's, where there are only two hundred and fifty men in the whole county, they were not so deluded as to suppose that they had Maryland in their grasp; and in Cecil on the 23d of April the people met and passed resolutions such as Cecil has always acted upon, professing not neutrality, as Kentuckians did, not a desire for the removal of "the Northern hordes," not that our soil should not be polluted by any individuals crossing it in arms, but declaring their determination to stand by and maintain the government of the United States (applause), branding as traitors the men who had attempted to gain the reputation of patriots, and themselves leading off in the chorus that swept all round the States in one unbroken jubilee over the failure of the attempted revolution. (Great applause.) And immediately following were the resolutions of Alleghany County consigning to the halter their representatives in the Legislature if they should dare to vote for an Ordinance of Secession; and then followed the resolutions of Washington County, just preceding their great election—itself held, I believe, on the second or third of May—declaring their unalterable devotion to the Constitution and the Union, and their determination to abide by it always, followed up two or three days afterward by casting 2300 out of the 3800 votes of the county for the Union candidate without opposition. And then followed the great meeting in Frederick; and intermediate here in our midst, all through our wards, when the Legislature ventured to attempt to fix on us a military despotism in the disguise of a bill of public safety, copying the provisions and the spirit of their infernal police law for the city to fix the yoke on the people of the State, as they fixed that on the neck of the people of this city, our people quietly met in their wards and passed their resolutions, which were followed up in so many of the counties of the State that even the Legislature let drop their infernal machine, and did not venture to put it to a vote. (Applause.)

And where were we, fellow-citizens, all this time, for it was dropped on the second or *third of May?* In whose power was the capital of the United States at that moment, on the hypothesis of the disloyalty of Maryland? There were six hundred regulars there on the 18th of April; there were one thousand Pennsylvanians, wholly without drilling and ununiformed; and that constituted the protection of the capital of the United States on the 19th of April. On that day one Massachusetts regiment marched through, its last company only having been assailed. From that day until the 26th of April there were no more troops in Washington than I have enumerated. Up to the second of May they could count only about 6000 troops for the defense of the capital, and there were at that time 6000 at Harper's Ferry, and cars there ready to bring them down, and 3000 men armed in the city of Baltimore.

Suppose the State of Maryland had been, as men now impudently say she is, disloyal, I ask in whose power was the capital of the United States? On that supposition, there can be no doubt that it was ours—ours by a march of forty miles—ours as long as we could hold it, it may be as long as the Southern Confederates have held Bull Run. And here, gentlemen, I desire to say that it is to the fault of the Confederates themselves, the remarkable lack of that quality which Danton said was the essence of revolution, audacity, *audacity*, AUDACITY—it is to their failure in that first and indispensable quality of revolutionary leaders, it is to the absence of that quality that we now owe (be Maryland loyal or disloyal) the possession of the capital of the United States. It was not saved by the promptness of Northern volunteers; it was not saved by the forecast of the administration, that during its first month labored under the delusion that peace and not war was before it; it was not by the forecast of that wretched old dotard Buchanan (hisses), who now mumbles about energy and activity from his home at Wheatland; it was neither one nor the other; but it was because revolutionists had undertaken the work, without having the quality of revolutionists, that we still hold it, and that the glorious emblem of the republic floats from its dome. (Applause.) Baltimore, so the myth goes by timid creatures in our city, who whisper to people in Washington and tell their fears for facts, and begrime the reputation of their native city, or spread in still more dangerous form their fancies through the columns of the Northern press to poison the minds of our fellow-citizens against us—these people would fain repeat that here is the very gate of hell; that its seething and boiling fire bubbles under our feet perpetually, and that nothing keeps it down excepting their sleepless vigilance—fit guardians for such a post! and "Lincoln's myrmidons." (Great laughter.) Where were these gentlemen that were to keep the peace in Baltimore City during that awful period from the 19th of April to the 14th of May?—time enough in the city of Paris, where revolutionists understand their work, to have gone through all the phases of a revolution, installed a new power, tried and beheaded their antagonists, and forgotten the thing as an old event. It was not until the 14th of May that General Butler marched into this "disloyal" city, teeming, as we are now taught to believe, with raging revolutionists, requiring 10,000 men more—so say some men of the last generation—to keep them down. General Butler marched one morning into the southern part of Baltimore, marched up to Federal Hill, comfortably encamped his men in the rain, issued a proclamation, in which he (understanding Baltimore better than those in it who delight to malign it) appealed to and trusted to the loyal men of Baltimore, having come, as he said, with little more than a body-guard—less than 1000 men in a hostile city of 230,000 inhabitants. That was the first appearance of troops here. Now tell me why (if there were the disloyal elements to the extent that is supposed), during all that period, nothing had been done. Why was there no array to resist his entrance? Why did it have no other effect excepting that Union men walked down the street and said, "Well, we are afraid it will have the effect of changing some of our weak-kneed brethren." That was the only doubt expressed about it, except that one despairing individual thought that the hill being in the possession of the troops of the United States would frighten all the market-women away, and we should have no lettuce for some time. (Laughter.)

How did the Legislature of Maryland understand the position

of affairs in the state? They had prayed and besought to be recalled again into existence. They had died a natural death in March the year previous, having signalized their short power by some events which were to form a remarkable antithesis to events to follow them. They had passed almost unanimously a resolution declaring that I, in voting Mr. Pennington into the speaker's chair of the national House of Representatives, in order to prevent the then incipient revolution, did not represent the people of Maryland. They had ejected the respectable members from the city of Baltimore in the last hour of their session, in order that they might make room for those who were to follow them, and be more fit companions for the majority. They had previously passed a Police Law, in which they had been careful to provide that "no Black Republican, or approver or indorser of the Helper book," should ever be a policeman under that law in the city of Baltimore. (Laughter.) And such is the poetical justice of time and Providence, that within a few months past we have seen a man set over the police of Baltimore by a "Black Republican" general, and N. P. Banks's name signed to an order to enforce the law; and some of the gentlemen who passed that law are now appreciating that, although a Black Republican could not be a policeman under their law, he might be a policeman over its authors and commissioners. (Great laughter.)

Thus ends the first act of the Maryland Assembly — more wretched in its character, more ignorant, more unfit for its position, less representing the dignity and the intelligence of the State of Maryland, more begrimed by filthy lucre than any Legislature within my memory. Men supposed that it had been carried to its burial and buried out of our sight forever, and if not out of our memory, at least out of our grateful recollection; and, doubtless, one great element in the pertinacity with which the governor refused to recall the Assembly was his distinct remembrance of their unfitness for their duty, and his unwillingness that the State should be degraded by their again assembling. (Applause.) But in an evil hour he assembled them. For what? According to the unanimous avowal of those who demanded it, to take the sense of the people of Maryland as to whether they wished to remain in the Union or to go out of it. They met, and an elaborate report was prepared and delivered before that body, making great complaints of divers acts of illegality and oppression that had been perpetrated within the territory of Maryland by President Lincoln, but ultimately coming to the conclusion that they were unanimously opposed to the assembling of a Convention at that time.

"At the time when the Legislature was called together," says this singular document, "there was certainly but little difference of opinion among its members of all parties as to the propriety of speedily adopting measures to secure the objects referred to. Since that time, the rapid and extraordinary development of events, and of the warlike purposes of the administration, the concentration of large bodies of troops in our midst and upon our borders, and the actual and threatened military occupation of the State, have naturally enough produced great changes of opinion and feeling among our citizens." (Laughter.) "They have no hesitation in expressing their belief now that there is almost unanimous feeling in the State against calling a Convention at the present time." (Laughter.) Since when? It goes on to assign the reasons. Now judge:

"To the committee, the single fact of the military occupation of our soil by the Northern troops in the service of the government, against the wishes of our people and the solemn protest of the State executive, is a sufficient and conclusive reason for postponing the subject to a period when the federal ban shall be no longer upon us."

It goes on to say: "The Constitution is silenced by the bayonets which surround us, and it is not worth while for us to fancy ourselves beneath its ægis. It would be criminal as well as foolish to shut our eyes to the fact that we will not be permitted to organize and arm our citizens, let our rights and Constitution be what they may."

That is to say, gentlemen, when there were not troops enough in Washington to defend it; when there were none to be spared from Washington, when there was not a single soldier within the limits of Baltimore, when there were not three or four thousand upon the soil of Maryland all told, these patriots, who tell us that the Constitution is silenced, that our rights are trampled down, that we are oppressed, think that these are the very reasons why they should not appeal to the people of Maryland for their own protection! They may be the fit representatives of what is called secession; they certainly are the representatives of that prudence which Maryland secessionists have always substituted for audacity; who will neither appeal to arms or the ballot-box against oppression unless the oppressor first stays his hand; but these men are not the representatives of the loyal and free men of Maryland. If affairs were as they represent them, *that* was the time to appeal to the people of Maryland. It matters not whence oppression comes, it matters not in what shape it be presented, it matters not how overwhelming may be its force, when oppression shall unsheathe the sword, I mistake the tone and temper of the people of Maryland if they would stop any more than the men of Lexington and Concord stopped to count their antagonists in 1775. (Applause.) I suppose that it was not the presence of the military which overawed the Legislature of Maryland; it was that they, like the Police Commissioners, like Marshal Kane, and like "Trimble commanding" (laughter), and like all his supporters and followers, adjutants and aids, had all found that, while the people of Maryland were almost unanimously opposed to calling a Convention, that unanimity resolved itself into these elements —a small minority of the people wanting the majority to vote with them, but knowing they would not, and therefore not wanting a Convention called which would reveal irrefutably their insignificance of numbers, and the overwhelming majority of the people of Maryland, who did not want to be pestered with a vote to put down such wretched revolutionists. (Applause.) Now, am I right, or am I wrong in my estimate of the causes? ("Right.") That was in May.

On the 13th of June a congressional election was held, to which both the mayor and the governor had referred the people as a fit opportunity to express their devotion to, or their abhorrence of, the government; and how did they express it? I have already told you that the Washington County men voted 4000 out of 5000 votes for their member of Assembly, and that Cecil County followed up her resolution at a special election by voting three fourths of her vote in favor it, and that is an index of what the State did. In the great upper district there was no opposition. In Mr. Webster's district there was no opposition. In the district now represented by Mr. Crisfield there was a candidate for peace, who attempted to oppose him. A peace man opposed Mr. Leary. A Union man with Southern sympathies claimed and received the suffrages of the 4th district. There was but one avowed secessionist throughout the State of Maryland that ventured to ask a vote, and that was in Mr. Calvert's district, and for the first time in many years one not a Democrat carried the district. (Applause.) How did the voting foot up throughout the whole State? If you give to the secessionists every vote not cast, making no allowance for lukewarm men, no allowance for the doubtful, hesitating, floating vote that had not made up its mind whether it would be for or against the government, the conditional men, all the people who are on this side to-day and on that side to-morrow, or all the time on both sides (laughter), separating all those men and giving them to the secession side of the question, the Union men of Maryland at that election, with no opposition in two of the districts, and no avowed opposition upon secession grounds any where excepting in one of the districts, cast a great majority of the whole vote of the State. (Great applause.) And, gentlemen, for whom? Not for men who are pledged to shun responsibilities, to avoid votes, to let the government bleed to death if need be, to talk about neutrality in Maryland, to join the governor in opposing the transit of Northern troops, but men pledged before their constituents, pledged before the Conventions that nominated them, pledged in every way that can bind honorable men to vote every man that the government should demand, and any amount of money that the government should say was needed—not for the purpose of making peace, not for the purpose of holding out the olive-branch, not for the purpose of making treaties with traitors, but to disperse them by arms. (Tremendous cheering.)

What followed? The arrest of Kane. (A voice: "They ought to hang him." Cheers.) They left him in power till after the election. Secessionists who were so fond of the truth can not say that they were frightened and coerced in the election! It was wise to do so. They fortunately have no excuse of that kind, because at the time of the election there were soldiers at Baltimore and soldiers nowhere else, and it was only in Baltimore that they were partially successful. But, after that was taken out of their mouths, Kane was arrested; and that was *one* great outrage (laughter); and then the loyal commissioners, who protested their loyalty, and supposed that other people had memories as short as their own, and had forgotten their acts of war from the 19th to the 24th of April—these gentlemen in the interest of

"Peace and Order," when Governor Banks, with wise discrimination, had stopped at arresting one mischievous man in the hope that other mischievous men, taking warning, would be peaceable —they in the interest of peace and order, or possibly hoping that a great city swarming with bad men, in the period of a great revolution, and with a great deal of revolutionary blood floating through the Irish of the 8th ward (laughter)—these stalwart reformers, and friends of peace and good government, supposing that all these elements with no police would be much more quiet than when they were aggravated into resistance by a police on their side—they told their policemen that they had no farther use for them at that time; they should continue to draw their pay, but they were not expected to do any duty. (Laughter.) General Banks, being a practical man, interpreted "no duty" to be any duty that they might see fit to do; and as they had some training in military matters, and had shown themselves pretty good instruments to begin a revolution, though their masters did not prove so good leaders in it after it was started, came to the very natural conclusion that possibly a vagrant police with nothing to do, with masters equally idle, might find something to do; and he took care of the masters, and that was another great and unspeakable "outrage." (Laughter.) A howl of indignation arose to the pitying heavens against the "outrage" of arresting men who only opened the door to civil discord in a city of 250,000 inhabitants! Every principle of American liberty was appealed to to insure traitors liberty for mischief; and they wrote their appeal to the Legislature, and their appeal to the Legislature found a fitting advocate in the gentleman whose name I have had occasion so often to refer to. A long, elaborate, insidious, and disingenuous report was after a while brought forward, in which all the history of the government was read backward; all the arts of special pleading were applied to the misconstruction of the Constitution; rash assertions as to the history of the Convention were strewn all through it; and we were called upon to believe that George Washington had framed and recommended the adoption of a Constitution which would be very good if every body would obey it, but would be very worthless if any body should say he did not wish to obey it; and that George Washington, and the other wise men who surrounded him in the Convention, having provided on the face of the Convention for the suppression of insurrection, and declared that *every* law of a State should be in subordination to the supreme law of the land, the Constitution and the laws of Congress made in pursuance of it, had yet left open this great, wide passage-way for all the evils that they had attempted to exclude, by excepting from that subordination that law which should annul the whole Constitution; that case in which a faction should get possession of the authorities of a State, should put their treason in the shape of law, array armies for its defense, and defy the government. I have no doubt that the author of that report is a respectable lawyer within a narrow sphere, and I think that those who read the report will come to the conclusion that he has, like a wise lawyer, confined his studies to his department. (Laughter.)

That Legislature raised the awful question as to whether the government of the United States could arrest men in arms against its authority! (Laughter.) They did not venture to reorganize the militia of the State. They found that it was dangerous. They could pass laws of indemnity for men who had been guilty of treason, as if an act of indemnity by the State of Maryland would bar an indictment in the United States Court; but that was out of their line of practice. (Laughter.) They thought they could debauch the minds of the people, a law-abiding and law-loving people, habituated to see the law enforced only through the tribunals, by the sheriff, the judgment of the court, the constable—unaccustomed to the short and sharp methods of military suppression equally constitutional against armed insurrection. They seized every opportunity to mislead the people of Maryland into the supposition that their rights were violated whenever the paramount law of the safety of the republic, embodied in that clause of the Constitution which authorizes Congress to call forth the militia to suppress insurrection, was required to be acted upon in lieu of the ordinary methods of enforcing the law through the judicial tribunals; and they attempted to delude and excite the people of Maryland by representing that as a violation of the fundamental law. The people of Maryland were not so ignorant as the majority of the Legislature, and understood the construction of their fathers better than the gentlemen of the secession school. They understood that just as the Legislature can take land against the will of the owner for the purpose of making a railway or other public improvement, so the United States can seize railways when necessary for the transportation of troops, so they can occupy sites for fortifications, and when men are in arms against the government, they can arrest them without process, just as when they see them in serried ranks opposed to them in the open field they can shoot them down without having inquired by a jury whether they be traitors or a loyal man. All their machinations fell harmless before the people of Maryland; and, adjourning from day to day, finally the fatal hour met the Maryland Legislature. It seemed likely to break the law of all things mortal and sit forever, when the administration, impelled by unfounded fear of mischief at their hands, silenced their harmless chattering by taking away their heads, and leaving their tails to writhe.

The people of Maryland saw with indifference or delight their dispersion, yet wondered at the importance attached to them. On the policy or legality of that measure I shall at present say nothing.

Now, gentlemen, that is the history of secession in Maryland; it is the whole history; it is the close of the history. (Applause.) It is going to let the election this fall go by default and by confession. It did not venture to nominate a man in this city the other day; it will not press the election of its candidate for governor in November; it will have no contestants for the House of Delegates in one half the counties of the State; it will make no contest for the Senate except in two or three counties which are doubtful, and there only for the purpose of holding a veto on the Union men in the Legislature, and it is that we are specially bound to take care of. But secession as an active, dangerous, and agitating element, I say, now lies writhing in its last agonies in Maryland. (Great applause.) I do not doubt that very nearly one third of the people of the State are disloyal—not that they will take up arms on the secession side, but they will not take up arms on the Union side; they are disloyal. In my judgment, that is a very large estimate of the strength of the secession faction in Maryland this day. It has found the limits of its power; the nature of the beast is the same, only it has been deprived of its fangs; it can now do nothing but mumble false prophecies about the coming of Jefferson Davis, and pray him not to falsify their predictions.

Maryland has been true in heart thus far. She has not furnished her quota of troops to put down the rebellion within or without Maryland. That is partly her fault; chiefly the fault of her governor, who paralyzed the energies of her citizens when they were ready to respond to the first call of the government. But those charged with military affairs at Washington are not without their share of responsibility; for when the governor refused to call forth the contingent of Maryland, and when the law was pointed out to them under which they could send their orders to any officer of the militia, and the names of officers holding commissions and ready to obey the orders of the government were laid before them, and the President had drawn in blank the order and directed it to be sent to the Secretary of War, it rested on his table unacted on. When subsequently, after the 14th of May, the governor determined conditionally to call forth the contingent of Maryland, and officers went to Washington and offered themselves ready to respond to the orders of the government, the War Department declined to receive them first under the call for men for three months, and when General Kenly offered, himself, to call forth his brigade if it would be accepted as a brigade for the war, that also was declined. (Applause.) It was quite apparent that the Department felt small confidence in the Union men of Maryland, and were not at pains to conceal their indifference touching their aid. After that, it was not to be supposed that others would be in a hurry to receive such a rebuff. These doubts of our loyalty were inspired by persons apparently who knew nothing of Maryland or of its men; who have not the confidence of its people, and are unknown in its affairs, and have constituted themselves the chief advisers at Washington with reference to Maryland affairs. These things are undoubtedly deplorable. We suffer —our reputation suffers by the conduct of the administration toward the State throughout the whole country at this time. It is our misfortune to have such citizens; it is the fault of the government to listen to their counsels. (Great applause.)

We have labored under peculiar disadvantages in common with all the central slave States. The peculiarity of the present crisis is the wonderful activity and energy of the people and the State authorities contrasted with the relative inactivity of the central government. In the free States the governments have been loyal, and they have organized and aided the enthusiasm of the volunteers. The central slave States, betrayed or deserted by their State governments, have been abandoned by the national government almost to their unaided resources—disarmed, unorganized, half defended.

But, gentlemen, a different state of affairs, I believe, now exists. I think now the ear of power is open to wiser counsels touching the military policy to be pursued in Maryland, and, I trust, in the central slave States generally. I know that now they listen to and act upon the representations of my friend, Mr. Purnell. (Applause.) I know that they now listen to Governor Thomas, of the Upper District. (Renewed applause.) I know that they listen to the appeals of Mr. Wallace, of Cambridge. (Continued applause.) I know that now they listen to the suggestions of Mr. Dodge, the Chief of Police. (Great applause.) I know that while for long months they refused to arm our Home Guard, even at the solicitations of General Banks, repeatedly pressed, at length they have come to think that it is perhaps a part of the duty of the government, in dealing with a great rebellion, to inquire for, and to organize and arm loyal men for their own defense in disturbed districts; and now we have the Purnell legion forming at Pikesville, Governor Thomas's brigade forming in the upper portion of the State, several regiments organizing around the city, two already in the service of the government, and others forming in the lower part of the State; and, in my judgment, so soon as the people shall, in November, have elected a governor and a Legislature that will do for the people of Maryland what every where has been done by the Legislatures of our brethren in the North for their volunteers, give them the aid, and countenance, and pecuniary assistance of the State, and the outfit that is necessary to facilitate enlistments, that Maryland will stand in this contest as she has always stood in every other contest, not lagging behind her brethren, but struggling with them for the foremost rank where glory is to be won. (Great applause.)

If I may be allowed to criticise the conduct of an administration which I did not help to make, but which I rejoice was formed —for John Bell is a traitor—and for whose success I am more earnestly anxious than for any that has wielded power in my day (applause)—an administration which, weak or strong, is the last and only hope of the American people, which must be supported let whatever else may fail (great applause)—in spite of the contempt with which it has treated the people of Maryland, in spite of that lack of magnanimous wisdom which would have taught it not to overlook the great body of the central States in high civil and military appointments—however much these things may grate upon our feelings, however much they may tend to dampen the spirits and slacken the energy of our people, however much the administration may find too late that it has weakened its power, however much already they may have expanded the theatre of war and advanced the frontier of the fight nearer to the national capital—just in proportion as these disastrous consequences have followed for that great error in point of public policy, just by so much the more earnest motives are we, men of Maryland, called on to forget the past, to obliterate its bitter recollections, to forbid any thing like pride to arise in our gorges, to put down at the bidding of patriotism every ill spirit that would paralyze our arms, and, forgetting the past, rush forward to the future, and take our revenge of those who have slighted us by heaping the coals of fire of repentance upon their head. (Great applause.)

That the administration chose to constitute itself on a strictly party basis in its higher department is not a just subject of complaint, especially after the President had tendered to Mr. Gilmer, of North Carolina, a place in his cabinet, which he declined. But it is a matter of complaint that the importance of securing support, organizing friends, arming loyal citizens in the great central slave States was so gravely underrated; and while the other departments are filled with men equal to their respective duties, it is a matter of great regret that those departments chiefly and directly charged with the military policy of the administration have fallen below the requirements of the times. They spent one month of precious time before apparently they took one step to meet the storm that was blackening the whole heavens before them. Then, while yet war was afar, ere Tennessee had yielded to the gentle pressure of the Southern bayonet, while yet Missouri was free from armed invasion, ere secession had grown to rebellion in Kentucky, they let pass the golden opportunity of feeling their way through these great States and finding friends over that great region. They left the friends of the Union not only unable to fight its battles, but unable to defend themselves. They left a majority of the people of Tennessee to be borne down by violence from abroad, and to be disheartened by the desertion of the national government. They allowed disaffection to spread in Kentucky, until Kentucky, in spite of her overwhelming Union majority, hung trembling in the balance, and was driven to repel invasion from her soil. They left Missouri without the aid of additional soldiers, and her own Home Guard only half armed, until she was nearly overrun. They left Maryland without a musket in the hand of one of her sons for four dangerous months after they were in power. Had they sought, as a wise policy would have dictated, friends in the midst of the doubtful States, they could have saved Tennessee; they could have commenced the war upon the northern borders of Alabama and of Georgia, where we know the partisans of the government, though now silenced, swarm by the thousands; they could have held possession of the great central nucleus of the Alleghany Mountains, filled with its freemen ready to descend in every direction upon the plains below, carrying with them the emblem of hope and peace to our oppressed brethren in the cotton districts. Had Maryland been properly armed, had her citizens been called out, had even that despised contingent of the three months' men been accepted, they might not now have been confined to one railway for all their Western communications; the loyal part of Virginia might have crossed the Alleghany Mountains and stretched to the Blue Ridge. The whole face and aspect of the war would have been changed by timely attention to the first elements of success in dealing with an insurrection—to find out the men on the spot, in the disturbed district, as near as possible to the focus of the rebellion, who are there interested in putting out the flames, and give them at least an opportunity of aiding in their own defense. The event of Bull Run has, I think, made the administration sadder and wiser men. They possibly have reflected that there the despised Maryland contingent might have turned that tide of battle, for it was just four thousand men that converted a victory into a defeat when brought against our exhausted brethren, borne down by the heat of that day's conflict. They have now begun—begun in earnest —I trust begun successfully—(applause)—to organize the men of the great central slave States, who to them are an elemeut of untold power. Equally brave with their Northern brethren, they are a thousand times more interested in suppressing the rebellion, for it touches their homes, their hearths, their lives. Massachusetts has her pride in the republic. So have Maryland, and Kentucky, and Tennessee, and Missouri, and Delaware. Massachusetts has her interest in the cotton region. So has Maryland, as well as her interest in her own fields. But, beyond all that, we of the central slave States have our liberty at stake; if we fail we are a conquered people; we pass from the glories of the American republic to be the suspected, watched, and chained subjects of a power we abhor, and which hates us.

Having already traced the position of Maryland, I need now but point your eyes for inspiration to the present condition of Kentucky. Betrayed by her treacherous governor, placed in the disloyal attitude of neutrality by her last Legislature, invaded by an armed force from Tennessee, deserted or assailed by such men as Breckinridge and his associates, she has, as one man almost, through her present Legislature, proclaimed her readiness to do her duty. When her energy was quickened into activity by actual invasion, then her Legislature met; made a loan for two millions of dollars, called out 40,000 volunteers; and then, as if to cover with contumely the men who speak only of "our Southern brethren," they passed by overwhelming majorities that touching vote of thanks to the men of Indiana, Ohio, and Illinois, who came rushing in arms ("Black Republicans" and "Lincoln's myrmidons" as they are) to protect Kentucky against her Southern brethren. (Applause.)

And there is Missouri, neglected by the War Department, defended by her half-armed and half-organized sons until they were decimated by superior numbers, and the gallant Lyon fell a sacrifice to his unsupported heroism; and then, when they came to rest on the support of the government of the United States, two thirds of their state was overrun, and a large body of troops and Home Guards captured right on the great highway of the Missouri River for lack of timely support.

It is vain to inquire who is responsible for such disasters—the War Department, charged with organizing the force, or the military officer commissioned to lead them; it lies between them, and this country will hold both responsible. I fear that the man to whom the destinies of Missouri are committed is fitter to issue proclamations violating every principle of the law of the land, and looking only to one purpose—his political elevation—than he is either to organize a force to repel invasion, or, it may be, to lead it after it is organized. He is not able (such is the last account) to move yet over ground where Lyon moved with none but Missourians at his back (applause)—not able yet to move because of lack of transportation, surrounded by loyal people and by loyal States—not able to move for lack of subsistence, in the very midst of the great granary of the United States. No man can believe, if these things be true, that a heavy debt of responsibility does not rest at somebody's door, to be answered for at some not very distant day. I feel for the men of Missouri, for they have not lain supinely down and waited to be defended; but they have been overborne; I say they are entitled to look to the government not merely for willing troops—they have been furnished by the thousand with that spontaneous enthusiasm which finds no equal in the history of the world—they are entitled to a leader who will not lack transportation, nor food, nor means to reach the enemy. (Applause.) Instead, they have a man who publishes gasconading proclamations fitter for a European despot than an American officer, such as "I do hereby extend and declare established martial law throughout the State of Missouri," two thirds of it in the possession of the armed rebels; "the lines of the army of occupation in this state are for the present declared to extend from Leavenworth, by way of the posts of Jefferson City, Rolla, and Ironton, to Cape Girardeau on the Mississippi River," within which they took Lexington from him the other day; and then followed by the *brutum fulmen* of a threat at the bottom—"all persons who shall be taken with arms in their hands within these lines shall be tried by court-martial, and, if found guilty, will be shot"—in the face of the solemn provision of the American Constitution that no man out of the military service can be condemned except by a jury of his peers before a court of the State or district in which the crime was committed, with an indictment and evidence, and the right to have counsel and all the precious guards of the common law thrown around to protect his life. He is to be tried and shot at the will of General Fremont, and whoever he may see fit to appoint to try him over a drum-head court-martial. It received its fit reward in having the very country over which he usurped despotic power swept from beneath him. And then, of course, it was impossible for a man who has high political as well as military aspirations, to overlook in this agitation the Negro Question as an element of popularity, and thereupon we have this lord and master of the free people of Missouri dealing thus with their property: "The property, real and personal, of all persons in the State of Missouri who shall take up arms against the United States, and who shall be directly proven to have taken active part with their enemies in the field, is declared to be confiscated to the public use, and their slaves, if any they have, are hereby declared free."

The President, with a straightforward honesty that has marked his every act, seized the earliest opportunity to rebuke that usurpation of illegal authority. I only regret that he did not go farther, and mark with his disapprobation that clause declaring martial law, and that he did not punish the usurpation by revoking the commission of the officer who, charged with high and responsible command in the midst of a slave State, gave the enemies of the government so serious a ground on which to impeach their policy, and who treated the representatives of the people with so much contempt as in the face of the very law which they had passed scarcely one month before, declaring exactly how the property of rebels should be dealt with, dared thus flagrantly to usurp legislative powers, and deal out wholesale confiscation and emancipation as if he were above all law. I think that the interests of the people of Missouri would be safer if we had some one who could be content with high military command, without playing the dictator, who would confine himself to marshaling his hosts, removing armed opposition, vindicating the authority of the government, and, like George Washington, be content to obey the laws, and not either violate them or attempt to make them. (Applause.)

Gentlemen, I have detained you already too long ("Go on"), and I have only one or two observations farther to submit to you. The policy of the administration and Congress in dealing with this rebellion has been eminently liberal. The policy of the people in the rebellious States has been eminently illiberal and barbarous. The men who pass along our streets and talk about oppression, are careful never to refer to the enactments of the Southern usurping Legislature; they never refer to that law which authorizes and directs the President of the Confederate States to imprison every alien enemy, meaning *our* fellow-citizens—which banishes every citizen of the United States who will not acknowledge their authority—which sequesters every cent's worth of property of every man living in any of the Northern States—which dooms to the halter, or to exile or imprisonment, every resident who, however peaceable, refused to acknowledge their usurping domination. Were we to apply that rule to the gentlemen who insult our moderation, how quickly should we in Baltimore be freed from the scowling looks, and the averted glances, and the insolent tones, and the menaces of retaliation that meet us every day and every where. How different, gentlemen, is the policy of the government of the United States. It confiscates nobody's property, even although taken in arms against the government. Fremont's proclamation presumed, in the face of the act of Congress, to do that. The law had forbidden it; the law condemns only property which has been used for rebellious purposes; it sets free only slaves that have been used to prosecute the war; it confiscates only property that has been used in the course of commerce between the rebellious States and the loyal States, and there it stops; lays hold of the thing that sins; it confiscates nothing beyond: it leaves the estates of the gentlemen who have left Maryland to wage war against their native State untouched by the law of confiscation; it leaves the negroes, however powerful an element they might be made of embarrassment in the slave-holding States, untouched, save where their masters have first used them to aid in breaking down the authority of the United States. Moderation, liberality is every where manifested by the government of the United States, just as vengeance, illiberality, a disposition to grasp and seize every thing within their power, to strip honest, innocent people, widows and children not less than men in arms, of their last support, even of the money that was confided to the faith of their States by being invested in their public securities. Gentlemen, that is the liberality, the respect for property, that these people show toward our fellow-citizens. It may be the foundation of a serious appeal for more stringent measures if events do not speedily render them unnecessary. (Applause.)

Gentlemen, there is nothing of such hopeful augury as the moderation of the United States in dealing with this great rebellion; and on that one subject of the freedom of the slave, tempting as it is to political aspirants, tempting as it is to men who wish a short method of dealing with a great rebellion, those in power have felt the responsibilities of power, and know that they are wielding power only to support the laws. They know that they are just as much bound to protect that property as any other property, and that no citizen's property can be taken at the will of the government otherwise than according to law and the Constitution. Only ignorant fanatics prate about decrees of emancipation. Therefore it is that every where wherever the arms of the United States have penetrated any of the slaveholding States, you have found no servile rebellion following their ranks or breaking out to meet them. A few stragglers find their way into the camps, a few seek protection, a few seize the opportunity of running away from their masters, but any thing like a servile insurrection has not been heard of any where in the presence of the armies of the United States. That is the short reply to every imputation upon the faith of the government. (Applause.)

But the great question remains, Can the government succeed in maintaining its authority? ("Yes.") That question events alone can answer. In my judgment, if the wisdom which wields the power be only equal to the enthusiasm, the devotion, the liberality with which the people and the States have lavished men and money in the cause of the republic, then there is no doubt as to what the result will be. (Applause.) It may be that here now, as heretofore in the history of the world, a great cause may fail in the field for lack of great ability to guide it in the proper departments of the cabinet. We humbly and earnestly trust that that will not be the case. Rashness has already been punished; disregard of high military advice has already met humiliation; humiliation has probably brought forth repentance, and repentance is the beginning of wisdom. I have reason to believe that hereafter military questions will be left to military men, and military men with heads upon their shoulders will be allowed to organize and direct the military power of the United States. (Great applause.) I know, fellow-citizens, that great changes have been wrought lately in both the military departments. Up to this time the blockade has been a mockery; the Secretary of the Navy, after six months' experience, has found it out, and there has been there a change. He has found out that age and decrepitude are not indispensable for command, and that Southern birth and residence are not disqualifications. Maryland and Delaware have been honored by high and responsible commands in the persons of Goldsborough and Dupont, who are about to sail from our ports with great expeditions under their charge—already too long delayed—but, in their hands, sure to prove fruitful of high enterprise and great results. (Applause.)

The wisdom of their selections redeems many of the delays and blunders which have led to them. The administration have shown no greater knowledge of men, no greater determination to subordinate unjust suspicions to the necessities of the public service and sound policy, than when from the bosom of two slave-holding States they selected the leaders of these great expeditions, which, uniting under the same command officers of high merit from Massachusetts and South Carolina, together with men from the slave and men from the free States, fitly represent the unity of the national power whose banner they are charged to restore on the Atlantic coast. (Great applause.)

The War Department has been taught by the misfortune of Bull Run, which has broken no power nor any spirit; which bowed no State, nor made any heart falter; which was felt as a humiliation, and which strung men's nerves to retrieve in, that has brought forth wisdom. They now know, if they did not know before, that a half-equipped army is not fit to deal with the desperate powers arrayed against the government. They now know that equality of forces is not a becoming proportion for a government in the face of a rebellion it is about to suppress; it looks too much like a struggle between a strong government and a weak one. They know now that it requires military knowledge to lead a host; that it requires months to convert a crowd into an army; that without artillery a modern army is nothing, and that without cavalry it is a bird without wings; that, without the means of following up a victory, victory is worthless. They now know that victory at Bull Run would have been disaster and not success; that, had they beaten the enemy finally as they had beaten actually from the field at one period in the day the Confederate forces, they could not have followed up the victory; that if they had attempted to follow it up, they would have found themselves in the midst of Virginia with an army melting like snow beneath the sun; that the three months' volunteers, as their terms of enlistment expired, would have left a remnant in the centre of Virginia to be a prey for the rebels' swollen power. How earnestly true was the exhortation of the great military leader and adviser of the administration appears by this—that Bull Run having been fought upon the 20th of July, the army of the United States, under a commander of relentless activity and energy, and of ability equal to the highest in the army, is still drilling, going through its parades, being organized, waiting for its material of war, within five miles of the City of Washington. All that they gained by the battle of Bull Run was that, instead of being able to march in October, as Winfield Scott told them, they would if they let him alone, and did not push him on before he was ready to go; they are not yet ready, and we are past the middle of October itself, and probably will not be ready before November. But, gentlemen, when that movement takes place, it will be no array of straggling regiments hunting up a commander over a vast field of battle (laughter); it will be no disorganized body of regiments never bound together in a brigade, and which hardly saw their commander's or their companion's face until the day of battle, but it will be the best men of the American people —as good, ay, better than ever faced an enemy in the same numbers before (applause), accustomed to all the evolutions of modern warfare, having profound confidence in their young and brilliant leader (great applause), accustomed by continual reconnoissances and skirmishes to meet the enemy in arms and learn what battle is, blended into that compound of steel and fire which makes an army ready to be launched like one of God's bolts upon the enemies of the country. (Great applause.) We may fail again, for war is a game of blended skill and chance whose determination is with the Most High (applause); but I earnestly trust and believe we shall not fail. The activity and energy with which those in power are now endeavoring to second the efforts of military men to organize a force before encountering the chances of defeat are of good augury for the republic.

When the banner once more points forward, it will proudly advance until the rejoicing soldier shall, like Xenophon's Greeks at the aspect of the Euxine, after their weary march, greet with the cry of "The sea," "The sea," the glancing waves of the Gulf of Mexico (applause); penetrating at more than one point, armies of deliverance shall march, not to subjugate, but to free; not to violate any law of the land, but to enforce them all; to put down rebellion and its armed insolence; to restore to loyal hearts the security that for long months they have not known; to restore the ancient boundaries of the republic; to wipe out from the escutcheon of the nation the stain of our failing arms; to restore our reputation before the nations of the world; to teach men that liberty is not a mockery, and a republic is not another name for feebleness or anarchy; to teach the jeering tyrants of the Old World that their day is not come yet; to let them know that the Bulwer Lyttons can prophesy in vain, and see false visions in their hopes of the overthrow of the great rival of England, and that Alison does not comprehend the greatness of this people, nor the peculiarity of their genius, when he indites puerile epistles about an Established Church and a limited monarchy for the free men of America. (Laughter and applause.)

Gentlemen, we do not want the assistance of the people across the water. We do not fear their hostility. We shall be glad of their good will; we will not mourn if it is withdrawn. We know that we owe them nothing but good will, and that we are ready to reciprocate. It is our duty to take care of ourselves. We mean to be fully up to that duty. We rely upon their interests, and not upon their love, to let us alone. We know that the South is disappointed in the expectation of having the blockade broken merely because John Bull counted the cost, and found that a war with the United States would cost more than the Southern cotton would pay for. We know very well that Louis Napoleon prefers not to pick any quarrel with this country, among other reasons because the navy of England overmatches his own, and he sees the time when possibly the sailors of America may be needed to balance the power of England. (Applause.) We know that while one interest would prompt him to embarrass, another, a greater, a near one, compels him to let us alone; for he is surrounded by revolutionary fires, stifled but not extinct, and if he turns from home he may find that "fire in the rear" uncomfortably girding his revolutionary throne. (Laughter.) There is some sympathy, strange to say, and it has more than once been manifested, by the great despot of Russia for this great democracy. They seem to have a kindred feeling in their youth, their newness, their growing strength, their freedom from most of the embarrassments of other governments, and the boundless regions of space that invites them to expand their empire. They feel that to them belongs the future, however different the form of empire; and although we may seek our advancement in different methods and in different forms, yet each, in his appropriate sphere, in his appointed time, in his own way, is working out the great problem of human destiny—we of human freedom on this side the Atlantic, he of human civilization among the half-civilized men of Asia.

But, while we accept the courtesy of the Autocrat's good wishes, we trust nothing to his good will; our fate is in our own hands; on them alone we must rely. There is now no prospect of foreign intrusion, but no man can tell what a day may bring forth. We shall, I think, meet with no disturbance from beyond the Atlantic at present. To-morrow it may suit the policy of England, or France, or Russia to fling their sword into the scale of our destinies, and that might decide them. Now is the time, at once, without delay, unitedly for us here in Maryland, as well as those in Kentucky and those in Missouri, with our brethren in the North, to scatter and destroy at one blow the armed array of our enemies, ere delay consolidates their power or foreign complication embarrasses our arms. We must not merely defeat, we must destroy the army before Washington. That will break the military power of the rebellion, and whenever the sword shall be stricken from the hand which lifted it against the Union, the terrors of despotic power will vanish from the land, and grateful eyes will turn in tears to greet the unforgotten banner of the republic.

CONSTITUTIONAL POWERS SUFFICIENT FOR REPRESSION OF REBELLION.

WHILE thoroughly upholding the government in all lawful and proper efforts to put down the rebellion, Mr. Davis freely criticised those acts of doubtful expediency, and still more doubtful lawfulness, which were, perhaps, almost unavoidable amid such confusion of affairs and such uncertainty as to men, especially at the outbreak of hostilities.

He condemned from the first the use of the word "blockade," as applied to our own ports held by rebel insurgents, whereby belligerent rights seemed impliedly conceded, or, at any rate, whereby an argument was afforded to those who did concede such rights to those insurgents. He condemned the virtual suspension of the *habeas corpus* by the President, which could be authorized by act of Congress alone. He condemned the proclamation of martial law in districts where the execution of the United States laws was not impeded by insurgent force. He condemned the permission by the government of such outrages against law, and such blunders in policy as Fremont was daily committing in Missouri; and he boldly set forth what he thought the proper course in such respects to be pursued by a government restoring law and order in regions where both had been subverted by insurrection.

For these utterances Mr. Davis was condemned by those extreme partisans who held that all things which could be wreaked on the insurgents were fair and lawful, although the attempt should involve the extinction of rights not less dear than the preservation of the Union itself. Yet, in thus condemning certain mistakes, Mr. Davis certainly offered that support of the administration which comes from the judicious reproof of a friend, and therein he showed himself a truer supporter than those incautious men whose rash advice, or worse than rash actions, only added to the number of its enemies.

Mr. Davis availed himself of an opportunity to speak on these points as early as November, 1861, at Brooklyn, in the following address:

MR. PRESIDENT AND GENTLEMEN OF THIS ASSOCIATION,—In the corner-stone of the southern wing of the Capitol at Washington, in the hand-writing of Daniel Webster, are these words: "If, therefore, it shall be hereafter the will of God that this structure shall fall from its base, that its foundation be upturned, and this deposit brought to the eyes of men, be it then known that on this day the Union of the United States of America stands firm, that their Constitution still exists unimpaired, and, with all its original usefulness and glory, growing every day stronger and stronger in the affection of the great body of the American people, and attracting more and more the admiration of the world." That deposit is hardly ten years old. Daniel Webster has not been gathered to his fathers ten years, and that stone is rocked by the earthquake of revolution. Those institutions, whose success he supposed he was announcing to a distant futurity, seem now already to be losing their hold on the affections of the people and the respect of nations abroad. Were he now called on to rewrite that solemn proclamation to posterity, he would lower its lofty tone. He would say,

"The Union of the United States of America is now assailed and shaken to its foundations; their Constitution has ceased, in a great measure, to command the confidence of the people of America or the admiration of the world, and the people themselves seek after a master."

The path of a nation in search of a master is broad enough and of varied aspect. Nations have sought him in the imperfections of their national institutions; in the madness of civil strife; at the hands of foreign intervention; in the degeneracy and corruptions of their own manners; in appeals from the ballot-box to the sword at the bidding or for the advancement of personal ambition. The people of America now exhibit more than one of the symptoms of that fatal hunt. One great region is marching in the path of Mexico to the overthrow of a government it has ceased to control. The other great region is following in that deadly path—unconsciously perhaps, not so palpably, but not less surely, not less fatally—by the blind madness with which they throw down every barrier liberty has erected against arbitrary power in their reckless eagerness to preserve the integrity of the nation. They see the gulf, and think nothing too precious to fill it. They are ready to lay their liberty a sacrifice on the altar of victory.

When Daniel Webster died, American liberty looked strong and was boastful of its strength; when President Buchanan left the White House, American liberty was like Herod, eaten of worms beneath his royal robes, and ready to give up the ghost.

The foundations of the constitutional edifice were already secretly sapped; the mortar was already picked from the stones; and when the judges of the Supreme Court pronounced the Dred Scott judgment, the very caryatides of the Constitution were seen to bend beneath the unusual pressure, and the whole edifice seemed, to thoughtful eyes, to rush to its ruin. The sap went on more earnestly, more vigorously; and as the catastrophe approached, all the energy and audacity seemed on the side of the assailants; all the doubt, all the hesitation, all the timidity on the side of the defenders—paralyzed at the awful aspect of the national dissolution. Then it was that the enemies of the republic thought their day was come; they rushed openly to the assault of the breach they had been so long and so secretly preparing. In their exulting confidence they boastfully shouted,

> "York is joined to Bolingbroke,
> And all your northern castles yielded up,
> And all your southern gentlemen in arms
> Upon his party."

And the sovereign people thought their power doomed when breathless messengers from the South gasped out,

> "White beards have armed their thin and hairless scalps
> Against thy majesty; and boys with women's voices
> Speak big, and clap their female joints
> In stiff, unwieldy arms against thy crown;
> Even thy beadsmen learn to bend their bows
> Of double fatal yew against thy state;
> Yea, distaff women manage rusty bills
> Against thy seat; both young and old rebel."

Bold men thought the last day of the republic was come. Bad men withdrew to seize their part of the dismembered heritage. Timid friends gathered round the bed of the dying patient, and talked hopefully of peaceful dissolution; and when rash men whispered, even with bated breath, of coercive remedies, they were put far off, lest the shock of the suggestion might hasten the catastrophe.

And then an unaccustomed sound echoed over the land—a strange event—a new thing under the sun—American arms pointed cannon at American breasts—American shot shattered an American fortress—American hands dragged down the standard of the republic, and boasted that they first had trailed it in the dust.

That touched a nerve of exquisite sensibility which vibrated to the heart of the nation; and it rose from its bed of death, and cast off its premature grave-clothes, and challenged its right to be a nation of history. From the Pacific to the Atlantic, living men stretched forth eager hands for arms to defend the republic.

And then the people passed from atomy to paroxysm in a day. Action—action was the cry!

The people were summoned to action—action upon a new theatre—action upon new principles and for new purposes—action on new paths, different from the recognized and used paths over which the American people had in this generation trodden—action at the bidding of one stern and irresistible impulse that seemed for an instant—nay, for months—to blind the American people, and make them forget the salutary principles of the Constitution, which was framed after the experience of one revolution, and is competent to carry the nation through another revolution. They supposed, because they had not hitherto been called to deal with the great question of the suppression of insurrection—the guarantee of republican government to the States—the assertion of the supreme authority of the United States—they supposed that laws were meant for times of peace, that constitutions were only to be obeyed in courts of law—that now fury might minister arms, that wrath might be the measure as well as the instigation to what is allowable to might. The maxims of the hour, urged by the press and the people on those in power, were, "Give them as good as they send—do as they do—make those acts against which you protest the measure of your conduct—we can not afford the protection of the laws to traitors—the laws are silent in the midst of arms—necessity is above all law—the safety of the people is the only law." And these maxims, unheard of before as American law, unheard of before upon American hustings, unheard of in the councils of legislation—I need not say never dreamed of in the courts of justice—these maxims have in a great measure ruled the government in its dealing with the existing troubles—ruled the government, in a great measure, in the modes in which it has attempted to deal with the great and terrible rebellion that we are called upon to suppress—ruled it, not at its own suggestion or inspiration—not against the will of the people; but the people leading the government on, urging it on, prompting it, rejoicing over every arbitrary act, calling for more vigorous measures, when the vigor had already, in more than one instance, overstepped the bounds of law; seeing nothing but the enemy before it, and supposing that enemies of law might be subdued by disregard of the fundamental principles of the government. I do not think I have overstated the case.

Certainly it is not my disposition to overstate the case. I do not know any one who is more interested—no one here, certainly, is so much interested—in the suppression of this rebellion as I am personally. You see the conflagration from the distance; it blisters me at my side. (Applause.) You can survive the integrity of the nation; we in Maryland would live on the side of a gulf, perpetually tending to plunge into its depths. It is for us life and liberty—it is for you greatness, strength, and prosperity.

If you are interested, still more am I; if illegal measures are necessary for salvation, I am more tempted than you to resort to them; and yet I desire to say that there is no circumstance connected with all the difficulties we are called upon to deal with—nothing, in my sight, so threatening in the future—nothing which I find myself so unable satisfactorily to contemplate, as the temper of the public mind in dealing with this great rebellion. Not that I have any tenderness for the parricidal hands that have lifted weapons against the heart of the nation—let them perish! (Applause.) But in their grave I do not wish to see American liberty buried. It is time that the energy of the nation, having now been aroused, her embattled hosts lining the whole border, flaming with the conflict, by whose light we read that the nation will not die a dog's death and will not perish of rottenness off the face of the earth—it becomes us now to turn our eyes to the principles upon which the contest is to be waged—to hold those in authority responsible, not merely for energy, but for legality and constitutionality—to silence the sneer with which men are met when they recall their rulers to the limits of law and the Constitution. Let them understand that the American government will not be so degraded in the eyes of history as to be driven to the necessity of inaugurating revolution for the purpose of suppressing insurrection. (Applause.)

They who speak about extraordinary methods—of the necessity of usurpation—of the necessity of neglecting the "technicalities of law," as they politely term them—the necessity of departing from all "red-tapeism," which is the ordinary phrase to describe now the regular operations of the government, conducted by wise men —these men must be taught (and it is for gentlemen like you to teach them) that it does not prove a man is disloyal because he thinks the Constitution better than they do, not only powerful in peace, but powerful in war; that its ægis is not only so broad as to protect the people in times of peace, but in the midst of civil war the surest protection; in the face of national disaster, the surest refuge. (Cheers.)

Let us review some of the measures which have been resorted to by the government in the name of the suppression of the rebellion, and with the accord of the people, and see where in six months we have drifted before the storm of war. If it is usurpation, it is usurpation against a willing people. If it is illegal, it is illegality prompted by the people. But it is equally certain that the acclaim of the people is the most dangerous symptom.

We have seen in the midst of the American republic, in the midst of the nineteenth century, after more than eighty years of republican rule, under a plainly-written Constitution—we have seen a republican administration assume the right to declare and execute martial law. We have seen a military commander in charge of a great and important district, within two months, I believe, after Congress had adjourned, issue a proclamation inaugurating, formally, martial law over two thirds of the State of Missouri—threatening with death, at the dictation of a drum-head court-martial, any one caught in arms within the district prescribed by his will. We have seen him assume the right to disregard the act of Congress ere the ink was fairly dry upon the parchment, and to confiscate property which Congress, by omitting, said could not be confiscated. We have seen (and those who have seen them must have laughed) deeds of manumission signed "John C. Fremont, Major General Commanding." (Applause and hisses. A cry, "Three cheers for Fremont!" and cries "for shame!")

Free speech exists where I speak. (Tremendous applause.)

I have seen tempestuous assemblies before in my day. Nay, more, I have seen, likewise, statements that three or four freemen of America have been convicted before a court-martial in the State of Missouri, presided over by a colonel of Illinois volunteers—that is the judicial tribunal—convicted of being in arms against the United States—that is treason—and sentenced to hard labor during the war.

The President, with the advice of the chief law officer of the government—a gentleman for whom I entertain, personally and politically, the very highest regard—has, under the pressure of the emergency of the times, asserted a right in the President, and the President has acted upon it in various instances, to suspend the writ of *habeas corpus*. (Applause.) And under this usurped power the President has arrested or allowed to be arrested many freemen who were not in arms, and had not been in arms, against the United States, and therefore were not fit objects of the military power vested in the President by Congress; has refused to submit the causes of their arrest to the judicial tribunal, even in New York, and has incarcerated them in fortresses that they might be out of the way of process.

We have seen a judge of the highest court of record in the District of Columbia held prisoner in his house, with a soldier marching up and down before the door, with bayonet on his shoulder. (Cries of "Serve him right! serve him right!")

We have not yet reached the question whether it has served him right or not. (Applause.) About the fact there is no doubt; that there was no sworn statement against him, there is no doubt; that the ordinary formalities of law were not pursued, there is no doubt. If he was guilty, let him be punished by law; if he was bearing arms, or about to bear arms, let it be known, and the world will justify the act. (Applause.)

We have seen likewise (and when we remember that it is the middle of the nineteenth century we may very well be startled at the very reference), we have seen at least one newspaper—probably more than one newspaper—stopped because of the character of its articles. We have seen more than one newspaper—(they do not express my sentiments)—we have seen more than one newspaper excluded from the benefit of the mails without authority of law.

We have seen a provost-marshal—the police-officer of a camp—inaugurate a civil court in Alexandria, Va., and (I presume I address not a few of the mercantile gentlemen of New York), if the papers have not again misled me, I think I saw a few days ago that the Chamber of Commerce had suggested to the President that he should vest authority in the provost-marshal to continue that illegal and usurped jurisdiction. (Cries of "Good," and applause.)

We have seen executed—as nothing of the kind has been executed in any despotic country of Europe, and with a completeness and precision, secrecy and dispatch, that would have done honor to the chief of police of France—the seizure of all the telegrams in all the telegraph offices, from one end to the other of the American republic, I believe, in one day. (Loud applause.)

We have seen, I believe, without any authority of law—we have seen an order from the Secretary of State saying that no man shall leave the United States without a passport—that is, by his leave. (Renewed applause.)

Now these things are not cast in the teeth of any body, nor stated for the purpose of crimination. I use them historically; I use them for the lesson they teach; I use them to bring before you, men of America, where you this day stand after your republican government has been in full and blessed operation for over eighty years.

These measures have been executed without any authority of law. Some of them might have been authorized by Congress; but Congress had just adjourned without having authorized them.

Over these measures of the executive there is a strange agreement between the friends and the enemies of the government.

The enemies of the United States have taken the Constitution under their special protection, the more easily to destroy it. They deny the constitutionality of every measure for the suppression of the insurrection, and confound the arbitrary and the legal in one indiscriminate outcry against usurpation and oppression.

The friends of the government apparently agree with them in their denial of the sufficiency of the Constitution for the crisis, and propose to eke out its omissions by the law of necessity.

I agree with neither of them. Both are wrong, and either view is equally fatal to the existence of the government.

The Constitution does vest in Congress adequate power to suppress every insurrection.

The Constitution does not vest in Congress or the President arbitrary or unlimited power for that or any other purpose. Now, if the constitutional powers of the government are not sufficient for the suppression of the rebellion—I mean the constitutional powers of the government, not construed by the standard of South Carolina, but measured by the standard of Daniel Webster, measured by the standard of Henry Clay (applause), measured by the standard of Abraham Lincoln, who differs in nothing from either of those great men (applause)—if the Constitution of the United States does not confer power upon the government to deal with a great rebellion like this, then, gentlemen, I wish you to draw your conclusion. Mine is, that the government of George Washington has failed! (Hisses, and cries of "No!") If the government that he founded can not deal with the events before it, it is not an inference of logic, it is the verdict of history, it has failed. (Hisses.) And hissing don't change the verdict. (Laughter.) Or else the hiss is to be interpreted in this sense—that the government has not failed, although it does not afford power to deal with the rebellion, which yet it is its duty to suppress. That argument is worthy of a hiss! I say, gentlemen, *if* the Constitution does not furnish these powers, then the people of the United States are in the face of another revolution. If you can not find, within the limits of the law written down, the mode and method by which you are to stamp out this rebellion, by what law is the President to be guided?

A VOICE. The law of self-preservation.

Mr. DAVIS. That is the law of Louis Napoleon.

A VOICE. The law of military power.

Mr. DAVIS. Yes, the law of Julius Cæsar—the law of the master over the slave. I do not know what you think of George Washington, but I shall not scandalize his memory by such a suggestion until, with all the lights before me, I shall have read the law he proposed for the government of the republic, and see, with the light of experience, the rulings of the courts, the opinions of great men, and the necessities of national life, whether we can not find on the face of the Constitution, without making ourselves slaves (for it is to be a slave to be bound to obey the will of any body beyond the limits of law), a republican way to preserve at once the nation and the liberties of the people. (Applause.)

And I say, in the first place, that martial law, whatever else is allowed—and while, in my judgment, the authority vested in the United States, applied in its proper forms and described by its constitutional language, is ample—I say that martial law, in any sense in which it is known to the history of the world, is something which is excluded from our system, and which we ourselves and our forefathers have been careful to exclude, because an arbitrary exercise of discretion could not be safely vested any where in our government. Why, what is martial law? The people are all of them crying out for martial law. If they mean the direction of military power against armed opposition—the direction of the military power to disperse military resistance—why don't they use the language of the Constitution, and speak of "calling out the militia to suppress the insurrection?" But if they use the words "martial law," men of the sword will interpret it in the only sense in which it is known to the history of the world; and Wellington has defined it, "It is the will of the commander-in-chief." Does the President, of his will, possess the power to declare, to inaugurate, or to enact martial law? Unless it is the perpetual law of the republic, it can not be enacted by him, nor declared by him, nor declared by any body that he may authorize to declare it, because the Constitution says—and this is a war for the Constitution as well as for the Union—the Constitution says that "all legislative power herein granted is vested in Congress." Then the President can not proclaim it. Can Congress proclaim it? Why, what is martial law? Mere will, limited by no definition—controlled by nothing except the will of the commander-in-chief—his discretion under the circumstances—his determination to allow and to forbid any thing—the right to judge people by court-martial—the right to order men to be shot down by a file of soldiers for wearing a red and white cravat—the right to disregard the limits of the Constitution. It is blind fate. It is enacted at the dictation of necessity, and necessity owns no law. It is proclaimed in the name of the public safety—it is the annihilation of every guarantee of the public liberty. With us our Constitution, framed by George Washington, is the great safeguard of the country. The safety of the people is the supreme law; but that Constitution *is* the safety of the people—the Constitution is that supreme law. Above it there is no necessity, beyond it there is no law, outside of it there is no security. That Constitution does not use the word martial law. It does not vest authority to declare martial law any where, in any body, under any circumstances. It professes to provide for every necessity of national life, and it forbids martial law; for it forbids arbitrary trials, it forbids any conviction for crime but by a jury, any trial but before the judges and courts it has provided, yet martial law has tried freemen for treason by a court-martial. It forbids arbitrary confiscations of property, yet martial law has already executed arbitrary confiscations. It forbids arbitrary invasions of the right of personal freedom, yet men who had offended against no law *now* are held by martial law, and in spite of the law of the land.

Yet the Constitution has not overlooked grave crises such as that we are now passing through. It provides, under proper sanctions and with proper limitations, for such emergencies; but it carefully forbids this arbitrary discretion, which British freemen found incompatible with their safety in the hands of the king, and which our fathers knew would be *fatal* to our liberty in the hands of the President, and too dangerous to be intrusted even to the discretion of Congress. They knew what martial law was, for they rebelled against it as their English ancestors had.

Martial law is not now for the first time supposed to be necessary; it has been often imposed under that pretext in the old home of liberty, and there it has been repealed by arms and forbidden by laws written in royal blood. Martial law had been thought *necessary* to prevent the dispersion of papal bulls or traitorous libels against the queen. It had been thought necessary for the suppression of sundry great unlawful assemblies, that such notable rebellious persons be speedily suppressed by execution of death, according to the justice of martial law; and Charles I. had thought it necessary for his purposes to issue commissions to try not only soldiers, but other dissolute persons who might commit murder or other outrage or misdemeanor whatever—just as Fremont thought it necessary for the quiet of Missouri to suppress such outrages—by the justice of martial law. But the Commons of England, by the Petition of Right, compelled the revocation of such commissions, and forbade them for the future, because no man ought to be "judged to death but by *the laws established in the realm.*" And our fathers were fresh in this history when they formed our Constitution, and incorporated among its solemn enactments these great prohibitions of arbitrary power which is the spirit of martial law.

The Commons of England had prohibited to the crown the arbitrary right to seize the property of the subject, or withdraw his personal liberty from the cognizance of the courts even on a commitment by the special command of the king, or to try him by commission of martial law, contrary to the laws of the land; and our fathers took from that petition their great safeguards, and placed them beyond and above even the legislative will of Congress.

The Constitution declares that the "judicial power *shall* be vested in our Supreme Court, or in such inferior courts as *Congress* may ordain."

The President, then, can't establish courts-martial.

"The judges of *both* the Supreme and inferior courts *shall* hold their offices during good behavior."

Neither Congress nor the President, then, can make a military officer a judge during will, nor a provost-marshal a civil court.

"The judicial power shall extend to *all* cases under the Constitution and laws."

The courts of law, therefore, alone can take cognizance of *any* crime against the United States.

"The trial of all crimes, except in case of impeachment, shall be by jury."

An Illinois colonel can not, therefore, try any one for any crime.

"No one shall be held to answer for a capital or otherwise infamous crime, unless on a presentment or indictment of a grand jury, *except in cases arising in the land and naval service.*"

A man can not then be tried by any court-martial, unless a soldier or sailor; and Congress is especially authorized to make rules for the government and regulation of the land and naval forces; and but for *this*, no soldier could be tried otherwise than by a court of law.

"Congress shall make no law abridging the freedom of speech or of the press."

Even Congress is prohibited from suppressing any newspaper; how can the executive claim the right?

The fathers of the Constitution assumed that the *habeas corpus* would protect our liberties; but they were unwilling to leave *that* to the discretion of Congress, and they therefore made *it perpetual* by *prohibiting* its suspension even, except when in cases of rebellion or invasion the public safety may require it.

Congress has not suspended it; it is therefore the right of every man confined contrary to law.

It is perhaps to be regretted that Congress did not at its late session suspend that writ in a portion of the United States, and give the President a wider power of arrest than the laws now allow—subject to such safeguards as might protect innocent people from vexatious, or mistaken, or malicious arrests; but Congress thought *otherwise*, and that confined the President to the limits of the *military* power conferred on him for the suppression of the rebellion, and that extends only to persons in arms, or those actively aiding and abetting them against the government. *Such* persons are liable to arrest by military authority under the *law of Congress*. Every one else is amenable only to the *judicial* tribunals and under *judicial* forms.

These provisions exclude martial law and all arbitrary discretion—all exceptional and temporary tribunals—all executive power over the liberty of the citizen.

If the government can not meet the necessities of the time without transcending these limits, then American republicanism has failed.

If a discretionary power over the liberty of the citizen, or a right to try him by exceptional tribunals is to be tolerated, then we are on the eve of a more dangerous revolution than the one we have undertaken to suppress.

We have abandoned the attempt to reconcile liberty with a government of law, national existence with the supremacy of law; we have been driven to invoke the principle of executive discretion in the last resort, and at its will to suspend every guarantee written down in the Constitution to protect the liberty of the individual against executive power.

If it were clear that the national existence demands this sacrifice, while it might be yielded, it would be not the less certain that our system of government has failed.

But if it be not so demanded, and yet the people from negligence, or indolence, or weariness of the perpetual demands on their time and attention for the actual conduct of the government by law and on its own principles, tolerate or invite these intrusions of arbitrary will on the domains of law—whether those intrusions result from the indifference of those in power, or their obedience to popular clamor, then it is not less certain that our government has failed in fact—failed because the people lacked republican spirit, energy, and vigilance.

And if this system of *law* have failed, there is but one alternative. We pass from the constitutional freedom of America to the democratic despotism of France. To *that* all free government tends in this age. Only England and the United States have avoided it of all modern free nations, and they have done so because their liberty was organized in institutions approved by experience, improved by reason, and adhered to by inveterate habit and national pride. Those institutions exclude every element of arbitrary power, and define by law the rights and duties of every man; and when those laws are abandoned, we become as France is. Necessity will be the supreme law—the President its supreme interpreter—its only rule his will—his only limit what he thinks the people will bear. He will still speak in their name, but he will not execute their written will, but what he divines to be theirs.

This is *democratic* government, but it is not *American republicanism.* It is the system now being inaugurated by the connivance or the blindness of the people.

We are treading the path of the Roman republic, the history of whose freedom is unconsciously summed up in a single paragraph of Justinian's Institutes, defining the sources of Roman law. Its whole history is there from the day of its vigor and vigilance, when the *law* was the only rule of action, down to its day of lassitude and corruption, when the weary people had accepted the will of the prince as their only law.

Lex est quod populus Romanus, senatorio magistratu interrogante, veluti consule, constituebat.

Plebiscitum est quod Plebs, plebeio magistratu interrogante, veluti Tribuno, constituebat.

Senatus consultum est quod senatus jubet atque constituit. Namquum auctus est populus Romanus in eum modum ut difficile esset in unum eum convocari legis sanciendæ causa, æqum visum est SENATUS VICE POPULI CONSULI.

Sed et quod Principi placuit legis habet vigorem, cum LEGE REGIA, *quæ de ejus imperio lata est,* POPULUS ROMANUS *ei et in eum omne imperium suum et potestatem* CONCESSIT!!

We have taken our first steps in this downward road. The last six months have laid up a mass of dangerous precedents for future ambition. And after your and my day, when our children shall have inherited the soil without the institutions of their fathers—when it shall have become the settled conviction that the

Constitution is made for times of peace, that necessity is paramount to its prohibitions, that the President's discretion is the judge of the necessity and of the measures required to meet it, the learned jurist of some American Justinian will enumerate as of the past the old sources of the law of the republic—the Constitution and the laws passed in pursuance thereof by Congress—but will tell us that the frequent necessities of the case, the defects of the written law, the inconvenience of consulting Congress—the greater convenience of presidential rescripts, epistles, edicts made for the emergency, in the confidence that the people will approve them—these have become the settled substitutes for constitutional legislation; and he will close his summary by those significant words:

"SED ID *quod Presidenti placuit legis habet vigorem!!*"

We are taking our first steps toward that dark cavern into which the steps of all free nations before us have strayed, and from which only a few have ever returned, and they seared by the fires of revolution and scarred by the chains of their servitude.

These dire calamities we may avoid if we resolutely adhere to the limits of the Constitution.

Let us appreciate the vast difficulties with which the administration is called to struggle; let us not judge harshly their errors; let us accord them a generous confidence; but let us require them to grapple with the difficulties according to law—forbid their recurrence to discretionary devices—rigidly repel usurpation under any pretext, at any instigation, even that of the people themselves.

Consistently with our Constitution there can be no such thing as martial law.

Has the Constitution, then, omitted or excluded any thing necessary to carry the republic through this great crisis?

Let us turn to its arsenal, and survey its arms.

We make the war in the name of the Constitution; that Constitution provides that Congress shall guarantee to each State of the Union a republican form of government. Wicked men in all the seceded States have flown in the face of that great fundamental law, and violated the fundamental principle of all republican government, and inaugurated governments in defiance of the supreme law of the land. It is the case in which the Congress of the United States—not by the law of necessity, not by the law of self-preservation, not for the safety of the people, not because the President or the people think it advisable, but according to the written law of the land—are bound to intervene with all their powers of every kind, and guarantee to the people of those States, loyal or rebel, a republican government, controlling the people under the forms of law; and Chief Justice Taney and the Supreme Court have told us so.

"Unquestionably," they say, "a military government established as the permanent government of a State *would not be a republican government*, and it would be the *duty* of CONGRESS *to overthrow it.*"

It is therefore the duty of Congress *now* to OVERTHROW the usurping governments in ten rebellious States. And how should it be done? Congress is vested with power to call forth the militia to execute the laws of the Union and to suppress insurrection, as well as to repel invasion. The critical gentlemen who impeach the authority of the government to use force, acutely distinguish between the rebellion in the Southern States and an insurrection. That is done under the authority of State sovereignty; it is done at the bidding of sovereigns, and therefore it is not insurrection. The Constitution of the United States, and all laws made in pursuance thereof, are the supreme law of the land, any thing in the Constitution or the laws of any State to the contrary notwithstanding. Let them be as sovereign as they please, when they pass an ordinance of secession it falls before that sovereign clause of the Constitution, and is so much waste paper. (Applause.) Their laws are the acts of a mob, transcending the limits of their power, and flying in the face of the supreme government of the land. If that be supreme, they are subordinate. If Congress is to declare the supreme law, the Ordinance of Secession is an inferior law. If the judges are to be bound by the laws of Congress, any thing in the Constitution or laws of the States to the contrary notwithstanding, then the judges are bound to annul and disregard the Ordinance of Secession, and Congress is bound to interfere the moment a State attempts to override the supreme law of the republic. And how? By authorizing the President to use the military power of the republic to compel the *submission* of its enemies, and by such reasonable penalties and forfeitures as will not exasperate and indurate the hostile population. The

President, of himself, has no power to do any thing. He is the executor of the laws. He has authority to command the army when the army exists, but it can only exist by the law of Congress. He is directed to see that the laws be faithfully executed, but he can execute no law until it exists. Until the laws give him authority to act, he has just as much power as you or I. He is not our master. He has no discretion vested in him. He is bound by the limitations of the law. What that allows him to do, he can do; what it does not allow him to do, he can not do. That is the principle of our republican government. That is the example set by Washington. He was compelled to suppress the Whisky Insurrection, and he did it in spite of the imperfection of the law, but according to law; yet there are some people who think that George Washington did not make a government that would conduct us through an insurrection. The law of 1795 was passed in his administration and at his instance, he having found in the Whisky Rebellion in Pennsylvania that the preceding laws upon the statute-book were inadequate for the purpose. Has any historical gentleman here present ever heard that Washington thought the inadequacy of the law a sufficient reason for usurping a power which the Constitution did not grant? No; he did the best he could. He bewailed the inefficiency of the existing law, but he did not venture to supply it by the law of the public safety, by his own ideas of the public necessity, by usurpation. There would have been no difficulty then, if usurpation could always supply a deficiency. But he, the great Father and founder of the Constitution, went to the Senate and House of Representatives, and laid before them, in his formal message, the deficiency of the law under which he had been obliged to struggle with the rebellion which then threatened the existence of the national republic as much as this threatens its existence, and begged them to relieve his successors from the embarrassment to which he had been subjected. And they did it. They who impeach Mr. Lincoln for usurpation shut their eyes to that law. They who say that the government has no legal authority to use military power to suppress the rebellion, overlook that law. I read to-day the message of the self-styled President of the Confederate States, in which he audaciously says that the President has made war upon them without the authority of Congress. And that very man, when he was Secretary of War, under that very law of 1795, organized those infernal proceedings in Kansas.

What has Congress done? If it has not done enough, it will meet in the course of a few days, and may do more. If it has omitted important measures, it can supply deficiencies. But what it has authorized up to this time is the limit of what it is allowable for the executive power to do. It has passed a law confiscating part of the property of rebels, and therefore nobody has the right to confiscate all their property. Be it right or wrong, wise or unwise, it is not in the law, and therefore it is forbidden. It has authorized, and in my judgment wisely, the confiscation of property used to promote rebellion, and there it stops—there the President is bound to stop—there the military commanders are bound to stop, whether on a foraging party or otherwise. That is the impassable limit of their power. It has enacted that there shall be a blockade of the Southern coast, a cessation of commercial intercourse. That is the greatest stretch of power that Congress has undertaken to exercise touching this subject. In my judgment, it is within its full competency. In my judgment, it was necessary to the accomplishment of the great purpose of preventing military and other supplies from reaching men in arms. It doubtless bears hardly on the loyal men of the South, who swarm there, as I am proud to know, by thousands, but disarmed, and therefore powerless. (Applause.) And I know that, while they feel the privations, they submit cheerfully to the restriction, for over the glare of the conflagration they still see the dawn of the coming day of liberty. (Applause.) These are two things that Congress has done. What else has it done? Placed a magnificent army at the disposal of the President of the United States, charged to guarantee a republican government to those who now no longer know its blessings, and to extinguish the last spark of rebellion.

Is that army an idle pageant—a holiday parade, or may it smite with the sword it bears?

The *law* is the only criterion; the law assembles it—the law defines its rights and duties.

Obedience to the Constitution and laws is all the government has a right to demand.

If individuals refuse obedience, the courts, and juries, and marshals will compel it.

If numbers combine to resist, the law vests the marshal with the right to summon the power of the county to dispel the array.

But when the unlawful combination swells into insurrection, and overmatches and defies the marshal and his powers, is the government to submit? When the ordinary civil, judicial, and legal modes of proceeding have failed, the enemies of the government say that it must stand with its hands by its side and see itself torn limbless. But does the law say that because the courts can render no assistance they can not be opened? On the contrary, when they have been closed, then the law lifts the banner of the republic, draws the sword, and, still waiting and giving its erring children time for repentance, forbids the use of the drawn sword till the President shall have issued his proclamation directing the unlawful combinations—not seceded States, but unlawful combinations of men too strong to be dispersed by the marshal—to go to their respective homes. And that Abraham Lincoln did. (Applause.) And when they did not go to their respective homes, when all the stages of republican forbearance had been passed, when all the forms of law had been duly invoked, and the last remedy was all that remained, he solemnly put forth his proclamation, and by the written law of the land called the children of the republic to its defense—and they answered by the million. (Applause.) Now, what are they charged to do? What is the reason that military force is allowed at all? Because the civil process has been overborne. What is the purpose of the military force? To disperse armed opposition, that arrests the progress of the marshal, that closes the court of justice, silences the judge on the bench, and renders impossible the ordinary and peaceful enforcement of the law. And what do you want the army to do? To hunt peaceful people, quietly residing at home, whom a marshal with a writ can arrest? Are six hundred thousand men, your sons and brothers, in arms for that? How wretchedly inadequate is the cause! For what, then! It is to scatter the array of armed men; it is to break down a combination of armed force—to break the military power arrayed against the republic. When that is broken, what stands between the marshal and the person that the law would punish? The right to draw the sword comes from the fact that the law is arrested. The sword must go into its scabbard when the law no longer meets with opposition beyond the power of the marshal to disperse it. This is not martial law; it is the solemn written law of the republic that armed men shall meet armed men—that they who lift the banner of rebellion shall be met by the banner of the republic—that they who appeal to arms shall be met in arms. And then when they quote to you, as they do, the language of the Constitution, that no person shall be deprived of life, liberty, or property without due process of law, I reply that against those in arms against the government the bayonet is the process of law. (Applause.) A bullet speeds on its mission just as legally as the marshal with his writ. (Applause.) The order to fire on men arrayed against the government is as much the language of the Constitution of the United States as the order of the marshal to arrest the man named in his process. (Applause.) Let them disperse if they do not wish to be dispersed, and if they will not disperse when commanded, then they draw the fire of the government—they call down its thunder upon their heads—they necessitate an appeal to the sword. Let them who draw it perish by it. (Applause.) Why talk about that word which is unheard of in republican lands, but is the home companion of the despots of Europe—martial law; a state of siege—the will of the commander—the necessity of dooming people to death after they have been arrested by the military authority, because vengeance can not wait the lagging process of trial? When the military array is dispersed, they no longer present opposition to the enforcement of the laws; the necessity of the military force ceases with the dispersion; the right to use it ceases with the necessity; the necessity is limited by the language of the law to combinations too powerful to be suppressed by the ordinary processes of law. That is the true, legal, and constitutional position. Is it not better to keep to the statute-book and the Constitution, than to insult the memory of Washington by supposing that the machinery of his government has failed on its first trial?

And when the army is assembled, what may it rightfully do? Is it subject to the caprice of private owners for ground to encamp on, for positions to fortify, for fields to fight on? Must it confine its march to the public highways? stop to pay toll? (Laughter.) Ask leave to trespass on a gentleman's ground before it ventures to deploy against an advancing foe? Is it to assess damages for treading down grass before it can throw up a breastwork to protect it from an advancing foe? If the Legislature repeal, or the company surrender the charter for the road, is the force stationary, or driven to violate the right of property which the Constitution so formally guarantees? So argue the enemies of the republic who profess to be the friends of the Constitution, but their argument displays their ignorance only.

The same right which takes land for a railway track against the owner's will subjects the whole territory to the burden of war at the will of the military authority. It is not a violation of a private right—it is the assertion of the right of eminent domain over the national territory. Is the authority to take a man's property for a railway more imperative than that which allows the government to defend itself against military power? Before the supreme right of the government to wage war—foreign or domestic—State lines are obliterated (applause), every division of private property is obliterated, every individual right is subordinated. It is the right of eminent domain of the republic, asserted in time of war by the highest political authority, the Constitution of the United States. The right to use military force granted in the Constitution must find its interpretation in the laws of tactics and strategy, of projectiles and defenses against them, the formal evolutions of troops on the march and on the battle-field, for these things *are war;* these things are the employment of military force; these things are what they meant who framed the Constitution. Every political authority so construes the Constitution, and the judicial agrees with the political department of the government. The Supreme Court, in sustaining the appeal to arms by Rhode Island, said, "It was a state of war, and the established government resorted to the *rights and usages* of war to maintain itself, and to overcome the unlawful opposition."

The same principle vests a military commander with the right to seize personal property for the use of the government on sudden and pressing emergencies, when recourse can not be had to public supplies—a right which Butler exercised when he seized the Annapolis railway.

He may destroy property to prevent it falling into the enemy's hands, even when he could not take it for his own use.

But beyond these and the like cases, private property of the citizen, loyal or disloyal, is as sacred in civil war as in foreign war or in peace. Rebellion gives no rights of robbery; but Congress may legalize confiscation—it is not a right of war, it is a penalty attached to crime.

But the right to seize and hold persons in arms, or aiding and abetting them, *is* a right involved in the right to use military force. On that the political authority and the judicial authority agree.

"In that state of things," say the Supreme Court (in a state of civil war), "the officers engaged in its military service might lawfully arrest any one who, from the information before them, they had reasonable grounds to believe *was engaged in the insurrection.*"

But when arrested, is he to be discharged at the bidding of any judge on a *habeas corpus?* and can that be prevented only by admitting the President's right to suspend it? On whom does the Constitution confer the right to suspend it? War does not suspend it. Can the President? Blackstone says that in England it is suspended only by act of Parliament. The writ of *habeas corpus,* so far as it is applicable, is issued under the language of the statute, and as long as the act is on the statute-book, there is no power in the United States that can arrest the progress of the writ, except in Congress, which may repeal or suspend the privilege for the time being. Where do they get the authority? If it were not prohibited therein specifically, it would result from their right to repeal a statute which they had enacted. You need go no farther than that. But the Constitution was careful to secure to us the right to the writ paramount to the will of Congress, except in cases of invasion and rebellion, where the public safety might require its suspension. When, therefore, those circumstances occur, that writ ought to be suspended. In my judgment, it was a serious oversight or neglect in Congress at the last session not to have suspended it in some parts of the United States, and in respect of some classes of persons. They did not do it; that is their fault. But that does not vest any right to supply their omission in the head of the executive department of the government. On this great topic the bar of the United States has been smitten with barrenness or vertigo. Only one discussion of it worthy of the subject and the bar has met my eye, and that was from the justly distinguished Professor Parker, of Harvard University. It is greatly to be regretted that so distinguished a jurist should have dropped an ambiguous doubt of the President's right to suspend the writ—that is, to repeal an act of Congress! Blackstone denies the right to the crown; Story confines the right to Congress. But no one has quoted the solemn judgment of John Marshall—a man of some repute in his day, and not entirely without weight among men in our times—respecting the Constitution, which he consolidated on the foundations of Washington. The writ was moved for in behalf of Bolman and Swartwout—arrested by a military officer at New Orleans, brought to the District of Columbia, and there, by President Jefferson, delivered to the court, and committed for trial for treason. The right of the court to award the writ was denied, and, after argument, the court, by John Marshall, thus delivered the judgment on the authority to suspend the writ:

"If at any time the *public safety* should require the suspension of the powers vested by this act in the courts of the United States, *it is for the Legislature* to say so.

"That question depends on *political considerations*, on which the *Legislature* is to decide. Until the legislative will be expressed, this court can only see its duty, and *must obey the laws.*

"The motion, therefore, must be granted."

I think hereafter it will be a stain on any lawyer's reputation to have ascribed to the President that dangerous and unconstitutional discretion.

I presume that argument may be dispensed with after that great authority, but what then? The enemies of the government draw from that an argument to paralyze the military force of the government. The President can not suspend the writ of *habeas corpus*, therefore it can be used to discharge every body! But is there no Congress? or, is it less trustworthy than the President? The business—according to those who wish to destroy the government—of the writ of *habeas corpus* is to let traitors out; its great merit is to turn out those who ought not to be free. I respectfully submit that they have overlooked some very material distinctions. Who is discharged by the writ of *habeas corpus?* The person who is not confined by law. If, therefore, he ought to have been confined, although he come up under the call of the writ, he will be sent back by the judge. An apprentice, a sailor, a soldier can not be *discharged* by a writ of *habeas corpus*. Their error is the assuming that there can be no legal confinement except that which results from legal process. I say that there can be legal confinement which is not the subject of judicial examination and which is not by process of law; and yet unlimited discretion does not exist in the President to arrest any person of whom he may have suspicion; but there are rules prescribing the limits of that power of arrest without judicial process, addressed to the President and not to the courts. That gentlemen who profess to be of the straitest sect of the Republicans should prefer to rush to the dangerous discretion of the martial law and indiscriminate authority in the President without limitation, rather than take the trouble to scan the settled law of the republic as it has been declared by its greatest lights, is one of the dangerous symptoms of the times. The President is authorized by the act of Congress to exercise military power, not against quiet people at home, nor against people who entertain treasonable sentiments, but against *men in arms*, against men aiding and abetting them; that is, against men engaged actually in the insurrection, men conveying military information or military stores, men sending them provisions—against men doing any *act* of any kind to aid the actual accomplishment of armed rebellion. The military force is directed against *them*. Chief Justice Taney, in a case which has become celebrated, and always unfortunate for the doubt which in some minds it has thrown over the law, previously well settled by both political and judicial authority, by his judgment in the case of Merriman, alarmed and astonished the country by declaring that there is no authority to hold a prisoner otherwise than by the leave of the courts under judicial process on judicial evidence. Jefferson Davis is now at Bull Run or Manassas Gap. In the course of a few weeks we trust the bayonets of the republic will point in that direction. (Applause.) We hope that superior numbers, great military organization, abundant military materiel, directed by superior military skill, and inspired by the love of the Constitution as well as the Union, will soon unite and destroy the Confederate army; and when it is destroyed, if Mr. Jefferson Davis shall happen to be taken prisoner, together with 50,000 of his soldiers, we may expect a writ of *habeas corpus* issued from the Circuit Court of the United States at Richmond, under the protection of United States bayonets, to call all the 50,000 before that court and discharge them, because there is not a magistrate's warrant to hold them. (Laughter.) You may shoot a soldier, but if you do not shoot him you can not hold him! Why, has every body forgotten the Dorr rebellion!! On a small scale, in a small but very patriotic State, men raised the arm of rebellion, and the Legislature declared "martial law." That is the first time those ill-omened words—"*martial law*"—can be found in an American statute; the weed has since spread and is eating out better grass. The governor understood it to mean—not discretionary despotic power above law, but the right to use military power to suppress that insurrection, and he did so; and in the course of his efforts, he forced open a house without a warrant of search, and arrested a man who was aiding in the insurrection without a warrant.

The question of the right to do so in this case was taken to the Supreme Court of the United States, and there a judgment was rendered which has acquired more significance by subsequent events than by those which brought it forth. He was arrested by military authority; he was held without process; he was held by a military officer. Was that a violation of the law of the land? What does Chief Justice Taney say in that case—for it was his fortune to pronounce the judgment of the Supreme Court in that case—a judgment which has acquired more significance by recent events than by those which brought it forth.

"It was a state of war, and the established government resorted to the rights and usages of war to maintain itself and to overcome the unlawful opposition. And in that state of things, the officers engaged in its military service might lawfully arrest any one who, from the *information before them*, they had reasonable grounds to believe was engaged in the insurrection, and might order a house to be forcibly entered and searched when there were reasonable grounds for supposing he might be there concealed. Without the power to do *this*, martial law and the military array of the government would be mere parade, and rather encourage attack than repel it."

No wiser words than those have been said on this delicate subject. First, we learn that when military power has been authorized by law—as Congress has authorized it now—the "military officers" might lawfully arrest—the lawful right is therefore *not* confined to a civil magistrate—"any one who, upon *information* before them"—that is, without *sworn* statements of any kind—without legal or sworn testimony—any one "whom they had reasonable grounds to believe"—not any one *proved legally* before a magistrate—"was *engaged* in the insurrection"—not any one of suspicious *opinions*, or *dangerous influence*, or uttering treasonable *sentiments*—but any one *engaged* in the insurrection—that is, when hostility had passed from a mental disposition into the external *act* of hostility; and such persons may be arrested, not merely when openly on the field in arms, but a house may without warrant be *forcibly* broken open and searched, where there were not *sworn* but *reasonable* grounds to believe them concealed.

The rights of the people and of the individual are all defined and guarded in this remarkable judgment; the military power is emancipated from judicial shackles and judicial blindness, and in another passage it is freed from *judicial revision.*

Now, one step farther. The court is speaking of the precise case that we have before us—of a declaration on the part of the President of the existence of circumstances requiring the use of military force—and the question is, whether they are cognizable by the courts at all. The courts proceed according to judicial forms; the political power does not proceed according to judicial forms; it proceeds in an administrative manner, which is equally legal and constitutional, for the Constitution authorizes both. What was Merriman's case? He had aided to burn bridges and prevent the advance of the national troops to Washington, and was actively engaged in that most efficient method of arresting their progress. That case, then, comes within the military right of the President to make a military arrest. What does the chief justice of the United States say touching the right of the court? What was the case of the Baltimore mayor and police commissioners, and their marshal of police? They were at the head of an armed force hostile to the United States, which they had actually used for hostile purposes in aid of the insurrection. *They* were subject to military arrest; but after arrest, were they subject to the results of a judicial process for their delivery, or were they liable by *law* of equal dignity to be held in spite of the courts and beyond their jurisdiction, and by a right of which *they* were not entitled even to judge? Read the judgment of the court limiting its own powers.

"After the President has acted and called out the militia, is a Circuit Court of the United States authorized to inquire whether his decision was right?"

"If it could, then it would become the duty of the court, provided it came to the conclusion that the President had decided incorrectly, to *discharge* those who were arrested or detained by the troops in the service of the United States. If the *judicial power* EXTENDS SO FAR, the guarantee contained in the Constitution of the United States is a guarantee of *anarchy*, and not of *order*.

Yet, if this right does not reside in the courts when the conflict is raging, if the judicial power is at *that time* bound to follow the decision of the political, it must be equally bound when the contest is over."

It can not, when peace is restored, punish as offenses and crimes the act which it before *recognized*, and WAS BOUND TO RECOGNIZE, AS LAWFUL.

A military arrest, therefore, of a person engaged in the insurrection is not only *legal*, but is beyond the cognizance of the courts.

It is true this judgment was rendered when President Tyler was suppressing an insurrection in a free State, and it may be thought doubtful if the same law apply to President Lincoln suppressing an insurrection in a slave State. The learned reader will, under Lord Coke's advice, note the diversity.

There are those who think against a Southern State the government has no rights; there are those who think against a Southern State there are no limits to the authority of the government. But these sentences cover the whole case; not by reasoning on my part from the language of the Constitution, not from judges supposed to be favorable to our side of the case, not in a case made in the heat of the time and in the midst of this controversy, but in a case decided under the presidency of John Tyler—decided when Southerners had the possession of every department of the government; when they had the balance of power in the Supreme Court itself; when it was their power that was arrested and defied, and when they were charged to execute the law and use the military power of the United States to enforce the laws of the United States. This judgment, rendered by one, perhaps, not too friendly to the United States in this hour of peril, is now the very foundation of the law of the republic; put there in the administration of John Tyler, as if to provide for the very case—to exclude controversy under changed circumstances. It does not say that if a man is arrested by the military authority and brought before the court, that the court, after inquiry into the justification of the arrest, would remand him, but that the court has a right to inquire into the legality of his arrest. It does not say that the court is entitled to inquire by the oath of witnesses, by the process of a magistrate. It says, when the President has acted and men are arrested, that the courts have no right to inquire into the subject at all.

The order of the President is conclusive on the courts; he is exercising a political discretion vested constitutionally by law in him, and for that he is responsible by impeachment in Congress. Now we begin to understand the power which resides within the Constitution of George Washington, as well as the limitations which, as with bands of iron, bind it down to the necessities of the public service, limiting and excluding every thing like mere discretion, every thing like mere arbitrary power, and subjecting the liberty of the citizen only to the *written law of the land.*

If, then, after the President's proclamation commanding rebels to disperse and ordering out the militia, a man arrested by the President's order, because engaged in the insurrection, apply for a *habeas corpus*, how shall the law be administered?

By the settled course of the courts, if he show the facts on the petition, the court will refuse the writ.

But if he state a case of illegal arrest, and the court award the writ on the false suggestion, is the military officer to produce the prisoner?

Assuredly not; his duty is to return to the court the simple fact that the person is held by the order of the President for being engaged in the insurrection. *That* is a legal and technical answer to the writ; and the court is bound to take official notice of the proclamation declaring the existence of the insurrection, which carries with it by law the right to use military power.

What if the courts attempt to *enforce* the production of the prisoner? It is the legal duty of the officer to resist force by force. Where one is held by authority paramount to the courts, that *fact* is the legal return. It has been so declared by Judge M'Lean, whose loss the jurisprudence of the country will long feel and deplore; and the eminent tribunal of which he was at once the ornament and pillar, by the mouth of the chief justice, has only four years ago instructed us on this momentous question.

A court of Wisconsin, infected by the theories of South Carolina, undertook to compel by *habeas corpus* the discharge of a person held by the United States marshal. The Supreme Court unanimously declared it "the duty of the marshal to make known to the judge or court, by a proper return, the *authority by which* he holds him in custody."

"After the return is made, and the State judge or court judicially apprised that the party is in custody under the *authority of the United States*, they can *proceed no farther;* and, consequently, it is his duty not to take the prisoner, nor suffer him to be taken before a State court or judge upon a *habeas corpus*, issued under State authority."

But what if the State court appeal to force?

"It would be his duty to resist it, and to call to his aid any force that might be necessary to maintain the authority of law against illicit interference."

"No judicial process, *whatever form it may assume*, can have any lawful authority outside of the limits of the jurisdiction of the court or judge by whom it is issued; and an attempt to enforce it beyond their boundaries is nothing less than lawless violence."

That is the condemnation of the proceedings in the Merriman case; the asserted right to suspend the writ by the President was justly disregarded by the court; but the return showed a military arrest in time of insurrection, of a person engaged in it, by order of the President, and such an arrest was by law beyond the jurisdiction of the court; and the officer was not bound to obey the writ to bring up and hold him for the judgment of the court, and take the chances of adjudication for want of legal evidence, although the man might have been arrested upon secret information which would be sufficient to move an army or fight a battle upon, yet not recognized by a court of justice—it was his duty to give the court information of the *authority* under which he was held, and that excluded the right to inquire whether he was held rightfully or wrongfully.

Now that is the precise condition, in every particular, of the President of the United States, who has seized men in arms against the government, or men who have been aiding those in arms, and is holding them pending the war. There is no hardship in holding a man who is engaged in arms against the government; and the right to determine who is in arms against the government is necessarily exclusively vested in the President when he is directed by law to suppress the insurrection; for, before that can be done, he must ascertain who is making it. He can punish no man for *treason*, but he can slay thousands on the field of battle; he can arrest no man because he has committed treason, but he may seize and hold thousands engaged in the insurrection till it is extinguished!

It is the difference between suppression of rebellion and punishment for treason; the power over persons and property incident to military operations allowed by law, and usurpations of power not granted or forbidden.

The President may occupy my house with armed men for defense, he may pull it down to prevent its sheltering the enemy, but he dare not quarter a single soldier in it without my consent, for the Constitution forbids it. He may pull down a printing-office if required by military operations; he may, if Congress make seditious articles a crime, prosecute an editor; but there is *no* power in the government to prevent him, or others for him, continuing to publish his paper, or controlling its contents by censorship, for the Constitution forbids it.

The property of rebel and loyal are alike subject to the sudden necessities of war; but the President, in conducting the war, has no right over property because it belongs to a rebel, more than he would have if it belonged to a loyal citizen. He is to make war for suppression, not for punishment; *that* belongs to the *courts*.

But within the scope of warlike operations, the President, by the law of Congress, is paramount to the courts. He is charged with a high discretionary political power, of the propriety of whose exercise the courts are incompetent to judge, as they have repeatedly declared; the courts take the law from the political departments in all such cases. They can recognize no government unless the President has recognized it. They can entertain no question of boundary of the United States other than that recognized by the political departments. They can not question the conduct of the President in declaring a state of insurrection or in ordering the militia to suppress it; and it is merely another application of the same principle which forbids them to control, arrest, or judge of the justification of any military acts done within the scope of the military authority confided to the President by Congress. The same law which gives the courts their jurisdiction, exempts such acts of the President from their cognizance.

I pray your indulgence for these dry details; but the foundation-stones of the republic are not polished as the columns and cornices which glitter in the sun, and it is those deep foundations I am exploring.

Gentlemen of the Association, I trust that I have made myself intelligible, but I fear I have wearied you by the dryness of a mere legal discussion, before a mixed and popular audience; but we all profess to be citizens of a great and free government, now engaged in one of those rare crises that every nation has to pass through at some period of its career, and it is well that we should look to the great charter of our liberties, and elevate it, if necessary, in our own estimation, by contemplating the wisdom with which it has foreseen every danger, the amplitude of the powers which it has provided to deal with every contingency, and the discretion it has exhibited in confiding powers to Congress, some with limitations and some without, providing in that way for every contingency that can arise. We may very well spend an hour or two, even if it be in the laborious pursuit of a dry argument, to rid our minds of an impression which has so settled into public conviction among great masses of our countrymen that the legal authority is not sufficient to deal with the existing danger. It takes away half our republicanism to feel that we put down rebels by a violation of the law. It takes away from the elevation, the dignity, and the superiority of the government in dealing with them. It is impudently flung into our faces by the message of Jefferson Davis, who speaks about the tyranny of men who are assailing him. I wish the war to be conducted as a war ought to be conducted, which is to determine the life, and not only the life, but that which is more, the freedom of the American people, the reputation of republican government, its respect, its enduring power, and its influence over the nations of the world. There are those abroad who would rejoice at our fall—there are few who would not, except the oppressed of the Old World. In their name I appeal to you—let not the name of the republic go to Europe humbled by the confession of its own failure. Let it not go shorn of the glory which has made it an ever-present terror to the enemies of liberty abroad. Let it stand glittering in armor, but the armor of the law. Let it stand the emblem of the power of the people to govern themselves according to laws wisely foreseeing danger, without putting their liberties, their lives, and their honor at the discretion of men no wiser or better than themselves—dictators to supply the want of foresight in the people. (Applause.) I am as humble as any man in this assembly, but there is no man here good enough to be my master. I respect and confide in the wisdom, resolution, and uprightness of President Lincoln; but President Lincoln is not good enough for my master. (Applause.) I will trust him with the administration of the laws, but I will not trust him to make them, nor beyond them. I will trust him with all the great deposit of power that the Constitution has placed in his hands—that vast power which, when it is called forth in the magnificence of its military array, blinds the eye accustomed only to the habiliments of peace; but I will not add to it a dictatorship—arbitrary and discretionary powers without the guidance and above the control of *written law.* I protest against it in the name of republican liberty. I protest against it in the name of every limitation in the Constitution under which we live. I protest against it in the name of those Englishmen who defied in arms their king, because he claimed over them discretionary, unlimited power; and of those fathers of the Constitution who in this country followed in their footsteps, were lighted by their wisdom, were guided by their example, and embodied in a law paramount to the varying will of the people the necessary restrictions upon the frailties of human nature. I turn with reverence to the great Northern light of the Constitution, the Newton of this great system—which is heaven while it is order, but will be chaos if discretion rule it—to guide my footsteps in this hour of darkness, and with him I read, inscribed on the foundations of the government, these cardinal principles: first, government by representation; next, that solemn declaration that the will of the majority—not of newspapers nor of public meetings—the will of the majorito—not in a fright, not in a panic, not divined from apparent necessity, but solemnly declared according to the forms of law—shall have the force of law; then, that there shall be a written Constitution, defining and carefully limiting the powers conferred upon the men charged to represent the people, and restricting their discretion. In that great, last legacy of the great Northern statesman, when he was speaking, as it were, to future ages, and telling them, by the grandest enumeration that ever summed up a nation's progress, of the elements of our prosperity, our power, our advancement, and the glories of our achievements—in that great oration he thought it important to call to the minds of his fellow-citizens that these glorious results were not the offspring of mob law, or of arbitrary discretion, of despotism disguised as democracy, which rules across the water, or of military law, or of law made for the exigency by executive usurpation, or of the law of necessity, or of the law of the safety of the people, but that the fountain from which all flowed was the rigid adherence to *written law, to the will of the people proclaimed in constitutional forms.* It was law so enacted that he proclaimed to be supreme. It was the result of a government so contrived and so administered, one that had attracted the admiration and the envy of the Old World, and was the foundation and prosperity of the New, which he celebrated; and in this his great parting legacy to his countrymen, when he prophesied the endurance of the republic, it was because these principles were its foundation, and he thought they would not be shaken. It is because these principles have been departed from that the edifice of the Constitution now reels around us. We must recur to them, cling to them, act upon them, if we would maintain the government that we have received from our fathers. It is our liberty that makes us respected and envied, powerful and glorious—our liberty of law in contrast with that which is democratic license, that mere unchecked, uncontrolled, absolute will of a floating majority, rolling over every barrier, where demagogues lash the people into fury in order to accomplish their ambitious purposes. The peculiarity of the American people has always been its adherence and obedience to law; its hesitation, even under the greatest emergencies, to step across the lines of the law. It is only the revolutionary fever of this latter time that has driven for a moment these American ideas and these American feelings from the American heart. It is now time that we should be enabled to show that we not only have the military power to suppress insurrection, but that we can do it clad in the panoply of law. It is only weighty to those who are not yet habituated to wear it. We have proved it on many a field; let us not throw it off in the day of battle.

The nations of Europe fail in their efforts for republican government because they are not habituated to the restraints of law self-imposed; they are not habituated to subordinate their will of the moment to the calm judgment which has foreseen and provided for the exigencies of the case. They fail because they admit the law of necessity to control the law of the land, and leave a discretion which is despotism to provide for the emergencies of the moment. It is self-control that is the greatness of the American people. (Applause.) It is obedience to their own law that is their power. It is because they have declared that their Constitution is the *salus populi*; it is because they adhere to the rule that the *written law* is the voice of the people; it is because they appeal from the hour of passion to the day of calm reflection, that they have proved themselves worthy of the liberty that their fathers conquered for them. When they shall neglect to adhere to that great rule, when they shall no longer be masters over themselves, when they can not stop in a moment of passion to reflect upon the limits they themselves have placed around their passions for their own good, and reverently bow before the holy laws, they can no longer be the peaceful, orderly, progressive, and powerful republic of Washington. Till now the current of our life has rolled on, quiet and powerful as the Gulf Stream. The storm of party strife has rippled on its surface; the foam of passion has vanished with the storm that caused it; and the great deep, undisturbed, has rolled still, quietly, majestically, and reflecting from its surface the image of liberty robed in law. When you shall upheave its lower depths by the earthquake of revolution, you will have changed its majestic course; you will have dried up the current of your prosperity; you will have closed the sources of your power; and in the place of the vanished waters will appear the lava and scoriæ which strew the soil of revolutionary Europe. (Applause.)

CONFISCATION OF THE PROPERTY OF THOSE ENGAGED IN REBELLION.

Two Letters to the Hon. Justin S. Morrill, a Representative in Congress from Vermont.

MR. DAVIS closely followed, and watched with interest the proceedings and discussions of the Thirty-seventh Congress, for a seat in which he had been defeated, under the circumstances already stated. During the debates in Congress in regard to the "Confiscation Bills," he frequently conferred with his former associates in Congress in relation to those measures, and to one of them he addressed the following letters:

Baltimore, Md., June 6, 1862.

MY DEAR SIR,—I have followed with great interest and some surprise the course of argument in opposition to the Confiscation Bills.

Their opponents seem inclined to trifle with the people, or else they have forgotten the simplest elements of law.

I observe that some respectable lawyers confound the Confiscation Bills with bills of attainder or of pains and penalties!

Congress is rightly forbidden to pass a bill of attainder; and I would forever maintain that inhibition. But what is a bill of attainder?

It is a law performing the office of a judgment. It is a Legislature doing the work of a judge. It is an act of Congress or of Parliament, declaring a particular person guilty of a specified act, and ordering his punishment. The passage of the law places the person just where a conviction and judgment of a court places him; nothing remains but *execution.*

It is ridiculous to call the bills before Congress bills of attainder. They have no one of the penalties of a bill of attainder, and the word can be applied to them in no sense ever recognized in a law-book. They who do so apply the word are either ill-informed, or invoke a prejudice to do the work of argument.

The bills before Congress *name* no particular persons, therefore they *punish nobody.* They declare that certain acts, committed after their passage, shall be punished by confiscation; but, till the act is committed, no one can be declared guilty of it; they do not therefore attaint *any one.* A bill of attainder relates to the *past,* and nothing but punishment remains after its passage. The bills before Congress relate to the future—declare the future consequences of future acts, and leave both the person and the fact to be ascertained after the law declaring the punishment shall have passed.

What excuse is there to confound such a law with a bill of attainder? a legislative judgment on a past act with a legislative penalty on a future act?

The same gentlemen invoke against the bills the clause of the Constitution which declares that "Congress shall have power to declare the punishment of treason; *but no attainder of treason* shall work corruption of blood or forfeiture, except during the life of the person attainted." But what has that clause to do with laws which confessedly provide for confiscation *without* conviction of the person for treason. The most plausible objection to the confiscation laws is that they *do not* make the forfeiture dependent on a previous conviction; it is therefore clear that the clause which defines the consequences of a *conviction* of the *person* can have no bearing on a law which prescribes *other* modes of ascertaining and enforcing a forfeiture. It may be that those methods are forbidden, and, if so, the law must fail of execution; but it is irrelevant to quote a rule of judgment defining and limiting the consequences of a conviction for treason against a law which contemplates neither conviction nor judgment for treason.

It is certain that Congress can pass no law whereby a person convicted of treason can be *sentenced* to forfeit his property, beyond his life, as a consequence of the conviction. Such a law would be void. Such a judgment would vest no title in the government, and the heirs of the owner could eject any one claiming his property under the United States.

But the provision does not say Congress shall not make forfeiture the penalty of any act, nor even that Congress may not make forfeiture a penalty of treason itself; it merely says that forfeiture beyond the life shall not be one of the consequences of a conviction of the *person* for *treason.*

Now the pending bills do not connect confiscation and conviction of the person for any crime, still less for treason.

This clause therefore, whatever it meant and whatever be its effect, has no relation to bills such as those reported by Mr. Eliot. *That* clause does not prove Mr. Eliot's bills to be unconstitutional.

Is there any other clause of the Constitution which forbids such legislation?

It seems to me the lawyers are especially at fault when they refer to the provisions relating to the trial of all crimes by jury.

No *person* can be convicted of any *crime* but by a jury; but these bills do not contemplate any conviction of any person, any proceeding against the person whatever.

Still less can any argument be deduced from the fifth amendment, declaring that "no person shall be held to answer for any capital or other infamous crime, unless on presentment of a grand jury," etc.; "nor be deprived of life, liberty, or property, without due process of law;" for no one is "held to answer" under these laws at all; and the question is whether this mode of depriving them of property is *not a due process of law for that purpose.*

There are various processes of law for depriving persons of life, liberty, and property, and one method does not exclude another method, but each is good in its particular case, while some are forbidden, and therefore are unconstitutional in all cases. A bill of attainder and an ex post facto law are *forbidden.* No person can be held to answer for any crime unless on the presentment of a grand jury, nor tried otherwise than by a jury of the State and district. If, therefore, Congress pass a bill of attainder against Jefferson Davis, or should enact that a Court of Admiralty should try and convict for murder, without a jury, or indictment by a grand jury, that law would be unconstitutional, for it is forbidden. It is a *trial* and a *conviction* without due process of law, and death under it is murder, and imprisonment under it an illegal violation of the liberty of the citizen. But it would be a gross error to say that no one can be deprived of liberty or life otherwise than under criminal prosecution, for then the President has murdered many men in the field, and enslaved many men in the military prisons. For men in *arms*, a bullet is due process of law; seizure by military power is due process of law; they are not conviction, nor trial, nor punishment of the *persons;* they as assuredly deprive them of life or of liberty as a conviction and a sheriff, and they are just as legal as conviction and hanging.

So there are methods of depriving persons of property which

are not connected with criminal proceedings against *the person*, and provisions which define the modes of proceedings against the person, and limit the consequences of such proceedings, have no relation to processes of law not against the *person*, which yet do deprive the person of his property.

Taxation deprives the person of his property, not by any judicial process, but by an administrative process; yet it is a *process of law*, essential to the existence of the government. It is just as rational to quote the prohibition against taking private property for public use without compensation, to prove the unconstitutionality of taxation, as to invoke the prohibitions against making confiscation a consequence of conviction, to prove that there could be no confiscation without conviction.

If taxes be not paid, the failure is followed by seizure and sale, without judicial process; for a small amount of taxes a large estate may be sold; and that is a consequence annexed to the illegal act of failing to pay the amount assessed. Not unfrequently a percentage is added for delay, and levied with the principal of the tax itself. When the sheriff, or the marshal, or the collector sells the property for taxes, that *is due process of law*, and the change of property is in the nature of a *penalty*, and the expenses of the proceedings are veritable forfeitures for illegal acts.

It is, therefore, a wholly unfounded assumption that property is liable to be taken for the defaults of the owner only upon or after conviction for an offense by jury and court. Yet it is this confusion between criminal proceedings against the person and proceedings against property because of a person's acts, which alone lends plausibility to the argument against the Confiscation Bills.

But, so far from being a new method of proceeding, intended to evade the securities thrown around the person against criminal prosecutions, it is one of the oldest forms of proceeding known to our laws.

The slightest examination of the revenue laws of the United States will show that, from the foundation of the government, forfeitures for illegal acts have always been enforced in the courts, irrespective of the conviction or prosecution of the guilty person. The fact has been investigated by the judge without a jury, and the confiscation enforced for eighty years, without any one dreaming that citizens were being punished without either grand or petty jury.

The act of 1799 declares goods entered under fraudulent invoices shall be forfeited; and the forfeiture is enforced by proceeding against the goods, and not the person committing the fraud. Surely the men of 1799 knew what *their* Constitution meant.

By various acts of Congress, goods imported in certain foreign vessels are forfeited, together with the vessel, and the forfeiture is enforced against the goods and vessel, and not by conviction of the owner or importers.

By our navigation acts, licensed vessels are forfeited for being employed in the foreign trade, or when found using a forged or altered license, or if sold to one not a citizen; and all these forfeitures are enforced against the vessel directly, and not by conviction of the owner whose property is confiscated.

It is a highly penal offense to sell spirituous liquors in the Indian country, and the law not merely punishes the person who carries liquor there by fine on conviction, but the boats, stores, places of deposit, and packages of the trader are directed to be searched, and if liquor or wine be found there, all the goods, boats, packages, etc., of the trader shall be forfeited to the United States; and the forfeiture is enforced, not by conviction of the person, but by seizure and condemnation of the articles confiscated in proceedings against *them*. The manner of proceeding for forfeiture under the revenue laws is expressly extended to confiscations under the Indian trading laws.

The laws for suppressing the slave-trade abound in pointed illustrations.

Every person concerned in the trade is declared guilty of a crime punishable by indictment, the penalty varying from a heavy fine to death, according to the acts committed; and side by side with these penalties, to be enforced by indictment and conviction, are classes of forfeiture to be enforced by libel against the thing forfeited. The forfeiture of confiscation depends on the *fact* of a crime committed, but not on the *conviction* of the person for the crime. The fact is ascertained by the appropriate tribunal in either case independently; and it is quite possible that the criminal may be acquitted while the vessel may be confiscated.

No citizen can hold any title or interest in any vessel engaged in the slave-trade; and if he do, it is forfeited by proceedings against the vessel, and the owner is liable to a penalty besides.

The United States vessels are authorized to seize vessels engaged in the traffic, and the vessel and every thing found on her is forfeited except the slaves. *They* can not be claimed by their owner, even though really slaves by the law of the owner's country. It would seem that the slaves are freed by the law; for the owner can not claim them, and no one else can show a title to them. These laws do not apply merely to the African slave-trade, but the same penalties and forfeitures attach to transporting from Brazil or Cuba into the United States persons who are slaves by the laws of those countries. The owner loses his vessel, the master his slaves on the vessel, and the persons engaged in the traffic or in navigating the vessel commit a crime for which they are punishable on conviction; but their conviction is not essential to the condemnation of the vessel or the discharge of the slaves.

In some cases, persons engaged in the slave-trade are guilty of piracy, and suffer death; yet in those, as in other cases, the vessel and cargo are confiscated by process against them, and wholly irrespective of any conviction of the guilty persons.

The precedents of the slave-trade laws are of special interest in relation to the confiscation of the *slaves* of rebels. The necessary form of confiscation is emancipation. The temper of the country would not tolerate the sale of slaves by the United States; still less would it tolerate the exemption of this species of property from any consequences the law may attach to *any* property of rebels. Slave property is the pretext of the rebellion, and the chief instrument by which the revolutionists have *coerced submission to their will.* Sound policy requires that a weapon of such power be broken or wrested from the hands of the enemies of the government, and nothing ought to arrest the blow but the plain prohibitions of the Constitution; for subordination to the supreme law is the condition of national existence. Fortunately, its wise provisions strip the government of no power which a free government ought to wield; least of all does it forbid the confiscation of slaves, and emancipation is an inseparable incident of ownership. Of course, they who call confiscation laws bills of attainder, will call emancipation of confiscated slaves abolition of slavery in the States by Congress. But no *loyal* people will confound the release of the government's title in *the slaves* confiscated with a prohibition against holding *any slave in the State.*

But Mr. Eliot's bill is in one particular wholly indefensible. It violates all constitutional principles of American law in requiring persons to *prove* their innocence. It places the title to negro property of loyal people at the mercy of the government, for it strips the owner of all power to prevent confiscation unless he can prove that he *has not* aided the rebellion, and *that* it is impossible for *any one* to *prove*. Require an *oath* that he has not been so engaged, but do not stain American law with a provision that a man shall be presumed guilty!!

The bill is defective in another particular. It gives the freedman *no* legal protection. He can, the bill says, *plead the law;* but the master will never *sue* him, but *seize* him. The freedman must be the *actor*, and the law gives him no standing in court. The United States is in duty bound to extend to him the habeas corpus in a United States Court which *now* no law gives him; and if these be not done, the act of emancipation will give *no* real freedom, but will be merely a source of endless confusion. Men freed by the law of the special session are *now* suffering in Maryland for want of such provision.

The slave-trade laws were passed in 1794, 1800, 1807, 1818, 1819, and 1820, in the administrations of Washington, Adams, Jefferson, and Monroe. They involve every principle now assailed in the Confiscation Bills, from the confiscation of property for criminal acts of the owner, without conviction of the guilty person, by process of law against the thing and not against the person, to the freeing of slaves for the violation of law by their owners.

It is therefore frivolous to assail these laws on the ground of unconstitutionality. If *any* principle is settled by the uniform practice of the government, it is this principle of confiscation for criminal acts by direct process against the property confiscated, and wholly without regard to the conviction or prosecution of the guilty person.

This review of Congressional enactments may well increase our astonishment at the hardihood of the assailants of these laws. They treat the precedents of the founders of the government with no more respect than they do the Constitution they made. Their objections to the bills are plausible only when the language of the Constitution is perverted and misapplied; and that distortion can only escape exposure by carefully abstaining from all consideration of the contemporary exposition of the Constitution by its authors.

It appears, therefore, from this investigation:

I. That there is no prohibition in the Constitution against making confiscation a penalty for any crime.

II. There is nothing in the Constitution which makes confiscation dependent on the conviction of the person on indictment.

III. There is nothing in the Constitution which limits all confiscations to the life of the guilty person.

IV. The only clause relating to the subject simply forbids Congress to make forfeiture beyond the life of the convict a consequence of *conviction* for *treason.*

V. But it does not say that Congress may not by law confiscate absolutely the whole property of persons who do the acts specified in the bills reported by Mr. Eliot, by proceedings against the property, and not in consequence of a conviction of the person.

VI. And the whole course of legislation of the country has sanctioned the distinction by laws passed under the auspices of the fathers of the Constitution.

If any one ask, *Why* prohibit confiscation in pursuance of conviction, and allow it without conviction?

I reply, The burden of showing the unconstitutionality of the law lies in those who affirm it. They can not defeat it by showing that the Constitution has forbidden it in cases not now contemplated. The question is what the Constitution says against confiscation *without* conviction of the person; and I say it is silent. It limits confiscation as the consequence of conviction, and there it stops.

It is possible a reason may be found for this limitation in connection with a conviction, in the spirit which dictated the definition of treason while other crimes were left to the definition of Congress.

Treason had been the pretext of many bloody judicial murders in English history; constructive treasons were the contrivances of jealous tyrants, or greedy applicants, or fierce opponents.

To limit the crime to open war, to require double proof, to remove the temptations of cupidity from among the motives of prosecution of the person, were *thought* correctives to the political or personal passions which might prompt unjust or revengeful prosecutions to the death. The temptation of covetousness was removed when *conviction* could involve forfeiture only between judgment and execution!

But a confiscation enforced by other process of law than a conviction of the person followed by a bloody end was subject to no such objection, and it was justly left to the wisdom and moderation of Congress for emergencies like the present.

It is quite certain that the restriction of confiscation in consequence of conviction and attainder to the life of the person convicted is not restricted to lands, and still more certainly has no reference to estates tail. They were liable at common law to forfeiture by attainder under their form of conditional fees, though singularly enough a distinguished senator assumes the contrary; they were exempted for a while by the construction of the statute "De donis conditionalibus," but lost their exemption in the reign of Henry VIII.

Such attempts to escape a constitutional difficulty merely discredit all defense of the Confiscation Bills.

The Constitution means just what it says, and the opponents of confiscation try to make it mean what it does not say. Leave that style of argument to them, in common with those strict constructionists who have found the denial of powers to Congress the most effectual way of leaving the government disarmed and powerless in the face of rebellion in arms.

The real explanation of the restriction, as well as of the careful definition of treason, I think I have above given. It indicates the desire to exclude *political persecution*, but not to deprive the government of any power essential to the maintenance of the government against the temptation of ambition or the violence of insubordinate factions.

It is quite certain that neither of the provisions respecting treason prevents the punishment of acts which amount to treason under other names and free from those restrictions. The traitors who burned the Maryland bridges and shot the Massachusetts men on the 19th of April were guilty of treason, but they were also guilty of resisting the laws of the United States, and of a riot, and of obstructing mail routes, and for any of those crimes *any* punishment, *any* confiscation may be constitutionally imposed as the *consequence* of the *judgment*, and one witness may prove them.

Still, the constitutional provision is a salutary admonition in favor of moderation specially suited to these times.

Very sincerely your friend, HENRY WINTER DAVIS.

Hon. Justin S. Morrill, Washington.

Baltimore, Md., June 15, 1862.

MY DEAR SIR,—In the hasty note of the 6th of June, I singularly enough forgot to mention the most pointed and conclusive authority for confiscation by emancipation.

The laws of the United States in the District of Columbia prohibited the importation of slaves for sale or residence, declared the slave imported *free*, and punished the importer by *fine*.

These laws were adopted by Congress from the laws of Virginia and Maryland. They have been repeatedly enforced in both those States. Every gentleman practicing in the courts of the district has enforced the freedom vested by those laws. I have myself, in more than one instance, successfully asserted the claim before the courts of the District and of Virginia, and the Supreme Court has sustained, in repeated instances, the validity of the law. The most recent case that I recall is that of Rhodes *vs.* Bell (2 Howard, 397), decided in 1844.

Those are old laws, passed in the good old times, before men were smitten with madness. But the compromise acts of *Mr. Clay*, passed in 1850, embody the same principle. The law of 1850 forbidding the introduction of slaves into the District of Columbia for sale, declared the slave so imported *liberated and free.* No greater name than Mr. Clay can be cited on any constitutional question, and the name of President Fillmore ought surely to satisfy the most timid of conservatives. Never were laws more keenly contested, more gravely considered, or adopted by abler men than the famous compromise acts of 1850; and it would seem that a Republican Congress might safely err in company with the men of 1850, than be right with the doubtful friends or secret foes of the republic in 1862.

These laws and these judgments of the courts under them dispose of the whole question of confiscation by emancipation, without indictment and conviction of the guilty person, but by civil process on behalf of the *person* freed for the master's illegal act.

The process for enforcing the freedom of the slave was by *suit* in the name of the negro against the owner *for freedom*, in the form of an ordinary action of trespass, and the title to freedom was *vested* by operation of law immediately on the consummation of the act of forfeiture, and the suit was merely the judicial form of authenticating the title the law had vested.

If you see fit to publish this note in confirmation and illustration of the views formerly presented, you are at liberty to do so. Had I thought of this case, so very familiar in my legal experience and in that of every gentleman of the bar in this region, I should have spared you a long dissertation by this decisive authority.

Very sincerely your friend, H. WINTER DAVIS.

Hon. Justin S. Morrill, of Vermont.

THE DEMOCRATIC HUE AND CRY A SHAM.—CONFISCATION AND EMANCIPATION.

ON the 30th of October, 1862, Mr. Davis addressed a very large meeting in Concert Hall, at Newark, New Jersey, on the condition of the country, and directed his argument especially against the "Peace and Recognition" party, then growing up, and threatening to carry the Northern elections. In the course of his remarks (of which only an incomplete account has been taken or published) he said:

"In arms, they (the rebels) will defy you; disarmed, they will beg for terms. But there are persons who are opposed to waging a war of subjugation! With the usual cunning of friends of traitors, they attempt to delude you into the supposition that because the South may be beaten in arms, therefore it will be reduced to slavery. That is at its option. If it shall persistently refuse to accept the benefits of free government under the Constitution of the United States, then the question is presented to us, If men perversely refuse to govern themselves under our laws, whether we shall therefore sacrifice our nation and our independence, permit anarchy because of their refusal, or govern them by law? The question will be then, Shall we be destroyed, and the government broken into a divided territory, or shall we, when there is no other way, subject and keep in subjection those who will neither govern themselves under the laws nor submit to them? I have no hesitation in saying, put what meaning you please on subjection, that *their* subjection means *my* freedom."

Referring to the threats then made that the army would rebel if General M'Clellan were removed from command, he said:

"Democrats tell us that they alone can carry on a successful war. But the War of 1812 had Mr. Clay for its civil leader, and General Scott for one of its military leaders, and neither of them was thought to be much of a Democrat. We then had an Indian war, and that was managed by General Harrison. Then came the Mexican War; and the civil mismanagement of it was done by Mr. Polk, while what was *done in the field* by military chiefs, who won it, was done by Scott and Taylor.

"The nearest approach to a war conducted by Democrats is the present rebellion. *They* got it up, *they* began it, and the generals now in highest command *on both sides* are Democrats. Whether they, or either of them, have been successful up to this time, you can judge as well as I.

"And I will say, on my own account, although it may not be popular to say it, that in my opinion SLOWNESS is not the way to prostrate this rebellion. And say what you please of 'military science,' I think the audacity and perversity of Zachary Taylor at Buena Vista would have stamped out this rebellion a year ago."

Mr. Davis then referred to the Democratic clamor about *habeas corpus*, and recalled the case of General Jackson at New Orleans, of Jefferson in Wilkinson's case, of General M'Clellan's arrest of the Maryland Legislature, and of the late proceedings in Baltimore by Generals Dix and Wool, *all Democrats.*

"All such hue and cry was a sham. They mean *to stop the war.* These men are insidiously referring to particular instances of interference with rights, which, indeed, are, in my judgment, illegal and unnecessary, and hereafter to be rebuked, but which can not *now* be rebuked without endangering the public cause and the safety of all.

"Oh! but they say the President is an 'Abolitionist.' He and his party have abolished slavery in the District. Do *they* mean to re-establish it there? If so, let us know it; if not, why howl? 'Oh! but it is a great outrage upon private rights; and the Proclamation!—it tends to disturb and overthrow all the foundations of society in the Southern States!' Suppose it does. Are *we*, at this time, to prevent any such disaster which *they*, the rebels alone, have rendered possible? I have my difficulties about the Proclamation, but not upon *their* grounds. *Their* objection is not that it is unconstitutional, not that it is illegal, but that it is *dangerous to their friends*, and *our enemies*, in the South. And on those grounds on which *they* oppose it I am in favor of it. 'Unconstitutional!' 'illegal!' grant it. 'Imprudent!' concede it. I always like to concede every thing they say, and then deduce the proper consequences from that with which they attempt to deceive the people. Suppose it is unconstitutional—it is an unconstitutional act that hurts no loyal State. Grant that it is illegal—its illegality does not touch any man in any State *not now in rebellion.*"

Referring to the Emancipation Proclamation, he said:

"If that proclamation is to be effectual, it must have the force of *law*—it must have the force of a national guarantee—not merely of the President's intention. Those who are to be emancipated thereby must *know* that they will be sustained in their refusal to do their masters' bidding. They must know that they are to refuse for *their own profit.* If we give them no *interest* in the result of the war, they can take none. They must be made to know that by the *law* of the land; by the *duty*, not merely by the intention of the President; *guarantees*, not offers of freedom; not declarations of freedom if they can snatch it, but reality of freedom if they will help to win it, shall be maintained to the full extent that the government maintains the integrity of its territory. Until that is done, you have nothing but promises on paper; when that is done, you have four millions of allies on the territory of your enemies." "If Congress at its coming session will recommend the adoption of an amendment to the Constitution declaring that no State shall tolerate slavery within its borders, extinguishing slavery throughout the United States, with a provision, if they see fit, for compensating the owners in loyal States, and such amendment is finally ratified, then you will have gone to the root and core of the matter.

"In my judgment, we ought also to have a Confiscation Bill—one going deeper into the skin than the flimsy thing passed by the last Congress—a bill that will touch the *lands* of the *leaders* of the rebellion; not for life, but in the fee simple. Then why not distribute those lands, as public lands, to the negroes who shoulder the musket? Have they not received bounties before for services in the Revolution, and prize-money for service in the navy? You can not bribe the negroes to fight for nothing, with the certainty of being re-enslaved after the war. He is better off in slavery than that. But wild 'Abolitionists' do not talk in this way. They seem to think you have but to utter a proclamation, and the negro will straightway rise to the clouds and sit in freedom at once. Then there are some, and the President is among them, who labor under the delusion that you can free the negroes and send them off at once to a foreign land. The thing is an impossibility; and if it were practicable, it would not be desirable. The lands in the Southern States must be cultivated, and the negroes will remain there, and will have to cultivate them, even if it were possible, or in the power of the nation, pecuniarily or physically, to remove four millions of them from the country. They will remain until the natural course of emigration in a long series of years may transfer them to some other clime which *they* shall think will be better for them, unless, indeed, collision and a war of races should ensue in the Confederate States if they can accomplish their independence, and in that case they may have another St. Domingo.

"But let us go on with our heroic soldiers, and let such changes be made as the President shall see fit, and with the devotion already shown by a people that has so far transcended in resources the devotion of their authorities in disposing of them—with that indomitable resolution never to submit, or to be content with any thing less than the subjugation of rebellion, the defeat of rebels, and the victorious maintenance of the whole republic, we shall, to-day or to-morrow, or sixty days hence, or in the spring, or next year, or two or three years hence, utterly and forever stamp out this rebellion."

NO PEACE BEFORE VICTORY.

It was in February of 1863 that the movement in favor of emancipation in Maryland began to take definite shape in active political movements to that end. It could only be accomplished by a change in the Constitution of the State, for which purpose the Legislature to be elected in November of that year would have to favor the submitting to the people the question of call of a Convention; and the canvass of the State previous to that election would have to be carried on against all the influences and power which slavery in Maryland could bring to its defense. In these movements Mr. Davis took a principal part; and to that part, and to the efforts of the Hon. J. A. J. Cresswell, was due, in great measure, the complete success of the movement. Mr. Davis visited various parts of the State, and spoke to large meetings at Elkton on the 6th of October, at Towsontown on the 15th, at Salisbury on the 24th, at Snow Hill on the 27th, and at Baltimore on the 28th of October. The election in November resulted overwhelmingly in favor of the measure. At the same election Mr. Davis was returned without opposition from the Baltimore district to Congress, and Mr. Cresswell from the district composed of the eight counties on the Eastern Shore.

Of the speeches made by Mr. Davis during that campaign in favor of emancipation no adequate report was made, or record or account sufficient to enable us to reproduce them in this collection. A *résumé* of some of these speeches may be found in some of the Baltimore papers of the 9th, 16th, and 29th of October, 1863.

In September Mr. Davis had been invited to take part in the canvass in Pennsylvania for the gubernatorial election there. In compliance, he delivered the following speech at Concert Hall, in Philadelphia, on the 24th of September:

Fellow-Citizens of the United States,—The election that is now pending in Pennsylvania and that which is now pending in the State of Maryland will go very far, though perhaps in very unequal degrees, to determine the presidential contest of next year. In my judgment, the election of a Democratic President, or, if he prefer the term, a *Conservative* President, will be the end of the war, and with the end of the war, in my judgment, the end of the Union of these States. It will be the end, likewise, of that great result, though not the original object of the war—the change of the social relations in the rebellious States, which have occasioned our present disturbances. (Applause.)

If it be of any moment to any one here that the conduct of the national affairs shall remain in the hands of those who represent the principles which now preside over their conduct—if there be any one here who thinks that the war ought to be continued until every rebellious weapon sinks in submission to the national authority—if there be any one who thinks it is worth while, after having had experience of the mischiefs that grow from a vicious social organization, that we shall not be twice jeoparded by the same cause when we have the opportunity to root it out, let that person bear in mind that on the vote of Pennsylvania this fall depends, in a great measure, that result. (Applause.)

The gentleman who is competing with your present distinguished and patriotic executive for the position of governor of this Commonwealth does not leave you in the doubts with which Mr. Seymour, and other gentlemen less candid or more prudent, veil their opinion. Here, we understand our opponents formally declare that the Democratic party alone can restore the Union; that it can not be restored by arms; that it can only be restored by peace and conciliation; and that they are the only persons who can so restore it. They were in power when the rebellion broke out. Why did they not arrest it? (Great applause.) They had all the factions that called themselves Democratic united—could have prevented the election of the gentleman who they now say has brought on the war. Why did they not subordinate their internal party differences to the patriotic purpose of averting an otherwise inevitable war? (Applause.) They say that they alone can restore the Union, and by peace. Then why did they break it up? ("That's it," and applause.) They are very fond of asking who is responsible for the war, and I take great pleasure in responding, the Democratic party that ruled the country for thirty years. (Great applause.) And I say that, with the kindliest regard, with the utmost respect, with the greatest deference for the honest members of that party, who, whatever may have been their judgments before the rebellion broke out, saw by the flames of civil war the dangerous path they trod, and joined their life-long political opponents in the right path. They who now arrogate to themselves the reputation and the name of the Democratic party are the mere refuse that remained behind when the patriotic elements withdrew for the defense of the nation. (Great applause.) If, when numbering many of the great men, many of the good men, many of the patriotic men, many of the eminent statesmen of the country, wise in council and firm in action, they could not prevent the war, who will believe that this wretched remnant can stop the war? (Laughter and applause.) Why did the South rebel? Because they had lost the majority of the North. There were a majority still at the North calling themselves Democrats, but they were Democrats that would not do what the Southern men desired. They committed themselves so far in favor of the Southern policy at the North that they lost the confidence of their fellow-citizens of the North, and with their confidence lost their votes; and when they lost their votes, the Southern men could no longer depend upon them to protect their peculiar interest—they smote those that had been their humble servants for two generations past. (Applause.) They taught Southern Democrats that they could ask no humiliation which would not be yielded; and that all who were not Democrats were Abolitionists—stood compurgators for every lie, and enabled them to imprint their hate and fear on the minds of the Southern people; and now that they are spurned by their masters—now the wretched remnant of these discarded allies (laughter), these worn-out tools of a despotic power that has been driven to rebellion—these men venture to assume to lift the mighty mace of the old Democratic party, and say, "We can restore the broken and shattered Union that all combined could not preserve." (Laughter and applause.) Why, men of the United States, what is the rebellion? The Democratic party in arms in the South and in sympathy in the North. (Great applause.) What Democrat does not sympathize with his "Southern brethren?" What Seymour does not speak of them as his "friends?" (Applause.) They restore the Union by pacific means! That means that they will stop the war. We need no one to tell us that. They opposed it in its beginning; they have maligned it to the present day; they have embarrassed its progress; they have vilified those that conduct it; they have struggled against every measure essential to its conduct. Place them in power, would they not effectuate their own purpose, and let it drop? Of course, peace is their policy!

Opposed to the war! Of course they are. James Buchanan,

and those that stood around him, and those that followed him, said, "It is unconstitutional." (Laughter.) Are they honorable men, and can they disavow the words of their chief; or, considering the value the Democrats have always placed upon consistency when consistent with their interest, are they likely to evade the obligation that they have assumed, to treat it as unconstitutional, and therefore to stop it?

Who is their candidate for governor in Ohio? Is Vallandigham for restoring the Union by suppressing the rebellion? Who was their candidate in Connecticut? The namesake of the New York Seymour, and, better than the namesake, an honest avower of the opinions which the other dishonestly concealed. He said that peace and not war, the arrest of bloodshed and not the suppression of rebellion, were the highest purposes that any statesman could proclaim for himself. Where have they elected a Legislature that has not let the cloven foot appear? What say my friends from New Jersey, that I see around me—is Governor Parker for the war or against it? Is the Legislature of New Jerfey for or against peace resolutions? Is the Legislature of Illinois for or against the war? Is the Legislature of Indiana for or against the war? Where have the resolutions in favor of an immediate armistice come from? Where have the resolutions proposing the meeting of a disloyal Convention in the city of Louisville come from? What great leading man, calling himself a Democrat and not now supporting the administration, avows himself in favor of prosecuting the war to the bitter end, till the banners of rebellion trail in the dust? Let him be named—who is he?

John Van Buren thought it would be worth while to go to Richmond, and then to proclaim an armistice. And what is to be done with the armies beyond it?

They all have profound, perfect confidence in an amnesty. An amnesty to men in arms, your equals on the battle-field, as often victorious as you are, inferior in numbers and resources, but nerved to desperation in a gigantic conflict! What is an armistice but something for them to laugh at?

Peace! Scarcely had Mr. Seward put forth another circular of ill-starred prophecies, than, as if to show you how far "our Southern brethren" are from dreaming of peace, they rush two to one upon Rosecrans and make him struggle to hold his ground even. Judge Woodward, I suppose, would appear upon the battle-field at Chattanooga with a laurel wreath on his head and an olive-branch in his hand (laughter) bidding back the foe from that terrific strife. Do they suppose, gentlemen, that the American people are born fools? Do they suppose that their word, instigated by the desire to attain power, will make the people believe what every man in all the rebel region, in every place of authority, loudly denies. Vallandigham told us that every where in his progress through the nether regions he heard nothing but cries of peace and union. Why did he not name the man in authority that hinted at any terms that they were willing to accept or even to consider? Did he not know from the temper of the people of this country, their earnest desire for peace, their weariness of the war, the exhaustion of their resources, the harrowing of their affections by the desolation of the family circle, that any man who would go to the South and bring back terms of peace of any kind, even touching on and bordering upon humiliation, would receive the acclaim of two thirds of the American people. Would he be now skulking over the border in Canada, or would he not rather be treading triumphantly over the heads of thousands of admiring fellow-citizens, as they hail him the harbinger of the peace that he proclaimed? His silence is the falsification of his wretched invention. (Applause.)

Somebody whispered over the Rappahannock the other day that peace was near. They found out the only officer that had been upon the banks that day, and language can not exceed the epithets of scorn and hatred with which he received the mere suggestion of peace—except upon terms that every Democrat is willing to receive to-morrow. (Laughter and applause.) The line of the Ohio, and the Mississippi, and the Potomac, the payment of the expenses of the war and damages for our outrages—who is ready for that here? ("None," "None")—the surrender of Western Virginia and her heroic loyalists? ("Never")—the yielding of Kentucky, that they have insolently called a member of their Confederacy, though no officer would dare set foot within her loyal limits?—the return of the disenthralled and rescued martyrs of Eastern Tennessee? (great applause)—now that daylight is dawning on North Alabama and North Georgia, the plunging them into hopeless and endless night—the return of Missouri to the domination that undertook to drive her from the ægis of the Union!

These are the terms, and the only terms any man has ever heard uttered above a whisper within the Southern country? If Judge Woodward and his like mean that in the face of these terms they are ready to stop the war, then eternal will be the disgrace of Pennsylvania if, knowing that, she elect him for her chief magistrate. (Applause.) If he do not mean to accept these, the only terms that have ever been uttered, then the people of Pennsylvania deserve to be placed in their own hospitals if they accept a man to regulate and govern their Commonwealth who says he is for peace and an armistice when these are the only terms that are possible. (Applause.) An armistice for what purpose? To argue with maniacs? to debate on the field of battle? or to realize the darling idea of the Democratic disunionists to palsy the arm of the United States, to arrest the impetus of its onward advance, to give the people in rebellion time to breathe, the men stricken to the knee time to gain their feet, the men whose resources are exhausted an opportunity to replace them, to break up the blockade, to open their ports to foreign commerce, to give them the recognition that could never be withdrawn, not merely of belligerents, but of parties holding a position competent to deal on equal terms with the United States. How long after an armistice would the recognition of the Southern Confederacy be delayed by England or France? How would they remain idle during the conferences, how long delay to make their arrangements, not merely to mediate between powers, but to intervene in arms? The mere proposal of the armistice reveals the traitorous purpose that remains behind it.

My friends, the reception that you have given our soldiers of the Army of the Potomac shows that you at least are for no armistice (great applause)—that you at least appreciate, without the necessity of argument from me, that an armistice is equivalent to the end of the war, and that the end of the war leaves the South independent. We can all now see where our opponents stand. They are opposed to every measure for conducting the war. Ah! they are opposed to the Conscription Act; yet they do not volunteer. How can we get soldiers? They are opposed to the $300 clause in it; yet they have generally paid the $300. (Laughter.) They are opposed to negro soldiers; yet negro soldiers are the poor man's substitute, who can not pay the $300. (Applause.) They are opposed to confiscation; yet confiscation alone can break the power of the leaders of Southern politics. (Applause.) They are opposed to emancipation; yet emancipation alone can break the oligarchy that has brought on the war. (Great applause, and "Three cheers for emancipation.") They are opposed to discretionary arrests, which they call arbitrary arrests. They opposed them first because the President could not suspend the writ of *habeas corpus*—which was all true. They oppose them now, though Congress has suspended the writ of *habeas corpus*, which nobody denies their right to do. (Cheers and applause.) They opposed them, not because they were illegal, nor because they were arbitrary, but because, though legal, the discretion of the President might think rebel sympathizers suspicious characters. (Cheers and applause.)

They are, then, opposed to all the means of conducting the war; they are, then, in plain English, opposed to the farther conduct of the war. That means that they are in favor, whenever and wherever they can get in power, of throwing themselves against the government in the conduct of the war. They attempted in Illinois to take the military power from the hands of a loyal governor. They have attempted every where to elect disloyal governors pledged to embarrass the United States in the enforcement of the laws. Seymour, knowing that the riot would embarrass the government of the United States, stood paralyzed and powerless before his "friends." (Laughter.) They discussed the propriety of recalling from the army the contingents of the various States. The candidate for Governor of Maine, lately so overwhelmingly beaten by that patriotic State (applause), was asked whether, in the event of his election, he would recall from the armies the troops of Maine. Instead of repelling with indignation a question which was a humiliation to any man except a traitor, he said, "When Governor Seymour recalls the troops of New York, and the Governor of New Jersey recalls the troops of New Jersey, then I am ready to recall the troops of Maine." That marked him for a traitor; but he is mistaken in supposing that any regiment or any company of the troops of Maine would obey his illegal and treasonable order. (Great applause.) Doubtless he thought they would obey, and that order would have been issued the day after his election. The people took care that he should not have the opportunity. (Laughter and applause.) Let them get the control by any accident, by any thoughtlessness, by any cowardice or timidity, by any weariness of the war or impatience of taxation, in the House of Representatives, and instantly every war measure will be clogged in that House; appropriations will be resisted; conditions will be annexed; the repeal of the laws that they have been assailing will be compelled by refusing supplies to the government; the government will stand paralyzed in the presence of its armed enemies.

If these are their purposes, then how are we to treat them and how are we to conduct the government? In my judgment, fellow-citizens of the United States, we all have a common interest in this great struggle, and what is the interest of Pennsylvania is the interest of Maryland. (Applause.) The line that so long has been of ill omen, I take it, was abolished by the day of Gettysburg. (Great applause.)

The current of events is daily sweeping away the only mark of disunion between Pennsylvania and Maryland—their internal recognition of slavery, or their refusal to recognize slavery. We stand together, and ought to stand together as one man in maintaining the integrity of the government, which more entirely crushes us than any other portion of the Confederacy if it fall in ruin about our ears. How, then, shall it be maintained? I say, first, by filling up the depleted ranks of the Army of the Potomac. (Great applause.) Whether the government see it or not, from the beginning of the war to this day there has been but one decisive point upon which one decisive battle could end the war, and that has been Virginia. It has never been a question of marching to Richmond; it has been a question of dispersing and destroying the army of General Lee, and that has never been difficult to find. What the government has needed is a singleness of purpose, bending its unbroken energies to the annihilation of that army, and with it would crumble the Southern republic. (Applause.) Victories on other points are victories of detail; victory on that point is decisive, final, and overwhelming. Peace will follow the destruction of that army; the war will endure until that army is destroyed. An armistice will not annihilate it; a mediation will not paralyze it; no election of a Democrat will do any thing except accomplish its purposes, without bloodshed, for it. The war drags its length now along because a Presidential election is only a year off, and the rebels of the South count on having their friends in office. ("Never, never.") If they have to make terms, they know the terms will be better with a Democrat than with men who are devoted to the integrity, and the power, and the perpetuity of the republic, and therefore they mean, so long as there is a man left in the Southern country, and as much as in them lies, that there shall no semblance of peace appear until a Democrat mount the presidential chair.

The way to peace, therefore, fellow-citizens, is over the battle-field, and there is no other path. If a lion lie in that path that you are afraid to meet, or one too powerful for you to meet, then give up the war. If you are unwilling to make that admission, then prosecute it with every energy that you can summon, of money and of men; with no hesitation; no stinting; no critical spirit; no inclination to find fault: mourning errors, not casting them in the teeth of those in authority; countenancing them with your earnest support, with the firm conviction that because there are traitors in the North, every loyal man must double himself in strength, energy, and devotion. (Applause.) And when they menace you with insurrection here, tell them the sooner it begins the sooner it will be ended. (Great applause.) Let them understand that it is wholly immaterial to you whether they begin the civil war now, or two years hence, when, having under false pretenses crept into power, betrayed the nation, negotiated a hollow semblance of peace with the Southern Confederacy, and brought discord to every Northern door, the beginning of desolation, the introduction of civil war, the impossibility of keeping the residue of the States together, will be manifest to all men—the sooner the better. That party has always been magnificent in bullying—do not be frightened by their violence. (Applause.)

But how else, gentlemen, shall you end the war? More than a million of men of the white race have volunteered their services in defense of American liberty against an oligarchy of slave-holders, and until recently their farms have been cultivated in quiet, their laborers have been untouched; they have suffered by the blockade, they have suffered by invasion when our armies touched them; the great mass of their agricultural labor has gone on as regularly as in the halcyon days when cotton was king. I propose to invade the quiet realm of this discrowned king. (Applause.) There are four millions of men in those regions on our side. (Applause.) Who opposes the arming of them except the *Democratic Conservatives?* They are slaves. The President has proclaimed them free. (Applause.) That paper confers no title; it can only be made a title by arms. The negro's arm is ready to execute it. Why shall he not be allowed to do it? (Applause.) "It is humiliating to white soldiers to serve in the same ranks with the negroes!" What say the Army of the Potomac to fifteen or twenty thousand to help them in the next great fight? What said General Banks at Port Hudson? What said General Gilmore at Fort Wagner? (Great applause.) Just what George Washington of the Revolution said. (Applause.) Just what Andrew Jackson at New Orleans said. (Applause.) Just what Perry on Lake Erie saw. (Applause.) Just what Barney, with his negro men mingled in with his white men at Bladensburg, saw, when other men ran away. Men are men in spite of the skin, and deeper than the skin. (Applause.) The first martyr of the Boston massacre in 1770 was a negro slave leading the white men. (Applause.) One of the heroes of the battle of Bunker Hill, living forever in the historic canvas of Trumbull, and living more immortally on the page of Bancroft, was a negro. (Applause.) No battle-field of the Revolution that was not stained by their blood. The men of that day shrank at first, and came to it afterward. They formed no separate regiment; they mingled in with the rank and the platoon of their "white fellow-countrymen," as Andrew Jackson called them. (Applause.) From the days of the Revolution to the days of the War of 1812, prejudice was silent before reason—national necessity and national interest. It was only when the cotton aristocracy arose that common sense was driven from the minds of men. What do they fear half so much as a negro army marching through the cotton-field?

Gentlemen, without a negro army an attempt at emancipation is idle. The President has proclaimed emancipation. A proclamation is a breath, or printer's ink. It dies of itself unless there be something living behind it. In point of law, no court will hold it a valid title to freedom; that is my judgment as a lawyer. I may be wrong, but it is my judgment. If the negroes of the South are to render us any material aid in the suppression of the rebellion, they must have a title to freedom that they will understand to be effectual, and they know that the proclamation is not effectual without something following it—a law of Congress and arms. They must farther be relieved from the idea, which has been most unfortunately countenanced in certain high quarters, that after they have fought the battles of liberty, and have aided us to win back our territory and consolidate our empire—that after an indefinite period of service upon public works in the malaria of the South, and on the canals of the Northwest, they are to be banished from the land in which they were born and which they have aided to save. Banish, gentlemen, from your minds that humiliating and unworthy idea. (Applause.) Make up your minds that if they are to be soldiers, they are to be freemen, with the rights of free laborers, protected by the laws, recognized by the United States in their position, guaranteed the remedies of the courts of the United States, and armed and drilled to make their rights effectual. (Great applause.) And how shall that be done? On the theory of our "conservative" fellow-citizens? They say that, true, the South is in rebellion, but the State governments remain; their governments are in existence; they have the right, the moment they lay down their arms, to be recognized by the United States as the only persons entitled to speak in behalf of the Southern States; that the men now in authority are the governors, the legislators, the judges, the magistrates, the sheriffs of the rebel States; and that what the President should do is merely to offer an amnesty to screen individual offenders, and open his arms to receive those who have just now had the sword pointed at our bosoms, not merely as citizens obedient to the law, but as the representatives and constitutional governors of the loyal people of the rebel States. That is the Democratic theory of the restoration of State government in the rebellious States. Where does that lead you? Suppose it to be accomplished; that is what they mean by "the Union as it was," with the old coalition of the Southern secessionist and the Northern Democrat to govern the country and divide the spoils. "The Union as it was" is their watch-cry. Do they mean that they will restore Western Virginia to Eastern Virginia, bound hand and foot? Do they mean that they will recognize the fugitive Harris as Governor of Tennessee, and his scattered legislators as her Legislature? Do they mean that they will recognize the men who assume to represent Kentucky in the Southern Confederacy as the proper representatives of the people of Kentucky? Do they mean that they will bring back the fugitive Governor of Missouri? That would be "the Union as it was." That would be to recognize as the parties entitled to govern the rebel States the rebels who now govern them. They are the people who, the Democrats say, are now entitled, and only entitled, to be listened to. I pray you pause and consider gravely this great subject of the restoration of State governments under the Constitution.

Are the American people ready for such a restoration as that? ("No, no.") Is all that the Union has accomplished by a hundred thousand of its dead sons, and hundreds of thousands of desolate men and women at home mourning them, to recognize an insolent pretense, which never for a moment has been a fact? If that be not so, then "the Union as it was," in the sense of the men who call for it, is an impossibility. (Applause.) They delude the people with vain words when they speak of "the Union as it was." Call the dead to life; clothe his bones with his dissolved flesh; restore the soul to the soulless eyes of the thousands that have fallen martyrs upon the battle-field, and then you can restore the Union as it was. (Great applause.) The attempt is to begin a new civil war. When you order back West Virginia, she will turn to you the points of her bayonets that are now on your side—and justly. When you recognize the butchers of East Tennessee for its republican government, the very ghosts of the murdered dead will lead the living men to battle against you. (Great applause.) When you talk of recognizing Kentucky and Missouri as States of the rebellion, you will be overwhelmed by ridicule that no man can stand up against. And that is "the Union as it was," in the words of the Democratic orators. Why will they perpetually come before the people with a lie in their mouth and delusion in their right hand?

"The Constitution as it is, and the Union as it was!" I am for the Constitution as it is, and that has altered the Union from what it was, and it will stay altered until eternity. (Great applause.) If the "conservative" gentlemen attain to power, it will stay altered in fragments of shame to us and our posterity. If those who are now in power, and their successors, continue to retain the management of the government on its present principles, it will continue as it is, excepting so far as it is bettered, according to the Constitution as it is. (Applause.) And when I speak of the Constitution as it is, I mean as it came from the hands of George Washington, and Alexander Hamilton, and James Madison, not the wretched, crippled humpback that has been presented before our eyes, the result of a cross between the Northern and the Southern Democrat, an ill-begotten and shapeless monster that they have contrived for their purposes. Born without arms to use or legs to move with, and with a head that could only contrive mischief, and for every thing else was impotent; but that Constitution, in the full vigor of its humanity, as it came from the hands of George Washington, adequate for every contingency of national life, speaking so plainly that those who run may read, and only the perversely blind can misinterpret. (Great applause.) Ay, the Constitution as it is, which says that Congress may call forth the militia and use the armies of the United States to suppress insurrection, and therefore the war is constitutional according to the letter of the Constitution as it is. That Constitution says that Congress shall guarantee to every State in this Union a republican form of government, and it is under the Constitution as it is that the armies now march to remove oppression and restore republican liberty. (Great applause.) And it is the Constitution as it is which declares that Congress shall have a right to pass all laws necessary and proper to carry into execution all the powers vested in it or any other department of the government; and, therefore, whatever Congress may think in its judgment is necessary to restore and guarantee republican forms of government in the rebel States, that law, according to the Constitution as it is, Congress may pass. (Great applause.) I am for exerting the power. I do not believe, my friends, that there is any arbitrary power vested any where in the government of the United States. I think the Constitution a provision made for the great necessities of national life by men who had just come out of a war of seven years, and anarchy of twelve years—wise men who knew the necessities of public life, and were not careful to bind the arms of the nation when its being is at stake; and they provided that in the event of invasion or rebellion, or public danger, the writ of *habeas corpus* might be suspended. That meant, not that the President should be vested with an arbitrary and reckless power to arrest any man at his will and pleasure, irresponsible to the people and answerable only to himself, but that the exigencies of national life, in the conduct of war, rendered it impossible to rest on the mere judicial process for enforcing the laws. It is impossible to let the public safety depend upon the possibility of proving by legal evidence a participation with public enemies; and, therefore, as the lesser of two evils, as anarchy stood upon the one side, and discretionary power, under the guardianship of the people, temporarily vested in their chosen officer by them, was the only danger to be encountered upon the other—as they trust the President to determine who are in rebellion, and with the command of the armies for its suppression upon the field of battle, and to sacrifice the lives of thousands because they are dressed in gray uniform, and not as we are, in blue, so they give him the discretionary power if in his judgment any one, Democrat or Republican, is dangerous to the public peace from any reason, he may not *punish* him, not try him by court-martial, not incarcerate him in the penitentiary, but he may arrest him to prevent mischief, and hold him till the danger is past. (Great applause.) That is the Constitution as it is, and not as the Democrats construe it; and I am in favor of applying its powers to the letter and in the spirit, and to the bitter end of the war.

I warned the government a year before they got an act of Congress to suspend the writ of *habeas corpus*, that undertaking to do it without that authority would raise a storm that they could not meet. Gentlemen, no man deplores more than I do the accuracy of my reading of the tenderness of the American people for the forms of law. It has cost us, and we are this day suffering from it, the State of New York, the State of Pennsylvania last year, the State of Ohio, the State of Indiana, and the State of Illinois. Now the power is upon the just basis of law. Rational men will yield obedience to it. None but traitorous conservatives will continue to howl against it. (Great applause.) Every loyal man knows the President will not use it for oppression.

I turn to consider that other great power and duty—the guarantee of republican governments to the States. That touches a question which ought to have been decided by the last Congress, which our friends are singularly timid about meeting. In my judgment, the sooner it is met the better, and the sooner the grounds upon which we act are ascertained, the better for all parties. I regret that, in dealing with the question of reorganizing the State governments, eminent gentlemen have used words which they, I think, will regret hereafter. They speak of the Southern men in arms as being alien enemies. The President has never so called them. Congress has never so called them. No law upon the statute-book so treats them. No official document has ever hinted at that character. To call them alien enemies admits that their secession was effectual to give them the right of independence in the eye of the world. It admits they are not traitors, but enemies. I say they are traitors and not enemies (applause); citizens under the law, against which they are illegally waging war, not foreigners waging a war upon equal terms with men who are foreigners to them. They war with the rope around their necks. (Applause.) Their victory can be decorated by no laurel in history. Where she speaks of their deeds of valor, it will always be with a melancholy tear over the cause in which it was exhibited. It will always be accompanied with the bar sinister, to mark that the cause was illegitimate, the purpose iniquitous, the object unjust. You sanctify them when you call them alien enemies. Keep them to their real character—traitorous enemies of their country. (Applause.) And when the right of conquest is referred to, as it has been by a very distinguished and a very able gentleman, to find out the methods of dealing with the reorganization of the State governments, I desire to say that any man or any party that claims over the Southern States, after the insurrection has been repressed—that is the legal language, gentlemen, of the statutes of the United States—any party that after the insurrection shall have been repressed shall attempt to consider them a conquered people, that party will destroy itself, or, if it be successful, it will destroy republican liberty. It is a doctrine unknown to the Constitution of the United States; it is beyond the purview of American principles of government; it recognizes what no responsible statesman has heretofore recognized or ought ever to recognize, the possession of absolute, arbitrary, despotic power in the government over a portion of the States as the result of its military operations to suppress an insurrection. It places the government above the law to enforce the law! The law speaks differently; the Constitution speaks differently. Under them both we have to act. We owe it to the wisdom of our forefathers to recognize that they have left our hands as free to deal with rebellion as wisdom will sanction, and every power in our hands which tends to accomplish the object. We must deal with it in their mode. The States are, by rebellion, extinguished and become Territories! says a very distinguished and eloquent statesman. Then how can it be that the Constitution requires Congress to guarantee to every State a republican form of government, if the destruction of a republican form of government in the State converts it into the condition of a Territory, and subjects it to the arbitrary power of Congress? They did not so deem it. They regarded the States as continuing, perpetual elements of our Union, and their citizens always beneath the Constitution. But they draw the broad and marked discrimination between the individual rights of the citizen, the existence of the State as a body politic, and its capacity by reason of its want of organization to exert its political powers. If a man in South Carolina comes to Philadelphia, no lawyer can plead "alien enemy" to his suit. If I go to South Carolina, I have all the rights of a citizen of South Carolina. The officers of the United States, their postmasters, their collectors, their marshals, are still provided for by law, and some exist; the statutes are still upon the statute-books; it is still illegal to import any thing within those limits without paying the duties; the courts exist wherever the President names judges. They are in every particular still under the laws of the United States, described on their statute-books, nowhere except as States of this Union. When men are to be tried for treason, they can only be tried in the courts of the United States, according to the laws of the United States, by juries summoned according to the laws of the United States, under the Constitution of the United States. But these clauses do not fetter the hands of the Government, as stupid Conservatives say when they quote the Constitution to prohibit the marching of an army to remove opposition to the execution of the laws. When the opposition is dispersed, then the reign of the courts is restored and the day of punishment may come. But with reference to their political franchises, the wisdom of our forefathers has placed them a step farther off. Our "Conservative" friends are altogether too eager to have their votes for the next Presidential contest when they propose to regard the existing authorities in the rebel States as entitled to be recognized as the authorities of the States within the Union. That, doubtless, would be very convenient if they could get the votes of half a dozen of the Southern States, and make up their deficiency of votes in the North in that way, and thereby elect their "Conservative" President. Fortunately, the law is not so unwise. There can be no electors of President from any State, unless there be a government organized in it recognized by the government of the United States, whose officers have sworn obedience to the Constitution of the United States. (Applause.) Till that, there can be no authority any where exerted. Do those men now in authority in the Southern States constitute the State governments under the Constitution that they repudiate, that they say is annulled, that they have taken up arms to destroy? On the contrary, the very first act in secession was not to carry their territory from beneath the laws of the United States, but to tear down their own State governments and institute others. Those that they tore down were republican governments in the sense of the Constitution. Those that they have established are a mob in the form of the government, and the rebellion organized to execute its purpose, entitled to recognition by nobody. To participate in their government is, by the laws of the United States, the crime of high treason. Their governor, by merely accepting his position, renders himself liable to trial, conviction, and hanging. Every officer of theirs is aiding to promote the war. They are a band of traitors, usurping rights over citizens of the United States. The armies of the United States move to strike that power from their hands, and restore it to loyal men; and in doing that, the only arbiter of what government shall be recognized, the only arbiter of who shall be treated as a governor, or a legislator, or a judge of a rebel State, is the United States in Congress assembled. (Applause.) Till they shall recognize another government, there is no government. In the absence of a State government, there must be either anarchy, or a legislative and executive power somewhere. Those that have abdicated can no longer be the government of the State. The right and the duty to guarantee a republican government is vested in Congress. Congress is therefore charged to take every measure that is necessary to restore republican government. Pending the interregnum, Congress is the only legislative power for the State, the President is the only executive power for the State. They can, under a provision which I have already quoted, pass any law in their judgment necessary to consolidate the republican government which they are about to establish, and they have the sole and absolute discretion of determining who shall and who shall not be recognized as the government of the State. Nay, gentlemen, so far is this from being mere theory or a fanciful disquisition, it is now the policy on which the administration has acted. John Letcher was playing governor at Richmond when the President of the United States recognized Pierpont as the Governor of Western Virginia, and the Senate of the United States and the House of Representatives admitted their representatives to the floors of Congress. When men speak of any other mode of adjustment, they fly in the face of the actual conduct of the government. It is not my theory; it is the policy of the administration. They have already solved the problem; they have already pointed out their course of action; they have already declared their interpretation of the Constitution to be that which I have put upon it, that they are acting as the guarantors of republican government in States where Republican government has ceased to exist, and that they alone are at liberty to re-establish it, that they alone are entitled to determine who are the legitimate possessors of power, and that they have done in the case of Western Virginia. Had John Letcher been the Governor of Virginia, and merely an erring mortal, going a little too far in the tracks of treason, as our "Conservative" opponents would lead you to suppose, then there could be no recognition of any other State government any where within the borders of Virginia. The President and Congress did not so treat him. They treated him as the head of the Richmond mob; they treated him as the leader of the Virginia rebels; they treated him as a traitor who had pulled down his own State government, and then undertook to usurp illegal authority over his fellow-citizens. It is in that light, and that alone, that he stands before the government of the United States.

Now, gentlemen, let us see how this will work out, and whether this is not the safer law and the only one possible path for us who mean to accomplish something practical, permanent, and blessed by the suppression of the rebellion to pursue. The President has proclaimed the abolition of slavery. (Applause.) If it rests on that proclamation, let us trace it out a little. Suppose the war to be ended, and our "Conservative" friends to be in power, and Mr. John Letcher to be recognized as the Governor of Virginia, and Mr. Bonham as the Governor of South Carolina, and so on through the rebellious States; the existing Legislatures remain; the existing distribution of political power remains; the existing Southern courts remain; the existing organization of the Southern militia remains; the existing debts, the war debts that they have incurred to fight us, remain. They will be at liberty to assume, as most of them I believe have already done, the Confederate debt of the rebel States. That, therefore, becomes a permanent burden upon the people of the United States in common with our State debts and with our national debt. Those men thus reinstated in power by our act are the only persons that can have a word to say on the subject of whether the proclamation is or is not valid as law. What do you suppose the judges of South Carolina would say on that point if a negro were to claim his freedom under it? It makes it at once a dead letter. It is altogether frivolous; I say farther, gentlemen, it is something very much like a cowardly evasion when men who wish to avoid that inevitable consequence of that form of reconstructing the governments in the rebel States say, "If the proclamation is valid, it will be held valid by the courts; and if it is void, it can not be made valid." Neither proposition is of the courts of the rebel States in the hands of the true. If it were as valid as any law upon the statute-book of the United States, if it remain a mere proclamation and be left to the tender mercies of rebel judges, it will be annulled and disregarded, for they are the only judges of what is the law of their own State, and therefore when you shall have turned the negro free, if he should attempt to assert his freedom, their process will hang him; their process will shoot him; their process will hunt him down by the bloodhound; their process will drag him backward into slavery. If he attempt to rebel and show himself too strong, they will call on the government of the United States to send the Army of the Potomac to reduce him to slavery under the laws of the States; and a "Conservative President would only be too happy to have the opportunity of manifesting in that manner that he was opposed to '*negro equality*.'"

Neither is the other hypothesis true that if it be invalid it can not be helped. As it now stands, in my judgment the Supreme Court of the United States will not recognize it as law; the United States courts can not enforce it. But it can be helped by an act of Congress under its power to legislate for the States pending the execution of the guarantee; it can be helped by an act of Congress in the execution of its guarantee of republican government if it considers that the continuance of these men in slavery, and the power of the masters over them, is incompatible with a permanent consolidation of republican institutions in the States. (Applause.) That is a political, and not a judicial question. That will be decided by the Congress of the United States and the President of the United States, and the courts of the United States will follow the judgment of Congress and the President. Make it an act of Congress, and then you have made it a law. Place on the statute-book judicial process, and then you have given the freedmen the courts of the United States to protect them against the local tyranny. Make it a law of the United States, and then the armies of the United States stand, not to return them to their masters, but to repel their masters from them under the law. (Applause.)

Let the Conservative howl; this *is* the Constitution *as it is;* this is the execution of the guarantee that George Washington placed in the Constitution; this is the condition to which the States by rebellion have brought themselves within the legitimate, express legislative power of Congress, to deal with them and their property, and the organization of their society, on such principles as Congress shall judge to be not incompatible with the permanence of republican government. It is frivolous to say that we can arm a million of men to prostrate half a million in the dust, taking away precious life, to restore republican government, but we can not restore freedom to slaves in the same cause. Life is protected against illegal aggression in the Constitution as well as property, even of the most unquestionable character. Life is not less sacred than slavery. Can we destroy life to repel from power those who have usurped a power to create unrepublican forms of government in the rebel States? and are we to be told, if Congress shall be of the opinion that the continuance of these men in slavery is an insuperable barrier to the restoration of republican government, if they shall be of opinion that the resources of the government are not enough to put down the rebellion without their aid, if they are convinced that they can not get their aid without promising and securing to them freedom, and that they can never be free unless their wives and their children, their old and their young, are free with them—are we to be told that the power of Congress is limited with reference to that species of property—that it must stand a perpetual obstacle to free government? Why, fellow-citizens, it is to construe the Constitution in the interest of the rebellious faction that by coalition with Northern Democrats has governed the country to its ruin for thirty years, to adopt it. (Applause.) They have always been the strict constructionists. George Washington was the rational constructionist. They have been always in favor of tying the government of the United States hand and foot, because they saw that it had strong feet to trample down rebellion, and long arms to reach it. (Applause.) Their rebellion has, I think, removed the cobwebs from before the peoples' eyes. They now begin to see the policy that lay at the bottom of the strict construction of the Democratic school. They begin to understand that they were barriers thrown up to protect the institution of slavery. They begin to understand that they were the deliberately prepared bulwarks for a premeditated rebellion. They now begin to see that James Buchanan was only repeating the lesson he had heard from Jefferson Davis when he said there was no power to invade a State, no power to make war against a State, no power to coerce a State; the States must be left to their good pleasure, to do ill if they so pleased. That was not the Constitution that George Washington framed, nor the one that the early men of the republic acted upon, nor is it the one that we now, in the presence of a great national necessity, will act upon. We will restore it to its power, and act upon *that*. Oh, but they say, if you refuse to recognize the existing State governments, they will refuse to lay down their arms. Nobody but a fool expects them to lay down their arms till they are knocked from their hands. (Great applause.) They are out of Eastern Tennessee now. How did they get out? They are out of Western Virginia. How came they out? They are out of one third of the residue of Virginia. How came they out? If the re-enforcements pour on rapidly enough, they will soon be out of Georgia and Alabama as well as Mississippi. (Applause.) Where would a "Conservative" President go to find the Governor of Mississippi or Louisiana now? When we are done with the rebellion, there will be no governments, even in form, to recognize, if the President do his duty. (Applause.) The traitors will be hunted from their hiding-places. If the President executes his duty, the first men to be sought out and arrested are those who have held civil office in the rebellious States. He will seize on the governor first, and the constable last, in the order of their precedence, and, when he shall send them to jail, he will tell them not to stand upon the order of their going, but to go at once, and go quickly (laughter and applause), and then the Conservatives will be in great trouble, for there will be no government, rebel or loyal. What are we to do then? The execution of the military powers of the President brings the States back to where I say they are by law—people forming a State without a political organization, called State government. That they can only receive under the auspices of Congress, and in accordance with the forms and by the laws that it, and it alone, shall see fit to prescribe. (Applause.) When proper provision shall have been made for these things, then there will be something else necessary, for to all liberties a guarantee is necessary. Our great forefathers had none of our foolish, sentimental belief in the impeccability of the people—not a bit of it. They thought that, as a general thing, and in the long run, the great mass and body of the people were wise, and liberal, and honest, and would conduct their affairs well; but they knew that bad men could get into power; that great masses of men could be inflamed by passion; that injustice might be perpetrated by mobs as well as by a tyrant; that a republican government could be overthrown and a despotic government erected; that a minority, with superior arms or superior intelligence, could trample down a majority disarmed and out of possession of the government. They foresaw, as the pages of the *Federalist* will prove to any man who has read it, when they framed the Constitution, exactly what we now see with our eyes in these days of blood and carnage, that a great interest acting together as a unit, covering a great region of country, antagonistic to the other interests of the country, might combine, and by foreign aid, and the possession of the local governments, create a great rebellion, overthrow the republican government, and establish something that was not republican; and therefore they created the power to suppress insurrection, and imposed the duty on Congress to guarantee republican governments. We, unlike those who have to deal with most great rebellions, without hurting any one great permanent legitimate interest of society, can strike from under the faction its only foundation. Heretofore civil strifes have arisen between the poor and the rich; those who have, and those who have not, property; between those who are in power and those who are out of power, to acquire what they have not. Those are revolutions difficult to be dealt with. It is difficult to get at the cause and to remove it. You can not destroy property. It is difficult to change the form of a political organization. Here the foundation is a social institution—the right by law, contrary to the law of nature, for one man to hold another in servitude.

You cut up the roots of the rebellion by striking the shackles from the slave. (Prolonged applause.) How shall it be done? Congress passed two laws in 1862 authorizing the President to use as many persons of African descent as he might see fit, to aid him, organized in such manner as he might think best, to suppress the rebellion. The President now, late in the day—in my judgment much later than it ought to have been—has commenced in earnest the organization of the negro regiments from the slave element of the country. The "Conservatives," North and South, cry aloud against it. No man who does not mean to aid the rebellion will lay a straw across the track of that march. (Applause.) We are informed "slaves can not be soldiers!" There is mighty little of the slave left in the man who has a musket upon his shoulder. (Laughter and applause.) "Slaves can not be soldiers." They who have taken leave of absence are likely to keep it. "Slaves can not be soldiers." Then make them free by law of Congress, and let us stop the argument. (Applause.) "You can not take private property for public use without compensation." No; but every man in the United States owes military service to the United States paramount to all laws of the States; and if the negro owes the service, the master has no right to claim pay for it. (Applause.) The burden passes with the property. The master has been voting upon the negro's personality for eighty years. We will let the negro fight a little now upon his personality. (Laughter and applause.) But it is said, white soldiers will not fight in the same ranks with the negroes. Where have the soldiers said they did not want their aid? Where have they turned their backs upon an enemy because a negro stood facing the same enemy? What officers have thrown up their commissions because they are humbled by being in the same ranks? Are they rather not rational enough to say that the musket upon the shoulder of the negro elevates him to the dignity of man? The *Federalist*, in its wisdom, foresaw this day in something of its brightness when it said that commotions might make a race of unhappy beings emerge to the level of manhood. (Applause.) But we are told, "You will disorganize your armies." Was Rosecrans's army disorganized four days ago because negroes had been introduced into the army? "The Union men of the loyal slave States will be disgusted, and they will rebel." Where? Western Virginia has abolished slavery since this system has been initiated and proclaimed. (Applause.) Missouri has passed her act of emancipation, made gradual by her Copperheads, because her loyal men would otherwise have made it peremptory and immediate. In Maryland, that surrounds your capital, and more than once has felt the tramp of the invader—such is the unanimous sentiment of her people, that her governor has been compelled to hasten up his lagging opinions and proclaim himself in favor of emancipation—and a Convention next year to effect it; and the only question is whether the enlistment of the slaves will leave any to emancipate. (Laughter and applause.) Who has rebelled? Who that was loyal to the government has become disloyal? Somewhere, where the negro fever has been lurking under the skin, of course it has broken out; but the fever was there before; it only required a hot day to bring it out. (Laughter.) No sound loyal man has a symptom of that in him.

"But there will be servile insurrections, outrages upon women, massacres of masters, burning down of houses, destruction of great regions of country," every thing that the Apocalypse describes before the last day. That mass of freedmen has done no such iniquity any where. They have submitted with more than angelic patience to the torments of their masters, till the United States has given them an opportunity of freedom; and then, murdering no one, outraging no one, insulting no one, they have marched quietly through the streets of Baltimore to the negro camp, and undertaken the obligations of the military oath. (Applause.) The guarantee that you want is, enough of them—that is all. Organize one hundred thousand, or two hundred thousand, or three hundred thousand, and plant them as a beacon-light and a tower of strength in the middle of the Southern country, and that, with an act of Congress, makes freedoms not only law, but fact; and till that is done, the President's proclamation is not worth the paper on which it is written. ("That's so," and cheers.) Your declaration that you are going to set the slaves free is a mere delusion; their rushing to join the army is merely preparing their necks for the halter; the recognition of the existing rebel authorities is merely handing them over to the stake and the torture. Humanity, Christianity, the highest principles, the most ordinary honor, combine in crying shame on thus complicating the fate of that innocent people with yours, if you do not mean to make their fate also yours. (Applause.) Let them stay at home, doomed to the inexorable lash and eternal labor, rather than drag them out to incur the deadly hate and hostility of their masters, and then return them defenseless to their tender mercies. There may be execrable humiliations yet connected with the adjustment of this great revolution, but the pen of the historian will steep itself in gall of equal bitterness for no other act as for calling negroes into the field, and abandoning them afterward to slavery. That, fellow-citizens, is one of those steps which, once taken, can never be recalled. "The Union as it was" can never be after that step. But when the negroes shall be organized, armed, disciplined, decorated with the uniform of the United States, and taught the manœuvres of the field, an act of Congress which proclaims them and their like free will be an act that will be respected. Then the United States will have acquired four millions of people in the rebel States whose liberty depends upon the perpetuity of the Union, and for the first time you will have a guarantee such as you never had before. You will have converted the element of your weakness into the element of your strength. You will have wrested the sword from your antagonist, and will wield it over his defenseless head. Your friends are camped eternally among them, and they are on their good behavior. If they attempt to reduce them to slavery, the law calls the men of the North to vindicate the right they have conferred, not to meet in arms the men they had previously armed against the Southern rebellion. That is the legal way that that problem will be accomplished. Then, if we hear the wretched cry, coming from the lowest of the populace, chiefly that which floods us from abroad, about negro equality and the intrusion of negro labor upon white labor, mention to them one or two things which may even meet their intellect. In the first place, if any body is afraid of negro equality, he is not far from it already (laughter); in the next place, if God has made him equal, and only accidental circumstances have made him unequal, you can not help it; and if He has made him unequal by the laws of nature, and independnetly of accidental circumstances, then no amount of demagoguism, no amount of abolition enthusiasm can make one hair black or white, or add an inch to his stature, intellectual or moral. When you talk about expelling him from the country, you talk simple craziness. Expel four millions of people! Where are the ships? Where is the land that will receive them? Where are the people that will pay the taxes to remove them?

Who will cultivate the deserted regions that they leave? Who will indemnify King Cotton for the loss of his subjects? (Laughter and applause.) What will the cotton-planter do—represented to you as a gentleman who, like Apollyon in the Pilgrim's Progress, eats and spouts nothing but fire; but you will find a little common sense at the bottom of it all. Let him understand that the negro is free, and that he has to deal with him as a free laborer, or let cotton go uncultivated, and he will hasten to pay him wages, and the negro will be glad to receive them. (Applause.) But he will run up North, say this same class of people, and compete with us for our labor. Who ever heard of a free negro running away from where he was free? Who ever heard of a negro running at all, if he could help it? (Laughter.) They don't run from Maryland to Pennsylvania—why from South Carolina to Louisiana? "But they are lazy and idle." Those who want to keep them as slaves say so; nobody else. We in Maryland have more experience on that subject than any body else. We have about 200,000 negroes; one half of them are free, the other half are slaves. We find that the slaves are lazier than the free negroes. We find that the free negroes have schools, educate their children, lay up money in the Savings' Banks, and do not crowd the court of my friend Judge Bond as much as the class of white people from across the water. Every body talks against them who wants to keep them down below the level of the slave. It is the interest of the people who own the slave property with which they come in competition to do it; but when there was an attempt made a few years ago to expel them from Maryland, the leading landholders and negroholders protested against it, and stopped it because it would destroy the agricultural industry of the State. If we in Maryland did not want to lose one half of our agricultural population, how will they of South Carolina live if they lose it all? (Applause.) Gentlemen, necessity is a teacher that we in this country have yet to learn to respect. We have been in the habit of doing what seemed to us good in our own eyes; frequently it was very bad. We have to learn, and our Southern brethren have to learn more bitterly than we, that sometimes people have to do what they can do, and not what they prefer to do. When the Southern master is taught that the question is not whether he will have the negro free or slave, but whether he will have him free or no cotton, he will take the negro free. (Applause.) No rebel State will vote to emancipate their slaves. Do not be under any such delusion for an instant. They mean to hold them as long as they can. No rebel State will vote to come back to the Union—rest assured of it—as long as there is an army in the field; but state the question, Do you prefer, now belonging to the United States, to govern yourselves or be governed by Congress? and they will hasten to reorganize a proper State government. So with reference to the negro: if you ask them whether they would rather have the negro free or slave, they will say unanimously "slave;" but if you say "the negro shall be free; will you pay him wages as a workman, or will you not have cultivators for your fields," they will say, "We will pay him wages;" and that is no speculation either, gentlemen. At this moment large plantations in Louisiana are cultivated under bargains made between the master and the slave for a reasonable compensation. To such an extent has the depletion of the slave population of the western shore of Maryland gone, that some of the most violent secessionists have gone to their slaves and offered them higher wages than heretofore they would have had to pay white men if they would stay at home and not enlist. (Applause.)

Gentlemen, the world moves palpably to the eye in this latter day, and the man who supposes he can stand still in the midst of the great moral movement of this world might as well plant his feet firmly in the mud and say, "The world may circle around the sun, but I will not go with it." You are parts of the current, and are borne on with it against your will. Day after day you accept what yesterday you would have scouted, and the day before would have thought craziness. Men's interests are sometimes blinded by their passions, but when their passions are chastised their interest resumes the supremacy. Crush the rebellion, and cotton will be again cultivated. Crush the rebellion, and the question of labor will revive. Crush the rebellion, and the interests of the planter will be a matter for his consideration. Crush the rebellion, and he will make the best terms he can with his emancipated and armed fellow-countrymen of the African race. (Applause.) And, on the other hand, if this wretched, cross-eyed, and double-faced conservatism (laughter) shall get into power; if the men who delude the people, and lie to their own consciences where they are not dishonest, shall crown themselves again, as for thirty years they have hitherto crowned themselves for evil, with the powers of the government of the United States, and shall proceed to act on their view of the Constitution, and recognize the rebel leaders as the masters of their loyal fellow-citizens, whom now for two long years they have illegally oppressed, restore them to the seats of power, admit into the Congress of the United States their representatives, leave the conduct of the local elections under their dictation, and allow their armies to stand guard over the ballot-box, and their laws to regulate who shall elect and who shall be elected, and their Constitution to determine how the balance of power shall be distributed between the white regions of the State and the slave regions of the State—then, I say, although the Union may be restored in that way, it will be at the loss of all the fruits of the war; there will be no permanent peace; it will be a treacherous and shifting sand on which no permanent structure can be laid, over which no great march for improvement can pursue its unobstructed way. We merely restore to power those that have rebelled, to subjugate the North by the old coalition to abide their time till undying hate, still fostered and kept alive by the perpetuation of political power, shall awake amid some great national collision from abroad; to leave our ranks in the day of battle, to lift the banner of rebellion in the midst of national disaster, with combined armies tear in pieces the republic that they are now vainly struggling to overthrow. I say that now, when our armies have advanced to the very heart of the Confederacy, let us press it home and rest nowhere. (Great applause.) Our armies now gird all the rebellion; the leaders of the rebellion begin to feel the inward tortures of conscious guilt, and they begin to feel the searching throes of the fire that we are heaping around them. Press forward only a little more, and they will be consumed in the conflagration that they themselves have created. (Applause.) We have now possession of the Mississippi; we have possession of all west of it substantially; we have all of Mississippi in our possession; we have nearly all Louisiana in our possession; we have all of Tennessee in our possession; we have one half of the State of Virginia in our possession; we have one full half of all the population that rebelled in our possession; we have crippled their resources, in great measure disorganized or paralyzed their armies; we have still fighting to do, but we have less of it to do than we had a year ago; and now, with one combined and energetic effort, if with our feet we can stamp down the "conservative" revolutionary reaction at home, and launch as a bolt of fire upon the enemy our unbroken ranks, a year more and possibly we shall begin to see the end of the war. (Applause.) But, gentlemen, rest assured that they who are ready to make peace first will not dictate the terms of it; rest assured that they who are determined to see no end of the war, excepting under the crown of victory, will wear that crown. (Applause.) It is tenacity, it is endurance, it is patience, it is the resolution never to stop fighting until your enemy yields, that constitute the great qualities of nations born to rule. We now are on trial before the nations of the world. If the sword drop from our wearied hands, they will say, "Go, ye nation of shop-keepers and weavers; work, navigate, be ingenious, build houses, weave fabrics; make arms for the rest of the world, leave other men to bear and wield them; you are not the legitimate descendants of the men who wrested their independence from the power of Great Britain." Maintain your power intact, scout down and stamp down any man who speaks of any terms of peace at all. (Great applause.) Tell him that this is no foreign war to be terminated by a treaty; it is a domestic rebellion to be stamped in the earth, and the only treaty is the Constitution of the United States as it is and as we construe it (great applause); the only privileges of the rebels are the laws of Congress as we have passed them and will execute them over them till they submit; their only right is to a legal trial and mercy afterward, if the President sees fit. (Applause.) They are not alien enemies, they are traitors whose lives are forfeited. When we deal with them, gentlemen, on these terms, they will understand that they have begun a work which they know now is not easy, they will then know is impossible; they will find that they set out to avert death in old age, and they encountered suicide at the threshold; they will begin to understand what might there slumbers in the heart of the American people, wielded by wisdom, backed by energy and resolution, and by that instinct which is never wanting to any people destined to greatness—the instinct of power that leads them never to yield as long as a man or a dollar remain, as long as there is an acre to be defended or an inch to be restored to their domination. Never allow the god Terminus to recede across the boundary of any State—let that be the watchword of the

American republic. Then it will be as great, as glorious, as beneficent, as long-lived, yea, more long-lived than the immortal example of republican government, the Rome of the ancient world. On these terms we shall stand respected before the nations of the world.

Every despot in Europe curled his lips when the rebellion broke out at the feeble, wretched, vacillating, dilapidated government that undertook to restore its authority over this immense and magnificent region. When the men of the North and of the loyal slave States commenced to develop their power, they paused in their determination to recognize, they paused in their more than half-formed resolution to intervene and throw the weight of their arms on the other side. When our arms were at a low ebb a year and a half ago, Louis Napoleon thought it a convenient opportunity to march in and take possession of Mexico—to limit our expansion. He would not do it to-day; and, by the blessing of God, when this rebellion shall be suppressed, I take it there is a long account to settle with two great nations of the European world. (Long-continued applause.) I never said a word, my friends, to any body in this house on that subject before, but I knew what I thought, and I guessed what every American thought. (Great applause.) The sailing of the Alabama and the Florida—the organization of companies to supply arms to shoot down our brethren—the organized attempt to break through the blockade with every material of war and every comfort of life for our enemies; under the guise of a neutrality violated at every step—the moral power and force given to the rebellion by the countenance of the governments of France and England, whose fear of the consequences alone prevented formal intrusion into our domestic quarrel—the thorn in our side of Nassau—the prying eye that watched our every movement at Halifax—the long thorn that France has planted in our side in Mexico—these things fester and rankle till the day of account. (Great applause.) I used to be opposed to foreign conquest, opposed to the acquisition of that territory, opposed to foreign war. I have learned something in two years. I take it that the sailing of the Alabama has unsettled the Northeastern frontier. (Applause.) I take it that the intrusion of a monarchical power into Mexico has made us feel that Mexico is a republic, and our safety requires its expulsion. (Tremendous cheering.) I take it that we feel uncomfortably bound in by the Bahama Islands, and that hereafter Nassau will not be the pirate's nest, to prey on us. (Great applause.) When this giant shall have recovered the use of all his faculties, not now like a man cloven from head to foot, and wielding scarce any of his native power, but restored to his whole manhood, united in his absolute vigor, I look with glorying to the day when the black regiments shall stream to the capital of the Montezumas, while the Army of the Potomac, becoming the Army of the St. Lawrence, shall march to Quebec and Montreal. (Enthusiastic applause, with great cheering and waving of hats.) And if by the blessing of God, and the wisdom that shall preside over the Navy Department, our navy shall reach the magnificent proportions of our army, and the navy of England shall meet her equal on the seas, if it shall only be the will of God that the nation's great admiral, Dupont, shall live to lead it on the ocean (applause), then I trust to live to hear of the explosion of the bombshells over the dome of St. Paul's, and of the arches of London bridge sent into the air. (Great applause.)

Y

REMARKS AT THE RECEPTION OF RUSSIAN NAVAL OFFICERS.

On the 12th of October, 1863, a dinner was given at the Astor House in New York by prominent gentlemen of that city in honor of the Russian minister, and the Russian Admiral Lisovski, commanding the Russian fleet then in New York Harbor. This entertainment had a peculiar significance, from the fact that at that moment our relations with England and France were by no means cordial, growing out of the temper excited in the United States by the disposition of the French government to recognize the "Confederate States," and, conjointly with England, to interfere forcibly to break the blockade of Southern ports. Russia alone of the European powers had shown a friendly regard and disposition toward the federal government. The occasion of a visit by the Russian fleet to the United States waters was eagerly taken advantage of to manifest the appreciation here of that feeling.

Mr. Davis was invited to the entertainment, and to respond to the second regular toast—"The President of the United States, the elected leader of the nation which is solving the problem of self-government and universal freedom"—which he did in the following words:

Mr. President and Gentlemen,—I regard it as one of the privileges of my life to have been selected on this occasion to respond to a toast to the President of the United States. There are others who, by long association with that gentleman, earlier his political supporters than myself, more closely connected with him in the administration of great affairs in this great crisis of our history, might have had that task more appropriately confided to them. But to none could it have been confided who would have with more pleasure and more heartiness borne his testimony to the earnest uprightness of purpose and far-seeing sagacity with which, in affairs more gravely complex and weighty than this nation, since the Revolution, had ever been called upon to deal with, the President has discharged his high duty. None can speak with more profound reverence than I do of that exalted office, as exalted as any known among men, conferred by the suffrages of his fellow-citizens, and to whose power obedience is yielded, not because of his power, but because of the veneration for the laws which raised him to his high post. So far I am not willing that any one shall claim more earnestly to represent the President of the United States than I do. I may be pardoned for saying that the following clause of the toast I must be permitted to criticise: "The elected chief of the nation." Certainly. "Solving the problem of self-government." No. We take it that this nation has solved that problem. (Applause.) That day of experiment has passed. This vessel was launched on the waters with many a trembling hope and many a prayerful utterance that it might survive the storms of life, and continue to be the light to other nations of the earth. Those fears are now dispelled—dispelled by more than eighty years of such success as has attended no experiment of human wisdom. After three generations now mouldering in the grave under the ægis of the republic, having lived in peace and died in blessedness, shall we call that an experiment? Whose affairs have been conducted with more regularity and order? Where in the civilized world has order been more secure? Where has personal liberty been less violated? Where the rights of religious conscience and free speech so much respected? Where has yet the first drop of blood for treason to be shed in the civilized world? And, until this rebellion broke out, where in all the world have arms not been drawn by citizen against citizen to maintain or to prostrate the experiment of the law? No; it is no experiment. It is a reality, vindicating now the right, in the success of eighty years, to continue to eternity to bear the torch of human freedom." (Great applause.)

Speaking of England's hostility to the United States, Mr. Davis said:

National hostility carried away men's hearts to swell the ambition of commercial triumph and rivalry, turned away the high thoughts of the great Anglo-Saxon nation. Her aristocracy rejoiced that the prophecies of our passing greatness were coming to be truths, and they thought that they might as well give a push to help the prophecy to its accomplishment. That we have tried to be friends with all the world is notorious. That we have tried to forget these things, and that we have forgiven them, is especially in the memory of all you gentlemen of New York; for how long has it been since—for the representative of that power which within the last two years has inflicted deeper wounds on your body than all the rest of the civilized world—your streets were swarming with multitudes, and resounding with hosannas to the prospective heir of the crown of the three islands? And our reward has been the Trent impertinence, the Florida, the Alabama, the pirate nest around our coast. Another great nation we thought we were entitled to the sympathy of—ay, and we have the sympathy of the nation, though, perhaps, not of its ruler. It is the proud peculiarity of the American people that their heart is so large, and touches humanity at so many points, that, however the rulers of the world may be jealous of a power hostile to her greatness and desiring her overthrow, the people in their secret heart pray for her success.

The last part of the toast to which I am called on to respond speaks of universal freedom. (Hurrah.) History will show no example of an equal struggle within the limits of any one nation, met with equal power, sustained with equal endurance, crowned with equal success, promising equal triumph with that in which we are engaged. But I turn to another subject—the palm of triumph belonging to the empire of Russia. There serfdom—covering twenty, thirty, forty millions of subjects, by the fiat of one man, and the assent of the great majority of the people, peacefully, quietly, deliberately, with compensation to injured interests, with provision for the serf converted into a freeman—has vanished like the morning clouds (applause); and this day, from one end of the empire of Russia to the other, the sun rises in the east and sets in the west only on freemen. (Loud applause.) Now, the men of America, having faith in an overruling Providence, know that that retrograde motion which planets sometimes seem to have is because we regard them from wrong points of view; but when we take the central situation in the universe, we recognize that they are circling round the centre of light. And so it is destined to continue until nations shall roll up like a scroll, and all created things shall be wrapped in the bosom of the Creator.

NO PEACE TILL AFTER REBEL SUBMISSION.

On the evening of the 9th of October, Mr. Davis, in response to an invitation, addressed a large meeting at the Cooper Institute, in the city of New York, upon the condition of public affairs. He urged the vigorous prosecution of the war inaugurated by the rebels in the South, and his argument was especially directed against the "Peace" party, which now was endeavoring to instill hopes of a settlement of the great controversy in any other mode than by victories in the field. He maintained then that there was *no government* in the rebellious States—no lawful government—none that the federal authorities could in any manner recognize. When their armed opposition shall be swept away, it would then be for the Congress to reorganize those States, establish there and guarantee a republican form of government. He said that

"Before next year Maryland will have wiped out slavery from her soil; and if the Congress to meet in December should do its duty, we should have a free republic from Maine to Florida in less than two years. Let those who think the negro not good enough to serve by their side remember that they served in the ranks of George Washington and of Andrew Jackson.

"I never sympathized with the radical Abolitionists, for I thought them one hair's breadth this side of craziness. I know that, with only a feeble influence, they have been used by Northern Democrats and Southern Secessionists to smut and blacken all the rest of the people of the North. Now, when the nation is on the point of triumph; now, when the only thing that fires the Southern heart is the success of the opposition here, and the hope that Mr. Seymour will come to their aid; now, when the last appeal is being made; now, even, some men begin to prate about 'negro equality,' and revive the old prejudices which the enemies of the republic alone use for our mischief, and which no man can use for our good. And I say—as little regard as I have for the Abolitionists—that the man who now utters a word for the purpose of awakening prejudice against *any man on the side of the government*, is either a traitor at heart, or so low in intelligence that he does not know the consequences of his acts."

There is no complete report of the speech. The extracts and account given above are from the New York papers of the following day (October 10th).

The Thirty-eighth Congress met on December 7, 1863. On the 14th Mr. Davis was named Chairman of the Committee on Foreign Affairs, and chairman of a special committee of nine, to which was referred "so much of the President's Message as relates to the duty of the United States to guarantee a republican form of government to the States in which the governments recognized by the United States have been abrogated or overthrown."

On the 14th of January, 1864, a joint resolution was before the House "explanatory of an act to suppress insurrection, punish treason and rebellion, to *seize and confiscate the property of rebels*, and for other purposes." After a speech from Mr. S. S. Cox, of Ohio, in opposition thereto, Mr. Davis addressed the House in the following speech:

CONFISCATION OF REBEL PROPERTY.

The House being in Committee of the Whole on the State of the Union, and having under consideration the bill to confiscate the property of rebels, Mr. Davis said:

MR. SPEAKER,—With whatever pleasure the gentlemen upon this side of the House may have heard the very novel declaration of the gentleman from Ohio, that he contemplated supporting in all proper measures the administration in the prosecution of the war and the suppression of the rebellion, it is perhaps fortunate that the result of the political elections in the central slave States has placed the administration beyond the necessity of relying upon his support. Were it not so, I incline to think that the kind of support the administration would receive from the great majority of gentlemen on the other side of the House was indicated early in the session in that resolution proposed by a gentleman from New York [Mr. Fernando Wood], which pronounced this an inhuman war. For myself, sir, relying on the fact that the people have sent enough of us here for the purpose of supporting the administration, I would suggest that perhaps gentlemen on the other side of the House had just as well execute the mission with which the constituents that elected them charged them—to oppose, to embarrass, to libel, and to break down the administration—and leave the support of it to gentlemen whom the people sent here to maintain it. With all due respect to the patriotic purposes, the eminent ability of the gentlemen on the other side, when they tender support I shall look at it with something of suspicion, and, for myself, shall say, "*Non tali auxilio, nec defensoribus istis.*"

A specimen of that support, Mr. Speaker, is exhibited by the mode in which the bill brought in by the Chairman of the Committee on the Judiciary has been received on that side of the House. It relates to what is now the settled policy of the administration, which gentlemen say they intend to support in the suppression of the rebellion. Whether one degree or another of confiscation be expedient, whether it be extended to the lower actors in this great scene, or, as in my judgment is proper, it be confined to a few of the leaders, still, that the confiscation of property shall attach to some portion of the people engaged in the rebellion is now the settled, resolved policy of the administration. The bill introduced by the Judiciary Committee is in furtherance of that policy. A joint resolution, in my judgment a very unwise one, of the last Congress, limited the operation of the Confiscation Law to life estates. This bill contemplates the obliteration of that limitation. I think its language does not accomplish that purpose, and therefore I shall vote for the amendment of the gentleman from Pennsylvania [Mr. Stevens], which goes directly to the object sought to be accomplished by repealing the limiting resolution.

But there we are met by the new supporters of the administration with the suggestion that this is uprooting the fundamental law of the republic. I ask where? What word in the Constitution does it violate? What principle does it in the least degree impeach? They quote the clause of the Constitution declaring that Congress shall have power to declare the punishment of treason, but that no attainder of treason shall *work* corruption of blood or forfeiture, *except during the life of the person attainted.*

If I have read aright the Confiscation Law of the last Congress, it nowhere attaches any confiscation or forfeiture to a *conviction* for treason or to an *attainder* of treason. Am I right or am I wrong? There is no word in the law of the last Congress that attaches confiscation of property to conviction of the *person* for treason, to attainder of *the person* for treason, on a criminal proceeding in any court of justice. If that be so, then the quotation of the clause from the Constitution is simply irrelevant to the matter in debate, for it is that no ATTAINDER of treason shall work corruption of blood or forfeiture except during the life of the party; so that, if there be no proceeding by indictment, there can be no attainder; and if there be *no attainder*, there is nothing on which the residue of the words in the Constitution can operate. That simple observation disposes of the whole argument. It is wholly immaterial whether, in the event of the party's being convicted of treason, Congress can or can not make a *consequence* of the judgment the forfeiture of lands in fee simple, or is confined to a forfeiture limited in duration by the life of the convict.

The question here is whether there is any process of law, however this provision be construed, by which we can effect a forfeiture of the whole fee in lands. That question gentlemen have nowhere met.

If, however, the Constitution limits the consequences of a conviction to a forfeiture for life, to assume that it limits *every other form* of process of law in like manner is simply begging the question. The Constitution speaks for itself. It limits the operation of an attainder. It limits nothing else. When, therefore, gentlemen accuse us here of uprooting the settled law of the land, they interpolate language not in the law, and quote it to condemn us. But even if the meaning of the Constitution itself were doubtful in a case of attainder, where the question would be whether the judgment of the court should be for the forfeiture of the land for life or in fee, no decision on *that* could affect any other process of law for confiscating lands without attainder. The doubt upon that question can not apply to a subject beyond the purview of the question.

Still it is worth while to hazard a suggestion touching the real meaning of those words so confidently invoked by our new allies for our confusion. I desire to speak with all modesty in solving this problem, for difficulties beset every solution, and while it is quite clear that its meaning is not that assumed by our new allies, it is perhaps not so easy to give a demonstrably right solution. I speak with hesitation, because their confidence surprised me into assuming once before the correctness of their interpretation. I think, however, the technical language of the clause, read in the sense it bore in the English law, may light us on our way. I think it points to a very different meaning from that which the honorable gentleman from Ohio [Mr. Cox] supposes.

No attainder shall *work* corruption of blood or forfeiture except *during* the life of the person attainted. Now I take it that the meaning of that clause is that the forfeiture worked must be effected during life. The honorable gentleman from Ohio, and those who think with him, would construe it to be that the forfeiture, when worked, shall only *endure* for the life of the party. Palpably the latter is the incorrect and the former the legal meaning. The purpose assumed is the protection of the offspring from punishment for the guilt of the ancestor. But a fine is equally taken from the offspring, as land; yet no one denies the right to fine a person attainted. There was, however, an effect of attainder that did punish the offspring, and the offspring alone. Every student of Blackstone knows that the judgment convicting a person of treason operated a corruption of blood. The corruption of blood stopped the transmission of hereditable blood to any heir of the person attainted; so that the legal effect of conviction for treason under the law of England was, first, to forfeit all the property, real and personal, of the person attainted, and, secondly, to corrupt his blood, destroy its heritable quality, so that he could neither take land by descent himself, nor transmit heritable blood to the persons who would, but for his attainder, have been his heirs. He could, in the language of the law, neither be heir nor have heirs.

Now, suppose the father of any person attainted for treason died the day after the execution, owning lands, they could not pass to the traitor's son, nor to any collateral relation claiming by descent through him, because the operation of the judgment, besides forfeiting the land owned by the party in his lifetime, had corrupted his blood, and no one could trace descent through him. He was a bar, cutting off the relationship between grandfather and grandson. Land which would have come to the grandson if the father had not been a person attainted, instead of going to the heir, was arrested in its transit to the heir by the corruption of blood, and passed either to the lord of the fee or to the king.

So that the Constitution deals merely with corruption of blood and its operation. There shall be no corruption of blood or forfeiture worked by attainder except during the life of the person. Attainder worked no forfeiture after the death of the party except by the corruption of blood. The forfeiture of a fee-simple estate was not a forfeiture after the life of the party; the whole fee was in the person attainted; his heirs had no interest in it, and no lawyer would ever dream of describing a forfeiture for life by the words of the Constitution, or describe the forfeiture of a fee-simple estate as a forfeiture worked by attainder after the life of the party. It was one of the settled laws of England at that time, and which also prevailed in some of the States of this Union, that the corruption of blood did, what the gentleman from Ohio so properly execrates, operate upon innocent persons with reference to their rights coming from a different source after the criminal had expiated his crime. Now, without meaning to say positively that that is the meaning and operation of the section, I say that in my judgment it comes nearer an intelligible exposition of it than any such theory as this, that you can not take lands in fee, but you may take all his personal property absolutely, which was the ground of the President's threatened veto of last year; that you can fine a man to the extent of his estate, but you can not take his lands to pay the fine. And being unintelligible, with all respect to our recent friends, they are driven to say that in the punishment of treason the Constitution has been guilty of this intolerable folly: that for robbing the mail, or piracy, for any ordinary offense, or murder on the seas, or in the army or navy for any other crime, Congress may prescribe what punishment they please; take the land in fee; in their sense make a forfeiture after death; but in providing for the punishment of treason, the greatest crime, the most dangerous crime, it has feebly attempted to protect innocent offspring by saving the lands of the convict, but leaving his life and all his personal property at the mercy of the law; that it has been guilty of sanctioning the unrepublican discrimination between real and personal property, and adopting the aristocratic idea that land was something that must not be taken, but preserved for the heir, to come down to him by a perpetual constitutional entail. And this anti-republican view is urged to fetter us in breaking the power of an aristocratic rebellion founded on land in large bodies and on negroes. Were there no other objection in this, that simple *reductio ad absurdum* disposes of the argument.

But, Mr. Speaker, the question here, as I have said, is not, what forfeiture does it allow an attainder to work, but does it declare that no forfeiture, that no confiscation under any process of law shall affect land for a longer period than the life of the owner? Does it apply to any case where there is no attainder, no conviction?

The law of the last Congress prescribed a different process from conviction in a court of law of the person guilty of the crime. It provides that upon proceedings *in the District Court in the nature of proceedings in admiralty* the lands of certain classes of persons, and all their personal property, shall be forfeited for the use of the government.

And the Constitution provides that the property of citizens shall not be taken without due process of law. Now, the question which gentlemen on the other side of the House have to argue is, not the law of attainder, but whether the process in the District Courts of the United States to confiscate the property of persons proved to be of the specified classes is *due process of law for depriving a man of his property under the Constitution.* If they can not maintain that it is not due process of law within the meaning of the Constitution, they can not throw the least doubt on the constitutionality of this mode of procedure.

If this were a new question, possibly there might be room for argument. But from the first administration down to this day there has never been a day in which, on the statute-books of the United States, exactly this process to forfeit property for crime without first convicting the owner on indictment has not been prescribed. The law of 1799, among the first of the revenue laws, forfeited property brought in under fraudulent invoices, without proceeding against the individual personally; and all the revenue laws from that day to this enforce these provisions by forfeitures and proceedings *in rem.*

The navigation laws of the United States, from the earliest days of the republic, inflict forfeiture in the District Court on proceedings against the vessel for violation of those laws without prosecuting the owner, though liable to indictment. Who ever heard that a vessel could not be forfeited unless the master or owner were indicted, or until after they had been indicted? Our laws regulating trade with the Indians make it penal to carry ardent spirits among them, and they punish the persons guilty and forfeit the property by process *in rem* in the District Court. Is that unconstitutional?

The law for the suppression of the slave-trade makes the parties violating it guilty of piracy, and they are liable either to be hung or confined in the penitentiary, according to the grade of the offense. But yet the vessels caught are always forfeited, whether owner or master be prosecuted or not. Was it ever heard that the person must be convicted of the crime before the vessel could be forfeited in the District Court? These things are of every-day practice, as every gentleman at all familiar with the ordinary administration of the laws of the United States knows. In a word, indictment and conviction of the person is not the only due process of law by which a person may be deprived of his property. The daily process of levying taxes proves that. And Congress has pleased to authorize confiscation without conviction, but in the time-honored forms of the early republic.

And another species of property about which gentlemen upon the other side of the House usually show more interest than about lands—property in negroes—affords a more striking illustration. We have in that case the same principle of confiscating property before conviction of the delinquent, settled by the laws of Maryland and of Virginia, adopted by Congress as the laws in the two counties of the District of Columbia, from the earliest days of the republic down to the day on which I am speaking. The law of Virginia goes as far back as the days of Jefferson. It prohibited the introduction of slaves into Virginia from any other State and from foreign countries; and while it prescribed the penalty on the party so introducing them, it also declared the slave free. The gentlemen from Maryland here know very well that was the law of Maryland down to within a few years, and, in some cases, it is so now. When Congress adopted the laws of Maryland and Virginia, both of those statutes were the laws of this district, and they were in force down to the time of the emancipation of slaves in this District.

Now, what was the ordinary process in these cases? I do not remember in my experience while practicing as a lawyer, either in Virginia or the District of Columbia or in Maryland, of an indictment or action for the fine or forfeiture against a party introducing negroes. It was the every-day practice when I came to the bar that negroes brought into that part of the District which was on the south of the Potomac River contrary to law, should apply to the court and bring a suit for their freedom; and it was in the ordinary form of an action for trespass, complaining that the master had illegally imprisoned them, and the judgment of the court was one cent damage against the master for the imprisonment. The question really involved was freedom or slavery. The law vested freedom; the court authenticated it. In other words, the operation of the law was that the act of bringing a negro across the line invested him with his freedom; that it deprived the master of his property, and invested the negro with the right to sue the man for the wrong committed by continuing to hold him. That has been adjudged again and again by the courts of Virginia and by the courts of Maryland; and though writs of error have more than once carried such cases in this District to the Supreme Court, that tribunal never dreamed that this was a forfeiture of property without due process of law. If gentlemen will take the trouble to run through the volumes of the Supreme Court Reports, they will find several cases; one so recent as 2 Howard, in which that form of proceeding was recognized as a competent mode in which to assert the right of freedom, which was a forfeiture of the master's right. The man who was a slave on the other side of the line became a freeman by being brought this side of the line; his master was not indicted, nor was his freedom a consequence of the conviction of, nor of a judgment against his master, but he acquired his title to freedom by the act of the Congress of the United States, which inflicted forfeiture on his master for violating it.

Congress, during the administration of Mr. Jefferson, I think, in organizing the Territories of Louisiana and Mississippi, in like manner forbade the introduction of slaves from abroad, and freed them when introduced by the master. And if we are to be told that this was antique legislation, and not fit for the light of these modern days, I ask gentlemen to read the compromise measures of 1850, brought in by the illustrious Kentuckian, Henry Clay, and passed by a Congress which thought fondly they had averted the agony that we now writhe under; let them read the law forbidding the slave-trade in the District of Columbia, where the hand of Henry Clay traced the words of forfeiture—that if any slave should be brought into this District by its owner, contrary to the provisions of the act, he should *thereupon become liberated and free.*

Now that covers all the Confiscation Acts of the last Congress. It is wholly immaterial whether it relates to land or to personal property, whether you forfeit lands or negroes. The forfeiture of slaves would even meet the technical objection of the gentleman from Ohio, because formerly in Virginia, as every body knows, slaves were real estate, not personal estate, passing to the heirs, and not to the executors; and it is only of late years that they have been treated as personal estate, though in the widow's share of them the traces of their *real* character still remain visible. Now the question that is involved in the Confiscation Law is not whether attainder can work corruption of blood affecting the heirs; of course it can not; it is not whether attainder can operate forfeiture of lands descending after the death of the attainted person, nor whether an attainder is confined to carving a life estate by forfeiture out of a fee; that is not the question. The question is whether, by other process of law not connected with indictment of the person, not following upon attainder, the United States government can say that those who have been in arms against it shall forfeit their property, and that the tribunals of the country shall enforce it *in rem;* and *this* is settled by the traditional laws of the republic.

DRAFT AND COMMUTATION.—COLORED TROOPS.

During the discussion of the "Conscription Bill" Mr. Davis opposed exemption from military service by payment of commutation-money, "except in favor of ministers of religion actually in charge of some congregation—of men having a wife or child dependent on them for support, and not having an income of twelve hundred dollars independent of their industry—of members of the religious society of Friends, or other religious denominations conscientiously opposed to bearing arms."

He also moved (February 10) to strike out from an amendment proposed so much as provided for the payment of three hundred dollars to the owner of any drafted slave, on the ground that if slaves were liable to military duty at all, they are so precisely as all who owe obedience to the laws are liable. To the objection that otherwise the government would be taking the *property* of the owner (in the labor of the slave) without compensation, he said:

"I beg pardon, sir. The son owes to the father labor, by the law of every State in the Union, as assuredly as the slave owes the master labor. We do not necessarily make the slave a freeman by taking him for a soldier. We *may* make provision that he shall be free thereafter. When the son is taken, when the apprentice is taken, somebody is taken who is quite as dear, quite as necessary, quite as valuable to the father and to the employer as when the slave is taken from the master. In other words, where the obligation of military service rests, the law pursues it, and insists upon it, leaving the burden of other losses to follow the necessities of the times."

Next day (February 11) Mr. Davis moved as an amendment "that the Secretary of War shall appoint a commission in each of the slave States represented in Congress, charged to award a just compensation to each loyal owner of any slave *who may volunteer* into the service of the United States, payable *out of the commutation-money received*," etc. In support thereof, he said:

"Mr. Chairman, I submit this amendment, not because I think it due at all to the owner of the slave, but because the President and the Secretary of War, in executing the law of 1862 allowing the President to use and organize persons of African descent to suppress the rebellion, have seen fit to appoint a commission, which is now in session in Maryland, for the purpose of estimating the value of, and awarding reasonable compensation to the loyal owners of, slaves who may volunteer into the United States service under the law of 1862. That brings the volunteering of slaves into some sort of correspondence with the established policy of the government in paying bounties to volunteers, the difference being that in the case of the slave the *bounty* is paid to the master instead, on *freeing his slave*, whereas the bounty in the case of the white volunteer of course goes to himself.

"It is a very different thing to impose on the government, when it is *driven to draft*, the necessity of paying to every slaveowner a compensation for any slave that may be drafted. The poor man, whose son works for him on his ten acres, receives no compensation for that son when he is drafted into the service, while the wealthy slaveholder, who may have three or four hundred slaves alongside, is to receive a compensation of three hundred dollars for every one of his slaves who may be drafted. It is apparent that if the government has the right to draft slaves into the service, and if the government has the right to take the slave, it has the right to take him exactly as it takes the son, the father, or the brother of any citizen of the republic, with no more compensation and no less compensation for discharging the duty he owes to the country."

FREEDMEN'S BUREAU.—DISPOSITION TO BE MADE OF FREE NEGROES.

On the 25th of January, the House having resumed the consideration of the Bill to establish a Bureau of Freedmen's Affairs, Mr. Davis said:

Mr. Speaker and Gentlemen,—The bill which is now under consideration involves a subject forced on us by the events of the war, and which must be determined one way or the other—the disposition of the freed negroes in the rebel States. The range of debate has naturally been very wide upon a bill of this character, and topics not perhaps at first sight very directly related to it have been dragged into the discussion.

The votes of the gentlemen from the loyal slave States cast a new light on the mind of the gentleman from New York [Mr. Brooks] respecting the fate of the negro race on this continent. But, while he justly appreciated the great and decisive weight of that vote upon the speakership of this House, he took occasion to discredit the moral power of that vote by impeaching the election of the representatives who cast it. He thinks they speak words not authorized by the people. He said:

"I know that the people of Maryland and of Delaware, if they had been allowed to vote, intended no such decree"—

That is, of emancipation.

"And I know that it is said those two States are better represented by the honorable gentleman from Ohio [Mr. Schenck] than by their representatives here."

If this were merely meant as a compliment to my distinguished friend from Ohio, I would be among the first to admit that any district of Maryland, as well as any in New York, would be better represented by him than by any gentleman representing either State—even the gentleman from New York. But when it comes in the shape of an imputation upon the validity and moral force of the election, it questions the legitimacy of the administration majority in this House, and must not pass unanswered. When the gentleman from New York says "*it is said* those two States are better represented by the honorable gentleman from Ohio than by those who represent them here," no person who cares to have any respect for his knowledge of the public affairs of the day has so said. And when the honorable gentleman says that "*he knows* that the people of Maryland and Delaware, had they been allowed to vote, intended no such decree," I desire to say that the honorable gentleman from New York does not know any such thing, and knows no fact that makes the error excusable.

"Had they been allowed to vote!" Who hindered them from voting? Where were they stopped from voting? "The people of Maryland!" If the gentleman means to say that because *the people of Maryland* determined that *the traitors* of Maryland, who disavowed their allegiance to the government, should not tarnish the ballot-box by their votes, we differ about the terms, but not about the facts. We *did* mean *they* should not vote, and we so meant because by the laws of Maryland such men are not entitled to vote. They who disavow, deny, and disown their allegiance to the United States, and declare and avow they are not citizens of the United States, have no right to vote; and so the judges of election held, almost from one end of Maryland to the other. If that is not good election law, this House can say so; the General Assembly of Maryland can say so; and if both be silent, the law is confessed.

If the gentleman referred to the complaints which are made of the interference of the military in the election, I desire to say that that complaint comes from nobody but heated partisans who howl because they are beaten. Even they confined the complaint to one single Congressional district out of five, and to four out of eight counties in that Congressional district; and therefore, conceding every thing that is complained of, and every thing that is inferred from the complaint, we have an undisputed election in four fifths of the State, which the gentlemen who make the complaint do not dispute. No one questions the election of the honorable member from the Fifth Congressional District [Mr. Harris], where the divided Union vote was overborne by the united secession vote, and where the aggregate vote of the district fell only a little below the normal vote of the district before the rebellion attracted many of its young men to the rebel ranks. My honorable friend in my eye from the Second Congressional District [Mr. Webster] could find no competitor to meet him before the people. The distinguished gentleman, the senior of the delegation [Mr.

Thomas], from the Fourth Congressional District, is here for the second time an unopposed candidate. And I am here because my political opponents did not care to take the responsibilities of a canvass, although aided and urged to oppose me by a distinguished adviser of the President up to within a week of the election. So that of all the State of Maryland, whose election is here impeached, in three fifths of it there was no contest whatever; in one fifth there was a contest in which our opponents had so free an election that they have their representative on this floor; and in the other fifth the contest is only impeached in four of the eight counties; and if the whole vote which was not cast in that district be added to the aggregate vote of our opponents, the emancipationists will still have a majority of thirteen or fourteen thousand in the State. And yet, in the face of such facts, a gentleman, who is entitled to be regarded as an intelligent observer of public affairs, rises here and says that *he knows* that if the people of Maryland had been *permitted to vote* they would not have allowed the emancipation candidate for Comptroller to carry the State by twenty thousand majority!

In Delaware the case is still more absurd; for, after an animated canvass, the opponent of the representative from that State withdrew on the eve of the election; and yet the vote for the gentleman from Delaware was the *largest* ever cast in that State for any candidate, and a majority of the whole vote of the State.

Mr. Speaker, the Legislature of Maryland is overwhelmingly Union, but not overwhelmingly for emancipation. There is a majority in the Senate opposed to it, and there is a majority in the House who were not in favor of it when they came to Annapolis; because, though elected by emancipation constituencies, they were nominated before their constituents had developed their views upon the subject. But this election which the gentleman from New York wishes to impeach carried with it such moral power that its enemies in the Senate and its lukewarm and doubtful friends in the House of Delegates are dragged backward over their prejudices and compelled to pass just such a bill as we dictated to them, and it stands now the law of the State of Maryland by the votes of a majority of both houses of the Legislature. They confessed that moral power which the honorable gentleman ignorantly denies.

"Slavery is dead," says the honorable gentleman. "Slavery

is dead" is echoed by some on this side of the House. "Slavery is dead" is echoed from the too sanguine people of the country. He may be a very sick man, Mr. Speaker, but I assure gentlemen of this House and the country that he is not dead; and if he is not done to death he will be your master again. That is my opinion, and I think my friend from Kentucky in my eye [Mr. Mallory] agrees with me.

Slavery is not dead in Maryland. We have to carry a majority of the Convention on the old slavery apportionment, where one fourth of the population ties the body; and whether the hostile influence that presides near the President's ear will allow Maryland to become a free State, or will fail her in her hour of need, remains yet to be seen. Up to this day Maryland is under no obligations to the President of the United States for the great strides that the cause of emancipation has made there. A Convention of the loyal men, the emancipationists of Maryland, on the 22d of this month, while declaring themselves in favor of immediate and unconditional emancipation, and while expressing their confidence in the President and their appreciation of his services, added this significant admonition, worthy of the State and of the people that uttered it:

"*Resolved*, That this Convention is in favor of the entire and immediate abolition of slavery in this State and in the States in rebellion, and is opposed to any reorganization of State governments in those States which do not recognize the immediate and final abolishment of slavery as a condition precedent. That this Convention express their sympathy with the radical emancipationists in Missouri, and in Arkansas, Tennessee, and Louisiana, and regret that influences in the cabinet have, in Maryland and those States, depressed the efforts of the radical friends of the administration and of emancipation, and given prominence to those who are the unwilling advocates of emancipation."

I trust that that admonition will have its weight, and that these sinister influences will cease to be the controlling element near the presidential ear in this grave crisis of emancipation in Maryland; and I desire that the country shall understand that, being under small obligations to the President for what has been done in Maryland up to this time, the people of Maryland thought it wise, while expressing their confidence in the President, to put that significant resolution before him for his serious consideration, so as to show that their devotion is not personal, but to principle; that their interest is in the cause and not in a man; and that while they will support the man as long as the man supports the cause, if the cause fail by any failure elsewhere, there may be a revision of their judgment respecting the person.

But "slavery is dead in the *rebel* States." No, sir. No, sir. Far from it. If our honorable friends on the other side elect their President in the coming fall, slavery is as alive as it was the day that the first gun blazed against Sumter. If we lose the majority in the next Congress, slavery is as powerful as it ever was. We are, it is true, in the condition in which we can not stand still. We must go backward or we must go forward. My face, sir, is to the future. I wish so to look at it, and so to say, to the men of my day and generation, what I think about the great measures which now touch the salvation of the country, that, whether I be on the winning or on the losing side, whether the nation triumph or fail, whenever any body shall by accident hereafter rake about among the ashes of the past and find my name, he will find at least that I did not fear to say to *friend* and foe what the times demand; and it may be that it will be well if it were heeded.

Slavery is not dead by the proclamation. What lawyer attributes to it the least legal effect in breaking the bonds of the slave? Executed by the bayonet, legally valid to the extent of the duration of the war, under the law of 1862, which authorizes the President to use the people of African descent as he may see fit for the suppression of the rebellion, it is undoubtedly valid to the extent of turning them loose from their masters during the rebellion. So long as the military power is engaged in suppressing resistance, they are free from their masters. Re-establish the old governments, allow the dominant aristocracy to repossess the State power in its original plenitude, how long will they be free? What courts will give them their rights? What provision is there to protect them? Where is the writ of *habeas corpus?* How are the courts of the United States to be open to them? Who shall close the courts of the States against the master? Does the master resort to the court against the slave? No; he seizes him by the neck. The law of last Congress freeing a few slaves provides that that act may be pleaded in defense. But when is the slave sued by his master? When is the time to plead in any such process? Gentlemen legislate without a knowledge of the country or of the people they are legislating for. Their laws are on the statute-book, and the opinions of the dominant faction conspire to perpetuate the master's rights and the slave's wrongs. Nothing but the resolute declaration of the United States that it shall be a condition precedent that slavery shall be prohibited in their Constitutions, and that the United States shall give judicial guarantees to the negroes, freedom in fact, and that the United States shall be kept under the control of men of such political views and purposes that the law will be executed as a constitutional law and imposed on reluctant people—nothing else can accomplish the death of slavery.

Supposing that to be done, Mr. Speaker, what then? This bill relates to the other grave social problem of the destiny of the negro race when their bond is broken. Now, many of them are thrown on our hands. We have to take care of them. To that extent the bill is right, and I shall vote for it for that purpose. How well it will answer, how far it must be modified after the national cause shall triumph, remains to be seen. Let the things of the future be cared for by the future. But it is necessary now to determine our policy respecting the negroes when freed; to form some definite ideas as to what shall be the future of the negro race; in other words, what dispositions we will make of them when we have broken the master's yoke, when Maryland shall have broken it hereafter, when Missouri shall have finally broken it, when West Virginia shall have finally broken it, and when slavery in all the rebel States shall have been destroyed and broken up in fact.

There are on that subject two, and only two, theories. The President says, "Colonize and pay for them." The people say, "Leave them where they are." In favor of colonization, and compensation to all loyal persons in the rebel States, we have the declaration of the President of the United States, which naturally carries with it great weight. He has formally proposed it for the consideration of the people as his preferred policy. It is for that reason that it is the more important to look at it directly in the face, and to deal with it, subject to the conditions which it involves, if it be adopted as the policy of the nation. It has been discussed and commented on by a distinguished gentleman, a member of his cabinet, supposed, on that and other subjects, more accurately to represent his opinion than any other person. (The Postmaster General.) These comments throw a flood of light on the views which prevail in high quarters on the practical execution of the scheme of colonization, and the industrial and social reasons which prompt or justify it. These comments have been published broadcast over the country as comments upon the emancipation policy of the President of the United States. Those comments have never been disavowed. They are entitled to our grave and respectful consideration, both from the high position and character of the gentleman from whom they emanate, and his peculiar relations to the President, and the concurrence of view between him and the President asserted and not disavowed. Those comments are in the form of an attack upon the "radical abolitionists;" but, while that is the form, the substance is a vindication of the colonization policy of the President, a demonstration of its necessity to the success of the emancipation policy proclaimed by the President, and the "radical abolitionists" are all who differ from the President and his commentator! I am one of them.

What are the grounds? First of all it is said that the "radical abolitionists" wish to change the Constitution of the United States and all of our laws, to elevate to an equality this race, which is wholly untrue; and, in the next place, that unequal races can not live together on terms of equality and peace, and therefore that it is necessary to prevent the massacre of the negro that he should be expatriated. Mr. Speaker, what is the foundation of this view? The negro must be colonized if he be free, or a war of races will exterminate him! What justifies this alternative? Will gentlemen tell me where in the history of the world they find the fact upon which they base that astounding generalization? Civilized people have overborne savages, men of one religion have borne down men of a different religion, ambition has overturned one nation by another, but where in the history of the world is there any case of a nation going to work to exterminate a large portion of its people of another race living in the midst of it, of the same religion, civilized in the same manner, conforming to its laws, subject to its will, willing to work for its wages, not ambitious, and not disturbing the public peace, because they are of a different race? Where is the instance in the history of the world of the subjugation and massacre of a different race under these circumstances? In earlier times great masses of people poured from Central Asia over Europe. They were of a different race from the inhabitants of the Roman empire, in any ethnological sense in which the word can be used. I do not know that they enslaved the whole mass of the people of the Roman empire. My impression is that the conquered civilized the conqueror, and that it did not end in the social war such as is contemplated here, but the descendants of both form now the people of Europe.

The distinguished commentator on the colonization views of the President refers to the Moors of Spain. In an ethnological sense they were far from kin in point of race to the Spaniards. But race was not the ground of war; it was religion; and every decree which undertook to expel them gave them the alternative of baptism or exile. The Spaniards wanted them to stay, and Ferdinand and Isabella would have been glad if they had remained to decorate the southern portion of their empire, the perpetual glory of their missionary zeal.

Then we are referred to San Domingo. That is exactly what gentlemen on the other side of the House are preparing for us in the future. There was no revolt of slaves against their masters, there was no war of one race against another, unwilling to live in peace and industry; but the French Assembly, having freed the slaves of San Domingo, undertook to reduce them to slavery again. They revolted against the authority which attempted to reduce them to slavery, and under Toussaint L'Ouverture, whose military genius Thiers thinks it worth while to commend, defeated both France and England in their attempt to reduce and hold the island.

These are the examples of wars of race! But why do they pass over the peaceful example of emancipation of Jamaica and the French colonies, where the circumstances would be more analogous? Why do they not invoke the great example of Mexico and South America? The Indian of those countries is as far removed from the Spaniard as our Indians from us, and as we are from the negro. The Spaniard gained and wielded the empire over them, but neither is exterminated; the two races are not blended, neither is reduced to slavery, and in Mexico both unite against the common foe. Race has nothing to do with the question. The Indian and Spaniard live together because both are civilized, and both are Christian, and both are interested in the same laws, and government, and industry.

I wait patiently till the gentlemen adduce their historic facts upon which to rest their theory of the necessary contest of races to reply to them. I have dealt only with those they have furnished.

The honorable gentleman from New York [Mr. Brooks] arraigned the harsh, hard-hearted conduct of Massachusetts toward the Indians. The war of Massachusetts on the Indians was that of a civilized and Christian people against a people of different religion, and which refused every form of American civilization. The same differences of religious and social organization prevents the toleration of a Mormon people in any of our States hitherto. He might have found an example nearer at home. The only example upon the American continent of a war on the peace and quiet of the negro is the riots in New York city last summer, when Seymour's *friends*, the Pahdees, undertook to show their Democratic mercy to the wretched negro. I agree that it is possible that such a class of population as that might be tempted to oppress the negro, but no class of American population would condescend to do it. There was more of Democratic hostility to the government than Celtic hostility to the negro. An argument without a fact is not likely to carry conviction; but the gentleman from New York did not venture to use the only one pertinent to his purpose, which bad men had prepared at his very threshold.

Then what are you going to do with them? The President and the commentator say, go to kindred races and congenial climes. Where? To Texas? That is abandoned. To Central America, for the purpose of making a connection between the great oceans? That was respectfully declined. To South America? I have not heard that the President has been successful there in finding a kindred race willing to receive them. Back to Africa? Won't you ask as a matter of kindness to transplant the Irish back to Ireland, to a kindred race and congenial bogs? Who inhabit Mexico? Who inhabit Central America? Who inhabit South America? I take it the Indian of this peninsula is farther removed from the negro of the African peninsula than we are who come more directly from the common stock of Central Asia. Then to transplant them there would be putting a greater diversity of races together to come into collision. Or will they love each other, though alien in race, because of their color? Is skin deep the depth of their philosophy?

In the imagination of the commentator, Cuba is the central empire of the negro; and strange as it appears, while one party of colonizationists are talking of transplanting the negro to the coast of Africa, the commentator on the President's policy grows enthusiastic over the vision of the negroes settled in the American tropics inviting their brethren from Africa to this Western world—a new Canaan for that outcast and rescued race? What becomes of the Spaniard and his rights? What becomes of the rights of the white population? What becomes of the aristocratic Spaniard, who has been crushing generation after generation in Cuba to enhance his wealth? How is he to receive the African in spite of the diversity of race? Is the Spaniard nearer in blood because Spain is nearer geographically to Africa? The theory of the incompatibility of different races has no foundation in history. The moment you come to state it in words, and ask what it means, all the theory, all the philosophy, and all the facts break down, and there is the end of it. Its very advocates discard it in their dreams.

But we are ourselves interested a little in this question of exportation of the negro. The President proposes to pay loyal owners for loss of slaves by the acts of the United States. That is part of his scheme of settlement. But who will submit to additional millions of taxation for slaves freed by the United States? Such a debt would equal the war debt: it would prostrate the resources of the country for generations: it would inflict the scourge of perpetual debt on a land destroyed by civil war, and made a desert by the deportation of its laboring population. The free men of the free States will not mortgage the labor of their sons and daughters for such a purpose; and the loyal men of the South must, and will, find their indemnity in the increased value of their lands, if they are not deprived of their labor.

But if the schemes of colonization be persisted in, who will pay the cost? Who will pay for the transportation? Who will supply the depleted labor of the country? Who is going to pay the increased price of bread to the poor mechanic? Who is going to pay the increased price of cotton? Who is going to fill up the enormous vacuum of labor swept away by this insane and unchristian philanthropy? What is the negro to do in the mean time? You can not take them away to-morrow or in a generation. The schemers propose to build canals and fortifications, connect the Mississippi with the lakes—*for a generation!* Under whose supervision, at whose expense, by what new forms of socialism will you sweep a whole region of country of three or four million people, and concentrate them upon the banks of the Mississippi to eat bread and dig ditches, while the cotton-fields are unplanted, and men and women starving? When you undertake to colonize the negro, you will meet the master, who says, "Do not leave me to starvation." The master will offer the negro more to stay than the government will offer him to go. Two generations can not fill up his place; and if we can stand his presence two generations, perhaps Christian philosophy will enable our descendants to reconcile themselves to the permanence of what has been found tolerable so long.

Why should they consent to go to barbarous countries? Why should they love the people of Ashantee? Would the King of Dahomey protect them from the cannibals of Africa? They prefer to stay where they are. You can not offer them as good homes; you can not offer them as good wages; you can not give them as good treatment; you can not give them as good churches, nor as good houses, and food, and clothing for their children. Why should they consent to go?

Now deal with the problem under the conditions which exist. The folly of our ancestors and the wisdom of the Almighty, in its inscrutable purposes, having allowed them to come here and planted them here, they have a right to remain here, and they will remain here to the latest syllable of recorded time. And whether they become our equals or our superiors, whether they blend or remain a distinct people, your posterity will know, for their eyes will behold them as ours do now. These are things which we can not control. Laws do not make, laws can not unmake them. If God has made them our equals, then they will work out the problem which he has sent them to work out; and if God has stamped upon them an ineradicable inferiority, you can not make one hair white or black, or add a cubit to their stature. Let us leave such questions for gentlemen of the school of Wendell Phillips to talk of; but I earnestly pray gentlemen in high positions, in view of the excited and feverish state of the public mind, in dealing with this delicate topic of the welfare of millions of whites and blacks, not to add to the inherent difficulties of the problem prejudices drawn from fancies, not facts, which we may never be called upon to deal with, and which can only exasperate the very feeling which we ought to allay, and instigate the very collision we all deprecate.

Sir, I am a Marylander, not a "Northern fanatic." My father was a slaveholder. I was myself for years a slaveholder. I have lived nearly all my life in Maryland. I know the temper of her people. I have lived for years in Virginia. I know the temper of her people; I know the relations of the white and black population in those States, and I am going to state some facts to the House nearer home than those cited by the dreamers.

In Maryland we have more free negroes than any other State in the Union. Virginia stands next. She has some fifty thousand among five hundred thousand slaves, and we have eighty-three thousand among eighty-seven thousand slaves. One eighth of our population is free negro. In 1859, just before the rebellion, there was what was called in Maryland a "Slaveholders' Convention"—a phenomenon under the sun—fit precursor of the slave confederacy! Nobody could be admitted who did not own slaves; and their purpose was, as their resolutions indicated when introduced, to put an end to free negroism in Maryland for the advantage of the white population. There was one man in that assembly who was not crazy, and that man was an old Whig whom I honored, and whom my friend from Kentucky [Mr. Mallory] knew and honored. His name was James Alfred Pearce, always a statesman, always a gentleman, however wandering into errors in his last days. He was placed upon the committee to which this subject was referred, and being a gentleman and a large slaveholder, and knowing something about political economy, and the effect of tampering with the laws of industry, he embodied his sane views in a report to that Convention, a part of which I will read for the benefit of the House:

"The existence of so large a number of free blacks in the midst of a slaveholding State is believed to be of itself an evil, and this evil is readily perceived to be greater when it is considered that a portion of them are idle, vicious, and unproductive. This, however, is not the case with the majority of them, and their removal would, as the committee believe, be far greater than all the evils the people of Maryland ever suffered from them. In the city of Baltimore it is estimated that there are more than twenty-five thousand of them, employed chiefly as domestic servants or laborers in various departments of industry. In many of the rural districts of the State, where labor is by no means abundant, they furnish a large supply of agricultural labor, and it is unquestionable that quite a large portion of our soil could not be tilled without their aid."

How much of South Carolina or Mississippi could be tilled without their aid?

"In some districts they supply almost all the labor demanded by the farmers. Their removal from the State would deduct nearly fifty per cent. from the household and agricultural labor furnished by people of this color, and indispensable to the people of the State; would produce great discomfort and inconvenience to the great body of householders; would break up the business and destroy the property of large numbers of landowners and landrenters—a class whose interests are entitled to as much consideration as those of any other portion of our citizens; would be harsh and oppressive to those people themselves; would violate public sentiment, which is generally not only just, but kindly, and would probably lead to other evils which the committee forbear to mention. We are satisfied that such a measure could not receive the legislative sanction, and would not be tolerated by the great body of the people of Maryland, even with that sanction."

That is from James Alfred Pearce, a slaveholder. Even the secession Legislature of Maryland, then about to meet, had it passed that law, James A. Pearce tells them the people of Maryland would not tolerate them in doing it. I beg you, gentlemen, observe the strength of the language:

"The committee, therefore, can not recommend their expulsion from the State. Still more unwilling should they be to favor any measure which looked to their *being deprived of the* right to freedom which they have acquired by the indulgence of our laws and the tenderness of their masters, whether wise or unwise, or which they have inherited as a birthright."

Then, sir, in Maryland a free negro has some rights.

The policy of the report prevailed in this Convention of slaveholders, and the iniquitous purpose was not by them pressed on the Legislature.

Some of the people in that Convention were in the Legislature, and a Mr. Jacobs was one of them. He introduced a law to hire the free negroes out to the highest bidders; and if they should be disobedient after being hired out, then they were to be sold as slaves for life. The bill could not be passed. It was objected to by county after county. It was only allowed to become a law with reference to four or five counties—St. Mary's, Charles, Somerset, Worcester, Baltimore County, and perhaps one or two others; and it was not allowed to be operative till approved by the people of the counties respectively. The friends of the infamous scheme went before the people at the presidential election in those counties; for the Legislature would not allow the law even to apply to those counties unless a majority of the people willed it. In

Howard, one of the slaveholding counties, they got just 55 votes for it, and against it 1397. In Baltimore County they got 681 votes for, and 5364 against it. In Kent County they got 74 votes for, and 1502 votes against it. It passed in no county except in one, and there by an accident. That is the judgment of the people of Maryland on the relations of the laboring free colored people living among them, essential to their industry, a part of their social system, filling well their place in life, without whom their interests can not be protected, and which we neither will expel ourselves, nor encourage to go, nor allow other people to expel.

If gentlemen want to know still farther how Maryland regards the free negro population, I desire to say that the emancipation movement of Maryland is indebted very much to the commencement of negro enlistments in Maryland for the same economic reason. Colonel Birney was sent there with general orders to enlist negroes. He was not instructed to take slaves. He commenced the enlistment of free negroes. Gentlemen found at once that that was a discrimination between the loyal people who do not own slaves and the disloyal people who do own slaves; and my friend Judge Bond wrote to the Secretary of War remonstrating against the inequality of taking from the Union men their labor, and leaving with the secessionist his labor. He pointed out the law of 1862, authorizing the enlisting of one as well as of the other. The Secretary of War agreed with him. Birney acted under the implied, if not the express authority of the Secretary of War, and commenced to levy from the slave population, in order that the Union men might have the free colored population to hire. So the beginning of slave enlistments was a question of political economy which the President and his commentator propose to solve in one way, but which the people of Maryland mean to solve in another way.

But it was also apparent that every slave enlisted was a poor white man's substitute. It was that, more than any thing else, that brought directly before the people of Maryland at the last election the burdens they were suffering from the existence of slavery, and that aided more than did the bayonets to which the gentleman from New York refers, more than all proclamations, more than any other argument urged, in bringing on our side the people of the slaveholding counties of Maryland, who had voted at the beck of the slaveholders for generations. They said, "If we are to have a draft, and if our rich neighbor's plantation is to be cultivated while we are dragged off to fill the quota of the State, we think that an injustice. We are for slave enlistments, and in favor of relieving the white people from the disproportionate burdens of the draft." It was that, sir, and no proclamation; it was that view, carried home by my honorable friend who represents the First Congressional District [Mr. Creswell], urged upon every husting, in every fence corner, that dragged out men in homespun to cast their first independent vote, and my honorable friend from the first district is the representative of that independent vote.

Such was the telling power of the enlistment of slaves that my colleague got in the county of Worcester, one of the great slaveholding counties, several hundred more votes than his predecessor, Mr. Crisfield, a most able gentleman, got when he was candidate of the united Union party.

If we are to be treated, Mr. Speaker, to speculations on equality, and prejudices of race, and matters of that kind, to bewilder and mislead the public judgment upon this grave and important topic, allow me to beseech gentlemen to recollect that we people in America are not the only ones who have prejudices, and that negroes are not the only proscribed race in the world; that other nations have been as unjust and as inclined to oppress, and that we, in some regions of the world, would fare no better than negroes do here. How long has it been since "dog of a Christian" was the most polite word to us in the Moslem's mouth? How long has it been since a Brahmin would condescend to sit at table with the most aristocratic Englishman? How long has it been since the nobles of Europe refused to mingle their blood with the blood of the *villain*, or the peasant of Continental Europe? Have we forgot the first example—that the Hebrew was *an abomination to the Egyptian-African?*

These are arguments to prejudice, and not to the merits. They are intended to mislead, not to enlighten. I beg gentlemen on the other side, whatever their views or purposes may be, let us combine, whatever the result, that the least damage may be done to the public service. Let us decide the question, not upon suggestions of prejudice, not on questions of hostility to race, but on the great *politico*-economic argument, if I may use the expression. Those forces which must determine it will determine it peacefully if we are wise, or in blood if we are unwise. Those, and those alone, in my judgment, are the alternatives.

REPUBLICAN GOVERNMENT IN THE REBELLIOUS STATES.

On the 22d of March, 1864, the House refused to recommit the Bill for the Government of the Rebellious States reported from the Select Committee, and the question being upon ordering the bill to be engrossed and read a third time, Mr. Davis, as Chairman of the Select Committee, addressed the House as follows:

Mr. Speaker,—The bill which I am directed by the Committee on the Rebellious States to report is one which provides for the restoration of civil government in States whose governments have been overthrown. It prescribes such conditions as will secure not merely civil government to the people of the rebellious States, but will also secure to the people of the United States permanent peace after the suppression of the rebellion.

The bill challenges the support of all who consider slavery the cause of the rebellion, and that in it the embers of rebellion will always smoulder; of those who think that freedom and permanent peace are inseparable, and who are determined, so far as their constitutional authority will allow them, to secure these fruits by adequate legislation.

The vote of gentlemen upon this measure will be regarded by the country with no ordinary interest. Their vote will be taken to express their opinion on the necessity of ending slavery with the rebellion, and their willingness to assume the responsibility of adopting the legislative measures without which that result can not be assured, and may wholly fail of accomplishment. Their vote will be held to show whether they think the measure now proposed, or any which may be moved as a substitute, is an adequate and proper measure to accomplish that purpose. It is entitled to the support of all gentlemen upon this side of the House, whatever their views may be of the nature of the rebellion; and the relation in which it has placed the people and States in rebellion toward the United States, not less of those who think that the rebellion has placed the citizens of the rebel States beyond the protection of the Constitution, and that Congress, therefore, has supreme power over them as conquered enemies, than of that other class who think that they have not ceased to be citizens and States of the United States, though incapable of exercising political privileges under the Constitution, but that Congress is charged with a high political power by the Constitution to guarantee republican governments in the States, and that this is the proper time and the proper mode of exercising it. It is also entitled to the favorable consideration of gentlemen upon the other side of the House, who honestly and deliberately express their judgment that slavery is dead. To them it puts the question whether it is not advisable to bury it out of our sight, that its ghost may no longer stalk abroad to frighten us from our propriety.

It does not address itself to that class of gentlemen upon the other side of the House, if there be any, nor to that class of the people of the country who look for political alliance to the men who head the rebellion in the South, and say to them, let us

> "Once more
> Erect the standard there of ancient knight,
> Yours be the advantage all, mine the revenge."

It purports, sir, not to exercise a revolutionary authority, but to be an execution of the Constitution of the United States, of the fourth section of the fourth article of that Constitution, which not merely confers the power upon Congress, but imposes upon Congress the duty of guaranteeing to every State in this Union a republican form of government. That clause vests in the Congress of the United States a plenary, supreme, unlimited political jurisdiction, paramount over courts, subject only to the judgment of the people of the United States, embracing within its scope every legislative measure necessary and proper to make it effectual; and what is necessary and proper the Constitution refers, in the first place, to our judgment, subject to no revision but that of the people. It recognizes no other tribunal. It recognizes the judgment of no court. It refers to no authority except the judgment and will of the majority of Congress, and of the people on that judgment, if any appeal from it. It is one of that class of plenary powers of a political character conferred on Congress by the Constitution, such as the authority to admit new States into the Union, the authority to make rules and regulations for the government of the Territories of the United States. With reference to that class of cases, the Supreme Court, renouncing all right to judge on political questions, has said that these sections vested in the Congress of the United States plenary power over the subject-matters mentioned, subject only to the limitations contained in those sections. In the section to which I refer there is, and almost from the very nature of the case there can be, no limitation. It is intended to meet all the emergencies of the national life. It is intended to apply to events which human imagination could scarcely have pictured. And yet the great wisdom of the framers of the Constitution has in no particular been rendered more remarkably apparent—although their imagination could scarcely have reached the belief in the possibility of events that are to us familiar as household words—than in their having laid by, in the arsenal of the Constitution, the weapons to deal with this great danger.

What is the nature of this case with which we have to deal—the evil we must remedy, the danger we must avert? In other words, what is that monster of political wrong which is called secession? It is not, Mr. Speaker, domestic violence within the meaning of that clause of the Constitution, for the violence was the act of the people of the States through their government, and was the offspring of their free and unforced will. It is not invasion in the meaning of the Constitution, for no State has been invaded against the will of the government of the State by any power except the United States marching to overthrow the usurpers of its territory. It is, therefore, the act of the people of the States, carrying with it all the consequences of such an act. And therefore it must be either a legal revolution which makes them independent, and makes of the United States a foreign country, or it is a usurpation against the authority of the United States, the erection of governments which do not recognize the Constitution of the United States, which the Constitution does not recognize, and, therefore, not republican governments of the States in rebellion. The latter is the view which all parties take of it. I do not understand that any gentleman on the other side of the House says that any rebel government which does not recognize the Constitution of the United States, and which is not recognized by Congress, is a State government within the meaning of the Constitution. Still less can it be said that there is a State government, republican or unrepublican, in the State of Tennessee, where there is no government of any kind, no civil authority, no organized form of administration except that represented by the flag of the United States, obeying the will, and under the orders of the military officer in command. It is the language of the President of the United States in every proclamation, of Congress in every law on the statute-book, of both houses in their forms of proceedings, and of the courts of the United States in their administration of the law. It is the result of every principle of law, of every suggestion of political philosophy, that there can be no republican government within the limits of the United States that does not recognize, but does repudiate, the Constitution, and which the President and the Congress of the United States do not, on their part, recognize. Those that are here represented are the only governments existing within the limits of the United States. Those that are not here represented are not governments of the States, republican under the Constitution. And if they be not, then they are military usurpations, inaugurated as the permanent governments of the States, contrary to the supreme law of the land, arrayed in arms against the government of the United States; and it is the duty, the first and highest duty, of the government to suppress and expel them. Congress must either expel, or recognize and support them. If it do not guarantee them, it is bound to expel them; and they who are not ready to suppress them are bound to recognize them.

The Supreme Court of the United States, in declining jurisdiction of political questions such as these in the famous Rhode Island cases, declared by the mouth of Chief Justice Taney, in the presidency of John Tyler, during the Southern domination, in support of the acts of John Tyler, that a military government, established as the permanent government of a State, is not a republican government in the meaning of the Constitution, and that it is the duty of Congress to suppress it. That duty Congress is now executing by its armies. He farther said in that case that it is the exclusive prerogative of Congress—of Congress, and not of the President—to determine what is and what is not the established government of the State; and, to come to that conclusion, it must judge of what is and what is not a republican government, and its judgment is conclusive on the Supreme Court, which can not judge of the fact for itself, but accepts the fact declared by the political department of the government.

We are now engaged in suppressing a military usurpation of

the authority of the State government. When that shall have been accomplished, there will be no form of State authority in existence which Congress can recognize. Our success will be the overthrow of *all* semblance of government in the rebel States. The government of the United States is then, in fact, the *only* government existing in those States, and it is there charged to guarantee them republican governments.

What jurisdiction does the duty of guaranteeing a republican government confer, under such circumstances, upon Congress? What right does it give? What laws may it pass? What objects may it accomplish? What conditions may it insist upon, and what judgment may it exercise in determining what it will do? The duty of guaranteeing carries with it the right to pass all laws necessary and proper to guarantee. The duty of guaranteeing means the duty to accomplish the result. It means that the republican government shall exist. It means that every opposition to republican government shall be put down. It means that every thing inconsistent with the permanent continuance of republican government shall be weeded out. It places in the hands of Congress the right to say what is and what is not, with all the light of experience and all the lessons of the past, inconsistent, in its judgment, with the permanent continuance of republican government; and if, in its judgment, any form of policy is radically and inherently inconsistent with the permanent and enduring peace of the country, with the permanent supremacy of republican government, and it have the manliness to say so, there is no power, judicial or executive, in the United States, that can even question this judgment but the PEOPLE; and they can do it only by sending other representatives here to undo our work. The very language of the Constitution and the necessary logic of the case involves that consequence. The denial of the right of secession means that all the territory of the United States shall remain under the jurisdiction of the Constitution. If there can be no State government which does not recognize the Constitution, and which the authorities of the United States do not recognize, then there are these alternatives, and these only: The rebel States must be governed by Congress till they submit and form a State government under the Constitution; or Congress must recognize State governments which do not recognize either Congress or the Constitution of the United States; or there must be an entire absence of *all* government in the rebel States; and that is anarchy. To recognize a government which does not recognize the Constitution is absurd, for a government is not a Constitution; and the recognition of a State government means the acknowledgment of men as governors, and legislators, and judges, actually invested with power to make laws, to judge of crimes, to convict the citizens of other States, to demand the surrender of fugitives from justice, to arm and command the militia, to require the United States to repress all opposition to its authority, and to protect it from invasion—against our own armies; whose senators and representatives are *entitled* to seats in Congress, and whose electoral votes must be counted in the election of the President of a government which they disown and defy!! To accept the alternative of anarchy as the constitutional condition of a State is to assert the failure of the Constitution and the end of republican government. Until, therefore, Congress recognize a State government, organized under its auspices, there is no government in the rebel States except the authority of Congress. In the absence of all State government, the duty is imposed on Congress to provide by law to keep the peace, to administer justice, to watch over the transmission of decedents' estates, to sanction marriages—in a word, to administer civil government until the people shall, under its guidance, submit to the Constitution of the United States, and, under the laws which it shall impose, and on the conditions Congress may require, reorganize a republican government for themselves, and Congress shall recognize that government.

These, therefore, are the things which are involved in the duty of Congress to guarantee a republican government to the States. But we have not yet suppressed the insurrection. We are still engaged in removing armed rebellion. Is it yet time to reorganize the State governments? or is there not an intermediate period in which sound legislative wisdom requires that the authority of Congress shall take possession of and temporarily control the States now in rebellion until peace shall be restored and republican government can be established deliberately, undisturbed by the sound or fear of arms, and under the guidance of law?

What is the condition of the rebellion at this time? I do not know that I express the opinions of gentlemen in this House, but, in my judgment,

> "Doubtful it stands
> As two spent swimmers, that do cling together,
> And choke their act."

Our arms have advanced deep into the regions of the rebellion; we have occupied a vast area wrested from its power, but to this day we have not expelled the rebels from *any State* they ever held.

There is no State some portion of whose territory is not pressed by rebels in arms whom we have not expelled, or whom we can not expel. There is no portion of the rebel States where peace has been so far restored that our military power can be withdrawn for a moment without instant insurrection. There is no rebel State held now by the United States enough of whose population adheres to the Union to be intrusted with the government of the State. One tenth can not control nine tenths. Five tenths are nowhere willing to undertake the control of the other five tenths. Nowhere does such a proportion exist willing to do so, or, if willing to do so, who can safely be trusted with the great powers of a State government, carrying with it the right of taxation, the existence of courts, the appointment of officers, the command of the militia, and, besides the supremacy of the internal concerns of the State, the right to participate in the government of the United States by representatives, senators, and electors appointed by their uncontrolled dictation. In West Virginia that authority exists and has been recognized. In no other State—the only one in respect to which a doubt can exist is Tennessee—in no other State is there such a portion of territory held, or any such portion of population under our control, or any such portion of it which is in our control inspired by such sentiments toward the government of the United States, so free from fear of the returning wave of rebel invasion, so assured of the continued supremacy of the United States, that we ought to be willing to intrust them with this power. You can get a handful of men in the several States who would be glad to take the offices if protected by the troops of the United States, but you have nowhere a body of independent, loyal partisans of the United States, ready to meet the rebels in arms, ready to die for the republic, who claim the Constitution as their birthright, count all other privileges light in comparison, and resolved at every hazard to maintain it.

The loyal masses of the South, of which we hear so much, what was their temper at the outbreak of the rebellion? what is their temper now? They did not want rebellion; they voted against secession; they acquiesced in the vote which decreed it; *they went with their State;* they were content to accept what they did not prefer, but were unwilling to resist; they preferred Union with peace, but when Union and peace could not exist together, they yielded up the Union rather than make war to maintain it; and when the question was Union and war for it or disunion and war for it, they preferred war against the United States to war against the South. Whether it was that the doctrines of secession had ground themselves into the minds of men and become unconsciously the foundations upon which their thoughts rested; or that they thought the interests of slavery must necessarily be sacrificed in the event of a war, and they were not willing to sacrifice it; or that the long strife on the Negro Question had deadened their national feeling; or that they had ceased to regard the people of the free States as fellow-citizens, and the horror of joining them against their Southern brethren oppressed them like a nightmare; or the fear of making war at their own doors, and the drawing of the sword against their own friends and neighbors, or a conviction that the United States was no longer a power, but a mere semblance of authority—a Roi faineant, whose Mayors of the Palace were merely clothing the reality of power long wielded with the forms of sovereignty—whether each or all of these were the motive, *the fact* is that after they voted against secession, they acquiesced in the judgment of their friends and fellow-citizens. It is the most astounding spectacle in history that in the Southern States, with more than half of the population opposed to it, a great revolution was effected against their wishes and against their votes, without a battle, a riot, or a protest in behalf of the beneficent government of their fathers—a revolution whose opponents hastened to lead it, without a martyr to the cause they deserted except the nameless heroes of the mountains of Tennessee, or a confessor of the faith they had avowed save the illustrious Petigru of South Carolina!

Doubtful of the issues of the war, exhausted by bloodshed, anxious for peace—peace and *independence*—there are some who will accept peace and union, but they are not men who will draw the sword for the United States, and they would be equally content with peace and independence. When the overthrow of the rebellion is an accomplished fact, they will acquiesce; when there shall be neither hope nor fear of rebel supremacy, they will submit to what we judge to be necessary for their good and for ours if we will peremptorily declare the conditions necessary to secure republican government. But it is the veriest child's dream to suppose that, so long as this war lasts, so long as its flames blaze over the Southern country, any large portion of the Southern population is willing to cast in its lot with the United States for good or evil, and assume now the responsibility that they declined at the beginning, of standing with us for better, for worse, in ruin or in triumph.

There is no fact that we have learned from any one who has been in the South, and has come up from the darkness of that bottomless pit, which indicates such repentance. There is no fact that any one has stated on authority at all reliable that any respectable proportion of the people of the Southern States now in rebellion are willing to accept any terms that even our opponents on the other side of the House are willing to offer them.

It has been repeatedly asserted—Governor Seymour, of New York, in his message asserted—that peace could be had upon any reasonable terms. That was his *guess*; it was his wish; it was his fond, *vain* hope. In fact, there is no ground for such hope, and to-day no man can stand before the American people and say that there is the least reason to suppose that any public man in the South has declared himself willing to consider peace on any conditions but that of independence.

What, then, are we to do with the population in these States? To make "confusion worse confounded" by erecting by the side of the hostile State government a new State government on the shifting sands of that whirlpool, to be supported by us while we are there, and to turn its power against us when we are driven out? That would be to erect a new throne where

> "Chaos umpire sits,
> And by decision more embroils the fray
> By which he reigns."

In my judgment, it is not safe to confide the vast authority of State governments to the doubtful loyalty of the rebel States until armed rebellion shall have been trampled into the dust, until every armed rebel shall have vanished from the State, until there shall be in the South no hope of independence and no fear of subjection, until the United States is bearded by no military power, and the laws can be executed by courts and sheriffs without the ever-present menace of military authority. Until we have reached that point, this bill proposes that the President shall appoint a civil governor, to administer the government under the laws of the United States and the laws in force in the States respectively at the outbreak of the rebellion, subject of course to the necessities of military occupation.

It is the policy of an ancient soldier that I adopt:

> "Trust none;
> For oaths are straws, men's faiths are wafer-cakes,
> And hold-fast's the only dog, my duck
> Therefore coveto be thy counselor."

When military opposition shall have been suppressed—not merely paralyzed, driven into a corner, pushed back, but gone—the horrid vision of civil war vanished from the South, then call upon the people to reorganize in their own way, subject to the conditions that we think essential to our permanent peace, and to prevent the revival hereafter of the rebellion, a republican government in the form that the people of the United States can agree to.

Now, for that purpose, there are three modes indicated. One is to remove the cause of the war by an alteration of the Constitution of the United States prohibiting slavery every where within its limits. That, sir, goes to the root of the matter, and should consecrate the nation's triumph. But there are thirty-four States —three fourths of them would be twenty-six. I believe there are twenty-five States represented in this Congress, so that we, on that basis, can not change the Constitution. It is, therefore, a condition precedent in that view of the case, that more States shall have governments organized within them. If it be assumed that the basis of calculation shall be three fourths of the States now represented in Congress, I agree to that construction of the Constitution, which I understand to be that of the Chairman of the Judiciary Committee, the gentleman from Pennsylvania [Mr. Stevens], and not without countenance in high judicial quarters. I think it was never contemplated that the supreme political power should pass away from the government of the United States. But that view will probably encounter as much doubt as the bill before the House, besides involving serious delay; and, under any circumstances, even upon that basis, it will be difficult to find three fourths of the States, with New Jersey, or Kentucky, or Maryland, Delaware, or other States that might be mentioned, opposed to it under existing auspices, to adopt such a clause of the Constitution after we shall have agreed to it.

If adopted, it still leaves the whole field of the civil administration of the States prior to the recognition of State governments, all laws necessary to the ascertainment of the will of the people, and all restrictions on the return to power of the leaders of the rebellion, wholly unprovided for.

The amendment of the Constitution meets my hearty approval; but it is not a remedy for the evils we must deal with.

The next plan is that inaugurated by the President of the United States in the proclamation of the 8th of December, called the Amnesty Proclamation. That proposes no guardianship of the United States over the reorganization of the governments, no law to prescribe who shall vote, no civil functionaries to see that the law is faithfully executed, no supervising authority to control and judge of the election. But if, in any manner, by the toleration of martial law, lately proclaimed the fundamental law, under the dictation of any military authority, or under the prescriptions of a provost-marshal, something in the form of a government shall be presented, represented to rest on the votes of one tenth of the population, the President will recognize that, provided it does not *contravene* the proclamation of freedom and the laws of Congress; and, to secure that, an oath is exacted.

Now you will observe that there is no guarantee of law to watch over the organization of that government. It may combine all the population of a State; it may combine one tenth only; or ten governments may come competing for recognition at the door of the executive mansion. The executive authority is pledged; Congress is not pledged. It may be recognized by the military power, and may not be recognized by the civil power, so that it would have a doubtful existence, half civil and half military, neither a temporary government by law of Congress nor a State government, something as unknown to the Constitution as the rebel government that refuses to recognize it.

But, Mr. Speaker, let us regard its operation on a great fundamental measure, the existence of slavery, the condition of future peace. How does it accomplish the final removal of slavery?

How does it accomplish the reorganization of the government on the basis of universal freedom?

The only prescription is that the government shall not *contravene* the provisions of that proclamation. Sir, if that proclamation be valid, then we are relieved from all trouble on that score; but if that proclamation be not valid, then the oath to support it is without legal sanction, for the President can ask no man to bind himself by an oath to support an unfounded proclamation or an unconstitutional law even for a moment, still less till it shall have been declared void by the Supreme Court of the United States. It is the paramount right of every American citizen to judge for himself, on his own responsibility, of his constitutional rights; and an oath does not bind him to submit to that which is illegal. If, therefore, he shall have taken the oath, he can, in good conscience as well as in good law, disregard it the next moment; so that, in point of fact, the law leaves us where the proclamation does; it adds nothing to its legality, nothing to its force.

But what is the proclamation which the new governments must not contravene? That certain negroes shall be free, and that certain other negroes shall remain slaves. The proclamation therefore recognizes the existence of slavery. It does just exactly what all the Constitutions of the rebel States prior to the rebellion did. It recognizes the existence of slavery, and they recognized the existence of slavery; and, therefore, the old Constitutions might be restored to-morrow without *contravening* the proclamation of freedom. Those Constitutions do not say that the President shall not have the right, in the exercise of his military authority, to emancipate slaves within the States. They say nothing of the kind. They do not even establish slavery. There is not a Constitution in all the rebel States that formally declares slavery to be the supreme law of the land. They merely recognize it just as the proclamation recognizes its existence in parts of Virginia and in parts of Louisiana; so that the one tenth of the population at whose hands the President proposes to accept and guarantee a State government, can elect officers under the old Constitution of their State in exactly the same terms and with exactly the same powers existing at the time of the rebellion, and may, under his proclamation, demand a recognition. No man will say that there is one word in their laws that contravenes what purports to be a paramount, not a subordinate order. So soon as the State government is recognized, the operation of the proclamation becomes merely a judicial question. The right of a negro to his freedom is a legal right divesting a right of property, and is to be enforced in the courts; and then the question is what the courts will say about the proclamation. Is it valid or invalid? Does it of itself confer a legal right to freedom on negroes who were slaves? Is it within the authority of the executive? These are the only questions open under such a government; and how local State courts, created by the Southern people, will decide such a question, *no one* can doubt; for it is quite certain that the great mass of that population is devoted to the system of slave labor; and though, if the question be whether they will give up slavery as the condition precedent to the restoration of a State government, they will abandon it, yet if it be whether they prefer to maintain or abolish slavery, there is not the least doubt that their voice would be almost unanimous for its maintenance. If they have the decision, we know what it will be already. It is, therefore, under the scheme of the President, merely a judicial question, to be adjudged by judicial rules, and to be determined by the courts. It is a question whether each individual negro be free. It is a question whether the master has the right of seizure, or the negro can control himself. It is to be determined by the writ of *habeas corpus*. It is a question of personal right, not a question of political jurisdiction. Its fate in the State courts is certain. Its fate in the courts of the United States under existing laws is scarcely doubtful. I do not desire to argue the legality of the proclamation of freedom. I think it safer to *make it law.* But I wish to admonish gentlemen who rely on Dunmore's proclamation for the right of a military commander to free slaves in a civil war, that no slave is known ever to have claimed his freedom under it, though, if valid, there must have been many persons so entitled, and the Courts of Virginia and of the United States were all open to them for its enforcement and their protection. When they recite the opinions of John Quincy Adams, it must be remembered that he is on both sides of the question. He wrote instructions to our minister denying the right to emancipate, and claiming compensation of England for slaves carried off in the last war, and insisted upon the question being decided by the Emperor of Russia. And it is farther a material consideration that under that claim, by authority of the United States, and in the name of that predecessor of Abraham Lincoln, England paid divers pounds sterling to the citizens of the United States for negroes she took, as he alleged, in contravention of the laws of war. If the proclamation free a slave, it diverts a right sanctioned by a law which he can not repeal; and if it be not repealed, it would seem to protect the right it confers. Under the act of 1862 the President is authorized to use the negro population for the suppression of the rebellion; while the rebellion lasts, his proclamation in law exempts the slave from the duty of obeying his master; but after the rebellion is extinguished, the master's rights are in his own hands, subject only to the opinion of the courts on the legal effect of the proclamation, without a single precedent to sanction it, and opposed by the solemn assertions of our government against the principle worked to authorize it. Gentlemen are less prudent or less in earnest than I am if they will risk the great issues involved in this question on such authorities before the courts of justice.

By the bill we propose to preclude the judicial question by the solution of a political question. How so? By the paramount power of Congress to reorganize governments in those States, to impose such conditions as it thinks necessary to secure the permanence of republican government, to refuse to recognize any governments there which do not prohibit slavery forever. Ay, gentlemen take the responsibility to say, in the face of those who clamor for speedy recognition of governments tolerating slavery, that the safety of the people of the United States is the supreme law; that their will is the supreme rule of law, and that we are authorized to pronounce their will on this subject—take the responsibility to say that we will revise the judgments of our ancestors; that we have experience written in blood which they had not; that we find now, what they darkly doubted, that slavery is really, radically inconsistent with the permanence of republican governments; and that, being charged by the supreme law of the land, on our conscience and judgment, to guarantee, that is, to continue, maintain, and enforce, if it exist, to institute and restore when overthrown, republican governments throughout the broad limits of the republic, we will weed out every element of their policy which we think incompatible with its permanence and endurance. The purpose of the bill is to preclude the *judicial* question of the validity and effect of the President's proclamation by the decision of the *political* authority in reorganizing the State governments. It makes the rule of decision the provisions of the State Constitution, which, when recognized by Congress, can be questioned in no court; and it adds to the authority of the proclamation the sanction of Congress. If gentlemen say that the Constitution does not bear that construction, we will go before the people of the United States on that question, and by their judgment we will abide.

Gentlemen must deny the jurisdiction of Congress over the States where there are no recognized governments, or place a bound or limit to the discretion of Congress. Until gentlemen find such a limit to the discretion of Congress under the paramount duty imposed, not *conferred*, upon Congress to guarantee republican governments, until gentlemen draw their line of demarcation and show that Congress has not the jurisdiction to remove what it thinks incompatible with the permanence of republican governments, I shall rest the argument where it is now. When they shall have attempted to lay down their line of demarcation, I will be ready to meet them with such opinions of the founders of the government, and those who in their footsteps have most wisely expounded its provisions, as I may be able to find.

And if the sentiments of State pride and State rights be touched by the assertion of this wide discretion, which men may deny but can not expunge, I would admonish those who dislike it that it is a jurisdiction which nothing but the dereliction of the States can wake into activity, and they who wish to exclude it from their limits have only not to give occasion for its exercise by renouncing obedience to the Constitution and pulling down their own State governments. But now the jurisdiction has attached in all the rebel States. Until Congress has assented, there is no State government in any rebel State, and none will be recognized except such as recognize the power of the United States; so that we come down to this: whether we—and when I say we, I mean we upon this side of the House, who are firmly, thoroughly, and honestly convinced that the time has come not merely to strike the arms from the hands of the rebels, but to strike the fetters from the arms of the slaves, and remove that domineering and cohesive power without which we could have had no rebellion, and which now is its animating spirit, and which will die when it dies—whether we will exert the power which the Constitution confers upon us, and whether in our judgment—not in the judgment of our enemies—who have a majority in this House and a majority in the Senate; in our judgment, who now represent a majority of the people of the United States; in our judgment, who now support the executive in this great war; whether in our judgment it is not time to assert that authority.

And if it be time, then all I ask in conclusion is, that gentlemen will go and read that great argument of Daniel Webster in the Rhode Island case before the Supreme Court of the United States, where he met this semi-revolutionary attempt to count heads and call that the people, and maintained—and so the Supreme Court judged when it refused to take jurisdiction of the question—that the great political law of America is that every change of government shall be conducted under the supervising authority of some existing legislative body throwing the protection of law around the polls, defining the rights of voters, protecting them in the exercise of the elective franchise, guarding against fraud, repelling violence, and appointing arbiters to pronounce the result and declare the persons chosen by the people. And he says, greatly to the honor of the American people, it would take him to the going down of the sun to enumerate the instances in which almost every Constitution in the United States has been changed without one ever having been changed by a revolutionary process, not under the ægis of law, not guided by a pre-existing political authority. He maintained it to be the great fundamental principle of the American government that legislation shall guide every political change, and that it assumes that somewhere within the United States there is always a permanent, organized legal authority which shall guide the tottering footsteps of those who seek to restore governments which are disorganized and broken down.

This bill is an effort to inaugurate in this great emergency, and to apply to the benefit of ourselves and our posterity, this great principle of American political law, which was expounded by the first greatest expounder of the Constitution.

ON EMANCIPATION IN MARYLAND.

MEANTIME the Legislature of Maryland had authorized the submission to the people of the question of a Convention for altering the Constitution of the State, and the canvass was about to commence as to delegates to that Convention, if approved, in favor of emancipation.

A large meeting was held in the Maryland Institute, in Baltimore, on the 1st of April, 1864, in pursuance of a call by the Unconditional Union State Central Committee to hear these questions discussed. On that occasion Mr. Davis spoke as follows:

FELLOW-CITIZENS OF MARYLAND,—We are now, I think, about at the end of the canvasses which so long have agitated Maryland, in one aspect or another, of the Negro Question. Last fall the people of Maryland indicated by an almost unprecedented majority their conviction that the times required that Maryland should be put upon the same basis of free institutions which have wrought such miracles of prosperity among our Northern sisters. (Applause.)

They gave that desire by twenty thousand majority. Their will was very nearly defeated by the selection of their candidates. The people found themselves with a Legislature opposed to them upon every material point of interest; a doubtful majority against them in the Lower House; a decided and resolute majority against them in the Senate; the validity of the election attacked by its enemies, who ascribed its successes to the bayonets of "the tyrant Schenck!" The governor had thrown obstacles in the path of our success, and in his message to the Legislature he smeared the election all over with the imputation of illegality.

The enemy held possession of both branches of the Legislature, but they did not dare to unseat one man elected at that "void" election. They whined, they shuffled, they evaded, they struggled and held back, but they did not dare to adjourn without passing our Convention Bill; and now we have the question directly before us, and you, gentlemen, have the decision of it in your hands.

We have made our nominations; our enemies have made theirs; and the question is, which of the two are to fill the seats of the Convention? Are we to have a Convention opposed to emancipation, as the Legislature was opposed to emancipation, and trust to the moral power of the coercion of the popular vote to compel them to discharge their duties? Or shall we have a Convention composed of the gentlemen we have nominated, who go there for the purpose of executing the will that the people have expressed, and who, when they get there, will have the manliness and the resolution to act up to the duties that have been prescribed for them? That, and that only, is the question.

There are other questions that are thrown before you for the purpose of deluding you, as has been the habit heretofore in all political canvasses. You have been told that other questions than the real one are the real questions you are called upon to determine; and what little I have to say here to-night is mainly for the purpose of clearing up all misapprehensions on that subject—of simply stating the question to you for you to decide, and then leave to the distinguished gentlemen who have honored us by their company this evening the enforcement of the views which are appropriate to the occasion.

The slavery interest, of course, struggles vigorously to maintain its domination. It has been heretofore your master, as well as the master of its slaves. One fourth of the people of the State have ruled it by the existing Constitution. They have used their power to take to themselves the lion's share of our political honor, and to cast upon you the ass's share of every political burden. The political power has been down in the rotten-borough counties of St. Mary's, Charles, Calvert, Prince George's, and Anne Arundel, and over in Somerset, Talbot, and Queen Anne's. Their slaves have been exempted from equal taxation.

Their laws have compensated slaveholders every where for their slaves when they forfeited their lives by violation of the law. The taxes have been imposed upon the city of Baltimore; the taxes have been imposed upon the northern and western portions of the State. The laws have been passed at the dictation of the southern portion; the burdens have been borne by the northern portion. In the south, south of the Patapsco River and south of the Sassafras River, you have about one fourth of the white population of the State, and you have one half of all its political power.

I desire gentlemen in that part of the State to know that the first practical fruit we expect to reap from the breaking down of the slavery system is to break down the domination of the power in those masters (applause); to redistribute political power in the State; to reassert the right of numbers; to restore the disturbed balance of popular power; to make those who are in the minority obey the will of those who are in the majority, and not, as at present, permit them to hold a veto upon your will, and wield a majority in the event of their being able to buy, or coax, or bully one or two votes in the other House against you.

That is what we mean to accomplish in the first place. That they do not like, and therefore their game is upon divers pretexts to prevent the calling of a Convention, for they know perfectly well that there is small chance of their controlling the Convention if it shall happen to be called. They have set up the claim for State compensation for their worthless negroes, and they expect to sweep the slaveholding regions of the State, and cause the sixteen or eighteen millions of dollars of surplus that will be raised in the free part of the State to be scattered broadcast in the slave part of the State, and therefore they have a great interest to make it appear that slaves are property, not merely by the conventional law, but in the nature of things, and that they are entitled to compensation when that property ceases by the law to be property. That carries a very powerful influence in all the slaveholding parts of the State. Here in the city of Baltimore, and then in the large free counties of Washington, and Frederick, and Alleghany, they come with a more insidious plea: "You, gentlemen, here, are in favor of emancipation, and uncompensated emancipation, but the Convention is called upon the basis of the old apportionment, and we may elect a majority of it; therefore you had better vote against calling a Convention to save yourselves against the dangers of the burdens of compensation." And this is having its effect on the friends of emancipation every where.

Now all that I desire to say on that topic is this one plain, simple fact: If they carry every slaveholding county in the State they elect only half the Convention, and with half the Convention they can pass no ordinance. In the next place, whatever ordinance they may pass as part of the Constitution has to be submitted to the vote of the people for their sanction, and the vote of the city of Baltimore alone will defeat any bill for compensation.

(Great applause.) And, in the next place, they will not have half the Convention. (Renewed applause.)

That is their day-dream; ay, and it is their last dream, for the day of dreams has gone and the day of facts has come. Let the people remember that in the Africa of the Eastern Shore, my friend, Mr. Creswell, now fills the seat that Mr. Crisfield—that the Compensationists were obliged to abandon (applause)—and did it on open canvass in the face of the people, arrayed the interest and the power of the non-slaveholder against the wealthy slaveholder, teaching them that every man counts one at the polls, and a rich man counts no more. (Great applause.)

Upon that simple rule of political arithmetic, my friend Mr. Creswell occupies the seat that Mr. Crisfield competed for. From that fact, I desire our friends in the southern counties to estimate the chances of a tie in the Constitutional Convention. I aided in my humble way my friend Mr. Creswell in his canvass. I went down into the deep regions of the dominion of slavery (laughter), where manufactures are unknown, and money is hardly seen by poor men, who wear homespun and have to walk twenty miles to get to our political meetings, and it was these men who, for three generations—they and their ancestors—had been voting at the dictation of the leading gentlemen of their regions, who ride on their horses to the election, and used formerly to give out their wagons to carry their poorer neighbors there, but declined on this occasion, because they knew their opinions; it was in that region that by our aid those men came forward and cast their first independent vote, for their own freedom first, and the freedom of the negro afterward. (Applause.)

Now I commend to those gentlemen a hopeful aspect of their cause; look at the result. Twenty thousand majority in Maryland for emancipation on an issue forced upon us (applause); Governor Thomas elected for the second time without an opponent daring to meet him; Mr. Webster candidly coming to our platform, accepting our principles, and nobody finding pluck to meet him in his district; men in high position struggling for an opponent to me up to within a week of the election, and nobody willing to take the chance of beating me (applause); Mr. Creswell met by the ablest man of the Eastern Shore, a gentleman of large property, a large landholder, a large negro-holder, with a national reputation, leaning to the Copperhead style of politics, intensely conservative, fearful that the President and the administration were going too far, and might put down the rebellion too rapidly and too vigorously by rooting out its cause—that man representing in its milder and only presentable type before the people of Maryland the Compensationist, the tardy Gradual Emancipationist, the men who thought the offer of ten millions of dollars was an insult, and the other class of men who thought it ought to be "spit upon." This man was beaten by Mr. Creswell, who argued at every man's door that the time for emancipation, both of black and white, from the slavery domination was come. (Applause.)

And now they come before the people of Maryland, hoping that, under the mild rule which it was supposed might prevail at Washington, all the secesh, together with the pro-slavery part of the Union body of the citizens, might enable them to save their property, or burden you with paying their estimated value. I need only say to gentlemen what now every one here sees, that after all the clamor, after all the imputations, after all the insults, after all the wretched affidavits, after all the flimsy secesh certificates, after the howl in the Legislature against the last election, the principle stands as Maryland law, by the vote of our enemies in the Legislature of Maryland, that men who are traitors to their country, and can be found out, have no part in our political community. (Great applause.) That Legislature has more than ratified my declaration that when we speak of political power in Maryland, we do not count traitors as part of that people in Maryland; we do not mean that they shall be counted as part of that power (great applause), and that the only question the people of Maryland will listen to for an instant on that point is whether the individual who offers his vote is or is not faithful to the government of his fathers? If he is unfaithful, he can not be allowed to soil the ballot-box of Maryland. (Great applause.) If he is faithful, welcome, though he be perverse as Vallandigham. (Laughter.)

But, according to the opinion of certain persons, we who are for the Convention are in favor of "negro equality," in favor of negro political privileges; and these gentlemen—our enemies—are exceedingly exercised lest that should become the law of Maryland. Nay, they say here they are as good emancipators as I am —they know they can not be any better—so they take me as the standard (laughter), but they do not go quite as far. Of course not.

They were dragged thus far. They did not go at all; they were dragged, they were compelled, they were overborne by the overwhelming power of the popular vote to confess and profess what now they do not believe. If you trust them, they will cheat you. And these men have the inconceivable impudence to say they do not go as far as I do because they are not in favor of negro equality, and that I am, and that the gentlemen who act with me are. They do not know, when they speak of the gentlemen with whom I act, that they are libeling the great body of the people of Maryland. They do not know, when they speak of the gentlemen who stand with me, that they are the men who beat them by 20,000 majority last fall. (Applause.)

They do not know, when they attempt to speak of the opinions that I express, that they speak of the opinions ratified, against their libels, at the ballot-box by the people of Maryland; and if they want to know my opinion upon negro equality, I can tell them my opinion upon that as upon any other question without any trouble at all. I am perfectly content that the negro shall be equal with them, but not with me or my friends. (Tremendous applause.)

In my judgment, they that are afraid of negro equality are not much above it now. Do they understand that? (Laughter.) In my judgment, they that are afraid of marrying a negro woman had better go to the Legislature and petition for a law to punish them if they are guilty of that weakness. (Laughter.)

But when gentlemen presume, in any of their wretched political circulars or speeches to the people of Maryland, to say that they do not go as far as I because I am in favor of negro equality, they libel me. They know that it is one of the paltry, dirty tricks to cheat men who they suppose are fools enough to be cheated. They know that no man in Maryland, from one end of it to the other, raises that question excepting themselves. They know that they raise it merely to delude. They know that they raise that question in the hope that they can get some blacking to stick on the character that they have been persistently attempting to smear for ten years, and which they have not dimmed yet. (Applause.)

What then? "Compensation for the invaluable right of property"—the touching of the "inalienable right of property!" And who are they that have the insolence to make this claim? Men who stand upon the statute-books of Maryland for the last forty years as plunderers of the public purse for their private benefit; men who passed a law to say that the property which they now want to get within the protection of the law of property should not be brought within the limits of the burdens of property, for their special benefit—property which they by formal law exempted from the sworn appraisers of the law—property which in the counties they have said shall be valued at an arbitrary and a disgracefully inadequate valuation—property which now, after it is gone, they estimate at thirty millions of dollars, and two years ago, when it was to be taxed, the Comptroller's Report shows they estimated at fourteen millions of dollars. When they talk of the rights of property and of pay for their negroes, let them open their accounts with the Comptroller of the State of Maryland, and pay back the plundered arrearages of thirty years of partial legislation. (Great applause.)

I do not know that they will find a paymaster in this audience; I do not know that they will find one in the State of Maryland; and I rather incline to think that the stupidity that prevailed over them, the judicial blindness that rested upon them, made them spurn the only chance they ever had of receiving any thing as a ransom for their slaves. For, gentlemen, you will remember I have a maliciously long memory, unfortunately (laughter); these gentlemen forget every three months; I take it that the world whirls so fast that they become giddy and do not know which way they are looking now; but they forget that it has not been more than a year and a half since I endeavored to induce Congress to execute the proposal of the President and give $10,000,000 to the slaveholders of Maryland; and they seem to have forgotten that Mr. Anthony Kennedy, the representative of the pro-slavery interest, said that he would spit upon your ten millions of dollars, and that Governor Hicks said that it was an insult which he could not pocket.

Such is the course of events, so rapidly does the tide run, so swiftly do men and opinions change, that the result of our victory last year has been to drive every one of these gentlemen now to clamor for compensation, part from the State, but most of them from the general government.

Fellow-citizens, allow me to say that repentance on the day of judgment will as surely carry them to heaven as repentance now will bring them compensation from the general government. (Laughter and applause.)

The day of death is past. Between them and compensation the great gulf is fixed. The rich man now is on one side of that gulf and Lazarus upon the other, and I do not know that there is much communication between them. (Laughter and applause.)

Hopeless, wretched, miserable, praying to a god that once smiled on them and now frowns, they say, "Give us emancipation with compensation by the government." Of course they do; but the people are for emancipation without compensation by the government, and the people are the stronger of the two. (Great applause.)

And how are they going to get it? They have been so in the habit of working for themselves in political life that they forget that the proposal of the President to them in Maryland was a bargain that had two sides to it. It was intended to promote the suppression of the rebellion. The purpose was to save a thousand millions of dollars. The purpose was to save a year of anarchy and bloodshed. The year has gone. The thousand millions of dollars are sunk in the ruts of our artillery in the South. The blood is shed. The blood that pays the ransom of the negro is poured out, and the money of the government went with it. (Great applause.)

It is just as well to look facts in the face as not. I say they are going to have—in my judgment they will have, in my purpose they shall have—no compensation from the government of the United States if I can avert it. (Applause.) They refused the offer when it was made, and when the acceptance of it would have saved thousands of lives and shortened this desolating rebellion; they spurned it, scoffed at it, scouted those who proposed it, did their best to beat and defeat the project in the councils of the nation, and now they may eat the bitter fruits of their folly.

Why should the United States pay for a dead dog any more than the people of Maryland? They do not free their slaves now because they want to do so, but they free them because the people of Maryland have said they shall be free; and after that is said, "Oh, well, if they are to be free, we should like to be compensated for them." Compensated for what? For that which is nothing by the *fiat* of the people, which only awaits the forms of law—compensated for an absolute interest which only has six months of life remaining in it—compensated for slaves made valueless as a house is reduced to no value by a conflagration which burns it down!

Why should any body pay them? They have no claim in morals. The United States never granted them slave property. It merely said, "If it runs away it shall be delivered up," but not that if the people of Maryland see fit to repeal the law allowing slavery, the government will continue to consider as property what the people of Maryland refuse any longer themselves to consider as property, and that they will pay as property for what the people of Maryland say shall no longer be property. Upon what ground is it? It is a political institution. It is like the tariff which now, twice or three times in the limit of my life, has made and destroyed values infinitely greater than the value of the slave property of Maryland.

South Carolina and all the South have twice or thrice, within the limits of my life, rejoiced over the prostration of a tariff system, the mere repeal of which effaced millions and millions of dollars throughout all of New England and all the free States; but did ever any body think that because the course of politics had changed, because the current policy of the government had changed, because a law which the Congress placed upon the statute-book another Congress had seen fit to repeal, therefore we must compensate the broken manufacturers of Massachusetts and the iron-dealers of Pennsylvania or Maryland? Yet that is exactly what we are asked to do now.

Negroes are no more property by the law of nature than white men. White men agreed between themselves that they should be so regarded, and they took the chances of the insurance, and they insured themselves beforehand against the damage of the ultimate conflagration which is now consuming them, by robbing the State treasury of the taxes upon their real value. That is their compensation. Their compensation is the improved value of their lands. Their compensation is four generations of uncompensated labor. Their compensation is the cleared lands of all Southern Maryland, where every thing that smiles and blossoms is the work of the negro that they tore from Africa.

Because they have enjoyed his uncompensated labor for four generations, shall we now give them a commutation of value? I do not know what the people of Maryland will say on that subject, but I have a very definite opinion upon what I will help them to say, and that is, that they have had the value which they had no right to for four generations, and they may rest upon that. If they suppose that we are fools enough to go into the next presidential canvass with our necks burdened down by the mill-stone of compensation for all the property destroyed by the government in the course of this terrible war, slaves included, they are mistaken; the candidate that goes into the canvass upon that basis goes dedicated to the ruin; for no mass, no considerable, no respectable proportion of the people of the States of America will ever agree to double the war debt, for all slaveholders will persuade doubting commissioners that they were loyal, and should receive compensation for the very property which their brothers, and friends, and neighbors rebelled to secure. (Applause.)

There is scarcely a household where there is not one dead; there is scarcely a household where children are not lacking for some of the comforts of life by reason of this great war, and their wants must not be increased to give luxuries to the rich slaveholders. The negro is paid for by the hardships that men are now enduring. He is paid for by the increased price of labor, the increased price of land and bread, the withdrawal of labor from the free States, the converting of an immense population into an army. This is the pay for it. It is paid for by the iniquity of the rebellion, and they will get no other pay but the suppression of the rebellion. (Great applause.)

Now, my friends, as usual, I have said just what I think is coming to pass. I have no doubt that the cunning contrivers of future political platforms will in the course of a year or two have a wretched, shriveled party in some corner of Maryland called the "Anti-Negro-Equality Party," and they will be rushing out frantically into the streets of Baltimore, and to the cross-roads, and the groggery-shops of the southern part of the State, to get somebody to be foolish enough to elect a man because he is opposed to negro equality, without any body's proposing it on the other side; and, foreseeing that that is about to be the case, I have thought it might just be convenient at this time to say that they who are preparing for that canvass are attempting to delude people whom they can not delude, and are preparing for a canvass in which they will receive a worse castigation than in that of the last fall.

Fellow-citizens, only one word in conclusion. All that I beg of you is this: when the day of election comes round, you will take the trouble, you and your friends, to walk to the polls, so that Baltimore may have the benefit of the power of her enormous population, that she may be secure in carrying the Convention, which not merely rids her commercial wealth of the burden of being in a slave State, but restores to her her political equality with all the free regions of the State. It requires only that we shall *turn out*, and the result is accomplished; and if we do not turn out, we may remain as we are.

Gentlemen, I now yield in order that others may be introduced to you.

THE EMPIRE OF MEXICO.

On the 4th of April Mr. Davis reported, from the Committee on Foreign Affairs, a joint resolution declaring

"That the Congress of the United States were unwilling by silence to leave the nations of the world under the impression that they are indifferent spectators of the deplorable events* now transpiring in the Republic of Mexico; and that they therefore think fit to declare that it does not accord with the policy of the United States to acknowledge any monarchical government erected on the ruins of any republican government under the auspices of any European power."

In supporting this resolution, Mr. Davis said:

"We inaugurate another policy than that which characterized the Democratic party ere the power passed from beneath their feet. The Democratic policy in dealing with our Republican brethren in South America and in Mexico has been that of the wolf to the lamb. Their growl was to frighten foreign wolves from the prey they marked for their own; they hectored, bullied, and plundered them, without even stretching out the hand of republican sympathy to appease their dissensions or consolidate their power. I suppose the treaty made by Mr. M'Lane was intended to smooth the way for the intrusion into Mexico of the Southern interests, now in rebellion against the United States. It afforded Southern men the opportunity, after breaking away from the Union, to fasten themselves upon Mexico. The provisions of that treaty secured such a right of interference and intermeddling in the affairs of Mexico as would have been contrary to the policy of this government to exercise, unless it was with the farther purpose of reducing Mexico to the condition of a province. If my friend from Ohio had expressed his regret at the failure of the ratification by

* Alluding to the war between Juarez, the constitutional President, and the French, intervening to place and maintain there the Archduke Maximilian under the title of emperor.

the Senate of the treaty negotiated by Mr. Corwin, granting pecuniary aid to the government of Mexico, which would, in all probability, have prevented this European intervention, I should have heartily agreed with him.

"But, sir, that time has already passed. The war is going on, and we wish, before another usurper has placed his foot upon Mexican soil, to let him understand, whether he be of the house of Austria, or of the family which for the present disposes of the forces of France—both the well-known enemies of republican government, and the last now making war to overturn the republican government of Mexico and establish upon its ruins a monarchical government—that that government will not be recognized by us.

"Our policy is very different from the Democratic policy. We wish to cultivate friendship with our republican brethren of Mexico and South America, to aid in consolidating republican principles, to retain popular government in all this continent from the fangs of monarchical or aristocratic power, and to lead the sisterhood of American republics in the paths of peace, prosperity, and power."

The resolution was passed unanimously. Mr. Davis afterward moved (May 23) that the President be requested to communicate to the House any explanation given by the government to the French government respecting the sense and bearing of the above joint resolution; and the correspondence of the Secretary of State with the United States minister in Paris in relation thereto was communicated, by which it appeared that the Secretary had rightly stated the effect of such joint resolution, acted on by the House only, not having passed the Senate, and not having received the sanction of the President.

EXPULSION OF MR. LONG, OF OHIO.

On the 9th of April the Speaker offered a resolution for the expulsion of Mr. Long, of Ohio, "for having openly avowed himself, in presence of the House, in favor of recognizing the Confederate States, now in armed rebellion, and, in so avowing himself, having violated his oath as a member of this House, that he had given no aid, countenance, counsel, or encouragement to persons engaged in armed hostility to the United States."

On the 11th of April, 1864, Mr. Davis addressed the House on this resolution in the following speech:

Mr. Speaker,—A singular disposition has been manifested to avoid the question before the House. I desire to call your attention to that question before I follow the gentlemen on the other side in the rather irrelevant discussion in which they have indulged.

It is not whether in the House of Representatives of the United States of America freedom of opinion is secured by law, nor whether the freedom of speech and of the press is the constitutional right of the American citizen, but whether the gentleman who delivered the speech now in question is a fit and worthy member of this House; not whether, out of doors, in his private capacity, he would be entitled to entertain, and as an individual to express, the opinions which he has uttered here, but whether as a legislator charged to protect the interests of the people, sworn to maintain the Constitution of the United States, he has not avowed a purpose inconsistent with those duties, a resolution not to maintain but to destroy; a determination not to defend but to yield up undefended to the enemies of the United States what he was sent here to protect. That is the question, and that is the only question which has not been discussed by the defenders of the gentleman from Ohio.

They tell us words can not be the subject of animadversion under the rules of this House, nor under the Constitution of the United States! What becomes of the resolution declaring the member from Maryland [Mr. Harris] to be an unworthy member of this House, adopted by their votes on Saturday? What becomes of the solemn adjudication as far back as 1842, when a majority of this House asserted the right to censure Joshua R. Giddings, not for introducing a petition to dissolve the Union, but for offering resolutions for the consideration of this House declaring that the mutineers of the Creole were not responsible for any criminal act under the laws of the United States, interpreted by the resolution of censure into a justification of mutiny and murder?

It is the judgment of this House, and therefore not necessary to be argued by me, that words may prove criminality when they reveal a criminal purpose; and, if they are sufficiently criminal, that they may be visited first by censure, and, if they judge it necessary to the public safety, by expulsion from the House. I do not envy the gentlemen who refused to expel the gentleman from Maryland for language uttered in the presence of us all, which they immediately after voted to declare tended and was designed to give aid and encouragement to the public enemies of the nation, and therefore he was an unworthy member of the House. Sir, it would seem to have been the logical conclusion that, if he is an unworthy member of the House, he ought not to be suffered to remain in it, and that gentlemen who so thought would have so said on the first vote for expulsion. How gentlemen will reconcile that glaring inconsistency to their constituents; how they who have declared the gentleman from Maryland an unworthy member, but that he should remain a member—who asserted the right to punish by inflicting punishment, but refused the only adequate penalty for the offense of which they voted him guilty, will justify themselves in the face of their own votes, it is for them to consider. It would be cruel to aggravate their embarrassments by any observations. *Ab hac scabie teneamus ungues.*

But it remains conceded by the votes of our opponents that, in spite of the Constitution of the United States, in spite of the conceded freedom of opinion, in spite of the conceded freedom of speech, words are and may be here, not out of doors, but here in this House, here upon a subject before the House for consideration, here where every body has a right to express his views upon every measure before the House, words are and have been adjudged by the votes of our opponents to be criminal, to be punishable, and they have been punished within two days.

The measure of judgment is a matter of discretion. The Constitution says that with the consent of two thirds either House may expel a member; that means not capriciously, but for some wrong, for misconduct, for acts, for words, for purposes, for avowals inconsistent with his duty on this floor, tending to show that he is not a safe depositary of the great powers of a representative; and the only constitutional criterion of what is and what is not adequate cause of expulsion is the judgment of two thirds of this House.

If that be so, the only farther question we have to ask is whether the gentleman from Ohio, respectable as he is in his private relations, respectable as has been his conduct in this House, honestly as his convictions may be entertained, has not placed himself beyond the pale of that protection which this House accords to freedom of speech, not by speaking as he ought not to have spoken, but by avowing himself in favor of the destruction of the nation.

Now, what is the charge against him? That his judgment is that there are but two alternatives: one, the extermination of the enemies of the United States, and the other the destruction of the United States itself, which he puts in the form of a recognition of the Southern States as an independent government. And, not resting on that mere declaration of opinion and the alternative resting in his own mind, he goes farther, and says that of the two he preferred the latter. That means, "*I*, here a representative, charged and sworn to the extent of my whole influence in the legislation of this House to protect and maintain the integrity of the nation, have come to the conclusion, in the midst of a great war, when the existence of the nation is at stake, that, rather than exterminate the enemies of the nation, I will exterminate the nation." He proclaims himself the friend of the enemies of the nation, and an enemy himself of the United States. He avows it his purpose to destroy it at the first opportunity to the extent of his vote. The rebel chiefs proclaim independence or extermination the only alternatives. The gentleman from Ohio declares extermination or independence the only alternatives. The rebel chiefs prefer the recognition of their independence to their extermination. The gentleman from Ohio avows himself for recognition and against extermination; and recognition of the Southern Confederacy means the dissolution of the United States. The

Constitution proclaims the perpetuity of the Union; and that Constitution recognizes no dissolution, no end of its existence. Sworn to maintain that Constitution, he now says: "In violation of a solemn oath, in spite of the duty I am sent here to discharge, rather than maintain it to the extent of exterminating its enemies, I will destroy it."

Now, that is the case stated in plain language. It has not been stated here before to-day. And the question which we are bound as gentlemen and as legislators to determine is whether a gentleman, acknowledged to be respectable, believed to be sincere, entertaining and avowing purposes which do not differ from those of the chief of the rebel Confederacy, or of the men in armed array beyond the Potomac bent on ejecting us from this hall, is the fit companion of gentlemen here, a fit depositary of his constituents' vote, a safe person to be intrusted here with the secrets of the United States, a worthy guardian of the existence of the republic. Are we to be seriously told that the freedom of speech screens a traitor because he puts his treasonable purposes in words? Does the Constitution secure the right of our avowed enemies to vote in this hall? May a man impudently declare that his purpose here is so to vote as to promote the success of the rebellion, to embarrass and paralyze the government in its suppression, to secure its triumph and our overthrow, to bring the armed enemy to Washington, or arrest our army lest it exterminate that enemy? Then why do not the Congress at Richmond adjourn to Washington, push us from our stools, and by parliamentary tactics, under the Constitution, arrest the wheels of government? You could not expel them. Sir, that picture is history—recent history. In 1860 that side of the House swarmed with the avowed enemies of the republic. One after one, as their stars dropped from the firmament of the Union, they went out, some with tears in their eyes over the miseries they were about to inflict; some of them with exultation over the coming calamities; some of them with contemptuous lectures to the members in the House; some staid behind to do the traitor's business in the disguise of honest legislators in both houses as long as they dared. One disgraced the Senate for one long session after armed men were soaking their native soil with their blood, and now he is in the ranks of our enemies.

Are we to be told that gentlemen, entertaining not these opinions, but these purposes, resolved to the extent of their power to paralyze the government, and only limited in what they can do by what it may be safe to do, must be allowed not merely to be members of the House, but to rise and insolently fling in our faces the avowal of their enmity, and invoke the Constitution of the United States in order that they may stab it to the heart? Shall men rise here and be allowed to express, whether in one form of phraseology or another, as may best aid the public enemy, their desire for the triumph of the rebel cause, and that, being too tender-hearted to wish that the enemies of the United States may be exterminated, they prefer our ruin? And is it to be said that that comes within the sacred shield of the freedom of public opinion, the right of debate, the freedom of speech? Why, sir, it is not opinion that we complain of; it is not liberty of speech that we wish to restrict. On the contrary, I thank the gentleman [Mr. Long] for his speech, for it revealed an enemy, and an avowed is a more respectable than a concealed foe. He is more frank than the gentleman from New York [Mr. Fernando Wood], who, with similar sentiments, conceals them. He is more manly than that gentleman from New York who on Saturday rose before the House with a paper in his hand, declaring it to be the identical sheet from which the gentleman from Ohio read—read it flauntingly in the face of the House, and declared that he concurred in every word of it, and that if the House expelled the gentleman from Ohio it must expel him also; but to-day, frightened by the explosion of the indignation of the House on the head of the gentleman from Maryland, was careful to say that he did not at all agree with the opinions for which the gentleman from Ohio is called in question. Commend me, sir, to an open adversary. I can respect the one, I can not have so much respect for the other. It is not for the freedom of the avowal, it is the entertaining the purpose which he does avow; it is not that he violated the order of the House, it is because he violates the law of the country by his purpose to destroy it, that the gentleman from Ohio is arraigned. We do not punish him for saying what he did, we punish him for meaning what he declared he does mean to do; and that is what we are called upon to do by the highest considerations of public policy, the plainest dictates of patriotic duty.

Oh! but we are told that it touches the rights of his constituents. Let his constituents have an opportunity to pass upon that after this declaration of purpose. But we must have mutual consideration for each other! Why, certainly, sir. But how far? Is there no end to patience? Is there no avowal showing criminal intent which wisdom requires we should guard against beforehand? What do you suppose would be the fate of a man sitting in the Capitol at Richmond who should arise there and propose to recognize the supremacy of the United States? Do you suppose that the freedom of debate which gentlemen have enjoyed on this floor would have been tolerated, even if desired by any body? Is it not certain that he would have been expelled if he lived long enough for the vote of expulsion to be taken? Suppose that in the French Assembly, when the life of France was at stake, as the life of this nation is now at stake, and when heroic men were struggling to maintain it, some one had arisen and proposed to call back the Bourbons, and place the reins of government in their hands—how long would he have remained a member of that body? Suppose that the day before the battle of Culloden, or the day after the battle of Preston Pans, some Jacobite had arisen in the House of Commons of England and declared himself of the opinion that the Pretender could not be expelled without the extermination of the Jacobites, and that therefore they should place him on the throne of England! Do you think the traditional liberty of speech in England would have saved him from summary expulsion? Do you think there is any law in England that could have stood between him and, not expulsion, but death? Would not the act have been considered a crime, and the declaration of it in Parliament have been considered an aggravation of the crime, demanding his expulsion? Would not the vote of that body have been instantaneous, and his execution swifter than that vote?

Are we to be told here that men are to rise in this hall, where the guns of the impending battle will echo in our ears, when we sit here only because we have one hundred and fifty thousand bayonets between us and the enemy; when Washington is a great camp, the centre of thirty miles of fortifications stretching around us for our protection; are we to be told that here, within this citadel of the nation, an enemy may beckon with his hand to the armed foe, assuring him of friends within the people's hall, at the very centre of power, and we can not expel him?

Sir, let me say to this House that if it were a constitutional right so to speak, in my judgment this is one of those cases which so far transcends the ordinary rules of law, one of those cases which carries us so near to the original right of self-defense, one of those cases which appeals so directly to the inalienable right of self-protection, that without law and in spite of law the safety of the people requires his expulsion, and I would be one to do it. But, sir, I do not think the Constitution does confer the right so to speak. I think we are within the limits of written law which the wisdom of our forefathers gave us with which to protect ourselves in every emergency, and this among others; and the only question is whether the patriotism of this House goes to the extent of the two thirds of its members required to rid it of the presence of an avowed public enemy. That, and that alone, is the question.

But, Mr. Speaker, we are told that this is a question of opinion. If it be, it is one of those questions of opinion that nobody in this country has a right to be on more than one side of. On one side is patriotism, duty, and an oath. On the other is treason, crime, and perjury. Is it our duty, for the protection of a man in his opinion, to allow him to destroy the nation we are trying to defend? Where, in the record of nations, do you find an illustration of that position? By what examples in history do you defend it? By what precedent of statesmanship? The great name of Chatham has often, in this debate, been invoked and desecrated to cover this avowal of preference for the enemy over the country. His example is wretchedly misunderstood. Doubtless his voice was lifted in warning tones against taxation without our consent, and still fiercer against war to enforce it. His example might be pleaded for moderation and respect for the rights of our Southern fellow-citizens; but they have not been violated; but never, never to sanction a division of the republic. His example is the bitterest reproach to those who claim its protection. After years of war unjustly begun and weakly waged, when exhausted England sank before the combined arms of America and France, and the Duke of Richmond rose in the House of Lords to move for peace with America, the patriotic soul of Chatham was stirred within him at the thought of the humiliation and division of that empire whose limits he had expanded and whose name he had decorated; and, frail and dying, his legs swathed in flannel, his crutch in his hand, he was borne to the House of Lords in the arms of his great son to lift his last voice in execration of the folly which had brought England to such humiliation, and to enter his dying protest against the recognition of American independence, already secured in fact by the sword. His English heart had no fear of exterminating the enemies of England in the holy work of maintaining the integrity of her empire. Sir, I accept the example, and I commend it to the consideration of the patriotic gentlemen on the other side of the House. I beg them to read a little farther than they seem to have done the history of the English statesman. Freedom of opinion! Surely, sir, opinion is the breath of our nation. It is the measure of every right, the guarantee of every privilege, the protection of every blessing. It is opinion which creates our rulers. It is opinion that nerves or palsies their arm. It is opinion which casts down the proud and elevates the humble. Its fluctuations are the rise and fall of parties; its currents bear the nation on to prosperity or ruin. Its free play is the condition of its purity. It is like the ocean, whose tides rise and fall day by day at the fickle bidding of the moon; yet it is the great scientific level from which every height is measured—the horizon to which astronomers refer the motion of the stars. But, like the ocean, it has depths whose eternal stillness is the condition of its stability. Those depths of opinion are not free, and it is they that are touched by the words which have so moved the House. Men must not commit treason, and say its guilt is matter of opinion and its punishment a violation of its freedom. Men can not swear to maintain the integrity of the nation and avow their intention to destroy it, and cover that double crime by the freedom of speech. *That* is to break up the fountains of the great deep on which all government is borne, and to pour its flood in revolutionary ruin over the land. To punish that is not a violation of the freedom of opinion or its expression. It is to protect its normal ebb and flow, its free and healthy fluctuations, that we desire to relieve it from the opprobrium of being confounded with the declaration of treasonable purposes here in the high and solemn assemblage of the nation.

The free expression of opinion! I am at a loss to know how the opinions of Abraham Lincoln, or Horace Greeley, or Wendell Phillips, or the gentleman from Ohio [Mr. Schenck], or Mr. Chase, if truly quoted, and equally criminal with those now arraigned, can extenuate their guilt or shield their author from the indignation of the House. Their guilt is not his innocence. If he imitated their guilt, let him follow their repentance. The time which they have devoted to atoning for error by patriotic services he has dedicated to indurating his error and accomplishing his unpatriotic purposes. But I am not concerned to vindicate in them what I condemn in him. I execrate the avowal equally in every mouth; and if their guilt is beyond my judgment, that of the gentleman from Ohio is not. I can well understand how such examples may serve to screen the Democratic party, or to delude an ill-informed crowd, and teach them that treason is error of opinion and not a crime, but they can not be successfully urged here before the gentlemen of the House of Representatives to exculpate the gentleman from Ohio; nor even, sir, can it vindicate the Democratic party from the charge of more sympathy with the enemies of the country than with the country itself. The people will laugh at this attempt to impeach the loyalty of the friends of the administration. They will see in this zealous defense of the gentleman from Ohio only another proof of Democratic sympathy with his views and purposes, hitherto invariably manifested wherever they have been in power. Where have they had power that they have not exhibited their sympathy with the enemies of the republic? I admit there are honorable exceptions. I admit there are cases of honest delusion. I suppose there are cases of unconscious sympathy. I can not doubt the prevalence of a criminal interest in the triumph of the rebels. I shall not discriminate one from the other. I speak of the party and its conduct. Where, since the war broke out, from the time that James Buchanan disgraced the American name by his message declaring, as gentlemen on that side of the House declare now, that this war is waged in violation of the Constitution, that there is no power to coerce a sovereign State, down to this day, is there a Democratic governor or Legislature which, until warned by the indignant voice of the people, has not tried to embarrass and discredit the government, and to give aid and encouragement to its enemies? The disavowals of individuals can not extenuate the conduct of Legislatures and governors. The prudence or cunning of caucuses or Congressmen, since the chastisement of 1863, can not make the people forget the conduct which provoked it. Will they ever forget the Legislature of Indiana and its votes on the resolutions for armistice and peace, which swarmed before it; or the Legislature of Illinois and the bill to strip the governor of his just military authority; and the resolutions for an armistice and a Convention at Louisville of Western and rebel States, to dictate terms to the United States, actually adopted, I think, by one House; or the New Jersey Legislature, which sent Wall of Fort Lafayette to the United States Senate, and was ready to adopt peace resolutions but for an accidental adjournment which enabled the members to gather the whisperings of their indignant constituents? How have they expressed their sympathies on the side of the United States unless by attempting to array the State authorities against the United States, to excite the prejudices of the people against the necessary suspension of the habeas corpus, to represent the assertion of the supremacy of the United States courts and officers in the enforcement of United States laws as invasions of the rights of the States? What Democrat in Pennsylvania did not vote for Woodward? What Democrat in New York did not vote for Horatio Seymour? What Democrat in Connecticut did not vote for Seymour of Connecticut? What Democrat in Ohio did not vote for Vallandigham? It is vain to attempt to conceal it. The history of that party during the war proves the declaration made on this floor that there is no such thing as a Democratic party for the war: its elastic mantle covers equally those who, like the gentleman from New York [Mr. Kernan], have a love for the Union, and fail when he comes to vote on it, and those who, like the gentleman from Maryland [Mr. Harris], glory in the failure of the armies of the United States to conquer the States in rebellion.

The gentleman from New York [Mr. Kernan] who last spoke, and whose earnest tones all must have felt, declared himself ready to do all in his power to suppress the insurrection, and yet he failed to vote for the Conscription Bill, the indispensable condition to the prosecution of the war. That is the type of the War Democrat! Very earnest in vague generalities for the War, equally earnest in decrying the policy of the administration, but, having exhausted their earnestness on those topics, are so unable on any practical measure to tear themselves away from party association, so penetrated with valetudinarian views or perverse judgments on the Constitution of the United States, that their aid is more embarrassing than their opposition.

But, Mr. Speaker, if it be said that a time may come when the question of recognizing the Southern Confederacy will have to be answered, I admit it; and it is answering the strongest and the extremest case that gentlemen on the other side can present. I admit it. When a Democrat shall darken the White House and the land; when a Democratic majority here shall proclaim that freedom of speech secures impunity to treason, and declare recognition better than extermination of traitors; when Vallandigham shall be Governor of Ohio, and Bright Governor of Indiana, and Woodward Governor of Pennsylvania, and Seymour Governor of Connecticut, and Wall Governor of New Jersey, and the gentleman from New York city [Mr. Wood] sit in Seymour's seat, and thus, possessed of power over the great centre of the country, they shall do what they attempted in vain before in the midst of rebel triumphs — array the authorities of the States against those of the United States; oppose the militia to the army of the United States; invoke the *habeas corpus* to discharge confined traitors; deny to the government the benefit of the laws of war, lest it exterminate its enemies; when the Democrats, as in the fall of 1862, shall again, with more permanent success, persuade the people of the country that the war should not be waged till the integrity of the territory of the Union is restored, cost what it might; that such a war violates the spirit of free institutions, which those who advocate it wish to overthrow; that it should stop, for their benefit, somewhere this side of absolute triumph, lest there be no room for a compromise; when gentlemen of that party in New York shall again, as in November, 1862, hold illegal and criminal negotiations with Lord Lyons, avow their purposes to him, the representative of a foreign and unfriendly power, and urge him to arrange the time of proffering mediation with a view to their possession of power and their preparation of the minds of the people to receive suggestions from abroad; when mediation shall appear, by the event, to be the first step toward foreign intervention, swiftly and surely followed by foreign armed enemies upon our shores to join the domestic enemies; when the war in the cars shall begin, which was menaced at the outbreak of the rebellion, and the friends of Seymour shall make the streets of New York run with blood on the eve of another Gettysburg less damaging to their hopes; when M'Clellan and Fitz John Porter shall have again brought the rebel armies within sight of Washington City, and the successor of James Buchanan shall withdraw our armies from the unconstitutional invasion of Virginia to the north of the Potomac; when exultant rebels shall sweep over the fortifications, and their bomb-shells shall crash against the dome of the Capitol; when thousands throughout Pennsylvania shall seek refuge on the shores of Lake Erie from the rebel invasion, cheered and welcomed by the opponents of extermination; when the people, exhausted by taxation, weary of sacrifices, drained of blood, betrayed by their rulers, deluded by demagogues into believing that peace is the way to union and submission the path to victory, shall throw down their arms before the advancing foe; when vast chasms across every State shall make apparent to every eye, when too late to remedy it, that division from the South is anarchy at the North, and that peace without union is the end of the republic—THEN the independence of the South will be an accomplished fact, and gentlemen may, without treason to the dead republic, rise in this migratory House, wherever it may then be in America, and declare themselves for recognizing their masters at the South rather than exterminating them! Until that day, in the name of the American nation; in the name of every house in the land where there is one dead for the holy cause; in the name of those who stand before us in the ranks of battle; in the name of the liberty our ancestors have confided to us, I devote to eternal execration the name of him who shall propose to destroy this blessed land rather than its enemies.

But, until that time arrive, it is the judgment of the American people that there shall be no compromise; that ruin to ourselves or ruin to the Southern rebels are the only alternatives. It is only by resolutions of this kind that nations can rise above great dangers and overcome them in crises like this. It was only by turning France into a camp, resolved that Europe might exterminate, but should not subjugate her, that France is the leading empire of Europe to-day. It is by such a resolve that the American people, coercing a reluctant government to draw the sword and stake the national existence on the integrity of the republic, are now any thing but the fragments of a nation before the world, the scorn and hiss of every petty tyrant. It is because the people of the United States, rising to the height of the occasion, dedicated this generation to the sword, and pouring out the blood of their children as of no account, and avowing before high Heaven that there should be no end to this conflict but ruin absolute or absolute triumph, that we now are what we are; that the banner of the republic, still pointing onward, floats proudly in the face of the enemy; that vast regions are reduced to obedience to the laws, and that a great host in armed array now presses with steady step into the dark regions of the rebellion. It is only by the earnest and abiding resolution of the *people* that, whatever shall be our fate, it shall be grand as the American nation, worthy of that republic which first trod the path of empire, and made no peace but under the banners of victory, that the American people will survive in history. And that will save us. We shall succeed and not fail. I have an abiding confidence in the firmness, the patience, the endurance of the American people; and, having vowed to stand in history on the great resolve to accept of nothing but victory or ruin, victory is ours. And if with such heroic resolve we fall, we fall with honor, and transmit the name of liberty committed to our keeping untarnished, to go down to future generations. The historian of our decline and fall, contemplating the ruins of the last great republic, and drawing from its fate lessons of wisdom on the waywardness of men, shall drop a tear as he records with sorrow the vain heroism of that people who dedicated and sacrificed themselves to the cause of freedom, and by their example will keep alive her worship in the hearts of men till happier generations shall learn to walk in her paths. Yes, sir, if we must fall, let our last hours be stained by no weakness; if we must fall, let us stand amid the crash of the falling republic and be buried in its ruins, so that history may take note that men lived in the middle of the nineteenth century worthy of a better fate, but chastised by God for the sins of their forefathers. Let the ruins of the republic remain to testify to the latest generations our greatness and our heroism. And let Liberty, crownless and childless, sit upon these ruins, crying aloud in a sad wail to the nations of the world, "I nursed and brought up children, and they have rebelled against me." (Great applause on the floor and in the galleries.)

THE ENROLLMENT BILL.

On the 1st of July Mr. Davis moved to concur in an amendment to the Enrollment Bill, which provided—1, that no exemption should be attainable by payment of commutation-money; 2, that the enrolled should be divided into two classes, from eighteen to twenty-five years of age, and from twenty-five to forty; 3, that during the rebellion 250,000 men should be drafted from the first class, organized and drilled as a *corps de reserve*, and to supply deficiencies; 4, that all required beyond that in any one year should be from the second class; 5, that volunteers, with three hundred dollars bounty, should first be called for; 6, that every drafted man having those dependent on him, and not having three hundred dollars a year income, should be allowed not exceeding twenty dollars per month for such dependents; and 7, that a draft might be had in the rebellious States, as occupied, and volunteers procured there should be credited to the State procuring them.

Mr. Davis proceeded to explain his views on these points as follows:

Mr. Speaker,—Illness and its consequences have deprived me of the opportunity of assisting the deliberations of the House on this topic till this time, when it is not to be expected that any thing I may say shall at all influence the result. But I beg that I may be allowed to have their attention for a few moments to explain the propositions which I have offered, and which embody, in the shape of a bill, what I think the exigencies of the time demand.

I am not under any delusion respecting the fate of the proposition. *I know that the amendment is not likely to receive the vote of* a majority of the House. I despair of seeing the House rise to the height of the occasion, and show that degree of energy which the crisis demands. I do not presume to put my judgment against theirs; all I desire is, that I shall have an opportunity of spreading before the country briefly what I think the great cause of the nation demands at our hands, and leave it to the future and events to decide who is right.

We want *men*, not money. We want men to bear arms. Whatever stands in the way of getting men is striking directly at the existence of the republic, and therefore not a subject for consideration touching its political expediency. To allow men to buy by money exemption from personal military service, is to place money in the hands of the government, and not men. To commute service for money is to throw upon that class of the community which can not raise the requisite sum the whole burden of compulsory military service. No democratic government can defend any such provision.

It is new in the history of military organization. No aristocratic or despotic country has ever ventured to attempt it, and those who undertake to defend it upon principle, reason upon ground I can not understand. It allows one man to pay his obligations to the republic in money, and requires another to pay it in blood.

Therefore, the first provision of my amendment prohibits any commutation for personal service. It leaves open the right, which is secure in every compulsory military organization in the world, to furnish a substitute, which gives the government, at least, the requisite ability to meet and repel the public enemy.

The Senate bill is fatally defective, though it repeals the commutation clause, in limiting the draft to one year. That pushes a mob of raw recruits against veteran corps to encounter inevitable defeat, and shed useless blood.

The opposition to a vigorous draft is wholly incomprehensible. It is the republican, and the only republican mode of raising an army. The Roman republic placed her youth liable to military service in the Campus Martius, and the consul selected at will whom he chose.

The French republic saved the existence of the nation, and the principles of republican liberty, by the law of conscription.

And it has been the law of the American republic from the administration of President Washington, and the law I propose merely adds vigor to that system.

The next provision of my amendment relates to the classification of the military population. No civilized nation includes in one draft all the men from eighteen or twenty years of age to forty-five years of age. There is no inequality in that. The rule of all military powers is to make the army to consist of, and cause it to be drawn from the young men of the country. The men under twenty-five or twenty-six years of age, before they become involved in the responsibilities of life, before in a large proportion they are married, before families have accumulated around them, before they become entangled in the business occupations of life, before large masses of workmen and great capitals are dependent upon their personal attention and their capacity to manage business, every military nation makes that the first and preferred source from which to recruit its army. Older men, having passed that period of liability to active military service, form the national guard, or a reserve for great emergencies. I therefore have provided, in the second section of the bill, that the military population of the United States shall be divided into two classes, the first to consist of the men between eighteen and twenty-five, and the second to consist of those between twenty-five and forty-five.

The next thing we want is that there shall be a regular, constant levy of force to supply the deficiencies of our troops, the casualties of the service, the expiration of terms of enlistment, and to enable the government to advance with a steady, unvarying pressure upon the enemy, so that it shall not be hereafter, as it has been heretofore, that we shall send an army into the field, and wait till it is wasted by disease and by the fire of the enemy, and then rest on our arms till the enemy recruits his ranks while we are recruiting ours, and refreshed by repose, and strong in the fruits of their vigorous conscription, they stand with full ranks to dispute our advance.

Therefore, the third section of my substitute requires that every year during the rebellion the President shall cause to be levied two hundred and fifty thousand men, to be armed, trained, and organized provisionally, and sent to the front, or held as a reserve to be moved as the President may direct, according to the exigencies of the service.

The fourth section of the substitute provides that, if more men are needed for the service in any year, the President shall cause the rest to be levied from the men over twenty-five and under forty-five, which subjects them in their regular turn to the responsibilities and dangers of war.

Then, as there is an earnest feeling all over the country in favor of procuring them by volunteering rather than by draft, the substitute farther provides that, prior to and concurrently with the draft, until it shall be filled, the President shall call for and accept volunteers to fill the requisition to the extent of the draft; and he is authorized to pay them $300 for an enlistment for three years, and proportionally for a less period, to be designated by the government.

That will enable the government to procure, as far as volunteering and bounties can do so, the men it requires. It imposes no definite delay between the call of the volunteers and the enforcement of the draft, for no man can regulate the advance of the enemy; no man can determine the exigencies of war; no man can say how long a time may elapse before this capital is in danger; before retreating forces may require men to be moved rapidly to their support; and therefore I leave to the discretion of the President to call for volunteers as long before, or as shortly before the draft as prudence or the necessities of the case may dictate. The bill has this other provision, essential to the draft being intolerable to the poor men, that men who have parent or wife, child or sister, dependent on their labor for support, shall, when drafted, be allowed ten dollars a month for each such dependent, *provided* that the allowance shall not exceed twenty dollars in any one month on account of any one conscript; and the sum is payable, not to the conscript, but to or for the dependent person for whose support it is a charitable provision. These deserted persons must starve, or go to the poor-house, or be honorably supported by the nation which exacts the time and blood of their natural protector.

And then the final provision is that it shall be the *duty* of the government—not merely giving authority—but that it shall be the *duty* of the government to enforce the draft in every district in the rebel States occupied by the armies of the republic. A traitor in the midst of loyal men, with a musket on his shoulder, will make as good and as vigorous a soldier as any man. Napoleon prostrated Europe at his feet with men conscripted from hostile nations, who would, if they could, have cut the throats of the men by whose side they fought.

There is also another provision that any of the loyal States may send agents into the rebel States, and there procure volunteers, which shall be credited to the loyal State procuring them.

I have also provided that persons residing in one State who

shall enlist or volunteer in another State shall be credited by calculating the draft to the State in which they reside.

Now, sir, in my judgment, this bill, as I have proposed to amend it, will give to the government the power to create an army, which, if there be only wisdom and energy at the White House, will be able to stamp out the rebellion in another campaign. This campaign can not accomplish it; we have not men enough in the field, nor on the decisive points of the field, and we can not get enough in time to accomplish that purpose during this campaign. What I desire is to adopt a system that shall keep our armies full continually; that will enable them to pour a constant stream of fire upon the enemies of the republic till the last armed rebel shall be driven into the Gulf of Mexico.

MR. MALLORY. Did I understand the gentleman from Maryland to say that his bill provides for the enlistment of soldiers in the rebel States by the loyal States, to be credited to the States enlisting them?

MR. DAVIS, of Maryland. Yes, sir, it allows them to go into the rebel States and enlist. I have put that provision in in deference to the feeling which exists on this side of the House.

It is not a provision which meets my approval entirely; but I do not regard it as one of vital importance, and therefore, for the purpose of meeting the wishes of gentlemen on this side of the House, I have inserted it as one of the provisions of the bill.

The amendment proposed by Mr. Davis was rejected.

THE PRESIDENT'S SUPPRESSION OF THE BILL FOR RECONSTRUCTION IN THE REBELLIOUS STATES.—1864.

On the 8th of June, 1864, the National Union Convention met at Baltimore, and unanimously nominated Abraham Lincoln for re-election to the presidency, and Andrew Johnson, of Tennessee, with almost the same unanimity, for election to the vice-presidency of the United States. Undoubtedly those nominations, made without difficulty, and almost without opposition, were most acceptable to,* and were received by the American people as peculiarly significant of their firm resolve to prosecute the war to final triumph, to sustain the administration, to approve Mr. Lincoln's course, and to show their appreciation of the courage, constancy, and patriotism shown by Mr. Johnson under circumstances of peculiar difficulty.

Mr. Davis had opposed the renomination of Mr. Lincoln; he preferred Mr. Chase or Mr. Wade; but it was early seen in the Convention upon what the feeling of the country was resolved.

After these nominations had been made, and after the rebel raid around Baltimore in July, and when it was known that the bill for the reconstruction of the rebel States would not be approved by the President, it began to be asserted by many of the dissatisfied in the Republican party that his course in that respect, if General M'Clellan should be the nominee of the opposition party at Chicago, would lose the States of New York and Pennsylvania, while it became doubtful whether he could bring out the party strength even in New England. Under these fears, if real, or, at any rate, in hopes of inducing or compelling the withdrawal of Mr. Lincoln, certain members of the Republican party invited a conference of the dissatisfied at New York at the end of July. Mr. Davis took part in it, and was warmly in favor of such a change of plan and candidate. It was resolved to send a committee, or delegation, to Chicago to confer with the opposition Convention to meet there, in hopes of inducing the choice of such a candidate and declaration of principles

* Even Massachusetts gave her vote, on the first ballot, for Andrew Johnson, who had been a Democratic senator from Tennessee; and yet it was afterward declared by some principal men from that State that these nominations could not be carried, even in Massachusetts, where they feigned to believe that General M'Clellan, whose platform declared the war a failure, would gain the day.

—such a party platform in regard to the conduct of the war as would, with the nomination of some popular leader in the war, insure the defeat of Mr. Lincoln. This proceeding failed, through the resolution of the Democrats to submit to the nomination of General M'Clellan, in hopes that his personal popularity would outweigh the repugnance to their platform. This declared the war a failure, and that temporary submission, compromise, and peace were the only means to reunite the country.

The conference of the dissatisfied Republicans had adjourned to reassemble in New York on the 30th of August, then to publish an address to the people. But, when that day arrived, there were but two or three who met or wished to proceed.

Upon these facts alone can be explained the determination to publish, on the 8th of August, during the canvass and after the nomination, and while it was uncertain at least if the change could be made, to aid the plan just mentioned, the paper known as the "Wade-Davis Manifesto," being an address to the people, signed by Messrs. Wade and Davis (and written by the latter), as chairmen respectively of the Senate and House committees on the reconstruction of the governments in the States lately in rebellion.

The President had suppressed the bill for the reconstruction of those States, which was finally passed within a few hours of the final adjournment of Congress, and had afterward issued a proclamation on the 18th of July, in which he declared his intentions in respect to those States, and his reasons for not signing the bill.

Thereupon the following paper was published in some of the journals, while the proceedings in relation to the change or defeat of the candidates of the Republican party were going on at New York.

TO THE SUPPORTERS OF THE GOVERNMENT.

We have read without surprise, but not without indignation, the proclamation of the President of the 18th of July, 1864. The supporters of the administration are responsible to the country for its conduct, and it is their right and duty to check the encroachments of the executive on the authority of Congress, and to require it to confine itself to its proper sphere. It is impossible to pass in silence this proclamation without neglecting that duty, and having taken as much responsibility as many others in supporting the administration, we are not disposed to fail in the other duty of supporting the rights of Congress.

The President did not sign the bill to "guarantee to certain States, whose governments have been usurped, a republican form of government," passed by the supporters of his administration, in both houses of Congress, after mature deliberation. The bill did not therefore become a law, and it is therefore nothing. The proclamation is neither an approval nor a veto of the bill; it is therefore a document unknown to the laws and Constitution of the United States. So far as it contains an apology for not signing the bill, it is a political manifesto against the friends of the government. So far as it proposes to execute the bill, which is not a law, it is a grave executive usurpation. It is fitting that the facts necessary to enable the friends of the administration to appreciate the apology and the usurpation be spread before them.

The proclamation says:

"And whereas the said bill was presented to the President of the United States for his approval less than one hour before the *sine die* adjournment of said session, and was not signed by him—"

If this be accurate, still this bill was presented with other bills that were signed. Within that hour, the time for the *sine die* adjournment was three times postponed by the votes of both houses, and the least intimation of a desire for more time by the President to consider this bill would have secured a farther postponement. Yet the committee, sent to ascertain if the President had any farther communication for the House of Representatives, reported that he had none; and the friends of the bill, who had anxiously waited upon him to ascertain its fate, had already been informed that the President had resolved not to sign it. The time of presentation, therefore, had nothing to do with his failure to approve it.

The bill had been discussed and considered for more than a month in the House of Representatives, which passed it on the 4th of May. It was reported to the Senate on the 27th of May, without material amendment, and it passed the Senate absolutely as it came from the House on the 2d of July. Ignorance of its contents is out of the question. Indeed, at the President's request, a draft of a bill substantially the same in all material points, and identical in the points objected to by the proclamation, had been laid before him for his consideration in the winter of 1862–3. There is, therefore, no reason to suppose the provisions of the bill took the President by surprise. On the contrary, we have reason to believe them to have been so well known that this method of preventing the bill from becoming a law, without the constitutional responsibility of a veto, had been resolved on long before the bill passed the Senate. We are informed by a gentleman entitled to entire confidence, that before the 22d of June, in New Orleans, it was stated by a member of General Banks's staff, in the presence of other gentlemen in official position, that Senator Doolittle had written a letter to the Department that the House "Reconstruction Bill" would be staved off in the Senate to a period too late in the session to require the President to veto in order to defeat it; and that Mr. Lincoln would retain the bill, if necessary, and thereby defeat it. The experience of Senator Wade in his various efforts to get the bill considered in the Senate was quite in accordance with that plan, and the fate of the bill was accurately predicted by letters received from New Orleans before it had passed the Senate.

Had the proclamation stopped there, it would have been only one other defeat of the will of the people by an executive perversion of the Constitution. But it goes farther. The President says:

"And whereas the said bill contains, among other things, a plan for restoring the States in rebellion to their proper practical relations in the Union, which plan expresses the sense of Congress upon that subject, and which plan it is now thought fit to lay before the people for their consideration—"

By what authority of the Constitution? In what forms? The result to be declared by whom? With what effect when ascertained? Is it to be a law by the approval of the people, without the approval of Congress, at the will of the President? Will the President, on his opinion of the popular approval, execute it as law? Or is this merely a device to avoid the serious responsibility of defeating a law on which so many loyal hearts reposed for security? But the reasons now assigned for not approving the bill are full of ominous significance. The President proceeds:

"Now, therefore, I, Abraham Lincoln, President of the United States, do proclaim, declare, and make known that, while I am (as I was in December last, when by proclamation I propounded a plan for restoration) unprepared, by a formal approval of this bill, to be inflexibly committed to any single plan of restoration—"

That is to say, the President is resolved that the people shall not, by law, take any securities from the rebel States against a renewal of the rebellion, before restoring their power to govern us. His wisdom and prudence are to be our sufficient guarantees. He farther says:

"And while I am also unprepared to declare that the free State Constitutions and governments already adopted and installed in Arkansas and Louisiana shall be set aside and held for naught, thereby repelling and discouraging the loyal citizens who have set up the same as to farther effort—"

That is to say, the President persists in recognizing those shadows of governments in Arkansas and Louisiana which Congress formally declared should not be recognized; whose representatives and senators were repelled by formal votes of both houses of Congress, and which, it was formally declared, should have no electoral vote for President and Vice-President. They are mere creatures of his will. They can not live a day without his support. They are mere oligarchies imposed on the people by military orders, under the forms of election, at which generals, provost-marshals, soldiers, and camp followers were the chief actors, assisted by a handful of resident citizens, and urged on to premature action by private letters from the President. In neither Louisiana nor Arkansas, before Banks's defeat, did the United States control half the territory or half the population. In Louisiana, General Banks's proclamation candidly declared, "The fundamental law of the State is martial law." On that foundation of freedom he erected what the President calls "the free Constitution and government of Louisiana." But of this State, whose fundamental law was martial law, only sixteen parishes out of forty-eight parishes were held by the United States; and in five of our sixteen parishes we held only our camps. The eleven parishes we substantially held had 233,185 inhabitants; the residue of the State, not held by us, 575,617. At the farce called an election, the officers of General Banks returned that 11,346 ballots were cast, but whether any, or by whom, the people of the United States have no legal assurance. But it is probable that 4000 were cast by soldiers, or employés of the United States, military or municipal; but none, according to any law, State or national, and so 7000 ballots represent the State of Louisiana. Such is the free Constitution and government of Louisiana, and like it is that of Arkansas. Nothing but the failure of a military expedition deprived us of a like one in the swamps of Florida; and, before the presidential election, like ones may be organized in every rebel State where the United States have a camp.

The President, by preventing this bill from becoming a law, holds the electoral votes of the rebel States at the dictation of his personal ambition. If these votes turn the balance in his favor, is it to be supposed that his competitor, defeated by such means, will acquiesce? If the rebel majority assert their supremacy in those States, and send votes which elect an enemy of the government, will we not repel his claims? And is not that civil war for the presidency inaugurated by the voice of rebel States? Seriously impressed with these dangers, Congress, "the proper constitutional authority," formally declared that there are no governments in the rebel States, and provided for their erection at a proper time. Both the Senate and the House of Representatives rejected the senators and representatives chosen under the authority of what the President calls the free Constitution and government of Arkansas. The President's proclamation "holds for naught" this judgment, and discards the authority of the Supreme Court, and strides headlong toward the anarchy his proclamation of the 8th of December inaugurated. If electors for President be allowed to be chosen in either of those States, a sinister light will be cast on the motives which induced the President to "hold for naught" the will of Congress rather than his government in Louisiana and Arkansas. That judgment of Congress which the President defies was the exercise of an authority exclusively invested in Congress by the Constitution to determine what is the established government in a State, and in its own nature, and by the highest judicial authority, binding on all other departments of the government.

The Supreme Court has formally declared that, under the fourth section of the fourth article of the Constitution requiring the United States to guarantee to every State a republican form of government, "it rests with Congress to decide what government is the established one in a State;" and "when senators and representatives of a State are admitted into the councils of the Union, the authority of the government under which they are appointed, as well as its republican character, is recognized by the proper constitutional authority, and its decision is binding on every other department of the government, and could not be questioned in a judicial tribunal. It is true that the contest in this case did not last long enough to bring the matter to this issue; and as no senators or representatives were elected under the authority of the government of which Mr. Dorr was the head, Congress was not called upon to decide the controversy. Yet the right to decide is placed there." Even the President's proclamation of the 8th of December formally declares that "whether members sent to Congress from any State shall be admitted to seats constitutionally rests exclusively with the respective houses, and not to any extent with the executive." And that is not the less true, because wholly inconsistent with the President's assumption, in that proclamation, of a right to institute and recognize State governments in the rebel States, nor because the President is unable to perceive that his recognition is a nullity if it be not conclusive upon Congress.

Under the Constitution, the right to senators and representatives is inseparable from a State government. If there be a State government, the right is absolute. If there be no State government, there can be no senators or representatives chosen. The two houses of Congress are expressly declared to be the sole judges of their own members. When, therefore, senators and representatives are admitted, the State government under whose authority they were chosen is conclusively established; when they are rejected, its existence is as conclusively rejected and denied. And to this judgment the President is bound to submit.

The President proceeds to express his unwillingness "to declare a constitutional competency in Congress to abolish slavery in States" as another reason for not signing the bill. But the bill nowhere proposes to abolish slavery in States. The bill did provide that all slaves in the rebel States should be manumitted. But as the President had already signed three bills manumitting several classes of slaves in States, it is not conceived possible that he entertained any scruples touching that provision of the bill respecting which he is silent. He has already himself assumed a right, by proclamation, to free much the larger number of slaves in the rebel States, under the authority given him by Congress to use military power to suppress the rebellion; and it is quite inconceivable that the President should think Congress could vest in him a discretion which it could itself exercise.

It is the more unintelligible from the fact that, except in respect to a small part of Virginia and Louisiana, the bill covered only what the proclamation covered—added a congressional title and judicial remedies by law; to the disputed title under the proclamation, and perfected the work the President professed to be so anxious to accomplish. Slavery as an institution can be abolished only by a change of the Constitution of the United States or of the law of the State, and this is the principle of the bill. It required the new Constitution of the State to provide for that prohibition; and the President, in the face of his own proclamation, does not venture to object to insisting on that condition. Nor will the country tolerate its abandonment; yet he defeated the only provision imposing it. But when he describes himself, in spite of this great blow at emancipation, as "sincerely hoping and expecting that a constitutional amendment abolishing slavery throughout the nation may be adopted," we curiously inquire on what his expectation rests, after the vote of the House of Representatives at the recent session, and in the face of the political complexion of more than enough of the States to prevent the possibility of its adoption within any reasonable time, and why he did not indulge his sincere hopes with so large an installment of the blessing as his approval of the bill would have secured?

After this assignment of his reasons for preventing the bill from becoming a law, the President proceeds to declare his purpose to execute it as a law by his plenary dictatorial power. He says:

"Nevertheless, I am fully satisfied with the system for restoration contained in the bill as the very proper plan for the loyal people of any State choosing to adopt it; and that I am, and at all times shall be prepared to give the executive aid and assistance to any such people as soon as the military resistance to the United States shall have been suppressed in any such State, and the people thereof shall have sufficiently returned to their obedience to the Constitution and laws of the United States, in which cases military governors will be appointed, with the directions to proceed according to the bill."

A more studied outrage on the legislative authority of the people has never been perpetrated. Congress passed a bill, the President refused to approve it; and then, by proclamation, puts as much of it in force as he sees fit, and proposes to execute those parts by officers unknown to the laws of the United States, and not subject to the confirmation of the Senate. The bill directed the appointment of *provisional* governors by and with the advice and consent of the Senate. The President, after defeating the law, proposes to appoint without law, and without the advice and consent of the Senate, *military* governors of the rebel States. He has already exercised this dictatorial usurpation in Louisiana, and he defeated the bill to prevent its limitation. Henceforth we must regard the following precedent as the presidential law of the rebel States.

"Executive Mansion, Washington, March 15, 1864.

"His Excellency Michael Hahn, Governor of Louisiana:

"Until farther orders, you are hereby invested with the powers exercised hitherto by the Military Governor of Louisiana.

"Yours, ABRAHAM LINCOLN."

This *Michael Hahn* is no officer of the United States. The President, without law, without the advice and consent of the Senate, by a private note not even countersigned by the Secretary of State, makes him dictator of Louisiana. The bill provided for the civil administration of the laws of the State till it should be in a fit temper to govern itself, repealing all laws recognizing slavery, and making all men equal before the law. These beneficent provisions the President has annulled. People will die, and marry, and transfer property, and buy and sell, and to these acts of civil life courts and officers of the law are necessary. Congress legislated for these necessary things, and the President deprives them of the protection of the law. The President's purpose to instruct his military governors to "proceed according to the bill"—a make-shift to calm the disappointment its defeat has occasioned—is not merely a grave usurpation, but a transparent delusion. He can not "proceed according to the bill" after preventing it from becoming a law. Whatever is done will be at his will and pleasure, by persons responsible to no law, and more interested to secure the interests and execute the will of the President than of the people, and the will of Congress is to be "held for naught," unless "the loyal people of the rebel States choose to adopt it." If they should graciously prefer the stringent bill to the easy proclamation, still the registration will be made under no legal sanction; it will give no assurance that a majority of the people of the States have taken the oath; if administered, it will be without legal authority, and void; no indictment will lie for false swearing at the election, or for admitting bad, or for rejecting good votes. It will be the farce of Louisiana and Arkansas acted over again, under the forms of this bill, but not by authority of law.

But when we come to the guarantees of future peace which Congress meant to exact, the forms as well as the substance of the bill must yield to the President's will that none should be imposed. It was the solemn resolve of Congress to protect the loyal men of the nation against three great dangers: (1) the return to power of the guilty leaders of the rebellion; (2) the continuance of slavery; and (3) the burden of the rebel debt. Congress required assent to those provisions of the Convention of the State, and, if refused, it was to be dissolved. The President "holds for naught" that resolve of Congress, because he is unwilling "to be inflexibly committed to any one plan of restoration;" and the people of the United States are not to be allowed to protect themselves unless their enemies agree to it. The order to proceed according to the bill is therefore merely at the will of the rebel States, and they have the option to reject it and accept the proclamation of the 8th of December, and demand the President's recognition. Mark the contrast! The bill requires a majority, the proclamation is satisfied with one tenth; the bill requires one oath, the proclamation another; the bill ascertains votes by registering, the proclamation by guess; the bill exacts adherence to existing territorial limits, the proclamation admits of others; the bill governs the rebel States *by law*, equalizing all before it, the proclamation commits them to the lawless discretion of military governors and provost-marshals; the bill forbids electors for President, the proclamation and defeat of the bill threaten us with civil war for the admission or exclusion of such votes; the bill exacted exclusion of dangerous enemies from power, and the relief of the nation from the rebel debt, and the prohibition of slavery forever, so that the suppression of the rebellion will double our resources to bear or pay the national debt, free the masses from the old domination of the rebel leaders, and eradicate the cause of the war; the proclamation secures neither of these guarantees.

It is silent respecting the rebel debt and the political exclusion of rebel leaders, leaving slavery exactly where it was by law at the outbreak of the rebellion, and adds no guarantees even of the freedom of the slaves the President undertook to manumit. It is summed up in an illegal oath, without a sanction, and therefore void. The oath is to support all proclamations of the President during the rebellion having reference to slaves. *Any* government is to be accepted at the hands of one tenth of the people not contravening that oath. Now that oath neither secures the abolition of slavery, nor adds any security to the freedom of the slaves whom the President declared free. It does not secure the abolition of slavery, for the proclamation of freedom merely professed to free certain slaves, while it recognized the institution. Every Constitution of the rebel States at the outbreak of the rebellion may be adopted, without the change of a letter, for none of them contravene that proclamation, none of them *establish* slavery.

It adds no security to the freedom of the slaves, for *their* title is the proclamation of freedom. If it be unconstitutional, an oath to support it is void. Whether constitutional or not, the oath is without authority of law, and therefore void. If it be valid, and observed, it exacts no enactment by the State, either in law or Constitution, to add a State guarantee to the proclamation title; and the right of a slave to freedom is an open question before the State courts on the relative authority of the State law and the proclamation. If the oath binds the one tenth who take it, it is not exacted of the other nine tenths who succeed to the control of the State government, so that it is annulled instantly by the act of recognition. What the State courts would say of the proclamation who can doubt? But the master would not go into court, he would seize his slave. What the Supreme Court would say who can tell? When and how is the question to get there? No *habeas corpus* lies for him in a United States court; and the President defeated with this bill its extension of that writ to this case.

Such are the fruits of this rash and fatal act of the President, a blow at the friends of his administration, at the rights of humanity, and at the principles of republican government.

The President has greatly presumed on the forbearance which the supporters of his administration have so long practiced, in view of the arduous conflict in which we are engaged, and the reckless ferocity of our political opponents.

But he must understand that our support is of a cause, and not of a man; that the authority of Congress is paramount, and must be respected; that the whole body of the Union men of Congress will not submit to be impeached by him of rash and unconstitutional legislation; and that, if he wishes our support, he must confine himself to his executive duties—to obey and execute—not to make the laws; to suppress by arms armed rebellion, and leave political reorganization to the Congress.

If the supporters of the government fail to insist on this, they become responsible for the usurpations which they fail to rebuke, and are justly liable to the indignation of the people whose rights and security committed to their keeping they sacrifice.

Let them consider the remedy for these usurpations, and, having found, fearlessly execute it.

B. F. WADE, Chairman of Senate Committee.

H. WINTER DAVIS,
Chairman of Committee of House of Representatives on the Rebellious States.

VICTORY THE CONDITION OF SUCCESS.

On the 14th of October, 1864, the new Constitution of Maryland, submitted by the State Convention in June, abolishing slavery in the State, was approved and adopted by the people. Mr. Davis thus lived to see accomplished the work of emancipation, in which he had taken great interest, and in the advocacy of which he had also had an active part.

But an opposition to him in the ranks of the Union party in his own district, which had been confined at first to a few, had been increased by the policy he had advocated and by his votes on some occasions in Congress, and had not been diminished by the tone he had sometimes used toward such opponents. His opposition to the renomination of Mr. Lincoln, and to certain measures of his administration, had had the same effect in this district, and it had lately been increased among others by the publication of the "Wade-Davis Manifesto." It was asserted by some of the opponents of Mr. Davis that, while he thus did not completely support the administration, and furnished (by the Manifesto) arguments against it during the canvass, he was in some things more extreme than the Republican party; that his votes in Congress actually drove away Southern trade from Baltimore, and that his course and proposed action now tended to exasperate instead of winning back the States now (then) in rebellion.

Besides these allegations, a good deal of the opposition to Mr. Davis must be traced to the personal animosities and bitterness of feeling which in Baltimore of late years had been the invariable consequence of a difference, not merely of party and political views, but of opinions also, as to the line of party conduct even among its own adherents. It was farther asserted by some that Mr. Davis was then, and would shortly declare himself, in favor of "negro suffrage," whenever he thought the necessities of the political situation demanded its adoption.

Upon all these grounds and assertions, this opposition to him, which had proved itself important two years before, when he was last nominated for Congress, now showed signs of carrying with it the control of the Union party. This was confirmed in September by the defeat, for the

State Nominating Convention, of those who opposed the nomination of Governor Swann, and it was finally settled in October by the result of a municipal election in Baltimore. At the ward meetings in the district, held immediately afterward, for delegates to a Convention to nominate a representative to the Thirty-ninth Congress (1865–'67), the opponents of Mr. Davis carried almost every ward. The nomination was given unanimously to Colonel Charles E. Phelps, of Baltimore, who had served with gallantry during the war, had been wounded in action, and who was returned in November without opposition to the Thirty-ninth Congress.

It is not necessary to discuss here whether any different course, if it had been pursued by Mr. Davis, would have maintained the unity of the party strength, continued its support of him, and prevented those defections which had on previous occasions refused to him the united party vote. He always boldly avowed his opinions, and assumed their full responsibility. He made no compromises with what he thought a vacillating policy, and those even who condemned his course could not refuse to admit the sincerity and the fearlessness of his action. He declined, on more than one occasion, to make concessions, or to explain away any vote or act of his, even when he was assured that his defeat would be the penalty of his refusal; for in matters of this kind he was as much unaccustomed to yield to the persuasions of friends, or to considerations of "policy," as he was to the threats and imprecations of enemies. Indeed, he took no account of opposition, except to work the more resolutely; and he frequently disregarded the advice of those even to whom he was attached, unless it accorded with what he thought right, and so, always and every where, expedient. He followed the convictions and conclusions of his own judgment alone.

In consequence of this defeat, and the feelings engendered by it, Mr. Davis was not invited by the State Central Committee of the Union party in Maryland to take part in the canvass in this State.

He was invited, however, elsewhere, and among these invitations he accepted one to Philadelphia, where he spoke on the 25th of October, in National Hall, to a very large meeting under the auspices of the Union League, as follows:

Fellow-citizens of the United States,—The canvass in which the American people are now engaged is very much the most momentous that the history of the world or of free government has presented. If it succeed, as in my judgment it will succeed, in placing in power the men who have conducted the government through this awful crisis till safety begins to be visible, a result will have been accomplished which will forever place the capacity of the people of America for self-government beyond cavil—beyond the reach of question; for they are called to vote for the election of a man who has presided over the government in circumstances altogether unprecedented, during a time when vast sacrifices have been exacted, and vast sacrifices have cheerfully been made by the mass of the American people; when enormous taxes have been imposed; when enormous armies have been raised; when great results were expected, and great results have not always been achieved; when disaster has perched upon the national banner as often as victory, and when the great preponderance of our resources in men and money, while gradually and steadily eating toward the heart of the rebellion, have not reached it with that promptness, have not crushed it with that decisiveness, that our hopes led us to expect when the war broke out. Under these circumstances, judged by the history of the world, discontent, dissension, the lack of spirit and of energy, divisions at home, dictating tones from abroad, popular submission, popular bewilderment, were what we were entitled to expect—nay, what we were bound to expect. Instead of that, what do we behold? The great mass of the American people having, as it were, been surprised into the renomination of the present candidate—then for a moment pausing, as if frightened at what they had done—then listening to the first echo from Chicago, and forgetting every doubt, throwing aside every hesitation, subjecting every criticism to the dictates of the highest reason and the highest statesmanship, as one man turned to the candidate whom before they had doubted, with a resolution that they must make an election—not between two individuals—not between the personal qualities of Abraham Lincoln and George B. M'Clellan, not between the public services of the one or the other, but an election between the overthrow and the salvation of the republic. (Loud applause.) They exhibited, they are now exhibiting every where in this land, that great and highest mark of sublime statesmanship, the capacity of judging between things neither of which may be acceptable, but one of which is necessary—the great quality of a great statesman to subordinate personal dislikes, differences of opinion, upon subordinate points; great failures for whom none but those in power can be held responsible—to subordinate the natural and inevitable discontent which such events as those bring about in a people, and to raise the great practical question, "What do we men of America wish to accomplish?" and having determined what they wish to accomplish, to ask the other question, "Which of the two men before the people for their votes is on our side?" not which is the abler, not which is the most skillful administrator, not which is the better warrior, not even which is the more patriotic; but, conceding them to be equal on these points, or conceding our opponent to be superior to our candidate on any or all of these points, the American people have solemnly asked themselves "which of those two men is on our side?" and having determined that one plain, simple question of fact, they have determined, if need be, that the principle of our politics shall be, and that the safety of the nation requires that it shall be, that even the worst man on our side is better than the best man on their side. (Applause.) And that is the reason, gentlemen, that I, and thousands like me in America, support Abraham Lincoln for the presidency; not because we think his acts are all wise or all defensible—not because we regard him as the ablest among the men who stand by the republic in the hour of its need—still less for that most dangerous reason assigned by the Secretary of State, that this great contest in which the people are engaged is a mere contest for the presidency, and that it would be yielding the point in contest to select another, even an abler man on our side. The people of America would shed no blood in such a quarrel; the people of America would raise no army to fight out a question of the succession to the presidency on the principles of Mexican politics. We shall vote for Abraham Lincoln, not because of any of those reasons, but because, whether we will or no, even if we preferred another now, we can not have him; if we desire a change, we can not change without bringing ruin upon the republic (applause); and for that reason, every doubt is subordinated to the great necessities of empire.

It is not a question, fellow-citizens, for school-boys to debate; nor is it a question for men to attend, as heretofore, political meetings, to be decided by the wittiest speech or the best-told story. Blood rests upon that decision; the being of a nation rests upon your judgment. Great sacrifices heretofore made are to be thrown away if you come to one judgment, and are to be fruitful in blessings if you come to another judgment.

Sloth, and ease, and hesitation, and cupidity, and cowardice, all counsel you to take another candidate, for there are burdens in taking Abraham Lincoln; there are battles in placing him at the head of the government; there is war at least for one year more, very possibly for two, it may be for three years, and it may be for more than three; and, therefore, when men resolve to take Abraham Lincoln for their President, they must do it as they do in forming the holiest of the relations of social life—for better, for worse—with the consciousness of what is before them; knowing the burdens that they assume; knowing the consequences that follow from it; knowing that, peaceful as we are here, it dooms fifty thousand men to death, and that they have to come from your brothers and from your sons—not to do his bidding, not to determine the wretched question whether he or some other man shall be President, but whether the fabric of government reared by our fathers shall remain untouched—whether the integrity of republican institutions shall be preserved. (Loud cheers.) After this remarkable period of hesitation to which I have referred, when so many patriotic eyes looked to Chicago for comfort and support, why is it that every patriotic man that turned his eyes in that direction has now turned his back in that direction? For it was done in the twinkling of an eye; it was done within twenty-four hours; it was done as soon as the men of America read the Chicago Platform. (Applause.) I have never for a moment hesitated in my judgment that the mass of American people, taxation, bloodshed, failures, to the contrary notwithstanding, are for the war as the only path of safety. Not because they want bloodshed, but because they want peace; not because they want to subjugate their fellow-citizens, but because they are determined all shall be free. (Great cheering.) Therefore, when they read the Chicago Platform, and learned that there was even a doubt as to whether the war was to proceed, that settled their judgment on their candidate. What is that platform? First it begins by assuring us that the Democratic party is now for the Constitution and the Union, "*as heretofore.*" When we read those words we had a measure by which we could judge the intensity and the character of their devotion; and we remembered that in their hands, under their control, under the presidency of James Buchanan, and while Judge Black was Attorney General, and in Buchanan's cabinet, war was allowed to be made upon the United States with impunity; humiliating contracts for armistice were made with rebels with arms in their hands; the army of the United States was scattered from one end to the other of its vast territory, in order that it might be away at the critical moment; every sea possessed an American vessel except the waters of our own coast; no arms were prepared, no precautions were taken; the warnings of Winfield Scott were disregarded; every arsenal was left a prey to the insidious assaults of the enemy, whose designs were known to the President. The Democratic party having taken care of the Constitution and the Union in that way, we accept as the interpretation of their platform the "heretofore" of Buchanan's administration, and say that their defense and protection of the Constitution and the Union mean its submission to Southern dictation, its destruction before Southern rebellion, dissolution and death, and not preservation. (Great applause.) And when we go one step farther into that remarkable document, and read there that after four years of unsuccessful war—justice, humanity, and religion require that there should be a cessation of hostilities with a view to the calling of a Convention, or "some other peaceable means," to end the war and restore the Union, we have an explanation that needs no comment as to what the first declaration meant. "Cease the war" means to lay down your arms, to lift your blockade, to relax the sinews of your arm, to induce your people to believe that peace is here, to treat upon equal terms with the rebellious enemies of the republic, to open the door for foreign recognition, to prepare the way for foreign intervention. And, after all that has been done, if the rebels refuse your "Convention or other peaceable means," where are we? How will you ever take up the musket after it has been laid down? How will you ever collect your army when it has once been allowed to return or almost disbanded on furlough? How will you ever strengthen the sinews of the nation up to the height of reopening the war after once you have dropped the sword from your hands? Why, fellow-citizens, they who propose that know as well as I know that an armistice means peace—that the cessation of the war means the end of the war—that the end of the war means the end of coercive measures for the restoration of the republic; and when they once propose that an armistice shall be instituted, without even saying that if its purposes fail the sword shall again be drawn, they tell us, in the most distinct language, that their purpose is to stop the war and take the consequences; they tell us that their purpose is to stop the war and not look beyond at the consequences of the stoppage of the war. Peace is what they want, and that is all. And when we turn to the letter of acceptance of General M'Clellan, there is a repetition substantially of the platform, but with no addition to it. He is in favor, as the Convention is in favor, of "perpetuating the Union;" he thinks, as they think, that it ought to be perpetuated; but he nowhere says that after an armistice and a failure to agree, he is in favor of taking up the sword. It may be that he is. I can easily believe that a general might desire to be commander-in-chief of half a million of men. But who and what is M'Clellan? He is what his party friends make him —what the men are who elect him—what they are who stand behind him. Fernando Wood has told you that whatever the private opinions of the candidate may be, when he is once nominated and elected, he will think, and speak, and act as the body of the great party that elected him may desire that he should think, and speak, and act. "He will be," says Mr. Wood, "our agent, the creature of our voice." And you all know what the voice of Fernando Wood is. (Laughter and applause.) Fernando Wood, a man who in the better days of the republic nobody would have thought it worth while to name at a public meeting, has now become one of the mischievous and poisonous reptiles that are biting the republic to death. (Applause.) Alexander Long, of Ohio, Clement Vallandigham, of ill-omened fame—these are the men who are supporting him; these are the men who look to high offices under him; these are the men who represent the great mass and body of the so-called Peace Democracy; and if there be any thing but a Peace Democracy any where that is not now supporting Abraham Lincoln, I do not know who the man is, or where he is. (Applause.)

I never could find a Peace Democrat in Congress who would do any thing except swell a majority when his vote was not needed, and leave you to be defeated when his vote was required to make a majority. Place them in the majority, and they are all peace men. One would like the war to go on, for there are pickings, and stealings, and plunder in it; another of them would like it to go on because possibly he might have some chance of military fame; but the body of them, the men who must form the Congress, the men who must vote the money, the men who must organize the army, the men who stand outside of Congress and send them there, are for peace; they are against taxation; they are opposed to paying two cents a box for matches. (Laughter.) They are the people who are guilty of the wretched folly and hypocrisy of placing side by side the columns of taxation of Buchanan's administration and the present administration, as if every body were as big a fool as the poor Democrats whom they want to cheat by that contrivance. (Applause.) And yet they are the men whom you are to place in power with M'Clellan; they are the men who are to hold his hands in the struggle—who are to support him with men and money—who are to guide his policy! To repeal every law on the statute-book for the carrying on of the war would be their first act whenever they should get a majority of both houses. Having a majority of one House only, they would palsy the majority in the other House that might be desirous even of furnishing the government with the means for carrying on the war. They would strike immediately from your armies 150,000 or 200,000 negro soldiers for fear they would disband the rest of the army! They would remove the suspension of the *habeas corpus*, in order that Democratic traitors might walk at large and communicate with the enemy. (Applause.) There is no measure necessary to the conduct of the war that they are not already pledged to destroy. Their canvass is against the measures of the war, and the people of the United States have come to the solemn conclusion that they who are not in favor of the means of carrying on the war are not in favor of carrying on the war at all; that they who are for paralyzing the arm of the government by stripping it of the needful legislation for the conduct of the war, can not be trusted with the conduct of the war; and, as rational men, they turn their back on those who profess before high Heaven that that is their purpose, and turn to men who at least profess to be willing to carry on the war—who at least have struggled to the best of their ability, be it poor or great, for four years to carry it on—who at least have accomplished some results, and if they are not stripped of power now by men who, under the disguise of pretending to be in favor of the war, are really against it, will, in a reasonable time, put an end to it. (Great applause.) Is there any other way, fellow-citizens, of restoring the integrity of the republic than by the bloody path of war? Believe Jeff Davis when he tells you that his only terms of peace are "independence," and that is only a new word for the dissolution of the Union; believe the men from one end to the other of the rebel Confederacy who tell you that all they want is to be "let alone," and "let alone" means that the United States shall march out of and abdicate more than one half of its territory. They tell you that they are not struggling because of slavery; they are struggling for independence, and "independence" means the destruction of the American nationality. If, therefore, there be any way of persuading them to make peace on other terms than those of independence, let some one arise and point out the public man or the mass of the population any where in the South that has declared a willingness to make peace on those terms. (Applause.) They are now stretching a long finger all through the United States, intermeddling in our presidential election. They utter nightly prayers for the success of M'Clellan. They hope that the division upon the presidential election will ultimately place some one in power who will make terms that they will agree to. Has ever any body heard them say, "If you will elect M'Clellan we will submit to the terms of the old Constitution as it is," in the slang phrase of the modern Democrats; that they are willing to accept the old "Union as it was," in the slang phrase of the modern Democrats; that they are willing to take any compromise; that they are willing to take slavery in the whole of the Territories of the United States; that they are willing to take the incorporation of slavery forever into the Constitution of the United States itself; that they are willing upon any terms whatever to reunite with you? Their question, gentlemen, is that of severance and independence, and the Democrats are perpetually mumbling to themselves some unintelligible words about "compromise" with people who say "we want no compromise;" terms with people who say "our terms are independence"—concessions to people who say "we will accept no concessions from your hands;" union to people who say "death rather." (Applause.) Then there is, gentlemen, but one path, I say, out of this difficulty. I have said so from the fall of 1860 to this time. I said so before a sword was drawn. I said so after the secession ordinances were passed, and when the old fogy Convention was mumbling over terms of compromise in what they called a "Peace Congress." (Applause.) I said so when two great committees of tho two houses of Congress were straining their nerves to get something to force down the rebels' throats, which they swore they would throw up as soon as it was forced down. There has never been a day that any body, who could see beyond the length of his nose, since South Carolina took the first step in 1860, after the election of Abraham Lincoln, did not know that the only path to unity in this country is over bloody battle-fields; and, gentlemen, they are before you yet. (Great applause.) I pray you be under no more delusions. We have now this awful, desolating campaign because the government would persist in dreaming all last winter that the rebellion was ended. And if they put on the night-cap and dream again this winter, Lee will be before Grant as strong next spring as he was last spring. You may be near the end of the rebellion, but there is many a sharp struggle before you yet, and the only way to end it is to let the rebels have no rest, to press on them day by day, and night by night, filling up the gulf between you and them with your dead sons and brothers if necessary, but remembering that every week of armistice, every day of delay, every month of winter-quarters means other hecatombs to fill up the gap in your march. (Tremendous applause.) And now we hear from the advocates of M'Clellan grave objections to the conduct of the President and the conduct of his administration as reasons why the Republican party should not be trusted—not the particular individual, but the Republican party that stand at his back, defends what he has done well, deplores what he has done ill or failed to do, and is resolved that he shall do better in the future. (Applause.) The Republican party stands at his back and takes the responsibility of what has passed heretofore, and means to meet the objections that are made; and while they admit, as in my judgment they must admit, that there are many things that have been done which ought not to have been done, and which a wiser policy and greater acquaintance with statesmanship would have saved us from, yet the substantial things of government have been done (great applause)—done better than our antagonists could do them if they wanted, or would do if they were allowed to attempt. We hear dolorous objections about the violations of personal liberty; we hear objections about weak men placed at the head of the armies; we hear objections about the lack of vigor in the conduct of the war; and the only arguments to be deduced from such imputations as those is not that Mr. Lincoln is not so great, or so able, or so wise as somebody else, but that George B. M'Clellan ought to be put in his place. The question is not whether Mr. Lincoln has done the best that any mind could conceive, nor even the best that he himself could do, nor whether what he has done is absolutely right, or absolutely in accordance with law; but the question is whether his opponent would do better. "He has," says a distinguished senator of Maryland, in a most elaborate and able speech in Brooklyn the other day in behalf of M'Clellan, "appointed weak and incompetent men to the command of the armies." I say yes, and M'Clellan at the head of them. (Great applause.) They say that he has punished and excluded from office men merely because they were the friends of George B. M'Clellan. I say yes, and Fitz John Porter was one of them. (Great applause.) They say that the war has not been conducted with that energy with which it ought to have been conducted, and which ought long since to have stamped out the rebellion. I say yes, and the greatest of all failures was the failure of George B. M'Clellan, who wasted the largest army the republic has ever assembled, in idleness, in and around the City of Washington, for nearly eight months, when not one third his number of enemies were within thirty-five miles in his front, and he did not dare to feel them with a regiment of his cavalry to ascertain their number. (Applause.) Yes, opportunities have been lost. There was no opportunity equal to the opportunity of George B. M'Clellan in the fall of 1861 and the spring of 1862. "Lost opportunities!" Ay, a greater one when a broken and flying army, with a vast river in its rear, was allowed to escape without pursuit, and that was by George B. M'Clellan after Antietam. (Applause.) It may be that the war has been badly conducted. It is certain that the worst parts of its conduct have been those parts which have been attributed to George B. M'Clellan. It is certain that there have been failures. There have been no failures so disastrous, so continued, so inexcusable as the failure of the Peninsular campaign. (Applause.) There have been failures. There has been no failure that rested on the good faith of any officer, excepting Buell's in Kentucky, and M'Clellan's and Fitz John Porter's failure at the second Bull Run battle. (Great applause.) Concede that the conduct of the war has been weak; agree to every thing that our antagonists say; the fact that the war has continued for four years without the rebellion being broken is because George B. M'Clellan, with the uncontrolled disposition of all the armies of the United States for nearly a year, left it, as it is, unbroken. (Applause.) We are told of violations of the right of personal liberty! Personal liberty has been invaded! If they had said that the personal liberty of somebody, whose liberty ought to be respected, had been invaded, there would have been some point in it. (Applause.) If they had said that somebody had been confined who ought to have been at large, I would have listened to the argument. If they had said that some loyal man had been maliciously arrested and maliciously confined, without a doubt upon the President's mind, and without a pretext of public reason, then I would agree that the President ought to be impeached. But when they say that the right of personal liberty has been invaded because men have been arrested without legal process, I beg leave to say that there is no law or Constitution in the United States which says that nobody shall be arrested excepting by judicial process. The solemn language of the Constitution of the United States is that "no man shall be deprived of life, liberty, or property without due process of law." "Property" and "liberty" stand in the same category with "life." How many men has Abraham Lincoln shot down according to law because they stood in gray clothes before men in blue clothes? What sheriff's precept goes before Grant's cannon balls? What marshal of the United States is required to give him liberty to fire? What jury of inquiry is summoned to ascertain whether the flag that is floating on the horizon is an innocent rag, or the emblem of rebel armed force? What antecedent judicial securities took place before 20,000 men laid down and died at Gettysburg, or 60,000 men were killed or wounded in the campaign from this spring to the present time from the Rapidan down to Petersburg? Then, so far as life is concerned, there is a law that is above judicial process. Nobody is fool enough to deny that. Is there a law above judicial process, with reference likewise to liberty? If there be not, why do you not turn loose the rebel prisoners? Why do you keep them confined for a day? What precept has ever ordered their confinement? Who sends the officers up to the lakes? Who crowds them into our forts? Who makes them swarm below here in Fort Delaware? Is there a judgment upon them, or is it that the law of the land says that men found in arms and seized shall be held, and that the President, finding them in arms, shall hold them upon his own judgment? (Applause.) Are we to be told that only those actually caught in battle array shall be so treated? May men furnish the enemy with munitions of war, or clothes, or information, or give them aid and comfort, or send them medicines, and yet not be within the range of indictment for treason, or, at the option of the country, the military security of a discretionary arrest? From George Washington's time down to the present day no man has ever doubted the legality of these things until the modern Democracy, having too many traitors in its midst, found it convenient to have these principles applied in practice. (Applause.) "But," it is said, "the *habeas corpus* has been suspended illegally by the President." I agree that it was suspended illegally by the President the first year of the war, and I warned him and his party friends of the illegality of, and the inevitable reaction in public opinion which would come if that were not corrected. The reaction came in the fall of 1862, and they supplied the omission early in 1863 by going to Congress to ask them to pass the requisite law to suspend it; the law was passed, but still the howl goes up the *habeas corpus* is illegally suspended! But, gentlemen, suppose the President has oppressed, has illegally arrested individuals, has committed all the oppressions that are ascribed to him, our opponents propose to place George B. M'Clellan in his place on his "record," ostentatiously referred to in his letter of acceptance as indicating the course of his own policy hereafter referred to, to supply the deficiency, to get rid of the different points of the Chicago Platform, and the first man that took a step in the direction of arresting without judicial process was George B. M'Clellan himself. Here is his order to General Banks, in September, 1861:

"Major General N. P. Banks:

"GENERAL,—After a full consultation with the President, Secretaries of State, War, etc., it has been decided to effect the operation proposed* for the 17th. Arrangements have been made to have a government steamer at Annapolis to receive the prisoners and carry them to their destination.

"Some four or five of the chief men in the affair are to be arrested to-day. When they meet on the 17th you will have every thing prepared to arrest the whole party, and be sure that none escape.

"It is understood that you will arrange with General Dix and Governor Seward the *modus operandi*. It has been intimated to me that the meeting might take

* The arrest of the members of the seditious Legislature of Maryland.

place on the 14th; please be prepared. I would be glad to have you advise me frequently of your arrangements in regard to this very important matter.

"If it is *successfully carried out it will go far toward breaking the back-bone of the rebellion.* It will probably be well to have a special train quietly prepared to take the prisoners to Annapolis.

"I leave this exceedingly important affair to your tact and discretion—the absolute necessity of secrecy and success.

"With the highest regard, I am, dear general, your sincere friend,

"GEORGE B. M'CLELLAN, Major General U. S. A."

The reason assigned was that the arrest would "go far toward breaking the back-bone of the rebellion." We who support the President think so too. (Applause.) While there have been cases of arrests which ought not to have been made, and some which, in my judgment, were not justifiable, and many which were indiscreet, in my opinion more men have been improperly discharged than have been improperly arrested. (Great applause.) But it is certain that on M'Clellan's "record" he is not the man to impeach the conduct of the President in that particular. "State rights," too, were here defied, and a sovereign Legislature arrested—arrested by George B. M'Clellan, whom his friend Mr. Attorney General Black only last night was defending and advocating in this city; and he imputed to the administration an entire deviation from every thing that had a precedent in American history, especially upon the subject of State rights and personal liberty; and he did that to induce the people to take George B. M'Clellan for President, who set the only example that has been exhibited any where on the American continent of the arrest of a Legislature in solemn session, in time of peace, at that place, and in that State; for there was no armed foe in Maryland when that Legislature was arrested. It was swarming with traitors, but traitors are the men they want to be free from arrest. They were not armed; they were not levying war; they were not threatening to levy war; they were too pusillanimous to attempt it; they were passing resolutions, receiving reports, declaring that the oppression of the government was too great to be resisted. They were safe traitors, and they are the men that George B. M'Clellan arrested. But there is another objection. It is stated in the Chicago Platform that military power has been brought to bear illegally upon elections. That is the imputation made by Mr. Senator Johnson, in his speech in Brooklyn the other day, arguing in behalf of George B. M'Clellan. Who set the example? On October 29, 1861, this order was issued from the head-quarters of General M'Clellan, by his order:

"Head-quarters Army of the Potomac, Washington, October 29, 1861.

"GENERAL,—There is an apprehension among Union citizens in many parts of Maryland at an attempt of interference with their rights of suffrage by disunion citizens on the occasion of the election to take place on the 6th of November next.

"In order to prevent this, the major general commanding directs that you send detachments of a sufficient number of men to different points in your vicinity where the elections are to be held, *to protect the Union voters*, and to *see that no Disunionists are allowed* to intimidate them, or in any way to interfere with their rights.

"He also desires you to arrest"—

By what writ?

"He also desires you to arrest and hold in confinement till after the election all Disunionists who are known to have returned from Virginia recently, and *who show themselves at the polls*, and to guard effectually against any invasion of the peace and order of the election. For the purpose of carrying out these instructions, *you are authorized to suspend the habeas corpus.* General Stone has received similar instructions to these. You will please confer with him as to the particular points that each shall take the control of.

"I am, sir, very respectfully, your obedient servant,

"R. B. MARCY, Chief of Staff.

"Major General N. P. Banks."

That was the first example in the United States, during this war, of an attempt to prevent rebels from voting. He uses a phrase there wider than any order that has ever been issued heretofore. He speaks of "Disunionists;" that is, men who entertain disunion opinions. No other order has ever gone farther than to say that men who have been in arms against the United States, or who have given aid, comfort, or encouragement to the enemy, shall be allowed to vote. Of Disunionists, we have twenty thousand in Maryland; of men who have given aid and comfort, we have only perhaps two or three, or four thousand. General Schenck's order stopped at the latter. General M'Clellan's order covered them all (applause); and at that election Senator Johnson was himself a candidate for the Legislature, and was elected, and never complained of the order. By that Legislature he was chosen to the seat in the Senate of the United States that he now holds, and never complained of that order. And yet he is the gentleman who makes that imputation against President Lincoln in behalf of the originator of the invasion of the freedom of the elective franchise in Maryland! (Great applause.) Military at elections! Were I an advocate of M'Clellan I would seek some other topic of imputation; were I a Democrat I would never mention it, for fear the bloody ghosts of the thirty men and women who were shot down while peacefully walking in the streets of Washington, in 1857, by the orders of James Buchanan, would rise and point their ghastly fingers at me. Still less as a Maryland Democrat, if I were one, would I ever refer to it, when I remembered that Governor Ligon, finding it impossible to control otherwise the indomitable spirit of the American party of Baltimore, summoned six thousand soldiers to control them on the day of election, and failed. And of all the men in the wide world to urge that argument, the last man is the Hon. Reverdy Johnson, who gave the opinion to Governor Ligon that it was legal to do so! If any one has any curiosity in reference to that sort of literature, here is the opinion. Of what sort of stuff are these men made, that they venture to fling in our faces their own vices, or their complicity with ours? It is the most overwhelming of defenses of the conduct of the administration against things that I myself think unadvisable and frequently illegal, to find that its antagonists are steeped up to their elbows in the only crimes they can cast upon it. If they, not responsible for the supreme direction of affairs, yet entertained the opinion that these things were allowable when the pressure of the necessity of the public administration was not on them, how can they blame with any reason those who, being responsible for the conduct of affairs, have resorted to the very measures that they have themselves executed and vindicated? (Applause.)

"But," our opponents say, "we will carry on the war on Christian principles!" (Laughter.) The only principle of war that I remember to have read of in the Christian dispensation is that, if one smites you on the right cheek, you should turn unto him the left also. I take it that is the Christian principle upon which the Democrats contemplate carrying on this war. (Laughter and applause.) "Christian principles." When they refer to the conduct of Christian nations in war, they must be taken to refer to some of the great nations that have waged war under great emergencies like these; and if so, I ask their historians (for they are learned every now and then) whether they remember the rebellion in India, when Christian England shot the King of Delhi in cold blood, in his own palace, unarmed, after the capture of the city, and blew from the mouths of their cannons men who had only rebelled to get their natural rights, against a foreign nation. (Applause.) Or, if they do not like the morals of Protestant England, do they remember the day when Catholic France by her marshals smoked to death in an Algerian cave an army of her rebel enemies? Or, if they do not like Catholic France, will they take Greek Russia, and tell me whether they wish to apply the Christian principles that now make Poland smoke with blood of her sons for claiming their national right? Or, if these are not the "Christian principles" to which they refer, will they point to some other war conducted by greater and more Christian nations upon more humane principles, and point out to us the way that we shall follow them? Which of these things have we done? Gentlemen, after some small reading of history by way of amusement, I desire to challenge those learned pundits, and I say that they can produce nowhere, in all the range of history, sacred or profane, ancient or modern, any war of four years' duration where one half the men were arranged on either side that have here been ranged in battle, any one year of which did not exceed all the atrocities that the United States troops have committed in four years of war—none—none whatever. (Applause.) I have mentioned the recent instances. Who would think of mentioning the great desolation of the Thirty Years' War, that left Germany a waste? Who would mention the seventy years' war of the Netherlands, where the gallows followed the advancing Spanish troops? In the civil wars of England, did not execution and blood follow victory? There never has been a war conducted upon principles that could be called so nearly Christian, excepting that the only Christian principle I can apply to the conduct of war is that it shall be short, and sharp, and merciful. (Applause.) And the danger of this war has been that the President could not rise to the height of the emergency, and steel his heart against what was pity in the individual, but cruelty in the ruler. Ay, many a man sleeps this day in a soldier's grave because the President would not execute military law upon deserters; and many a bloody battle has been lost, and many a regiment torn to pieces, because traitors were allowed to go free in the open day, and carry information of the march of our troops, and of their numbers, to the enemy. Gentlemen, war is war. No other word is its equivalent. It needs no definition. It is the greatest destruction in the shortest time. That is mercy, and that is wisdom.

Now, gentlemen, I have one other word to say to you about the Chicago Platform. It proposes, in certain contingencies, that the Democrats shall rebel, and I do not think that an idle threat. I desire to treat it as I feel with regard to it—as a contingency that may not be very far off. We have the Democratic party in arms at the South; we have had them here in sympathy with the armed Democrats of the South ever since the war broke out, and if the leaders get the opportunity, they will, as they have heretofore tried to do, put the Democratic party of the North in arms with them. There have been some efforts in that direction already. We know that when M'Clellan was removed from command, such was the temper of a certain portion of his officers, so contemptuous were they with regard to the government at Washington, so devoted personally to M'Clellan, so outraged at the exertion of the simple prerogative of the President, that they advised him to march to Washington; and these men were not denounced, and have not been punished to this day; but his friends claim it as a virtue that he did not do what they suggested! Judge of a man who requires that his virtue should be found in refusing to violate his oath and draw his sword against the government that placed it in his hands, and who could be silent about such a suggestion! Then, on the eve of the battle at Gettysburg, we had the rebellion in New York—they call it mob, I call it a rebellion — Seymour's rebellion; the rebellion that Seymour's "friends" and M'Clellan's friends got up to resist the arms of the United States, or perhaps it was to help carry on the war by aiding the draft. (Laughter.) That was stamped out rudely, "illegally," our Democratic friends would say, for men were shot without a sheriff's process. But, legally or illegally, it was extinguished effectually. (Cheers.) The next thing we hear of is a tremendous struggle in Indiana and Illinois, a political struggle for the possession of those States. Gentlemen acquainted with them said, "The loss of Indiana is not the loss of an election, it is the loss of a State to the Union;" and scarcely had a gentleman made that remark to me, being himself a resident of Indiana, than arms hidden were discovered, the tracks of a great conspiracy were developed, and they were found to be standing on the brink of a volcano, prepared doubtless for the day of the millennium of the Chicago revolution! And they, not yet taught by the resolute determination of the American people to deal with traitors by force, and supposing that men who have met the Southern people in arms would be frightened by the Democrats in arms in the North, passed a resolution declaring that if the violation of the elective franchise in Maryland, and Kentucky, and Delaware was repeated, they would regard it as cause of revolution, and they adjourned their Convention to meet upon the call of their National Committee or President. Some persons thought that was with a view to the possible refusal of the nomination by M'Clellan. I think any body who so thought was very short-sighted in public affairs. It meant to keep a recognized representative of the rebellious element of the Democratic party together, so that if they failed by a small vote, and the impatience of taxation, and the weariness of the war, and the languor of the administration would allow them an opportunity, they could call their Convention together, and spring to arms, and make a war for the presidency. That was what they meant. The interference with elections in Maryland! Why did they slap their own candidate in the face? They would not have done that without a cause. They knew what he had done, but they wanted to make the preparation for a rebellion. They knew that the American people are tender upon the subject of the elective franchise. They knew that there was great discontent, just or unjust; great impatience; great weariness of the war; great disappointment at the failure to obtain great results after great means had been granted. They thought that if they could only show an immense power in the Northern States, carrying a majority of the free States, and they should happen to be overbalanced by the vote of the border States, they could persuade the people that the vote of the border States which saved the Congress last time was not a legal vote, and precipitate them into rebellion, and they are waiting now that chance. Whether they will have the bad boldness to execute it remains to be seen; but the people of the United States have taken the best security against the opportunity. A lesson has been read them in Indiana that they are not likely shortly to forget. (Great applause.) It has been re-enforced in Ohio under the odium of Vallandigham. (Tremendous applause.) And Pennsylvania, though stripped of thousands of her voting population, has responded to the Western voice. (Great applause.) What New York will do nobody knows; but let New York look to her port if she dare to wriggle even under what the majority do.

(Applause.) They have tried, gentlemen, more than once to bully the United States, and they found it a hard bulldog to bully. (Laughter and applause.) All through the campaign of 1862 the government was taunted with its hostility to George B. M'Clellan. They thought the government did not dare to remove him, or they thought if it did that he would have the pluck, and his soldiers would have the villainy, to follow him in a march on Washington; and it was met then as it will be met now, with a very short intimation to them that there are other generals in the United States besides M'Clellan, and other armies besides M'Clellan's. (Vehement and long-continued applause.) They can begin, gentlemen. Perhaps they will not end the strife that they begin. But the only way to deal with events of this kind is not to do as Mr. Buchanan did, and encourage them to grow suddenly from infancy to manhood, and endow them with gigantic power before you strike them, but take their first threat for an act, and smash them to the brain. (Great applause.)

But, gentlemen, the policy of the President, it is said, has divided the North and united the South! So say the advocates of M'Clellan—so said Senator Johnson. Will any body do me the favor to tell me when the North was united? Was it at the presidential election of 1860? Was it in the winter of 1860–61? Was it when Sumter was fired on, and Pennsylvania sympathizers with the South said, "Send troops to conquer the South, and we will begin the war in the cars!" There are gentlemen who have heard that, I know. It was told me when I was in Philadelphia at the time that Butler's regiment was passing through to go to Annapolis. "Go South and we will begin the war in the cars," was the unity of the North in 1861. Who that was ever for the prosecution of the war and with the administration is now against it? Name him, some one of the thousands here. (Applause.) There never was a day that the great mass of the Democratic party and its chief leaders were not opposed to the war, as Buchanan was opposed to the war. They had a majority in the lower house of Congress, and in the Senate at that day, all Democrats, and all opposed to war. Nay, they were afraid to breathe the word "war." How is it with the people out of doors? Many patriotic men forgot their Democratic relations and rushed to the war; but where are they now? What Democratic vote has come up from the army? They have joined "the crusade against the South." (Great applause.) But those that staid at home, those that carped at the administration, those that sneered at the obscurity of its members and the incompetency of its head, those who prated about "negro equality" and an "Abolition war," have they now, for the first time, divided the North? Or are there more of them now to-day than there were in 1861? Or are there not now ten radicals for one that existed then?—then a minority, now a majority of the supporters of the administration this day. (Applause.) Things that men shrank from then, they now regard as the dictates of the holiest patriotism and the sublimest wisdom; for they have been taught by the teacher Experience, and none have gone back excepting those sows of the Democracy that go back to wallow in the mire from which they never were washed clean. (Laughter.) Divided the North! What divided it? United the South! When was it not united? On the 4th of August, 1861, General M'Clellan wrote thus to the President of the United States:

"The object of the present war differs from those in which nations are engaged mainly in this: that the purpose of ordinary war is to conquer a peace, and make a treaty on advantageous terms. In this contest, it has become necessary to crush a population sufficiently numerous, intelligent, and warlike to constitute a nation. We have not only to defeat their armed and organized forces in the field, but to display such an overwhelming strength as will convince all our antagonists, especially those of the governing, aristocratic class, of the utter impossibility of resistance."

Now what has occasioned that unity?

"Our late reverses make this course imperative."

It was Bull Run that united the South, or rather consolidated what before was united, welded into one unbroken mass the iron which hitherto we have vainly striven to rend asunder. That is the testimony of General M'Clellan.

"The contest began with a class; now it is with a people—our military successes can alone restore the former issue."

I can quote no higher authority upon this point—certainly not to our antagonists—none higher to myself, for it conforms entirely with my own judgment. From the day of Bull Run to this day there has never welled up by accident any where in the broad region of the South one bubble of discontent. The South was made a unit by the firing on Fort Sumter. It antedated Bull Run; and any body who has ever conversed either with gentlemen of the United States army, or others resident in the South who have found it necessary to fly from there, knows that that collision in arms sunk every opposition in the State of Virginia, made North Carolina instantly a unit, as instantly as the Chicago Platform united the dividing fragments of the Republican party within a month or two past. Then we did not unite the South. They united themselves to gain their independence, and they are struggling now for it. They will be disunited when the band of iron that clasps them is torn asunder. They will be disunited when Lee's army is beaten and dissolved. And when they are disunited you will find that there will be no difficulty in reorganizing loyal governments and bringing them back to their normal relations to the national government. But we did not unite them; they united themselves. But now what caused the divisions of the North? We are told that the "negro policy" has divided the North. Well, what part of it, and when? In 1861 the war began. I have shown you that then the North was divided. Every body who has lived in the North knows it; but it became patent to every eye in the summer of 1862. Then was the canvass in Pennsylvania, in Indiana, in Ohio, in New York. I think there are gentlemen present who remember that there was a division in Pennsylvania at that time, and that some Congressmen were lost. I think there are gentlemen who remember that Ohio was swept, and that only five Republican members survived in the lower house of Congress. Indiana and Illinois were stripped of their previous majorities, and overwhelming majorities were cast against the administration. Governor Seymour was elected in New York. There was division then, and divisions upon the identical ground that it is now alleged to have arisen upon; and up to that day what had the government done that was not sanctioned by the express words, the formal advice of George B. M'Clellan, on the Negro Question? What one law was passed, what one executive act was done, that he did not in writing and in print formally advise and approve?

I beg your pardon for quoting again from a letter written by George B. M'Clellan at a very significant date, on the 7th of July, 1862, at Harrison's Landing, when one would have supposed that the care of his army and military operations would more appropriately have occupied his mind than penning political instructions to the President of the United States. Here is his advice:

"Military arrests should not be tolerated except in places where active hostilities exist."

That, I suppose, was intended as a comment upon his arrest of the Maryland Legislature.

"Military power should not be allowed to interfere with the relations of servitude, either by supporting or impairing the authority of the master, except for repressing disorder, as in other cases."

On the 13th of March, 1862, Congress had passed an act forbidding officers of the army to be concerned in returning fugitive slaves to their masters. George B. M'Clellan did not disapprove that law.

"Slavery, contraband under the act of Congress, seeking military protection, should receive it."

On the 6th of August, 1861, Congress declared that slaves allowed by their masters to be used in any manner to aid the rebellion should be free. George B. M'Clellan thinks they ought to be free, and ought to be received within the military lines of the United States. So he did not disapprove of that act of Congress.

"The right of the government to appropriate permanently to its own service claims to slave labor should be asserted, and the right of the owner to compensation therefor should be recognized."

That was written on the 7th of July, 1862, and on the 17th of the same month, as if in obedience to that very letter, in perfect conformity with its precise provisions, Congress passed a law authorizing the President to accept and use as many persons of African descent as he might see fit to aid in suppressing the rebellion. (Great applause.) If M'Clellan disapproved of that law after it was passed, he advised it before it was passed.

"This principle might be extended."

Now, gentlemen, you will hardly believe your ears when I read to you the next words:

"This principle might be extended upon the grounds of military necessity." (Laughter and applause.)

Did you ever hear those words impeached as savoring of despotism?

"Upon grounds of *military necessity and security*."

To whom?

"To all the slaves of a particular State."

The government to confiscate to its own use all the slaves of a particular State, with compensation, on the ground of military necessity! (Applause.) Why, gentlemen, he was three months ahead of the Emancipation Proclamation. (Applause.) And what is his comment? What is his purpose? To serve the United States!

"Thus working manumission in such State."

Thus working manumission in such State on the ground of military necessity, by the paramount authority of the government of the United States, confiscating to its own service only for form's sake, in order that manumission might be carried throughout the whole State. And where? In the rebel States, where men were in arms against the government, where there was some excuse for the authority of Congress to do what he intimated? No. "And in Missouri"—a loyal State of this Union. "Perhaps in Western Virginia," just organizing as a new State. "And possibly even in Maryland; the expediency of such a measure can only be a question of time."

Now, gentlemen, is it not the arch-fiend's mock, a man like that to talk about the President's having divided the North on the Negro Question? (Great applause.) The President, in my judgment, overstepping his legal authority—I do not agree with M'Clellan any more than I do with him on that—on the 22d of September, 1862, issued his monitory proclamation of freedom, promising thereafter to make it peremptory. He never dreamed that his power went into a loyal State with an existing State government; he never dreamed that "military necessity" would justify him in turning the slaves of Maryland and Kentucky, and Western Virginia and Missouri, free; yet George B. M'Clellan, the "Conservative" candidate for the presidency, the candidate opposed to "negro equality," the candidate who represents that party who impute to the President the division of the North on the Negro Question—while Mr. Lincoln was wrestling with the Western parsons on the question of emancipation, screwing his courage up to the sticking-point, and endeavoring to find his way through the mists of his conscience to do what the people wanted him to do, and what he could not see his way to do, M'Clellan is already in the seventh heaven of emancipation, and tells him to do it by virtue of military necessity. (Great applause.) We only made one mistake, gentlemen; we did not take George B. M'Clellan for the Emancipation candidate for the presidency. (Laughter.) That brings us up to 1862, in September, and October, and November. Was there division in the North then? Was Pennsylvania with the administration? or New York with the administration? or Ohio? or Indiana? or Illinois? Was not the whole body of the great central States of the republic with the enemies of the republic? Did you not lose every State government where there was a contest at that time? Then there was division—division when the President was stepping tenderly and slowly along behind the longer strides of George B. M'Clellan on the Negro Question toward emancipation. Who divided the North? Gentlemen, the Origin of all Evil divided the North when he put "Democracy" in it, and until he is bound with that chain which Revelation speaks of, that division will be here. And you must be just as much upon your guard against it politically as you must be against the great enemy of mankind spiritually, and pray God to preserve you from it, or it will bind and chain you yet. But something has taken place since 1862. We are divided now; but how? In 1862 the division was on their side, they being the majority. To-day, in this day of wretched radicalism and awful taxation, this day of blood and waste, there is division; but the majority is on our side. (Great applause.) The "crazy men" have turned out to be the prophets; the "radical maniacs" have turned out to be wise statesmen. Energy for the thousandth time has been shown to be stronger than hesitating weakness. When a thing is to be done, the shortest way is the best way to do it, and brings strength and energy with it. (Cheers.) The country to-day stands committed to this: the end of the war, the integrity of the government, and the extinction of the cause of the war, slavery. (Tremendous applause.) Our strength has grown in proportion as the "black Abolitionists" have got near the President's ear (cheers), and the men of the Blair school have got far from it. We want no division around that ear. (Laughter.) Why, gentlemen, trace the progress of events and see if there be not, as plain as daylight, the tracings of the finger of God working out chastisement for the iniquities of ourselves and our fathers, and blessings for our posterity. First, with timid steps, Congress passed a law saying that negroes employed to aid the rebellion should be free. Then they enacted that officers of the army should not return fugitives. Then they abolished slavery in the District of Columbia, and on M'Clellan's advice paid the masters for their emancipated slaves largely more than their average value.

Then, in the same year, they passed a law authorizing the President to employ negroes to aid in suppressing the rebellion. Then came the premonitory proclamation of freedom. Then, on the 1st of January, 1863, came the proclamation of freedom, which has rested to this day a mere declaration, and will not be more until the President shall approve an act of Congress making it law. But it was an utterance, though illegal, in the right direction. Then came the admission of West Virginia, upon condition that she should abolish slavery. (Applause.) And that expunged from the political law of the United States the great principles of the Missouri Compromise, which was that Congress could impose and should impose no conditions upon the admission of a State. It was another step in the progress toward the supremacy of the national authority. And then followed emancipation in Missouri, first moved by her radical men, and then, when they were about to be successful, seized on by the "Conservatives," and converted into a temporary and remote emancipation. Still it was emancipation. And then, under the auspices of Colonel (now General) Birney, and General Schenck, and Mr. Stanton, with the sympathy of Mr. Chase, but against the opposition of every body else connected with the government in Washington—by the assumption on their part of grave responsibilities—commenced the great system of negro enlistments in Maryland, the recruits to be used as substitutes for the whites, which began the great emancipation contest there. (Applause.) And then came the law of the last Congress, which declared that bond and free owed themselves—not by reason of their masters, but themselves—military service to the United States; formally placing it upon the statute-book that they were entitled to volunteer, and, as volunteers, should receive such bounties as the United States government was in the habit of giving, and that the slaves should be subject to draft, put upon the same rolls, and drawn from the same box, according to the same proportions as the white subjects of the republic (cheers), and now more than 100,000 are in arms for our defense. On the 12th and 13th of October the State of Maryland sealed emancipation, and made herself free (great applause)—made herself free without the aid of those in power in Washington—free by her own act, in the face of strenuous opposition to the particular forms that it assumed—cheered on by the energetic countenance of a citizen of your own State, the Secretary of War, and, beside him, none—aided at the dead point of the machinery by liberal gentlemen here and in Boston—elsewhere receiving no aid—free by the untouched and untrammeled vote of her own citizens, although Mr. Attorney General Black had the insolence last night to say that the great majority of her people had been placed by the administration, and by outrageous frauds, under the control of a "corrupt and venal minority." Gentlemen, the corruptest of the corrupt traitors in Maryland would stand above him in political honesty. (Applause.) He, the apologist of the Lecompton villainy, is a pretty person to criticise the free conduct of the Maryland people, who have just decided for freedom by a vote as close as yours at the late election, and as free as yours, with traitors perjuring themselves to vote, and voting every where, without any body to touch them. The imputation came from an appropriate source. One of the ministers of the infamies of Buchanan's administration, stained with the blood of the Washington massacre and the fraud and blood of Kansas, taunts the people of Maryland with being under the influence of a corrupt and venal minority! Why, he can teach corruption and venality to the inhabitants of our penitentiary. (Laughter and applause.) But there we are. It is possible that the gentlemen of Chicago may rebel; I don't see any other remedy for it than that. (Laughter.) It is done. Now, at this day, when we have brought the whole mass and body of the Republican party—I use a more comprehensive phrase, all men who are supporting the administration in the conduct of the war and its general policy—when we have brought the whole body and mass of them up to that point, to these radical measures, these great regions won to freedom, these great steps toward the maintenance of the equality of the rights of all mankind, these steps in national wisdom, these steps which have brought a vast population of a different color but great patriotism to the support of the government—after these steps, I say, we stand to-day more united, stronger, agreeing better in opinion, more resolutely determined to meet the public enemies, more united about the instruments that we shall use to smite them down than at any other period—and the people are with us! I rather think that, instructed by the lessons of this latter day, the men who slipped secretly to the President's ear and advised him to pocket the bill that was carried through both branches of Congress by the whole mass of his supporters to consolidate the legal freedom of the slaves of the rebel States, and give them judicial guarantees—the men who gave that secret advice and pushed the bill off in the Senate until it could be defeated without the responsibility of a veto, will not repeat the advice at the coming session of Congress. (Great applause.) The thunder of the coming majorities will reach even their dead hearts and dull ears. The fact that the mass of the American people are resolved that no slave shall breathe American air will become intelligible to every mind. (Tremendous applause.) Trembling and doubting Conservatives, with their gouty feet, will cease to stand in the way of the march of the nation to universal freedom. (Great cheering.) They will be walked over, or pushed aside, or forgotten, or left to mumble with toothless gums over the old women's tales of their boyhood. Wise men, firm men, in the vigor of their years, with reason unimpaired, and eyes that can see the teachings of the time, and who have read deep in the bloody lesson of this day, will apply the lesson for the benefit of themselves and their children, and go down honored and rejoicing to the grave that closes over them, but buries them in a free land. (Great applause.) Trust not conservatism—the wretched respectability that covers up every corruption—that defends every iniquity—that maintains every wrong—that sanctifies it by appealing to the past, and subordinates every moral consideration to maintaining what is, because they have grown up in it, and grown fat by it, and profited by it, and been in the habit of bowing down low before it. It is to the young generation that have stood in the front of flaming rebellion, and extinguished its fires, that the republic looks to hereafter to guide it in civil as well as in military affairs. (Great applause.) And when, gentlemen, the people shall have elected their President, they will let him know that whatever his proclivities or disposition may be, whatever doubts may encumber or hang around his mind still, whatever may be his private opinions, they must be subordinated to the will of the American people. (Great applause.) If he does that, then he will have a peaceful, quiet, glorious, magnificent administration, with the sun of peace blazing over its declining days; and if he do not, woe to him before the tribunal of history and in the minds of his countrymen.

Gentlemen, I have said almost all that I want to say. ("Go ahead," "Go on.") All that I wish to add is this: We are now on trial for our lives before the tribunal of history. Nations that are born to empire must be content to go through grievous trials, and we are going through ours. Whether a people with popular institutions can conduct great wars, bear great burdens, submit to great disasters, and still keep their government intact, submit to rulers whom they do not approve, and whose conduct is not always equal to the emergency; whether a people can rise to the height of that enormous self-sacrifice, the subordination of their passions, and their impatience, and their interest to the great paramount interest of simply standing together (for that is the meaning of nationality), simply doing what their leaders direct, submitting and not rebelling, whether their judgment accords with what is ordered or not—whether this people shall rise to that height or not, I was going to say is a question that depends on this canvass. I beg pardon of the American people; it has been proved already. The nations of the Old World—phlegmatic John Bull or any of them—suffering what we have suffered, would have torn their own government to pieces in a furious effort after some short way to relief. The people of America have exhibited the wisdom of the highest statesmanship, that which would have added another flower to the garland of such a statesman as Richelieu or Chatham, by their patient submission to the grievances of the time, and their acceptance, quietly and submissively, of the necessities of empire, the necessary losses, the necessary inconveniences, the necessary agony and bloodshed. All that they have now to do is resolutely to determine that, having gone through the greater part of the suffering which they will be called upon to endure during the war, they will only endure a little longer; they will only not fail in the very hour and crisis of victory, for he that holds out the longest is sure of the victory. The only criterion of a great nationality is the capacity of endurance. There are many nations that have exhibited brilliancy upon the battle-field, great soldierly qualities, great capacities for industry; but none is born to empire, none is born for long life, none will live in history, none will vindicate the right and the power of the people to govern themselves, excepting those that are endowed with the old Roman instinct of never submitting while disaster prevails, never yielding till victorious peace has sanctioned the power of the republic to maintain its integrity. (Great applause.) If we but bear that great example in mind, we shall more than equal the duration in time, the extent in territory, the greatness in power, the magnificence in resources, and infinitely surpass in the beneficence of our influence the first great example of free republican government that the world ever saw. (Enthusiastic applause.)

JOINT RESOLUTION ON MEXICAN AFFAIRS.

THE joint resolution, adopted unanimously on the 4th of April by the House of Representatives, declaring what should be the policy of the government in relation to the French interference in Mexico, had not been concurred in by the Senate. It was thought there unnecessary and imprudent to publish any such declaration in the existing condition of affairs during the still pending rebellion, and while its passage might complicate our relations with France. It was supposed it might wear the appearance of a threat, and it was deemed safer to allow the French government to retreat from any position incautiously assumed, and only because of supposed or expected results of the rebellion here, when that government should find out its own mistake, not less in that respect than in regard to the practicability of building up a Mexican empire. Previous to the rising of the first session of Congress (July 4, 1864), the House Committee on Foreign Affairs, to which was referred the communication of the Secretary of State containing the correspondence with the United States Minister at Paris in relation to the House joint resolution, had, on the 27th of June, made a report in relation thereto. At the subsequent session (December 15), that report and resolution appended (written by Mr. Davis as chairman), of the House Committee on Foreign Affairs, was presented to the House as follows:

The Committee on Foreign Affairs have examined the correspondence submitted by the President relative to the joint resolution on Mexican affairs with the profound respect to which it is entitled, because of the gravity of its subject and the distinguished source from which it emanated.

They regret that the President should have so widely departed from the usage of constitutional governments as to make a pending resolution of so grave and delicate a character the subject of diplomatic explanations. They regret still more that the President should have thought proper to inform a foreign government of a radical and serious conflict of opinion and jurisdiction between the depositories of the legislative and executive power of the United States.

No expression of deference can make the denial of the right of Congress constitutionally to do what the House did with absolute unanimity other than derogatory to their dignity.

They learn with surprise that, in the opinion of the President, the form and term of expressing the judgment of the United States on recognizing a monarchical government imposed on a neighboring republic is a "purely executive question, and the decision of it constitutionally belongs, not to the House of Representatives, nor even to Congress, but to the President of the United States."

This assumption is equally novel and inadmissible. No President has ever claimed such an exclusive authority. No Congress can ever permit its expression to pass without dissent.

It is certain that the Constitution nowhere confers such authority on the President.

The precedents of recognition, sufficiently numerous in this revolutionary era, do not countenance this view; and if there be one not inconsistent with it, the committee have not found it.

All questions of recognition have heretofore been debated and considered as grave questions of national policy, on which the will of the people should be expressed in Congress assembled; and the President, as the proper medium of foreign intercourse, has executed that will. If he has ever anticipated its expression, we have not found the case.

The declaration and establishment of the independence of the Spanish American colonies first brought the question of recognition of new governments or nations before the government of the United States; and the precedents then set have been followed ever since, even by the present administration.

The correspondence now before us is the first attempt to depart from that usage, and deny the nation a controlling deliberative voice in regulating its foreign policy.

The following are the chief precedents on recognition of new governments, and the policy of the United States government on that topic:

On the 9th of February, 1821, Henry Clay moved in the House of Representatives to amend the Appropriation Bill by the following clause:

"For an outfit, and one year's salary, to such minister as the President, by and with the consent of the Senate, may send to any government of South America, which has established and is maintaining its independency on Spain, a sum not exceeding $18,000." It failed.

On the 10th of February, he moved that the House of Representatives participates with the people of the United States in the deep interest which they feel for the success of the Spanish provinces of South America, which are struggling for their liberty and independence, and that it will give its constitutional support to the President of the United States whenever he may deem it expedient to recognize the sovereignty and independence of any of the said provinces.

A motion to amend by the proviso

"that this resolution shall not be construed to interfere with the independent exercise of the treaty-making power,"

and another,

"that the House approves of the course heretofore pursued by the President of the United States with regard to the said provinces,"

were negatived.

The resolution was adopted, and a committee appointed to lay it before President Monroe.

The committee, on the 17th of February, reported

"That the President assured the committee that, in common with the people of the United States and the House of Representatives, he felt great interest in the success of the provinces of South America, which are struggling to establish their freedom and independence, and that he would take the resolution into deliberate consideration, with the most perfect respect for the distinguished body from which it had emanated."

So the House of Representatives took the initiative toward recognizing the new republics. The amendment to the Appropriation Bill would have been a legislative recognition. The resolution was a formal statement of the opinion of the House to the President, which he did not think beyond their constitutional authority.

At the first session of the next Congress, the House of Representatives, on the motion of Mr. Nelson, of Virginia, resolved

"That the President of the United States be requested to lay before this House such communications as may be in the possession of the executive, from the agents of the United States with the governments south of the United States, which have declared their independence, and the communications from the agents of such governments in the United States with the Secretary of State, as tend to show the political condition of those governments, and the state of the war between them and Spain, as it may be consistent with the public interest to commmunicate."

President Monroe answered the application on the 8th of March in an elaborate message, of which the following extracts sufficiently show that he did not think recognition "a purely executive question, and that the decision of it constitutionally belongs, "not to the House of Representatives, nor even to Congress, but to the President of the United States:"

"In transmitting to the House of Representatives the documents called for by the resolution of that House of the 30th of January, I consider it *my duty* to *invite* the attention of *Congress* to a very important subject, and to communicate the sentiments of the executive on it; that should *Congress* entertain similar sentiments, there may be such co-operation between the two departments of the government as their respective rights and duties may require."

"This contest has now reached such a stage and been attended with such decisive success on the part of the provinces, that it merits the most profound consideration, whether their right to the rank of independent nations, with all the advantage incident to it in their intercourse with the United States, is not complete."

After narrating the events, he proceeds:

"When the result of such a contest is manifestly settled, the new governments have a claim to recognition by other powers which ought not to be resisted."

"When we regard, then, the great length of time which the war has been prosecuted, the complete success which has attended it in favor of the provinces, the present condition of the parties, and the utter inability of Spain to produce any change in it, we are compelled to conclude that its fate is settled, and that the provinces which have declared their independence, and are in the enjoyment of it, ought to be recognized."

"*In proposing this measure*, it is not contemplated to change thereby in the slightest manner our friendly relations with either of the parties."

"*The measure is proposed* under a thorough conviction that it is in strict accord with the law of nations, and that the United States owe it to their position and character in the world, as well as to their essential interests, to adopt it."

"Should Congress concur *in the view herein presented*, they will doubtless see the propriety of making the necessary appropriations for carrying it into effect."

It is quite apparent that President Monroe was far from countenancing the opinion that the form and time in which the United States would think it necessary to express themselves on the policy of the recognition is a purely *executive question*, and that he did not think the decision of it *constitutionally* belongs, not to the House of Representatives, nor even to Congress, but to the President of the United States, to the exclusion of Congress. Had he so thought, he would have refused the production of the papers, as President Washington did the diplomatic instructions relative to the English treaty.

He would have announced his purpose to recognize the republics, and left it to Congress to provide for diplomatic intercourse with them.

Far from that, he proposes for their consideration the policy of recognition; and, if they concur in *that*, asks them to make the necessary appropriations to carry *it* into effect.

He consulted the *will* of the nation at the mouth of Congress, and proposed to concur in its execution.

So Congress understood him, for the papers and message were referred to the Committee on Foreign Affairs. That committee considered, in an elaborate report, the question of independence of the republics, the policy and principles involved in their recognition, and on the 19th of March, 1822, they submitted it to the House. It concluded as follows:

"Your committee, having thus considered the subject referred to them in all its aspects, are *unanimously* of opinion that it is *just* and *expedient* to acknowledge the *independence of the several nations of Spanish America* without any reference to the diversity in the form of their governments; and in accordance with this opinion they respectfully submit the following resolutions:

"*Resolved*, That the House of Representatives concur in the opinion expressed by the President in his message of the 8th of March, 1822, that the American provinces of Spain which have declared their independence, and are in the enjoyment of it, *ought to be recognized by the United States* as independent nations.

"*Resolved*, That the Committee of Ways and Means be instructed to report a bill appropriating a sum not exceeding $100,000 *to enable the President to give due effect to such recognition.*"

It is therefore equally apparent that the House of Representatives of the 17th Congress was clearly of opinion with President Monroe that the question of recognition was not purely executive, but that it constitutionally belongs to Congress as well as to the President; that the Legislature declares the will of the United States, which the executive gives effect to, each concurring in the act of recognition according to their respective constitutional functions.

In obedience to that resolution, the following bill, recognizing the new nation, was reported, and passed, and approved on the 4th of May, 1822:

"That for such missions to the *independent nations on the American continent* as the President may deem proper, there be, and hereby is, appropriated a sum not exceeding $100,000, to be paid out of any money in the treasury not otherwise appropriated."

The approval of that law completed the recognition of the new nations. The sending ministers to some or all of them was matter of executive discretion, not at all essential to or connected with the fact of recognition. Ministers were appointed to Mexico, Colombia, Buenos Ayres, and Chili, on the 27th of January, 1823. None was appointed to Peru till May, 1826; yet it is certain Peru was as much recognized by the United States as the other governments from the 4th of May, 1822.

This great precedent has governed all that follow it.

The acknowledgment of the independence of Texas stands next in our history. It is a most instructive precedent, strictly following the forms respecting the governments of Spanish America.

On the 18th of June, 1836, on the motion of Henry Clay, the Senate adopted the resolution

"That the independence of Texas ought to be acknowledged by the United States whenever satisfactory information shall be received that it has in successful operation a civil government capable of performing the duties and fulfilling the obligations of an independent power."

The House of Representatives, on the 4th of July, 1836, adopted a resolution in the same words; and added a second:

"That the House of Representatives perceive with satisfaction that the President of the United States has adopted measures to ascertain the political, military, and civil condition of Texas."—Congressional Globe, 1st session 24th Congress, p. 453, 486.

Those resolutions were not formal acknowledgments of a government of Texas; the report of the Senate committee showed the circumstances were not sufficiently known; and both Senate and House awaited farther information at the hands of the President.

On the 2d of December, while communicating the information, President Jackson accepted the occasion to express to Congress his opinion on the subject. The following passages are very instructive, touching the authority to recognize new States:

"Nor has any deliberative inquiry ever been instituted in Congress, or in any of our legislative bodies, as to whom belonged the power of recognizing a new State; a power, the exercise of which is equivalent, under some circumstances, to a declaration of *war;* a power nowhere expressly delegated, and only granted in the Constitution, as it is necessarily involved in some of the great powers given to *Congress,* in that given to the President and Senate to form treaties and to appoint embassadors and other public ministers, and in that conferred on the President to receive ministers from foreign nations."

"In the preamble to the resolution of the House of Representatives, it is distinctly intimated that the expediency of recognizing the independence of Texas should be *left to the decision of Congress.* In this view, on the ground of expediency, I am disposed to concur; and do not, therefore, think it necessary to express any opinion as to the strict constitutional right of the executive, either apart from, or in conjunction with, the Senate over the subject. *It is to be presumed that on no future occasion will a dispute arise, as none has heretofore occurred, between the executive and Legislature in the exercise of the power of recognition.* It will always be considered *consistent with the spirit of the Constitution, and most safe* that it should be exercised, when probably leading to war, with a previous understanding with that body by whom war can alone be declared, and by whom all the provisions for sustaining its perils must be furnished. Its submission to Congress, which represents in one of its branches the States of this Union, and in the other the people of the United States, where there may be reasonable ground to apprehend so grave a consequence, would certainly afford the fullest satisfaction to our own country, and a perfect guarantee to all other countries, of the justice and prudence of the measures which ought to be adopted."

After forcibly stating why he thought "we should still stand aloof," he closed with the following declaration:

"Having thus discharged my duty by presenting with simplicity and directness the views which, after much reflection, I have been led to take of this important subject, I have only to add the expression of my confidence that if Congress should differ with me upon it, their judgment will be the result of dispassionate, prudent, and wise deliberation; with the assurance that, during the short time which I shall continue connected with the government, I shall promptly and cordially unite with you in such measures as may be deemed best fitted to increase the prosperity and perpetuate the peace of our favored country."

The concurrent resolutions of the Senate and House of Representatives, and that message of President Jackson, leave no doubt that the views which presided over the recognition of the South American governments still prevailed, and that the President was as far from asserting as Congress from admitting that the recognition of new nations and the foreign policy of the United States is a purely executive question.

The independence of Texas was finally recognized in pursuance of the following enactment in the Appropriation Bill of the second session of the Twenty-fourth Congress, which appropriated money

"For the outfit and salary of a diplomatic agent to be sent to the *Republic of Texas* whenever the President of the United States may receive satisfactory evidence that Texas is an independent power, and shall deem it expedient to appoint such minister."—5 Statutes, 170.

That law was approved by President Jackson.

Not only is this exclusive assumption without countenance in the early history of the republic, but it is irreconcilable with the most solemn acts of the present administration. The independence of Hayti is nearly as old as that of the United States; it antedated that of the South American republics, and the republic of Liberia has long been recognized by European nations. Both were first recognized by act of Congress, approved by President Lincoln on the 5th of July, 1862, which enacted

"That the President of the United States be, and he is hereby *authorized*, by and with the advice and consent of the Senate, to appoint diplomatic representatives of the United States to the *republics of Hayti and Liberia* respectively. Each of the representatives so appointed shall be accredited as commissioner and consul general, and shall receive the compensation of commissioners," etc., etc.

That was a formal recognition of those republics by *law*, whether the President sent diplomatic representatives or not.

Quite in the spirit of these precedents is the well-considered language of the Supreme Court:

"Those questions which respect the rights of a part of a foreign empire which asserts and is contending for its independence belong more properly to those who can declare what the law shall be, who can place the nation in such a position with respect to foreign powers as to their own judgment shall appear wise, to whom are intrusted its foreign relations, than to that tribunal whose power as well as duty is confined to the application of the rule which the Legislature may prescribe for it."

But the joint resolution of the 4th of April does more than declare the refusal of the United States to recognize a monarchical usurpation in Mexico. It declares a general rule of policy, which can be authentically and authoritatively expressed only by the body charged with the legislative power of the United States.

"*Resolved by the Senate and House of Representatives of the United States of America, in Congress assembled,* That the Congress of the United States are unwilling, by silence, to leave the nations of the world under the impression that they are indifferent spectators of the deplorable events now transpiring in the Republic of Mexico; and they therefore think fit to declare that it does not accord with the policy of the United States to acknowledge a monarchical government erected on the ruins of any republican government in America under the auspices of any European power."

The committee are of opinion that this authority, to speak in the name of the United States, has never, before the correspondence in question, been considered a purely executive function.

The most remarkable declaration of this kind in our history, which events seem now likely to make of as grave practical interest as when it was uttered, is President Monroe's declaration in his message of the 2d of December, 1823:

"With the governments which have declared their independence and maintained it, and whose independence we have, after great consideration and on just principles, acknowledged, we could not view any interposition, for the purpose of oppressing them or controlling in any other manner their destiny by any European power, in any other light than as the manifestation of an unfriendly disposition toward the United States."

But, though always the accurate expression of the feelings of the American people, it was not regarded as the settled policy of the nation, because not formally declared by Congress. By the administration of President John Quincy Adams, which followed, it was treated as merely an executive expression on behalf of the people, which Congress alone could elevate to the dignity of a national policy by its formal adoption.

In 1826, Mr. Poinsett, the minister to Mexico, having used language supposed to commit the United States to that policy in behalf of Mexico, a resolution was promptly introduced into the House of Representatives and adopted on the 27th of March, 1826,

"That the Committee on Foreign Affairs inquire and report to this House upon what authority, if any, the minister of the United States to the Mexican Republic, in his official character, declared to the plenipotentiary of that government that the United States have pledged themselves not to permit any other power than Spain to interfere either with their (the South American republics) independence or form of government," etc., etc.—2 Cong. Deb., 19th Con., 1st sess., p. 1820.

Mr. Poinsett hastened to explain by his letter of the 6th of May, 1826, to Henry Clay, then Secretary of State:

"I can not rest satisfied without stating explicitly that, in the observations I made during my conference with the Mexican plenipotentiaries, I alluded only to the message of the President of the United States to Congress in 1823.

"That message, declared, in my opinion, by the soundest policy, has been regarded both in Europe and America as a solemn declaration of the views and intentions of the *executive* of the United States, and I have always considered that declaration as a pledge, so far forth as the language of the *President* can pledge the *nation*, to defend the new American republics from the attacks of any of the powers of Europe other than Spain. That *the people of the United States are not bound by any declarations of the executive is known and understood as well in Mexico, where the government is modeled on our own political institutions, as in the United States themselves.* But, in order to correct any erroneous impressions these words might have made on the minds of the Mexican plenipotentiaries, I explained to them, in the course of our conference this morning, their precise meaning: that the declaration of Mr. Monroe in his message of 1823, to which I had alluded, indicated only the course of policy the executive of the United States was disposed to pursue toward these countries, *but was not binding on the nation unless sanctioned by the Congress of the United States;* and when I spoke of the United States having pledged themselves not to permit any other power than Spain to interfere with the independence or form of government of the American republics, I meant only to allude to the above-cited declaration of the President of the United States in his message of 1823, and to nothing more."

This explanation is the more significant from the fact that Mr. Clay's instructions to Mr. Poinsett directed him to bring to the notice of the Mexican government the message of the late President of the United States to their Congress on the 2d of December, 1823, asserting certain important principles of intercontinental law in the relations of Europe and America; and, after stating and enlarging on them, Mr. Clay proceeds:

"Both principles were laid down after much and anxious deliberation on the part of the late administration. *The President, who then formed a part of it, continues entirely to coincide in both,* and you will urge upon the government of Mexico the propriety and expediency of asserting the same principles on all proper occasions."

And in reply to the resolution of inquiry of the 27th of March, Mr. Clay accompanied his instructions with the declaration—entirely in the spirit of Mr. Poinsett's letter—

"that the United States have contracted no engagement, *nor made any pledge* to the governments of Mexico and South America, or either of them, that the United States would not permit the interference of any foreign power with the independence or form of government of those nations. * * * * * * *

"If, indeed, an attempt by force had been made by allied Europe to subvert the liberties of the southern nations on this continent, and to erect *upon the ruins of their free institutions monarchical systems,* the people of the United States would have stood pledged, *in the opinion of the executive,* not to any foreign State, but to themselves and their posterity, by their dearest interests and highest duties, to resist to the utmost such attempt; and it is to a pledge of that character that Mr. Poinsett above refers."—2 Cong. Debates, 19th Congress, 1st session, App. 83, 84.

Such were the views of the administration of President John Quincy Adams, whose Secretary of State was Henry Clay, and whose minister to Mexico was Mr. Poinsett, upon the supremacy of the Legislature in declaring the foreign policy of the United States, the diplomatic execution and conduct of which is confided to the President.

It is impossible to condense the elaborate message of President Adams of the 15th of March, 1826, dedicated to persuading Congress to concur in and sanction the Panama mission; but that message, and the great debate which consumed the session in both houses, are unmeaning on the assumptions of this correspondence with the French government; and the consideration and approval of its recommendations elevate President Monroe's declaration to the dignity and authority of the policy of the nation solemnly and legally proclaimed by Congress.

That message was in reply to a resolution requesting the President to inform the House of Representatives "in regard to what objects the agents of the United States are expected to take part in the deliberations of that Congress"—of Panama.

Among other subjects of deliberation, the President enumerated the declaration of President Monroe above quoted, and on that topic said:

"Most of the new American republics have declared their entire assent to them; and they now propose, among the subjects of consideration at Panama, to take into consideration the means of *making effectual* the assertion of that principle, as well as the *means of resisting interference from abroad* with the domestic concerns of the American governments.

"In alluding to these means, it would obviously be premature at this time to anticipate that which is offered merely as matter for consultation, or to pronounce upon those measures which have been or may be suggested. The purpose of this government is to concur in none which would import hostility to Europe, or justly excite resentment in any of her States. Should it be deemed advisable to contract any conventional engagement on this topic, our views would extend no farther than to a mutual pledge of the parties to the compact, to maintain the principle in application to its own territory, and to permit no colonial lodgments or establishments of European jurisdiction upon its own soil; and with respect to the obtrusive interference from abroad, if the future character may be inferred from that which has been, and perhaps still is, exercised in more than one of the new States, a joint declaration of its character and exposure of it to the world would be probably all that the occasion would require.

"Whether the United States should or should not be parties to such a declaration may justly form a part of the deliberation. That there is an evil to be remedied needs little insight into the secret history of late years to know, and that this remedy may best be considered at the Panama meeting deserves at least the experiment of consideration."

Upon this message, after elaborate debates, Congress passed in May an appropriation "for carrying into effect the appointment of a mission to the Congress of Panama;" and the President, by and with the advice and consent of the Senate, appointed ministers to that Congress, and furnished them with instructions in conformity with the message, and in execution of the policy approved by Congress.

Accident and delays prevented the arrival of our mission before the dissolution of the Congress; but President Adams thought the gravity of the precedent justified him in communicating to Congress, in 1829, Mr. Clay's instructions to the ministers for our information; and the precedent remains forever to vindicate the authority of Congress to declare and present the foreign policy of the United States.

The great name of Daniel Webster is justly considered authoritative on any question of constitutional power; and in that debate, when the enemies of the administration strove to insert *particular instructions* to the diplomatic agents sent to *that Congress*, he clearly defined the limits of executive and congressional authority in declaring the policy and conducting the negotiations to effectuate it.

On the 4th of April, 1826, he is reported to have said in the House of Representatives:

"He would ask two questions: First, Does not the Constitution vest the power of the executive in the President? Second, Is not the giving of instructions to ministers abroad an exercise of executive power? Why should we take this responsibility on ourselves? He denied that the President had devolved, or could devolve, his own constitutional responsibility, or any part of it, on this House. The President had sent this subject to the House for its concurrence by voting the necessary appropriation. Beyond this the House was not called on to act. We might refuse the appropriation if we saw fit, but we had not the power to make our vote conditional, and to attach instructions to it.

"There was a way, indeed, in which this House might express its opinion in regard to foreign politics. That is by resolution. He agreed entirely with the gentleman that, if the House were of opinion that a wrong course was given to our foreign relations, it ought to say so, and say so by some measure that should affect the whole, and not a part, of our diplomatic intercourse. It ought to control all missions, and not one only.

"There was no reason why the ministers to Panama should act under these restrictions that did not equally apply to other diplomatic agents—for example, to our minister at Colombia, Mexico, or other new States. A resolution expressive of the sense of the House would, on the contrary, lead to instructions to be given to them all. *A resolution was, therefore, the regular mode of proceeding.* We saw, for instance, looking at these documents, that our government had declared to some of the governments of Europe, perhaps it has declared to all the principal powers, that we could not consent to the transfer of Cuba to any European power. No doubt the executive government can maintain that ground only so long as it receives the approbation and support of Congress. If Congress be of opinion that this course of policy is wrong, then he agreed it was in the power, and, he thought, indeed, the duty of *Congress* to interfere and to express dissent. If the amendment now offered prevailed, the declarations so distinctly made on this point could not be reported, under any circumstances, at Panama; but they might, nevertheless, be reported any where and every where else. Therefore, if we dissent from this opinion, that dissent should be declared by resolution, and that would change the whole course of our diplomatic correspondence on that subject in all places. If any gentleman thinks, therefore, that we ought to take no measure, under any circumstances, to prevent the transfer of Cuba into the hands of any government, European or American, let him bring forward his resolution to that effect. If it should pass, it will effectually prevent the repetition of such declarations as have been made."—2 Cong. Debates, 19th Congress, 1st session, p. 2021, 2022.

This view is, in the opinion of the committee, at once the just view and the traditional practice of the government; the will of the people expressed in legislative form by the legislative power can declare authoritatively the foreign policy of the nation; to the President is committed the diplomatic measures for effecting it.

The constitutional authority of Congress over the foreign relations of the United States can hardly be considered an open question, after the concurrent resolutions of Mr. Senator Sumner, adopted in the last Congress, it is believed, at the suggestion, certainly with the approval of the President, and by him officially notified to foreign governments, as the most authentic and authoritative expression of the national will respecting intervention, mediation, and every other form of foreign intrusion into the domestic struggle in the United States.

The committee are not inclined to discuss theoretical questions of relative power. The Constitution is a practical, and not a theoretical instrument. It has been administered and construed by men of practical sagacity, and in their hands the voice of the people has been heard authoritatively in the executive chamber on the conduct of foreign affairs.

But this correspondence requires us to say that, in view of the historic precedents, it is not a purely executive question whether the United States would think it necessary to express themselves in the form adopted by the House of Representatives at this time; it does belong to Congress to declare and decide on the foreign policy of the United States, and it is the duty of the President to give effect to that policy by means of the diplomatic negotiations, or military power if it be authorized.

The President is not less bound to execute the national will expressed by law in its foreign than in its domestic concerns.

The President appoints all officers of the United States, but their duties are regulated, not by his will, but by law. He is the commander of the army and navy, but he has no power to use it except when the law points out the occasion and the object. He appoints foreign ministers, but neither in this case are they, by reason of their appointment, any thing but the ministers of the law. If it be true that the appointment of an embassador to a nation implies the recognition of the nation, it is just as sound logic to argue that none can be appointed to a nation that does not exist by the recognition of Congress, as that the President can recognize alone, because he can appoint.

But we prefer to waive the question. We are anxious not to depart from the approved precedents of our history. Our desire is to preserve, not to change. We will not inquire what would be the effect of a recognition of a new nation by the President against the will of Congress. We prefer to indulge the hope, so wisely expressed by President Jackson, that

"it is to be presumed that on no future occasion will a dispute arise, as none has heretofore occurred, between the executive and Legislature in the exercise of the power of recognition."

Hitherto new nations, new powers, have always been recognized upon consultation and concurrence of the executive and legislative departments, and on the most important occasions by and in pursuance of law in the particular cases.

Changes of the person or dynasty of rulers of recognized powers, which created no new power, have not been treated always with the same formality; but usually the general law providing for diplomatic intercourse with the power whose internal administration had changed remained on the statute-book and conferred a plenary discretion on the President, under the sanction of which he has accredited ministers to the new possessors of power. It is not known that hitherto the President has ever undertaken to recognize a new nation or a new power not before known to the history of the world, and not before acknowledged by the United States, without the previous authority of Congress.

It is peculiarly unfortunate that the new view of the executive authority should have been announced to a foreign government, the tendency of which was to diminish the force and effect of the legislative expression of what is admitted to be the unanimous sentiment of the people of the United States, by denying the authority of Congress to pronounce it.

Of the prudence of that expression at this time Congress is the best and only judge under the forms of the Constitution, and the President has no right to influence it otherwise than in the constitutional expression of his assent or his dissent when presented to him for his consideration.

It is vain to suppose that such a declaration increases the danger of war with France. The Emperor of the French will make war on the United States when it suits his convenience, and it can be done without danger to his dynastic interests. Till then, in the absence of wrong or insult on our part, there will be no war. When that time arrives we shall have war, no matter how meek, inoffensive, or pusillanimous our conduct may be, for our sin is our freedom and our power, and the only safety of monarchical, imperial, aristocratic, or despotic *rule* lies in our failure or our overthrow.

It postpones the inevitable day to be ready and powerful at home, and to express our resolution not to recognize acts of violence to republican neighbors on our borders perpetrated to our injury. That declaration will encourage the republicans of America to resist and endure, and not to submit. It is not perceived how an attack on the United States can promote the establishment of a monarch in Mexico. It might seriously injure us, but it would be an additional obstacle to the accomplishment of that enterprise. It is fortunate that events in Europe in great measure embarrass any farther warlike enterprise on this continent, and the ruler who has not thought fit to mingle in the strife of Poland or Schleswig-Holstein will hardly venture to provoke a war with the United States.

The committee are content to bide their time, confident in the fortune and fortitude of the American people, but resolved not to encourage by a weak silence complications with foreign powers inimical to our greatness and safety, which, in the words of Mr. Webster, "a firm and timely assertion of what we hold to be our own rights and our own interests would strongly tend to avert."

The committee recommend the adoption of the following resolution:

"*Resolved*, That Congress has a constitutional right to an authoritative voice in declaring and prescribing the foreign policy of the United States, as well in the recognition of new powers as in other matters; and it is the constitutional duty of the President to respect that policy, not less in diplomatic negotiations than in the use of the national force when authorized by law; and the propriety of any declaration of foreign policy by Congress is sufficiently proved by the vote which pronounces it; and such proposition, while pending and undetermined, is not a fit topic of diplomatic explanation with any foreign power."

Mr. Davis demanded the previous question upon the passage of the foregoing resolution, which was seconded, and the main question ordered. The adoption of the resolution by the House would of course have been equivalent to a public censure of the conduct of foreign affairs by the Secretary of State, under the direction of the President. It would have implied that the management of those affairs in relation to the French interference in Mexico, and the course adopted by the Secretary of State, were, in the opinion of the House, improper, and too obsequious toward the Emperor of the French. To avoid a rejection of the resolution reported by the committee, and the expression of any such censure which the House was not prepared to make, a motion to lay the resolution on the table was adopted.

Mr. Davis thought that in this difference of opinion on the part of the majority of the House was involved the propriety of his continuing as Chairman of the Committee on Foreign Affairs, and, immediately upon the adoption of the motion laying the resolution on the table, he asked the House to excuse his farther service on that committee in the following speech:

FOREIGN POLICY OF THE UNITED STATES IN REGARD TO MEXICAN AFFAIRS (1864).*

MR. SPEAKER,—I rise to a privileged question. I desire to be relieved by the House from farther service on the Committee for Foreign Affairs. I am willing, sir, to take all of the responsibilities that are connected with any service upon which the House of Representatives shall place me; but when, in the course of the discharge of those duties, I find myself unfortunately differing in opinion from the majority of the House, I do not consider it is proper I should longer continue to hold any such position. The vote which has been just passed by the House is one which will allow of no other construction.

The House, on my motion, on the unanimous recommendation of the Committee on Foreign Affairs at the last session, passed a resolution declaring the policy of this government touching the republics of America. It was adopted unanimously. It went to the Senate, and there it lies. It had not been passed three days before the officer charged with the foreign correspondence of this government directed our representatives abroad virtually to apologize to the French government for the resolution adopted by the representatives of the people, and in that correspondence presumed to impeach Congress of usurpation in undertaking to prescribe to the President the rules which should guide him in the foreign policy of the United States.

That correspondence was made the subject of a circular by the French government, and to all of the governments of the world, to let them understand that the Congress of the United States had no right to speak with authority in the foreign affairs of the government, and that nothing was to be regarded except the will and declarations of the executive. In the debates that took place in the French Assembly, the world was given to understand, by the member representing the emperor, that the passage of the resolution touching Mexican affairs and the French intrusion into Mexico was a momentary outburst of passion on the part of the

* See note on preceding page.

representatives of the American people, like that which occurred when Messrs. Mason and Slidell were arrested on board the Trent, but which did not prevent the federal government from giving up the two prisoners. The world was given to understand, on the authority of the Secretary of State, by the imperial government, that Congress is such a thing as the French Assembly—the docile reflex of the executive will—its resolution a *vain and presumptuous usurpation.* The letter of the Secretary of State was in a tone that was not respectful to the dignity and the authority of the House of Representatives. And if that letter lays down the law of the land—and this House by its vote to-day says it does—then you have no right to a committee on foreign affairs, and I am no child to play at doing that which you have no right to do.

The Secretary of State, before all Europe, in a matter of the greatest moment, slapped the House of Representatives in the face, in his correspondence with the French government, and the House of Representatives says it will not even assert its dignity. The House of Representatives is the appropriate and adequate guardian of its own dignity.

Sir, I am the only guardian of my own dignity, and, after this vote and that correspondence, I, most humbly but respectfully, ask to be excused from farther service upon the Committee on Foreign Affairs.

Mr. Speaker, I regret that, in the discussion that has taken place, several topics have been introduced that were not very intimately connected with the simple and earnest application made to the House to relieve me from farther service on the Committee on Foreign Affairs.

It was made in all earnestness and simplicity, from a profound sense of duty, and not from any personal feeling of discontent with the vote of the House.

I was not in the least degree ruffled in my temper by the circumstance that the House has now, as it has done on so many occasions, differed from me in judgment.

I have been brought up in defeats, I have lived in minorities; I always submit, and, I trust, with perfect humility, to the better judgment of the House. If any gentleman, in the course of my eight years' service in this House, has ever seen any manifestation of personal spleen or personal disappointment, then may the observations of the gentleman from Massachusetts [Mr. Dawes] be justified. If no man has on any occasion seen that, then I shall be pardoned for taking no farther notice of the mean malice that prompted them.

But I do not wish to be misunderstood upon another point. It has been repeatedly stated that this resolution assails the President. Well, sir, I am ready to assail the President, or any body else, who stands across the broad track of republican principles. I need not say that in this House, and yet, sir, there is no word in that resolution which assails the President, nor was it contemplated to assail him. It was carefully, deliberately, critically prepared, and received the approval of every member of the Committee on Foreign Affairs, with the dissenting voice alone of the gentleman from New York [Mr. Pomeroy].

I beg the attention of the House to the language of the resolution. The rights that it asserts I do not now pretend to debate. The judgment of the House has been rendered, to which I shall bow, and bow without argument. The resolution was not a cobweb of my brain, brought there to hang fine dissertations upon about the abstract rights of different departments of the government. This House has asserted its authority in matters of the gravest national importance—events which had arrested the attention of the civilized world, and made anxious the heart of every friend of liberty in it. A free nation on our borders lay bleeding in the talons of the French eagle, and a vagrant adventurer, who had never seen the soil of Mexico, called himself her emperor. The American House of Representatives had declared that it did not accord with our policy to recognize any monarchical government erected on the ruins of any republican government in America, least of all in Mexico, our neighbor and our friend. It did not relate to remote or possible contingencies, but to a bloody, awful reality—the ruin of a free nation by European violence, under false pretexts, and with an insolent hostility to our power; a ruin now more nearly consummated, and by *our* fault—ay, and still more by the fault of those charged with the conduct of our diplomatic intercourse. But that resolution had rested in the Senate. We had done all that we could, and we were obliged to rest in silence.

But when the Secretary of State of the United States sent abroad a dispatch to a foreign government relative to a matter then pending within the legislative department of the United States, where the executive eye has no right to penetrate, respecting the vote on which, until communicated to him in the regular form, he has no right to know any thing—when at that stage the Secretary of State saw fit to enter into diplomatic communication with a foreign government, in order to rob the vote of this House of its legitimate and moral power before it had acquired any legislative authority, and, in doing that, not only questioned the wisdom and expediency but the right of this House, and of both houses, to say one word upon the subject, I could not sit in silence; and the House will find, I think, that they will be unable to do so, if they have a due regard to their dignity as one of the branches of the government.

And it was in deference to that practical, actual case, that the resolution was drawn—drawn carefully, drawn critically, drawn with a studious avoidance of every innuendo against the personal character either of the President of the United States or of the distinguished gentleman who presides so ably over the Department of State; and the language of his letter, to which the language of the resolution refers, will show how carefully it was adapted to this object, and how completely it accomplished it. The Secretary of State says:

"It is, however, another and a distinct question whether the United States would think it necessary or proper to express themselves in the form adopted by the House of Representatives at this time."

If it be another question whether the United States would think proper to express themselves at this time, and in the form that the House of Representatives have seen fit to use, who speaks for the United States?

The Secretary says:

"This is a practical and purely executive question."

Here the executive speaks for the United States:

"And the decision of it constitutionally belongs not to the House of Representatives, nor even to Congress, but to the President of the United States."

Then the President is the United States! Do gentlemen now understand how the word "President" came there? It was because the Secretary of State had told the French government, with a view to break the force of the vote of the House of Representatives, that it belonged not to the House of Representatives nor to Congress, but exclusively to the *President of the United*

States to declare what the United States thought, and when it was expedient to declare what it thought in reference to our foreign affairs; and foreign affairs mean war, and peace, and alliances, and recognitions, and neutrality, and every interest and every right by which we touch the nations of the world; and that in the face of the formal words of the Constitution ascribing those functions, in whole or in part, to one or both houses of Congress.

It was that declaration, in conflict with all the precedents of the United States, that the Secretary of State saw fit merely to express here in the ordinary intercourse between the departments of the government, but to send abroad to our minister in France and lay before a foreign government, and to impeach and discredit the judgment of Congress before it has pronounced, which imperatively required to be rebuked.

And it was at that language that the resolution was pointed. Now judge ye whether it be true or not that Congress has a constitutional right to an authoritative voice in our foreign affairs. That raises the issue directly, does it not, with the language, not with the person of the Secretary of State, whether "Congress has a constitutional right to an authoritative voice in declaring and prescribing the foreign policy of the United States, as well in the recognition of new powers as in others matters; and it is the constitutional duty of the President to respect that policy, not less in matters of negotiation than in the use of the national force when authorized?"

It was no blow aimed at the President. But a right had been asserted for the President by the Secretary of State. He first impeached the right of Congress to do what it has always done, and usurped its right for one of the flowers of the presidential prerogative. I deny his law and his fact. I make the question of right and not of person, either with the Secretary or with the President.

"And then whether the United States would think it necessary or proper to express themselves in the form adopted by the House of Representatives"—

the Secretary tells the world is an executive question! We can not allow our votes to be received other than in a constitutional form of a veto by the President; then he has the right to approve, or refuse to approve, them in the forms of his constitutional authority.

But I have yet to learn that it is the right of the President to say what is necessary or proper, or what is wise and what is unwise, with reference to any vote of this House, or of both houses of Congress, except when our votes are communicated for his approval; therefore, to make the issue direct with the other portion of the Secretary's letter, this clause is introduced:

"And the propriety of any declaration of foreign policy by Congress is sufficiently proved by the vote which pronounces it."

That is the assertion that our vote is not the subject of executive criticism; that it is the right of the people of the United States to say what they will upon the foreign policy, and it is the duty of the President to veto or obey it. But, sir, if Congress have sunk so low that it must look beyond the limits of its own halls to vindicate the necessity and propriety of this solemn declaration of national policy at this time in the form we adopted, perhaps we can find no arbiter between us and the executive government which it will recognize so readily as the Baltimore Convention; and that body, forced by public opinion, thought it necessary and proper to echo the resolution for which the Secretary apologized—only, attempting to give a rebuke the form of a compliment, they converted it into a sarcasm.

That is the substance of the resolution. Now, sir, I say again that I do not mean to debate the policy of the resolution, or any matter connected with it. Nobody except the gentleman from Maine [Mr. Blaine] has impeached it here upon historical grounds. With great respect to that gentleman, I say that the precedent which he quotes is frivolously irrelevant; and that, from the beginning of the government until this day, there is no vote of either house of Congress, there is no claim by any President of the United States, there is no expression by any respectable public man of any party, that it does not belong to the Congress of the United States to declare and prescribe the foreign policy of the United States; and from the time of the Panama mission, when John Quincy Adams asked and obtained the authority and support of Congress for that great mission which we must soon repeat, until this day we have vote on vote of Congress, under almost every administration, affirming, implying, asserting, or exerting that prerogative, without question from any quarter; and under this administration more than one act, approved by President Lincoln himself, to add to the unbroken law of precedents.

The recognition of Hayti and Liberia was not the spontaneous act of the President; but he, like his predecessors, waited till Congress had authorized him to open with them international relations.

Sir, there is but one judgment and one course of precedent from the beginning to the end of American history. Monroe concurred in it. The messages of John Quincy Adams are replete with it. General Jackson, in the case of Texas, recognized it. Mr. Clay asserted it. Mr. Webster asserted it. What other authorities are worthy of notice after we have named these? That, sir, is all I have to say on the subject.

Now, sir, one other word. I have said that, in asking to be excused from farther service on the Committee on Foreign Affairs, I act from no feeling of personal pique. I make that request from a sense of public duty, in view of the relations that the chairman of the committee necessarily bears to the House of Representatives. It is possible, sir, for the House to differ on many occasions, not only with the chairman, but with the committee. They are bound to take the instructions of the House; they are bound to conform to such instructions; they are bound by the judgment of the House, and they must act in conformity with it.

But the position of chairman of a committee means that he stands there as the representative of the political views of the majority of the House of Representatives. He is to the House what a member of the cabinet is to the President. An absolute conformity on all essential principles between the chairman of a committee and the House on a subject respecting which the committee is raised, is essential to a due discharge of his duties, just as a similar relation between a cabinet officer and the President is essential to the due conduct of executive affairs. *I am not the representative of the House upon this question.* The vote of this morning places a great gulf between me and the House of Representatives. I cheerfully admit that I may be wrong and they may be right, but the criterion of my conduct must be my own judgment, and I can not separate myself from the history of America to conform to the vote of the House of Representatives.

And, sir, I go a step farther; not only is it impossible that I should continue to represent the House in that responsible situation without misrepresenting myself, but, insignificant as I may be personally, I am unwilling, when this matter crosses the ocean, as it will cross it, I can not consent to seem to submit, or to acquiesce in, or have part or lot with this grave surrender of the power of the people; for, Mr. Speaker, whatever the insignificance of the person who moves this question, his connection with this vote elevates him to *its* importance; and I will tell you there is more than one crowned head in Europe that now looks anxiously to the conduct of this House upon this very question, and a shout will go up from one end of despotic Europe to the other when it is known that the House of Representatives has confessed that its resolves are vain breath before the dictation of the President, and that the President is the United States, as Louis Napoleon is France.

Insignificant though I be, I am not humble enough to allow my name to be associated with that humiliating abdication.

With all kindness to the gentlemen who have so kindly expressed themselves here to-day—a kindness which overwhelms me sensibly, a kindness frequently expressed heretofore in private, but never before so publicly—I beg they will not let that kindly feeling enter into consideration on this vote, but will do as I ask them—simply relieve me from acting longer in this responsible position where I so gravely misrepresent the House which has honored me.

ADMINISTRATION OF THE NAVY DEPARTMENT.—MONITORS AND ARMORED SHIPS.

On the 3d and 6th of February the House resumed the consideration of the Naval Appropriation Bills. Mr. Davis had on previous occasions expressed his dissatisfaction with the management of the Navy Department, not only in regard to its conduct toward and disposition of officers, but particularly respecting the expenditures for monitors and iron-clad ships. On this occasion he expressed his views at length on those points in the following speeches:

The House resolved itself into the Committee of the Whole on the State of the Union (Mr. Washburne, of Illinois, in the chair), and resumed the consideration of the bill (House of Rep., No. 676) making appropriations for the naval service for the year ending June 30, 1866, the pending question being the amendment submitted by Mr. Davis, of Maryland, to add to the bill the following:

Provided, That no money appropriated for the naval service shall be expended otherwise than in accordance with the following provision, so far as it is applicable; that is to say, that the President, by and with the advice and consent of the Senate, shall appoint a Board of Admiralty, which shall consist of the vice-admiral and one rear admiral, one commodore, one captain, one commander, and one lieutenant commander, over which the Secretary of the Navy or the officer highest in rank present shall preside; and when the subject under consideration shall appertain to the duties of any bureau in the Navy Department, the chief of such bureau shall be a member of the Board, and entitled to sit and vote on the consideration of the subject.

Sec. — *And be it further enacted*, That the Board shall deliberate in common and advise the Secretary on any matters submitted by him relating to naval organization, naval legislation, the construction, equipment, and armaments of vessels, navy yards, and other naval establishments, and the direction, employment, and disposition of the naval forces in time of war. All such opinions shall be recorded.

Sec. — *And be it further enacted*, That no vessel of war shall be built or materially altered, nor any guns of new construction ordered or adopted, nor any engine for any vessel of war adopted or ordered, nor any permanent structure for naval service executed, until the plans, estimates, proposals, and contracts for the same shall have been submitted to the Board, and its opinion and advice thereon communicated in writing to the Secretary; nor shall any patented invention be bought or adopted for the naval service without first the opinion of the Board thereon having been taken; and all experiments decided to test inventions, and naval plans and structures, shall be conducted under the inspection of the Board, or members thereof named by the Secretary, and submitted to the Board for its opinion thereon.

SEC. — *And be it further enacted,* That all invitations for plans or proposals for any of the works above mentioned shall be prepared by the Board, subject to the approval of the Secretary; and all bids or offers, or proposals for the same, shall be opened in the presence of the Board, and the award made by it, subject to the approval of the Secretary.

SEC. — *And be it further enacted,* That the Secretary may add to the Board, from time to time, other officers of the navy eligible to the position of chief of bureau, not exceeding three at any time, for consultation on any of the above subjects. The Board may take the opinion of eminent practical engineers, mechanics, machinists, and architects, in their respective branches of art or industry, when in their opinion the public service will be promoted by it, and pay them such reasonable compensation as the Secretary may approve.

Mr. Davis, of Maryland, said:

MR. CHAIRMAN,—I should have been glad, but for the importance of this subject, to have allowed the vote to be taken upon the amendment which I have offered without making any observations on it; but the condition of the navy, and its great importance in the adjustment of accounts which we will have to adjust with other nations so soon as the rebellion shall be suppressed, make it a matter of vital moment that we should not be deluded by any apparent strength, that we should not allow weakness to be covered up under great numbers, whether of vessels or of guns, nor allow ourselves to be persuaded by articles adroitly inserted in newspapers in various portions of the country, into the belief that we are a naval power of the first magnitude, till that illusion is dispelled by some day of disastrous memory. For these reasons I desire to offer a few observations in support of the amendment which I have proposed.

This amendment is not introduced upon my own judgment, is not one hastily drawn and brought before the House to provoke a discussion, but it was introduced after great deliberation—not deliberation in my own mind, but deliberation in connection with the first officers of the navy of the United States, the men who must bear our flag, navigate our ships, fight our guns, and maintain the honor of our country with the means we place at their disposal. They are the men who tremble at the present condition of the navy.

The honorable gentleman from Ohio [Mr. Spalding], on the Naval Committee, was prompt and anxious to thrust aside, unconsidered, this amendment when it was introduced the other day, because it was *under consideration* before the Naval Committee. But it is proper to say that the bill was referred to the Naval Committee at the last session — not late in the session — three months before its close. And if they have not considered it, it is because they do not wish a vote upon it, or do not consider it worthy of consideration. I have more than once applied to one or two gentlemen upon that committee to take the bill up and consider it, and report it, even if they reported unfavorably upon it, so that the country might have an opportunity of having the judgment of this House and the vote of this House upon that measure.

Perhaps the House will understand why that report is made now, when it can be no longer delayed. At an earlier stage, as an independent measure, there would have been a chance of having a consideration of the bill. When I saw that there was a purpose that there should be no consideration of it, I moved it as an amendment to the Appropriation Bill. *The Naval Committee were not then ready* to express their judgment upon it. Now that it is here, and the House *must* act upon it, they have suddenly made up their opinions—upon what consideration it is for them to say —and throw the weight of their judgment against it when it is before the House. Sir, their judgment will, of course, not have the weight and consideration of a committee, but that they have deliberated for nearly a year without deciding on it looks as though their opinion were given now for the purpose of accomplishing what they did not accomplish by smothering the bill.

There are, I agree, grave objections to incorporating important measures in the appropriation bills. But, before this amendment was moved, the House, by an almost unanimous vote, had greatly changed the organization of the navy by increasing largely the number of cadets allowed at the Naval Academy. And the objection urged to incorporating this amendment upon the Appropriation Bill struck me as very remarkable, when an amendment of that kind had already been adopted within half an hour before I made my motion, on the motion of the honorable gentleman now in the chair [Mr. Washburne, of Illinois], amended and enlarged upon the motion of the chairman of the Committee on Ways and Means [Mr. Stevens]; so that there are circumstances in which grave and important measures may with propriety be put into an

Appropriation Bill; and while that precedent fully justifies this amendment in point of parliamentary law, there is an additional consideration why this should be incorporated here. The declaration of the gentleman from the Committee on Naval Affairs sufficiently shows that this measure does not meet with favor at the other end of the avenue; that the people whose hands are to be tied by the presence of responsible advisers prefer that the fetters should not be put upon them. And we have experienced more than once in this Congress that measures of national moment, passed unanimously by this House, have rested unacted upon elsewhere. Sir, there is small prospect of securing the passage of any measure which has to be forced upon opponents at the other end of the avenue. It is impossible to get even a vote upon such measures unless they are placed upon bills that put them before the public eye, and require a vote either in the affirmative or negative. I avow, sir, that it was not to insure the passage of the amendment, but to compel a vote on it, that I moved it when I did.

Mr. Chairman, we are creating a navy at enormous cost; not increasing a navy; not merely continuing the ordinary expenses of a navy; we are creating one. We are driven to the necessity of passing from a second or a third rate into the class of a first-rate naval power, and the question we have to decide is under what responsibility, by whose advice, under whose auspices, shall that great change be made? We have now had the experience of four years of war. The changes made have been made under the auspices of the Secretary of the Navy and his irresponsible assistant secretary, who is the real and acting Secretary of the Navy, and of the chief of the Bureau of Engineers; and beyond that responsibility there is no responsibility to the people or the country for any thing that has been done heretofore or any thing that may be done hereafter.

What has been the result? We are taught to believe that we are a great naval power. We have the semblance certainly; whether we have the reality is something that remains to be seen. We are told by authority that we have 671 vessels of war, and that we have 4610 guns afloat, or for which vessels are being built. If that be so, then we are a great naval power, though perhaps not the first class. But, sir, it is important to analyze that statement, and see what there is of substance in it—how many guns there are afloat that must go down in the first collision, how many that can bear the flag of the republic in the face of a great naval power. When we scan the figures given us by the Department, and analyze in the light of the reports of the Department the origin, structure, and speed of the vessels which bear the guns, and apply to it the judgment of naval men, the laws and conditions which are to be observed in the construction of naval vessels—matters upon which I am not entitled to express an opinion, but on which I may quote the opinion of those who are professionally competent—we find that these figures dwindle to more modest proportions; that the real navy of the nation is greatly less than the apparent navy of the report.

The aggregate given by the Secretary's report is 651 vessels, with 4610 guns. But there are 112 sailing vessels, with 850 guns. The Secretary of the Navy tells us that sailing vessels are useless for the purposes of modern war. It is useless, after that authority, to quote any other; for if the Secretary of the Navy knows it, then every midshipman at least knows it, and every body else in the country. Then 850 guns are to be taken from the apparent power of the navy. We have, besides, 174 paddle-wheel steamers bought; that is to say, merchant vessels, with all their machinery exposed, so that a single shot subjects them to the fate of the Hatteras, exploded and sunk by the Alabama in the Gulf of Mexico. They are not war vessels, built for naval service, but ordinary mercantile vessels, purchased by the United States for the purposes of the blockade. Now, sir, I do not criticise the propriety of those purchases; on the contrary, I think they were eminently wise when they were made. Whether they were made as economically as possible is a matter that I do not propose to consider. But to place them among the war vessels of the navy, and to think that those 174 vessels, carrying 921 guns, are to be accounted part of the naval strength of the United States in the event of a naval war, is a delusion that must result in disaster.

There are, besides, 149 screw vessels, light propeller vessels, likewise bought from the mercantile marine. Every naval man knows that no vessel constructed for mere mercantile purposes is or can be made a vessel of war fit to be placed in line of battle in a great naval struggle. They answer to catch blockade-runners; they will answer possibly to cruise after the commerce of the enemy. But when the flag of England shall float over a fleet representing in this day that which Nelson commanded at Trafalgar, the nation that meets such a fleet with vessels built for the merchant service is doomed to disaster; and when we have a statement which includes such vessels as a part of the naval strength of the country, no man who values the honor of the country, or its safety in a day of naval battle, can permit such a statement to pass without saying that it is a delusion and a snare. When you sum up those vessels, you find, from the aggregate of 671, you have stricken off 435 vessels and 2385 guns, and left 236 vessels bearing 2225 guns.

But let us go a step farther. There are likewise of the vessels built for naval purposes, under the auspices of the Department, 47 paddle-wheel steamers — double-enders, as they are called — ferry-boats, river steamers, hawks to catch blockade-runners; but for a day of naval battle no naval man will allow them to be called war vessels at all. Their machinery is all exposed, their very boilers are exposed. Whatever may be their availability for blockade purposes, though they escape a chance shot from a rover, as part of the naval force of the United States they must be stricken from the list, for it is not possible they could survive a collision with vessels of equal armament constructed on naval principles. And we must also deduct five paddle-wheel steamers of the old navy. These two classes of paddle-wheel steamers carry 524 guns; and if they are deducted from the 2225 guns, there remain 1701 guns on 184 vessels of war properly so called. So, when we have analyzed the real naval force of the country that stands between us and aggression from abroad, we are reduced to the number of 184 vessels and 1701 guns—a respectable increase, but an increase which leaves us exposed to overwhelming disaster if we stop there; a difference between the official statement and the real condition of the naval force of the government to which the attention of the people should be called.

In order to give a clearer idea of the real force existing and what has been added by the Department since the rebellion broke out, it is necessary to say that of these 184 vessels, 25 are screw steamers of the old navy, which I suspect can sink all the wooden vessels which have been added of the new navy by the mere weight of their batteries; 62 iron-clads, of which 22 are not afloat, leaving only 40 in service; and 97 wooden vessels, mostly of small size; none at least of large size; none beyond the grade of a sloop-of-war of moderate size, at present afloat; for 28 vessels included in that 97 are, I believe, now upon the stocks, and that 28 include all the larger cruisers mentioned in the Secretary's report; so that our fleet actually afloat is reduced to about 134 vessels, bearing 1150 guns. And there we stand to-day if we have a declaration of war with England to-morrow.

The organization of the Navy Department, as I have already said, leaves the whole responsibility of the construction of all naval vessels, their forms, structure, armament, machinery, and materials, limited only by the amount of money appropriated for their construction, at the irresponsible discretion of the three persons I have named; for the organization of the Navy Department is a secretary who administers it, an assistant secretary who administers him, and the chiefs of bureaus who are the ministerial fingers and hands of the gentleman at the head of the Navy Department. Such an organization of a Navy Department exists nowhere else in the civilized world among naval powers. In our fast American style, we sneer at the slow motions and grave deliberation that mark every step of the great naval powers of the world, France and England, yet to-morrow we are unable to cope with either of them with one half of their force in ranged battle on the ocean.

Their organization, Mr. Chairman, is a different one. In England we know that the office of Lord High Admiral is exercised by a board of six commissioners, who are called Lords of Admiralty, and a chief Secretary of the Admiralty. The First Lord of the Admiralty is a member of the cabinet, and the Secretary must be a member of the House of Commons, where he is charged with the naval estimates. The powers which are exercised in England by the Board of Admiralty are here exercised by the Secretary of the Navy. The Board of Admiralty in England is charged with the responsible and discretionary administration of the Navy as the Secretary is here, both having ministerial officers under them which with us are called chiefs of bureaus.

The French navy is administered by the minister Secretary of State for the Marine and the Colonies. He is surrounded by a Council of Admiralty, composed of three naval officers of high grade, vice or rear admirals, and three high officers of colonial administration, named by the crown, presided over by the minister, and charged to give its advice on all measures relating to maritime and colonial legislation, the administration of the colonies, the organization of the naval force, the modes of supplying it, naval structures and buildings, and to the direction and employment of the naval force in time of war. This council is intended for advice on the higher matters of legislation and administration. But the minister is provided with another Council of Naval Works, composed of the inspector general of naval construction, the inspector of artillery, the inspectors general of hydraulic constructions, two captains of the navy, a director of naval constructions, and an engineer of the navy, acting as secretary, with a deliberative voice, the whole presided over by one of the Council of Admiralty, and charged to give its advice on matters submitted to it by the minister, on the plans and estimates for naval constructions, hydraulic works, material of artillery, and all works in navy yards, on the preparation of regulations for the execution of naval works of all kinds, on the preparation of proposals for contracts for any of the above objects, on the adoption of inventions, and every thing relating to improvements of naval structures, artillery, or hydraulic works. Thus the minister Secretary of State for the Marine and Colonies, aided by a large naval staff of professional officers for professional advice, is charged with the responsible administration of the French navy. They deliberate in common, constitute the council of the Secretary of the Navy, as we should call him, his cabinet, whose advice is to guide and enlighten the administrative discretion of the minister. It is to the minister, aided by the deliberations of those responsible bodies, that the great duties of creating and employing the French navy is confided.

What I propose is this: that we shall create a Board of Admiralty, adhering to the American idea of the unity of the executive or administrative officer, but surrounding him with responsible advisers, appointed by the President, not depending upon the caprice and will of the Navy Department; men of professional standing, competent ability, and of high and permanent rank, without whose knowledge and advice nothing can be done within the purview of the bill; not that their assent shall be necessary to any order or act, but that no material step shall be taken with reference to the various subjects included in the bill without their advice having been previously taken in writing and spread upon the records of the Department. The general effect of that is, that there can be no such thing as mere improvidence, mere charlatanism, mere ignorance, or the mere application of civil ideas to military matters. We have learned something during this war; we have learned that every man is not born a soldier or a sailor: he may be born a President of the United States, but he is not born with the special knowledge belonging to and required of this Department. What is necessary in order that there shall be a navy created is that there shall be men of competent professional knowledge, who shall advise in a responsible form, authentically, in writing; and if their advice be neglected, the responsibility will lie with those who neglect it. The mere existence of such a responsible body of advisers infinitely diminishes the chances of error, or corruption, or ignorance, or plausible and dangerous charlatanism, or rash and improvident conduct. It will be to the Secretary what the cabinet is to the President—an aid, not a hindrance.

We have repeatedly resorted to temporary boards of this kind; one of them was adopted in 1860 to consider the application of steam to our sailing vessels; another was organized by the Department to devise the plan of blockade; another was organized under a law of Congress for experiments in iron-clads; and another, summoned by the Department, was called to advise upon the engines of the navy. Others are now, we are informed by the report of the Secretary of the Navy, engaged in investigating various questions respecting steam machinery. But boards of this kind are made *pro hæc vice*—are liable to the particular influence prevailing at the moment; made rather to accomplish a particular purpose than to give independent advice; and if created under the authority of Congress, and therefore of an independent character, they are temporary in their purposes, their influence is not permanent, and the effect of their opinions passes off the moment they are dissolved.

What I propose by the bill is that there shall be a board composed of men of the first responsibility in the navy, which shall be headed by the vice-admiral, who is neither an old fogy, nor a charlatan, nor an enemy of the Secretary, but one of the great officers of the navy, possessing the confidence of the Department, whose opinion they ought to be bound to consult and respect, for whom the nation has created a new title and new grade, whom all the officers of the navy will cheerfully follow, and constituted of the other officers of designated rank, to be appointed by the President and confirmed by the Senate, to advise the Secretary in all matters relating to naval organization.

While I can not go into the details of the condition of the Navy Department at this time, I think that the opinion of the naval officers is that it is a failure as a machinery for successful administration. There is no responsibility any where to be found; every thing is managed by a subordinate in the name of the Secretary, and it is more to that than any intentional abuse of power or neglect on the part of the Secretary that I attribute the rash empiricism, the scandalous improvidence, and the costly failures which mark the administration of that Department. The way to avoid that is not to howl about them in Congress, but to provide the Secretary with responsible advisers on naval construction and the armament and machinery of vessels, on the organization and location of navy yards.

The House has been deprived of the services of the Committee on Naval Affairs a large portion of the last year, while they were engaged in investigations to advise the Navy Department on the selection of a navy yard for iron-clads—a matter which, if they were competent to determine, I submit any one single experienced officer of the navy was more competent to determine. And when my friend, the honorable gentleman from Ohio [Mr. Schenck], who accompanied them on one trip, was a little sensitive at my doubts of their competency, he could not refuse his assent to my avowal that I would take with more confidence the opinion of his distinguished brother of the navy than his own upon that subject. I think, if there had been a board of competent advisers to the Secretary of the Navy on the topics embraced in the second section of this bill, that there are some expeditions that would not have been undertaken by the Navy Department; I think the nation would have been saved from some failures; and I think some successes would have been followed up, and the fruits of victory reaped which to this day are barren. I think half a dozen rebel cruisers could not have swept our commerce from the ocean, or driven it to take refuge under foreign flags, and destroyed many millions of property, and lighted every sea with the conflagration of our ships for three years with absolute impunity, had any body of competent naval officers been invited to devise a systematic plan for their pursuit and capture. I think that the great day at Port Royal would have produced something more than a secure foothold for the blockading squadron. With proper advice around the Secretary when Savannah and Charleston were exposed half armed, that blow would have been followed up by others which should have reduced those places; we should have been spared the humiliation of a fruitless bombardment before Charleston for a year and a half—a bombardment utterly ineffective, leaving the rebel fortifications there to-day as absolutely beyond the reach of our naval forces as they were before Gilmore battered Sumter. It would not have been left for Sherman and his army, after three or four years of war in the West, to march across the continent and take Savannah, but it would have been taken long ago by forces actually there. But, without any competent advisers, the Navy Department rested upon the laurels of Port Royal, and left it barren to the nation of half its rightful fruits which the victor was so eager to gather. I think, if the head of the Department had had proper advisers, there would have been no such thing as an attack upon three hundred guns in Charleston Harbor by thirty-six guns, if any naval opinions, good or bad, retired or active, had been listened to or even asked in the Navy Department. It would not have been reserved to the Department to vindicate naval opinion and condemn its own rash presumption on that occasion by sending four hundred and fifty guns to batter Fort Fisher with its fifty or sixty guns, after sending thirty-six guns to tear in pieces the enormous fortifications of Charleston bristling with three hundred guns. One or the other is an unspeakable folly; and history has already declared which.

But what I wish more particularly to remark upon is what has been accomplished by the Navy Department. Where are we now, and how did we get there? I desire that it should be borne in mind that I am not now seeking to cast imputations upon any one, to show his incompetency, but to expose the evils of a merely personal and irresponsible administration of the Department, and to demonstrate the necessity of a remedy. I make no suggestions for which I do not propose an adequate remedy. I state the failure that gentlemen may be enabled to judge of the propriety of the remedy. If they can say that a lack of advice does not exist, then let them say so. But if they admit the results, then give me a judgment upon my remedy.

The first great thing that we are called upon to deal with is the subject of iron-clads. Congress was conscious that it was going into a new department of naval expenditure; but it failed in the drawing of the act which it passed upon that subject. It created a board of skilled and eminent naval officers, and upon their advice the Secretary of the Navy was authorized to cause *one or more* iron-clads to be built. That board, of which Admiral Charles Davis, of Boston, was the scientific head, met and advised the construction, upon a consideration of multifarious plans of *one* of each of *three* types of vessels, which are now known to history as the Galena, the Ironsides, and the Monitor. They were constructed merely as experiments, their value to be subsequently determined; to be determined, I take it, not by acts of Congress, not by the irresponsible and unscientific judgment of the Secretary of the Navy, however honest, respectable, and praiseworthy, but by competent men to advise after the idea had been embodied in a vessel of war, and was ready to be tried or had been tried in action.

Now what were the facts? Had the board existed which I propose, we would not be suffering as we now are from the neglect of those precautions. How came it that the monitors which we know now to be failures were multiplied, while the Department neglected the Ironsides, the only one of all the iron-clad vessels, with perhaps one doubtful exception, that has met the approval of naval officers.

The Monitor accidentally came into Hampton Roads as the Merrimac was trying to destroy, as it had already destroyed, some of our vessels. A collision took place. Neither party was destroyed; neither vessel was sunk; neither party was crippled, it is said; and the country ran wild over two guns in a cheese-box on a raft having done any thing, and not been defeated. People forget that our vessels were either sailing vessels at anchor which were destroyed, or steamers which had run aground in the narrow channel; that the Merrimac drew more water than they and could not reach them, and was no stronger than the Minnesota, her duplicate, and therefore weaker when burdened by her armor, and liable to be run down by our steamers when afloat, which were beyond reach of the Merrimac when aground. And upon the simple fact that the Monitor and the Merrimac exchanged shots and did not sink, without consultation with one single naval officer any where, without the judgment of any one professional man upon the floating or the fighting qualities of this class of vessels, without any additional consideration except that the Department tells us it had been well persuaded in its own mind beforehand by the spirit of prophecy that that type of iron-clad was to be successful and had proved itself successful, the Secretary orders twenty of them at a cost of from four hundred thousand to four hundred and sixty thousand dollars, amounting to $9,200,000. This was done upon the fight between the Monitor and the Merrimac, and no other consideration whatever. So the Department tells you in its report.

From that day to this monitors have been a gold mine for iron contractors, and to doubt their perfect success is as much as any naval officer's chances of command or promotion are worth.

That is the consideration that was given to this great topic. On an accidental collision between one vessel and another, without any of its scientific bearings having been adjudged and considered by competent officers, $9,200,000 were spent in constructing upon that type, without any material change, twenty vessels of that character. And so closely did they stick to the model, that one of the most distinguished officers of the navy, who now enjoys the highest considerations of the Navy Department, told me that he had to battle day after day with Ericsson and the men who were building them to get them to put upon those vessels the most ordinary naval appliances to fit them to be used at all in Charleston Harbor.

Following up that, the Department proceeded likewise, without any naval advice or investigation, to order the Dictator and the Puritan, under the authority of Congress, which improvidently left every thing to the Department and the contractors and speculators, at a cost of $2,300,000. Each monitor was to carry about two guns, which would make each gun cost about two hundred and fifty thousand dollars. The Dictator and the Puritan were to carry, I think the former about two, the latter four guns, which would make the cost of each gun of the Dictator $575,000, and of each gun of the Puritan $287,500. Then they ordered the Dunderberg, not yet completed, but on the plan of the casemated batteries of the rebels, likely to be more formidable than the vessels on the monitor principle, for she will have a battery of ten guns. So that just at one breath, by one stroke of the pen, the Department expended in this type of vessels, without any other consideration or advice whatever, $13,000,000. I submit, sir, that after the resolution of this House, passed last year, to make additional compensation to the constructors of the Dictator and Puritan in addition to the enormous contract already made with them, the honor and dignity of the country required that more consideration should have been given, more scientific advice should have been asked, before such enormous sums were expended in forms so totally new, which no experience had justified, which no naval opinion had then advised, and which no naval opinion at this day now advises.

Then, sir, there were others built, I suppose at the navy yards. I do not see any details respecting them in the reports, and I can not speak in regard to them. That, sir, was the work of 1862, as the Department informed us.

In 1863, when the additional monitors were ordered, to which I am now going to refer, there had been no trial of the original monitors excepting that one accidental and partial experiment in Hampton Roads, in smooth waters, a drawn battle, and excepting the failure on the Ogeechee to silence a land battery that mounted four guns, and the experience of the attack in Charleston Harbor on the 7th of April, 1863, when one half of the monitor force was silenced in forty minutes. On that discouraging experience, listen to the Secretary's account of new contracts for more monitors.

"The pressure for iron-clads of light draught, which could ascend the rivers, and penetrate the sounds and bays along our coast, was felt to be a necessity."

That is, the *pressure* was *felt* to be a *necessity*. Well, so it was. The pressure of iron contractors, I take it, not of naval officers.

The Secretary proceeds,

"The operations of our armies in the vicinity of the inland waters and adjacent to the rivers required the constant presence of gunboats. But the men thus employed, as well as the magazines and machinery of the vessels, are exposed, especially in the narrow streams with high and wooded banks. Some vessels and not a few valuable lives have been lost by these exposures, and in order to afford all possible protection to the gallant men who encounter these dangers, the Department considered it a duty to provide armored vessels of light draught for their security. Contracts were entered into for the construction of twenty vessels on the monitor principle, each to carry two eleven-inch guns in order to be efficient, and to draw but seven feet of water."

Now contracts for those vessels were made in the course of 1863, from March to August. They cost from $386,000 to $395,000 each vessel, amounting in the aggregate to $7,800,000!

Upon what advice? Upon whose opinion? Upon what consideration? Upon what specification? Upon what calculation? To accomplish what purpose? Let the gentleman who represents the Department answer. So carelessly, so absolutely without scientific consideration that the Department has been forced in its report at this session to confess and smooth over its failure in the construction of vessels—utter, absolute, ridiculous, disgraceful—a failure, Mr. Chairman, which is inexcusable, because, irrespective of the naval or fighting qualities of a vessel, the weight of iron, the weight of water, the ratio of displacement, and exactly how the vessel will float, when dimensions and material are given, is a question of mathematical and physical research, settled for centuries, that no school-boy would hesitate at if the conditions of the problem were placed before him. Yet so carelessly were these vessels, at those enormous sums, ordered, that there was an absolute failure of the whole fleet. All of them had to be materially altered. Some nearly sank when they were launched, and I learn had to be shored up with barrels in the harbor before the workmen would go on them in order to complete them. One at Pittsburg sank—went straight to the bottom when launched. But I do not pretend to official evidence in these things. These are the rumors. But here is the *official confession* of the *failure*, which is more than enough. The Secretary tells us, "It was ascertained, however, when the first two approached completion, that their draught of water was more than was intended." Had the weight of water changed, or the weight of iron, or had the laws of arithmetic changed? Was the calculation proved to be false after it was made? Or, indeed, was there any calculation? Did Mr. Fox sit in his office, and when a man came in with the model of a monitor of light draught and heavy cost, ask him, How much water will that draw? So much. Then build me that thing. Is that administration in time of war, and debt, and danger?

The report says:

"The heavy armor and the two eleven-inch guns, with the machinery to give them proper speed, involved the necessity of enlarging the capacity of each of them."

There was another question of arithmetic, and of the twenty not one could carry their machinery or their guns. Who devised their machinery? I suppose the head of the engineering department. Who advised the form, capacity, or weight of the monitors? It is nobody, or Mr. Fox.

"When making these necessary alterations, it was deemed advisable, under application from some of the commanders of squadrons for boats that should present but a small rise above the surface of the water, to dispense with the turrets in five of these light-draught vessels, with a view to special operations. The remaining fifteen were ordered to be enlarged by raising their decks, thereby giving them additional tonnage and greater draught, and making them more efficient, but in other respects carrying out the original design. This work is now being performed, and most of the vessels are near completion."

So the Secretary informs us that he dispensed with the turrets upon five of the light-draught vessels. Why? Because, with the turrets, they were *not light-draughts.* The only thing in which a monitor differs from an iron box is this revolving turret, and when the turrets were taken away they failed to be *monitors* at all. Yet the monitor price was paid, with a large addition to cover the official blunder. The remaining fifteen were ordered to be *enlarged* to make them draw less water! Their decks were raised in order to give them additional tonnage—an official euphuism, in which raising them above the water is put for sinking them deeper in the water to get them to float at all. They had too much draught before, and they would not float unless they had more cubic contents to buoy them up! The Department wanted light-draughts, not heavy-draughts. Those built before were too heavy to get into shoal waters. The Secretary says that in *all other* respects the original design is being carried out—they have only been made more efficient. But the original design was for light-draught monitors and nothing else; yet the light-draught has been abandoned *on all* for heavier draught, which excludes them from answering the original design wholly; and on five the turret is gone—so they are neither monitors nor light-draughts! What part of the original design remains but to give $7,000,000 to iron contractors to be invested in worthless iron? If there was any consideration on that subject, if any advice was taken, the officer who gave it ought to be cashiered. If there was not any consideration, no professional advice asked, I leave it to the Naval Committee to say what judgment should be pronounced upon the Department.

We come next to the consideration of the sea-going iron-clads, because even the Secretary of the Navy will not allow American genius to be chained to our own coast. For that purpose we are told by the Department—I beg to be understood that I am using official information, obtained from official documents, and nothing else—we are told by the Department that they wanted two swift sea-going iron-clads that should be able to cross the ocean and dictate the law abroad, and therefore one was called the Dictator and the other was called the Puritan—a singular mingling of the religious and warlike element, I suppose in memory of the great Puritan Dictator. But when he dictated, it was to kings on the field of battle; but the things they have made here, and marked with the names of power, will dictate nowhere except at the bottom of the ocean. The two were to cost $2,300,000. I think the Dictator was to carry two guns of enormous calibre, and the Puritan four, I think. Divide, and you will find what each gun costs. They are to go to sea. Sir, the Dictator can not carry more than six days' supply of coal with her armament, ammunition, and necessary provisions for sea, without going to the bottom. "Swift to pursue the enemy!" Why, sir, she can not go over six miles an hour, I believe, burning fifty-four tons of coal a day at that; for that, I am told, has been proved by the result of her trip from New York to Fortress Monroe. But in this matter I am outside of the record and official information. I make this statement upon what I suppose good authority; the log of the Dictator can correct it if erroneous. She started from New York to join in the attack on Fort Fisher. I have not official authority for saying, but I think it will not be controverted, that she did not go there because her machinery broke down in going from New York to Fortress Monroe, and I understand she is detained there undergoing repairs. Then that is not a sea-going iron-clad, nor a swift iron-clad, nor one available for offensive warfare. However destructive she may be if the enemy consult her convenience by taking position within her range, yet the swiftest vessel has the choice of field, and the enemy will not stay within her range unless it is to close on and board her, or to shut up her port-holes by rapid, and concentrated, and continuous fire, which will prevent her using the enormous shots which go once in seven or eight minutes, or crush her thin decks with shot as heavy as her own.

But these are matters for navy men to settle; all that is now known is that the Dictator is as useless for a sea-going vessel of war as the light-draught monitors are to go in shallow water.

A moment as to the providence with which the contract was made. I remember to have heard—and the records of the Department will correct me if I am not correctly informed—there were claims made for extra compensation on those two vessels, and a board was summoned, consisting of officers whose names I will not mention. I do not know how much, but perhaps two hundred thousand dollars were demanded. The board declined to recommend it. Another board was summoned of more pliant material, and they recommended the allowance not only of what was asked, but greatly more; and, if I am not misinformed—and here again the Department has the record—the award was so much beyond what was asked that application was made, formal or informal, to withdraw the original application!

The Secretary of the Navy shrank from acting under the advice of such a board. The claimants then came here to Congress, and Congress at its last session, upon the motion of the honorable gentleman from Massachusetts [Mr. Rice], passed a resolution making material additions to the compensation awarded; how nobody knows. The result has been that the Puritan remains, I believe, upon the stocks, uncompleted, and nobody knows when, if ever, she will be completed. The Dictator lies with her machinery broken on her first trip from New York to Fortress Monroe.

Such is the investment of the Department in sea-going iron-clads, and there it stops. When the Dunderberg comes out we shall know more about her; but she is not of the monitor class. Her engines are not of bureau device, but by the builders; she will bear ten guns, and may be a powerful floating battery, hardly any thing more. We are without a single sea-going iron-clad capable of cruising, the Ironsides alone excepted.

Now, sir, to what purpose are these vessels of the monitor type adapted? They have no ram. Their engines are so weak that in collision they can do no harm. Their draught is eleven and a half feet, perhaps twelve, instead of ten. They have no sails; they can not attack; they can not escape if attacked; they can not batter forts with any success; they have never yet silenced a sand-battery, or shaken a stone of a casemated fort, any where, at any time. It does not appear that in the course of a year's operations before Charleston, any impression has been made there upon any fortification of any kind. At Fort M'Allister, the rebel officers mounted the ramparts and smoked their cigars between the shots. They can not stand heavy and continuous battering, for, though the turrets be not pierced, their machinery for turning the turret, closing the ports, and working the guns, is so delicate as to deprive them of half their fire by constant derangement; and if a line-of-battle ship has half her guns silenced, it is supposed she is materially damaged in the conflict, though hull and engine survive. Of the seven monitors that went into action in Charleston Harbor, four of them were partially or wholly disabled in forty minutes. That is a proportion of loss that Trafalgar did not show.

Safe? Why, sir, their liability to sink, whether from a torpedo or the storms of the ocean, when going down the coast, is more fatal to life than an ordinary general action. Four of them, including the original Monitor itself, have already sunk, out of the twenty that have been built and launched, carrying down nearly all the crews. The Weehawken went down in perfectly quiet water in Charleston Harbor, carrying thirty men with her; one nearly sank lying at the Washington navy yard; the original Monitor went down on its way to Port Royal; the Patapsco was sunk the other day by a torpedo in Charleston Harbor, and carried down some seventy men, it is said; and the Tecumseh sunk in the action at Mobile, burying Craven and all but three or four of her crew. The unpublished health reports exhibit disastrous and unprecedented results. The ratio of loss, taking the liability to sickness, the chances of sinking, together with the chances of losses in action, shows that they were not safer, and are less effective in fight, than ordinary wooden vessels. Every body will appreciate the remark of Admiral Porter when he intimates that he had rather stand behind his wooden walls and take what comes, than be confined in one of these iron coffins. And it is remarkable that this class of vessels has nowhere received, and can not now get, the suffrage of any respectable proportion of the American navy as any part of the national defense at all, unless it be behind obstructions across the entrance of a port where they can not be reached; and casemated batteries, with numerous and equally heavy guns, not costing $250,000 a gun, can do that duty with equal effect. And any one who will read, what I have not now time to read, the special report of Admiral Porter on these vessels at Fort Fisher, will find that, while he complacently decorates them with words of vague eulogy, yet his criticism leaves them nothing of peculiar value, and his consent never could be gotten to build another monitor. The single exception is the Monadnock, whose sailing qualities he speaks highly of; but her engines were not built under the auspices of the Navy Department, and she is not a monitor at all in point of fact. He did not venture to put the ammunition on board these vessels before they started; he did not venture to put their coal on board, but towed every one of them down the coast to Beaufort, and when they got there their ammunition and coal were placed on them for the first time. And any one who will compare the results in Mobile Bay with the results at Fort Fisher will find that the effective instruments in each case were the broadside vessels, with their concentrated and rapid fire, covering the whole field of battle with their shells, rendering it untenable to any one; while, as I have already mentioned, when the monitors alone were engaged at Fort M'Allister, the officers did not hesitate to stand upon the ramparts and smoke their cigars between the shots. Admiral Farragut is entitled to be heard upon the question of naval armament, and he did not ascribe any decisive influence on the result at Mobile, one of the great days of our republic, to our iron-clads. He did not think that the monitors defeated the enemy in that conflict, the most serious conflict between vessels during the rebellion. Hear his report:

"Our iron-clads, from their slow speed and bad steering, had some difficulty in getting into and maintaining their position in line as we passed the fort, and, in the subsequent encounter with the Tennessee, from the same causes were not as effective as could have been desired; but I can not give too much praise to Lieutenant Commander Perkins, who, though he had orders from the Department to return North, volunteered to take command of the Chickasaw, and did his duty nobly.

"The Winnebago was commanded by Commander T. H. Stevens, who volunteered for that position. His vessel steers very badly, and neither of his turrets will work, which compelled him to turn his vessel every time to get a shot, so that he could not fire very often; but he did the best under the circumstances.

"The Manhattan appeared to work well, though she moved slowly. Commander Nicholson delivered his fire deliberately, and, as before stated, with one of his fifteen-inch shots broke through the armor of the Tennessee, with its wooden backing, though the shot itself did not enter the vessel. No other shot broke through the armor, though many of her plates were started, and several of her port shutters jammed by the fire from the different ships."

That is not my judgment nor the judgment from an officer at war with the Department, but the judgment of an officer whose name in history will rest on that day. It is not magnanimous to depreciate the merits and power of vessels and arms which did his work, and he could not have penned the report if the monitors were the dominant power in the battle. He was on board his wooden vessel, with his other wooden vessels; their rapid and powerful batteries converging on the Tennessee from every quarter and silencing her fire, and their rapid rush, or, as a gentleman very appropriately said, the mobbing of the Tennessee by the wooden vessels, determined the contest, and not the slow, unmoving, helpless, powerless monitors that were there to look on at a battle in which they barely participated. The same thing has been experienced elsewhere; but I quote Admiral Farragut because his testimony is in print, and because there can be no question as to its meaning; because every body knows that he is a naval man, and one who would make use of every means placed in his hands, and fairly distribute the merits of the result.

Again, at Fort Fisher, monitors mingled their fire with the heavy fire of broadside vessels, and none is so competent to speak of the value of the monitor as Admiral Porter. He says:

> "Compared with the Ironsides, their fire is very slow, and not at all calculated to silence heavy batteries, which requires a rapid and continuous fire to drive men from their guns; but they are famous coadjutors in fight—"

Why, certainly, any thing will help upon a pinch,

> "and put in heavy blows which tell on casemates and bomb-proofs."

But they never yet destroyed a bomb-proof or tore to pieces a casemate. After a bombardment of two days at Fort Fisher, when it is said all the guns were dismounted, and the work torn to pieces, twenty-five hundred men with whole skins rose from beneath the ruins ready to dispute the possession of that fort, and held it during five hours of hand-to-hand conflict with the army led by the heroic Terry.

If that were all the effect of four hundred and fifty guns of the whole fleet, how much is to be ascribed to the ten guns of the monitors? And how much was effected by the *first* bombardment of two or three days with the same enormous force, if so soon the fort was ready for defense?

But Admiral Porter proceeds:

> "*The smaller class of monitors*, as at present constructed, will always require the aid of a steamer to tow them and take care of them. In smooth water they ought to go along by themselves, and when towed the tow-rope should never be less than two hundred fathoms in length. It strains them very much to have a short tow-line."

Then he thinks them worthless as sea vessels, incapable of independent action as at present constructed—that is, as monitors built at a cost of $250,000 a gun.

He proceeds:

"I do not know yet what their real durability is or would be in a continuous fire against their turrets. Solid eleven-inch or two-hundred-pounder rifles are apt to break something when they strike, and I should be much better satisfied myself to be behind wooden bulwarks, and take what comes, than to be shut up in an iron turret, not knowing whether it is properly constructed. This, though, is the prejudice of an old sailor, and should have no weight whatever."

So he thinks not much more of their defensive than of their aggressive qualities, and prefers the risk with the power of broadside vessels. That is the naval opinion, not my judgment, upon the monitors at Fort Fisher.

The Monadnock, a turreted vessel, but not a monitor, alone attracted Porter's good opinion:

"As to the Monadnock, she could ride out a gale at anchor in the Atlantic Ocean. She is certainly a most perfect success so far as the hull and machinery are concerned, and is only defective in some minor details, which, in the building of these vessels, require the superintendence of a thorough seaman, and a practical and ingenious man. The Monadnock is capable of crossing the ocean alone (when her compasses are once adjusted properly), and could destroy any vessel in the French or British navy, lay their town under contribution, and return again (provided she could pick up coal) without fear of being followed."

But her speed is no merit of the Department, for her engines were not on their plans. If she could work such wonders abroad, why not try her on Charleston? And the coal question seems to interpose an insuperable barrier to transatlantic exploits, unless she is to remain there.

The admiral turns to the Ironsides:

"I have never yet seen a vessel that comes up to my ideas of what is required for effective operations as much as the Ironsides. The most important is the comfort with which the people on board of her live, though she would be no match for the Monadnock in a fight, the latter having more speed.

"The accuracy of fire is, I think, in favor of the Ironsides, judging from what I have seen here. The turrets get filled with smoke, and do not clear as quick as the Ironsides, though that defect could be avoided by not firing both guns so near together."

Yet this class of vessels, of which the Department have, I believe, but one, which was built upon the recommendation of the original commission, has not been multiplied. They propose to build no more. She can go abroad; she can make her cannon heard on the shores of Great Britain; she can sail as well as steam; and she can carry coal enough to enable her to steam to any extent that may be necessary for the success of her operations. She cost only $780,000, just $80,000 above what the Department paid for a single engine in 1863!!

Now, sir, it is material to observe that as the judgment of a navy man upon this iron-clad, the Ironsides. It was one built upon the advice of naval men. She is one that has not been repeated. She is the one that has not been accepted by the Department. Why? No one can tell, unless it be that the Navy Department had gone crazy on monitors, and was so deeply engaged in their construction that no money or thought remained for any thing else. Can any one doubt but that others of the Ironsides class would have been built if naval men had been consulted?

Now, sir, I pass from that to the other question, on which I have something to say. I can not say as much upon this as I desire. I come to the great question of machinery; no corruption in contracts—nothing of the kind—but to the responsible advice on which the existing machinery of the navy has been made; simply as a business transaction, treating it as a question of prudence and common sense in the administration of the government. We have twenty-three screw gunboats of the Unadilla class, twelve double-enders of the Miami class, ten of the Juniata class, twenty-seven double-enders of the Utah class, and one or two other vessels made of iron, and I believe likewise of the double-ender class, whose machinery was built on the plans and designs of the Bureau of Engineering, as the head of the bureau tells us in his report. There are likewise four other vessels built by the Department, the Oneida, the Tuscarora, Wachusett, and Kearsarge, duplicates of the Iroquois, the Mohegan, the Wyoming, and the Seminole. Their machinery was not devised by the Bureau of Steam Engineering, but was copied from the machinery of the other four vessels of which they were duplicates, and on principles which the Department discarded in the machinery designed by the bureau, and placed in the vessels of the four classes above mentioned.

In the course of the year 1862, as the screw sloops of the Juniata class and the paddle-wheel double-enders were being completed and put afloat, a serious question arose as to the efficiency and durability of machinery. The Department summoned a board of the first engineers of the United States to take their opinion on what the Department had done without the advice of any body. That board was requested to convene and investigate the machinery of the screw steamers of the Juniata, Monongahela, and Lackawana class, and of the paddle-wheel steamers then building, and report to the Department upon a series of questions. That report was made, printed, and a copy of it has been handed to me. Now the first thing to be observed is, that on page 69 of that report, this commission of civil engineers, summoned by the Secretary of the Navy to judge his machinery, say the ability to propel naval vessels of proper model at a high rate of speed is an essential point in designing the machinery, and not less than twelve knots per hour for *screw vessels* should be attainable on emergencies, under favorable circumstances AT SEA. They then proceed to give their opinion upon the machinery. I will read for the instruction of the committee a few passages to show how great was the divergency of judgment between the engineers selected by the Department and the engineer officers who constructed the machinery, at a cost of $12,000,000, which now renders our naval vessels the laughing-stock of every blockade-runner. It says:

"*Interrogatories.*

"1. On the valve gear, whether it admits of using the steam with such degree of expansion, or is usual or desirable with marine engines for the naval service, and whether it is a proper one for screw and paddle-wheel engines, as the case may be?

"In reply to the first interrogatory, we separate our opinion in relation to the screw and paddle-wheel engines. For the screw engines it is considered by the board (with the exception of two members named hereafter) that the principle adopted in admitting and exhausting steam by one side-wheel valve, actuated by the link motion, though not deemed the best in all cases, is, all things considered, proper in the present case, combining simplicity of construction with such a range of expansion as is usual or desirable in the naval service. But the use of very large steam ports, so much in the excess of the proportion adopted by the best builders, while, by permitting a free exhaust, it may afford a slight advantage, has involved a serious loss of steam, in our opinion overbalancing such an advantage. It has also entailed all the evils of great travel of valve, namely, difficulty of reversing, increased friction and wear, and a system of gear to work it of excessive size, weight, and cost, both in construction and maintenance.

"For the paddle-wheel steamers, it is believed that, although it would have been better to have adopted a form of valve gear, having an arrangement for adjusting while in motion, yet that the principle adopted must be considered a proper one for the purpose, since the admitting and exhausting of the steam are accomplished by different valves and different movements, which in the use of slowly reciprocating engines for marine purposes is very desirable. It is also believed that little if any loss of fuel will result from controlling the engine by the throttle in those cases of emergency when it is ordinarily deemed proper to quickly alter the rate of expansion. We are, however, compelled to object in this case, as in the other, to the great and unnecessary size of ports used, much in excess of that which, in our judgment, is requisite, entailing, as it does, a great loss of steam as well as additional expense of construction."

"2. On the boilers, whether they are superior, equal, or inferior to others in use in compactness, durability, efficiency, and proper adaptation to the conditions of the naval service ? * * * * * * * *

"1. In regard to compactness, to obtain an equal amount of evaporation under ordinary circumstances, the boiler used in the steamers under consideration is inferior to the horizontal tubular boiler, requiring about ten per cent. more cubular space. 2. In regard to durability. We regard the boiler used in these steamers as equal in this respect to the horizontal tubular boiler, proper care and attention being bestowed in each case. 3. In regard to efficiency, including economical effect and evaporative power, with natural draught. In the former particular, economy, taking all the conditions of the use of the naval boilers into consideration, we think the vertical tubular boiler used in these steamers is equal to the horizontal tubular. A farther note on this subject, by five of the members, will be found in a subsequent part of the report. As to the second particular, namely, evaporative power under natural draught, irrespective of economical effect, the vertical tubular is inferior to the horizontal tubular boiler, requiring one third more cubical contents to produce the same amount of steam. 4. In regard to accessibility for cleaning and repair. In this respect, taking into consideration the liability to derangement from carelessness, and the facilities for cleaning fire and water spaces, and for effective repairs, both at sea and in port, we consider the vertical water tube boiler in use in these steamers as, upon the whole, inferior to the horizontal tubular boiler. 5. Power of producing large evaporation with least sacrifice of economical effect by artificial means. In this respect we consider the vertical tubular as inferior to the horizontal tubular boiler. The former is in this respect open to serious objections. It requires the use of artificial means to produce an evaporation which is ordinarily obtained with ease in the horizontal tubular ; and when these means are employed for any length of time, the flue spaces become clogged.

"We reply, therefore, to your second interrogatory, that, on the whole, we are compelled to consider the type of boiler used in these steamers as inferior to the horizontal tubular boiler which is generally used by other nations, and by this country in the mercantile marine."

* * * * * * * * * *

"4. On the general design and arrangement of the machinery in the different cases, and whether, on the whole, all the conditions of the naval service being duly considered, there is any other arrangement in use that would give superior results?

"In reply to this interrogatory we have to report that the general design and arrangement of machinery for the screw steamers is inferior to that of other types in the following particulars: 1. Compactness. It occupies more cubical space than either the ordinary back-acting engine (this phrase objected to by Mr. Everett), or the direct-acting engine, either of which, with the same stroke, could have been gotten into these vessels. 2. Liability to derangement. It is more liable to derangement than either of those types, owing to the great number and weight of the moving parts, and comparative inaccessibility of some of them. 3. In reference to economy of fuel. The consumption of steam as applied to the propulsion of the vessel must be proportionally greater in these engines than in those of ordinary proportions, owing to the excessive weight of the reciprocating parts to be put in motion at each alternation of movement, involving additional friction, and also the employment of such large steam ports, involving loss of steam even after allowing for the gain by free exhaust so obtained, as well as the expenditure of power due to great travel and friction of the valves. 4. Owing to the peculiar arrangement of the smaller pumps and of the valve gearing, they are more inaccessible for care and adjustment when in motion and for repairs either at sea or in port. Taking all these points into consideration, we believe, first, that the direct-acting engine presents the greater number and amount of advantages for marine service in the navy, and can state that the space allotted for the machinery in these vessels would have permitted the introduction of the direct-acting engine in place of that adopted, having the same stroke of piston, a sufficient length of connecting-rod, and ample surface in the journals to bear the same maximum strain brought upon the reciprocating parts without sacrificing any of the essential elements of a successful performance; second, that the saving of cubic contents occupied in the vessel, due to such change of type, would have been not less than twenty per cent.; and, third, that the employment of the proportions used by the best practice for the various parts of these engines would have resulted in a saving of weight amounting to not less than sixty tons, involving reduced cost, other conditions being the same.

"With regard to the paddle-wheel engines, we consider the general plan adopted as not open to serious objection, inasmuch as the space to be occupied in these vessels is of secondary importance. It affords the necessary accessibility for care and adjustment during operation, and for repairs at all times. It is not peculiarly liable to derangement, and has superabundant journal service. We object, however, to the weight of some of the parts of the engine proper, which, judged by the proportions used in the best practice, is excessive. This objection applies especially to the first paddle-wheel boats. In both classes, however, it is believed to be of importance, as involving additional displacement to carry it and increased cost of construction. We object also to the large proportions of the condensing apparatus (except the condensers *proper* in the second class of engines) as being in our opinion unnecessary, and to the size of steam ports, valves, etc., about double that of the best practice hitherto, on account of the loss of steam caused thereby. The overhanging wheels and their constructions are approved. We approve also of the adoption of single engines for vessels of this class."

"5. Whether, had the drawings and specifications of this machinery been submitted to you before their construction, you would have objected to any thing in it as likely to render its performance in any way inferior to other machinery in use for the same purpose and under the same considerations?

"We should have objected to many of the points of arrangement and details in these plans and specifications, as giving results inferior to what might, in our opinion, have been obtained had changes been made in them."

"6. You will please also give, in the event of your disapproving of all or any part of the machinery, the reasons therefor, and state what, in your opinion, it should have been.

"In compliance with this request, we have to state that we should have placed more power, both of engines and boilers, in the screw steamers, recognizing the great importance to naval steamers of having the capability to maintain continuously a high rate of speed when desired; and believe that in both respects the power could have been proportionately increased by a change in type and detail—as indicated in previous replies—to the extent of at least one third more, without adding to the space occupied by the whole, reducing the coal space, or equaling the total weight.

"By such a change, obtained without sacrifice of room or displacement, a higher rate of speed would have been attainable; while in ordinary cruising, both engines and boilers could have been worked at a less pressure of steam, and managed in a manner most conducive to economy of fuel and their greater durability.

"We should have objected to certain points of detail and proportion, as indicated in our replies to previous interrogatories. A farther objection and proposed change is submitted by four members of the board in a subsequent part of this report. * * * * * * * * *

"Objections to answer the first interrogatory by Messrs. Coryell and Wright, who object to so much of the foregoing answer as relates to the principle adopted for the valve gear used in the Juniata class of engines, for the reason that it will not allow of the proper motion of the steam valve for an engine working expansively, in combination with a proper opening of ports for the exhaust; in other words, all engines should have a separate valve and motion for working steam expansively. The type of valve motion used on the Iroquois, Wachusett, and vessels of that class, though not combining every thing desired for an efficient expansive gear, is in every respect superior to that in use in the Juniata class of engines." * * *

"Addition to answer to sixth interrogatory by Messrs. Hibbard, Wright, Loring, and Coryell, who add to the foregoing answer by stating that they regard the diameter of the cylinders of the Juniata class of engines as too small to develop in the most economical manner the power of the steam that can be generated by the boilers, as they require the steam to be admitted at a pressure of thirty to thirty-five pounds per square inch above the atmosphere for about three fourths of the stroke, to develop their ordinary full working power. With large cylinders, fifty-four inches in diameter, cutting off the steam at about three eighths the stroke, and using the same pressure and volume of steam, would, in their opinion, develop more power from it, and at the same time, by cutting off a larger point, enable the engines to work for a limited time with a large excess of power in an emergency, or at full power with a lower pressure of steam, as would be very desirable in case the boilers were weakened by wear or other causes, or if the pressure of the steam became accidentally lower, or if from leaking or other derangement of the fresh-water condenser it became necessary to work the boilers with salt water, and that such increased size of the cylinders would not materially increase the cubic space occupied. The size of cylinders used do not in our opinion permit the best rate of expansion that the valve gear will give, except at a low rate of speed of the vessels."

The Board make this important statement on page 97:

"It is true that the best screw vessels in the navy for speed and efficiency are provided with an independent cut-off apparatus; but this superiority is not necessarily due to the use of an independent cut-off. We believe there are no vessels built for the Navy before the date mentioned [1861] without an independent cut-off."

Then we have on page 127 of the supplemental report this remark of the Board:

"We did not, for example, in our report allude to one disadvantage of the form of boiler now used in the naval service, although it was fully discussed, namely, the impossibility in the gunboats or sloops, of reducing its height so that the crown of the boiler can be below the main load water-line of the vessel. This can be done by other forms of multitubular boiler, either horizontal or vertical, while the ordinary horizontal tubular somewhat occupies less height, when *properly designed*, to give the same effect."

Now, the effect of having the steam machinery exposed in action was disastrously illustrated when the Sassacus was exploded in Albemarle Sound, and the Hatteras disabled by the Alabama in the Gulf of Mexico, by a single shot passing through a portion of their steam machinery.

And then we have another significant fact on this point in the remark they make, that the engines differ from those of the best practical engineers. They were mere innovations. However they may be justified hereafter, they were against the opinion of the profession when adopted, and against the experience of the best vessels in the United States service as the commission of engineers report, and they are different from these vessels which now make the best time at sea under the ordinary conditions of the application of machinery to the propulsion of vessels. They were mere innovations—ideas that came across the head of the chief of the Bureau of Steam Engineering; and *they*, engines and boilers, stand condemned by this commission, which was summoned by the Department to pass its judgment upon them.

On one innovation, made without experiment or any proposed advantage, the Board speak as follows:

"Both in the naval and merchant marine large sums of money have been expended in constructing elaborate machinery, especially required to accomplish long ranges of expansion. On the other hand, during the past two years, some twenty-five or thirty vessels (mostly in the navy) have been provided with machinery constructed on a different theory, namely, that it was more economical to make the steam cylinders of such dimensions that a small range of expansion could be used.

"We respectfully submit that a knowledge of the fact of which of these systems is the most economical would be productive of so great a moneyed economy to the government that we can not but earnestly recommend that you will authorize the necessary experiments to determine this question, particularly as an expenditure not to exceed from fifteen to twenty thousand dollars only would be required, which, in comparison to the importance of the subject, is insignificant."

Then the Board advised experiments to test the relative values of the horizontal and vertical tubular boilers, chiefly out of deference to the Department's partiality for the latter, which they had condemned in the form used by the Bureau of Engineering. This report was made in February or March, 1863, and it condemned every thing that had been done at that time, every engine that had then been placed by the Department in a naval vessel. We are told that these investigations are now going on, in the report of the Secretary to this session. The Bureau of Steam Engineering informs us that *now*—that is to say in December, 1864, when the report came in, commissions were sitting to determine those two problems proposed for solution in February, 1863, and were carrying on their investigations in November and December, 1864, to advise the Department what course it should pursue in creating new engines.

Now, what has been the course of the Department while that investigation was going on? Why, sir, I hold here a report of the chief of the Engineer Bureau of the 28th of November, 1864, which, after eulogizing the form of boiler which that Board of Engineers condemned, and giving us his assurance that his subsequent experiments quite justify his opinion, condemned by the Board of Engineers, informs us that, on the 28th of November, 1864,

"A Board, consisting of the principal steam-engine builders of the country and the chief of this bureau, is now experimenting with critical accuracy on two boilers of the respective types for the purpose of definitely determining their relative merits for the naval service under every variety of circumstance and of proportion. It is believed the results will be of the utmost importance to all engaged in the manufacture and use of steam machinery.

"Another Board, consisting of three members of the Franklin Institute, three of the Academy of Sciences, and three on the part of the Department, are now experimenting with the utmost precision on machinery devised by Mr. Horatio Allen, of the Novelty Iron Works, New York city, one of the Board, to determine by practical results the economy of using steam with different measures of expansion, under different conditions of mechanism, pressure, and back pressure. It is believed these experiments will give a correct practical solution to a very vexed problem, and be of incalculable benefit."

That is to say, experiments of vital moment proposed in February, 1863, to guide the Department in the expenditure of millions, and to determine the value of the whole machinery of the navy, have been cleverly protracted from February, 1863, till November, 1864, that is, during *twenty-one months*, nearly two years; and while this was going on, we are informed that the Department has solved those problems in its own sense; and in the face of this report of the Board of Engineers, and its judgment upon the machinery of the Bureau, it has ordered machinery of its own condemned types to the amount of millions of money, for I can not tell how many vessels! The statement of contracts for steam machinery made by the Bureau of Steam Engineering since the 1st of August, 1863, that is, six months after the report of the Board of Engineers, shows contracts for twenty-one engines at $400,000 each, four at $580,000 each, two at $600,000, and two at $700,000 each, amounting to about twelve millions of dollars; all after August, 1863; all after the condemnation by the Board of Engineers; all pending the experiments which were to determine their structure! In what year the last were ordered is perhaps not quite certain, for the dates are not very distinctly set forth; but all seem to be in 1863.

What I ask the attention of the committee to is the fact that a Board of Engineers, summoned by the Department, condemned all the machinery the Department had placed in any wooden vessel up to the date of its sessions, and that the Department, instead of changing its course, goes on and constructs machinery upon identically the same principle, as the Bureau of Engineers informs us. I speak now upon the report; and then, as if to add mockery to this abuse of the public confidence, they tell us that now, after the time which has elapsed between February and March, 1863, and November, 1864, they are diligently pursuing investigations to settle questions which they have practically solved by the expenditure of millions of dollars upon work which has been condemned by a Board authorized by the Department itself more than a year ago, and pending experiments intended to determine some of the most vital points of the machinery! If that is wise action, then let others explain it. If there are differences of opinion so grave as that, then it is time to stop until the problem is solved, and not say that, after having built a whole navy at such stupendous sacrifice of money, they are now diligently pursuing investigations for the purpose of solving a problem which they have practically solved by this great expenditure. That is a trifling with the country which should bring down upon them the indignation of this House. And if no other fact existed, that should be a sufficient reason to surround the head of the Navy Department with responsible advisers, whose opinions he can not disregard, whose opinions he can not push away in the pigeon-holes of the Department, as he did those of the Board of Engineers, where they may lay until they were brought out after weeks of investigation by our committees, but who would command respect from the head of the Department, or bring down condign punishment upon his head if neglected. It is to prevent such an abuse of the public confidence as is shown by the report of the Board of Engineers on the one side, and the report of the Engineer Bureau on the other, that I have drawn the proposition I have offered; and in drawing it I have embodied in it as nearly as I could, and as the system of our government would allow, the provisions which have, by the experience of other countries and our own, from time to time been found useful to guide and aid the discretion of the Secretary when novel ships or great expenditures on new forms of naval defense were about to be hazarded, and to prevent this great squandering of the public money. In my judgment it will be a guarantee of an efficiency of service hereafter such as we have never had heretofore.

I have already detained the House longer than I intended. I merely wish to say now that, so far as I can get information from any source whatever, the speed of the engines placed in the naval vessels constructed by the Department on its type up to this time falls three miles short of what they ought to have attained according to the Board of Engineers. A defender of the navy has furnished a striking proof of this great failure. When the question was raised upon that subject in the newspapers some time ago, the statement that the screw sloops of the Department could not exceed between nine and ten knots drew out a reply from a distinguished officer in the navy, who said that it was very far from being true that none of the vessels of the navy could go more than nine or ten miles an hour under steam continuously, under the conditions of the naval service—not running down the Potomac without armament, or coal, or ammunition, or water, or provisions, and in smooth water, *but at sea.* It is the only direct, authentic published statement that I have ever seen from any naval officer respecting the speed of any of the vessels of the United States built by the present Department which carried their speed above ten miles an hour. But the contradiction is solved by noting the *names* of the vessels forming the exceptions. Captain Craven, the heroic officer who went down with the monitor Tecumseh in Mobile Bay, is the officer referred to, and his card, in answer to the suggestion that none of the Department vessels would go more than ten knots an hour under naval conditions, stated that he had commanded both the Kearsarge and the Tuscarora, and that they could go thirteen knots an hour. But the Kearsarge and the Tuscarora *are not provided with machinery built by the Department or the Bureau of Engineering*, but they are two vessels of war which were duplicates in structure and machinery of the Iroquois, the Mohican, and the Seminole, vessels constructed by the last administration, *whose engines are constructed on the principle that the new Bureau of Engineering has condemned*—principles which it has discarded in the construction of the new engines, but which prevailed in the structure of the old vessels of the United States Navy, and of the vessels constructed in navies abroad. And I say that this is evidence in corroboration of the fact that none of the vessels whose machinery is devised by the Bureau can approach the speed which it is said by the Board of Engineers ought to be attained, and can be attained, with proper machinery, under naval conditions for naval vessels. The number of revolutions of the screw, not exceeding sixty or sixty-two a minute, and the pitch of the screw, limit the speed of the screw sloops to less than ten knots an hour, unless a vessel can go faster than her propeller; and that such is the limit appears officially by the report that the Monongahela, in rushing full speed against the Tennessee, made sixty-two revolutions, manifestly the utmost limit of her power; and that they are under twelve knots an hour is implied by the Board of Engineers assigning that as the desirable limit, while they condemn the machinery, and say it might, by change in type and detail, have in the screw steamers been increased in power to the extent of one third. It is plain they thought the speed of the sloop *not over nine knots*. The impunity of the Alabama and her consorts for three years is the practical result; while the official report adds to the confirmation by showing that of ninety steamers captured during the year, not over five or six were taken by vessels built on the Department plans.

Now, sir, without going farther into detail upon this subject, for I desire to stop where official data stop, I submit that the course of the Department with reference to the iron-clads, and its course with reference to the construction of machinery, all other matters being laid aside, show the necessity of some supervising board, some advisory power beyond authority which is at the head of the Navy Department, and to secure to the nation the benefit of the money that it is now expending in the structure of vessels. We have spent already, sir, over $280,000,000 on our navy, and yet at this day there has been accomplished scarcely any thing which ought to be satisfactory to the nation, or which materially adds to its security. I trust, sir, that by the adoption of this amendment a security will be provided for the future, for nothing can remedy the squandering of the past.

Messrs. Rice, Pike, and Griswold, of the Committee, and Mr. Blow, having opposed the amendment, Mr. Davis said on the 6th of February,

Mr. Chairman,—Had the gentlemen of the Naval Committee treated the proposition I had the honor to present with ordinary fairness, or exhibited in the course of their discussion of it that they had read the bill and amendment which they rejected, and understood that which they attempted to induce the House not to adopt, I should not have indulged in a word of reply; for, sir, no fact I have adduced from the public record of this or the last session has been controverted or can be controverted by them; nor, indeed, if those facts stand, is there any reply possible to the considerations urged by me. But, instead of meeting the argument I addressed upon a measure introduced upon grave deliberation, and referred to that committee for its consideration now nearly a year ago, both honorable gentlemen commenced their observations by remarking on the personal feeling and temper of my remarks.

Now, sir, whether that temper was that of a May morning or of a November night scarcely affects the value of the measure before the House. Whether I am pleased with or disgusted with gentlemen who preside over the Navy Department is not an argument either for or against the measure I presented. My wrath did not sink the light-draught monitors, and the puffs of the Boston Advertiser can not float them. If the gentlemen meant to intimate, for the purpose of weakening the weight of any observation I made here, that the measure I introduced is prompted by any personal feeling relative to the gentlemen who control that Department, I desire to say it is their invention, and nothing else, which gives foundation to the suggestion. I have not the honor of an acquaintance with either of those gentlemen. I have neither been refused, nor asked, nor received any favor at their hands, and that is more than the two gentlemen [Mr. Rice and Mr. Pike] upon the committee can say for themselves.

If I am in ill temper, and that ill temper is to affect the judgment of the House upon the argument I presented, it is only fair to say—though I mention matters of this kind with great reluctance—that the devotion to the Department of the honorable gentlemen upon my right may be supposed equally to affect the weight of their arguments; and so far as the gentleman upon my left [Mr. Griswold], who adduces his testimony to the efficiency of the machinery and the structure of the Dictator is concerned, I may be permitted to say that the gentleman, if I am not misinformed, has had interest in the construction of the iron-clads which may naturally be supposed to warp his judgment upon that subject at least as much as my disgust biases mine; so that, when the collateral facts are made, I submit, be my temper what it might, my argument is entitled to weigh equally with the arguments of gentlemen on the other side, irrespective of the temper that dictated or pervaded them.

But another step; and it is to the gentlemen I refer. He spoke about my inaccuracy touching the consideration of the bill before the committee, and said, if I understood him correctly, that it had been considered promptly by the committee after I had requested the honorable gentlemen and some others to have it considered, whether at the last session or the present session I do not remember. When that consideration took place I do not know, and the honorable gentleman does. But if I was misled by the statement of the distinguished gentleman from Ohio [Mr. Spalding], a member of the committee, who, when I moved this amendment formally, said to the House, as an objection to its consideration, that it "*is now undergoing investigation before that committee*," and if it was decided before that time, I was not at fault in supposing it had not been decided. If it was decided since that time, I am right in supposing that the judgment was made while my amendment was pending, in order to affect the judgment of the House unfavorably and unregularly upon it.

But how have the gentlemen treated the measure itself? From beginning to end as if I had introduced this bill to annex the British system of a Board of Admiralty to the organization of the Navy Department. There was no other ground of objection or point of observation made by either of those gentlemen, so far as I could understand them. I desire to say that gentlemen who are arguing from the Board of Admiralty of England against this bill do not know what that Board is, or they never have read or understood this bill. The Board of Admiralty is the Navy Department of England. The six lords administer the navy; they do not advise a single head. They are the executive body itself, not a council to advise another head. It is formed upon the old system of the government of England, which is ministerial, by a board of ministers, and not by the nominal head, the king. The Board of Admiralty is the organization of the ministry in the administrative department of the navy. That is the peculiarity of the system. Against that peculiarity the objections to the Board of Admiralty in England are directed alone. It is that peculiarity which I *do not* propose to adopt, and it is upon this peculiarity of that Board that these gentlemen have argued here against that which I introduce.

The gentleman who is chairman of the Naval Committee stated that a Board of Naval Commissioners was appointed under a law passed in 1815, and that was repealed, and the bureau system was adopted in 1842. The burden of his argument was that the Naval Commissioners of 1815 was such a Board as I propose now. Why, Mr. Chairman, does not the gentleman understand the history of the organization of the Department which he here represents and attempts to defend? The Navy Commissioners of 1815 were the ministerial organization of the Department, for which were substituted the present bureaus, now the ministerial portion of the Department, executing the instructions of the Secretary of the Navy. What I propose—and now, at least, I shall be able to make myself understood—what I propose is not to remove the bureaus, not to substitute any other organization to discharge their ministerial duties, nor to interfere with the free discretion of the Secretary, but to interpose, on the French system, between the administrative discretion of the Secretary and the ministerial obedience of the bureaus a council of naval officers, whose advice the Secretary may command on all matters, whose opinions he must take on some matters, but which, when taken, he is free to disregard. Is that intelligible? As the President has his cabinet, so the Secretary shall have his advisers. I would have the Secretary, without restricting his executive discretion, surrounded by advisers of competent professional knowledge, who would prevent blunders, expose errors, and furnish light if the Secretary have only eyes; or, if he had light, give him greater light. The weaker he is, the more he wants it; the wiser he is, the more he will prize and profit by it.

The very foundation of the American system of government is an executive head, with a council of advisers around him. In view of the great errors and blunders that have been committed by the present administration of the Navy Department, I endeavor to apply that same system to the Secretary of the Navy so as to surround him with professional advisers who may save him from repeating the errors of the past by mere caprice, by mere blundering, or by mere carelessness or haste. If he had the genius of Napoleon Bonaparte he would need advice, and if he were as wise as Napoleon before empire crazed him he would seek and not decline it. Those who are familiar with the great history of the Consulate and Empire know that in his earlier and better days, when he exhibited greater administrative capacity than any man who had ruled France since the days of Richelieu, he adopted no great measure of war or peace, of diplomatic policy or internal administration, until it had been debated fully, freely, and deliberately by his council around him. The fruits of that consultation appeared in the judgment which closed the sitting, and in the event which consolidated France and revolutionized Europe. It was only when an insane ambition—as a smaller ambition here leads people to discard advice and avoid professional advisers, and inflict on this land all the evils of personal rule—only when an insane ambition had lured him on to the conquest of Europe, and his projects would not stand discussion even in his own private councils, that the campaign of Russia and the invasion of Spain were determined on, without consultation, in spite of remonstrances now sunk to whispers, on mere fancies of his own imagination; and he followed them to his ruin. It is thus all merely personal government must end, and it is from mere personal irresponsible rule the navy is now suffering. If Napoleon could take advice, certainly Mr. Welles should not be above it.

If he needed counselors around him, I submit that Mr. Fox is not a sufficient counselor for the Secretary of the Navy.

Now, what do I propose? First, that professional officers shall be appointed by the President. Next, that they shall advise the Secretary of the Navy on every matter relating to naval administration, naval legislation, and the application of the naval force in time of war. It does not compel him to follow, it gives him the privilege of taking the advice of this Board. But on the great subjects that involve vast expenditures, the organization of navy yards, the structure of new vessels, the forms of iron-clads, the adoption of new machinery, the pursuit of new investigations in new departments of inquiry, on these subjects the bill says, not that the Secretary shall be bound to come to the same conclusion with the Board, but that he shall come to no conclusion, and shall make no order, until he has taken the advice of this Board. Tell me what harm advice can do him. It does not divide the responsibility. It does not delay his judgment. It does not control his conclusions. It puts light around him, and then leaves him to take the way to ruin if he sees fit to do so, on his responsibility before the American people, with the advice which he has had, and which we have provided for him, lying printed beneath his eyes to condemn or to justify him.

The honorable gentleman who heads the Naval Committee [Mr. Rice, of Massachusetts] has informed us that boards have been organized from time to time by the Navy Department for its assistance, and that that is done continually. Then, sir, if the Department, at its discretion, feels the necessity of advice, why should not the country have the benefit of the experience of men responsible to it, appointed under the law by the President and confirmed by the Senate, whose opinions shall stand before the country, instead of having a commission, packed for the occasion, responsible to no law and no person, but simply executing the Secretary's will or caprice? Why should we not have this Board, instead of one to be summoned, as in the case of the additional expenses of the Dictator, for the purpose of revising the decision of another Board, and of coming to a conclusion more satisfactory to the Department—the results of their adverse judgment known only by accident, and after Congress, in ignorance of their findings, had improvidently ratified the reckless extravagance of the Department for "the honor and interest" of the government?

The committee treat my observations on their hunt for a navy yard as an imputation on them. Nothing is farther from my meaning. My complaint at the loss of their services in the House was wholly playful; but the argument which pointed my remark was sharp and direct, and that they evaded under cover of a personal complaint. Gentlemen have treated this measure as an imputation on the Committee. Perhaps they did not understand the point of my argument; they did not answer it. It was that the Committee on Naval Affairs conceded, last session, the necessity of advice by constituting themselves a Board of Admiralty for the Secretary of the Navy. If they thought he needed advice, and that they were competent to advise him on the choice of navy yards, is not a board of naval officers as competent and as necessary to give advice upon the great questions of naval administration?

But, in the pursuit of their argument, derived from the experience of the Board of Admiralty in England, the honorable gentlemen brought themselves, I think, into divers inconsistencies. They even attempted to play on our prejudices in favor of American genius. They are not more American than I am. They attempted to awaken the susceptibilities of this House by imputations that I had depreciated the enterprise of the American navy. Mr. Chairman, every officer of the American navy knows that I am pleading his cause; and if I do not give the names of officers of the first position in the navy who hang breathless on the passage of the measure, it is because the Assistant Secretary of the Navy says that courts-martial are organized *to convict.*

But, sir, let us pursue the argument on the question of the English Board of Admiralty. Notwithstanding this perpetual American gasconade about the performances of the Monitor in Hampton Roads, which, we are told, according to English authority quoted here, has made all their ships useless, neither France nor England has built a single monitor; and that was in 1862, and we are now in 1865. Russia has built thirteen monitors, we are boastfully told. When did Russia become a naval power whose opinions could instruct Americans on a question of naval armament? Sir, I may have said bitter things in the course of my observations, but I said nothing so bitter and so insulting to the American navy or the Navy Department as that.

But the honorable gentleman from Maine [Mr. Pike] informs

us that English authorities declare "that all their broadside vessels of the iron-clad class, like the Warrior, will have to be built over." Yet there they stand unchanged. England still adheres to her system of broadside iron-clads as tenaciously as she holds to the "exploded" Board of Admiralty. I suppose that we shall next be told that England is no naval power, because she has changed neither the organization of her Navy Department nor the structure of the iron-clads that she has built.

The honorable gentleman has cited another authority, Sir Charles Napier, one of the Napiers so proverbial for their quarrels in both branches of the English service. But what does he complain of? Unfair promotion and lack of responsibility. Will the gentleman ask any officer of the navy of the United States whether he thinks the promotions in our navy are fair? That is a most unfortunate topic for the honorable gentleman just now, that the Department has organized the Board of promotions, on which its malice has excluded the officers of the South Atlantic Squadron from the representation accorded every other squadron. Where is any responsibility? Who is responsible for any thing that is done? For we have a head that does nothing, and the active power under him, irresponsible, that does every thing.

Then the same honorable gentleman quoted a high English authority as saying that it would be an outrage to send men into action in wooden vessels. Why does he cast such an imputation upon the head of the Navy Department, that sent Farragut to Mobile and Porter to Fort Fisher in wooden vessels, and is now building a whole fleet of them, with engines alone costing $400,000 and $600,000 each?

But a word on the question of iron-clads abroad. The "American idea," as it is called, embodied in the Monitor and the Dictator, has hitherto produced nothing that will cross the ocean. The New Ironsides, that will cross it, is not on that American idea, but a copy of the Warrior. And, whatever opinions of magazines or officers the gentleman from Maine may quote, it is not true either that England or France has adopted the American idea, or abandoned as failures the Warrior or La Gloire. Against those hasty suggestions I quote and prefer the opinion of an American naval constructor, whom the gentleman from Maine so justly eulogized, the great naval constructor of the United

States, Lenthall, to whom we are indebted for our great superiority in the structure of our wooden vessels. He does not think that the iron-clads of either England or France are a failure, but does think that we have nothing to oppose them. Here are his words:

"For the protection of our coasts and harbors we are probably well prepared; but we have only three vessels that can pretend to cope with the sea-going iron-clad vessels of European nations, and these have not yet been tried. It is a problem to be yet resolved whether a large steam vessel, with her deck a foot or two above water, and without sails, can be effective and use her guns as a cruising ship. Experience has shown that as ships increase in dimensions and weight there must be a certain relative portion above the water—that is, the height of the guns from the water should be increased; but this may, to some extent, be modified by making sacrifices in some other qualities.

"The accounts we have of the performances of the iron-clad European vessels, if to be relied on, show that the elevated position of their armor-plating has not seriously affected the motion of the vessels, and some of them are represented as being easier than ordinary vessels. Their large dimensions have much influence in this; but our principal harbors do not permit us to have so great a draught of water as European vessels have, which is stated to be from twenty-six to twenty-seven feet."

Now, sir, with reference to the iron-clad navies of France and England, abandoned upon the mere rumor of the impossible Dictator, let me read again:

"Until such time as it becomes the policy of the government to build iron-armed vessels for sea service—and, whenever commenced, it will require some years to have them in sufficient number to keep an enemy from our coast—we must have recourse to plating wood vessels, of which the first cost may appear less, though it is certain to be more expensive in the end.

"Unless we have armored sea-going ships"—

not Monitors, not Dictators, not Dunderbergs, but armed sea-going ships—

"we must give up the expectation of engaging our foes on the ocean, and must limit our operations to attacks on their commerce with fast and light-armored vessels."

That is the judgment of our great naval constructor upon the extent to which the *American idea* of *monitors* has affected the sea-going iron-clads of Europe. He declares that we must go to work and build iron-clads of the same class, if we contemplate meeting them on the ocean in battle array.

I will not repeat what I quoted from Admiral Porter about the New Ironsides—the only vessel of that kind in the navy—

the best he ever saw for aggressive purposes, the counterpart of the Warrior; so that the Warrior class can not be a failure, if she is not. But I can not refrain from invoking against the Department and the gentleman from Maine the judgment of Dahlgren, who went to Charleston to do impossibilities, and staid there two years without accomplishing them;. who went there to show that monitors could take forts, and has taken none. Though he was pledged by his appointment to a judgment in favor of the administration wherever it was possible, his scientific judgment could not be so deluded as to overlook the great power of this form of vessels. He ventures no opinion on the monitor form for sea-going cruisers, apologetically refuses a judgment on the general merits of iron-clads of that class, but gives the palm of superiority for aggression to the form which the gentleman from Maine supposes the monitors have superseded.

"The Ironsides is a fine, powerful ship. Her armor has stood heavy battering very well, and her broadsides of seven eleven-inch guns and one eight-inch rifle has always told with signal effect when opened on the enemy. Draught of water about fifteen and a half to sixteen feet. Speed six to seven knots, and crew about four hundred and forty men.

"Just as they are, the Ironsides is capable of a more rapid and concentrated fire, which, under the circumstances, made her guns more effective than the fifteen-inch of the monitors."

He, pledged by his appointment to a judgment in favor of the administration of the Navy Department, as far as it is possible to bend his scientific judgment to meet the expectations of the Department, can not be so used as to put out of sight the great power of this form of vessel, or to venture an opinion in favor of monitors beyond the special circumstances of war. He says this corroborates in every particular the statement of Admiral Porter read by me, that that vessel, constructed on that model, came more perfectly up to his idea of those intended for aggression than any other he had ever seen.

Now, sir, I agree with the honorable gentlemen of the committee that we can not adjust these conflicting authorities. But here stands the great fact, that while the great clamor across the water exaggerates the effect produced by the attack of the Monitor upon the Merrimac, it has not changed the course of European structure; it has not produced a single monitor in the ports of France or England; and the judgment of our naval officers is in conflict with the opinions quoted from abroad, responsible or irresponsible, by the gentleman from Maine, but conforms to the official judgments of France and England, that vessels of the Ironsides class are neither a failure, nor inferior to the American idea embodied in the monitors. I prefer the judgment of American naval officers to the judgment of English naval officers, and still more to the clamor of English magazines; and in any legislation for the benefit of the navy I should consult their judgment, and not a criticism of the English Board of Admiralty, which is not analogous to the one I propose. Arguing from one to another is merely for the purpose of misleading the judgment of the House, or because gentlemen did not understand the bill they are criticising.

Now, Mr. Chairman, I do not contemplate following either of the gentlemen through their arguments, in which they evaded every thing that was to be answered, and controverted many things which were not asserted. But I desire to say, when my honorable friend on my right [Mr. Rice, of Massachusetts] spoke of the swiftness of the Eutaw—as if that in the least degree controverted my statements in reference to war vessels of the navy, and not to those river boats, as I termed them—he was introducing a topic I had not touched. I did not mean to say one word in respect to the speed of those vessels, because I considered them set out of the account as naval vessels. But the honorable gentleman must not suppose that I can allow to pass his statement of the performance of this vessel in smooth river water, without her provisions, without her ammunition—I do not know whether she had her armament—certainly without her full load of coal, under none of the conditions of a vessel going to sea, subjected to no collision with the waves, as if I accepted that as a test of the power of the same vessel at sea.

Mr. Rice, of Massachusetts. Does the gentleman want to hear the report of Admiral Porter in reference to sea-going of that vessel?

Mr. Davis. The report will show what I state to be correct; but no form of machinery of a paddle-wheel steamer can be protected, and therefore none of these vessels are war vessels.

But, sir, what I meant to refer to now, though not covered by my former remarks, is this: that it will appear that after the explosion of the Chenango in New York Harbor, killing and wounding nobody can tell how many of our sailors, an investigation took place before the Coroner, who, after a full investigation upon the evidence, stated the result of the evidence to the jury; and it went to show conclusively that the boilers placed in this vessel, and others of her class, which were condemned by the Board of Engineers summoned by the Navy Department were so liable, by their peculiar structure, to exhaust the water in the boiler, that it was dangerous to run the vessel with open ports or full power. And that was proved by the officers of the vessel themselves.

I now send to the Clerk to be read an extract from that investigation.

The Clerk read as follows:

"It is apparent that the engineer corps of the navy, as well as the persons whose plans are involved, have a deep interest in assigning some other cause than low water, since, if it were low, it must have been so either from the carelessness of engineers, or from inherent defects in the organization which baffled the ordinary skill of such persons as had the machine in charge; yet no attempt has been made to explain away the melted lead, or to reconcile its presence with the fact that there was enough water in the boiler. And as this is the ordinary cause of explosion, it would seem consequently the true one here, particularly since no evidence of any sort has been produced to substitute any other cause; and we are left to the mere suggestion, without proof, that possibly the braces might have been taken out by Mr. Cahill and not replaced, or possibly the cold-water test, which experience has shown to be infallible, has in this case proved a snare. Unfortunately there are other facts, which point out very clearly the existence of an organic disease in these vessels, requiring the utmost vigilance to guard against, the presence of which is abundantly proved. A number of these vessels are just now coming out, and it so happened that on Saturday, the 16th, the day after this explosion, the Pautuxent, having been run for ninety-six hours at the dock, was taken out on a trial trip from Providence. In the course of the run it became necessary to shut off the steam from the engine from some cause, and thus the fact appeared that the water, which had seemed to be abundant in the gauges, was low. Mr. Baker, an experienced engineer, who sat up and ran the engine on her ninety-six hours' trial, at once had the fires drawn from the furnaces as a measure of safety, the necessity of which, under the circumstances, Mr. Sewell admitted to you when on the stand; and it was found that the steam-pump required twenty-two minutes to resupply the boiler with the water found wanting, although the gauges had given no warning of its absence. But for Mr. Baker this accident would have probably had its counterpart; and so convinced of the danger of the machine was Mr. Baker, that he refused to come to New York in the vessel unless he had the control given him; and he has told us these facts, and sworn to the danger.

"On the Chenango, the experienced engineers who ran the engine at the dock have told us that they considered their lives in danger from the liability to low water, and so convinced were they of it that they refused to open wide the throttle valve, though the United States engineers who were present insisted that the contract required the engine to be run wide open. Mr. Smith, the engineer who erected and ran the engine of the Metacomet, another of the same class, has proved here that the water could only be kept in her boilers by so setting the valves that when those valves were ordered by Mr. Sewell to be set so as to open wider, and the vessel was run from the shop to the navy yard, the water worked so that the valves had to be put back to the original position, which was done by himself at the navy yard, under orders from the chief engineer of the ship. The drawings of these engines have been produced before us, and the measurements made of the cubic feet of vacant space which existed in these cylinders between the valves when they are closed and the piston when at the extreme end of the cylinder nearest the closed valves, and it appears that these spaces are great enough to hold more than sixteen hundred pounds of water at a revolution before they will be filled so as to arrest the motion of the piston as it approaches the end of the cylinder, and compel the opening of the relief valves, which are placed in each end of the cylinder to prevent the destruction of the engine by the confinement of the solid water in the cylinder; yet it appears here that even more than this quantity of water would at times come over from the boiler at a revolution, and that these self-acting relief valves had to be opened constantly by hand, to permit the escape of this enormous quantity of water more freely than it could be voided by the self-acting valves. When it is considered that only about nine pounds of water in the shape of steam are needed to make the ordinary revolution of these engines, and that at times they draw even more than three quarters of a ton of water at a revolution, it is very easy to show how the boilers might be robbed of their water in a very few minutes, and the attention of an ordinary man be eluded.

"The coal burned by the Chenango on her trial has been proved, and the amount of steam which that coal produced has been measured on the indicator diagrams which were taken on the trials, by which it is proved that in the form of steam these boilers only evaporate from three to four pounds of water to the pound of coal, whereas if they did not use up the heat by carrying it off from the boiler in hot water, they would evaporate seven or eight pounds of water into steam; and it is testified to here, and the calculations show upon the indicator diagrams themselves, that these engines must have been working out of the boilers, in water, on an average, during the ninety-six hours of the trial, about six times as much hot water as steam. Of the accuracy of such calculation, based upon comparing the weight of coal burned with the cubic feet of steam used by the engine, you are perhaps better judges than I am; but it is to be remarked that these calculations have been on the table for several days challenging contradiction, and that they are not disputed. It is farther proved here that a considerable number of these vessels, exactly like the Chenango, have been recently built and tried, and that they are now awaiting orders for sea; yet no witness has appeared before us to say that any of the other of these vessels have operated differently from those whose performance has been proved; although there is no want of proof that when these boilers are arranged with a high steam space above the ends of the tubes, and a steam chimney, they do not work out their water. It would have been much more instructive to us if the engineers who have run so many of these low-roofed boilers had been produced, instead of those whose only experience has been with boilers not liable to that difficulty.

"It is not very surprising, perhaps, that among the great number of vessels used by the United States and placed in the hands of young men who have had but little experience, and who are employed when there is a scarcity of engineers, on account of the great demand for the services of such men suddenly made by the navy, that an explosion should occur at some time; and if the machinery were of the ordinary kind, the accident would excite no unusual interest. But when it occurs on machinery peculiar in its construction, and which had been condemned as inferior by an official board of the most eminent engineers in the country; and when it appears that those peculiarities have so exhibited their dangerous qualities as to alarm practical and scientific men, and to induce them to foretell an accident of this kind; and when we find these peculiarities existing on a greater number of other vessels just coming into use, upon which the lives of our fellow-citizens are to be intrusted, then it is of serious consequence, and demands of us to raise a voice of warning in time to prevent any more such horrors as we have witnessed. Our brave men, who are willing to expose their bosoms to the enemy's shot, ought not to be subjected to the chances of a horrible death at the hands of their own friends, and in their own floating homes."

Mr. DAVIS, of Maryland. So much for the boilers of the double-enders.

Two gentlemen of the Naval Committee have made great complaint that I imposed upon them last year a burden too heavy to be borne in the resolution of inquiry I introduced relative to steam machinery. Mr. Chairman, when I referred that resolution to the Naval Committee, I thought I was paying them the highest compliment I could bestow, for I supposed I was sending a resolution to a committee which, from its connection with the Department, would have the best means possible of information, and from their devotion to the interest of the navy would prosecute their inquiry with energy and thoroughness, and give us the full benefit of their judgment. It related to the same matter investigated in part by the Board of Engineers organized by the Department in 1863, and disregarded by the Department. It was intended to save the ruin of the machinery of the navy, to bring it to the test of science and knowledge; and the topics which were to be inquired into could have been inquired into effectually as well in the course of two weeks as in the time which has elapsed from the day that resolution was brought in down to the day the committee brought in their report about a week ago. There was a few topics, and only a few, requiring investigation, which the examination of half a dozen engineers would have settled almost immediately, and the Department and this House would have had the results of this investigation upon that subject in time to act upon it.

But, on the contrary, what do we find? The stupendous diligence of the gentlemen of that committee had absorbed all their leisure time from the day of the reference of the resolution down to the day, I think, before the motion made by me to append this amendment to the Navy Bill. An immense mass of testimony—twenty hundred pages—was introduced, which nobody can possibly read, which nobody can possibly consider. Their report came here, and has not yet been printed. It is worth now substantially, no matter how wise or correct the resolution to which the committee came, just as much as the paper upon which it will be printed, because during the time that the investigation was being carried on the Department had been building the very machinery that it was intended to test, and correct, and examine. Just as the Department has kept an investigation going on to verify the results of the engineers appointed in February, 1863, still diligently at work in November, 1864, and all the time, the Department, since February, 1863, has been building the machinery; so that, without its being intended to have that effect by the gentleman making that investigation, exactly the same result has been accomplished—that is to say, the government does not get the advantage of that investigation at all; but, while the investigation has been lumbering on, every machine-shop in the country has been ringing with the construction of the very machinery which is in question. In a word, both investigations have been a mere screen to the Department, giving impunity to its gross abuse of the public confidence.

Mr. GANSON. I would ask the gentleman if it would not be a more direct and reliable mode of obtaining information to have the head of the Naval Department upon this floor?

Mr. DAVIS, of Maryland. I answer that question with very great pleasure. If the information were in the head of the Department, I would say yes. (Laughter.)

Mr. GANSON. I would ask the gentleman if he has found that it is *out?* (Laughter.)

Mr. DAVIS, of Maryland. I fear the gentleman does not give me credit for as much acuteness as I flattered myself I possessed. I had found that out long ago. (Laughter.)

I take leave of this digression.

Sir, I submit that this measure must be determined on its merits. Gentlemen can not escape responsibility before the country by saying that I proposed it out of ill temper; nor that a vote for it might disturb *their relations* with the Department; nor that their appointments might be interfered with; nor that it might diminish their capacity to serve their constituents with the head of the Department, whom the gentleman from Missouri [Mr. Blow] eulogized so strenuously, I take it, in order to procure favor for his navy yard at Carondelet. These arguments can not support them before the country, and they are dangerous arguments to go into a political contest on. I ask a vote upon the measure I propose, not upon my disgust at the Department; I ask the vote upon the public considerations which must determine the judgment of the country that the measure is right or wrong. I ask gentlemen to say whether they think the Navy Department has been managed so during this war that no advice can improve it. I ask whether they are content that the American commerce shall have been swept from the ocean by five rebel privateers, with six hundred cruisers in our navy to catch and destroy them. I ask them if they think that American commerce can live if this is what we call an energetic and wise management of the Navy Department. If we give the navy a chance to live, and a voice in its own preservation, we may rescue our commerce from destruction; and when we are called upon to meet a grand naval power on the ocean, we shall not be driven to imitate the plundering warfare of the rebels, and, shunning our armed enemies, go mousing over the ocean for their defenseless commerce, but, like a great power, meet our foes in arms, and dictate terms of peace on the water as well as on the land. When gentlemen shall take steps to do that, America will be a power; but as long as Congress will not assert its supremacy over the Departments, and prescribe such organization of them as will give this nation the benefit of its resources, so long as Congress stops to inquire what the Departments wish instead of imposing on them what the interest of the nation requires, we will be powerless before the nations of the world.

Mr. Chairman, I wish to say that I am here to-day pleading the cause of the American navy against the Navy Department. I am saying what four out of five of the officers of the navy would say had they a voice in this House. I say what the ablest and leading men of the navy would say to-day through the newspapers, were it not that the fear of exposure makes the Department despotic. Gentlemen quote here the opinions of the officers of the British navy against the administration of their navy; but who in our navy dare say any thing against our Navy Department? Have we not seen one of the most distinguished officers of our navy, Admiral Wilkes, for controverting statements in the report of the Department seriously affecting his honor as an officer, dragged before a court? Was that court organized "to convict," in the language of the Assistant Secretary of the Navy? He was dragged before a court for vindicating himself and his own administration of the squadron under his command, and subjected to three years' suspension from service—a cruel and disgraceful persecution, such as has never before tarnished the administration of the American navy. Sir, this system of tyranny in the Department deprives the country of the benefit of the opinion, and advice, and judgment of the officers of the navy upon the structure and organization of the American navy. They are always ready to risk their lives and shed their blood on any thing that will float, but they shrink from advising the country for the benefit of the navy at the expense of a trial by a court organized to convict. Let them have a voice in the making of the vessels they are to navigate; let them have a voice in the selection of the artillery they are to use; let them have a voice in advising where they shall be sent. Had this been done, the Alabama's career would have been shorter and less disastrous. The coal dépôts and other necessities of navigation, the lines of commercial transit, the passes of the seas pointed out where the rebel cruisers must go from any given point, and any competent board could have devised a plan to meet and destroy them. Under the spasmodic guesswork by which the Alabama was pursued by this Department for four years, our commerce was swept from the ocean, sent to the bottom, or driven under foreign flags. Rebel cruisers burnt our ships not merely on distant seas, but almost within sight of the American coast; and then the Department telegraphed to the navy yards, and all the newspapers were filled with eulogies of the marvelous diligence of the Department in setting vessels afloat to catch the rebel cruisers. The seas swarmed with vessels sent to the spot where the burning took place, and came back to report that the rebel cruisers were not there, and that nothing was found but the ashes of the conflagration. That system, sir, is one which could not have existed had there been competent professional advisers around the Secretary. His own patriotism; his feeling for his country's cause; the vain clamor of New York merchants; their cry to him to spare their commerce, would have compelled him to listen, if the law had only clothed a board of officers with the right to speak, free from the danger of courts-martial organized to convict. It is that great deficiency that I am now trying to remedy. I am not influenced by any estimate of the personal value of the present Secretary, or of any other Secretary of the Navy. Be he as respectable as he may, be he as able and upright as he may, be he as honest and efficient as he may, I would not waste five minutes of the precious time of this House in eulogizing or condemning him. I look beyond men to measures. I look beyond the head of the Department to the great country which that Department represents. I look beyond the brief and flitting moments of his official life, now rapidly drawing to a close—if the prayer of every naval officer can be heard—to the day when the American nation will have to vindicate its power before the nations of the world now insidiously seeking our ruin, not by stealthy depredations on unarmed traders, but with a navy bearing proudly the banner of the republic over the seas, worthy to meet in arms the armed foes of the thirty millions of united Americans whose freedom and empire it guards, and able to prove on some great historic day that the republic can neither be torn asunder by internal dissensions nor browbeaten by the coalesced monarchies of Europe. (Applause on the floor.)

RECONSTRUCTION OF THE REBEL STATES.

On the 21st of February, 1865, the bill for reconstructing the governments in the States lately in rebellion, reported from the joint committee on that subject, was under consideration in the House. Various amendments were offered, proposing that senators and representatives should not be received from those States until *Congress should first declare that a just local government* had been organized therein, and such State entitled to representation in Congress, or until a Constitution had been adopted, guaranteeing to *all persons* freedom and equal rights before the law. A motion was then made to strike out the enacting clause of the bill. The bill, as reported by Mr. Davis from the committee, provided for the appointment of a provisional governor by the President in eleven States declared in rebellion, who were to carry out in those States, by the military aid of the United States, the provisions of the act. It provided for the assessment and collection of taxes from the year next preceding the overthrow of the recognized State government; for the complete freedom—*in fact*, enforced by United States authority—of *all persons* heretofore held to labor; for the enrollment of all white male citizens over twenty-one of such States, with a view to the election of a Legislature, when the *majority of such citizens* should take the oath prescribed, and not before; and the reconstruction, through such Legislature, of its relations with the federal government.

Various substitutes and amendments were proposed, and finally, in lieu of the bill, another was offered by the committee, providing that *all citizens of the United States* of the age of twenty-one years (omitting the words white residents of the State), and all such honorably discharged from the military or naval service of the United States, together with the loyal citizens enrolled as aforesaid, and who shall take and subscribe the oath of allegiance to the United States, shall be electors, and may vote for delegates for the Convention (to restore the relations of the State), but excluding therefrom any person who held *any* office under the rebel usurpation, and from voting also at such election.

Upon this bill and amendments offered, Mr. Davis closed the debate, on the 21st of February, 1865, as follows:

Mr. Speaker,—I merely rise to state the case for the House. If I can find voice enough to do that, I shall have accomplished as much as I expect.

The bill, which is now the test to which amendments are pending, is the same bill which received the assent of both houses of Congress at the last session, with the following modifications to suit the tender susceptibilities of gentlemen from Massachusetts: 1st, the sixth section, declaring rebel officers not citizens of United States, has been stricken out; 2d, the taxation clause has been stricken out; 3d, the word "government" has been inserted before "trial and punishment" to meet the refined criticisms of the two gentlemen from Massachusetts, who suppose that penal laws could be in force, and operative, when the penalties were forbidden to be enforced; that discriminating laws could survive the declaration that there should be no discrimination between different persons in trial and punishment. There has been one section added to meet the present aspect of public affairs; that section authorizes the President, instead of pursuing the method prescribed in the bill in reference to the States where military resistance shall have been suppressed, in the event of the legislative authority under the rebellion in any rebel State taking the oath to support the Constitution of the United States, annulling their confiscation laws, and ratifying the amendment proposed by this Congress to the Constitution of the United States, before military resistance shall be suppressed in such State, to recognize them as constituting the legal authority of the State, and directing him to report those facts to Congress for its assent and ratification.

With these modifications, the bill, which is now the test for amendment, is the bill which was adopted by this House at the last session.

I shall not reflect upon the gentlemen of this House so far as to go into any argument to prove its authority to do what this bill proposes to do; its vote of the last session for this bill, word for word, is the sufficient proof of the right of this House to adopt it.

It is only the House itself that can reverse that judgment, and impeach the assertion of its own powers. Nor need I trouble myself to answer the arguments of the gentlemen who in the last session voted for this bill, who, in the quiet and repose of the intervening period, have criticised in detail the language, and, not stopping there, have found, in its substance, that it essentially violates the principles of republican government, and sanctions the enormities of the laws with which the existence of slavery has covered and defiled the statutes of every rebel State.

That these discoveries should have been made since the vote of last session, is quite as remarkable as that they should have been overlooked before that vote. But they were neither overlooked before, nor discovered since. The vote was before a pending election. It is the will of the President that has been discovered since.

It is not at all surprising, Mr. Speaker, that the President, having failed to sign the bill passed by the whole body of his supporters by both houses at the last session of Congress, and having assigned, under the pressure of events, but without the authority of the law, reasons, good or bad, first for refusing to allow the bill to become a law, and therefore usurping power to execute parts of it as law, while he discarded other parts which interfered with possible electoral votes, those arguments should be found satisfactory to some minds prone to act upon the winking of authority.

The weight of that species of argument I am not able to estimate. It bids defiance to every species of reply. It is that subtle, pervading epidemic of the time that penetrates the closest argument as spirit penetrates matter that diffuses itself with the atmosphere of authority, relaxing the energy of the strong, bending down the upright, diverting just men from the path of rectitude, and submitting the will and favor of the power for the will and interest of the people as the rule of legislative action.

It is an evil which can be remedied only by the people of the United States in the selection of their representatives; and when they send representatives here of stuff impenetrable to that subtle essence, then reason and not the executive wishes will eliminate them on the merits and necessity of legislative measures. Till then I despair of reaching the source of their conduct.

All I desire now to do is to state the case, and predict results from one course to the other. The course of military events seems to indicate that possibly by the 4th of next July, probably by December, organized and armed rebellion will cease to lift its brazen head in the land.

Disasters may intervene, errors or weaknesses may prolong the conflict, the proverbial chances of war may interpose their caprices to defer the national triumph, but events now point to the near approach of the end. But whether sooner or later, whenever it comes, there is one thing that will assuredly accompany it. If this bill do not become a law, when Congress again meets, at our door, clamorous and dictatorial, will be sixty-five representatives from the States now in rebellion, and twenty-two senators, claiming admission, and, upon the theory of the honorable gentleman, *entitled* to admission, beyond the power of argument to resist it; for peace will have been restored, there will be no armed power but that of the United States, there will be quiet, and votes will be polled under the existing laws of the State, in the gentleman's views.

Are you ready to accept that consequence? For if they come to the door of the House, they will cross the threshold of the House, and any gentleman who does not know that, or who is so weak or so wild as to suppose that any declaratory resolution adopted by both Houses as a condition precedent can stop that flood, had better put his puny hands across the flowing flood of the Mississippi and say that it shall not enter the Gulf of Mexico.

There are things, gentlemen, that are possible at one time, and not possible at another. You can now prevent the rise of the flood, but when it is up you can not stop it. If gentlemen are in favor of meeting that state of things, then do as has been so distinctly intimated in the course of this debate: vote against this bill in all its aspects, leave the door wide open, and let "our brethren of the South," whose bayonets are now pointed at our brothers' hearts, drop their arms, put on the seemly garb of peace, go through the forms of an election, and assert the triumph of their beaten faction under the forms of political authority, after the sword has decided against them. I am no prophet, but that is the history of next December if this bill be defeated, and I expect it not to become a law.

But suppose the other course to be pursued. Suppose the President sees fit to do what there is not the least reason to suppose that he desires to do; suppose that after he has destroyed their armies in the field, he should go farther, and do, as I think he ought to do, and what the judgment of this country dictates: treat those who hold power in the South as rebels, and not as governors and legislators, disperse them from the halls of legislation, expel them from executive mansions, strip them of the emblems of authority, and set to work to find out the pliant and supple "Union men," so called, who have cringed before the storm, but who will be willing to govern their fellow-citizens under the protection of the United States bayonets; suppose that the fruitful example of Louisiana shall spread like a mist over all the rest of the Southern country, and that representatives like what Louisiana has sent here, with such a backing of votes as she has given, shall appear here at the doors of this hall, whose representatives are they? I do not mean to speak of those gentlemen now here from Louisiana in their individual character, but in their political relations to their constituency. Whose representatives are they?

In Louisiana they are the representatives of the bayonets of General Banks and the will of the President, as expressed in his secret letter to General Banks. If you admit such representatives, you must admit, on the same basis and under the same influences, representatives from every State from Virginia to Texas. The Common Council of Alexandria—which has just sent two senators to the other House, and has ratified the amendment to the Constitution abolishing slavery in all the rest of Virginia, where none of them dare put his portly person—would be entitled to send ten representatives here, and two senators, to speak for the indomitable "Old Dominion." If the rebel representatives are not here in December next, you will have servile tools of the executive, who will embarrass your legislation, humble your Congress, degrade the name of republican government for two years, and then the natural majority of the South, rising indignantly against that humiliating insult, will swamp you here with rebel representatives and be your masters. These are the alternatives; there is no middle ground.

To meet that state of the case, the honorable gentleman who so ably heads the Judiciary Committee [Mr. Wilson] has proposed a *declaratory resolution*, and *that is all*—a declaratory resolution, with no provisions of law to execute it, with no power to arrest the flood at our door, a very bubble born amid the hubbub of the waters, and floating with the flood—that senators and representatives shall not be received from any State heretofore declared in rebellion, until a joint act or resolution of Congress shall have declared that they have organized a new government.

If they have elected their representatives, there is no power to prevent this House from admitting them, if they see fit to do it.

I hope I answer the gentleman intelligibly. But if such an election is held any where in any such State, it is an assertion of sovereign power without authority of law—it is rebellion itself; and this bill directs the President to disperse the electors, and prevent the election being held. If this law should be passed, and the President should sanction such an election, it would be an impeachable offense; and if he did not sanction it, the question would never be here to trouble us. I trust I have answered the gentleman intelligibly. Now a word upon the criticisms upon this bill, and I have done. Provisional governors are to be appointed. That is a point of objection to the gentleman from Massachusetts [Mr. Eliot], who first spoke, why such governors are appointed *now without law;* and all that we propose is that they *shall be under the responsibility of law*, and subject to the control and *confirmation of the Senate.* Provisional governors illegally appointed, and judges of provisional courts unknown to the law, and whose appointments have never been submitted to the Senate, are now usurping authority in Louisiana. The very landmarks of the law are swept from the land; my effort is to restore them, and to that the gentleman objects.

Why, sir, suppose this bill be not passed, suppose this machinery be as objectionable as the gentleman supposes, what is the alternative? The President remains in power, with no law to guide him. I am attempting to lay down a law for his guidance. The gentlemen prefer arbitrary will to a written law, and they can not avoid that statement of the issue.

Sir, when I came into Congress ten years ago, this was a government of law. I have lived to see it a government of personal will. Congress has dwindled from a power to dictate law, and the policy of the government to a commission to audit accounts and appropriate moneys, to enable the executive to execute his will and not ours. I would stop at the boundaries of law. When I look around for them I seem to be in a waste; they are as clean gone as the division-fences of Virginia estates from here to the Rapidan.

But the gentleman from Massachusetts [Mr. Dawes] said yesterday that by this bill we are reviving the hateful black laws of the South.

I drew the section that refers to that subject, and I am content to take upon my shoulders all the responsibility connected with the revival of all the laws that are revived by the bill which I had the honor at the last session to report, which both houses of Congress approved by their votes, which to-day I am here to maintain; I took some credit to myself for putting in a brief space the shortest possible declaration that all men should be equal before the law, when I drew the clause declaring that no law which recognizes the right to hold men in involuntary servitude shall be recognized, and that the laws for the trial and punishment of *white* persons shall apply to the trial and punishment of *all persons whatever*.

I had ignorantly supposed that if the negro had to be tried by the same court, under the same law, upon the same evidence, for the same crime, for no other crime, upon no other evidence, and by no other tribunal, I had come in those words as near annihilating the black laws of the South as gentlemen could have done if they had spent tomes in writing out the provision for that purpose.

But in order to meet the refined criticism of the gentleman from Massachusetts [Mr. Dawes] upon this bill, my friend from Ohio [Mr. Ashley] put our heads together, and, after great contortions of the brain, we thought we might possibly make the effectiveness of the law visible to gentlemen whose eyes had failed to discover the difficulties of the law of the last session, by inserting before the words "trial" and "punishment" the word "government." And as "government" means the provisions and execution of the law which defines the rights of persons and property, and other responsibility of men to the law, I take it that the gentleman will withdraw that objection now, and vote for the bill, because it does effectually, and even to his satisfaction, annul the laws to which he has objected.

But, says the gentleman [Mr. Dawes] who spoke yesterday, and the one who spoke several days ago [Mr. Eliot], "There is no time fixed within which the provisional governor must call upon the people to elect whether they will organize a State government or not." Certainly not, nor can there be any. It is necessarily left to the judgment of those whom we charge with the execution of the law. If the President shall appoint provisional governors who will not execute his bidding, nor take his word for it that the rebellion is suppressed, and that the people have sufficiently returned to their allegiance, then there is no remedy except to change the President, and that remedy, I fear, is impracticable.

I take the men we find in power, the men who must execute all the laws we pass, if they be executed at all, but the real grievance is not expressed. I prescribe a rule, and it is my imposing any rule that is the offense, and not the execution of it, nor any doubt about its meaning, still less the uncertainty of its beginning. There is no uncertainty. The bill says there shall be no government organized until armed resistance is suppressed, and the people have sufficiently returned to their allegiance, the test of which is to be, that a majority of the people have taken the simple oath to support the Constitution of the United States. But there are those who would leave one tenth of the people govern all the world. There are those who would organize into oligarchies, like the Common Council of Alexandria, to sack the blood of great States, degrade the character, and exasperate the temper of the people of proud commonwealths, and send their tools here to legislate for my constituents. Sir, my successor may vote as he pleases. But, when I leave this hall, there shall be no vote from the Third Congressional District of Maryland that recognizes any thing but the body and mass of the people of any State as entitled to govern them, and to govern the people that I represent. And they who may wish to substitute one tenth, or any other fractional minority, for that great power of the people to govern, may take, and shall take, the odium. Ay, I shall brand it upon them that, in the middle of the nineteenth century, in the only free republic that the world knows, where alone the principles of popular government are the rules of authority, they have gone to the Dark Ages for their models, reviving the wretched examples of the most odious governments the world has ever seen, and propose to stain the national triumph by creating a low, wretched, vulgar, corrupt, and cowardly oligarchy to govern the free men of the United States—the national arms to guarantee and enforce their oppressions; not by my vote, sir, not by my vote. If the majority of the people will not recognize the authority of the Constitution of the United States, what does the gentleman say who proposes these declaratory resolutions? That they shall come here without it? No, sir; but I would govern them for a thousand years first by the authority of the Constitution which they have defied, and will not acknowledge. And govern them how? Not by the uncontrolled will of this or any other President that ever lived, George Washington included. I would govern them by the laws that in the hours of their sanity they enacted, unaltered, excepting so far as the progress of events require that they should be altered, to the extent we have proposed to alter them in the bill, and no farther. I leave their own rules for their government—make the President appoint, under his official and public responsibility, the officers who are to execute them; and if they do not like to be governed in that way, let us trust that the prodigal will one day come to his senses, and, humbly kneeling before the Constitution that he vainly defied, swear before Almighty God that he will again be true to it.

That is my remedy for the grievance, that is what we propose. It is for this House to say whether it prefers arbitrary discretion or legal rule; whether it prefers that anarchy shall reign, or that law shall be supreme; whether it prefers that we shall be overrun by men who do not recognize the government, and who yet insist on taking part in our legislation, or whether it will erect a barrier now at this time to prevent the question being forced on our successors, who, wiser, it may be firmer, better republicans than we, will, from the mere fact of the pressure of the times and the clamor of the day, be absolutely incompetent to deal with those things which we now, before the event, can calmly and deliberately adjudicate. Sir, I have done.

A motion was then made to lay the bill and amendments on the table, which was carried by 91 to 64—27 not voting. A motion to reconsider this vote was laid on the table by 92 to 57. So the bill was finally disposed of.

SPEECH ON PROPOSING AN AMENDMENT TO THE MISCELLANEOUS BILL PROHIBITING THE TRIAL OF CITIZENS BY MILITARY COMMISSIONS.

THE trials of citizens by military commissions, especially within the States not in rebellion, where the courts of the United States were open, had from the beginning been opposed by Mr. Davis. He had, as early as December, 1861, in his speech at Brooklyn, protested against such misuse of power as tending to increase the strength of the enemies of the government, and to bring the administration into disrepute through an implied avowal on its part that the *laws of the land* did not provide an *adequate* remedy and punishment for those offenders, in favor of whom their mere trial by a military commission raised a sympathy, and the desire to relieve which inseparable from a view of oppression.

At the close of the Thirty-eighth Congress (March 2, 1865), when the Miscellaneous Appropriation Bill was on its final passage, Mr. Davis moved an amendment thereto (given below) prohibiting such trials, and spoke in support of his proposition as set forth in the following speech, being the last delivered by him in Congress:

SEC. —. *And be it further enacted*, That no person shall be tried by court-martial, or military commission, in any State or Territory where the courts of the United States are open, except persons actually mustered, or commissioned, or appointed in the military or naval service of the United States, or rebel enemies charged with being spies; and all proceedings heretofore had contrary to this provision are declared vacated; and all persons not subject to trial, under this act, by court-martial or military commission, now held under sentence thereof, shall be forthwith discharged or delivered to the civil authorities, to be proceeded against before the courts of the United States according to law. And all acts inconsistent herewith are hereby repealed.

I wish to say merely a few words in explanation of this amendment.

Mr. Chairman, I do not desire, at this period of the session, to detain the House even by an argument in favor of the amendment I have submitted. I desire to state merely what it contemplates, and to beg the House to give a direct vote upon it. It is a measure which touches the very foundation of republican government, the liberty of the citizen, nothing more, nothing less.

I do not think it is exclusively, perhaps not chiefly, the fault of those in authority that military commissions have tried, contrary to the Constitution and laws of the United States, many of its citizens. It began first in the rebel States, then spread to the border States, the theatre of armed conflicts, then invaded Pennsylvania, Indiana, and New York, amid the general acclaim of the people; and now that it reaches as far north as Boston, we hear the first murmur of its advocates or instigators. What that amendment contemplates is, not to cast imputation upon any administration or any officer, but, recognizing the error which the people, as well as the government, have in common committed against the foundation of their own safety, now, before the very idea of the supremacy of the law has faded from the country, to restore it to its power.

This amendment is confined rigidly to the loyal States, to the States in which the courts of the United States are open, to the States whose governments the United States guarantee, so that it does not strip the government of any power, legal or usurped, which it has thought necessary in its efforts to suppress the rebellion. It leaves every body to be tried by court-martial who is actually in the military service of the government, or who, being a rebel enemy, is arrested as a spy. But it annuls every thing that has been done heretofore under illegal military commissions, directs all persons now in illegal confinement under sentence of illegal military commissions to be either discharged, or delivered to the civil tribunals, to be there proceeded against according to law. There the amendment stops.

I desire to make an imputation on no one. This amendment is proposed for the benefit of every party and of every administration; and I trust that the House will allow it to be incorporated into this bill, that it may become the acknowledged, as it is now the supreme, law of this land and the right of the citizen.

Tellers were ordered; and Messrs. Washburne, of Illinois, and Davis, of Maryland, were appointed.

The committee divided; and the tellers reported—ayes, 50; nays, 65.

So the decision of the Chair was not sustained.

The question was upon the amendment of Mr. Davis, of Maryland, who spoke as follows:

Mr. Chairman, I appreciate the weight of the criticism of the distinguished gentleman from Pennsylvania [Mr. Stevens], and I am sure that nobody will say that I have ever embarrassed the proceedings of this House by any pertinacious adherence to schemes of my own. I have never embarrassed the House week after week by motions to tax or exempt whisky on hand. That would have been a more appropriate subject of criticism than such an amendment as this, which is never too early, and can never be too late, until the voice of liberty shall cease to be heard in the United States. Then it will be impertinent to arrest the progress of supplies for the government by calling the attention of the representatives of the people to the freedom of their constituents. Let this bill perish a thousand times rather than that any vote should go on the records of this House declaring that the protection of the liberties of the citizens of Massachusetts and citizens of Maryland are not of paramount importance to a vote of money for the violators of their rights. There has been no other period, sir, at which I could obtain the ear of the House on such an amendment. I have had my eye on the gradual intrusion of the military authority on the rights of the citizen from the outbreak of the rebellion. It was first instigated by the people; and the most eminent jurists of the land converted their clamor into the semblance of the voice of the law by maintaining the right of the President to suspend the *habeas corpus* without the authority of Congress—in the face of John Marshall's judgment. Gentlemen of the opposition, on this topic, have no right here to cast imputations on the administration. George B. M'Clellan first set the bad example in an order illegally suspending the writ of *habeas corpus* in Maryland. I refer to that not as an imputation on them, but because it shows that it is no party question with which we are dealing to-day, but an American question, a question of republican liberty endangered by the common madness of government and people. The evil has gone so far that to-day every man feels, without the necessity of an argument, that there must be a stop put to military trials of citizens in the States here represented, or there is no law or liberty in the land.

The honorable gentleman from Pennsylvania has said that these convictions have taken place under laws passed by Congress. I admit it in some cases; but that proves only that Congress is also guilty of the usurpation. And the honorable gentleman from Massachusetts [Mr. Dawes] has told us that the law which he introduced has failed to serve the purpose contemplated, while it has developed consequences of which he did not dream. The honorable gentleman says that it ought to be repealed; and if it ought to be repealed, then carry the remedy to the root of the grievance, and discharge the men who were convicted under what was in form a law, but in fact a usurpation which had not the authority of the Constitution.

But, sir, have prosecutions stopped within the limits of the acts of Congress? If they had, I could have heard with more patience the appeal of my honorable friend from Pennsylvania. But every one knows that they have not. We in Maryland have known it by sharp castigation now for three years. It is now being known in New York. And in Boston men have turned gray under persecutions not according to those laws.

But, sir, what do you say of trials for things that are not crimes under any law, for things that are not defined to be crimes, civil or military? What do you say to the trial of a loyal citizen in the city of Baltimore upon the charges and specifications which I hold in my hands, for forging Jefferson Davis's currency? One of my constituents *is now in jail under those specifications*, having been tried and condemned by a military tribunal for attempting to break down the rebel currency! I can state no other fact that will better illustrate the insolence of irresponsible military tribunals, known to no law, appointed under no law, restrained by no law, authorized by nobody, bound by no law but the will of the men who sit in their uniforms to try the rights of American citizens according to the law of the sword.

Mr. STEVENS. Do I understand the gentleman to say that this man was convicted on the ground of having counterfeited rebel currency?

Mr. DAVIS, of Maryland. He was condemned for that, and is now in jail.

Mr. STEVENS. Well, I think that a man who was fool enough to spend his time in such work ought to suffer some severe punishment.

Mr. DAVIS, of Maryland. If all fools are at the mercy of the military courts, and they are to judge of it, they have a wide jurisdiction. (Laughter.)

Then there is the case of Weisenfield. This man was not

charged with defrauding the government under the act of Congress; he never placed himself within the reach of the law to which the gentleman from Massachusetts has referred. He was charged, and in my judgment charged falsely, and convicted on testimony which no jury in the world, of any political complexion, would weigh an instant, of having sold a few hundred dollars' worth of goods to a government spy to be sent across the lines to the Southern Confederacy. That trial by military commission was authorized by no law known to any statute-book in the United States. The crime of trading with the rebel States is punishable by law only as giving aid and comfort to the enemy, and that is expressly directed to be tried and punished by *indictment* before the United States courts for a misdemeanor merely; but he now lies in a New York penitentiary, herding with felons, murderers, and thieves, though, if legally convicted before Chief Justice Chase, he could by law have been sentenced only to fine and imprisonment in jail!

I am daily beset by letters and solicitations of loyal gentlemen, my firmest and best personal friends in the world, to go to the President and beg as a boon that this man be *pardoned!* I have had no stronger pressure brought upon me since I have been in public life. My reply is, If a petition is gotten up for Mr. Weisenfield to pardon the President for his illegal oppression, I will sign it; but I will not degrade the name of an American citizen by signing a petition to beg as a favor the personal liberty of an American citizen, illegally and oppressively condemned by a military commission, and that at the hands of the President, who twice refused to refer his case to the courts of the United States, wide open for his protection, and in the face of the laws and Constitution of the United States subjected him to this illegal persecution.

Sir, let him stay where he is till the voice of public indignation or the whispers of conscience compel his honorable discharge—not his pardon. Till they who illegally confined him shall beg him to come forth.

Mr. Chairman, the alarming fact is this—military commissions do not even profess to be governed by the laws of the United States enacted by Congress. They have created a department of jurisprudence unknown to the laws of the United States, nowhere embodied in statutes or decisions, called the "customs of war." They try loyal men in loyal States, where no war rages, for a violation of what they call "*the usages of war.*" *Here are the pandects of the future empire of the United States*—the rulings of the Judge Advocate General on "the usages and customs of war," applied to peaceful citizens in loyal States where the courts are open, where the law alone ought to be the rule of every judgment and every conviction.

This invention of the law of "the usages of war" and "military offenses," applied to citizens and friends instead of enemies, annuls every act of Congress.

In vain does the act of the 3d of March, 1863, punish the aiding a soldier to desert by one not in the military service on legal conviction in the courts of the United States; in vain does the act of the 3d of March, 1863, punish fraudulent claims, false oaths, forged signatures, forging papers, embezzling United States property, false receipts for arms, purchasing arms from soldiers, when committed by a person in the military forces of the United States, on conviction by court-martial, and at the discretion of the court-martial, but in the third section declares that any person *not* in the military forces of the United States guilty of those acts shall forfeit certain fines and be subject to certain imprisonment on conviction in the courts of the United States; for the military commissions presume to punish every one of these acts committed by citizens in defiance of the law securing them a constitutional trial.

By the act of the 2d of March, 1831, forging pay certificates is punishable by the courts of the United States in the District of Columbia; yet a military commission punishes it within sight of the open court-house and of the President's mansion!

In vain the act of March 3, 1863, expressly directs a person guilty of resisting the draft to be arrested by the provost-marshal and to be forthwith delivered to the civil authorities, and, on conviction by them, subjects him to fine and imprisonment; the military commissions have annulled that law, and, instead of delivering the person to the civil authorities for trial, themselves hold and try, convict and punish him; and this where the courts of the United States are wide open, in this district where Congress sits in peace and enacts the laws which are thus defied!

If these things be not arrested, there is no law but the sword, no judge but the majority of a military commission holding their commission at the will of the President.

Now, sir, I have a word for the gentleman from Kentucky [Mr. Yeaman], who moved to include persons engaged in violating the rules and customs of war. Does that mean citizens of the United States in loyal States, where the courts of the United States are open, where their act is treason, for which the statutes of the United States say they shall be tried, on indictment, before the courts of the United States, and who, the Constitution says, shall be tried no otherwise than by a jury of the State and district in which the crime was committed, and convicted only on the testimony of two witnesses?

If it is notorious that they are guerrillas, why, in the name of conscience and common sense, can not that be made to appear to a jury of their loyal fellow-citizens, to be summoned by a marshal appointed by the President himself; prosecuted by a district attorney that he appoints; adjudged by judges who hold their office during life; many of them now even appointed by Mr. Lincoln, and all liable to impeachment by us and conviction by the Senate if not fit to administer justice? If it be a matter of doubt, then the prisoners are entitled to that doubt; and if it is so plain that there is no doubt, then any tribunal will convict. That is my answer to that proposed amendment.

In the first place, if three fourths of the State of Kentucky are subject to incursions of guerrillas, the other fourth is not, and that will furnish jurors enough. If there is room to hold a military court there is room to hold a civil court. If men are not afraid to go to testify before a military court they will not be afraid to go before a civil court. If bayonets are needed to protect them before a military court, bayonets can protect them before a civil court. Sir, this hankering after military courts is not because they can not be tried and convicted before the courts of the United States if guilty; but men mad with civil war want a sharper and easier way to deal with criminals as enemies. It is the cry for vengeance and not justice! That is what it is, and nothing else.

I live in a State that has never disgraced itself by rebellion, but it has been disturbed by internal dissensions; and I know the rancorous hostility which has grown up between men even of the same family. I do not wish military tribunals to apply their harsh, sharp vengeance between men who live on adjacent estates, at the instigation of personal revenge, of malice, without local public trial, unprotected by the rights secured to them by the

Constitution and laws of the United States, when a whispered lie may stain innocence with the penitentiary by the vote of two out of three of a military commission. If they have committed acts which render them dangerous, but are not criminal or can not be proved, we have authorized the suspension of the *habeas corpus*, and the President can *hold* them; not try, not convict, not disgrace, not degrade, not kill, but *hold them* under the precautionary discretion conferred by law, and rendered secure by the military power. If they have committed crimes known to the law which can be proved, and which it is desirable to punish, the President can prove it before the courts of the United States in Maryland, and they can be convicted in the courts of the United States in Maryland.

Now a word touching the amendment of my honorable friend from Ohio [Mr. Schenck], with whom I always differ with the greatest hesitation. Yet I think that his logic will bring him to this conclusion, that if the Constitution of the United States says that no one shall be tried for an infamous crime otherwise than by a jury of the State and district, except cases arising in the military or naval forces of the United States, any enactment which authorizes any one to be tried in any other way in the States where United States courts are open is itself void. The tribunal which tries a case not arising in the military forces in any other way is a trespasser, and the party who was convicted has a private remedy for the injury he has sustained if the court had no jurisdiction. No one can violate the right of the citizen to immunity from military trial safely, whether we declare it or not, and every one has his remedy to-day in the courts of the United States, in spite of any enactment, for every oppression.

Why, then, place a provision in the law declaring these proceedings to be void? In order that a loud voice should go out from this hall to the American people, ringing over the land, to announce by authority that their representatives recognize and declare the nullity of the proceedings of these military tribunals, and to encourage the people to seek redress in the courts of the country, not by crawling solicitations at the hands of the President of the United States, but of right, by law, before the courts, which are the glory and the safety of the American republic.

My honorable friend also wishes me to strike out that part of my amendment which provides that those not liable to trial by military courts now held under their sentences should be discharged, or delivered to the civil tribunals for trial. Sir, if it will satisfy any gentleman here, or remove any doubt or hesitation, I will most cheerfully agree that the word "discharge" shall be stricken out; so that the provision will stand that these men shall be delivered over to the civil tribunals to be proceeded against according to law—the American's birthright.

But it is objected by my honorable friend from Ohio [Mr. Schenck] that these men, having first disputed the jurisdiction of the military court, will, when brought before a civil court, plead their former conviction in bar. I know the eminent legal ability of my friend, and if he will run over in his mind the form of plea that must be made in such a case, he would find that it would be this: On a given day, at a given place, before A, B, C, a military commission convened by order of the President of the United States, I, a citizen not in the military service of the United States, was convicted for a violation of "the usages of war," or some crime known to the law, but punishable by statute only in the courts of the United States, and sentenced to punishment. My learned friend would be the first to put in a demurrer to such a plea. On the record it would appear that the military commission had no jurisdiction of the party; that he had not been *convicted* at all; that he had never been in jeopardy of life or limb; for the Constitution forbids such a tribunal to try such a person. The jurisdiction of every court, especially one of limited and exceptional jurisdiction, may be impeached collaterally, or must appear on its record; and the appearance of generals, and colonels, and captains, sitting at the will of the President, in place of venerable judges, whose tenure is good behavior, and the absence of a jury, show that it is not a court at all, but an unlawful combination of trespassers usurping the functions of a court, guilty of a crime, and not exercising an authority. Any court of the United States will, on *habeas corpus*, discharge a citizen confined under sentence of such a tribunal.

Let those now in illegal confinement seek that remedy; and if it be denied them, let an impeachment by the representatives of the people vindicate the rights of the people.

Mr. Chairman, the public safety never has required these illegal and summary trials; it now requires that they cease. The past men are ready to forget, the American people most of all; they instigated or tolerated the usurpations of those in authority; but they now have felt the sharpness of military justice, and demand of their rulers a return to the Constitution and laws. If heretofore they have violated the law and Constitution—I do not say criminally, I do not say with intent to oppress, I do not say even knowing it to be criminal—it was the common error; and they may plead the error of the people which misled the leaders of the people at the beginning of the rebellion. More firmness, more knowledge, more coolness in high places, might perhaps have arrested the popular current, and silenced the popular tumult, and kept the torrent within the bounds of law. It was not found in places of authority; all bowed before the storm; all floated with the current. It is in the power of the representatives of the American people alone to stop it before every vestige of American liberty is buried beneath the waters.

Sir, I am not willing to change one word of my amendment. It was not framed out of my own head, of my old-fashioned whims and fancies, now out of fashion in this era of gold lace and military vertigo. I had frequent consultations with some of the ablest members upon this side of the House, those most conspicuous for the ardor of their support of the administration, and they think with me that obstinate adherence to these abuses must destroy either the administration or the republic. If it would satisfy any one to strike out the word "discharge," I have no objection, because an American citizen is safe when delivered into the custody of the civil authorities, to be proceeded against according to law; but beyond that I do not feel disposed to modify my amendment in any particular.

Least of all can I accept the amendment of the gentleman from Iowa [Mr. Kasson], which enumerates the offenses for which citizens shall not be tried by military courts, and yields the whole principle by admitting that persons not in the military forces, in the States where the United States courts are open, may be tried for violating the "usages and customs of war;" it recognizes the category of military offenses committed by a citizen, an exception which would place your liberty and life, and mine, at the beck and call, at the will and pleasure of any military commission of officers too worthless for field service, ordered to try us, and "organized to convict." That amendment involves a total misapprehension of the whole question. It is not what offenses military courts may try, but what persons they may try for any offense. The Constitution forbids them to try any citizen for any offense.

I will not detain the House by narrating the individual cases of oppression that are fresh in my memory. There is no gentleman who does not know of such cases in his own neighborhood, and who has not felt this atmosphere of oppression around him. If there be, they are happier than we are in Maryland, or than they are in Massachusetts.

This measure is demanded by the feeling of the country, and in my judgment, if the House will now say that the liberty of the American citizen is of equal moment with the Miscellaneous Appropriation Bill, and will pronounce by such a vote as that by which it referred the resolution of the gentleman from New York [Mr. Ganson], with only three dissenting voices, to the Military Committee, that law is still supreme, every man in the United States will breathe freer, and bear himself more loftily, and look with assured joy to the day when armed rebellion shall be destroyed, to be followed, not by armed despotism, but by the peaceful reign of liberty and law; by submission, but not by servitude. (Applause on the floor and in the galleries.)

Mr. Farnsworth. Mr. Chairman, I rise for the purpose of opposing these amendments. In desperate emergencies vigorous measures are required. I am here for the purpose of sustaining with my voice and vote those measures adopted and put in force by the War Department in the punishment of culprits in any manner connected with the army. The gentleman from Maryland [Mr. Davis] has dilated largely on those things that have occurred in his own State. He has referred to the act of General M'Clellan. It is not necessary that I should say here that that act of his rendered his name more popular, brought him into more favor, and attracted to him more of the affection of the people of the country than any other act of his life. Is it not well known that when he ordered the arrest of the Maryland Legislature, that Legislature was convened for the very purpose of hurrying the State into secession and involving it in civil war? The gentleman refers to the arrests made in the city of Baltimore, and in Maryland. Has not the gentleman from Kentucky [Mr. Yeaman] told us that in many counties in his own district the civil law could not be enforced; that they have neither judges nor jurors who will enforce it, nor court-houses in which to hold their courts;

that they have been burned by secessionists? So it was in the city of Baltimore up to within two years since. I believe that two years ago a rebel could not be convicted in any court in that city. Those vigorous measures of the President and of the War Department are what saved Maryland from civil war and the country from destruction.

Mr. DAVIS, of Maryland. The gentleman will allow me to say that there would be more fear that a disloyal man could not have a fair trial in Maryland before a civil court, so intense is the desire to punish any thing looking like treason.

Mr. FARNSWORTH. That may be now, and is a very healthy feeling, but two years ago it was not so.

Mr. DAVIS, of Maryland. There was never a moment, sir, in which it was not so.

Mr. FARNSWORTH. There was a moment, sir, when any thing looking to the suppression of the rebellion was very unpopular in Baltimore. There was a time when both the civil and military arms of the government were powerless to preserve peace and order in the gentleman's own city. There was a time when Massachusetts soldiers, marching peacefully through that city to the rescue and defense of the capital, were ruthlessly set upon by the mob of secessionists, and murdered in the streets of Baltimore, and there was no power there to suppress the riot. There was a time when the authorities of Maryland, through their governor, made application to the President of the United States that no more troops should pass over the soil of Maryland, because the civil and military power of that State could not preserve order. Without the suspension of the *habeas corpus*, and without the vigorous measures put in force by the government, where would that State be to-day? Probably in the Union, but she would have been the seat of war, and her fair fields would have been desolated as are now the fair fields of Virginia.

Mr. DAVIS, of Maryland. Will the gentleman allow me to correct him?

Mr. FARNSWORTH. Certainly.

Mr. DAVIS, of Maryland. I desire to say that there never was a day when the people of Maryland were not masters of her fortunes, and masters of the capital of the United States, *and that Mr. Lincoln was inaugurated here only because they were loyal.*

Mr. FARNSWORTH. If that is the case, it seems to me there is a monstrous lie going the rounds of the country.

Mr. DAVIS, of Maryland. I think there is. The people of Maryland have been libeled from one end of the country to the other.

Mr. FARNSWORTH. It is well known that when the President came here to be inaugurated, four years ago, he was obliged to flee through the city of Baltimore like a stranger, in disguise, to avoid assassination.

Mr. DAVIS, of Maryland. The gentleman says the President had to flee through Baltimore. I say it may be that he *did* so; but a man of heroic mould would have marched through it safely.

Mr. FARNSWORTH. I regret exceedingly, Mr. Chairman, that my friend from Maryland, who has been, in the main, right, should now, in the last days of the session, surround himself by those who have been heretofore his enemies, and who now beslobber him with their praise. When a man on this side of the House puts himself in such a position as that the unworthy member from Maryland [Mr. Harris] congratulates him and smiles his praise on him for the speech he makes, and when the gentleman from Indiana [Mr. Voorhees] marches over here and takes him by the hand, and congratulates him for his assault on the administration, he ought to raise his hands toward heaven, and say, "My God! what have I done, that my enemies and the enemies of my country should praise me?"

Why, sir, how long is it since, in the city of Chicago, only the day before the last general election, a stupendous conspiracy was discovered? Among the plotters were persons of that city. They had conspired with the rebel prisoners in Camp Douglas, and with emissaries from the South, to release all the prisoners in Camp Douglas, put arms in their hands, and then sack and destroy the city of Chicago. Those men are now being tried before a military commission, and such facts have been proved against them; so thoroughly have they been fastened upon them that one or two of them have put an end to their own existence in despair, and in anticipation of their deserved doom.

Gentlemen are mistaken, it seems to me, as to the manner of conducting these courts-martial. Every particle of evidence taken before them is preserved in writing. The defendants have subpœnas issued for their witnesses, whose attendance is compelled, and all the testimony, *pro* and *con*, is taken by the judge advocate and the counsel of the defendants, for they are allowed to have counsel, and the testimony is preserved, and with the specification and findings is filed in the War Department, where it undergoes the careful supervision and review of Judge Holt, one of the ablest, most honest men in the country. The findings are thoroughly reviewed, and approved or disapproved, and the sentence carried out or not, according to that decision. These records go into the archives of the government, and can at any time be called for by this House, and be published to the world.

Now this amendment of the gentleman from Maryland [Mr. Davis] would let loose upon the country some of the very worst characters we ever had among us. It is not long since a resolution was introduced into this House, and adopted, instructing the Military Committee to examine into the military prisons in this city. The Military Committee made that investigation; they examined the prisoners and took testimony. And upon my soul—and I think every member of the Military Committee will agree with me in this—I do think that of all the rapscallions, of all the miserable, devilish tribe I ever saw in my life, they are those in the military prisons in this city. I have not heard of one of them, no matter how arbitrarily he may have been arrested, but he was properly arrested, for he was guilty.

[Here the hammer fell.]

March 3. The Committee of Conference having failed to agree, and the Senate insisting on its amendment, in the House the bill was defeated as follows:

Mr. DAVIS, of Maryland. I rise for the purpose of making a report of the Committee of Conference on the disagreeing votes of the two houses on the amendments to the Miscellaneous Appropriation Bill. If it be required the report can be read, but perhaps I can accomplish the same purpose by stating briefly and more intelligibly the substance of it.

Mr. Speaker, owing to an error on my part in reference to the chairmanship of the committee, it so happens that I took the notes of the conference instead of my honorable friend from New York [Mr. Littlejohn], and by his courtesy I make the statement of the result.

Having passed over the amendment which was the subject of controversy in the House until we reached this point, we then reverted to it, and found that there was a radical diversity of opinion, and perhaps an irreconcilable one, between the representatives of the House and those of the Senate. The gentlemen on the part of the Senate stated that while a majority of the Senate concurred in the principle involved in that amendment, yet that the majority of the Senate had refused *upon two votes, had deliberately determined not to pass the amendment as a part of this bill.* It was then proposed to them that they should take the section in the form in which it had passed the House, carry it into the Senate and pass it immediately as a separate bill, and send it to the House in order that we might act upon it immediately, upon which condition we were ready to have agreed to recommend the House to allow the bill to pass without this amendment. The gentlemen thought they could not accomplish that in the present state of feeling and temper of the Senate, and declined to make the effort.

Under these circumstances, it remained for a majority of the House committee to determine between the great result of losing an important appropriation bill, or, after having raised a question of this magnitude touching so nearly the right of every citizen to his personal liberty and the very endurance of republican institutions, and to insure its consideration fastened it on an appropriation bill, to allow it to be stricken out as a matter of secondary importance. The committee thought that their duty to their constituents, to the House, and to themselves, would not allow them to provide for any pecuniary appropriations at the expense of so grave a reflection on the fundamental principles of the government.

The situation is a grave one. The President has now by law—a law insanely passed by the last Congress, to repeal which this House early in its first session unanimously passed a bill which to this day the Senate has refused even to consider—the absolute authority to deprive every officer of the United States of his commission at his will, on his own judgment, and at his pleasure, or caprice alone. The law does not merely authorize, but it requests the President to use the power conferred.

There are laws upon the statute-book which subject to trial by courts-martial, composed of these officers, thus dependent upon the will of the President, large classes of our fellow-citizens.

The practice of the government has introduced into the jurisprudence of the United States principles unknown to the laws of the United States, loosely described under the general term of "the *rules and usages of war*," and new crimes, defined by no law, called "military offenses;" and without the authority of any statute, constitutional or unconstitutional, pointing these laws—confined by the usage of the world to enemies in enemies' territory—against our own citizens in our own territory, the government has repeatedly deprived many citizens of the United States of their liberty, has condemned many to death, who have only been redeemed from that extreme penalty by the kindness of the President's heart, aided doubtless by the serious scruples he can not but feel touching the legality of the judgment that assigned them to death.

There have been many cases in which judgments of confinement in the penitentiary have been inflicted for acts not punishable either under the usages of war or under any statute of the United States by any military tribunal; crimes for which the laws of the United States prescribe the punishment have been visited with other and severer punishments by military tribunals; violations of contract with the government, real or imputed, have been construed by these tribunals into frauds, and punished illegally as crimes; excessive bail has been demanded, and, when furnished, impudently reduced; and the attempt of Congress to discriminate between crimes committed by persons in the military forces and citizens not in those forces has been annulled, and the very offenses it specifically required to be tried before the courts of the United States have been tried before military tribunals dependent upon the will of the President.

The President, when petitioned humbly, has refused or neglected more than once to stop the illegal proceedings and submit the case to courts of the United States.

"*Courts-martial are organized to convict*" is the sinister declaration of the Assistant Secretary of the Navy, and the President still tolerates his presence!

That hand inserted, under the innocent title of a bill to increase the paymasters of the navy, a section subjecting every agent and servant of the Navy Department to trial by court-martial, which passed the Senate and the House without discovery or exposure, and now hangs on a motion to reconsider.

It was the settled purpose of oppression disclosed by that

act which occasioned this amendment, and forbids its abandonment.

The committee remember that such things are inconsistent with the endurance of republican government. The party which tolerates or defends them must destroy itself or the republic. They felt they had reached a point at which a vote must be cast which may break up political parties, or if it do not, will break up or save a great republican government. Before these alternatives they could not hesitate. They thought it best now, at this time, to leave this law standing as a broken dike in the midst of the rising flood of lawless power around us, to show to this generation how high that flood of lawless power has risen in only three years of civil war, as a warning to those who are to come after us, as an awakening to those who are now with us.

They have, therefore, come to the determination, so far as the constitutional privileges and prerogatives of this House will enable them to accomplish the result, that this bill shall not become a law if these words do not stand as part of it—the affirmation by the representatives of the States and of the people of the inalienable birthright of every American citizen; and on that question they appeal from the judgment of the Senate to the judgment of the American people.

Mr. LITTLEJOHN. Believing, sir, as I do, that this great republic could not have been given to posterity except by the exercise of the very power of which the amendment of my friend from Maryland [Mr. Davis] seeks at this time to deprive the executive, I agreed with the Senate committee, and it was our desire to report unanimously, advising that the House recede from its amendment. We could not agree, however, and hence we have narrowed down the question as much as possible. I propose therefore, if it be in order, that the House concur in the report of the Committee of Conference upon all except the amendment known as the Winter Davis amendment, and upon that I move that the House recede, so as to bring the question to a direct vote. And upon these motions I move the previous question.

Mr. DAVIS, of Maryland. I am in earnest in this matter, and am determined that not one item of this bill shall pass without the whole of it.

Mr. KASSON. I appeal to the gentleman to allow the appropriation for the insane to be made.

Mr. LITTLEJOHN. I agree with the gentleman from Maryland. I object to any such proposition. This whole bill must pass through, or none of it.

A determination being thus manifested that the bill should not become a law without the amendment securing citizens against trials by courts-martial, the House, after one or two dilatory votes, proceeded to other business till adjournment *sine die.*

LETTER ON RECONSTRUCTION.—UNIVERSAL SUFFRAGE.

To the rising of the Thirty-eighth Congress rapidly succeeded the events which astounded the country—the surrender of the rebel armies under Lee, the assassination of the President, the attempts to assassinate the Vice-President and the Secretary of State, and the final dispersion of the armed rebellion in the Southern States.

Mr. Davis had left Congress, with health impaired by labors and exposure there, but he still continued his efforts in relation to the matter of reconstruction of the governments in the Southern States.

In May he wrote to a friend in Washington upon that subject the following letter, which contains the first formal declaration of his opinion as to the necessity of conferring the right of suffrage on the colored race in those States.

Baltimore, May 27, 1865.

MY DEAR SIR,—Please accept my acknowledgments for your kind note.

I wish I could give you a short and satisfactory answer to your brief and pregnant question touching our prospects under President Johnson.

The future of the nation is summed up in the restoration of political power to the States lately in rebellion.

Of what the President's policy is on that topic I know nothing.

The conditions of the problem are plain, and the consequences of the several possible solutions follow with logical certainty. It rests with the President, in the state in which Congress has left the question, to take the initiative, and the mode in which that is done will determine all that follows. Whatever State governments he allows to be organized, and to elect representatives and senators to Congress, will be recognized by Congress in December in all probability.

None exist now in any State which rebelled; none can be organized legally without the assent of the United States, and no steps to secure that assent can be taken without his permission.

The President's only power over the question rests in his right to refuse permission for any Convention or election to be held, unless on terms satisfactory to him; but that power is decisive. If he refuse to permit any election or any Convention to be held, things will await the solution of Congress.

If he permit the aggregate white population of the South, qualified to vote under the old governments abrogated by the rebellion, to organize the State governments, that installs the revolutionary faction in power in the States, and fills Congress with their representatives and senators.

That is to place the sceptre in the hands from which we have just wrested the sword.

If the President attempt to discriminate the loyal from the disloyal, and exclude from voting all who have given aid and comfort to the rebellion, a mere handful of the population will remain, wholly incompetent to form or maintain a State government, and sure to be overwhelmed by the political counter-revolution at the next election, which will restore power to the leaders of the rebellion. While it stands under the protection of the United States it will constitute an odious oligarchy, disposing of the lives and property of the great mass of their fellow-citizens, without any responsibility, and controlling the national legislation by the people for whom they vote.

This result is unavoidable. The whole mass of the population of the South has given aid and comfort to the rebellion. The war was made by the accession of the Union men to the rebel faction. It is idle to talk of a quiescent mass of loyal men overborne by violence. It was the Union men who passed the Ordinance of Secession in Virginia, and who made it effectual after it was passed. In no State was the rebellion dangerous without the active aid of those opposed to secession.

But the United States had no friends in the rebel States against those States, and they have none to-day.

The Union men of the South preferred union and peace to disunion; they deplored the outbreak of the war, but they never hesitated a moment which side to take. If there was to be war, they were for their States and against the United States. There was no respectable number of Union men willing to aid the United States in compelling submission to the Constitution, and there are none now. All submit to force. Many are willing to acquiesce in the unavoidable. All are willing to govern the United

States again, since independence is impossible; but all were also willing to aid the rebellion; and not an assault and battery was committed for the United States from the Potomac to the Gulf of Mexico.

The Union men of the South did not merely bow to overbearing force, but they hastened to seek places in the Legislature, the Congress, the executive mansions, and gave it a countenance and support, without which it must have fallen in a year; and when its cause was hopeless, they were quiet and submissive, and did not rise to aid the United States.

It is certainly to this class of the white population that we must look for aid in restoring civil government in these States, but it is a great delusion to suppose them either bold or strong enough to meet and defy the united and energetic faction of revolutionists which drove them into rebellion. If they be in power, they will again do the will of the resolute and reckless men who stood behind and around them, and no legal line discriminates them from the rebel mass.

If this discrimination be attempted by the oath to support the Constitution of the United States, every body will take it, and nobody will be excluded.

If the leaders of the rebellion, civil and military, be excluded, though willing to submit and take the oath, the mass of the rebel faction will be admitted, and that will be the controlling and determining element in selecting representatives and senators, and the practical result is the same as if nobody were excluded.

If either of these forms be accepted by the President and recognized by Congress, it will instantly change the balance of political power in the United States.

It is probable that the people who saved the nation are not content to accept its consequences without a murmur.

None of the white population of the Southern States is interested in paying the public debt or imposing taxes to meet its interest. They hold none of it. It was created to subjugate them to the laws. It has been consumed in their overthrow. It is to be paid, in great part, out of their substance. It has annihilated their public debt. It has filled the land with ostracized officers, with wounded soldiers, with an odious free negro population, lately their slaves, and still under their political control.

If the whites be restored to political power, their representatives are interested in repudiating that public debt, in refusing to pay its interest, in restoring their officers to the army and navy, in placing their wounded on the pension roll, in indemnifying their friends for losses by war, or confiscation or forced tax sales, in restoring slavery under the form of apprenticeship or fixed wages and compulsory service and discriminating and oppressive legislation. The effort has already been made in Tennessee, and the spirit which dictated it pervades the whole South, and will find statutes ready to its hand in every State. In Congress a minority can arrest legislation. A majority of either House can compel submission to any terms, under penalty of arresting or disorganizing the government.

The representatives from the States lately in rebellion will form a powerful and hostile minority, and if they do not find enough enemies of the government from the States now represented to give them a majority in one House for some of the purposes above indicated, the near past throws no light on the near future. The prospect of political disorganization will present few terrors to people still hot with rebellion, smarting with overthrow, and quite as content to ruin as to rule the country.

To expect them to join in electing a Republican President would be an amiable delusion which the first election would dispel; and they might find it some indemnity for emancipation if the increased vote they would cast in the name of their freed slaves should happen to decide the contest and elevate them to power.

If the people are ready for these consequences, then there is no difficulty in restoring political power to the Southern States. Louisiana or Virginia will serve as models, or other forms will grow with mushroom rapidity.

But if it be important that the friends and not the enemies of the government shall continue to govern it, other measures must be taken.

The State governments in the South must be placed in hands interested to maintain the authority of the United States. It is not enough that conquered people are willing to submit to entitle them to govern us. The United States must find friends interested and able to suppress hostility to its authority and to discharge all the functions of government, state and national, in the face of every disloyal or hostile power. And the power of those who rebelled must be curbed by those who did not rebel, aided by those who joined the rebellion reluctantly, and are anxious to atone for their error or weakness.

This can be done only by recognizing the negro population as an integral part of the people of the Southern States, and by refusing to permit any State government to be organized on any other basis than universal suffrage and equality before the law.

Whatever anomalies may have been winked at during the era of slavery, it may well be doubted if, without a serious blow at our principles, any government can be recognized as republican in form which excludes from suffrage and equal laws a majority of the citizens of the States, as would be the case in South Carolina and Mississippi, or half the citizens, as would be the case in Alabama, Georgia, Louisiana, and Virginia, if the negro citizens be disfranchised.

It is certain that governments which declared them equal before the law, and recognized universal suffrage, would be republican in form and substance also. It is equally certain that such a constitution in the Southern States is the only one consistent with the national peace and safety; and Congress has the right, and, I think, ought to refuse to recognize any State governments in those States not on that basis.

But the white people of the States which rebelled will not organize governments on that basis. No considerable portion of the white population of those States is in favor of it. The loyal are as much against it as the rebel leaders.

None will adopt it of themselves, nor will they adopt it on the request and under the influence of the President; but all will submit to it if exacted, and accept it if unavoidable.

To submit the question to the loyal voters of the State assumes the existence of a State government and a Constitution defining the right of suffrage, and making loyalty a condition.

But there are no such Constitutions in any State which rebelled. The United States have refused to recognize any State governments in *any* of those States. There are, therefore, no State governments and no voters in any of the rebel States.

There are *States*, and people of those States, both known to the Constitution of the United States. And the negroes are as integral a part of the people of the State as the whites. Both are citizens; neither has a right to exclude the other; neither can speak in the name of the State for the other; it is the equal right of both to be heard and represented in constituting their common government, and any proposal to submit the question of the political or civil rights of the negroes to the arbitrament of the whites is as unjust and as absurd as to submit the question of the political rights of the whites to the arbitrament of the negroes—with this difference, that the negroes are loyal every where, and the great body of the whites disloyal every where.

The problem, therefore, is solved by a simple appeal to the people of the State.

No election can be held, no Convention assemble, no political authority be legally exercised in any of those States but by the will of the United States, and for the present, till Congress speak, by the will of the President.

If, therefore, the President will declare that no election shall be held unless the negro population have a free and equal voice, that no Convention shall assemble which they have not helped to elect, that none shall proceed to frame a government unless in the beginning universal suffrage and equality before the law be declared its fundamental basis, the problem is solved.

If those conditions be accepted, the Constitution will be presented to Congress and the government recognized which it forms.

If they be not accepted, the President will hold the States till Congress declare how they shall be governed.

If the problem be not dealt with in this way, or in some such way, it will be solved in an adverse sense.

If it be not solved *rightly*, it threatens to generate a barren and bitter agitation, sure to result disastrously to those who propose the political enfranchisement of the negroes, and to consolidate the union of the enemies of the government in the loyal States into an irresistible power, which must wrest the government from the hands of those who had saved it. This coalition is probable in any event; but on this question it is certain and fatal.

The negro population must be recognized by the President and Congress as an integral part of the *people* of the State in the view of the Constitution of the United States, without whose concurrence and full participation of power no State government will be recognized in any State which rebelled, or it will remain ostracized and outcast for another generation, and the enemies of the government will wrest it from the hands of those who saved it.

To permit the whites to disfranchise the negroes is to permit those who have been our enemies to ostracize our friends. The negroes are the only persons in those States who have not been in arms against us. They have always and every where been friendly and not hostile to us. They alone have a deep interest in the continued supremacy of the United States, for their freedom depends on it. On them alone can we depend to suppress a new insurrection. They alone will be inclined to vote for the friends of the government in all the Southern States. They alone have sheltered, fed, and pioneered our starved and hunted brethren through the swamps and woods of the South, in their flight from those who now aspire to rule them.

The shame and folly of deserting the negroes are equaled by the wisdom of recognizing and protecting their power.

They will form a clear and controlling majority against the united white vote in South Carolina, Mississippi, and Louisiana.

With a very small accession from the *loyal* whites, they will form a majority in Alabama, Georgia, and Virginia.

Unaided in all those States, they will be a majority in many congressional and legislative districts, and that alone suffices to break the terrible and menacing unity of the Southern vote in Congress.

If organized and led by men having their confidence, the negroes will prove as powerful and loyal at the polls as they have already, in the face of equal clamor and equal prejudice, proved themselves under such leaders on the field of battle.

To those who say they are unfit for the franchise, I reply they are more fit than secessionists.

If they be ignorant, they are not more so than large masses of the white voters of the South, or the rabble which is tumbled on the wharves of New York and run straight to the polls.

However ignorant, they know enough to be on the side of the government, and the intelligence of the master has not yet taught him that wisdom.

They may be influenced by the master, but the master must touch his hat to them at least, and it will be an open question whether they will vote with the master any more than they fought on his side. It is certain the Northern immigrant will find the negro a safe ally, and arguments on his lips will lose no weight by their Yankee origin.

It is said not to be safe for masters to visit their plantations in Georgia; when they do they will hardly carry much influence politically.

I repeat that in this problem are involved the issues of life and death.

If the negro population be recognized as an integral portion of the people of the States which rebelled, and governments can be organized on the basis of universal suffrage and equality before the law, Congress ought to recognize them, and the problem is solved forever.

If governments be allowed by the President to be organized on the basis of the exclusion of the mass of the negro population, then Congress ought to refuse to recognize them; but I fear it will not refuse.

If the question be submitted to the vote of any portion of the white population, the negroes will be excluded from power.

That result entails on us a barren agitation instead of a beneficent settlement. It carries with it a division of the friends of the government, and threatens to elevate its enemies to power.

For premature agitators I have small sympathy. They are cocks which crow at midnight; they do not herald the dawn, but merely disturb natural rest by untimely clamor.

But this is a question of political dynamics, which presses now for solution, and on it depends the chief fruits of the war.

If it be not rightly solved *now*, it will find no solution for a generation, and possibly none then without renewed civil commotions. Over the result I have no power. I can only hope and fear.

Your obedient servant,

H. Winter Davis.

LESSONS OF THE WAR. — THE AMERICAN CONTINENT REPUBLICAN.—SECURITY FOR THE FUTURE, AND SELF-GOVERNMENT BY LAW, WITH LIBERTY GUARDED BY POWER.

MR. DAVIS was invited to deliver the oration at the civic celebration of the 4th of July, 1865, by the city of Chicago. He complied with this invitation, and on that occasion the proceedings took place, and the oration was delivered, as set forth in the following account:

Never in the history of our country was the National Anniversary more generally and heartily observed than at its recent occurrence. The war had just closed. The troops were coming home. The people and the returned veterans had well earned, by the patriotic sacrifices of four years, and by its splendid result in a rescued nation, the right to make the ovation of patriotic rejoicing memorable. In all parts of the country, in all the cities, in the larger towns, and in the rally by counties, festive celebrations took place on a large scale. The best talent of the country was enlisted for the intellectual portion of these occasions, and the utterances of not a few of these orators will possess a more than transient importance. The subsidence of the war has left important and vital questions of national polity and humanity to be decided in our day. Utterances which throw light on the path of the people, and are an aid to public duty, are worthy to gain a wider circulation than in the single locality of their origin. It is with this view that it has been decided to preserve in the present form the oration of Hon. Henry Winter Davis, of Maryland, the orator of the day in Chicago. It is not necessary to claim for it the characteristics all loyal men will accord it on perusal. An extended reference to the other accompanying features of the day is scarcely called for. It was a general observance by our citizens, probably the first that ever united all classes of our community, all nationalities, and all organizations, in a common patriotic purpose of Fourth of July observance. The procession was in this respect representative. The officers of the day were Col. John L. Hancock, Chief Marshal, with Col. J. M. Loomis, Col. James H. Bowen, Chief Engineer Harris, John Durkin, and Jacob Koch, as marshals of the several divisions. In the proceedings of the day our returned war heroes bore prominent share. The audience-room was the largest that offered shelter to any gathering in the United States on that day. It was the mammoth Hall of the Sanitary Fair, then just closed. Probably not less than ten thousand were comfortably accommodated within reach of the speaker's voice. The following were the officers at the Hall:

President of the Day—Hon. J. B. Rice, Mayor of Chicago.

Vice-Presidents—Hon. Lyman Trumbull, Hon. Julian S. Rumsey, Hon. J. R. Jones, Daniel Brainard, Hon. J. B. Bradwell, Philo Carpenter, A. J. Galloway, James Miller, C. B. Blair, Michael M'Auley, Hon. Thomas Drummond, Fred. Letz, Hon. F. C. Sherman, Joseph Lane, Luther Haven, H. D. Colvin, Hon. Van H. Higgins, Geo. Schneider, Perkins Bass, Hon. S. S. Hayes, Saml. Hoard, Philip Wadsworth, Jonathan Burr, Hon. John C. Haines, Hon. Perry H. Smith, General J. B. Turchin, M. D. Ogden, Walter Kimball, D. D. Driscoll, J. Linton Waters, Robert Forsyth, A. V. Towne, A. Shuman, J. L. Scripps, George C. Bates, J. C. Fargo, Colonel G. W. Smith, Charles Randolph, W. W. Boyington, General S. P. Bradley, W. F. Tucker, Benj. Lombard, W. C. Coolbaugh, A. D. Tittsworth, Benj. V. Page, J. L. Reynolds, John V. Farwell, H. E. Sargent, E. C. Larned, C. Wahl, Maj. Gen. Webster, Brig. Gen. Stolbrand, I. Y. Munn, F. A. Hoffman, J. K. Pollard, J. Y. Scammon, C. N. Holden.

Secretaries—Joseph Medill, Charles L. Wilson, L. Brentano, J. W. Sheahan, and A. Worden.

The exercises were the reading of the Emancipation Proclamation, the Last Inaugural, the Declaration of Independence, and the delivery of the Oration. A magnificent feature of the day was the grand chorus of one thousand singers, with a monster orchestra, who gave, with thrilling effect, the patriotic songs on the programme. A grand banquet to the returned soldiers, in the adjoining Horticultural Hall, and a splendid exhibition of fireworks in the evening, were the closing observances of the day.

With this preface, we leave the reader to the enjoyment of the main feature of the occasion, preserved in the pages which follow. THE COMMITTEE.

ORATION.

The President introduced the orator of the day, Hon. Henry Winter Davis, as one who hailed from Maryland, but whose reputation was national; one who for many years has served his country faithfully in the councils of the Union.

Mr. Davis spoke as follows:

FELLOW-CITIZENS,—It is with unspeakable joy that I to-day congratulate you upon this auspicious return of our national birthday, proclaimed in the midst of doubt and the clash of arms, celebrated at the close of the Revolution when independence was accomplished, and now celebrated with additional joy, additional heartiness, and overflowing exultation at the second foundation of the American republic; for to-day that Declaration, then a promise, spoken in the spirit of prophecy, belied by the facts that were all around it—to-day that Declaration is true in right and true in fact from one end of this broad land to the other—true now not only in Virginia, and in Maryland, and the Carolinas; not now limited to the Alleghanies and the coast; but true for the whole American people, from the Atlantic to the Pacific, and covering every inch of territory from Maine to the Gulf of Mexico—every where true in right and true in fact—bought with precious blood wrung from reluctant hands, strengthened by the heart's blood of many of your brothers and many of your sons, through good report and through evil report, in the day of darkness and in the day of hope, till glorious light has crowned the cause with its final victory, and we meet here to-day to celebrate its jubilee.

Fellow-citizens, the American republic rested, in the fall of the year 1860, as peacefully and as quietly as the infant on the mother's breast, not dreaming of war, with no weapons to grasp, with no arms provided, with no army organized, with no generals to lead us save those at the plow, with no leaders but their enemies, in power, while a deep and wide-spread conspiracy, organized for years, was preparing to strike what it fondly hoped was the final blow at the integrity of the American republic and the glory of the American name. It proposed to expurgate the Declaration of Independence, and to declare that all men were *not* born free and equal; it proposed to repeal the Constitution of the United States, which embodied one government for all of these States forever; it proposed to defy the power of the government, and to assail the authority of the ballot-box with the sword; without a grievance, without a wrong, without a well-founded complaint, the conspirators against its existence had held the places of honor, had filled the positions of power, had dictated the policy of the government, till they aimed that blow at its being, so swiftly, so sharply, so deadly, that it had almost accomplished its purpose before you, in the great centre of the American republic, knew that the deadly blow was aimed, before you knew that the arm was raised to strike it. It was difficult for men to believe; it was long before the idea sank into men's minds that such wickedness and such bloody purposes actually existed. But gradually the light dawned upon the public mind, and the people found that it was not mere braggadocio, that it was not all a game of brag. They then found that it meant a struggle of no ordinary magnitude, a determination on the part of the South to stab the nation in a vital part; in a word, that it was what we now know it to be. They found that the rebels had a thoroughly-prepared, a well-considered, a perfectly-adjusted plan to tear in pieces the Union;

and instantly, as if by magic, from one end of this land to the other, men arose in arms to offer their lives for the salvation of their country. Generals were improvised, and regiments raised, and armies created, until men were bewildered with their numbers, scarce believing in the magnitude of the power the republic was disclosing to put down its enemies.

And yet, amid all this, there was a hesitation, a doubt in the minds of many, so deeply had it been grounded in the minds of the masses throughout the North, that whatever else might be touched, there was one emblem of royalty, one sign of aristocratic domination which must not be interfered with—that was slavery. So thoroughly were they convinced that the rebellion could not touch its strong-hold, that men were found picking their way tenderly and carefully through the South, as if they were marching through a powder magazine with a lighted candle, and were guarding it carefully for fear of an explosion, which would hurt their enemies. While we were divided, they were united; we hesitated, while they were decided; we sought to strike without doing them damage, they were aiming blows directly at the heart of the people; they fought to conquer, to destroy, we fought to save them; we fought tenderly, carefully, dealing with them as our fellow-citizens, who we fondly supposed were misled in an evil hour—accidentally as it were—and that suddenly a sense of their iniquity would break in upon them, and that by-and-by they would return, and we should all repose again peacefully under the shadow of the old patriarchal institution. But gradually the popular heart caught the real spirit of the rebellion, and their inspiration breathed itself in song. Around the camp-fires, from the solitary sentinel to the soldiers drawn up in battle array, the chords of the American heart were touched by the spirit of "Rally round the Flag, Boys," and that other inspiring heresy, "John Brown's Soul is Marching On," until the hearts of the people were warmed with its magic spell, and the people's voice reached and inspired the dull ears of those in power. Then, as the nation knew it was struggling, not only to retain reluctant States, but to expunge from its institutions that which made the Declaration of Independence a lie and a vain thing—then it was that the patriotic men rallied to the support of the government; and, though badly led, and badly directed, and often defeated and involved in disaster, still was heard the cry, "We come, three hundred thousand more." They were ready to fill the graves on every battle-field till those who defied the national emblem should be laid low. Then it was they found that if there was division at the North, there was unity there too; that the day of doubt had passed; that if there had been hesitation it was gone, and merged into a strong, sober, stern resolution—that resolution of a great people to die, but never to yield—the spirit that breathed in the men who stood at Marathon, and died on the field of Cannæ that liberty might survive—the spirit which fired the heart of the French Republic when it defied Europe in arms seeking its overthrow—the resolution, which is that of all nations born to greatness, to accept no peace *they* do not dictate, no peace that does not humble every rebel weapon that has been raised against the power and majesty of the republic. And from that day the defenders of the cause, inspired by principle, have pursued energetically the contest, in the face of the hostility of all the nations of the world, and loud predictions of failure here, till that glorious consummation has been attained which greets us here to-day. Not that blood has not flowed in abundance to secure it, for what family has not lost a brother, son, or husband, or some near bosom friend? This triumph has not been purchased lightly. It has been gained at the expense of much suffering and many tears; it is the end of a great tragedy. These triumphs are secured with our blood. Like all those great results which are won on the fields of history by the nations destined to immortality, our empire has been secured by the sacrifice of the best and noblest of the land. And who does not, when contemplating these sad and yet ever-glorious battle-fields, every where see—who does not deplore it with tears—that American blood has flowed *on both sides*; that it was our *brethren* who were led astray, ruined, scourged to destruction by the Nemesis of History, which drives men to work out themselves the punishment of their own errors? Who does not remember that they are sons of the same forefathers who fought for that very Union which they attacked and we defended? Any man who does not remember this lacks one half of the American heart. But, fellow-citizens, we have fought this fight once, and we have fought it forever. Every heart exultingly exclaims,

> "No more the thirsty entrance of this soil
> Shall daub her lips with her own children's blood.

No more shall trenching war channel her fields,
Nor bruise her flowerets with the armed hoofs
Of hostile paces. Those opposed eyes,
Which, like the meteors of a troubled heaven
(All of one nature, of one substance bred),
Did lately meet in the intestine shock,
And furious close of civil butchery,
Shall *now*, in mutual well-beseeming ranks,
March all one way, and be no more opposed
Against acquaintance, kindred, allies.
The edge of war, like an ill-sheathed knife,
No more shall cut his master."

If this be prophecy or prayer, let all the people say "Amen," and pray that it may be so.

We have passed, fellow-citizens, through the valley of the shadow of death; harm has come nigh us, but it has not overthrown us, and it is well now, as we pass out of the gloomy part of that valley, that we should, like the Pilgrim of the great "Progress," pause, as the sun has risen upon our steps, and look back to see the dangers from which we have been rescued, that we may be thankful for, and not proud of, the things we have accomplished.

Many a delusion, many a false prophecy, many a treacherous declaration has been dispelled by the harsh collision of arms, and they are buried forever among the errors of the past, to be remembered only that we may avoid them hereafter. Who now does not know that secession is not a peaceful remedy? Who now does not know that the rebellious South can not be conquered? Who now does not know that the way to preserve the bond of peace is not by compromise or concession, or by friendly proposals? Who does not know that the negro is a man? for he has proved his manhood at the point of the bayonet; not where the President proposed to place him, in forts or garrisons, but in the line of battle alongside of armed white men, charging just as deeply into the heart of the enemy's ranks as his white brethren, vindicating his right to manhood by the exercise of the highest prerogative of man—fearlessness in the presence of eternity, and of death which leads him there. We have learned something else: State rights are responsible to the bayonet. Those great organizations that insolently lifted their arms in the front of battle against the nation, where are they now? That

Virginia, the Old Dominion, with the master in its name, holding from George Washington till now hereditary power, the Mecca of Southern rights, the Palestine of the Southern religion, that "sacred soil," for violating which Ellsworth fell, where is now its proud motto, "*Sic semper tyrannis?*" Her old dominion rent in twain, she lies under the heel of Liberty, and "*tyrannis*" is that Virginia, her slavery clean gone from the earth forever. So let it perish. Pierpont, a name unknown to her aristocracy, not in the line of her rulers by descent, a common man from across the mountains, not a native of the soil he now rules, was picked up by the loyal Virginians and created her master at the bidding of national necessity, and because the nation required that the old government of Virginia should cease to exist. States are immortal, but State governments, that are organized by men, and may be used for selfish purposes, perverted to the purposes of treason to defy the Union, are by the laws of the United States not immortal, but amenable to the laws as men for their acts, and die by treason.

But, fellow-citizens, how have these results been accomplished? Not by great leaders; not by wise statesmanship; not by far-seeing advisers; not by generals of illustrious renown, known to the world, whom it was an honor to follow. We had George Washington provided to lead our steps in infancy, but we had no George Washington to guide us through these awful struggles. No William the Silent to lift the standard before the failing heart of the people in despair; no Richelieu or Chatham to organize victory by wise and efficient administration; no far-sighted Congress prepared victory by wise organization beforehand, anticipating the wants of the nation. We had, charged with the conduct of public affairs, honest, faithful, diligent, devoted, and now martyred servants of the republic. But they did not initiate the movement which led to this great consummation; it sprang from the popular heart, which compelled them to make war; the impulse came from the masses of the people, and they freely poured out their treasure and the blood needed to carry on the war. It was the people who anticipated it, their instinct dictated it, their treasure supported it, and they demanded every measure, and sustained, without a murmur, every disappointment, and supplied money to fill up every waste and every loss. It is the greatest example in history of a great people, without leaders, selecting its own instruments to accomplish the popular will. It was a great movement of the whole mass of the nation; one whose progress was like the roll of the great Mississippi onward to the Gulf, irresistible because of its impetus and volume, and guided to its end by the hand of God. It stands before the world as a solitary example, beside the struggle of the French Republic, against those who sought its overthrow.

We stand to-day before the nations of the world as the American people never stood before. All Europe was opposed to us; they hastened to vest our enemies with the rights of war; they threw open their ports for their privateers; they prepared in their machine-shops the materials for breaking our blockade; they prepared the arms with which our enemies fought us; and for four years they fitted out ships of war, and manned them with English sailors, to depredate on our commerce. They had an instinctive presentiment that our success was their overthrow; they knew well that if the republic came safely out from this struggle, it would not suffice to tell the people that imperialism alone could keep order, that aristocracy alone insured a permanent government, that hereditary thrones alone could peacefully transmit power in a government; for they would have, standing before them, unbroken in all its gorgeous panoply of war, and still more glorious in its civil garb than before, an illustrious example to the contrary. They would see thirty millions of American people choosing their own rulers, dictating their policy, redressing their own wrongs, plowing their own lands, forging their own arms, filling the ranks of their own armies, creating their own generals, fighting their own battles, compelling submission to the laws they had made, and defying all nations to arrest them in their progress. They were too sure of their game; they thought as the traitors *here* thought, that the South could not be conquered, and that the North would go to pieces in the collision, and therefore held their hands and did not intervene. They thought our day of doom was come, and it is not impossible that their error proved our salvation. But we will remember that it was their error and not their merit, and will visit its consequences upon them. No sooner did they suppose the terrors of the American people were gone, that the great ægis of our protection ceased to cover the republics of America, than they began their work. Spain seized upon San Domingo, her ancient colony, and invaded Peru, whose independence she had never recognized, reasserting her original title. France and England, under the pretext of playing the bailiff to collect dues for their subjects, conspired against the republic in Mexico, and, under the false pretext of carrying "*order*" into the midst of that distracted country, added new confusion to disturb the quiet which was settling down over that republic. Insidiously they wrought with an armed power. Under the false pretense of a desire to establish peace, they have destroyed the last remnants of it, and with it the most free and liberal government that had ever attained a permanent foothold in Mexico. The Mexicans had just passed through such a struggle as we have here passed through. Their collision was with the Catholic Church, with the power of the priesthood, which held three fourths of their territory, just as we have been driven into collision with the slave power, which owned so much of our territory. They had succeeded in divesting that church of its political power, secularizing its lands and distributing them among the people, and inaugurated a just government, when Louis Napoleon, with the purpose of limiting our expansion and strengthening his imperial throne by its counterpart in America, refused to recognize the government of Juarez, imposed on the people an Austrian for their master, supported him by French armies, boasted that order was founded in Mexico, and, with Mexico bleeding at his feet, referred to his name and history as a sufficient guarantee that he could impose no government on the Mexicans against the will of the nation. He thought the world had forgotten December and the Boulevards, or perhaps they are not in his history. That mission of "restoring order" was undertaken by our European foes, who tenderly, calmly advised that we should not press the South to desperation, but should haste to make terms lest we should be destroyed. We dissembled our indignation at this grave menace and insult—with difficulty, but for the present perhaps not unwisely; but that time of trial to the American republic is now over, and the people have not forgotten the insult, nor ceased to appreciate the greatness of the danger to republican institutions involved in the example of an imperial throne standing on the ruins of an American republic supported by European bayonets. If necessity imposed silence, to-day that necessity has ceased. When the armies of Sherman and of Grant paraded before the President's stand in Washington, in that grand review after their great victories, the representatives of foreign powers stood at the back of the President; and while every European face wore an aspect of polite resignation, our South American friends were radiant with joy, and avowed that our triumph was theirs. And whether it be to-day, or to-morrow, or next month, or next year; whether Louis Napoleon shall succeed or not in consolidating the throne of Maximilian; no matter who may be in power, or who may assume to control the destinies of this nation; no matter who may attempt to stop its onward march, or preach moderation or the danger of perpetual war, the introduction of a European prince into an American republic for the purpose of founding on its ruins a hereditary throne is an insolent defiance of the declaration of President Monroe, and the American people are pledged to resent it. It is vain to attempt to adduce to us evidence that Mexico assents; there is no dissent with the bayonet at the throat. No argument can be permitted to prove that submission to armed force is free choice. Let them withdraw their armies. Let them leave Mexico. If they don't like the state of anarchy which prevails there, let them leave it to its normal condition. It is not their right to interfere with the internal affairs of Mexico. It is a perpetual menace to us. If they need order, we prefer a different neighbor to Louis Napoleon, the *liberal* Emperor of France. We wish for no conquests, but we have established freedom here, and we will have freedom from here to Cape Horn. I desire no policy of conquest. I merely stand where President Monroe stood, where Henry Clay stood, where Daniel Webster stood, where the Congress of '26 stood, which sanctioned the Panama mission, in the application of this principle to Mexico, that the people are entitled to work out their own salvation in such form as they may see fit, and that European meddling with them is a menace to us. But we do not recognize a monarchical power as a good nurse to put a republic to. These are the first results of the war.

Fellow-citizens, we stand again in all our integrity and power before the nations of the world, desiring to war with nobody, but remembering that in our hour of need men tried to destroy us. Desiring to observe all the laws of neutrality, we are resolved that England shall accept and respect her own neutrality laws. Any rule will suit the American people except the insolence and caprice of a power presuming to domineer over us.

But, fellow-citizens, the war has taught other lessons than these.

It has taught us lessons we must perforce read and remember, whether we would or not. Why is it that the American republic, so peaceful, so just, so moderate, so wise, as it heretofore has been for eighty years of unbroken internal quiet, has been for the first time plunged into civil war? It is because we embodied in our institutions one which was not reconcilable with the principles on which they all rest. The unanimous declaration of the thirteen colonies of America consecrated forever as the groundwork of the nation the principles of personal freedom and government by law. Government by law we secured in the Constitution, personal freedom we sacrificed to an existing interest, supposed to be temporary, admitted to be wrong, difficult of remedy, but to be remedied. But the expansion of our territory inspired that interest as it grew in strength, first with a desire for permanence, then with a desire for power. The addition of the great regions of Florida and Louisiana to the domain of the United States fired the blood of its supporters with the determination of ruling. It was resolved by them to become a power, and cease to be merely an interest. It could be tolerated as an interest, it could not be tolerated as a power, which by political coalition became the dominant power of the nation. It first asserted itself as a power in the great Missouri Compromise so long worshiped by all men as the emblem of our peace. Texas was its conquest. The compromise of 1850 was the recognition of its equality with freedom in disposing of the fortunes and fate of the nation. The repeal of the Missouri Compromise was its assertion, not merely that it was a power, but that it had power to rule. The war in Kansas was its struggle to assert, against a reluctant people, its right to rule. The Dred Scott decision was the sanction of its most insolent claims by the supreme judicial authority of the nation, before which bowed every dissenting voice in the South. It had made for itself a permanent home in the South, a home full of ideas and arguments for its maintenance and advancement; it seized upon and taught the doctrine of State rights as one of its bulwarks; it cultivated submission to the local authorities, so that in case of collision the men of the South might prefer their State to the nation. Slavery was first wrong, then excusable, then defensible, then defended by scriptural, historical, and political arguments, then advocated and vaunted as the highest development of the social organization. Every principle of human reason was confounded in this deliberate attempt to make right of a wrong. It created a new theology, a new history, a new ethnology for itself. The Southern ethnology separated the negro from the human race; the Southern religion proclaimed the slave-trade a missionary enterprise; the new Southern morals proclaimed the duty of holding the negro, for his own benefit, as the highest of moral obligations; the new Southern theodicy deduced the highest proofs of the wisdom of God from his placing the black man in subjection to the white; the new Southern history made the chief purpose of the Constitution the protection of this interest; the new Southern political economy professed to have found in negro slavery that organization of labor for which the Old World had so long striven in vain; the new Southern political philosophy added to Jefferson's enumeration of the inalienable rights of man that of the negro to a master. Admitted to be wrong, it was weak; when merely excusable, the time would come when it would cease to be excused; admitted defensible, it was still on the defensive; but as a *power* it could control and assume its own position. Thus this interest, a flaw at first in the foundation of our great national temple of freedom, undermined its foundation, and threatened its overthrow. It was no longer an interest, but a power, ready to fight for empire, to assert in arms its authority. Fearful that the intrusion of new ideas might breed doubts, they surrounded their territory with Gorgons, hydras, chimeras dire, to repel Northern men: white men with free ideas could not work in the South; the Southern sun was fatal to the men of the North; the frightful pestilence walked in darkness to smite the stranger who ventured among them. They dreaded the intrusive eye of freedom, tolerated it only blindfold, and thus, firmly imbued with convictions scientifically and logically wrought into a social system, strong in arguments for its support, at peace with their consciences, given over to believe a lie, a territory equal in area to the greatest empire in the world, filled with an energetic, brilliant, brave, and devoted people, educated in the idea that the State is supreme and could secede at will, and that even if the State had not that right, it could sanction, and by its authority, which they were bound to obey, excuse all who under its bidding took arms against the nation; armed against moral reprobation by pride, strong against the laws of the land in arms, in the sympathy of many at the North, in a generation educated and devoted to those ideas for which they were ready to die, they drew the sword, throwing away the scabbard, to assert that slavery is the true corner-stone of freedom. That corner-stone on which they sought to raise a new empire now lies crumbled and shattered under the feet of advancing freedom.

In the stagnant East these ideas could have lain side by side for generations, sleeping quietly as twin brothers; for there, despotism and slavery are as eternal as its deserts, and as shifting as their sands; but in the fruitful and teeming West, the sun makes the tare grow as rankly and rapidly as the wheat. The same sun ripens the weeds and the corn together, and when the seed of the evil weeds are sown, they will come to maturity and destroy the good grain if the husbandman does not pluck them out. This has been our task for the four years past. During that time we have been persuaded by those who live far from the South, who know nothing of its moral atmosphere, nothing of the impulses which drive its people to action, that these men could be conciliated, that we could make compromises with them. They said, strike the arms from their hands and they would thenceforth quietly submit. It would suffice that the loyal men of the South should be armed, and the disloyal trodden down, to insure security for the future. What does history say of these views of Southern temper? There was not even an assault and battery committed on behalf of the United States, from the Potomac to the Gulf of Mexico. Where *then* were the loyal friends of the government? There were Union men; but you must translate that into the language of the South. There were many among them who preferred that the government should not be broken up, but if it were to be broken up they were for the South. They preferred that there should be peace; they were willing to vote that peace should continue, and with it the Union; but if it were to be broken, then they would not fight against their brethren at home for the maintenance of the Union. They preferred peace at home and war with the United States, to war at home and peace with the United States. They loved the government, but they loved their State better; they were devoted to the nation, but more to their State. "Our people" was the phrase by which they designated the men of their own State, and "our enemies" that by which they spoke of those born under the same paternal government with them, the loyal men of the North. This temper of mind has not changed, and any man, in authority or out of authority, who supposes that repentance has come by castigation, misreads the minds of the men of his own time, and is preparing ruin for himself and his land. If the question be submitted to the vote of the Southern people to-day whether they will remain a part of the United States and celebrate with us this glorious day, or expunge from their calendar the Fourth of July, expurgate the Declaration of Independence, restore their slavery system, and form an independent government, the vote would be overwhelming and unprecedented in favor of independence. If that is the sentiment of the Southern people, men of America, look well where you tread. There is doubtless a division among them, but it is a division of political parties, more or less devoted to Southern ideas and Southern power. Those who acquiesce readily, and those who acquiesce only under coercion—those who consider their cause hopeless and are disposed to put the best face they can upon it, and those who lie down to sleep with hatred in their hearts, and wake up to invite a French or English army to join with them in the destruction of the republic — these are the only divisions. I know the noble names of Petigru and Joshua Hill; and when I have named these men, and added to them John Minor Botts and Governor Aiken, I name all I know in all the Southern country who have been so far friends of the nation that they closed their mouths, bowed their heads, and allowed the waters of strife to pass over them, trusting to God whether they should survive or perish.

To that people our rulers are now proposing to extend the privilege of governing themselves and *us*—themselves and US!! There are precautions to be taken for the future, fellow-citizens. There is such a thing as "making haste slowly." There is such a thing as allowing men's tempers to cool, time to develop their purposes, time to pick out instruments on whom you can rely, to count heads and see where an election will land you. Do not then hasten it. Reinstated to-day in authority, read the transactions of the loyal Legislature of Virginia, and tell me how you are to get cordial support and sympathy from such men—men burning with the passion of the war in every branch; the men who are known enemies to the government every where elected to offices in every department of authority except the powerless, impotent, and deluded governor. Every attempt to discriminate loyal from disloyal was hooted down in the twinkling of an eye at the first session; mocking and jeering at the oath which was meant to separate the true from the false, the "test" oath was known as the "detested" oath in the vocabulary of loyal, reorganized Virginia. There are therefore precautions absolutely necessary.

We have disposed of the doctrine of secession by the bayonet; but that their acute legal suggestion—that although the State has not the right to rebel, yet the citizens are bound to obey it, and it will stand between them and responsibility incurred in fighting for it against the nation—may be effectually put down, it must be refuted, as it only can be, by the judgment of death on their leading traitor. I am not bloody-minded, gentlemen, and I think mere personal punishment at the end of a war in which two or three hundred thousand men have been laid in bloody graves has no relation to the ordinary purposes of punishment. If you could punish so as to break and destroy the power of the "aristocracy" which inaugurated the war, it were well; but Congress has refused to pass the law which deprived them of their citizenship, and now the supreme law of the land forbids it, the opportunity is gone, and gone forever. They have suffered, and suffered much, by the confiscation of their slaves. But the mere hanging of men has no power to prevent such a rebellion as this, wherein men have staked hundreds of thousands of lives on the issue and died glorying in their cause. By hanging them you would be only multiplying the number of martyrs without materially diminishing that of criminals. But they should be stamped with the foul brand of treason, not allowed to glory over their struggle against the nation, to remain the heroes of the South, as they are at this day. When the vanquished rebel can hang his sword over his door, and in after years boast of it to his grandchildren, you have left the seeds of future rebellion, the temptation of impunity for the future; and it is material that these great words of the Constitution, "that this Constitution, and the laws of the United States made in pursuance thereof, shall be the supreme law of the land," shall be understood to mean what they say, to be resisted by no wire-drawn pleas, to be avoided by no plea of State rights, to be stripped of authority by no impunity claimed under any obligation to obey the Constitution of the State; so that the man who takes his musket to resist it shall know that *he* commits the crime, and not his State. The judgment of the court will clear him of every delusion on the subject, so that hereafter he will not be troubled by metaphysical arguments on State rights, which are national wrongs, but he may go to his doom justly, as well as legally. The kindly advice of our English cousins and our French friends, preaching moderation in the hour of victory, is good, but we can not but remember that their friends are those who are to suffer. Hopes of foreign aid from those powers weighed heavily in causing the rebellion, and they naturally have an interest in preventing the extreme penalty of the law from falling on the heads of those they tempted and deserted. We can understand that they have an interest in still keeping open a cleavage in the fast-closing rock of the republic, wherein foreign powers may again force a lever to shake the republic to its foundations. Fellow-citizens, when we feel the need of it, we will ask their advice, but we look alone to *our laws* for the rule of our action, and to the moderation of the people to prevent the stain of useless blood upon our hands. Let England remember Napoleon, and Emmett, and O'Brien; the massacred Indians, who only fought to throw off a foreign yoke, which England feared we would impose upon the South. Let Louis Napoleon, too, remember Ney and Abd el Kader, the massacre of the Boulevards and the deportation of one half the members of the Assembly of France, as the measure of French mercy. We are to-day a nation in spite of their advice, their enmity, and their efforts: silence would better become them, saving us the trouble of flinging their crimes in their teeth, to expose the motives of their unasked advice.

That disposes of one great precautionary measure.

We can not govern this immense region by military power. That would be to create proconsuls to whom armies will become devoted, in whom the spirit of ambitious power will grow and become strong, and one of whom may, like Cæsar, march across the Rubicon on the insidious pretext of the public good, when America may be as Rome was. Military government in vast regions of territory, over great populations, is inconsistent not only with the principles of our institutions, but with the permanence and integrity of the American government, and therefore must be excluded from every body's mind. If you wish a temporary civil government, let it be organized *by law;* but we must recognize *not only personal freedom*, but the *principles of self-government*—the right of the PEOPLE to rule. We want no rebel State government; we want still less a military government; a rebel government is safer than a military government. We do not want oligarchies of professed Union men, who have been so low down out of sight that nobody can divine their relations to the rebellion, or men who treacherously sympathized with the power that was, and now meanly seek to serve the power that is. We want the free government of the loyal men of the South who are on our side, who will draw the sword for us, and will maintain our rights where they are threatened, and are powerful enough to maintain the authority of the State government at home. There is no white population at the South, no great mass of it any where, who will conform to these conditions. After you have erased from the list of voters every man you can clearly prove to have been a secessionist, after you have sifted clear all you can call the loyal men, you have men who have sympathized with rebellion, have given it their countenance, if not their active aid, by their arms and their money; can they be relied on in any emergency? The Secessionists of the South are the heroes of the South, toasted, fêted, worshiped. This day Robert E. Lee could carry every electoral vote of every Southern State for the Presidency of the United States, and I would not swear he could not carry some Northern States I could name. Under a reorganization on the basis of the white population, the South will be more united and powerful than when she drew the sword.

But there is a mass of population there that is on the side of the United States, against all white men at the South, whether Union or Secession, who to-day have a part in the Declaration of Independence which they never had before, and which they have earned on the battle-field by the side of these gentlemen bearing the uniforms of the nation. On many a bloody battle-field they have proven that they are men, not beasts. Will any body on this subject venture to moot the small paltry question that hitherto has divided Illinois, and wearied the people of other States, touching the voting of a handful of negroes lost in the midst of white millions? Is that the way to state a grave national question? or is it wise in these gentlemen of the abolition schools to be always talking of justice and humanity to the negro? as if justice or humanity ever determined any great question in the world, or as if it were the rights of the negro, not our safety, which is at stake! It is not a question of justice, but of political dynamics.

It is a question of power, not of right—a question of salvation, not of morals. The alternatives are before us of a republican friendly government, or a hostile oligarchy in the South.

No State government has ever been recognized which ostracized a majority or any great mass of the people. When slavery existed, slaves were merged in the master. But the right of the State to ostracize a great mass of free negroes has never been recognized. They were a handful every where but in Maryland—and *there they voted with the whites on the adoption of the Constitution of the United States.* If this precedent be set now, it is for the first time to be set. When negroes become free, they become a part of the people of the nation, and to ostracize them is to sanction a principle fatal to American free government.

In South Carolina there are twice as many negroes as whites; in Mississippi there are more negroes than whites; in Alabama, in Louisiana, and in Georgia they are nearly equal. They are now in sufficient numbers at the South to control the result of any election. "They will vote with their masters," insidious gentlemen tell us; then at least let their masters be under the necessity of touching their hats to them to get their votes. "They are not intelligent enough to vote," another says. They know, fellow-citizens, a gray uniform from a blue one. They know a Yankee from their masters. They have fought well under Yankee leadership; maybe they can vote as intelligently under Yankee leadership. They are not spread in equal masses over the Southern country, but they are congregated in particular districts that border the Atlantic, the Gulf, and the Mississippi, and are in immense majorities in fully one third of the congressional districts of the South. They can break the terrible unity of the Southern vote that plunged us into the rebellion. Men who are not capable of understanding considerations like these had better go and whine about negro votes. I have seen about as much of negroes as any of you, have lived as near them, and suppose I have as much prejudice toward them as any of you; but to talk of this after we have had to call them to our aid in putting down the rebellion, is either driveling folly or infinite meanness. If you did not wish to have the negro hereafter enjoy the rights of a man, why did you bring him on the battle-field? You, white men of Illinois, why did you not have the quota of your State increased, so that the negro should not be needed? We of Maryland carried emancipation by going to the poor white men in the southern portion of the State, and showing them that the negro could relieve them from military service. They did not stop to discuss his right to political privileges then. If he is their and your equal on the battle-field, in the service of the country, he is, and should be, at the ballot-box; and if he is not your equal on the battle-field, then you have cheated the United States, to the injury of the national cause, to save yourselves from service.

There is nothing in President Johnson's proclamation which assumes to conclude the judgment of the Congress of the United States on the recognition of State governments in the rebel States. He may have had more confidence in the white people of the South than I have—he may have desired to give them a golden opportunity of refuting every slander and silencing every doubt regarding their loyalty. He might have a hope that when they should be called upon to vote on their Constitutions under his proclamation, to be ready to present them to Congress in the form of petitions, for they would be nothing else; that, seeing the signs of the times, and what justice and humanity require, or rather what the people of the North will suppose their safety requires, they would incorporate universal suffrage as the basis of their Constitutions. I shall rejoice with him if that result shall come about, but I am far from expecting it. I will believe, until I learn the contrary, that that was his purpose. I will not believe the declaration of any person who says he is opposed to it. He knows that the only authority that can recognize State governments at the South is the Congress which admits their representatives and senators; that it must judge of the republicanism of their form of government. I turn to that august assembly with some doubt, but with earnest hopes, and I appeal to it to be ready for any emergency, to be caught by no snare, to yield to no solicitations; not to take any man's declaration as to the safety of trusting the whole mass of the rebels of the South with the control of the Southern States, but to remember that a revolutionary minority can and will throw almost insurmountable obstacles in the way of legislation; that the Southern delegations, joined with interested and discontented men from the North, may clog and even arrest the wheels of government on any bill; that they can organize a powerful opposition to the payment of our national debt, and the imposition of taxes, unless we agree to their demands to reinstate rebel officers, place their wounded on your pension lists, or indemnify slaveholders for their slaves. I pray these gentlemen to look this thing in the eye, and if they have no regard for "justice and humanity," I would say to them, I, like you, gentlemen, am no enthusiast. I am very little of a philanthropist. I am not convinced of the intellectual superiority of the negro over the white; but I know that his vote is important, and if I have not much respect for justice and humanity, I have great regard for the 5-20s; I have great respect for the integrity of the government and the possibility of carrying on its machinery. If the Constitutions do not give the mass of the negroes the right of voting on equal terms with the loyal white men (not those who can read, where it has been a penitentiary offense to teach one to read for twenty years—that is trifling with grave matters—but that mass of the negro population whom we subjected to the draft, and at whose hands we sought aid in our hour of weakness) the safety of the nation requires, republican principles require, that no such government shall be recognized as republican in form, that no representative or senator from such a State shall be admitted to either House, or even complimented with the privileges of the floor.

We need the votes of all the colored people; it is numbers, not intelligence, that count at the ballot-box; it is right intention, and not philosophic judgment, that casts the vote. More glorious still would it be for Congress to follow the great example we have just set, of abolishing slavery by an amendment of the Constitution. Let it pass by a two-thirds majority, in both houses of Congress, an amendment of the Constitution consecrating forever the mass of the people as the basis of the republican government of the United States, and submit it this very coming winter, before the Legislatures adjourn, for their ratification. And when it shall have received the assent of three fourths of those now represented in Congress, let Congress instantly proclaim it as the fundamental law of the land, valid and binding as the Constitution itself, of which they will thus have made it a part, under which they sit, of which no State caprice, no question of political parties, nothing in the future, except the triumph of slavery over free institutions, can ever shake or call in question. Then all the principles of the Declaration of Independence will be executed; this government will rest on the right of individual liberty, and the right of every man to bear a share in the government of the country whose laws he obeys and whose bayonet in the hour of danger he bears. And the personal freedom which the dark children of the republic have won by our blood and theirs will not be a vain mockery, exposed to violation at the caprice of their masters, enthroned in the Legislature, on the bench, and in the executive chamber, but, secured by the arms they hold and the ballot they cast, will be Liberty guarded by Power.

THE NECESSITY OF UNIVERSAL SUFFRAGE IN RECONSTRUCTION.

In October Mr. Davis again published his views in relation to the reconstruction of the States lately in rebellion, insisting on the necessity of suffrage for the colored race as an indispensable condition in re-establishing the federal relations of those States.

His letter was addressed to the editor of the (New York) *Nation*, and appeared in that journal in the form here following. It is the last paper on any public matter which he wrote or designed for publication.

To the Editor of The Nation:

My extreme reluctance to intrude on the public where I am not responsible for results has hitherto withheld me from offering to you the following communication.

The Connecticut vote has solved my doubts and removed my hesitations. It reveals the fact that the great body of the Republicans are true to their principles, but that there is an unreliable minority in our ranks willing to unite with the enemies of the country to prevent us from consolidating our victory and securing its fruits. These two elements will, I fear, be found to divide our friends in Congress. Our great majority there can be broken only by a great desertion. A few we may expect to be disloyal. We may trust, however, that enough will not join those who have vilified us for four years to place *them* in control of the houses. If they *do*, then Connecticut is the emblem of the fate of our cause, and the same coalition which perpetuated *there* the seeds of discord will prevent our rooting them out forever from the nation.

In Connecticut no practical importance attaches to the negro vote, and old prejudice was free to assert its power. But in the Southern States lately in rebellion the negro population is a *controlling power*, if properly organized, and endowed with arms and ballots. It is the only *power* on which the United States can rely there in the event of a renewed rebellion. It is the only body of people who can give the white minority of loyal men a voice in the nation, and prevent them from being overwhelmed and ostracized by the hostile majority. It is the only body of natural friends of the United States in all those States, for its freedom depends on the integrity of the Union. It is the only body from which a Republican vote can be expected in any of those States, for the mass of whites, loyal as well as disloyal, hate and vilify us, while the negroes know that their liberty is *our* gift, and that as surely as it would cease on disunion, so surely its safety and enjoyment would be jeoparded and impaired by the accession to power in the United States of the old coalition of their masters in possession of the Southern States, and the Democrats holding enough of the Northern States to elect a President or control either house of Congress.

The tone of the Southern press—now merely muttering between bayonets—is that of execration against the Republicans, while unanimous in supporting the President they elected; and to overlook this manifestation of Southern temper in dealing with their restoration to political power is to seal our own death-warrant, and secure the triumph of our opponents and of the enemies of the country for a generation. This grave question is to be settled within the next session of Congress, and probably in its earlier weeks. They who elected the President stood confounded and divided by the policy he has dictated to them for its solution. The North Carolina proclamation they tolerated as an experiment, till it has indurated into a policy executed in every State which rebelled, and supported by every Northern Democrat and every rebel pretending to loyalty. *In words*, the proclamations summon that "portion of the people who are loyal" to reorganize the State governments; but in *reality* they exclude the whole negro population, half the aggregate population, and nearly the whole of those who have always been loyal in those States. *Under these proclamations, therefore, no republican form of government is possible.*

The only alternatives are an oligarchy of loyal whites or an aristocracy of hostile whites. The one is loyal, but is not republican; the other is neither loyal nor republican. The former President Lincoln organized in Virginia and Louisiana; the President is organizing under his proclamations the latter. The legal effect of their recognition is to restore the State governments to those whom we have just expelled from them, to subject the emancipated negroes to the discriminating legislation of their masters, to continue their domination over the loyal minority, to guarantee to them the right to represent, now three fifths, and at the next census the whole of the disfranchised negroes, and to admit to Congress votes enough to compel equality, at the peril of anarchy, between loyalty and disloyalty. They were our armed enemies when Lee surrendered; they are now our disarmed enemies. They are now for independence and slavery, and against union and freedom; they acquiesce in both till time or disaster gives them opportunity to realize their hopes, and till then their interest and purpose are to obliterate every distinction between those who rebelled and those who put down the rebellion. In all the South the only mass of the population interested and able to foil these designs is the negroes whom the President has disfranchised.

Whatever his purpose may be, his policy is that of our enemies. His apologists say the President is *in favor* of negro suffrage, but that is small comfort if his proclamations exclude it. We remember his declaration that traitors should be punished, yet none are punished; that only loyal men should control the States, yet he has delivered them to the disloyal; that the aristocracy should be pulled down, yet he has put it in power again; that its possessions should be divided among Northern laborers of all colors, yet the negroes are still a landless, homeless class; that he was opposed to military commissions, yet they still defile the land, and others for higher victims are said to be in preparation! The President's words are, therefore, uncertain guides to his conduct. His apologists say, to the States alone belongs the question of suffrage, and the President left it to the people interested in it. But that is what the President did not do. The negroes of the States which rebelled form in some States a majority, in others a half, in all a vast, powerful, and loyal body of citizens, and to them he has not left it. On the contrary, he has left *them* to the will of their *masters.* It is true the President has no power to dictate who shall vote, but it is equally true that he has no power to dictate who shall *not* vote. He has as much power to *admit* as to *exclude.* His apologists assure us it was in obedience to the State Constitutions, which survive the State governments. But the President's proclamations do not say so, and his conduct says to the contrary. He did not obey the Constitution in making *the oath* a qualification of suffrage, nor in authorizing the provisional governor to determine the loyalty of voters, nor in appointing him to make rules for convening the Convention, nor in directing it to be convened at all, nor in requiring it to prohibit slavery; and it is nonsense to say if he was not bound on these points he was bound on negro suffrage. His whole conduct was a usurpation, but it was no more usurpation to direct his agents to *receive* than to *refuse* negro votes.

The suggestion that the Constitutions survive the governments is at once absurd and dangerous. The governments ceased to exist because they disowned their subordination to the United States in point of law. Our arms expelled them as usurpations in point of fact. The Constitutions were Constitutions of *those* governments, and of nothing else. If they did not constitute those governments they constituted nothing. A Constitution of nothing is nothing. A Constitution which does not constitute is a contradiction in terms. Such are the absurdities of this new form of Southern Constitutional metaphysics!

Our ordinary language is elliptical. We speak of a Constitution, but that means nothing till we add, of *what.* We mean a *Constitution of government;* and the moment we say what we mean, the folly of a Constitution surviving the government is apparent. When the rebellion usurped power in the States, the State governments ceased to exist; the Constitutions became dead forms; the line of official transmission of powers was broken; there ceased to be any person designated to renew the functions of government, and they could never be renewed till the people *constituted* anew the governments, or Congress, in executing its guarantee, directed such governments to be *constituted.* For a government is certain *men* charged with certain *powers.* A Constitution of government is the law creating the powers and designating the men to execute them; and without the men the government and the Constitution are alike nonentities.

But the view is also dangerous. For if the Constitutions continue in force, then the representatives and senators elected under them are entitled to appear in their seats, require their names to be called, and to vote on the simple production of their *certificates.* It is not necessary that Congress should recognize governments in those States; for the old governments which it has heretofore recognized continue, and to recognize others is to oust them by revolution. This has always been the view of the Democratic allies of the rebels; but it is now, for the first time, presented for the approval of the Republicans. The President had not thought of this view when he made the prohibition of slavery a condition of reorganization; and if he did not include negro suffrage in the conditions, it was not because he had not as much power, but less inclination to do it. Nothing is more true than that the question of suffrage belongs to the States, but it is equally true that Congress is the exclusive judge of the compatibility of their solution of it with republican principles. The States have the right to prescribe who shall vote, but they have no right so to exercise it as to create an oligarchy or an aristocracy instead of a republican form of government: and it is the right and the duty of Congress to judge this question; and its judgment is final and conclusive on all departments of the government. If Congress thinks the State has constituted an oligarchy or an aristocracy by its law of suffrage, it is entitled and bound to refuse to recognize it, to annul the law, rescue the people from its power, and prescribe measures and conditions for the organization of a government, republican in form *in its judgment*, on American principles. This judgment it is the duty of the President to *execute;* over it he has no power. It is the duty of guaranteeing republican government in the States which gives Congress this high jurisdiction; and the right of determining who are the representatives and senators carries with it the *exclusive* right of determining which is the constitutional, that is, the republican government of a State, for otherwise it might find itself compelled to admit representatives and senators of States whose governments are not republican in form or substance in its opinion.

It is therefore clear that the President is wholly beyond the sphere of his power in every step in reorganizing State governments; for each step is either legal and binding on Congress, or illegal and a nullity; and as it can not bind Congress, it is a nullity and an illegality. It is therefore frivolous to say the President could do nothing but what he did. He could have done *nothing*. It was his duty to have done *nothing*. His intermeddling has gravely *complicated* the question of what is republican government with the claims of persons to seats and of parties to votes. But this does not *vary* the question, and it must be met as it is presented. Republican principles and national interests alike forbid the acceptance of the President's plan. That is the recognition by Congress of the principle that State governments which ostracize a majority, or a half, or a great mass of citizens, and subject them to the absolute government of others, is republican in form. That principle has never yet been acknowledged by any Congress. No State government has ever been recognized by Congress which ostracized the great mass of the *people*, white or black. It is not the exclusion from political power merely which is the test, but the exclusion of *great masses* of citizens.

A State may arbitrarily exclude from power one man, or a family, or a thousand families; or it may exclude from power a greater proportion of those who have renounced their allegiance and defied its laws, and yet not affect the republican character of the government. But republican government in the American sense is the government by the mass of citizens through their representatives. Whenever, therefore, the mass of the citizens, or any great proportion of them, is excluded from political power, yet required to submit to its laws, the government ceases to be republican, and Congress can not recognize it as such. Here the question is not of the rights of man to a voice in the government, but of the meaning of republican government required to be guaranteed in the Constitution.

Connecticut has just refused to admit negroes to vote; but that does not touch the republicanism of her government, for the persons excluded form no material or appreciable portion of her citizens. But negro suffrage is one thing in Connecticut and another thing in South Carolina. In the latter State, the negro citizens form two thirds of the whole body of citizens. To deny them a vote and subject them to the will of the one third is absolutely in conflict with a republican form of government. It is not merely an aristocracy of race, it is an oligarchy. If the Constitution of the United States permits the ostracizing of two thirds of the citizens and their subjection to one third, the guarantee is one of mere form. A tenth may as well rule as a third, or one man as well as a tenth.

It is an *accident* that the line of disfranchisement and color are the same; it is not a question of race, but of republicanism. If two thirds who are black may be excluded in South Carolina, two thirds who are white may be excluded by the blacks in North Carolina, and one is just as republican as the other. The Constitution makes no distinction of color. Its only distinction is that between free *and slave* inhabitants. The slaves were always excluded irrespective of numbers, for they were not citizens. But free negroes were citizens of the United States. They were never declared by any State not to be citizens at the time of the adoption of the Constitution. They have never been declared not to be citizens by any department of the government. The Dred Scott case has been ignorantly quoted to settle that point; but it decided not that a *free negro* could not be a *citizen*, but that a *slave* is not a *citizen;* and nobody ever supposed he could be. But free negroes are citizens of the United States by the unanimous judgment of all departments of the government. That is now a settled point. And the Constitution draws no distinction between a black citizen and a white citizen. Congress has never acknowledged a State government to be republican which ostracized two thirds, or a half, or one third of its citizens. At the adoption of the Constitution the free negroes were in no state a *tenth* of the whole population. In Virginia they were one to thirty-six; in South Carolina one to seventy-seven; in Georgia one to one hundred and twenty-eight; and they voted in neither State, though in Virginia declared by law to be citizens. In Maryland they were one to twenty-five; in North Carolina one to sixty; and they voted in both. The largest proportion excluded at that time was in Delaware, where they were one to eleven. In Tennessee, the first State admitted, they were one to nine, and *they voted.* In Kentucky, the next State, they were excluded; but they were only one to *five hundred and twenty-six.* Even when Louisiana was admitted—the great prize of the ambitious slave power—the ratio was only one to seven.

But now Congress is asked to *guarantee* as *republican* such despotisms as these: In North Carolina 631,000 citizens ostracize 331,000 citizens. In Virginia 719,000 citizens ostracize 533,000 citizens. In Alabama 596,000 citizens ostracize 437,000 citizens. In Georgia 591,000 citizens ostracize 465,000 citizens. In Louisiana 357,000 citizens ostracize 350,000 citizens. In Mississippi 353,000 citizens ostracize 436,000 citizens. In South Carolina 291,000 citizens ostracize 411,000 citizens.

It would be just as republican to reverse the numbers; and if we have no respect for republican principle, common sense would require that we, holding the government, should vest our friends with the State governments and ostracize our opponents. The

President asks us to ostracize our friends and place our enemies over their heads! Either course leaves republican government without any guarantee of its substance. It is vain to attempt to cover such iniquities as those by the example of the freehold or property qualifications formerly existing in some States. They might doubtless be pushed to the extent of impeaching the character of the government; but hitherto they have never in the United States gone so far as to require the interposition of Congress. They never excluded any such masses of population as are ostracized by the President's plan, and they ostracized nobody. Every one could vote on getting the requisite property, and that was beyond nobody's reach. But the negro citizens are ostracized, they and their posterity forever, even where two thirds of the people. It is therefore impossible for republicans to recognize the President's governments. Nor ought they to feel the least hesitation in rejecting them, for the President's intermeddling is wholly illegal; it is an assumption to dictate to Congress respecting its members; and what has been done is a vain form, having no claim to legal authority till Congress by recognizing it gives it legal force. These mushroom governments *play* at governing the Southern States. It is plain the President treats them not as legal and authoritative governments, but as his puppets, whose acts he annuls when they don't suit him. Congress, then, is free, and bound to treat them as mere nullities—to brush them away as so many cobwebs, and on the cleared field to mark out the foundations of republican principles on which the government should be erected. The objects to be kept in view are to break the force and unity of the rebel vote in Congress; to rescue the States from its domination; and to place in the hands of the colored population political power for their protection and our safety. Retaining the States under military power postpones the first danger, but it involves a greater. Such rule continued long over such vast populations must destroy every vestige of republican government. The military commissions which still defy the law, under the authority of the President, and, without the frivolous apology of actual host lities, inflict punishments unknown to the law for acts *displeasing* to the President, are now fast unsettling the foundations of national freedom and personal security. If military government be continued in the rebel States, the idea of government by law will die out from the land, and the President's will be the only law. I prefer to risk the negroes under their masters and the country to the rebel vote in Congress, rather than subject loyal negroes and disloyal whites to the common despotism of military government, and expose the North to the dangers of tolerating and organizing such a despotism. Discarding, therefore, the horrible thought of military government as one the people ought not to tolerate, and will not tolerate, how can Congress paralyze the dangerous vote? It can amend the Constitution so as to apportion representation according to the persons who are allowed to vote. Mr. Sloan moved this last winter, but it never came to a vote. But that leaves the *States* in the hands of the disaffected. That could be avoided in the opinion of some by excluding disloyal men who have been engaged in the rebellion from power in the States. But the loyal white population are so mere a handful in the midst of the disaffected mass as to be wholly unable to administer the government and enforce submission to the laws, and the pressure of public opinion would compel them to open the door to the excluded mass. That attempt has so resulted in Virginia and Louisiana, where Governor Pierpont and General Banks pursued that policy. They merely created a temporary and powerless oligarchy. But it would fail in one other material object. The negro population would still be without a voice or a guarantee for any right. It is *necessary*, therefore, at once to *satisfy republican principles, rescue the States from rebel domination, secure Congress against their undivided and hostile vote, protect the rights of the negro population, and create a body of friends for the United States, interested to fight for its supremacy, that Congress should require the States to be reorganized on the basis of universal suffrage*, and that it should refuse to recognize any government which does not recognize that. It should then secure this permanent foundation of American republicanism against the mutations of political life and the local hostilities in the Southern States by proposing an amendment to the Constitution, consecrating it forever as the criterion and condition of republican government in every State.

These measures are the necessary buttresses for the support of that prohibiting slavery. Without them it will totter and may fall, and certainly must fail to secure real liberty and equality before the law. Power alone is security, and with it comes respect, and dignity, and education. They who propose to postpone negro suffrage till the negro is educated, need political education more than the negro. I think our only safety is in confining our efforts to *these measures.* It is too late to break the power of the Southern aristocracy by depriving their leaders of citizenship. Confiscation was never possible unless by partition of the lands among the negroes, and that Congress feared to enact. To sell a continent is impossible without a continent of buyers; and the laws are and will remain in the President's hands mere political thumb-screws to extort votes more powerful than all his patronage. All that remains open is to balance the power of the disaffected aristocracy by the resident mass of loyal negroes armed with the ballot and bayonet.

It is quite certain the President does not mean to insist on this. If his proclamations were an experiment on the temper of the white population, he is satisfied with facts which dismay his friends. He is so impatient of contradiction that loyal warnings are become "*pestilent* and *malignant utterances.*" He is experimenting *now* on nothing but the patience of the Republicans and the support of the Democrats. Of the latter he is receiving daily gratifying assurances. Of course, he is not thinking of joining the Democrats, for that would be going into a minority. But neither does he seem to be devoted to the Republicans. His policy is that of the Democrats, and his hope is to induce the Republicans to abandon their principles and unite with him in executing that of the Democrats. How many of the Republicans will unite with the Democrats to reinstate the representatives of the rebellion in power, in order that *they* may unite with the Democrats to expel *us* from power, remains to be seen. If enough to give the President a majority, a counter revolution is effected, which postpones the fruits of the war for a generation—it may be, then to be wrung from those in power by another civil war. It is possible the President may mean to disappoint the hopes of the Democrats, but it is not safe for Republicans to stake their cause on that doubtful and improbable chance. If he persevere, they must be ready to defy a most formidable coalition; for the Southern representatives, if admitted, will in this Congress meet many warm friends from the Northern States.

In the next Congress the coalition can hardly fail to be in a majority in the House, and to press so closely on our majority in the Senate that a few defections may destroy it. The loss of the next presidency is the natural sequel of the triumph of the President's plan, and, if once lost, will any one name a day when there is a reasonable prospect of our regaining it? The best we can hope for, therefore, under the President's policy, is, that the Southern representatives will subordinate their passions to securing their interests in the Union by the coalition as of old. It is not likely the Democrats will repel their advances.

It is possible that these people, so arrogant in rebellion, may be meek when in power over their enemies; that they will pay our debt, pension our soldiers, vote indemnity to loyal citizens; and vote against assuming their own debt, against pensioning their own wounded, against restoring their own officers to the army and navy, against compensation for their slaves, against annulling the confiscation acts or indemnity where the title can not be revoked; and that the Democrats will aid them in passing their self-denying ordinances, but it seems to me not wise to assume it. It is safer to take their view of their interests as the measure of what they will attempt, and what they *can* do as the limit of what they will do.

I do not fear a new rebellion now, but I will not shut my eyes to what men who have no interests but what are opposed to those who triumphed may do in power. Fifty-seven representatives and twenty-two senators are more than enough to arrest legislation in either House by tactics well known and often applied, and not hitherto pushed to revolutionary extremes, because the constituencies had an interest in the government the representatives did not venture to disregard. But here revolutionary constituencies stand behind representatives struggling for their interests against their conquerors. They will not restrain their representatives, and if they persist, will not Democrats hasten to rescue the government by granting their demands? If they fail in this, the life of nations is too fruitful of changes to justify us in excluding from our calculations contingencies where foreign war or civil discord may place the nation at the mercy of a hostile minority; when a Buchanan may be President, and refuse to strike while they divide the nation without the fear of the sword; or when a loyal President may rashly expel them from Congress, break the power of law by violence, and plunge us into the anarchy of civil war without a government recognized by all which alone carried us safely through the rebellion.

Against all these dangers, the refusal to recognize loyal oligarchies or disloyal aristocracies, and the recognition only of governments republican in form in the Southern States, are the sufficient and only guarantee. The mass of the loyal negro vote breaks the unity of the hostile vote in every State, and will absolutely control it in many.

In 1776 God gave us wise men who secured every point of victory possible. In this time of trial God has given us, for our sins, rulers who are not so wise, and the people grope toward their salvation and teach their rulers to secure it. By his blessing we are intrusted with two thirds of both houses of Congress, and that is the absolute legislative power of the United States. *What we think right we can do.* If the President deserts those who elected him for the votes and policy of their opponents, we must break the coalition at any cost. The President can have our support only by conforming his conduct to our principles. It is vain to argue, from the dangers of division, the necessity of submission to his will; that will itself, if unchanged, works the ruin more surely than any division. It is itself the division, unless we meanly sell a great cause for presidential patronage.

But it is vain to deny that failure now is final for this generation, for the people who want negro suffrage are in the North, and they who are to decide it are in the South, representing and voting for the negroes in more than one fourth of all the States, with a negative on any amendment of the Constitution, and absolute power in each State. It is insane to dream that the South will of itself ever give either suffrage or equality before the law, and now is our only time to compel it.

If men say God works slowly, yet will not let a good cause fail, they had better enlighten their piety by a glance at his ways in history, and reflect that he visits wasted opportunities, not less than wickedness, with ruin. I trust we may not be monuments of that wrath. Very sincerely, your obedient servant,

HENRY WINTER DAVIS.

BALTIMORE, October, 1865.

THE END.

www.ingramcontent.com/pod-product-compliance
Lightning Source LLC
LaVergne TN
LVHW021222110826
845150LV00002B/222
* 9 7 8 1 4 2 5 5 6 4 1 2 4 *